WEST AFRICA'S
SECURITY CHALLENGES

A project of the International Peace Academy

WEST AFRICA'S SECURITY CHALLENGES

Building Peace in a Troubled Region

EDITED BY
Adekeye Adebajo
Ismail Rashid

LYNNE
RIENNER
PUBLISHERS

BOULDER
LONDON

Published in the United States of America in 2004 by
Lynne Rienner Publishers, Inc.
1800 30th Street, Boulder, Colorado 80301
www.rienner.com

and in the United Kingdom by
Lynne Rienner Publishers, Inc.
3 Henrietta Street, Covent Garden, London WC2E 8LU

Library of Congress Cataloging-in-Publication Data
West Africa's security challenges : building peace in a troubled region /
   Adekeye Adebajo and Ismail Rashid (eds.).
   p. cm. — (A project of the International Peace Academy)
   Includes bibliographical references and index.
   ISBN 1-58826-259-6 (hardcover : alk. paper) — ISBN 1-58826-284-7
(pbk. : alk. paper)
   1. Africa, West—Politics and government—1960– . 2. Africa, West—
Economic conditions—1960– . 3. Africa, West—Military policy. 4. National
security—Africa, West. 5. Regionalism—Africa, West. 6. Conflict management—
Africa, West. 7. Peace-building—Africa, West. I. Adebajo, Adekeye, 1966– .
II. Rashid, Ismail O. D., 1963– . III. Series.
DT476.5 W48 2004
966.03'3—dc22   2003025704

British Cataloguing in Publication Data
A Cataloguing in Publication record for this book
is available from the British Library.

Printed and bound in the United States of America

   5 4 3 2 1

Contents

Foreword

David M. Malone
President, International Peace Academy

It is with great pride and pleasure that the International Peace Academy (IPA) presents this unique, scholarly contribution on West Africa's security challenges. This volume, the first comprehensive attempt to assess the subregion's security dilemmas after the Cold War, is edited by two outstanding young African scholars, Adekeye Adebajo, director of the IPA's Africa Program from January 2001 until September 2003, and Ismail Rashid, an academic at Vassar College and close collaborator of the IPA. In producing this volume, both editors worked primarily with African scholars and practitioners, who were joined by three non-African academics.

The IPA's Africa Program—initiated by my predecessor, Olara Otunnu, and by Margaret Vogt, both eminent African activists and scholars—has for many years focused on the means of enhancing African capacity to reduce the continent's tensions, resolve its conflicts, and prevent violence. During the 1990s, the IPA worked closely with the Organization of African Unity (OAU) to help conceptualize and operationalize its security mechanism. Africa is undergoing enormous transformation and its subregional security organizations are playing larger conflict management and peacebuilding roles. For these reasons, the IPA began to see the importance of working with subregional organizations such as the Economic Community of West African States (ECOWAS), the Southern African Development Community (SADC), the Intergovernmental Authority on Development (IGAD), and the East African Community (EAC) to enhance their capacity for conflict management. Between July 2000 and June 2003, the Africa Program consolidated its efforts at assisting subregional organizations to develop, establish, and operationalize their security mechanisms through a project on developing Africa's regional and subregional security mechanisms.

IPA staff have published extensively on security issues in West Africa. The IPA was also involved in conceptualizing the ECOWAS security mechanism of 1999. In partnership with ECOWAS, the IPA held a major seminar in Abuja, Nigeria, in September 2001. We examined various issues related to economic integration; small arms and light weapons; security sector reform; the lessons of the ECOWAS Cease-Fire Monitoring Group (ECOMOG) interventions in Liberia, Sierra Leone, and Guinea-Bissau; the conflict management role of civil society actors; governance and democratization; rebel movements; child soldiers; the significance for West Africa of the African Union (AU) and the New Partnership for Africa's Development (NEPAD); and the political economy of conflicts. Subsequently, the IPA and ECOWAS convened a task force meeting in Dakar, Senegal, in August 2002 with the explicit aim of exploring ways to strengthen the capacity of ECOWAS's security mechanism. In addition to its work in West Africa, the IPA has organized several major policy seminars in Botswana (2000), South Africa (2002), Uganda (2002), and Tanzania (2003) on southern, eastern, and central African security issues.

This volume, which is largely based on material presented at the Abuja seminar, also reflects some of the contributions and perspectives of the Dakar task force meeting of August 2002. It provides a context for understanding West Africa's security dilemmas by highlighting the links between the failures of economic integration and development, the challenges of democratization, governance and military insecurity, and cycles of violent conflict in West Africa.

Such an endeavor would not have been possible without the foresight and dedication of our funders. The IPA is deeply grateful to the governments of Denmark, Germany, the Netherlands, and Finland, as well as the United Kingdom's Department for International Development (DFID). Their support of the IPA's Africa Program and their commitment to policy development on subregional security issues throughout Africa have made it possible for my colleagues to explore these pressing issues.

We are also very grateful for the direct involvement of Mohamed Ibn Chambas, the dynamic executive secretary of ECOWAS, who has generously contributed a more substantive foreword to this volume. Mohamed Chambas worked closely with my colleagues in the Africa Program to help make the IPA's research and policy development on West Africa's security dynamics more meaningful. He helped to launch the report on the Abuja seminar in New York and participated actively in the Dakar task force meeting, both in 2002. Both of these interactions and his personal interest in bridging the gap between policy and practice have helped to strengthen the IPA's commitment to developing useful and innovative policy recommendations for managing conflicts in West Africa. This unique volume is intended for policymakers, activists, and scholars, both within and outside

Africa. We hope that this exciting contribution will advance efforts at strengthening the capacity of West African actors and institutions to manage their own conflicts, in close collaboration with the international community.

Finally, I am personally very grateful to the volume's contributors and editors. Adekeye Adebajo, after a tenure of rare achievement at the IPA over five years, left New York in fall 2003 to direct the Centre for Conflict Resolution (CCR) in Cape Town, an exciting new role in a preeminent institution, but a tremendous loss for the IPA. He will be much missed in our midst, but his move should reinforce the valuable cooperation initiated between our two institutions in 1996 by Laurie Nathan, former CCR executive director, and Olara Otunnu.

Foreword

Mohamed Ibn Chambas
Executive Secretary, Economic Community of West African States

This volume addresses contemporary issues that are of the utmost significance for managing conflict and building peace in West Africa; it also
examines many of the concerns of the Economic Community of West
African States (ECOWAS).

The International Peace Academy (IPA) is one of ECOWAS's collaborators in the area of peace and security. In September 2001 our organizations jointly convened a seminar in Abuja, Nigeria, where discussions centered on the West African security architecture, the role of ECOWAS in the
context of conflict management within our region, and the gains of our
newly evolved mechanism on conflict prevention and management. That
seminar brought together diplomats, military officials, academics, policymakers, and civil society actors and provided a forum for examining the
issues of security and governance in West Africa. Following the Abuja seminar, our two institutions jointly organized a task force meeting in Dakar,
Senegal, in August 2002, with the theme "Operationalizing the ECOWAS
Mechanism for Conflict Prevention, Management, Resolution, Peacekeeping, and Security." The Dakar meeting sought to find ways of enhancing the
roles of the key actors in subregional peace and security. These two auspi-
cious occasions were part of a series of activities that the IPA had pro-
grammed within a three-year period, targeted toward stimulating awareness
and discussions on regional security mechanisms within and outside Africa.
Based on discussions in Abuja and Dakar, and judging from this volume, I
do consider the collaboration between the IPA and ECOWAS to have been a
resounding success and must continue to thank the IPA for its keen interest in
the affairs of West Africa and ECOWAS. We look forward to a planned
collaboration in 2004 on ECOWAS-UN cooperation. In a commendable

demonstration of its interest in West Africa, the IPA provided me with several opportunities to interact with new collaborators over the security challenges of our subregion and ECOWAS's efforts at keeping abreast with and
managing these problems.

The member states of ECOWAS created their organization driven by
the need to transform West Africa's economies into an integrated economic
community that would be responsive to domestic needs and resources.
However, with the outbreak of the civil war in Liberia in 1989 and the
accompanying humanitarian tragedy, drastic measures had to be taken. A
standing mediation committee was therefore set up in 1990. This committee in turn established a cease-fire monitoring group, ECOMOG, which
immediately assumed the role of peace enforcer and peacekeeper in Liberia
and in the subsequent conflicts that arose in Sierra Leone and Guinea-
Bissau. What followed were several years of ad hoc conflict management
interventions by some of ECOWAS's member states in Liberia, Sierra
Leone, and Guinea-Bissau, where brutal fighting between the governments
and rebel forces resulted in the death of thousands of citizens and the displacement of hundreds of thousands of people.

As is to be expected, ECOMOG's exploits in these war zones prompted
discussions among member states that centered on the need to develop an
institutionalized mechanism for conflict management. The ECOWAS mechanism for conflict prevention is to be found in the Protocol Relating to the
Mechanism for Conflict Prevention, Management, Resolution, Peacekeeping, and Security, which was adopted by our heads of state on 10 December
1999. This mechanism makes it imperative that ECOWAS member states
promote and strengthen cooperation in the areas of preventive diplomacy
and sharing of information (of the early warning variety). All member states
are involved in peacekeeping and policing operations under a newly structured ECOMOG, which is now a multipurpose body made up of standby
forces that are permanently ready for immediate deployment. ECOMOG has
a multipurpose function that includes observation, monitoring, and peacekeeping. The force can also be deployed for humanitarian interventions or as
an enforcer of sanctions. Finally, the mechanism provides for joint control of
transborder crime, international terrorism, and proliferation of small arms
and antipersonnel mines.

As a necessary conflict prevention strategy, the mechanism is in the
process of setting up an early warning system: a regional observation network spread over designated states in the region—Benin, Burkina Faso,
Gambia, and Liberia—with a central observatory located within the
ECOWAS secretariat in Abuja, where economic, social, political, and
security-related data collected from member states are analyzed in a bid to
detect or unearth warning signals that may indicate areas of potential conflict. Our mechanism is also emphatic on the need for ECOWAS to develop

a capacity for postconflict reconstruction and peacebuilding in order to assist in the restoration of political authority, social and economic rehabilitation, and enthronement of the rule of law and respect for human rights in a postconflict environment.

This volume addresses the root causes of conflict in our subregion with depth and insight. Indeed, addressing the root cause of conflicts is one way of resolving these conflicts. It is for this reason that ECOWAS adopted, in Dakar in December 2001, a protocol on democracy and good governance, supplementary to the 1999 protocol on the mechanism for conflict prevention. This new protocol sets out guiding principles for intrastate relations that would help foster participatory democracy, good governance, the rule of law, respect for human rights, and a balanced and equitable distribution of resources, among a host of others—all issues the neglect of which often results in instability within states.

The contributors to this volume put forward recommendations for concrete ways of enhancing the ECOWAS mechanism for conflict management, which is still very much at an embryonic stage even after four years of implementation. They also highlight the diverse roles of local, national, subregional, and international actors that can be called upon to help prevent or manage conflicts. Some of these recommendations will help to engender more coherent and practical cooperation with the United Nations, the African Union (AU), and other subregional organizations in Africa. We need to create direct links between Africa's subregional organizations and the UN, improve the exchange and channeling of information, and establish a fast track for implementing our mutual conflict management and peacebuilding objectives.

I am delighted that so many distinguished African and non-African scholars and practitioners have brought their expertise and very rich experiences to bear on the diverse subjects addressed in this volume. I wish to thank the IPA, the editors, and the contributors for making this important scholarly contribution toward finding a lasting solution to instability in our subregion. This volume will certainly prove useful in guiding future practitioners and scholars in our mutual quest for consolidating peace, strengthening democracy, and promoting economic development and integration in West Africa.

Acknowledgments

We would like to thank all the contributors to this volume for their patience, good humor, and willingness to work through several drafts of their chapters. We must also thank the incredible staff at the International Peace Academy (IPA) for their impressive efficiency in completing this volume. We would like to thank in particular David M. Malone, IPA president, who was a consistent source of support and encouragement; John Hirsch, IPA senior fellow, who has been the most dedicated collaborator of the IPA's Africa Program over the past five years; Aida Mengistu and Angela Muvumba, senior program officers at the IPA, who were the backbone of the Africa Program; and Dorina Bekoe, IPA research associate, and Mashood Issaka, IPA program officer, who contributed to completing the volume. We would also like to thank Clara Lee, the IPA's publications coordinator, for liaising effectively with Lynne Rienner Publishers during the publication process. Sally Schramm, manager of the Peace Library at the Centre for Conflict Resolution in Cape Town, provided invaluable assistance in locating missing references. Lynne Rienner and her staff deserve much praise for their friendly efficiency. We would like to thank our family and friends as well, for their consistent support and understanding as we completed this project.

The volume is an outgrowth of a joint policy seminar between the IPA and the Economic Community of West African States (ECOWAS) held in Abuja, Nigeria, in September 2001. We would like to express our gratitude to the efficient and overworked staff at the ECOWAS secretariat who assisted with this seminar as well as former ECOWAS executive secretary Lansana Kouyaté and his team for supporting this project so enthusiastically. The initial papers from the Abuja seminar were edited, reviewed, and updated to take into account important developments that have occurred since the seminar was held. We must express our profound gratitude to the current ECOWAS executive secretary, Mohamed Chambas, his deputy, General Cheick Diarra, and the rest of their team, for the strong support of the IPA-ECOWAS collaboration. Mohamed Chambas presided over a joint IPA-ECOWAS task force meeting in Dakar, Senegal, in August 2002, which the president of Senegal and chair of ECOWAS at the time, Abdoulaye Wade, also attended. The Dakar seminar offered suggestions for strengthening ECOWAS's security mechanism of 1999 and its recommendations fed into several chapters in this volume.

We must also thank the many specialists who agreed to comment on the chapters for us: Dorina Bekoe, John Hirsch, Eboe Hutchful, James Jonah, David Keen, Christopher Landsberg, Kate Maegher, Peter Schraeder, Courtenay Sprague, Augustine Toure, and Margaret Vogt. Finally, we would like to thank the governments of the Netherlands, Germany, and Denmark, and the United Kingdom's Department for International Development (DFID) for supporting the IPA Africa Program's work with ECOWAS as well as the publication of this book. We hope that this volume, written mostly by African authors, will contribute to a less Eurocentric view of Africa and allow African perspectives a role in promoting a deeper understanding of West Africa's post–Cold War security challenges.

—Adekeye Adebajo and Ismail Rashid

*Our struggle will in no way be a limited struggle character-
ized by narrow nationalism. Our struggle is that of all peoples aspiring to peace and freedom. That is why we must
never lose sight of the qualities and the just aspiration
toward peace—a just peace, dignity, and genuine independence—of the peoples that surround us. Of course, they must
carry out their historic duty. They must rid themselves of all
the serpents that infest their territory, of all the monsters
who rob them of their happiness. We have shouldered our
responsibilities. Other peoples must do the same—their
youth, their patriotic and democratic forces, their civilian
and military personnel, their men and women alike.*

—Thomas Sankara,
head of state of Burkina Faso, 1983–1987

Economic Community of West African States (ECOWAS)

WEST AFRICA'S
SECURITY CHALLENGES

1

Introduction

Adekeye Adebajo

This volume is the first comprehensive attempt to assess West Africa's security challenges after the end of the Cold War. Written by a group of largely African scholars and practitioners, the book provides a context for understanding the region's security dilemmas by highlighting the link between the failures of economic development and integration—as well as governance and democratization—and military insecurity and violent conflicts. The study focuses on the important role and motivations of West Africa's soldiers, warlords, and rebels. The political economy of conflicts in the region is also assessed, as well as efforts to curb the proliferation of small arms and light weapons and the phenomenon of child soldiers. The role of key regional and external actors—the Economic Community of West African States (ECOWAS) Cease-Fire Monitoring Group (ECOMOG), the United Nations, the United States, Britain, and France—in foiling or fueling conflicts is also examined.

West Africa is among the world's most unstable regions. In the last decade, Liberia, Sierra Leone, Guinea, Côte d'Ivoire, Guinea-Bissau, and Senegal have been embroiled in an interconnected web of conflicts that have seen refugees, rebels, and arms spill across porous borders. Nigeria, Mali, and Niger have been plagued by internal conflicts that have weakened their capacity to provide security to their citizens. Democratization efforts have suffered setbacks in Burkina Faso, Gambia, Guinea, and Togo. The fifteen states that make up ECOWAS today—Benin, Burkina Faso, Cape Verde, Côte d'Ivoire, Gambia, Ghana, Guinea, Guinea-Bissau, Liberia, Niger, Nigeria, Mali, Senegal, Sierra Leone, and Togo—are among the poorest countries in the world. West Africa is also the most coup-prone sub-region in Africa: more than half of successful military coups d'état in

Africa since independence (forty-one out of about seventy-five) have occurred in West Africa, a subregion comprising less than a third of the continent's states. In the last decade, Liberia and Sierra Leone have been embroiled in protracted civil wars; Guinea-Bissau experienced a brief internecine conflict from 1998 to 1999; Casamance separatists have continued to battle the Senegalese government, as they have done for two decades; the Tuareg conflict has simmered in Mali and Niger; Liberia and Guinea have launched cross-border raids against each other's territories; and Côte d'Ivoire, previously one of West Africa's most stable states, became embroiled in civil conflict in September 2002.

But West Africa has also recorded some successes in the areas of democratization and regional security. Civil society actors pressured autocratic military regimes to leave power in Benin, Niger, and Sierra Leone in the 1990s. More open political systems have emerged in Benin, Ghana, Nigeria, Mali, Senegal, and Sierra Leone. ECOWAS has established one of the world's first security mechanisms to manage regional conflicts. More recently, Charles Taylor, Liberia's warlord-turned-president and the most destabilizing influence in West Africa's decade-long conflicts, was forced into exile in Nigeria in August 2003. Taylor had been indicted a few weeks earlier for war crimes by the Special Court for Sierra Leone. Two of West Africa's most notorious "spoilers"—Foday Sankoh, leader of Sierra Leone's brutal Revolutionary United Front (RUF), and Sam Bockarie, Sankoh's former battlefield commander—also died in 2003 before they could stand trial before the court.

The fact that regional actors took the lead in efforts to manage conflicts in Liberia, Sierra Leone, and Guinea-Bissau represents a significant trend in conflict management. The post–Cold War era has seen an increasing division of labor between regional actors and an overburdened United Nations. In his 1992 report *An Agenda for Peace,* former UN Secretary-General Boutros Boutros-Ghali argued that regional security arrangements should be used to lighten the UN's heavy peacekeeping burden as foreseen in Chapter VIII of the UN Charter.[1] Peacekeeping debacles in Somalia (1993) and Rwanda (1994) led to great reluctance on the part of the most powerful members of the UN Security Council to sanction new UN missions, particularly in Africa.[2] This situation resulted in efforts by African subregional organizations and the African Union (AU) to develop their own security mechanisms. It has further led to efforts by casualty-shy Western countries to strengthen the capacity of regional security organizations in Africa as a way of avoiding pressure to intervene themselves.

This book addresses traditional state-centric security issues such as the ones outlined above, as well as newer nontraditional human security issues including the role of civil society actors in managing conflicts in West Africa, the importance of governance and democratization to conflict prevention efforts, the phenomenon of child soldiers and the impact of armed conflicts on children, the proliferation of illicit small arms and light weapons in West Africa, and the implications for ECOWAS of initiatives to implement new norms of governance such as the Conference on Security, Stability, Development, and Cooperation in Africa (CSSDCA) and the New Partnership for Africa's Development (NEPAD).

Towers of Babel?
The Politics of Regional Economic Integration

West Africa currently has a population of about 230 million and an average per capita income of less than $500. There are considerable disparities in the subregion in the distribution of natural resources among countries and the distribution of wealth among citizens. Many of the states in West Africa are economically unviable and too small—only Nigeria, Ghana, and Côte d'Ivoire have populations of over 15 million—to achieve economies of scale without harnessing their efforts to a larger subregional market. ECOWAS was therefore established as an economic organization to create a common market, rather than as a security organization. The treaty establishing ECOWAS was signed in Lagos on 28 May 1975. The aims initially assigned to the organization by its charter were centered on the promotion of cooperation and development in all fields of economic activity. ECOWAS set out to achieve a common market in which goods, services, and people would move freely across West Africa, and in which members would derive benefits from increased trade and a common external tariff. But for the first two decades of its existence, ECOWAS's goals were hampered by a lack of political commitment and the rivalry between Nigeria and a French-led francophone bloc. This resulted in the establishment of competing regional organizations in West Africa that were often pursuing identical goals. Most ECOWAS states also lacked basic infrastructure and industries, and their economies remained dependent on primary commodities.

In Chapter 2 of this volume, Adebayo Adedeji, a visionary scholar-practitioner, embarks on a retrospective journey that seeks to explain why ECOWAS failed to achieve its integrationist goals in the past three decades. Adedeji is particularly well placed to undertake this assessment, having been described as "*le Père de la CEDEAO*" (the Father of ECOWAS).[3] He outlined the vision for subregional integration in West Africa in an article in the *Journal of Modern African Studies* in 1970 before turning theory into practice by convincing subregional leaders to adopt his vision of ECOWAS while serving as Nigeria's minister of economic reconstruction and development from 1972 to 1975.[4]

Adedeji blames West Africa's imperial powers for not prioritizing the building of indigenous leaders and institutions. He laments the balkanization of West Africa by European colonial powers who created continuing divisions between anglophone and francophone states and retarded efforts at regional integration. Adedeji argues that regional integration must be seen as an instrument for national survival and socioeconomic transformation, and should involve the creation of common agricultural policies and the establishment of regionwide communication and transport systems. He notes that an effective ECOWAS would strengthen the bargaining power of its members in international trade negotiations and debt relief efforts. Adedeji particularly blames political instability in Nigeria—the subregion's potential hegemon—for stalling ECOWAS's efforts at economic integration.

ECOWAS's renewed focus on institution building and subregional economic and monetary integration in the 1990s represents an important attempt to overcome a "credibility deficit" generated by programs that have had little impact on the living conditions of the majority of West Africa's citizens. However, ECOWAS's efforts at market integration through trade liberalization have failed to yield the desired results, as Adedeji's analysis clearly demonstrates. Intraregional trade still represents an insignificant portion of the total official exports of the ECOWAS subregion, having only grown from 4 percent to about 11 percent over the past two decades. The initial plan to create a single monetary zone by 1994 had registered little progress by 1993, when the Cotonou treaty postponed the deadline for a monetary union until 2009.

One complicating factor in monetary and trade integration in West Africa is the different and at times competing integration projects between francophone and anglophone West Africa. The different timing of independence in British West Africa (Gambia, Ghana, Nigeria, and Sierra Leone) and the actions of Ghana's Kwame Nkrumah—usually regarded as one of the leading fathers of pan-Africanism—in dismantling the common subregional institutions set up by the departing British colonial power had a negative impact on regional integration. French West Africa, in contrast, recognized the need to minimize the restrictions and constraints that fragmentation had imposed on its development through the vigorous and relentless promotion of cooperation and integration. Cooperation within the Communauté Financière Africaine (CFA) franc currency zone led to the creation of the largely francophone Communauté Economique de l'Afrique de l'Ouest (CEAO) in 1973, which later became the Union Economique et Monétaire Ouest Africaine (UEMOA) in 1994.[5]

In Chapter 3, S. K. B. Asante, one of Africa's leading political economists, assesses the travails of economic integration in West Africa, highlighting divisions between francophone states and other ECOWAS members. He analyzes prospects for a common currency in West Africa; the current efforts by Gambia, Ghana, Nigeria, and Sierra Leone to create an anglophone currency zone; and the future of the largely francophone UEMOA. Asante calls for the creation of a common ECOWAS currency and stresses the need to create popular support for the subregional body within West African civil society. Like Adedeji, he laments the proliferation of economic organizations in West Africa, noting that they have contributed significantly to the failure of regional integration. Asante therefore calls for the implementation of the decision by subregional leaders in July 1991 to declare ECOWAS the sole body responsible for economic integration in West Africa.

Understanding West Africa's security architecture also requires examining the patterns and prospects of regionalization in West Africa. In Chapter 4, Daniel Bach focuses on West Africa's efforts to confront the challenges of globalization through "developmental regionalism." The French scholar reviews ECOWAS's current integration strategies and programs, and assesses the supranational, hegemonic, and intergovernmental aspects of regional construction. Bach also analyzes ECOWAS's efforts to draw lessons from the European Union (EU). The attempt by ECOWAS leaders to import foreign models without thinking creatively of ways to adapt them to fit West Africa's specific circumstances is a theme discussed by both Bach and Adedeji. Bach concludes his chapter by focusing on issues involving the interactions within West Africa between de facto "informal trade" and institutional patterns of regionalization.

Friends and Foes: Regional and External Actors in West Africa's Security Complex

Dramatic changes on the West African security landscape since the end of the Cold War have contributed significantly to West Africa's new security challenges. Kaye Whiteman and Douglas Yates make clear in Chapter 15 that France, West Africa's traditional great power, appears to have reduced its high-profile military role in Africa and diversified its commercial relations in Africa beyond its former colonies. Adebayo Adedeji, Adekeye Adebajo, and James Jonah note in Chapters 2, 13, and 14 that France's historical rival, Nigeria, seems at the same time to have staked its claims to be a new subregional military power by leading three ECOMOG interventions, in Liberia (1990–1998 and 2003) and Sierra Leone (1997–2000). Between 1960 and 1990, France remained the principal obstacle to the realization of Nigeria's hegemonic aspirations in West Africa. Nigeria's leaders, as a result of French support for Biafran secessionists during the Nigerian civil war of 1967 to 1970, championed the creation of ECOWAS in large part as a way of reducing French influence in West Africa. At independence in the

1960s, France had established close military, political, economic, and cultural ties with its former West African colonies and maintained up to 12,000 troops in military bases in Senegal and Côte d'Ivoire, as well as in Djibouti, the Central African Republic (CAR), and Gabon.

With the end of the Cold War and policy debacles in Rwanda and Mobutu Sese Seko's Zaire from 1994 to 1997, the French military presence in Africa has been drastically reduced. Two military bases were closed in the Central African Republic in April 1998, though Paris still maintains its West African bases in Côte d'Ivoire and Senegal. France's failure to intervene militarily after a December 1999 military coup against the regime of Henri Konan Bédié in its wealthiest former West African colony, Côte d'Ivoire, was seen by many as a historic watershed. The event fueled much speculation about the prospect of France's apparent military disengagement from Africa drawing francophone states in West Africa into closer security cooperation with Nigeria and other nonfrancophone ECOWAS states. In March 2000 the all-francophone Conseil de l'Entente invited Nigerian president Olusegun Obasanjo to a meeting in Togo to discuss security issues— the first time a nonfrancophone state had attended such a meeting. But France currently has about 4,000 troops in Côte d'Ivoire, sponsored a largely francophone ECOWAS intervention into Guinea-Bissau in 1999, and also financed a largely francophone ECOWAS intervention into Côte d'Ivoire in 2003. The French gendarme may not be as ubiquitous a presence in Africa as in the past four decades, but the Gallic power may come to rely more heavily on African troops to pursue its strategic interests as its direct military role of the past becomes increasingly anachronistic and discredited.

As Adedeji, Adebajo, and Jonah note in their chapters, Nigeria, in a bid to fulfill a historic Pax Nigeriana, provided the bulk of the men, money, and military matériel for ECOMOG's efforts in Liberia and Sierra Leone. With over 50 percent of West Africa's economic might, half of its population, and a 94,500-strong army that dwarfs the combined total of those of its neighbors, Nigeria remains a potential hegemon in its subregion. But it is unclear whether Nigeria has the capacity and will to play this role. Nigerian casualties in Liberia and Sierra Leone were estimated at over 1,000, while the costs of both missions ran into billions of dollars. It is unlikely that the civilian government of Olusegun Obasanjo—which unlike Nigeria's military brass hats cannot ignore its parliament, press, and public opinion—will be able to sustain these casualties and costs without some loss of political support. There are also internal political and financial constraints on Nigeria's ability to undertake future peacekeeping missions. Nigeria's refusal to contribute peacekeepers to Guinea-Bissau in 1998 and its reduction of troops from Sierra Leone from 12,000 to about 4,000 by 2000 are clear signs of a growing wariness at the costs of protracted peacekeeping efforts in West Africa. Nigeria's insistence on the UN taking over its peacekeeping responsibilities in Liberia before it committed troops to that country in August 2003 was further evidence of this trend.

The changing French security role in West Africa and growing Nigerian frustrations with subregional peacekeeping have coincided with increased, though limited, U.S. and British security roles in West Africa, which have been described in a rich comparative analysis by Kaye Whiteman and Douglas Yates. The authors provide a historical background of the security roles of the three Western countries during the Cold War, noting that these countries largely collaborated in the grand strategy of halting the spread of communism in Africa, even while often pursuing more parochial goals. While the French and U.S. security roles in West Africa were prominent during this period and were sometimes marred by a "subterranean" rivalry, the authors note that Britain shunned a militarily interventionist role during this period.

Whiteman and Yates observe that since the end of the Cold War and the debacle in Somalia in 1993, the United States has desisted from playing an active military role in Africa, but has increasingly become an alternative source of military assistance for many francophone states. Washington has trained peacekeepers from Benin, Mali, and Senegal as part of its African Crisis Response Initiative (ACRI)—now renamed African Contingency Operations Training Assistance (ACOTA)—to strengthen the military capabilities of African states for regional peacekeeping. The United States also provided logistical support to ECOMOG's efforts in Liberia in 1996 and trained Nigerian, Ghanaian, and Senegalese battalions for participation in the United Nations Mission in Sierra Leone (UNAMSIL). In August 2003 the United States launched a limited military intervention into Liberia to assist a Nigerian-led force in establishing stability in a country with which the United States had deep historical ties, having been founded by freed American slaves in 1847. Washington had also provided $500 million to the autocratic regime of Samuel Doe during the 1980s as part of its Cold War strategy in Africa.

In a dramatic shift from its low-key military strategy in Africa during the Cold War, Britain sent a small military contingent to Sierra Leone in 2000, which helped to stabilize a crumbling UN mission and also led efforts at security sector reform. Whiteman and Yates explain the intervention as having been driven by key figures within the cabinet led by Prime Minister Tony Blair, who embarked on a historic visit to Nigeria, Ghana, Sierra Leone, and Senegal in February 2002. The authors describe the intervention in Sierra Leone as "probably . . . the most significant British intervention in Africa in recent years" and note the increasing coordination of the African security policies of London and Paris. But critical voices in Africa continue to argue that these external efforts have not been properly coordinated, that Africans have not been adequately consulted on these initiatives, and that emphasis on training is misplaced since logistical and financial support is more essential for African peacekeepers.[6]

Pax West Africana? The ECOWAS Security Mechanism

The task of coordinating and constructing a common security strategy has been initiated at the regional level. The ECOWAS Mechanism for Conflict Prevention, Management, Resolution, Peacekeeping, and Security was adopted at the ECOWAS summit in Lomé in December 1999. The mechanism borrowed from two previous subregional security initiatives: the ECOWAS Protocol on Non-Aggression in 1978 and the ECOWAS Protocol Relating to Mutual Assistance on Defense in 1981. The first protocol called on member states to resolve their conflicts peacefully through ECOWAS, while the second promised mutual assistance for externally instigated or supported aggression and called for the creation of an ECOWAS allied armed force consisting of standby forces from ECOWAS states. The force was never established.

The ECOWAS security mechanism of 1999, examined in detail in Chapter 13 by Adekeye Adebajo, proposed the establishment of three organs to implement security decisions: the Mediation and Security Council, the Defense and Security Commission, and the Council of Elders. The mechanism also called for improved cooperation among ECOWAS states in early warning, conflict prevention, and peacekeeping operations, as well as in stemming cross-border crime and the proliferation of small arms and narcotics. Local bureaus for gathering political, economic, and social information for the ECOWAS early warning system have been established. Many of these ideas were based on ECOMOG's experiences in Liberia, Sierra Leone, and Guinea-Bissau. Ten members are now elected to two-year terms on the ECOWAS Mediation and Security Council, with decisions being made by a two-thirds majority of six members. The council has met over ten times to devise regional responses to the crises in Liberia, Sierra Leone, Guinea-Bissau, and Côte d'Ivoire. The Defense and Security Commission, consisting of chiefs of army staff, as well as police and customs officials, is advising the Mediation and Security Council on mandates, terms of reference, and the appointment of force commanders for military missions. Members of ECOWAS's Council of Elders have observed elections in Gambia, Sierra Leone, and Zimbabwe.

All three ECOMOG interventions, in Liberia, Sierra Leone, and Guinea-Bissau, clearly exposed the logistical weaknesses of West Africa's armies. For the foreseeable future, such logistical support will have to come from external actors like the United States, the UN, and the EU, until the subregion develops its own capabilities. The issue of financing is particularly important to the building of a proposed ECOMOG standby force consisting of fifteen battalions, one from each of the fifteen ECOWAS states. The ECOWAS mechanism foresees troop-contributing countries bearing financial costs for the first three months of military operations, before ECOWAS takes over those costs. Under the new ECOWAS mechanism, a special peace fund has been established to raise revenue through a community levy.

The ECOMOG peacekeeping missions, however, clearly demonstrated the importance of securing financial support *before* embarking on military interventions. Such costs can prove a disincentive to future interventions in a subregion saddled with a crippling debt burden. Tanzanian and Ugandan peacekeepers withdrew from the ECOMOG-led peacekeeping mission in Liberia in 1995 in large part because their financial and logistical needs were not being met. The three Nigerian-led peacekeeping missions to Chad from 1979 to 1982 were crippled by a lack of funding and logistical support and eventually forced to withdraw. These points underline the significance of mustering financial and logistical support from the international community for future subregional efforts at conflict management.

Brothers in Arms? ECOWAS and the UN

Despite ECOMOG's determined efforts to keep peace in West Africa, it is important to emphasize that the UN Security Council has primary responsibility for international peace and security, but has often simply shifted its responsibilities to ECOWAS due to the reluctance of its powerful members to sanction UN peacekeeping missions in Africa.[7] In Chapter 14, James Jonah, a scholar-diplomat and former UN Undersecretary-General for Political Affairs who was intimately involved in many of the issues he writes about, notes that the ECOMOG interventions underlined the importance of an active UN role in subregional peacekeeping efforts. The UN's mission to Liberia in 1993 was the first time in its history that it had contributed troops to work alongside a regional organization's peacekeepers in the field.

As in Liberia and Sierra Leone, the UN eventually became involved in Guinea-Bissau, though it played different roles in all three cases. In Liberia, the UN's unarmed military observers played a very limited monitoring role to ECOMOG. The UN helped to organize and monitor Liberia's 1997 election and established a small peacebuilding office in Monrovia following this election. In Sierra Leone, UN military observers played a monitoring role in support of ECOMOG similar to that in Liberia from August 1998, until the UN took over ECOMOG's peacekeeping duties and subsumed some of its troops under UN command in 2000. In October 2003 the UN

Mission in Liberia (UNMIL) took over the peacekeeping responsibilities of the ECOWAS Mission in Liberia (ECOMIL), which had been deployed two months earlier. In Guinea-Bissau, the United Nations performed no military role, but was involved in development work through the UN Development Programme (UNDP), and helped to organize and monitor elections in Guinea-Bissau in 1999 and 2000. The UN currently has a peacebuilding office in Bissau and established a peacekeeping mission in Côte d'Ivoire in February 2004.

Following the May 2001 recommendations of its Inter-Agency Task Force on West Africa, the UN established an office in Dakar, Senegal, in 2002 and appointed Ahmedou Ould-Abdallah as the Special Representative of the UN Secretary-General to head this office. The UN office in Dakar has been asked to help strengthen ECOWAS's peacekeeping and electoral capacities, and to work with civil society groups in West Africa. The office is to perform the following specific tasks: assist the UN and its subregional offices in coordinating strategies in West Africa; monitor and report on political, humanitarian, and human rights developments; harmonize UN activities with those of ECOWAS; monitor ECOWAS's decisions and activities; and support national and subregional peacebuilding efforts.[8] But so far, the office remains chronically short-staffed and has yet to carve out a proper role for itself in West Africa's security complex.

West African Renaissance?
Governance and Democratization

Two important issues in the quest to achieve durable peace in West Africa are governance and democratization. Aside from the continuing instability in the Mano river basin—Liberia, Guinea, and Sierra Leone—governments in Benin, Côte d'Ivoire, Ghana, Mali, Nigeria, and Senegal continue to strive to achieve democratic consolidation after decades of military rule or one-party administrations. Governments in West Africa often have to mediate ethnic tensions and to reverse past discrimination in the distribution of positions in state institutions like the military and civil service. These tensions have often resulted in armed conflicts and have contributed to the current spate of instability in West Africa.

In all four of West Africa's major conflicts in the last decade, in Liberia, Sierra Leone, Guinea-Bissau, and Côte d'Ivoire, personalized autocracies were a significant trigger. Samuel Doe and Charles Taylor in Liberia; Siaka Stevens and Joseph Momoh in Sierra Leone; João Vieira and Kumba Yala in Guinea-Bissau; and the heirs who inherited Félix Houphouët-Boigny's crown in Côte d'Ivoire—Henri Konan Bédié, Robert Guei, and Laurent Gbagbo—have all displayed antidemocratic tendencies and often ethnic favoritism that alienated and threatened certain groups in the process. Placing ethnic kinsmen in senior political positions in multiethnic states has often fueled violent confrontations by disaffected groups. This points to the importance of the ECOWAS security mechanism of 1999 applying democratic principles consistently and sanctioning military and civilian autocrats. Only through such actions can ECOWAS's security mechanism avoid becoming a defense pact for autocrats to protect their friends—a fear often expressed by civil society actors in West Africa.

As Amos Sawyer and Christopher Landsberg argue in Chapters 5 and 6, understanding the link between democracy and security requires a nuanced and multidimensional approach. Sawyer, the president of Liberia's interim government from 1990 to 1994 and one of his country's leading intellectuals, argues that governance is not only closely related to security, but also is the central element in attaining human security. Democracy and security in West Africa are therefore closely related to issues such as poverty, disease, environmental degradation, and political and ethnic identities. Sawyer further notes that the only viable form of governance is one that is rooted in the citizens of a state. He calls for a strengthening of national parliaments and civil societies. While many states in West Africa are formal democracies in the sense of conducting elections at regular intervals, democracy throughout the subregion continues to face many tensions that could easily reverse the gains of the past decade. Pressures for greater freedom within states and for cooperation among them compete with troubling signs of antidemocratic behavior like the harassment of opposition parties, civil society groups, and the press, as well as the conducting of elections of dubious legitimacy. The seeds of democracy are sprouting in West Africa against the backdrop of growing economic difficulties and military conflicts.

Sawyer argues that the machinations of the Cold War and the failed economic policies promoted by the World Bank and the International Monetary Fund (IMF) over the last two decades have contributed significantly to eroding Africa's governance institutions. He notes that the absence of an indigenously inspired African democratization agenda has undermined the legitimacy of the state in many countries. An important trend in the post–Cold War era that has serious implications for democratic consolidation in West Africa is the shift in the balance between the respect for the sovereign rights of states and the respect for the human rights of citizens. As governments seek new ways to prevent conflicts and injustices within states, human security has become a new focus for international relations research and analyses. The international dimensions of democracy, also discussed by Sawyer, explore such changing norms as the promotion of democratization and the external dynamics surrounding it.

Christopher Landsberg investigates initiatives like the CSSDCA, NEPAD, and the AU—which he identifies as part of a "fifth wave of pan-Africanism"—in promoting norms of good governance and democracy that challenge the noninterventionist doctrines of Africa's four post-independence decades. Nigerian president Olusegun Obasanjo's proposal for a conference on security, stability, development, and cooperation in Africa was first discussed at a conference in Kampala in 1991. The final report of the conference proposed establishing a permanent CSSDCA, developing a continental peacekeeping machinery, promoting conflict prevention and military self-reliance in Africa, establishing an African peace council of elder statesmen to mediate conflicts, and drastically reducing military expenditures in Africa. Some of these ideas have been incorporated into the ECOWAS security mechanism of 1999. NEPAD has also been championed by Obasanjo, Senegal's Abdoulaye Wade, and most significantly South Africa's Thabo Mbeki. The plan is based on a straightforward bargain: external donors promise African leaders increased assistance and investment, as well as debt forgiveness and fairer trade, in exchange for the establishment by African leaders of good political and economic governance in a self-monitored peer review process. But NEPAD has its critics. Adebayo Adedeji, for example, notes in this volume that the initiative has not remained faithful to the ideals of the 1980 Lagos Plan of Action (LPA), which promoted the cardinal principles of self-reliance, self-sustainability, and the democratization of the development process.

The changing norms of democratization and sovereignty embodied by initiatives like NEPAD and the CSSDCA have not just remained in the realm of theory, but are also evident in practice. The 1999 Algiers declaration against unconstitutional changes of governments in Africa by the Organization of African Unity (OAU) led to the exclusion of the military governments of Côte d'Ivoire and Comoros from the OAU summit in Lomé in 2000. Within ECOWAS, its new security mechanism of 1999 explicitly permits humanitarian interventions to stem instability and proposes sanctions in cases of unconstitutional changes of government. This last clause was clearly inspired by the precedent of ECOWAS's nonrecognition of the military junta in Sierra Leone from 1997 to 1998 and the removal of the junta from power by a Nigerian-led ECOMOG force. The fact that the Nigerian military regime of autocrat General Sani Abacha led the intervention, however, raised troubling questions about the legitimacy of such interventions.

Vox Populi: Civil Societies as Peacebuilders

In tackling issues of legitimacy in regional interventions, the potential role of civil society has often been overlooked. Civil society actors in West Africa include religious organizations, women's groups, human rights activists, and the media. As Yasmin Jusu-Sheriff, one of the leading lights of Sierra Leone's women's movement in the 1990s, eloquently argues in Chapter 12, several West African governments continue to regard civil society organizations with grave suspicion. In extreme cases, some governments have dismissed such actors as foreign agents and unpatriotic enemies of the state. Several ECOWAS governments have, however, embraced the role of civil society actors in preventing and managing local conflicts and in reintegrating former combatants into local communities. Civil society actors in West Africa have also been useful human rights monitors and promoted democratization in their countries. The ECOWAS security mechanism of 1999 recognizes the role of civil society actors in two important areas: first, in gathering information for the local bureaus of ECOWAS's evolving early warning system; and second, in undertaking mediation efforts through the Council of Elders.

Jusu-Sheriff assesses the role of civil society actors in managing conflicts and promoting democratization in West Africa. In the 1990s, civil society actors in Benin, Mali, and Niger played an instrumental role in democratic transitions. In Liberia, the Inter-Faith Mediation Committee (IFMC) crafted the ECOWAS peace plan of 1990, while the Catholic Justice and Peace Commission monitored human rights issues during Liberia's civil war. In Sierra Leone, a cross section of women's organizations pressured the military government to hold democratic elections in February 1996, while the Inter-Religious Council of Sierra Leone (IRCSL) played a critical role during the negotiation of the Lomé peace agreement of 1999. In Senegal's Casamance region, human rights organizations like Rencontre Africaine pour la Défence des Droits de l'Homme (RADDHO) have sought to play a mediation role, while several traditional leaders and women's organizations led successful efforts to manage the Tuareg problem in northern Mali. But Jusu-Sheriff notes that, in some cases, coalitions of civil society groups in West Africa have failed to operate in a cohesive and effective manner. The lack of institutional capacity has sometimes led to strong personalities dominating these groups, some of which have also been accused of lacking transparency and democratic accountability.

The Men on Horseback: Civil-Military Relations

In a lucid examination by Jimmy Kandeh in Chapter 7, a critical issue that is closely related to governance and democratization is the role of the military in West Africa and the phenomenon of military regimes during the decade of the 1990s in places like Nigeria, Gambia, Ghana, and Sierra Leone. Of the fifteen ECOWAS states, only Cape Verde and Senegal have avoided the scourge of military coups d'état. In seeking to reform West

African militaries and to avoid future putsches, it is vital to explain why West Africa has been the most coup-ridden subregion on the continent. It is also important to understand how the military has exercised power in West Africa in ways that have either fueled or successfully managed conflicts.

Kandeh investigates methods for reforming the military in order to subordinate the institution under civilian control through such means as better recruitment, training, and education. But he also provides a critique of some of the traditional approaches that have been used by external donors to promote security sector reform in West Africa. According to Kandeh, there is a need to move the debate on civil-military relations beyond the issue of civilian control of the military. He argues that what is most relevant for West African societies is not just democratic control of the military, but also incorporating some of the institutional grievances of the military into the agendas of democratic forces.

In Kandeh's opinion, the military remains "uncaptured" by democratic forces, and forms of civilian control of the military in West Africa (payoffs, ethnic selectivity, political co-optation, external security guarantees, and security counterweights) have done more to invite than to prevent coups. In other words, undemocratic instruments of civilian control are inherently counterproductive. Kandeh argues that the engagement of the military by democratic forces can help to foster the attitudinal shift needed for the military's strategic disengagement from the political class. This may require radical strategies like the alignment of popular sectors in society with the lower ranks of the military—the lumpen militariat—in opposition to the political class and senior military officers.

Warlords and War Chests: Rebel Movements, Youths, and the Political Economy of Conflict

In both Liberia and Sierra Leone, the largest factions, the National Patriotic Front of Liberia (NPFL) and the Revolutionary United Front (RUF), aimed to win military victory and inherit the state by controlling its political institutions. In both countries, battles were often fought for control of areas rich in economic resources, including diamonds, gold, timber, bauxite, rutile, rubber, and iron ore. In Liberia, Charles Taylor is estimated to have earned $450 million from illicit exports of resources in territory he controlled during the civil war. In Sierra Leone, RUF rebels and rogue military officers and units controlled an estimated $250 million annual diamond trade. The existence of economic resources in these areas complicated peacemaking efforts, as rebels were able to sell these resources to enrich themselves and buy weapons to continue to prosecute their wars.

In Chapter 8, on rebel movements, by Ibrahim Abdullah and Ismail Rashid, and Chapter 9, on the political economy of conflict, by Eboe Hutchful and Kwesi Aning, the authors criticize what they see as the prejudiced and ill-informed scholarship of several Western authors such as Paul Collier, Richard Dowden, Stephen Ellis, Robert Kaplan, David Keen, and William Reno. They criticize this work for being overly economistic and/or culturally stereotypical. This scholarship is also criticized for lacking a proper political and historical understanding of the context in which conflicts occur in West Africa.

Abdullah and Rashid provide a rich analysis of the roles that the intelligentsia, urban youth, and popular culture have played in postindependence Liberia and Sierra Leone, and demonstrate how these factors have helped to shape national political discourses, the character of rebel movements, and the dynamics of both conflicts. According to the two West African scholars, despite the often brutal methods employed by rebel movements in Liberia and Sierra Leone and their plundering of resources to fund their wars, capturing political power remained their central goal. Hutchful and Aning share this analysis, and focus particular attention in an impressively and tightly argued chapter on the discourses around "greed" and the parochial economic agendas of warlords that authors like Paul Collier see as the key factors driving West Africa's conflicts. They suggest alternative explanations based on the political dynamics of conflict situations, political and economic marginalization (particularly of alienated youths), social exclusion, identity and citizenship, and the erosion of African states. The authors then provide brief case studies of Liberia, Sierra Leone, Nigeria's Niger Delta, and Ghana in support of their arguments.

The wars in Liberia and Sierra Leone both saw widespread human rights abuses and atrocities. Underfed and underpaid fighters, many of them drug-induced child soldiers, were often only nominally controlled by their leaders. The use of child soldiers to prosecute these wars and the exploitation of children as sex slaves by ruthless warlords (increasing the spread of HIV/AIDS) have brought devastation on an entire generation of West Africa's youth. Children constitute about half of all refugees and internally displaced persons from West Africa's wars. The growth in Nigeria of ethnic militia like the Oodua People's Congress, the Bakassi Boys, the Ijaw Youth Movement, and the Arewa People's Congress, often involving disaffected youth, has also become a major source of instability. The phenomenon of unemployed, disaffected youths in rural areas being recruited, sometimes forcibly, by warlords to fight their wars is another major issue of concern to security in West Africa.

These issues are discussed in Chapter 11 by 'Funmi Olonisakin, who worked in the office of the UN Special Representative for Children and Armed Conflict. Olonisakin focuses attention on the special needs of child

soldiers in rehabilitation and reintegration efforts, and the difficulty of convincing their local communities to take back these children, many of whom
have committed atrocities against their own people. She blames the "crisis
of youth" on the lack of capacity within many governments in West Africa
to create employment, provide welfare support, and rehabilitate juveniles.
Olonisakin also criticizes peacemakers in Liberia and Sierra Leone for
offering blanket amnesties to faction fighters, which she sees as fostering a
culture of impunity. In proffering possible solutions to these problems,
Olonisakin argues that any effort to address the plight of war-affected children in West Africa must adopt a coordinated, subregional, and holistic
approach that assesses the potential role of instruments like the ECOWAS
Child Protection Unit (CPU), national truth commissions, and special
courts in addressing these issues.

Swords into Ploughshares:
Small Arms and Light Weapons

West Africa's conflicts in the 1990s were particularly destructive due to the
unregulated spread of armaments throughout the subregion. In Chapter 10,
Comfort Ero and Angela Ndinga-Muvumba address the proliferation of
small arms and light weapons in West Africa. The authors note that these
weapons have escalated the intensity and impact of intrastate armed conflicts in West Africa. Small arms and light weapons are acquired through
legal and illegal channels of supply. An estimated 7 million weapons are
currently circulating in West Africa. In part because of the nature of today's
armed conflicts, the main victims of these weapons are civilians. Ero and
Muvumba note that the proliferation and easy availability of these weapons
often increase the lethality and duration of hostilities, and can adversely
affect postconflict peacebuilding, as current events in the Mano river basin
so clearly demonstrate.

Following the end of Liberia's civil war in 1997, ECOMOG worked
with the UN to collect nearly 20,000 pistols, rifles, and machine guns, and
over 3 million rounds of ammunition. Liberia's weapons destruction program in 1999 mirrored prior initiatives to reduce the impact of small arms
and light weapons like Mali's "Flame of Peace" in 1996, during which
3,000 weapons were collected and destroyed. A conference on conflict prevention, disarmament, and development in West Africa sponsored by the
Malian government in November 1996 culminated in a three-year ECOWAS
moratorium on the export, import, and manufacture of small arms and light
weapons, which was signed in October 1998 by ECOWAS leaders. The
moratorium was extended for a further three years in 2001. The agreement
is a voluntary commitment. It is, in essence, a confidence-building measure

aimed at tackling widespread instability in West Africa. Technical assistance to support implementation of the moratorium is being provided through the UNDP's Programme for the Coordination and Assistance for Security and Development (PCASED).

ECOWAS has been widely praised for declaring a moratorium on the flow of these lethal weapons. However, since the signing of the moratorium, progress in achieving concrete results has been patchy. ECOWAS and PCASED have found it difficult to effect change on the ground. Ero and Muvumba examine the constraints to the progress of the ECOWAS moratorium and consider the options available to ECOWAS and PCASED in influencing the implementation of the moratorium at the national and subregional levels.

* * *

In concluding this introduction, it is worth noting that there is a ray of hope in the birth of a new security mechanism in West Africa. ECOWAS has finally started to create an indigenous system for managing its own conflicts. The organization must now draw from its experiences in Liberia, Sierra Leone, Guinea-Bissau, and Côte d'Ivoire to build an effective security mechanism. ECOWAS's leaders will also have to develop the vision to promote economic integration and create political space for civil society actors to be involved in conflict management and democratization efforts. Subregional leaders must observe common norms of democratic governance that can help subordinate their militaries under civilian rule and prevent rebels from exploiting genuine grievances by taking up arms against the state. National resources will have to be better managed for the benefit of populations, and the proliferation of lethal weapons effectively controlled. Measures must also be taken to reduce the impact of armed conflict on children to prevent the emergence of a "lost generation" of child soldiers. Finally, external actors like the UN, the United States, and European powers, some of which have fueled conflicts and divisions in the past, must now contribute positively to peacebuilding efforts in this troubled region. It is these key challenges that this book seeks to address. We hope that this volume will contribute to academic and policy debates through chapters that are both intellectually rigorous and policy-relevant.

Notes

1. See Boutros Boutros-Ghali, *An Agenda for Peace* (New York: United Nations, 1992); and Boutros Boutros-Ghali, *Supplement to an Agenda for Peace*, UN Doc. S/1995/1, 3 January 1995.

2. See Adekeye Adebajo and Chris Landsberg, "Back to the Future: UN Peace-keeping in Africa," *International Peacekeeping* 7, no. 4 (Winter 2000): 161–188; Christopher Clapham, "The United Nations and Peacekeeping in Africa," in Mark Malan, ed., *Whither Peacekeeping in Africa?* (Halfway House, South Africa: Institute for Security Studies, 1999), pp. 25–44; Marrack Goulding, "The United Nations and Conflict in Africa Since the Cold War," *African Affairs* 98, no. 391 (April 1999): 155–166; and Agostinho Zacarias, *The United Nations and International Peacekeeping* (London: I. B. Tauris, 1996).

3. See S. K. B. Asante, *African Development: Adebayo Adedeji's Alternative Strategies* (Ibadan, Nigeria: Spectrum Books, 1991).

4. Adebayo Adedeji, "Prospects of Regional Economic Co-operation in West Africa," *Journal of Modern African Studies* 8, no. 2 (1970): 213–231.

5. On the rivalry between the CEAO and ECOWAS, see S. K. B. Asante, "ECOWAS/CEAO: Conflict and Cooperation in West Africa," in Ralph Onwuka and Amadu Sesay, eds., *The Future of Regionalism in Africa* (London: Macmillan, 1985), pp. 74–95; Daniel Bach, "The Politics of West African Economic Cooperation: CEAO and ECOWAS," *Journal of Modern African Studies* 21, no. 4 (1983): 601–621; Olatunde Ojo, "Nigeria and the Formation of ECOWAS," *International Organisation* 34, no. 4 (Autumn 1980): 571–601; and Omotayo Olaniyan, "Nigeria and ECOWAS: A Role and Problem Analysis," in G. O. Olusanya and R. A. Akindele, eds., *Nigeria's External Relations* (Ibadan, Nigeria: Ibadan University Press, 1986), pp. 126–140.

6. See, for example, International Peace Academy (IPA) and ECOWAS, *Toward a Pax West Africana: Building Peace in a Troubled Sub-Region,* Abuja, Nigeria, September 2001; and IPA and ECOWAS, *Operationalizing the ECOWAS Mechanism for Conflict Prevention, Management, Resolution, Peacekeeping, and Security,* Dakar, Senegal, August 2002; both available at www.ipacademy.org.

7. For interesting African perspectives on this issue, see IPA/Center on International Cooperation (CIC), *Refashioning the Dialogue: Regional Perspectives on the Brahimi Report on UN Peace Operations,* Regional Meetings February–March 2001, pp. 6–11.

8. Report of the Inter-Agency Mission to West Africa, *Towards a Comprehensive Approach to Durable and Sustainable Solutions to Priority Needs and Challenges in West Africa,* UN Doc. S/2001/434, 2 May 2001, p. 15.

PART 1

Context

2

ECOWAS:
A Retrospective Journey

Adebayo Adedeji

In this chapter, I have been specifically requested to be retrospective, to undertake an agonizing review of the past, to look back in order to be able to look forward. Indeed, it is a well-known saying among the Yoruba of southwest Nigeria that when a young person falls, he or she gets up and looks forward with a view to continuing the journey; but when the same fate befalls an elderly person, he or she looks back in retrospect. As the English poet T. S. Eliot has rightly reminded us, both the past and the future are organically linked with the present:

> Time present and time past
> Are both perhaps present in time future
> And time future contained in time past.[1]

Of course, there is no denying the fact that to undertake a retrospective journey of regional integration arrangements inevitably involves an analytical history of West Africa during the precolonial period, during the era of colonialism, and during West Africa's four postindependence decades.

Before the coming of Europeans, West Africa had been the home of some of the most remarkable achievements of early black civilizations, with such illustrious empires as Songhay, Mali, Ghana, the Sokoto caliphate, Benin, and Oyo. Education and the involvement of the people in governance, even during the colonial era, were quite advanced in West Africa, and agitation for political independence began virtually from the beginning of the colonial era. West Africans left the colonialists in no doubt that their rule would not last for long. Because the climate was considered inhospitable for Europeans, West Africa was spared the presence of white settlers, which complicated the decolonization process in eastern and southern Africa. It was not surprising, therefore, that West Africa achieved political independence before any other African subregion.

While there is no denying its self-evident geographical existence and the sometimes broad territorial reach of its ancient empires and states, the idea of "West Africa" in terms of a territorially organized Westphalian space is a modern development—a postindependence phenomenon. Before independence, West Africa for the British meant their four colonies and protectorates: Nigeria, the Gold Coast (now Ghana), Sierra Leone, and Gambia. In contrast, French West Africa was, until 1958, a "federation" of eight colonies: Mauritania, Senegal, French Sudan (now Mali), French Guinea, Dahomey (now Benin), Niger, Côte d'Ivoire, and Upper Volta (now Burkina Faso). The French-administered part of Togo, a trusteeship territory, had a separate status. As for Portugal, its colonies of Cape Verde, São Tomé and Principe, and Guinea-Bissau constituted its West African empire. So glaring were the different perceptions and definitions of West Africa that Senegal's founding president, Léopold Senghor, once advocated that the subregion be extended from Cape Verde and Mauritania to Zaire (now the Democratic Republic of Congo). This was an attempt to balance the future strength of the Nigerian colossus during negotiations for an economic union in West Africa in the early 1970s.

In discussing the origins of West African integration, due recognition must be accorded to the great foresight of the fifth pan-African congress, held in Manchester, England, in October 1945. The congress recommended the establishment of a West African economic union "as a means of combating the exploitation of the economic resources of the West African territories and for ensuring the participation of the indigenous people in the industrial development of West Africa."[2] But the West Africa that the conferees in Manchester had in mind was "British West Africa." This was to be expected of a predominantly English-speaking conference organized by leaders from British colonies in Africa, the West Indies, and the United States. A leading figure in organizing this congress was Ghana's first ruler, Kwame Nkrumah.

The definitive delineation of West Africa was undertaken early in the 1960s by the UN's Economic Commission for Africa (ECA). The ECA came to the conclusion that the most viable approach to regional integration was one that, as a first step, embraced narrower geographical areas as opposed to an all-embracing continental organization. Accordingly, the ECA divided the African continent into four subregions: eastern and southern, central, northern, and western. Following the ECA's regional structure, West Africa's sixteen member states established the Economic Community of West African States (ECOWAS) in 1975.[3] In taking this step, ECOWAS leaders had fully endorsed the precise ECA delineation of West Africa as a region extending from Cape Verde and Mauritania to Nigeria.

The Balkanization of West Africa

All sixteen ECOWAS states were the creation of colonialism, born out of the rivalries and geopolitical strategies of European imperial powers. Their artificiality has constituted the greatest obstacle to the achievement of more stable and dynamic statehood. Independent West African countries are effectively states that have struggled to transform themselves into more coherent nations. With regard to the objective of stable statehood, the colonial legacy of standing armies with their military machines and imported technologies of destruction made it relatively easy for a few ambitious men in uniform to coerce and subject their citizens to their authority. Military rule in Africa was facilitated by the fact that national political institutions had been hastily cobbled together by departing colonial rulers just before independence. The military, on the other hand, had been a permanent feature of colonial rule and the "men on horseback" were better organized and often better disciplined than the emerging political leadership in West Africa. It was clear that in any struggle for power, the military would have little problem in pushing the civilian leaders aside.[4]

We must not forget that throughout the colonial era, the imperial powers never put in place any proactive policy for indigenous leadership development. The "indirect rule" of Lord Frederick Lugard deformed and crippled traditional modes of governance in Africa. Traditional rulers, who were mostly illiterate by Western standards, were alienated from their people, particularly the rapidly emerging class of Westernized educated elites. The cumulative consequence of this process at the dawn of independence in the 1960s was the central dilemma of the struggle for power between the Westernized civilian political leadership and the postcolonial armed forces. As J. I. Elaigwu and Ali Mazrui succinctly put it, "During the colonial period, traditional rulers were on the defensive as they faced the challenge of the westernized intelligentsia. Since independence, the western-educated leaders have been on the defensive as they face the challenge of the military."[5]

The dismantling at independence of regional political integration processes removed all the vestiges of countervailing power that could have moderated the ambitions of West Africa's militaries. The French started the process of dismantling Afrique Occidentale Française (French West Africa) in 1956. Without consulting with African leaders—not even with Africans who were members of the French National Assembly—Gaston Defferre, the minister of Overseas France, completely reversed the long-standing policy of successive French governments in centralizing power at the "federal" level under the high commissioner. Arguing that the French West African federation was too large economically, administratively, and politically, Defferre pushed forward the *loi cadre* that launched the process of the balkanization of West Africa. When in 1958, under *enfant terrible* Sékou Touré, French Guinea rejected, by over 90 percent of votes cast, the constitutional proposals granting membership to colonies in a French community instead of outright independence, the death knell of the community was sounded.[6] In retaliation, President Charles de Gaulle abolished French West Africa as a political entity.

The different countries within the former federation reacted differently to de Gaulle's action. The richest country within the former federation, Côte d'Ivoire, welcomed the move, since Abidjan had always felt that Senegal and others benefited more from the federation. Senegal and Mali (then French Sudan) attempted to oppose the balkanization of French West Africa by creating the Federation of Mali, which initially also included Upper Volta (Burkina Faso) and Dahomey (Benin). But this new federation could not be sustained once independence had been granted separately to each of the constituent parts of French West Africa. Thus, by 1960, instead of one viable independent nation emerging from French West Africa— appropriately renamed, no doubt—there emerged eight independent states in addition to Togo. France, which had at first ruled out independence for its African colonies and had favored incorporating them into a French union and later into a French community, had radically changed course. Paris had opted for a policy of balkanization after Sékou Touré called its bluff in 1958. Had de Gaulle not overreacted to Touré's apparent affront to the "Mother Country," the history of West Africa would certainly have been very different. If the federation of the eight countries had been sustained into independence (as the Nigerian federation, for example, had been preserved by the British), the political fragmentation that was imposed by European cartographers in 1884–1885 at the Berlin conference would have been partially ameliorated, particularly since these French territories were less populated and developed than British West Africa.[7]

Britain, in contrast to France, entertained no illusions of a British community or union. London granted independence to its four West African territories separately. Ghana became independent in 1957, followed by Nigeria in 1960, Sierra Leone in 1961, and Gambia in 1965. This staggered pace of decolonization had a negative impact on the maintenance and sustenance of joint institutions established by the colonial authority. Ghana, which became independent first, insisted, under Kwame Nkrumah, on the disbandment of these joint institutions. The common anglophone West African currency was replaced by the cedi in Ghana, the pound and later the naira in Nigeria, the leone in Sierra Leone, and the dalasu in Gambia. West

African Airways, which had operated air services between the four countries, was disbanded, and national agricultural research institutions replaced
those established by Britain to cater for its four colonies. Nkrumah,
renowned historically as a visionary pan-Africanist, had thus paradoxically
inflicted great damage to the process of subregional integration in West
Africa.

The approach of the countries that emerged from the disintegrated
French West Africa was the opposite of the situation in former British West
Africa. With strong encouragement from France, they quickly recognized
the need to overcome, or at least minimize, the restrictions and constraints
that fragmentation had imposed on their development through the vigorous
and relentless promotion of cooperation and integration. Some of these initiatives predated independence, and France, after breaking up the federation, maintained close political, economic, and military ties with its former
colonies after independence (see Chapter 15). The Union Douanière de
l'Afrique de l'Ouest (UDAO, West African Customs Union), consisting of
Côte d'Ivoire, Senegal, Dahomey, Mauritania, Niger, Mali, and Upper Volta,
was created in June 1959. The UDAO was replaced seven years later by the
Union Douanière et Economique de l'Afrique de l'Ouest (UDEAO, West
African Customs and Economic Union). Both organizations failed woefully
in achieving their integrationist goals, and the Communauté Economique de
l'Afrique de l'Ouest (CEAO) was created in 1973, with strong French
encouragement (see Chapters 3 and 4). In addition to organizations encom-
passing all eight former "federating" countries and Togo, some initiatives at
the subgroup level were undertaken. The Conseil de l'Entente (1959),
whose members included Côte d'Ivoire, Upper Volta, Niger, and Dahomey,
and the Organisation des Etats Riverains du Senégal (1968) are two examples of such initiatives. The CEAO took the wind out of the sails of the
Conseil de l'Entente, while the Organisation pour la Mise en Valuer du
Fleuve Senégal (OMVS, Organization for the Development of the Senegal
River) replaced the Organisation des Etats Riverains du Senégal.

One striking feature of all these attempts at regional integration was the
perpetuation of the divide between francophone and anglophone West
Africa. This divide remained virtually intact and preserved the colonial
legacy. Thus, in spite of having achieved independence, West African
states, particularly the French-speaking ones, continued to depend on their
former colonial rulers for trade, investment, aid, and security. The few
attempts to break this neocolonial dependence occurred at the bilateral and
trilateral levels, involving the important experiments by Nigeria-Niger,
Ghana-Guinea-Mali, and Senegal-Gambia. All these initiatives, however,
failed to achieve their goals due to problems of political will and economic
balkanization. At the multilateral level, such initiatives as the River Niger
Commission and the West African Free Trade Area (1964), initiated by Côte

d'Ivoire, Guinea, Liberia, and Sierra Leone, were either ineffective or failed to take off at all.

Despite these disappointments, in retrospect the decade of the 1960s can be regarded as the halcyon years of African attempts at integration. The creation of interstate groupings fostered regional cooperation. However, there was no doubt that by the end of the 1960s, integration projects in West Africa were in serious trouble as the different groupings began to disintegrate. The attempt by the ECA in 1966 to establish an effective and sustainable regional cooperation grouping that would cut across the anglophone-francophone divide in West Africa came to nothing. This effort failed despite the holding of several meetings by West Africa's fourteen independent countries in Niamey, Accra, Dakar, and Monrovia to consider the draft articles of association for an organization to promote economic integration that had been prepared by the ECA secretariat in Addis Ababa, Ethiopia.

The ECOWAS Vision

It was the failure to achieve a breakthrough in establishing a sustainable process of regional integration in West Africa that transcended the colonial divide that led the Inter-African Public Administration seminar (an annual meeting of senior African mandarins) to devote its eighth annual meeting in Monrovia in November 1969 to the subject of regional integration. I was asked to present a paper on West African integration at the meeting. I started my presentation by noting the low volume of intercommunity trade in West Africa, the nonconvertibility of the various currencies, and the multiplicity of languages, ethnicities, and cultures. I went on to advocate pragmatism and prioritization as essential to economic integration, and identified six priority areas: the building of a regional road network; the creation of a regional airline that would absorb and replace all existing airlines; the provision of other regional infrastructure to facilitate trade and investment; the establishment of a clearing and payments union; the facilitation of the free movement of people, goods, and services within West Africa; and the abolition of foreign exchange controls. These priorities were to be underpinned by five essential preconditions: first, a coordinated regional approach to food, agricultural, and industrial development, particularly in the intermediate and capital goods industry; second, the establishment of sovereign control by each state over its economy rather than allowing it to be allied to outside forces; third, political goodwill, cooperation, and total commitment to regional cooperation were to be fostered at the highest levels of government; fourth, the linguistic division of the region into francophone, lusophone, and anglophone was to be overcome; and fifth, each state was to establish, within its government machinery, mechanisms such as a permanent secretariat and an interministerial party, to ensure the implementation of subregional protocols signed by heads of state. I recommended that every West African government should establish a ministry for West African economic cooperation and integration, to be headed by a cabinet minister whose success or failure as minister should be judged by how much effective cooperation was achieved in the subregion during his or her tenure in office. A revised version of the paper I presented in Monrovia was later published in the *Journal of Modern African Studies* in July 1970.[8] At the time of this publication, I was a pure academic. Since I did not have the gift of prophecy, I could not have foreseen that in early 1972 I would be challenged to take all the actions necessary to actualize the proposals in the paper.

Two years after the Monrovia seminar, I became minister of economic development and reconstruction in General Yakubu Gowon's government in Nigeria, responsible, inter alia, for regional cooperation and development. Without any doubt, my ministerial appointment in 1972 provided me with a historic challenge to put some of my theoretical prescriptions into practice. This was indeed a golden opportunity for translating the hypothesis of pragmatic developmental regionalism in West Africa into reality. And it was a battle royal—Herculean and daunting, as the forces of neocolonialism were more than ever determined to derail the effort.

Given my long-standing commitment to economic cooperation and integration, I accepted the challenge most enthusiastically, since I have always believed that economic cooperation among African states is a conditio sine qua non for the achievement of national socioeconomic goals and not an "extra" to be given consideration after the process of national development has become well advanced.[9] This commitment comes from my observation and deep concern about the conditions in virtually all of sub-Saharan Africa. West Africa suffers from inadequate supply of competent entrepreneurs in both the private and public sectors, scarcity of skilled manpower, lack of indigenous technological know-how to assess and access natural resource endowments, limited interindustry integration, and lack of regional infrastructural facilities and services (particularly banking). Life expectancy at birth varies considerably in West Africa—as low as 37.9 years in Sierra Leone and as high as 69.4 years in Cape Verde. Only in eight countries is the average above 50 years (see Table 2.2). Three of the countries—Niger, Burkina Faso, and Mali—are landlocked, and all but four—Nigeria, Côte d'Ivoire, Ghana, and Cape Verde—have been classified as least developed countries. Only Nigeria, Ghana, and Côte d'Ivoire have populations of more than 15 million people. Without exception, all fifteen ECOWAS states are currently heavily indebted. Regional economic cooperation must therefore be the backbone of *developmental nationalism,* a tool to combat and reduce the excessive external economic dependence of

developing countries.[10] Only by achieving a breakthrough in regional economic integration and development can West Africa make the transformation from being merely a "geographical expression" into an economic
region and common market.

Entente Cordiale: The Nigeria-Togo Initiative

In 1972, the initiative that culminated in the establishment of ECOWAS
was launched by Nigeria and Togo. Three years thereafter, on 28 May 1975,
the treaty establishing ECOWAS was signed in Lagos by fifteen heads of
state and government (Mauritania signed shortly after). Barely five days
after this historic event, I was on my way to Addis Ababa to take over as
executive secretary of the UN Economic Commission for Africa.

A heavy burden fell on my shoulders when I was asked to lead the
process of reactivating and reenergizing the economic cooperation and integration process in West Africa. This occurred in 1972 after both General
Yakubu Gowon and General Gnassingbé Eyadéma had, in the communiqué
issued after Gowon's state visit to Lomé during April 1972, announced
their decision to sponsor jointly the ECOWAS initiative. I was clear in my
mind that the overarching objectives of the project should be the ideas outlined in the paper I had presented at the Monrovia seminar, with "pragmatism" and "prioritization" as the key watchwords.

The joint sponsorship of the initiative by Nigeria, West Africa's largest
and most powerful state, and Togo, one of the region's smallest and poorest
countries—the one an anglophone country and the other a francophone—
conveyed a powerful message to the rest of the region. Gowon and Eyadéma gave Henri Dogo, Togo's trade minister, and me marching orders to
establish a community that would transcend linguistic barriers and include
all of West Africa's states. Our first task, therefore, was to establish a meeting of minds between Lagos and Lomé on all major issues and to agree on
a program of work. Accordingly, a joint Nigeria-Togo ministerial consultation took place in Lagos in June 1972 under my leadership. There was little
difficulty in reaching agreement on how to proceed. The ideas contained in
my 1970 journal article became our guiding principles. Accordingly, we
embarked on the arduous journey of taking our integration message to
every independent West African country to ascertain the reactions of their
leaders to our proposals and to build support for the ECOWAS project.[11]

The Nigeria-Togo joint ministerial delegation was well received in all
twelve countries that we visited.[12] Without exception, we were received by
the head of state and government in each country and held meetings at ministerial and technical levels. In virtually every country, the responses to our

proposals for a West African economic community were positive. Almost every leader agreed with the fundamental principle that the time had come for economic cooperation in West Africa to transcend inherited colonial divisions. Everyone naturally realized that the real task of negotiating the details of a future union still lay ahead

Even at this early stage, the Nigeria-Togo joint ministerial delegation was not in any doubt that, in the spectrum of support, Senegal's Léopold Senghor and Guinea's Sékou Touré were at opposite ends of the integration spectrum. Touré gave the initiative his unqualified support, and Senghor, while not opposed, wanted two conditions to be satisfied before francophone West African states could cooperate with their anglophone counterparts. First, the poet-president insisted that West Africans must be fluent in both French and English, and second, Senghor demanded that the West African subregion be extended geographically to Kinshasa to bring Zaire into the proposed economic community. Like France, Senegal has never been able to hide its fear of a strong Nigeria dominating West Africa. Senghor's idea of including Zaire in ECOWAS was an attempt to balance Nigeria's strength.

As leader of the joint ministerial delegation and its spokesman, I respectfully rejected both propositions. I asked Senghor whether his colleague and brother, Zairean president Mobutu Sese Seko, had indicated to him that his country would like to be part of West Africa rather than remain in Central Africa where geography had placed it. Regarding the precondition that all West Africans must be fluent in both French and English before cooperation could take place, I reminded Senghor that neither of these two foreign languages was important to the vast majority of people in West Africa. I noted that West Africa should emulate the example of East Africa by developing its own lingua franca as part of the process of cooperation and integration rather than as a precondition for it. I warmly congratulated President Senghor on his ambition to translate all the works of William Shakespeare into French. I added that, while this feat would admirably qualify him for membership in the Académie Française (French Academy), it would have very little effect on the life of the average Senegalese, not to mention the average West African, now or in the future.

At that point in the discussion, the president abruptly ended the meeting and sent the delegation "down" to then–prime minister Abdou Diouf (who succeeded Senghor as president in 1980). The prime minister never referred to Senghor's two conditions throughout the joint delegation's long discussion with him. Diouf was more forthcoming in his support for ECOWAS than Senghor and assured us that Senegal would be one of the founding members of any organization that emerged from our efforts. Indeed, when the Lagos summit of May 1975 took place, it was Diouf who represented and signed the treaty on behalf of Senegal. President Senghor had preferred to go to the United States to accept an honorary degree from one of the relatively unknown land-grant state colleges in that country!

At the other end of the spectrum was President Ahmed Sékou Touré of Guinea, who felt that the process of negotiations for an economic community should be accelerated so that an all–West African community could be established by 1973. Indeed, the Guinean leader, together with Mali's Modibo Keita and Ghana's Kwame Nkrumah, had blazed the integration trail when they founded the Ghana-Guinea-Mali Union in 1958 as a first step toward the Union of African States. In July 1959 a bilateral meeting in the Liberian town of Saniquellie had explored the possibility of the political and economic integration of Liberia and Guinea. This was a precursor of the Mano River Union, founded in 1973 between both countries and Sierra Leone.[13]

In the middle of this spectrum of integration "hawks" and "doves" was Ivorian president Félix Houphouët-Boigny whose anticolonial stance in the 1940s was less well-known because he had been pressured by the French in 1950 to disaffiliate his Parti Démocratique de Côte d'Ivoire (PDCI) from the French Communist Party. As a deputy in the French National Assembly, Houphouët-Boigny had ignored the opposition of French Socialist deputies to establish and lead, between 1946 and 1950, the Rassemblement Démocratique Africain (RDA, African Democratic Rally)—a coalition of African political parties dedicated to the anticolonial struggle. The RDA's deputies— seven in the French National Assembly at this time—were affiliated with the French Communist Party.

The French Communist Party was expelled from the French government in May 1947 and an attempt was made to restore colonialism through the reconquest of Indochina and the repression of the nationalist movement in Madagascar. Houphouët's RDA was not spared. In order to reduce the political weight and influence of Côte d'Ivoire within French West Africa, Upper Volta was excised from it in 1947. (Since 1932, Upper Volta had been integrated with Côte d'Ivoire by French colonial administrators.) In 1949, the French governor of Upper Volta resorted to violence in order to dismantle Houphouët's RDA. Many Ivorian leaders were arrested and brutalized. On the advice of such fellow socialists as François Mitterrand and René Pléven, minister of Overseas France, Houphouët decided to throw in the towel and undertook a tactical retreat. It was from this time that the Ivorian leader metamorphosed into a member of the French establishment and the main interlocutor between France and sub-Saharan Africa. But Houphouët's sense of African nationalism never disappeared.

The Ivorian leader's warm welcome of the Nigeria-Togo initiative did not therefore come as a surprise to those of us who knew about his anticolonial past. Economic integration would also facilitate the reunification of Houphouët's Baule kinsmen, a large number of whom lived in Liberia and Ghana. Houphouët was particularly delighted that Nigeria was leading this initiative and stated categorically that as long as Nigeria continued to play this leadership role, his country would fully support the process.

However, in Nigeria, Houphouët's support and assurances were received with mixed feelings because he had put his considerable diplomatic weight on the side of Biafra during the Nigerian civil war of 1967 to 1970. The Biafran rebel leader, Emeka Ojukwu, had also been given sanctuary in Abidjan after the end of the war.[14] It took much effort to persuade some of my cabinet colleagues in Lagos that without Houphouët and Côte d'Ivoire, there could be no genuine cooperation and integration in West Africa. Côte d'Ivoire was quite simply the richest and most important state in francophone West Africa and its leader was among the most influential members of the Francophonie. When early in 1975 the French government, under President Georges Pompidou, made the last attempt to prevent the birth of ECOWAS by convening an emergency summit of former French West African countries in Niamey to warn them about the elephant (Nigeria) and its appetite for grass (the francophone West African countries), it was Houphouët-Boigny who saved the day. He assured Pompidou that an all-inclusive West African economic community would neither pose a threat to continued French influence in West Africa nor affect the personal loyalties and allegiances of francophone countries to France. Houphouët argued strongly in favor of the Nigerian initiative, urging his fellow leaders to give their full support to the creation of ECOWAS.

After our joint mission to West Africa, the first-ever conference of West African ministers responsible for economic development and planning, as well as trade and commerce, was convened in Lomé in April 1973. In order to ensure that the private sector in each country was involved in the process, I urged my colleagues to include the representatives of the organized private sector in their respective national delegations. I included the late Chief Henry Fajemirokun, then president of the Nigerian Association of Chambers of Commerce, Industry, Mines, and Agriculture (NACCIMA), in the Nigerian delegation. The various representatives of national chambers of commerce took advantage of the Lomé ministerial conference to launch the process that eventually led to the creation of the Federation of West African Chambers of Commerce in 1974.

Not only was it unanimously agreed in Lomé that an Economic Community of West African States should be established, but both Nigeria and Togo were mandated to prepare the draft treaty that was to be sent to the various countries for study in preparation for a second ministerial conference. This meeting took place in Monrovia in 1974, and it was agreed that the summit to sign the ECOWAS treaty should take place during the first half of 1975 in Lagos. This meeting took place on 28 May 1975, and ECOWAS was officially born in Lagos. The cooperation efforts that resulted

from the Nigeria-Togo initiative had finally borne fruit with the creation of
ECOWAS.

28 May 1975:
The Dawn of a New Era in West African Integration?

The creation of an economic community in West Africa stretching from
Cape Verde and Mauritania to Nigeria exploded two myths—first, that differences in language, culture, and economic development necessarily render cooperation impossible in West Africa; and second, that cooperation
between relatively small countries and big ones is harmful and could therefore not occur in West Africa (see Box 2.1). Throughout the three-year
negotiating process preceding ECOWAS's birth, the all-or-nothing
approach to economic cooperation and integration was replaced by a pragmatic approach that argued that the long-term benefits that would accrue
to individual countries—small and large—would make short- and medium-
term sacrifices worthwhile. This approach further recognized that it would
be unrealistic to expect spectacular results from this integration effort in the
short to medium term. Pragmatism had triumphed over pessimism.

The enthusiasm with which ECOWAS was established was such that at
least two heads of state arrived in Lagos with their countries' instruments of
ratification of a treaty they had not yet signed! When this became known, I
was obliged to put pressure on Nigeria's attorney-general to prepare the
country's own instrument of ratification for submission immediately after
the signing ceremony so that Nigeria, as the host country, would be the first
to ratify the treaty. Indeed, within a few days after the signing ceremony,
more than half of ECOWAS's members had ratified the treaty. A few weeks
later, all sixteen countries had submitted their instruments of ratification.
By any international standard, this was an impressive feat.

By July 1976 the five protocols called for under Article 62 of the
ECOWAS treaty had been prepared by the newly established ECOWAS
secretariat in Lagos, working closely with the ECA and the International
Monetary Fund (IMF). These protocols were then submitted to the first
meeting of ECOWAS's Council of Ministers, which was held in Accra in
July 1976. The five protocols were:

- contributions of member states to the ECOWAS budget;
- reexportation within ECOWAS of goods imported from third countries;
- the Fund for Cooperation, Compensation, and Development;
- assessment of loss of revenue by member states as a result of trade
  liberalization within the community;
- definition of the concept of products originating from participating
  states.

Box 2.1 The Political Significance of the ECOWAS Treaty

The signing of the ECOWAS Treaty was quite a remarkable achievement. That 16 independent African countries stretching from Mauritania to Nigeria and bounded to the north by the Sahara, countries at varying levels of development, with different historical and cultural backgrounds and speaking different languages (and here I am not thinking only of the foreign languages—English, French and Portuguese—but also of the multiplicity of indigenous African languages, quite a few of which fortunately cut across political boundaries), that all these countries unanimously agreed to the establishment of an economic community that cuts across linguistic and cultural barriers was no small feat. Indeed, it was a visible demonstration of how far the West African Governments and leaders have developed in realism and political maturity since the early unsuccessful attempts to establish a similar economic grouping in West Africa in the 1960s. As General Acheampong, Ghana's Head of State, so rightly stated in his address to the first session of the ECOWAS Council of Ministers which took place at Accra last month, "by this single act more than 120 million people of West Africa, through their representatives who assembled in Lagos, put a seal on their determination to end the centuries of division and artificial barriers imposed on them from outside and to recreate together the kind of homogeneous society which existed before the colonialists invaded our shores."

Source: Adebayo Adedeji, "Collective Self-Reliance in Developing Africa: Scope, Prospects, and Problems," address delivered at the first international conference of the Economic Community of West African States, Lagos, August 1976.

The first three protocols were adopted at the Accra meeting, but the last two protocols proved to be controversial and contentious. Only after much hard bargaining did they reach ECOWAS's protocol statute book. It was really a shame that the ECOWAS Council of Ministers allowed itself, at its very first session, to get bogged down by the classic problems of trade liberalization, thus giving the impression that this was the organization's only concern. When all the principal goals of the ECOWAS treaty are taken together, it is clear that the overarching mission of the organization is the transformation of production and the reorganization of distribution at the national level in such a manner as to forge intercountry policy, as well as program and project development and harmonization. Through a misplaced focus due to a misunderstanding of the overall objectives of ECOWAS and the priorities required to achieve them, seven danger signals (see Box 2.2) began to rear their ugly heads. A static, classical approach to economic cooperation began to gain prominence within ECOWAS at the expense of a dynamic, pragmatic approach. Thus the optimism of May 1975 turned out to be short-lived. Within a short space of time, the bang of ECOWAS's creation had become a whimper because the skeptics, cynics, and orthodox market integrationists had replaced the visionaries, pragmatists, and developmental integrationists in determining the future course of ECOWAS.

Box 2.2 Seven Potential Danger Points in Economic Cooperation

- Half-hearted commitment to the goals of economic cooperation manifested *inter alia* by insufficient perception of the imperative of collective self-reliance and lack of sustained political commitment, particularly at the highest level of government.
- Placing too much emphasis on institutional arrangements at the expense of substantive definition of objectives.
- Absence of appropriate machinery at the national level to deal effectively with community problems, including having in the cabinet a minister responsible for regional cooperation.
- The often limited scope and authority of the Community's organs, the invariably low quality of the generality of staff and the lack of the observance of the principles of the need to enhance efficiency, effectiveness, initiative and innovation in the recruitment process.
- The non-involvement of all stakeholders—business, industrial and financial enterprises and institutions, professional associations and the civil society and community-based organizations—in policy formulation, implementation and monitoring.
- The insistence on a static and impossible demand for exact quantification of benefits accruing to individual partners. Focus is often narrowed down only to financial aspects, foreign exchange, and public revenue loss, to the neglect of critical real factors such as skill development, technology, the employment multiplier, production linkages, etc.
- Negative interference by external forces and exogenous factors which undermine the commitment of participating countries, or some of them, and consequently derail the process.

Source: Adebayo Adedeji, *Toward a Dynamic African Economy* (London: Frank Cass, 1989), pp. 288–289.

The Past Continues to Haunt the Present and the Future of West Africa

The optimism at the birth of ECOWAS in 1975 was short-lived because conventional wisdom and orthodox thinking had taken over the process of integration. Lateral thinkers who see everything only in orthodox and doctrinaire terms came to dominate the integration debate within ECOWAS. For such people, the raison d'être of economic cooperation and integration is trade liberalization, creating a customs union, and establishing a fund for compensation. This school of thought is not impressed with the argument that economic cooperation must be seen, first and foremost, as an instrument for national survival and socioeconomic transformation as well as a forum for forging common strategies and policies. Without accepting this principle, economic cooperation cannot bring about the transformation of national and subregional production. In other words, ECOWAS, in its formative years, should have focused on such activities as forging a common food and agriculture policy, a common approach and strategy to fighting drought and desertification, a coordinated industrialization strategy and program, joint efforts at developing regionwide communication and transportation systems (including air transportation), and a common approach to debt relief. In addition to providing mutual support in pursuit of national socioeconomic objectives, economic cooperation should have provided a forum for collective bargaining with third parties.

Unfortunately, the political commitment that had been built up during the three-year period of negotiations of the ECOWAS treaty (1972–1975) dissipated because of the failure to address the subregion's real sectors. This failure was captured most poignantly by Lansana Kouyaté, ECOWAS's former executive secretary, in his 2000 interim report:

> The integration process in West Africa has so far been such that attention has been focused on the choice of the institutions needed for integration, thus relegating the actual business of building the community to the background. Instead of asking with whom, in what context and under what conditions integration might be possible, attention has rather been on the institutions to be established and the measures to be promoted. Giving priority to identifying institutional arrangements completely diverts attention from the vital task of determining socio-economic objectives and setting priorities.[15]

In support of this contention, the silver jubilee anniversary publication by the ECOWAS secretariat titled "The Economic Community of West African States: Achievements and Prospects, 1975–2000" bluntly admitted that "an analysis of the West African experience of integration within the context of ECOWAS shows a poor record with regard to the Community programmes."[16] The publication also maintains that the principle of supranationality contained in the revised ECOWAS treaty of 1993 was not being applied. It maintained that several protocols were being contravened, especially those pertaining to free movement of goods and persons. The report concluded that the "situation shows clearly that a sense of belonging . . . is cruelly lacking."[17] The failure to address the real sectors has been aggravated by the lack of a breakthrough in trade liberalization and the failure to create a customs union. Thus today, ECOWAS has not fulfilled six of its most important goals. First, trade liberalization has not taken place, even though the original target date for its completion was January 1990. Second, there is as yet no ECOWAS common external tariff, which is a necessary step toward the creation of a customs union. Third, the goal of the harmonization of economic and fiscal policies remains unrealized. Fourth, although it had been decided, as early as 1983, that a single monetary zone was to be created within ECOWAS—a fundamental integration objective—this ambition remains unfulfilled. Turning the ECA-sponsored West African clearinghouse into an ECOWAS-led West African monetary agency would be one sensible way of facilitating this process. Fifth, ECOWAS, despite its current plans for a community levy to raise revenues to finance its work, has failed to design and implement a funding formula to replace the existing reliance on member state contributions that has resulted in the accumulation of arrears by many ECOWAS states (unpaid dues stood at $38.1 million in 2000). Finally, many ECOWAS countries have consistently failed to ratify and implement agreed protocols.

In other words, no effective integration has taken place in ECOWAS— not in trade, not in production, and not in laying the foundation for the economic transformation of West Africa. Even the free movement of persons is wracked by countless problems and obstacles. In spite of the praiseworthy abolition of visa requirements for ECOWAS citizens, West African travelers are still confronted by administrative harassment and extortion at border posts. Security checkpoints abound all along subregional routes. Nigeria is the worst offender, with seven checkpoints on every 100-kilometer stretch of the road between Lagos and Abidjan, while Togo and Burkina Faso each have four checkpoints on every 100-kilometer stretch of their regional highways. Benin and Niger each have three checkpoints on every 100-kilometer stretch of their own transnational highways.

With regard to production and economic transformation, the adoption in June 1987 of an ECOWAS four-year economic recovery plan (ERP) failed woefully to launch a process of sustained subregional development. The ERP was divided into two parts: one dealt with short-term policy reform, while the other concerned itself with the promotion of an integrated investment program in regional and national projects in key real sectors. The first part of the ERP was implemented under the aegis of the IMF and the World Bank as part of their structural adjustment program, while the integrated investment program was undertaken independently of ECOWAS. Unfortunately, the effort at promoting integrated regional investment failed. Less than 30 percent of the 136 projects proposed secured external funding, and only 3.5 percent of the resources required by the plan were raised.

All these failures imposed a heavy toll on the economies of West African states. As shown in Table 2.1, the gross domestic product (GDP) per capita incomes of ECOWAS states in 1999 were barely half of their 1981 levels. In the sphere of human development, most ECOWAS states have barely managed to survive. The average life expectancy in West Africa is 49.7 years, compared to the world average of 66.4. West Africa's infant mortality rate averaged 106 per 1,000 live births in 1999, compared to the global average of 56 per 1,000. The average under-five mortality rate in West Africa was 174 per 1,000 live births in 1999, compared to a global average of 80 per 1,000 (see Table 2.2).

Only two of West Africa's sixteen countries, Cape Verde and Ghana, are ranked as middle human development countries. All the others are in

Table 2.1 West Africa's GDP per Capita and GDP Growth Rate, 1981–1999

	U.S.$ per Capita	Growth Rate (%)
1981	724	–0.6
1985	551	–0.5
1988	658	0.9
1990	385	5.0
1995	328	3.5
1998	373	3.2
1999	378	2.7

Sources: United Nations Economic Commission for Africa (ECA), *Economic Report on Africa 1990* (Addis Ababa: ECA, 1990); African Development Bank (ADB), *African Development Report 2000* (Abidjan: ADB, 2000).

Table 2.2 Human Development Survival in West Africa: Progress and Setbacks

	Life Expectancy at Birth (years)		Infant Mortality Rate (per 1,000 live births)		Under-Five Mortality Rate (per 1,000 live births)	
	1970–1975	1995–2000	1970	1999	1970	1999
Benin	44.0	53.5	149	99	252	156
Burkina Faso	41.5	45.3	163	106	290	199
Cape Verde	57.5	68.9	87	54	123	73
Côte d'Ivoire	45.4	47.7	158	1.2	239	171
Gambia	37.0	45.4	183	61	319	75
Ghana	49.9	56.3	111	63	186	101
Guinea	37.3	46.5	197	115	345	181
Guinea-Bissau	36.5	44.1	186	128	316	200
Liberia	n/a	n/a	n/a	n/a	n/a	n/a
Mali	42.9	50.9	221	143	391	235
Mauritania	43.5	50.5	150	120	250	183
Niger	38.2	44.2	197	162	330	275
Nigeria	44.0	51.3	120	112	201	187
Senegal	41.8	52.3	164	68	279	118
Sierra Leone	35.0	37.3	206	182	363	316
Sub-Saharan Africa	45.3	48.8	138	107	226	172
Togo	45.5	51.3	128	80	216	143

Source: United Nations Development Programme (UNDP), Human Development Report 2001 (New York: UNDP, 2001), pp. 167–169.

Note: n/a = not available.

the low human development category, with six—Mali, Guinea-Bissau, Burkina Faso, Niger, Sierra Leone, and Liberia—being among the lowest of the low human development countries. Six factors are primarily responsible for the deteriorating human economic conditions in West Africa and the state of

---

Box 2.3 Crisis and Decline in West Africa

The Economic Community of West African States (ECOWAS) exhibits more common characteristics of underdevelopment and environmental degradation than diversity. . . . The multifaceted political economy of the subregion in its economic, political, social and environmental essence manifests the dominant common features of profound structural disarticulation, deep sectoral distortions, excessive external dependence, and a bewildering confusion of values and institutions. . . . These are reflected most graphically in the asymmetry between production and consumption patterns, the disproportionality between agriculture and the rest of the economy, severe rural-urban dichotomy and persistent political instability that is basically a crisis of legitimacy. These have been and continue to be tragically exacerbated by inter- and intra-country strifes.

Source: Adebayo Adedeji; "Economic Development Issues of West Africa," keynote address to the West African Conference on Economic Development and Environmental Sustainability, organized by Friends of the Earth, Accra, 1990.

---

paralysis that confronts ECOWAS. The first is the absence of an indigenous, coherent development paradigm and integration culture. The second is the proliferation of intergovernmental organizations and the lack of success of all efforts at rationalization. The third is the perception that, whenever any country is confronted with a national economic crisis, it should, in order to cope and survive, sacrifice its commitment to regional integration. The fourth is political instability, civil strife, and conflicts, which have been the Achilles heel of regionalism and economic integration in West Africa. The fifth is the resurfacing and reassertion of external influence and control, which have been a negative development in West Africa's integration process. The sixth factor retarding economic development and integration is that ECOWAS's goals have remained unfulfilled as a result of the lack of the kind of proactive and visionary political leadership that had been demonstrated at the birth of the organization in the early 1970s.

*Absence of a Coherent National Development
Paradigm and Integration Culture*

Perhaps the most basic hindrance to development in Africa—at the national, regional, and continental levels—is the lack of understanding of what development entails, who it is for, and how to achieve it on a sustainable basis. This lack of clarity has made economic progress extremely difficult. It has also rendered the task of forging Africa's future by Africans themselves virtually impossible.

If Africa's capacity to forge its own future is to be improved, two fundamental problems must be addressed. First, there must be a renewed understanding of the limitations imposed on Africa by colonial economic and political legacies and the imperative of seriously, as opposed to rhetorically, embarking on a process of economic decolonization. So far, African governments have failed to confront the past and to learn lessons from it to improve the future. Instead, there has been "a carry over of the disabilities from the slave trade era to the colonial period, and from the colonial period into the period after independence. This has often involved a loss of self-esteem, an undue willingness to substitute dependence on charity for self-confidence and self-reliance."[18] African leaders have generally failed to realize that trying to march toward the future without tackling the continent's colonial legacies has dimmed the prospects for the continent.

Second, even where attempts have been made by African governments and people to craft their own development strategies and policies, such efforts have invariably been rebuffed by the international financial institutions, with the connivance of the international donor community. During the 1970s and the 1980s, African leaders, intellectuals, and policymakers, with the support of their regional organizations, the ECA, and the Organization of African Unity (OAU), undertook serious and sustained initiatives to craft their own indigenous development paradigms. The Lagos Plan of Action (LPA) and the Final Act of Lagos (FAL) of 1980, the African Priority Program for Economic Recovery, 1986–1990 (of 1985), the African Alternative Framework to Structural Adjustment Program for Socio-Economic Recovery and Transformation (AAF-SAP) of 1989, and the African Charter for Popular Participation for Development of 1990 are all outstanding examples of African alternatives to the dominant development paradigm championed by the World Bank and the IMF. But these initiatives were all opposed, ridiculed, undermined, and discarded by the two Bretton Woods institutions.

Regrettably, the latest African initiative at crafting a development paradigm—the New Partnership for Africa's Development (NEPAD)—has, in the minds of many people, not remained faithful to the fundamental principles that animated earlier strategies, particularly the LPA and the FAL. The cardinal principles of self-reliance, self-sustainability, a transformation ethic, holistic human development, and democracy—particularly the democratization of the development process—have been practically abandoned by NEPAD. Little wonder that the donor community and the international financial institutions have warmly welcomed NEPAD. In contrast, in the 1980s the same donors rejected both the LPA and the FAL.[19]

The undermining of the ability of African governments to determine their own development strategies and policies has been successful because of the phenomenon that I described in June 1990 as Africa's "three-lenses syndrome."[20] First, Africans, particularly educated Africans, view industrialized countries through the distorted lenses crafted for them by rich countries.

Second, Africans also view themselves through lenses crafted for them by their former colonial masters. Finally, Africans see the rest of the world through Western lenses. Wearing these made-in-Europe lenses, educated Africans continue to see their continent's future only in relation to the West. Under such circumstances, economic decolonization becomes virtually impossible to achieve.

Closely related to the need for an endogenous self-reliant development culture is the fostering of an integration culture, since the one facilitates the other. For example, sound food and agricultural policies at the national level will sooner or later necessitate the imperative of a complementary regional food and agricultural strategy and policy. Not only are all West African countries agricultural economies, but they also produce identical crops since similar geographical conditions exist throughout the region. A common policy for crops grown by more than one country is therefore essential to the success of economic integration in West Africa.

Proliferation of Intergovernmental Organizations

A major obstacle to economic cooperation and integration in Africa is the existence of a large number of intergovernmental organizations. The proliferation of such organizations is more pronounced in West Africa than elsewhere on the continent. The most frustrating aspect of this phenomenon is that, while all ECOWAS governments recognize the need to rationalize these organizations, very little progress has been achieved in this area. If anything, the situation has become worse.

West African countries have flagrantly contravened Article 88(4) of the 1991 treaty establishing the African Economic Community (the Abuja treaty), which stipulates that "member states undertake, through their respective regional economic communities, to coordinate and harmonize their subregional organizations, with a view to rationalizing the integration process at the level of each region."[21] It looked as if a breakthrough was possible when, at the beginning of the 1990s, policymakers talked more openly than ever about making ECOWAS the only intergovernmental economic body in West Africa, thus absorbing the CEAO and the Mano River Union. The revised treaty prepared by the ECOWAS Eminent Persons Committee,[22] which conducted a review of the Lagos treaty in 1992, envisaged such a provision in the revised ECOWAS treaty. Unfortunately, within fifteen months of the adoption of the revised ECOWAS treaty in Cotonou in January 1993, the Union Monétaire Ouest Africaine (UMOA) was transformed into the Union Economique et Monétaire Ouest Africaine (UEMOA), while the ailing CEAO was dissolved in March 1994. The timing of these changes was exquisite. UMOA was doubtless transformed into UEMOA to get rid of the ailing CEAO, but also as a way of checkmating ECOWAS in a pernicious chess game. UEMOA has succeeded brilliantly in this mission. The francophone-dominated organization has thrown ECOWAS into a state of paralysis. ECOWAS now spends a great deal of its time trying to harmonize its programs with those of UEMOA (see Chapter 3).

In contrast to ECOWAS, UEMOA, whose eight members (Benin, Burkina Faso, Côte d'Ivoire, Guinea-Bissau, Mali, Niger, Senegal, and Togo) are also members of ECOWAS, has become a single market as of 1 January 2000. As such, all tariffs on goods produced inside the eight member states have been abolished, a single external tariff has been adopted, and there are ongoing efforts to standardize business laws and the registration of companies. Given the fact that all of these eight countries have a common currency—the Communauté Financière Africaine (CFA) franc—it is not surprising that UEMOA is being hailed in the West as the most impressive cooperation entity yet seen in Africa.

If, as is being rumored, Ghana—Nigeria's co–fast tracker on the wobbling ECOWAS rail track—has an interest in joining the UEMOA organ responsible for bringing about a unified business law regime, this might be a first step by an anglophone African state toward joining UEMOA. Ghanaian businessmen are reported to be favorably disposed to such a move. After the withdrawal of Mauritania from ECOWAS in December 2000, Nigeria, Cape Verde, Gambia, Guinea, Liberia, and Sierra Leone are the only member states left with undivided allegiances to ECOWAS.

Many African governments, peoples, and institutions have been particularly suspicious of UEMOA and its equivalent in Central Africa, the Central African Economic and Monetary Union (CEMAC). The African Development Bank 1993 development report expressed "grave concern" about the implications of these initiatives for the future of the Abuja treaty of 1991, as well as for the existing economic communities in West and Central Africa. As A. London put it in a paper for the Global Coalition for Africa's ministerial conference in 1993:

> If the more advanced Member States of an economic community proceed along a decision in which the remaining Member States of an economic community have not taken part, the variable geometry strategy can become a disintegrative strategy, splitting the community in two, as the remaining Member States of the community have only two options: implementing the decision taken by the "core community" or taking a direction more consistent with their joint interests. The variable geometry strategy becomes an especially important concern when the pace of progress of the core countries depends on the impetus carried into the community from outside the region. Indeed, an integrative strategy is unlikely to succeed if the steam for the locomotive is not generated by Member States forming the very community.[23]

Dumping Regional Integration in the Face of National Crises

In my first address to the ECA conference of ministers held in Kinshasa in February 1977, I argued that a new economic order must be put in place at the national and regional levels in Africa as a first step toward achieving the New International Economic Order (NIEO) that developing countries were clamoring for at the UN General Assembly at the time. At the national level, I argued that the economic order should be based on the principles of self-reliance and self-sustainability, recovery and establishment of self-confidence, and the freeing of national economies from the shackles of excessive external dependence. The new national economic order should maximize not only the rate of development but also social justice and equity. At the regional level, I argued for the pursuit of collective self-reliance among African countries and suggested that regional economic cooperation should be regarded as a conditio sine qua non for the achievement of national socioeconomic goals. In other words, national objectives should be compatible with regional ones and both should be pursued with equal vigor and commitment.

The preoccupation of individual African governments with urgent day-to-day national problems has slowed down the progress of regional economic cooperation. These governments have uniformly failed to put in place an efficient and effective national machinery for monitoring the consistency of national programs, policies, and projects with regional ones. As earlier noted, where there is neither clarity about, nor commitment to, development objectives and strategies, it would be too much to expect a virile integration culture in such an economic community. In any case, whatever sense of regionalism exists disappears once there is an economic crisis. Aided and abetted by the international financial institutions and the donor community, many African countries have pursued policies that contradict, or are inconsistent with, the principles and practices of regional economic cooperation.

Without doubt, the structural adjustment programs advocated by the World Bank and IMF since the 1980s have been a major constraint on regional cooperation. Macroeconomic measures required of individual countries by these institutions often have negative effects on neighboring countries. And since there is no national monitoring mechanism, there is no alarm system. The proposal put forward in my 1970 journal article that each West African country should establish a ministry for West African economic cooperation to be headed by a cabinet minister whose career would depend on the extent to which he or she succeeds in pushing the frontiers and intensity of cooperation was adopted by Nigeria only as recently as 1999. Burkina Faso, Guinea, Ghana, Mali, Niger, and Senegal have also now created ministries dealing exclusively with regional integration.

Regional Cooperation, Political Instability, and Conflict

Politics is the final arbiter in determining the prospects of any regional integration scheme. Regional integration has flourished best in a politically stable and democratic environment. Good governance, dynamic economic growth, transparency, and accountability are the pillars around which dynamic regional integration arrangements are built. Unfortunately, West Africa has been one of Africa's most conflict-ridden and coup-prone subregions. Nigeria, the most important country to the success of ECOWAS, has not been spared this instability. No sooner was the ECOWAS treaty signed in May 1975 than General Gowon, one of ECOWAS's chief architects, was removed from power through a coup d'état. Eight months later, his successor, General Murtala Mohammed, was assassinated. Between July 1975 and May 1999, Nigeria has had nine heads of state and government. If the eight years of General Ibrahim Babangida's rule (1985–1993) are excluded, the average duration of the eight regimes during this period was roughly two years. Political instability in Nigeria has been a primary cause of the paralysis of ECOWAS.

Unlike Nigeria, Togo has not, during this period, experienced any violent change of government, though it has experienced sporadic political unrest. General Eyadéma has doggedly retained power in spite of the destabilization that this has caused from time to time. After the death of Houphouët-Boigny in 1993, Côte d'Ivoire has suffered from periodic political instability, including an unprecedented coup in December 1999 and the outbreak of civil war in September 2002. Parts of Ghana and Senegal have been in rebellion against the central authorities for years, while Gambia and Niger have suffered from several bouts of violence and coups. Liberia and Sierra Leone, and to a more limited extent Guinea-Bissau, have been faced for years with armed conflict and civil strife. Mention must also be made of Benin and Burkina Faso, which currently enjoy some modicum of stability, but have had their share of violence and instability. Unlike the period between 1970 and 1975, when, after the Nigerian civil war, there was a Pax West Africana, the subregion has been faced with unparalleled challenges to its political stability, particularly throughout the 1980s and 1990s.

Unfortunately, the conflicts in West Africa have not been limited to internal conflicts. There have also been conflicts between ECOWAS members. Mali and Burkina Faso clashed in 1975 and 1985, and periodic violence has broken out between Senegal and Mauritania. The inherent dangers of such centrifugal forces have made the search for subregional mechanisms for mutual defense, cooperation, and nonaggression necessary. In June 1977, seven of the nine francophone countries blazed the trail when they successfully negotiated and signed the Agreement on Non-Aggression and Assistance in Defense—the Accord de Non-Aggression et d'Assistance en Matière de Défence (ANAD)—in Abidjan. Its seven signatories were Burkina Faso, Côte d'Ivoire, Mali, Mauritania, Niger, Senegal, and Togo. By this agreement, the seven francophone states committed themselves to resolving their disputes peacefully. ANAD also called for cooperation between the police and security forces of member states in order to combat terrorism, subversion, and other crimes. The organization further pledged to prevent any subversive acts by dissidents of any member state in the territories of other states. In the two conflicts that have erupted between its member states, ANAD has risen to the challenge. It was ANAD's quick intervention and mediation that brought about a cease-fire in the 1985 border conflict between Mali and Burkina Faso. ANAD also played an instrumental role in restoring good relations between Senegal and Mauritania after the murder of civilians from both countries following a dispute between Senegalese and Mauritanian residents of the Bekel zone on the Senegal river in April 1989. These two conflicts, involving four ANAD member states (Mali/Burkina Faso and Senegal/Mauritania), are a reminder of the fragility and precariousness of peace in West Africa.

Similarly, ECOWAS soon realized that economic cooperation and integration would be extremely difficult to achieve without an environment of peace and harmonious understanding among its member states. ECOWAS members consequently adopted a protocol on nonaggression in April 1978 that sought to outlaw aggression by member states, and gave primacy to the peaceful settlement of disputes. This protocol was further supplemented in May 1981 by a protocol on mutual assistance on defense that identified three cases of permissible armed intervention by ECOWAS. The first case concerns any armed threat or aggression directed against any member state, which shall constitute a threat or aggression against the entire community. The second case pertains to an armed conflict between two or several member states in which the settlement procedure of the nonaggression protocol has proved ineffective. The third case involves internal armed conflicts within a member state that have been engineered and supported actively from outside and are likely to endanger the peace and security of the entire community. It was this protocol that Samuel Doe invoked in July 1990, at the beginning of the Liberian crisis, when he requested in writing that an ECOWAS peacekeeping force be sent into Liberia to halt further bloodshed. The ECOWAS Cease-Fire Monitoring Group (ECOMOG) was the response to this request. This is not to suggest that the establishment of ECOMOG was free of controversy. There was disagreement among ECOWAS member states as to the competence of ECOWAS to intervene in the crisis on the basis that the situation in Liberia was purely an internal conflict.

Led by Nigeria, ECOMOG's original 3,000 troops were contributed voluntarily by four other member states—Ghana, Guinea, Sierra Leone, and Gambia. The intervention was funded almost single-handedly by Nigeria until peace was achieved, elections were held, and a new government was installed in July 1997. Before the creation and deployment of ECOMOG forces, Liberia was in a state of utter hopelessness in which bloodshed and destruction raged unabated and the international community seemed to be anxiously pleading for someone to do something about the crisis. Despite the controversy that surrounded its origins, ECOMOG was an outstanding success in both Liberia and Sierra Leone, where a military coup was reversed and democratic government restored by March 1998. The eventual support of all ECOWAS countries for ECOMOG and the full support of the OAU—now the African Union—and the UN for the subregional peace-keeping body testify to this success. Both military operations are estimated to have cost Nigeria about $8 billion, a huge sacrifice for a relatively poor country (some of these funds, though, were reportedly embezzled by some members of Nigeria's military leadership). It is indeed important to build on the valuable experience of ECOMOG so that it can be replicated in other African subregions (see Chapters 13 and 14). Nigeria led yet another peace-keeping mission into Liberia in August 2003.

Resurfacing and Reassertion of External Influence and Control

The transformation of UMOA, a francophone-dominated monetary union (lusophone Guinea-Bissau is the single nonfrancophone member) into an economic and monetary union (UEMOA) in 1994, a year after the ECOWAS treaty had been successfully revised and the new treaty adopted by heads of state in Cotonou in 1993, was reminiscent of the establishment of the CEAO in 1973. The establishment of the CEAO also occurred a year after the negotiations for an all-inclusive West African economic community had begun. The resuscitation of the principle and practice of an almost exclusive francophone organization set the hands of the integration clock back by undermining the ideal of true regionalism in West Africa. In the acronym-infested world of West Africa, this was a classic case of WALA: West Africa Loses Again!

In this connection, it is worth repeating what I said during my keynote address in August 2000 at the fortieth annual general meeting of the Nigerian Association of Chambers of Commerce, Industry, Mines, and Agriculture:

> So successfully has UEMOA check-mated and undermined ECOWAS that all that the latter now spends a great deal of its time doing is to harmonize its programmes with those of the former, hold joint ministerial meetings, seek the convergence of the economic and financial policies and the harmonization of the legal framework, accounting procedure and statistics of both ECOWAS and UEMOA. In any case, such convergence will for long remain a pipedream since UEMOA countries now constitute a majority of ECOWAS member countries and as such can play both judge and jury. In spite of the apparent unity that exists, ECOWAS is a house divided against itself.[24]

The former ECOWAS executive secretary, Lansana Kouyaté, also said as much, though using different words, in his 2000 interim report on the organization.

Lack of Proactive Leadership in West Africa

There is no doubt that the development of ECOWAS has suffered greatly from the lack of the kind of proactive leadership that led to its establishment in May 1975. The coup against General Gowon exactly two months after the historic triumph of his government in creating an organization to foster West African economic cooperation and integration sent the wrong signal to countries that had come to accept Nigeria's leadership of ECOWAS and had developed trust in its rulers. Matters were not helped by the fracture of the Nigeria-Togo alliance that had been instrumental in establishing ECOWAS. This was due partly to the fact that Togo provided refuge to General Gowon after his overthrow and partly to the rivalry between Lomé and Lagos over the hosting of the ECOWAS secretariat. In the end, the secretariat went to Lagos. After the fall of Gowon, the initial hostility of Generals Murtala Mohammed and Olusegun Obasanjo to the ECOWAS project also did not help matters. In the 1980s, the expulsion of 3 million mostly West African citizens declared "illegal aliens" from Nigeria contradicted the country's commitment to ECOWAS's 1979 protocol on the free movement of people.

The collapse in international oil prices and the adoption of the inappropriate and disastrous structural adjustment programs in the 1980s put paid to Nigeria's ambitions to be an economic success story in the eyes of its West African neighbors. No country that is confronted with a long period of political instability, economic stagnation, and regression, and is reputed to be one of the most corrupt societies in the world, has a moral basis to lead others. If it tries to, it will be resisted. Unfortunately, the bogey of domination by the Nigerian ogre was revived and sustained by the French, whose determination to maintain their sphere of influence in West Africa has remained strong. Sadly, there is no other country that is as well placed as Nigeria to play this leadership role. It overshadows every other country in the subregion, accounting for about half of its population, over half of its economic strength, and by far its biggest market and most bountiful natural resource endowment.

Toward a West African Economic Community

We must now bring this retrospective journey to an end. One theme that has recurred throughout the journey is that, in the final analysis, it is politics and not economics that will ultimately determine the fate of regional integration arrangements. Without a strong and sustained political commitment, re-gionalism will not take root in West Africa, let alone develop and prosper. Political leaders are therefore key factors to the success of regional coop-eration and integration processes. In the course of a retrospective journey spanning five decades, successes have only occurred where and when polit-ical commitment was present. It is when such commitment is absent, or is very weak, that decisions are difficult to reach, that their implementation proves even more difficult, that no consistent effort is made to align na-tional priorities with regional objectives, and that meeting financial and budgetary obligations becomes increasingly rare.

West Africa has been fortunate in occasionally having some leaders in a limited number of countries who have been committed to the ideal of regional integration. The subregion is also fortunate in having an organized private sector that has successfully set up its own forum—the Federation of West African Chambers of Commerce—which enables it to make periodic contributions to the development of regional cooperation. The time has no doubt come for civil society, community-based organizations, and the media to be fully mobilized and engaged in the promotion of a pervasive integration culture. Strong nongovernmental participation will be a critical factor in relaunching and accelerating the goals of regional integration in West Africa (see Chapter 12).

The revised ECOWAS treaty of 1993 makes adequate provision for the participation of civil society and nongovernmental groups in its institutions. We look forward to the day when these various stakeholders will be allowed by their governments to participate actively in community deci-sionmaking as well as in the implementation of community programs. For West Africa's many minuscule countries, there is no viable alternative to the type of regional cooperation and integration that inspired the establish-ment of ECOWAS in 1975. Without harnessing their efforts to a broader integration scheme, these tiny countries lack the population, resources, and markets to achieve the economies of scale necessary for industrialization and development.

The Final Act of Lagos of 1980 and the Treaty Establishing the African Economic Community in Abuja in 1991 require that regional economic co-operation and integration be organized around one central economic com-munity in each subregion. For West Africa, ECOWAS remains the obvious choice. All other integration arrangements in West Africa must be rational-ized to eliminate duplication and rivalry. Perhaps the apparent declining interest of France in Africa and the dissolving of the French franc into the euro may yet increase the commitment of francophone states to ECOWAS.[25] It is only by achieving genuine economic integration in West Africa that economic cooperation and regional security can be properly linked and armed conflicts eliminated or contained. Indeed, without an effective and dynamic ECOWAS, West Africa's security mechanism of 1999 will be ineffective and ineffectual, and Pax West Africana will remain an elusive dream.

Notes

1. T. S. Eliot, "Burnt Norton," in *Four Quartets* (London: Faber and Faber, 1955), p. 7.

2. Adebayo Adedeji, "Comparative Strategies of Economic Decolonisation in Africa," in Ali Mazrui and C. Wondji, eds., *Africa Since 1935: UNESCO General History of Africa,* vol. 8 (Oxford: Heinemann, 1993), p. 408.

3. The sixteen members of ECOWAS were Benin, Burkina Faso, Cape Verde, Côte d'Ivoire, Gambia, Ghana, Guinea, Guinea-Bissau, Liberia, Mali, Mauritania, Niger, Nigeria, Senegal, Sierra Leone, and Togo. Mauritania left the organization in December 2000.

4. See, for example, Samuel Decalo, *Coups and Army Rule in Africa,* 2nd ed. (New Haven, Conn.:Yale University Press, 1990); and Eboe Hutchful and Abdoulaye Bathily, eds., *The Military and Militarism in Africa* (Dakar: CODESRIA, 1998).

5. J. I. Elaigwu and Ali Mazrui, "Nation-Building and Changing Political Structures," in Mazrui and Wondji, *Africa Since 1935,* p. 436.

6. See Ladipo Adamolekun, *Sékou Touré's Guinea: An Experiment in Nation Building* (London: Methuen, 1976); and Claude Rivière, *Guinea: The Mobilization of a People* (Ithaca: Cornell University Press, 1978).

7. See, for example, Yves Person, "French West Africa and Decolonization," in P. Gifford and W. R. Lewis, eds., *The Transfer of Power in Africa: Decolonization 1940–1960* (New Haven, Conn.: Yale University Press, 1982).

8. Adebayo Adedeji, "Prospects for Regional Economic Cooperation in West Africa," *Journal of Modern African Studies* 8 (July 1970): 213–231.

9. Adebayo Adedeji, "Africa, the Third World, and the Search for a New Economic Order," Turkeyen Third World Lectures, Georgetown, Guyana, November 1976, p. 43; and S. K. B. Asante, *African Development: Adebayo Adedeji's Alternative Strategies* (Ibadan, Nigeria: Spectrum, 1991).

10. Edward S. Milenky, "Developmental Nationalism in Practice: The Problems and Progress of the Andean Group," *Inter-American Economic Affairs* 25, no. 3 (1971): 49.

11. For an insider's account by one of the key actors, see Yakubu Gowon, "The Economic Community of West African States: A Study of Political and Economic Integration" (Ph.D. thesis, Warwick University, February 1984).

12. Guinea Bissau and Cape Verde had not yet become independent.

13. See Amadu Sesay, "The Mano River Union: Politics of Survival or Dependence?" in R. I. Onwuka and A. Sesay, eds., *The Future of Regionalism in Africa* (London: Macmillan, 1985), pp. 125–148.

14. See Olusegun Obasanjo, *My Command* (London: Heinemann, 1980); and John Stremlau, *The International Politics of the Nigerian Civil War, 1967–1970* (Princeton: Princeton University Press, 1977).

15. ECOWAS, *2000 Interim Report by the Executive Secretary,* ECW/CM XLVVI/2, p. 70.

16. Ibid., pp. 70–72.

17. Ibid.

18. J. F. Ade-Ajayi, "Africa's Development Crisis in Its Historical Perspective," in Bade Onimode and Richard Synge, eds., *Issues in African Development: Essays in Honour of Adebayo Adedeji at Sixty-Five* (Ibadan, Nigeria: Heinemann, 1995), p. 41.

19. See my keynote address "NEPAD: A View from the African Trenches," in International Peace Academy, *NEPAD: African Initiative, New Partnership?* seminar report, New York, 16 July 2002, available at www.ipacademy.org.

20. Adebayo Adedeji, "Africa and the Single European Act 1992," paper submitted to the seminar "Europe 1992," organized by the Union Bank of Nigeria Plc, 12 June 1990.

21. Organization of African Unity, *Treaty Establishing the African Economic Community,* Abuja, 3 June 1991, p. 52.

22. The members of this committee were General Yakubu Gowon (chairman); Adebayo Adedeji; Abdulai Conteh, former vice president of Sierra Leone; Diaby Ouattara, first executive secretary of ECOWAS; Ide Oumaru, former OAU secretary-general; Ibrahima Fall, former foreign minister of Senegal; Pius Okigbo, former economic adviser to the Nigerian government; Pascal Zagre, Burkina Faso's minister of planning; Toga Mcintosh of Liberia; Jeghan Senghor of Gambia; M. B. Toure of Guinea; and Jack Wilmot of Ghana.

23. A. London, "Promoting Regional Economic Cooperation and Integration in Africa," paper prepared for the Global Coalition for Africa ministerial meeting, 9–11 June 1993, Cotonou, Benin.

24. Adebayo Adedeji, "The Role of the Private Sector in the Economic Integration of the West Africa Sub-Region," keynote address at the fortieth anniversary of the Nigerian Association of Chambers of Commerce, Industry, Mines, and Agriculture, 16 August 2000, mimeo.

25. See, for example, Adekeye Adebajo, "Nigeria: Africa's New Gendarme?" *Security Dialogue* 31, no. 2 (June 2000): 185–199.

3

The Travails of Integration

S. K. B. Asante

Economic cooperation and integration have been a major arena of debate among African leaders since the continent moved toward independence in the late 1950s and early 1960s. There was a realization that, while political independence had been the primary goal of African states—as evidenced by Ghanaian president Kwame Nkrumah's famous call for African leaders to seek first the political kingdom—these territories were largely artificial byproducts of the colonial scramble in the era of the Berlin conference of 1884–1885, at which European imperialists carved up the continent among themselves. Africa's present fragmentation and its small markets are a consequence of the specific political and economic conditions in which the continent found itself at independence. Many African states were too small to be economically viable, and the transformation of political into economic independence required concerted and united action. Regional cooperation and integration are therefore widely recognized and accepted as a necessary condition for the long-term sustainable development of Africa.

The Economic Community of West African States (ECOWAS)—whose current members include Benin, Burkina Faso, Cape Verde, Côte d'Ivoire, Gambia, Ghana, Guinea, Guinea-Bissau, Liberia, Mali, Niger, Nigeria, Senegal, Sierra Leone, and Togo—the francophone Communauté Economique de l'Afrique de l'Ouest (CEAO), and its successor grouping the Union Economique et Monétaire Ouest Africaine (UEMOA)—whose current members include Benin, Burkina Faso, Côte d'Ivoire, Guinea-Bissau, Mali, Niger, Senegal, and Togo—are the most concrete regional economic cooperation and integration experiments in West Africa. Since UEMOA emerged out of the dissolution of the CEAO and has roughly the same members, the two organizations will be assessed together. The creation of the CEAO and UEMOA was a major development in the institutional arrangements of economic integration in West Africa. Whereas such groupings as the Mano River Union—a subregional body involving Guinea, Liberia, and Sierra Leone founded in 1973—were regarded as building blocks toward a more integrated ECOWAS, UEMOA is, in many respects, a miniature ECOWAS, and may thus be less easy to accommodate within the organization.

Consequently, the continued separate existence of UEMOA and ECOWAS has posed a number of challenging questions about the process of West African integration. What are the differences between ECOWAS and UEMOA? To what extent does the parallel existence of the two economic groupings create a competitive rather than complementary model of integration in West Africa? In what way is UEMOA a threat to ECOWAS? (This question is particularly relevant since UEMOA is externally anchored by France and the Communauté Financière Africaine [CFA] franc and has been provided enormous bilateral and multilateral financial and technical assistance by the European Union [EU].) Is UEMOA, like the CEAO before it, not a major obstacle in ECOWAS's efforts to create a West African common market? Will the double membership of UEMOA states in ECOWAS not lead to a weakening of both cooperation experiments, and thus retard West Africa's integration process?

These are some of the thorny issues that I will address in this chapter. My main objective is to provide a critical analysis of the implications of the coexistence of ECOWAS and the CEAO/UEMOA for regionalization in West Africa, highlighting the potential contribution of regional integration to the alleviation of conflicts in the subregion. Without delving into the debate about the definitions of such closely related concepts as regionalization, regionalism, "new" regionalism, regional integration, and regional cooperation, I adopt Daniel Bach's definition of regionalization, which refers to "processes that may or may not be related to the emergence of institutional structures and patterns of transaction" (see Chapter 4). Following this brief introduction, the next section describes the socioeconomic conditions of postindependence West Africa and the emergence of ECOWAS and the CEAO/UEMOA. The third section provides a comparative analysis of the effectiveness of ECOWAS and the CEAO/UEMOA as schemes for West African economic integration. The fourth section highlights the current challenges and main obstacles to the West African integration process, while the final section analyzes the prospects for West African integration and proposes an agenda for action in this area.

The Socioeconomic Features of West Africa

Interest in the concept of economic integration in West Africa is closely related to the complex economic, political, and social features of the subregion, which is the most diverse in Africa in terms of the size of its fifteen countries, the degree of economic development, its linguistic diversity, and the internal and external links of its economies. While Nicholas Plessz observed in 1968 that West Africa "occupies a very particular position in so far as integration is concerned,"[1] Adebayo Adedeji aptly noted a year later that a "study of integration efforts in West Africa is inevitably a study in frustration."[2] If Africa as a whole is badly fragmented, West Africa must be the most fragmented subregion on the continent. West Africa represents the most heterogeneous conglomeration of states in Africa, and has the largest number of ministates, with populations too small in size to be viable individual markets. With the possible exception of Nigeria, none of the states in West Africa is a large enough economic unit to create and sustain an integrated modern economy with high levels of productivity.

Another important feature of West Africa's socioeconomic landscape is the artificiality of its national borders. If most of Africa's borders are artificial and arbitrary, West Africa's are absurd and capricious. These frontiers run inward from the coast, cutting across ethnic, cultural, and linguistic boundaries. As Adedeji notes in Chapter 2, the artificiality of West Africa's states "has constituted the greatest obstacle to the achievement of more stable and dynamic statehood."

Two other significant characteristics of postindependence West Africa are the subregion's abysmally high levels of poverty, and the generally low living standards of this area, which is among the poorest regions in the world. With such poverty exist widespread socioeconomic inequalities and perhaps unsurprisingly, West Africa is also among the world's most politically unstable subregions. The internal insecurity of many West African countries has been reinforced by the epidemic of military coups, counter-coups, and threats of coups (see Chapter 7). As noted in a recent study by Adekeye Adebajo, West Africa is "among the world's most unstable subregions: thirty-seven out of seventy-two successful military *coups d'état* in Africa (about 50 percent) between 1960 and 1990 occurred in West Africa, a subregion with less than a third of the OAU's (Organization of African Unity) members."[3] These unfavorable factors are compounded by limited infrastructure, new and fragile borders, and economies that are highly vulnerable to fluctuating world prices for imports, even as the prices of the exports of their cash crops continue to decline. In 2001, fourteen West African countries were ranked in the lowest category of the United Nations Development Programme's human development index scale.[4] Only two of West Africa's states—Cape Verde and Ghana—are ranked as middle human development countries. Life expectancy at birth in the subregion varies considerably, from 37.9 years in Sierra Leone to 69.4 years in Cape Verde. Only in eight of West Africa's countries is the average life expectancy above 50 years.[5] Thus, West Africa is arguably the subregion in the world where economic integration, or at least the avoidance of disintegration, is most imperative for economic development.

The Creation of ECOWAS

It was against this background that the creation of ECOWAS in 1975 was generally welcomed as the much-needed subregional economic scheme that would promote and enhance economic development through close cooperation among its member states in all fields of economic activity. ECOWAS, it was hoped by its "Founding Fathers," was a scheme that would also have the potential to meet the interlocking development challenges of West Africa, particularly in four key areas: first, expanding intracommunity trade; second, improving physical infrastructure (by increasing the existing transport and communications links between countries to promote the free movement of persons, goods, and services within the community); third, strengthening the weak production structures in the subregion in order to reduce its excessive external dependence and critical lack of productive activity; and finally, enhancing monetary and financial cooperation in order to create a single ECOWAS currency.

The creation of ECOWAS represented a culmination of many years of efforts by West African states to increase the economic mass and the bargaining base of their economies. Through a pooling of economic "sovereignty," West African leaders sought to transform their economies to improve the living standards of their citizens and to extend the struggle for political decolonization into a quest for economic decolonization. Having achieved Nkrumah's political kingdom, West African states now sought the economic kingdom. The creation of ECOWAS was also a response to the recognition by West African states that the fragmentation of the subregion—the product of colonial balkanization—into narrow domestic markets renders a shift in the pattern of production designed to reduce dependence both difficult and costly. In brief, therefore, the inauguration of ECOWAS must be seen as an attempt by West African leaders to enhance their economic opportunity and reduce their external dependence. They hoped thereby to overcome the existing structures of neocolonialism and underdevelopment in West Africa. Political economists have now widely recognized that the reduction of a high degree of external dependence is a necessary precondition for achieving basic structural development goals.[6]

ECOWAS, the most ambitious economic grouping in Africa, constitutes a geographical area larger than western Europe. It is the most heavily populated of all of Africa's subregions, with 236 million people and a total gross domestic product (GDP) of $82 billion in 2000. Per capita income for 2000 averaged an estimated $322. Cape Verde, with a per capita income of $1,300, was the "richest" ECOWAS country in 2000, while Sierra Leone, with a per capita income of $132, was the "poorest."[7] A comparison with other African subregions reveals that the per capita income of West Africa is lower than that of North Africa ($1,146) and southern Africa ($1,464). However, West Africa's per capita income is higher than that of East Africa ($234) and Central Africa ($270).[8] Until the withdrawal of Mauritania in December 2000, ECOWAS comprised all sixteen countries in West Africa. The organization thus has the special feature of transcending the linguistic and cultural divisions bequeathed to West Africa by its former colonial masters—Britain, France, and Portugal. Alongside ECOWAS have existed francophone regional groupings that since the early 1970s have complicated the course of West Africa's integration process.

The Birth of the CEAO/UEMOA

The CEAO, which a critic has recently stigmatized as France's "Trojan horse" within ECOWAS,[9] was created as a means of strengthening the cooperation of West Africa's francophone states before ECOWAS's birth. The CEAO was launched in April 1973 and began to function in January 1974. Twenty years later, in January 1994, UEMOA was created as a successor organization of the CEAO in order to pursue the goals of the all-francophone Union Monétaire Ouest Africaine (UMOA), which was established in 1962. Both UEMOA and ECOWAS aim to become customs unions. The treaties of both groupings also provide for free trade and free movement of persons, as well as a common external tariff. UEMOA was created at the very time when a larger West African market was required to meet the challenges posed by increasing globalization and liberalization, coupled with the emergence of trading blocs in Europe, the Americas, and Southeast Asia.

There remains a profound concern that West Africa's position, and indeed that of Africa as a whole, in the world economy will be further weakened if the subregion does not strengthen its institutional and managerial capacity in the integration process. This concern has been prompted by the recognition that, given the changes in the world economy, a failure to overcome or reduce the costs of market fragmentation in West Africa will mean that the subregion will be less well placed to attract the foreign investment, technology, and scientific know-how on which it will have to depend for its future growth. Therefore, UEMOA was seen by non-UEMOA ECOWAS members as a major challenge not only to the decision of the ECOWAS summit held in Banjul, Gambia, in May 1990, to reaffirm the wider subregional body's commitment to the establishment of a single economic community, but also to the highly significant July 1991 decision of the ECOWAS summit in Abuja, Nigeria, that designated ECOWAS the sole organization to promote integration in West Africa. UEMOA has subsequently been described by its critics as an organization with the potential to retard the West African integration process.

The creation of both the CEAO and UEMOA placed ECOWAS in a dilemma. The concerns expressed by nonfrancophone ECOWAS leaders about the two largely francophone organizations stem from four sources. First, the objectives of the CEAO and UEMOA were identical to those of ECOWAS, while the integration programs in all fields listed in the CEAO and UEMOA treaties were similar to those in both the 1975 ECOWAS treaty[10] and the 1993 revised ECOWAS treaty.[11] The second concern was related to whether the CEAO and UEMOA took regional cooperation initiatives into account in designing their own programs. Not only was there no explicit commitment by these organizations to working toward a merger with ECOWAS's integration programs, but the UEMOA treaty, unlike that of the CEAO, invites other West African countries to become full members of UEMOA and encourages other African countries to acquire associate membership in specific UEMOA sector programs.[12] Third, the UEMOA treaty provides for a parliament and a court of justice, which are to coexist alongside similar institutions called for in the revised ECOWAS treaty. Fourth, given the similar economic circumstances of West African states, the CEAO and UEMOA's rules of origin and their trade liberalization schemes could not realistically be different from those of ECOWAS. Four important questions flow from this analysis. First, since UEMOA members are also members of ECOWAS, which of the two treaties will UEMOA countries implement? Second, will there eventually be convergence between ECOWAS and UEMOA, or will the coexistence of the two schemes retard market integration in West Africa? Third, if UEMOA turns out to be more successful in its integrationist goals than ECOWAS, will other ECOWAS member states be granted most-favored-nation treatment within UEMOA? Finally, will the UEMOA common external tariff also apply to other non-UEMOA ECOWAS members? These are some of the complex issues that are increasingly obstructing ECOWAS's integrationist ambitions.

A Comparative Analysis of ECOWAS and CEAO/UEMOA Integration Schemes

A comparative analysis of the integration experiences of ECOWAS and the CEAO/UEMOA provides an opportunity to assess critically the institutional and operational strengths and weaknesses of these groupings and their achievements so far as economic integration schemes are concerned.

Institutional and Operational Strengths and Weaknesses

While the institutions of ECOWAS and UEMOA are not as elaborate as those of the EU, it is obvious that UEMOA places much more emphasis than ECOWAS on the development of adequate institutional machinery as an essential condition for the successful coordination of development policies.

Compared to the ECOWAS treaty and those of other regional economic communities in Africa such as the Southern African Development Community (SADC) or the Common Market for Eastern and Southern Africa (COMESA), the UEMOA treaty—unlike that of the CEAO—is striking in many respects. The provisions of the UEMOA treaty for establishing a "union" approach to regulating and managing the macroeconomic policies of its member states are elaborate, particularly in fiscal matters. Convergence rules are to be negotiated and enforced to foster policy harmonization and the emergence of common regimes in key sectors.

Besides the principal decisionmaking bodies that UEMOA has in common with ECOWAS, UEMOA's treaty contains some innovations that ECOWAS lacks. These innovations could accelerate UEMOA's integration process. One example of such an innovation is the key role that UEMOA assigns to its commission, the counterpart of the ECOWAS executive secretariat. UEMOA's commission is not only the union's executive but also its driving force. It is a vital cog in the institutional machinery of UEMOA. Unlike ECOWAS's executive secretariat, the regulations, directives, and decisions of the UEMOA commission are binding on all member states. Thus the obstacles involved in the tortuous process of ratification, which have greatly contributed to the failure to implement many ECOWAS decisions, acts, and protocols, do not exist in the case of UEMOA. Although the revised ECOWAS treaty of 1993 makes provision for the empowerment of the community to act as a supranational institution, not much progress has been made toward the enhancement of the autonomy of the ECOWAS secretariat.

At the national level, the UEMOA commission is assisted by well-established and effective National Policy Economic Committees, whose role is to monitor internal economic developments within UEMOA countries and ensure compliance of government policies with the commission's convergence criteria. These national committees are composed of high-ranking economic and financial administrators from UEMOA member states, as well as senior representatives of national agencies of central banks and key economic ministries. This is a far cry from the National Units of ECOWAS, most of which are underequipped and have inadequate staff of characteristically low quality and limited influence within their own national administrative structures and equally limited contact with their economic and social sectors.[13] On the whole, at both the national and the regional levels, UEMOA appears to be far better equipped institutionally than ECOWAS to meet the complex challenges of West African regionalism.

The Experience of Integration: ECOWAS and the CEAO/UEMOA

Trade and monetary issues have been the dominant concerns of both the CEAO and UEMOA, in stark contrast to ECOWAS. The different experiences of ECOWAS and the CEAO in the West African integration process in the 1970s and 1980s clearly show that, while the CEAO's interstate trade was showing some remarkable progress during this period, ECOWAS's activities were very much at a rudimentary stage. It is obvious that in the initial · implementation of treaty objectives, the CEAO, as an organized trade zone with a common currency, performed better during this earlier period than ECOWAS.[14] The activities of the CEAO created some complications and elements of conflict with ECOWAS that contributed to a slowdown of the latter's progress, particularly in the area of establishing a customs union. For while the CEAO sought to establish a customs union within twelve years, ECOWAS set a fifteen-year goal. Likewise, in recent years, while ECOWAS has been struggling with printing and distributing customs documents, not only has UEMOA achieved progress in the areas of institutional harmonization and functional cooperation, but its trade liberalization scheme became effective on 1 January 2000. Undoubtedly, UEMOA countries have performed better than the non-UEMOA ECOWAS members in the area of intraregional trade. Experts and nonexperts alike have concluded that UEMOA's trade liberalization scheme has been better organized, better managed, and better implemented than ECOWAS's scheme.

Although economic cooperation and trade are accorded high priority within ECOWAS, its track record in these two areas is more uneven than that of the CEAO/UEMOA. ECOWAS's programs, such as the free movement of peoples and goods, a trade liberalization scheme, and a trade compensation fund, have only achieved limited degrees of success. The level of intraregional trade within ECOWAS remains low, accounting for a paltry 11 percent of total trade with third countries. ECOWAS's trade liberalization scheme has scarcely taken off: goods continue to be subject to undue control, constituting a serious nontariff barrier, increasing the cost of transactions, and posing a major obstacle to the subregion's market integration process.[15] With the exception of infrastructural integration, ECOWAS's activities in the development and integration sectors have been abysmally weak. Only in the "hardcore" areas of economic integration has ECOWAS produced any results, and then only meager ones. This is despite ECOWAS's panoply of institutional structures and cooperation programs.

The Role of External Actors

The CEAO/UEMOA dimension of economic integration has been strengthened, sustained, and reinforced by the role of external actors in West Africa's integration schemes. Whereas, for example, ECOWAS was inspired mainly by African political leaders and was created and administered by African technocrats and bureaucrats, the reverse is true of the CEAO/UEMOA. Not only was the creation of the CEAO/UEMOA inspired by

France and the European Economic Community (EEC)—the EU's precursor—but the CEAO treaty, like that of the Union Douanière et Economique de l'Afrique Centrale (UDEAC), reveals the overpowering influence of Jacques David, a former French customs official, during the colonial era. CEAO/UEMOA members, like those of the UDEAC, are linked to the French system to a degree that makes them collectively dependent on Paris, and hence in need of its support. In reality, Africa has been an important economic partner for France as a source of strategic raw materials, as a market for its manufactured goods, as an outlet for its capital investment, and as a prop to its currency. This is aptly summed up in the important remark of former French president François Mitterrand in 1957: "Without Africa, France will no longer have a history in the twenty-first century."[16]

France and the EU provided substantial assistance to UEMOA right from its inception in the form of technical assistance and expert assessments; through provision of computer equipment, communications, and documentation; and through seminars, training modules, and information campaigns. The overall objective of the EU in relation to francophone West Africa is to contribute to the economic development of UEMOA countries and to their smooth integration into the world economy.[17] Thus on the whole, with stable and predictable funding arrangements and a flexible structure, coupled with the credible performance of UEMOA's institutional arrangements in the areas of economic cooperation and integration, UEMOA poses a threat to ECOWAS's integrationist goals.

Integration within UEMOA "appears inextricably tied to the future of the franc zone,"[18] which has since January 1999 been pegged to the euro. Certain problems may arise, however, as a result of the birth of the euro in January 2002. A fixed exchange rate may prove to be a disadvantage to UEMOA as soon as the euro appreciates against the dollar and other major currencies. While a strong euro is likely to curtail inflation in the franc zone, it is also likely to stimulate imports and penalize exports. That, in turn, would adversely affect the balance of trade and balance of payments of UEMOA states, thereby making their economies less competitive. It is still too early to tell how the euro will affect the CFA.

Challenges to West Africa's Integration Process

So, what are the reasons for the wide consensus over the disappointing results of the ECOWAS economic integration process, despite the continuous rhetoric about the need for regional cooperation and integration in West Africa? The complexity and sensitivity of the subject do not appear to allow for simple explanations. For besides UEMOA, which, as Adebayo Adedeji argues in Chapter 2, "has thrown ECOWAS into a state of paralysis," compelling it to spend a "great deal of its time trying to harmonize its programs with those of UEMOA," a multiplicity of other challenges would seem to have played a role in the poor record of the ECOWAS integration experience.

The Challenge of Political Commitment

There is no denying the fact that UEMOA's member states have demonstrated stronger political will and commitment to their organization than ECOWAS members have to theirs. While, in the case of ECOWAS, political commitment with regard to financial contributions, data provision, and implementation of directives is an identifiable obstacle to integration, there is in UEMOA—the newer, younger organization—clear evidence of a higher degree of political commitment. This point is clearly illustrated by the difficulties in obtaining agreement on the implementation of several decisions and protocols adopted by ECOWAS members to strengthen the ECOWAS integration process. The implementation status report of priority programs compiled by former executive secretary Lansana Kouyaté in September 1998 shows that an average of only 45 percent of ECOWAS programs have been implemented by ECOWAS member states, compared to 68 percent of UEMOA programs by UEMOA members.[19]

A comparative analysis in other areas, such as the level of involvement and participation of member states in institutional activities, reveals a low level of attendance, participation, and quality of representation at ECOWAS summits of heads of state and government and meetings of its council of foreign ministers. This contrasts sharply with UEMOA meetings, which often involve consistently high-level representation and clearly reveal more political commitment by UEMOA members than by ECOWAS members in their respective organizations. It is this glaring lack of political will and commitment by ECOWAS leaders to implement programs and protocols that are necessary for achieving their integration goals that compelled Ghana and Nigeria to adopt the much discussed fast-track approach in a bid to accelerate the ECOWAS integration process. The main objective of this approach is to create a second monetary zone in West Africa by 2003, which would be merged with the CFA zone to form a single currency zone in West Africa in 2004.[20] With the complications in creating this new monetary zone, this timetable proved to be over-ambitious.

The Challenge of a Common ECOWAS Currency

To perhaps a greater extent than in other areas, the existence of the separate monetary projects of ECOWAS and UEMOA has in many respects contributed to impeding progress in establishing a common ECOWAS currency.

Since monetary integration among franc zone countries is controlled by the French treasury in Paris and is accompanied by cooperation in the banking, fiscal, and budgetary fields, this may increase the difficulties of promoting trade within ECOWAS as a whole. This arrangement furthers the integration of the markets of the franc zone countries in favor of exports from France and other EU countries. Thus the coexistence of separate ECOWAS and UEMOA monetary integration schemes complicates the management of ECOWAS's single monetary cooperation program. There is thus considerable economic merit to the objective of the fast-track approach to establish a second program, the West African Monetary Zone (WAMZ), which seeks eventually to create a common currency within ECOWAS. The implementation of this program, involving a common central bank and a common monetary policy, would no doubt pose some formidable challenges of political commitment and leadership to Nigeria and Ghana as well as their partner states—Guinea, Sierra Leone, and Gambia.

The most immediate and pressing challenge facing WAMZ members is how to meet the four convergence criteria of the plan—a restriction of budget deficits (excluding grants) as a percentage of GDP to no more than 4 percent, a restriction on annual inflation rates of less than 10 percent, a ceiling on central bank financing of budget deficits of no more than 10 percent of the previous year's tax revenues, and a floor on foreign exchange reserves of at least three months of imports—within the prescribed timetable for creating a single currency. By the end of 2000, only two countries—Gambia and Nigeria—had met all of the program's primary criteria. Sierra Leone had met two, Guinea met only one, while Ghana had not met any.[21] By June 2002, none of the countries had fulfilled all four criteria. The monetary union could therefore not be launched in January 2003 as previously envisaged. Leaders of the WAMZ held their fourth summit in Conakry in November 2002, and extended the launch of the monetary zone for two and a half years. They thus committed themselves to launch the West African monetary zone on 1 July 2005. The implementation of the WAMZ will require its members to incur certain associated costs, such as the loss of sovereignty in the conduct of monetary policy, coupled with the loss of part of their import duties that would otherwise have accrued to their national treasuries.

These challenges, however, are not insurmountable with genuine commitment to the West African integration process and strong political will. The goals of the single currency envisaged by the WAMZ are not impossible to meet. The West African Monetary Institute (WAMI) was established in Accra, Ghana, in March 2001 to undertake the technical preparation needed for the smooth functioning of the West African Central Bank. The WAMI has made considerable progress in designing the framework for a monetary union for member states of the WAMZ currency zone.[22] Macroeconomic performance criteria and convergence monitoring systems for the zone have already been put in place. Intensified efforts are being made by WAMZ members to ensure that they attain the convergence criteria set by ECOWAS for its proposed monetary union. However, success in creating a common currency will depend heavily on the maintenance of regional peace and security.

Economic Integration and the
Challenge of Regional Peace and Security

Economic integration has a potential role to play in alleviating regional conflicts in light of the symbiotic relationship between peace, security, and economic development. Regional integration is not just an economic issue; it is a multidimensional issue in which integration is seen as a process of community building or social contraction and is not limited to the expansion of regional trade. It is within this context that the revised ECOWAS treaty of 1993 makes provisions for cooperation between its members in nonstrictly economic areas, as part of the enormous challenges that West African states face in their quest for development through subregional integration. These countries are fully aware that the absence of stable and compatible policies in noneconomic areas militates against the success of regional integration. It is therefore generally agreed that, in combating poverty and the various problems in the field of human development, economic growth cannot be durable unless accompanied by investments in human and social infrastructure, particularly in the areas of technical training, education, and health. These structural elements of development can only exist within a climate of peace, security, and stability.

Security, which is intimately linked to issues of poverty, disease, the environment, ethnic and political conflict, and political instability, has been a characteristic feature of the West African subregion, particularly over the last decade. Unbridled personal political ambition, unemployment, and underdevelopment, underpinned by low levels of education and political systems in which certain sections of the population are excluded from political and economic decisions that affect them: these are the root causes of West Africa's social breakdown and conflicts in the 1990s and early twenty-first century. Similarly, civil and political crises often erupt when governments are unable or unwilling to satisfy their citizens' most pressing needs. Put differently, the inability of some states to govern, to provide basic services, and to protect their citizens is the key to understanding the security dilemma confronting many West African societies (see Chapters 5 and 7).

These factors, together with the traditional understanding of security—meaning in large part the security of sovereign states and their borders rather than that of people and their rights—constitute the key challenges facing ECOWAS today. West African leaders must break out of the current vicious cycle of conflicts. ECOWAS members must initiate development programs that seek to implement sound macroeconomic policies and "good governance." Both are essential for the establishment and maintenance of an environment conducive to socioeconomic development, as the current ideas of the New Partnership for Africa's Development (NEPAD) make clear (see Chapter 6). In addition to transparency and prudent management of public resources, good governance must be underpinned by an economic and regulatory environment that allows for open competition and individual initiative, while encouraging economic growth. The importance that ECOWAS currently attaches to the role of good governance in its development policies is based on the realization that macroeconomic policy reforms on their own will not provide West African states with the means to achieve the sustainable growth necessary to reduce poverty. Thus ECOWAS's potential contribution to alleviating conflicts in West Africa will depend to a large extent on the progress of its economic development programs.

Prospects for the Future and an Agenda for Action

In spite of the somewhat negative impact of the CEAO/UEMOA dimension of regionalism on the ECOWAS integration process, there are several reasons for some guarded optimism in considering the prospects for economic integration in West Africa. Much more is now known in the subregion about the problems as well as the advantages of economic integration than in the past, and the main factors for successful integration have been identified more clearly than before, even if the lessons of regional integration have not yet been fully implemented. There is growing conviction in all ECOWAS member states among government officials, business executives, and civil society actors that the future of each national economy lies in successful regional integration. Evidence of this conviction has been manifested in the fact that several ECOWAS governments are enhancing institutional arrangements for integration by creating a ministry exclusively devoted to regional integration in Burkina Faso, Guinea, Ghana, Mali, Niger, Nigeria, and Senegal. The private sector, too, through the West African Enterprise Network and similar regional bodies, is getting more involved in the integration process. The establishment of ECOBANK, a private regional commercial banking group with twenty-four branches in twelve ECOWAS countries, is a further concrete manifestation of private sector–led cooperation in West Africa.

While not much has been achieved in the "core areas" of regional economic integration in West Africa, it must be noted that ECOWAS has recorded major breakthroughs in some vital areas. ECOWAS and the East

African Community are the only economic groupings in Africa whose members have abolished entry visas in order to facilitate the free movement of community citizens within their subregion. Further signs of progress involve the creation of an ECOWAS travel certificate, ECOWAS traveler checks, and harmonized immigration and emigration forms. A community-wide insurance scheme has been established for ECOWAS citizens, and a telecommunications project has resulted in improved communication among member states. A West African gas pipeline is being built to transport gas throughout the subregion. All this, together with the construction of interstate highways and interconnecting roads, will enable ECOWAS to make greater strides toward creating the regional infrastructure needed to stimulate trade and investment.

While plans for the creation of a single West African currency are making progress but have yet to achieve their goals, the long-awaited ECOWAS parliament and court of justice have now been inaugurated. The increasing spread of more democratic government in Benin, Cape Verde, Ghana, Mali, Nigeria, Senegal, and Sierra Leone has created new possibilities for West African populations to take a more active part in shaping their political and economic future. Problems of good governance, democracy, and human rights constitute the foremost preoccupations of most West African countries today. Though full-fledged democracy is still far from being entrenched in the subregion, the general picture shows that substantial progress has been made in establishing more transparent political systems. In most West African states, the old political order appears to be disappearing, with single-party systems having given way to multiparty systems, while the market economy is replacing previously government-dominated economies.

This progress has been boosted by economic reforms that have led to the increased participation of the private sector in national economies, and to productivity gains. These initiatives should improve the competitiveness of local firms in international markets. The widespread adoption and pursuit of wide-ranging economic reforms by ECOWAS countries is now a matter of record. These reforms provide an indispensable backbone for regional cooperation and integration. Specifically, the pursuit of bold structural adjustment programs and other economic reform policies should remove some of the rigidities in national economic policy, promote flexible responses to the dynamics of internal and international economic relationships, and remove distortions that have often obstructed positive approaches to integration. A number of favorable developments have taken place since the end of the Cold War—in particular, the adoption of the fast-track approach to monetary integration—that have not only given the integration process much needed impetus, but also provided the basis for future strategies that can be adopted to ensure an accelerated and sustainable integration of the national economies of

West African states. The fast-track initiative has already led to the first serious attempt toward harmonization of the integration programs of ECOWAS and UEMOA. This progress must be continued.

The most impressive success recorded by ECOWAS so far, however, is in the area of the maintenance of regional peace and security. The decision by West African leaders to launch the ECOWAS Cease-Fire Monitoring Group (ECOMOG) operation into Liberia, and subsequently Sierra Leone, Guinea-Bissau, and Côte d'Ivoire, represents an attempt by ECOWAS to employ peacekeeping and peace enforcement as part of its approach to finding a solution to subregional conflicts. With the realization that ECOWAS cannot fulfill its integrationist ambitions without a stable subregion, the decision to establish ECOMOG marked a strategic turn in the international approach to managing internal crises. ECOMOG is the first subregional, multinational peacekeeping effort by African countries to resolve an African conflict. It has earned international respect for the continent through its efforts to return Liberia, Sierra Leone, Guinea-Bissau, and Côte d'Ivoire to stability after a decade of bloody conflicts. Above all, the birth of a new security mechanism in West Africa in 1999 has given the subregion a glimmer of hope for the future (see Chapter 13).

Much needs to be done before the successful reduction or eventual elimination of the UEMOA complication in ECOWAS's integrationist ambitions. The need to rationalize regional integration arrangements in West Africa in order to establish ECOWAS as the sole motor of integration has become increasingly necessary to eliminate subregional duplication and rivalry. This should be done by absorbing UEMOA into ECOWAS under a common currency. This way, a large consumer market "could be created between now and 2020, with a population of 350 million with a consumption potential as great as that of France today."[23] Such a move would also help ECOWAS avoid the great deal of time it now spends on harmonizing its programs with those of UEMOA.

One major concern of this chapter has been the importance of political will at the highest levels of government in order for these integration efforts to succeed. The experience of the past four decades has demonstrated that it is the vision, will, and commitment of those directly involved, and especially of senior political leaders, that have proved to be the critical factor in the successes and failures of subregional initiatives in cooperation and integration. ECOWAS members should therefore demonstrate greater political will by implementing the decisions, acts, and protocols that they have willingly adopted. They should emulate UEMOA countries that created a free trade zone in less than two years and entered into a customs union by 2000. Meaningful action must be taken to overcome the problems of program implementation. To this end, ECOWAS should create a high-level multidisciplinary implementation group to pursue two goals: first, critically review measures taken by each member state toward ratification and implementation of ECOWAS conventions and protocols, as well as the legislative and administrative conventions that have been concluded for the implementation of ECOWAS priority programs; and second, periodically monitor and assess the progress of the ECOWAS integration process.

The success of any regional strategy for collective self-reliance hinges on the nurturing of common political will by national governments, which in turn requires support from political leaders and citizens in general. In this regard, ECOWAS institutions should be more rooted in the minds of West Africa's citizens, who should be constantly taught and reminded that whenever they use a telephone, cablegram, e-mail, fax, or the Internet, whenever they enter any West African country visa-free, whenever they are permitted to reside in a subregional state and establish a business there, they are using services and enjoying rights that have been facilitated by the existence of ECOWAS. By emphasizing the functional aspects of the community to its citizens, and by encouraging them to participate more fully in ECOWAS's development process, a greater commitment to regional cooperation and integration will develop.

One important lesson to be learned from past experiences of regional economic cooperation and integration in West Africa is that ordinary people are marginalized from the process of regionalism. Accelerated economic recovery in West Africa requires a new domestic order that emphasizes democratization and popular participation. The pervasive political instability, crises of legitimacy, and civil strife in West Africa are incompatible with successful economic cooperation and integration for accelerated recovery and transformation of the subregion. Since one of the most common sources of these political problems is often the perceived denial of democratic participation, West African countries must ensure the full participation of all sections of their societies in the process of developmental regionalism.

Closely related to this is the need to strengthen the popular base of West African regionalism to enable it to meet the challenges of integrating UEMOA into ECOWAS. There is an urgent need to create popular support for regionalism. This requires an increase of pressure groups for both participation in, and mobilization of, public opinion in support of ECOWAS's integration goals. Various stakeholders—the business community, market women, civil servants, and the private sector—must be made aware of ECOWAS's integration program through education on the benefits of cooperation, and through publicity campaigns to enlighten the public on the fruits of economic integration. Regionalism cannot be imposed by ECOWAS leaders from above. It has to develop from the grassroots and closely involve civil society. The effective implementation of these policy prescriptions would contribute significantly to meeting the challenges of integration in West Africa. The time for empty rhetoric and fruitless debate is over. It is now time for concrete action in the noble aim of achieving the lofty ambitions of ECOWAS's "Founding Fathers" to build an economically integrated community in West Africa.

Notes

1. Nicholas Plessz, *Problems and Prospects of Regional Integration in West Africa* (Montreal: McGill University Press, 1968), p. 13.

2. Adebayo Adedeji, "Problems and Prospects of Regional Cooperation in West Africa," in African Association for Public Administration and Management, *Problems and Prospects of Regional Cooperation in Africa* (Nairobi: English Press, 1969), p. 67.

3. Adekeye Adebajo, *Building Peace in West Africa: Liberia, Sierra Leone, and Guinea-Bissau* (Boulder: Lynne Rienner Publishers, 2002), p. 24.

4. UNDP, *Human Development Report 2001* (New York: Oxford University Press, 2001), pp. 146–147.

5. Ibid., pp. 167–169.

6. S. K. B. Asante, *The Political Economy of Regionalism: A Decade of the Economic Community of West African States (ECOWAS)* (New York: Praeger, 1986), pp. 2–3.

7. ECOWAS, *Annual Report 2001* (Abuja: Executive Secretariat, 2001), p. 10.

8. Ibid.

9. Adebajo, *Building Peace in West Africa,* p. 31.

10. S. K. B. Asante, "ECOWAS/CEAO: Conflict and Cooperation in West Africa," in R. I. Onwuka and A. Sesay, eds., *The Future of Regionalism in Africa* (London: Macmillan, 1985), pp. 77–82.

11. S. K. B. Asante, *Regionalism and Africa's Development: Expectations, Reality, and Challenges* (London: Macmillan, 1997), pp. 114–116.

12. S. K. B. Asante and Alex Abankwa, *A Study of the Impact of the West African Economic and Monetary Union (UEMOA) on Ghana,* consultancy report, Accra, October 1999, p. 10.

13. Ibid.

14. Asante, "ECOWAS/CEAO," p. 87.

15. ECOWAS, *Economic Community of West African States: 2000,* interim report by the executive secretary, ECW/CM XLVVI/2, Abuja, 2000, p. 70.

16. Cited in Christopher M. Andrew, "France: Adjustment to Change," in Hedley Bull, ed., *The Expansion of International Society* (Oxford: Clarendon Press, 1984), p. 337.

17. European Commission, *The European Union, the Countries of West Africa, and WAEMU* (Brussels: European Commission, 1997), pp. 15–19.

18. Asante and Abankwa, *Study of the Impact of UEMOA,* p. 74.

19. Cited in ibid., pp. 39–40. Compiled from *Status Report on Implementation of ECOWAS Priority Programmes,* ECW/CMXLIII/13, Abuja, September 1998.

20. S. K. B. Asante, "Ghana-Nigeria Fast-Track for the West African Integration Process: Problems and Prospects," paper presented at the workshop "West African Integration: The Way Forward," organized by the Legon Centre for International Affairs and Friedrich Ebert Stiftung, Ho, Ghana, November 2000.

21. David Asante, "The West African Common Currency: The Benefits to Workers and Employers," paper presented at a seminar for the Trade Union Congress (Ghana), Accra, 2001.

22. H. A. K. Wampah, "Future Plans for the ECOWAS Monetary Zone," paper presented at the seminar "European Monetary Union and the Euro: A Learning Experience for ECOWAS," Accra, April 2002.

23. John Igue, "Regional Dynamics in West Africa," issue paper presented at the workshop "Special Event Meeting of the Sahel and West African Club," Accra, 20–21 May 2002.

4

The Dilemmas of Regionalization

Daniel C. Bach

This chapter focuses on current attempts in West Africa to adjust to the challenges of globalization through the revival of developmental regionalism: the core component of the mandate of the Economic Community of West African States (ECOWAS). After an introductory discussion of the concepts of "new" regionalism and regionalization, the integration strategies and programs currently being implemented by ECOWAS are reviewed. This is followed by a discussion of the supranational, hegemonic, and intergovernmental dimensions of regional construction. The concluding section of the chapter examines the destructuring pressure of de facto regionalization and its implications for states and institutions in West Africa.

The literature on regionalization was once stigmatized for its lack of clarity in the use of such notions as integration and cooperation, or the interactions between regional organizations and regional systems.[1] In recent years, the renewal of debates on regionalism and regionalization has similarly been prone to laxity and fuzziness due to the growing global impact of, and increasingly broad agendas associated with, their interplay within the world economy. This process has involved such extensive transformations in the scope and patterns of previously existing regional arrangements as to warrant their encapsulation as "new" regionalism. Just as in the past, there is no clear understanding of what precisely "new" regionalism entails and how it fits into the post–Cold War international order.[2] In the introduction to a four-volume collection on "new" regionalism published in 2000, Björn Hettne defines the concept as "a multidimensional form of integration which includes economic, political, social and cultural aspects and thus goes far beyond the goal of creating region-based free trade regimes or security alliances. Rather the political ambition of establishing regional coherence and identity seems to be of primary importance."[3] This definition aptly reflects on the considerable broadening of agendas associated with regionalism. Its emphasis on state-centered projects, regimes, and processes remains extremely conventional insofar as it overlooks the cross-fertilization, and at times disjuncture, between institutionalized de jure spaces and strategies and informal de facto processes.[4]

Current African experiences stress the implications of a dichotomy between regionalism and regionalization so as to enable an appraisal of "new" regionalism in a comparative perspective, free of the imprint of European experience on the conceptualization of regionalism in the Third World. Regionalism refers specifically to ideas, ideologies, programs, policies, and goals that seek to promote an identified social space as the regional project. It involves the construction as opposed to the formation of an identity. Whereas the construction of this identity is premised on explicitly defined policy initiatives and objectives, formation addresses social processes and outcomes and often requires a longer-term perspective.[5] Regionalism postulates the implementation of a program and the definition of a strategy and is therefore often associated with institution building. Regionalization, on the other hand, refers to processes that may or may not be related to the emergence of regional institutional structures and patterns of transaction. Regionalization may therefore result from regionalism being put into practice, but it may also emerge irrespective of whether there is a regionalist project or not. Regionalization may simply be an outcome of the behavior of agents who are not motivated by regionalist concerns, as illustrated by transborder trade in West Africa, the strategies of transnational corporations in Europe, or the ability of the Chinese diasporas of Southeast Asia to build systems of production across borders inherited from the Cold War.

In Africa, "new" regionalism has become associated with two key features: the broadening of institutional agendas and the globalization of the world economy. The broadening of institutional agendas results from the unprecedented emphasis on security as a threat to states and a precondition for the implementation of traditional developmental concerns. This occurs in a context where the dissolution of the "overlay" effect of the Cold War and postimperial legacies on domestic and interstate conflicts has created a new space for the assertion of regional powers and regional conflict resolution mechanisms.

"New" regionalism is also closely related to the advancement of globalization. Domino effects were created by the deepening of European integration (through the single European act of 1986) and the creation of the North American Free Trade Agreement (NAFTA) in 1993, which simultaneously triggered a scramble for the (re)institutionalization of regionalism. By the late 1980s, in Africa, as in Eastern Europe and Latin America, regional integration schemes that set out to achieve "delinking" from the international system through import substitution or insulation from capitalism had failed to do so. Many developing countries were by then committed, at least in principle, to macroeconomic structural adjustment reforms, and the revival of regionalism as an economic project was conceived as the expansion of neoliberal national programs into neoregionalist policies. In Africa, this meant that new mandates and priorities were ascribed to, or imposed on, such major regional institutions as ECOWAS (the revised Cotonou treaty of 1993), the Southern African Development Community (SADC) (the Windhoek treaty of 1992), the Union Economique et Monétaire Ouest Africaine (UEMOA) (the Dakar treaty of 1994), and the Common Market for Eastern and Southern Africa (COMESA) (founded in 1993 in Lusaka as a direct continuation of the Preferential Trade Area for Eastern and Southern African States [PTA]). In 2001 the African Union (Lusaka treaty) also replaced the Organization of African Unity (OAU) as an all-embracing continental organization. Parallel to these processes, the classic conception of North-South and East-West interactions as necessarily antinomic has been challenged by the creation of interregional free trade and investment zones and the increasing integration of neighboring states and economies into "core regions."[6] This trend is vividly illustrated by Mexico's adhesion to NAFTA in 1994 and the enlargement of the European Union (EU) to include ten eastern and central European states by mid-2004.

Development Integration:
Is It Still ECOWAS's Primary Function?

The current focus on institutional capacity and restructuring within ECOWAS, and the organization's recently reiterated commitments to economic and monetary integration, represent valuable attempts to overcome a "credibility deficit" generated by programs that have had little impact on the living conditions of the majority of West Africa's 230 million citizens. As Jeffrey Fine and Stephen Yeo provocatively observed:

> In spite of . . . the establishment of many sub-regional entities and substantial expenditure on transport and communications, links among the economies of the [African] region are in certain respects even weaker than in colonial times. . . . In West Africa, neither the establishment of the ECOWAS nor the CEAO (*Communauté Economique de l'Afrique de l'Ouest*) has restored the economically efficient seasonal migration of labour to the cost of colonial times.[7]

Indeed, the brutal expulsion of about 3 million mostly West African "aliens" from Nigeria in the 1980s, or more recently, the violence generated by the instrumentalization of xenophobia in Côte d'Ivoire, has challenged the very patterns of migrations and settlement that ECOWAS and the CEAO/ UEMOA were mandated to guarantee and promote.[8]

As the ECOWAS treaty was being redrafted in the early 1990s, its executive secretary, Abass Bundu, seriously dampened expectations that this process would be sufficient to revive subregional integration: "The slow pace of regional integration in West Africa has almost nothing to do with the limitations [insuffisances] noted in the 1975 ECOWAS Treaty. The adoption of an ideal treaty is of little importance if member-states do not decide to consider regional integration as an important national enterprise" (my translation).[9] Bundu's pessimistic assessment regarding the lack of political will and commitment to regional integration was echoed by his successor, Lansana Kouyaté, a decade later:

> An analysis of the West African experience of integration within the context of ECOWAS shows a poor record with regard to the execution of the Community programmes. The provisions of the revised Treaty instituting the principle of supranationality are not being applied. Several protocols are contravened, particularly those pertaining to free movement of goods and persons. . . . The situation shows all too clearly that a sense of belonging to a plurinational Community is cruelly lacking.[10]

The 1979 ECOWAS protocol on the free movement of persons is often considered to be the most significant achievement of ECOWAS in the area of socioeconomic integration. Under the protocol, citizens from any ECOWAS state may travel and reside in another member state for a maximum of ninety days, provided that they possess valid travel documents, namely a passport or travel certificate and international vaccination certificates. The implementation of the protocol began in 1980, and it is now formally operational in all member states. Yet "nearly all the states still maintain numerous check-points and ECOWAS citizens are subjected to administrative harassment and extortion," an assessment all too often confirmed by news reports or anecdotal accounts by travelers in the subregion.[11]

The lack of market integration through trade liberalization is commonly presented as "the most glaring failure for ECOWAS."[12] Intraregional trade still represents an insignificant portion of total official exports in the ECOWAS subregion, having only grown from 4 percent to about 11 percent over the past two decades. In accordance with ECOWAS's trade liberalization program relaunched on 1 January 1990, a free trade area should have been established by 31 December 1999 through the progressive elimination of tariffs and barriers on unprocessed products, handicraft, and industrial goods originating from the ECOWAS countries. By the beginning of 2000, implementation of the scheme had hardly begun—only one country, Benin, was considered by the ECOWAS secretariat to have met the conditions of the program.

Nor have past commitments toward monetary integration materialized. ECOWAS's initial plan to create a single monetary zone by 1994 had made no progress by 1993, when the Cotonou treaty (Article 54) postponed the deadline for a single monetary union until 2009. Implementation of this schedule was lagging behind when the ECOWAS Authority of Heads of State endorsed a program of "remobilization" at their Lomé summit in December 1999. Officially described as a "fast-track" initiative toward economic and monetary integration, the program aims at the creation of a single market, the establishment of a common external tariff, and monetary cooperation based on the harmonization of economic and financial policies. Central to this process is the acknowledgment that "any group of countries may take concrete pragmatic measures to accelerate integration among themselves."[13] This resulted in a joint initiative by Nigeria and Ghana—the "Declaration of Accra"—toward the creation of a monetary union between the nonmember states of UEMOA by 1 January 2003.[14] Since April 2000, Gambia, Ghana, Guinea, Nigeria, and Sierra Leone have adhered to the establishment of the future West African Monetary Zone (WAMZ), which, once established, is expected to collaborate with UEMOA toward the creation of a single monetary union.

The main impetus behind this ambitious ECOWAS program is the implementation of domestic policies of macroeconomic adjustment, a precondition for the harmonization of ECOWAS economies on a subregional basis. Both UEMOA and non-UEMOA states have committed themselves to "adhere to the ECOWAS macro-economic convergence criteria and adopt a surveillance mechanism for macro-economic policies . . . streamlined with national economic policies and incorporated into the structural adjustment policies in member states."[15] This approach is strongly evocative of the post-Maastricht macroeconomic convergence exercise toward the European Monetary Union (EMU) after 1992.[16] Yet the domestic environment and conditions of implementation of the two processes are hardly comparable. The establishment of the euro zone came after much long-term preparation, planning, and public mobilization. The Werner report on the European Monetary Union was issued in 1970. There was widespread mobilization and consultation of citizens and civil society, a process that caused delay and, at times, dramatic setbacks, but also became a decisive step toward the legitimation of the project within member states. By 1989, much had been achieved within what was then known as the European Monetary System (EMS) in reducing inflation rates and maintaining a stable set of currency exchange rates when the Delors committee on the implementation of EMU released its macroeconomic and political blueprint. The conclusions of the Delors committee had considerable political weight because the majority of its members were central bank governors from EU states.[17] Most of their conclusions were eventually endorsed by national governments and found their way into the Treaty on European Union (TEU), signed in Maastricht in December 1991.

The Maastricht treaty was eventually ratified following a painstaking process fraught with uncertainties and policy reversals.[18] Implementation was not an easy task: Britain and Italy were forced to leave the EMS during Europe's financial crisis of 1992; in Belgium, France, and Germany, the convergence process resulted in governments having to adopt stringent and unpopular measures to control inflation, lower budget deficits, and maintain stable interest rates. The commitment to ensure domestic implementation of the criteria, however, remained undiminished, thus enabling a special European Council meeting in Brussels to endorse eleven of the twelve applications for membership in the monetary zone in May 1998.[19] The subsequent creation of the euro zone on 1 January 1999, and the replacement of European national currencies by the euro on 1 January 2002, could not have been undertaken without two decades of domestically enforced macroeconomic adjustment processes. The EMU is thus the outcome of a deepening and growing internalization of global macroeconomic adjustment constraints by member states, combined with their acceptance of a de jure empowerment of a new EU institution—the European Central Bank (ECB)—as the agency exclusively charged with the coordination of monetary policy within the euro zone.

A similar process of long-term planning, internalization of common economic policy objectives, and the empowerment of regional institutions has not yet occurred in West Africa. As Lansana Kouyaté noted in 2000:

> In its years of existence, ECOWAS has undertaken many cooperation and integration programmes in the key sectors of the economy, particularly with regard to trade promotion, trade liberalisation, provision of better road and telecommunication infrastructures. . . . However, such programmes have had minimal impact because most of the decisions taken by the ECOWAS policy organs are never implemented.[20]

The deficit of policy implementation that has affected ECOWAS for several decades is largely responsible for its de facto transformation into a multisectoral development agency. If left unchecked, this trend will, at best, restrict its role to identifying and mobilizing international support for projects toward the physical integration of West Africa through transport infrastructure, communication, and energy.

The Elusive Quest for Supranationalism

Policy formation and enforcement within ECOWAS and UEMOA reveal three patterns of power allocation and redistribution: supranationalism, intergovernmentalism, and hegemonic integration. Supranationalism is generally defined as a pattern of interaction between states and an international institution that is entrusted with the management of sovereign powers in specifically defined areas. Decisions "are taken by a majority voting system" as opposed to relying on consensus, "and their execution is supervised by the international institution, rather than by the state[s]."[21] Consequently, supranationalism involves "changes in the structure and powers of the international institution" and challenges two aspects of state sovereignty: "the exclusive competence of the state in its own territory" and "the relative independence of law-making entities from outside intervention."[22] Other factors conducive to the promotion of supranationalism include formal guarantees such as the independence and budgetary autonomy of the secretariat of the institution vis-à-vis member states, as well as "less tangible factors such as the quality of leadership in the institution."[23]

In the ECOWAS charter, signed in Lagos on 28 May 1975, the initial aim of the body was defined in Article 2 as the promotion of "co-operation and development in all fields of economic activity." No reference was made to "integration" nor to the notion of the supranational empowerment of ECOWAS (see Chapter 2). Reflecting concerns about the nonimplementation of decisions, ECOWAS member states revised their charter in July 1993 in Cotonou and broadened the subregional body's objectives to include "co-operation and integration, leading to the establishment of an economic union."[24] Despite the broadening of ECOWAS's mandate, the approach to regional integration remained cautious and tentative under the new treaty, and the process was described as one that "*may* demand partial and gradual pooling of national sovereignties to the Community" (my emphasis).[25] Throughout the text of the Cotonou treaty, "integration" does not clearly emerge as a major goal, unlike such notions as "co-ordination," "harmonization," and the development of "joint programs" or "common policies." The decisionmaking structures in the Cotonou treaty also reiterate the overall preeminence of intergovernmentalism: the Authority of Heads of State remains the "supreme institution" of ECOWAS.[26] However, the independent budgetary funding of institutions and the establishment of new institutions of control and arbitration—an ECOWAS parliament, court of justice, and economic and social council—may well produce some degree of supranationality.

The implementation of the decision to establish an ECOWAS levy providing an independent source of revenue for member states has been a slow and somewhat self-defeating process. In 1996 it was decided to levy a 0.5 percent tax on products imported from non-ECOWAS countries. By mid-2000 the eight ECOWAS states that had adopted the required changes were retaining total control over the resource allocation process. This led former ECOWAS executive secretary Lansana Kouyaté to complain that "the amounts collected are not paid directly into the Secretariat's accounts. They are first paid into government coffers from where Treasury officials transfer into the Community accounts the amounts they please."[27]

The recently established ECOWAS court of justice should be able to perform important supranational functions.[28] It is expected to carry out its mission "independently of the Member States and the institutions of the Community."[29] It will deliver rulings that are "binding on the member-states, on the institutions of the Community and on individuals and corporate bodies."[30] This new organ will require adequate funding and effective powers of enforcement in order to have any impact. In those areas under its competence, the court will be located at the apex of the hierarchy of judicial institutions in West Africa. Its effectiveness will therefore depend largely on the attitude of domestic courts toward the enforcement of community law. The empowerment of the court with a supranational level of jurisdiction will only make sense if its architecture is inclusive of decision-making structures within member states. The ability of ECOWAS to arbitrate and impose its rulings through a regional court of justice presupposes that, across the subregion, national judicial systems may be called upon when community law is being violated.

A decade after the revision of the Cotonou treaty, the empowerment of ECOWAS as a supranational institution and the enhancement of its autonomy are still being awaited. Such a situation is sadly the norm rather than the exception on a continent where the only working examples of supranational integration originate from the adaptation of schemes established under colonial rule and managed through a process of embedded hegemonic domination.

Hegemony as the Exclusive Pattern of Institutionally Endorsed Integration

Integration through hegemonic domination and regulation is a characteristic shared by regional groupings in sub-Saharan Africa. In South Africa, integration within the Southern African Customs Union/Common Monetary Area (SACU/CMA) is organized around a customs union and a de facto common currency: the South African rand.[31] In West and Central Africa, the Communauté Financière Africaine (CFA) franc zone provides the basis for UEMOA—known as Union Monétaire Ouest Africaine (UMOA) until 1994—and the Communauté Economique et Monétaire d'Afrique Centrale (CEMAC)—previously known as the Banque des Etats d'Afrique Centrale (BEAC). Integration within these three organizations is institutionally guaranteed by a core state as opposed to a supranational institution. Most significant, these guarantees are also formally endorsed by decisionmaking structures. Integration through a core state refers accordingly to a pattern of interactions as much as to a de jure status.

International hegemony as a pattern of domination is essentially, though not exclusively, based on the expression of power through consensus. This definition has the advantage of being inclusive of the criteria emphasized by scholars of international relations and international political economy who rely on significantly distinct theoretical premises. Robert Cox notes that hegemony requires "that the consensual aspect of power is in the forefront." Even though "coercion is always latent, [it] is only applied in marginal, deviant cases."[32] In order to act as a hegemon, Cox continues, "a state would have to found and protect . . . an order which most other states . . . could find compatible with their interests."[33] James Mittelman and Richard Falk characterize hegemony as a "mix of coercion and consent in which consent is the dominant element."[34] Hegemonic power does not depend on control through violence or territorial incorporation; it requires the ability to establish some degree of legitimacy through co-optive power. For this reason, hegemony cannot be reduced to such notions as "preponderance of power" or "imperialism," even though the line between hegemony and imperial dominance is at times tenuous. The characterization of imperial domination as "hegemony's evil twin" by the Greek historian Herodotus is a pertinent reminder that hegemony may represent a step toward direct territorial control or may refer to processes resulting from the dilution of imperial control.[35]

The discussion of South Africa's hegemonic status within the SACU/CMA does not fall within the scope of this chapter and has been adequately discussed elsewhere.[36] Within UEMOA and CEMAC, monetary union may be described as the founding stone and the cement of regional integration. Both groupings belong to the CFA franc zone, a monetary union of fifteen member states established before World War II and reorganized in 1972 and 1973.[37] Intraregional monetary integration is ensured through two regional central banks: the Banque Centrale des Etats de l'Afrique de l'Ouest (BCEAO) and the BEAC. These banks operate on a parallel basis and issue currencies that are freely convertible on a one-to-one basis through an interbanking system. The overall unity of the CFA franc zone and its stability and convertibility result from the role played by France: the CFA is pegged to the French franc at a fixed parity of 100 to 1, and its convertibility is guaranteed by the French treasury in Paris. The currency reserves of BCEAO and BEAC member states are kept in operation accounts in Paris, which may incur overdrafts.

The institutions of the franc zone have been celebrated as "an appropriate blend of penalties and rewards, of national participation and supranational discipline, and of African and donor power."[38] For African member states, the rewards of the franc zone include the benefits of collective reserve-pooling and the guarantee from France of financing aggregate deficits. The penalties entail the loss of the collective reserve-pooling capacity and loss of French aid implicit in its underwriting of the zone.[39] Paris's financial underwriting represents one of the functional characteristics associated with the notion of hegemonic domination and regulation.

France's role as a guarantor of the franc zone arrangements would not make sense without its ability to act as an "agency of restraint" on monetary issues.[40] This was most clearly illustrated when fiscal indiscipline and an overvaluation of the CFA led Paris to conclude that it was necessary to devalue the currency. Member states of the CFA franc zone had no other alternative but to follow suit at the Dakar meeting of 11 January 1994.[41] This process effectively recognized the inability of the franc zone's decisionmaking structures to instigate and ensure proper implementation of macroeconomic adjustments within the UMOA. Indeed, its larger member states had successfully "avoided direct controls on financing by borrowing from commercial and development banks which could obtain refinancing from the BCEAO at concessional rates. The lack of control over these credits opened the door to excessive lending to governments, despite respect of the formal ceilings on direct financing."[42]

For member states of the franc zone, the devaluation of the CFA in 1994 signaled a return to the classical tools of structural adjustment and a reduction of the opportunities for escapism generated by France's previous hostility to International Monetary Fund (IMF) prescriptions. Devaluing the CFA involved an acknowledgment by Paris of its inability or unwillingness to conceive of integration within the franc zone as an exclusively bilateral relationship. At the same time, the signing of the UEMOA treaty by francophone West African states in Dakar on the eve of the devaluation in 1994 also signified for France "an expanded role in a new international treaty for which it acts as the ultimate guarantor. . . . [T]he commitment is open-ended involving the establishment of new multilateral institutions and surveillance of macro-economic policies whose credibility ultimately rests on France herself. In short, France's role as a guarantor appears significantly greater than under the previous monetary agreement."[43]

Since UEMOA was established in 1994, it has achieved progress in the field of institutional harmonization and functional cooperation, and a number of new agreements have been completed. Yet the evidence points toward a limited internalization of the integration-through-norms approach ("*intégration par les règles*"). Even as a revised Convergence, Stability, Growth, and Solidarity Pact (CSGSP) was being adopted in Lomé in December 1999, progress toward macroeconomic convergence remained uneven within UEMOA due to "the lack of sanctions, the absence of a consultation process among members, as well as poorly designed indicators."[44] By the time trade liberalization became effective on 1 January 2000, private interest groups within member states had "pushed to have many locally produced goods moved into tariff categories with the highest protection."[45] Intrazonal trade continues to be hampered by nontariff barriers such as unnecessary roadblocks and administrative harassment by customs officials. In addition, despite substantial reforms in recent years, "financial depth remain[ed] relatively low [due to] the low level of competition among banks, the weakness of the judiciary system's enforcement of contracts and the extensive government involvement and management of banks."[46]

Integration within UEMOA appears inextricably linked to the future of the franc zone, which is now pegged, through the guarantee of the French treasury, to the euro. Indeed, the European Council agreed in November 1998 that the franc zone's monetary arrangements could continue as a quid pro quo for an empowerment of the EU as a multilateral agency of restraint. France's margin of maneuver is nowadays restricted by the need to inform the ECB and its financial and economic committee about any adjustment of the euro/CFA parity. Changes affecting the nature, scope, and membership of the franc zone also require prior approval by the European Council, acting on the advice of the ECB and the European Commission in Brussels. Although this was not necessarily initially envisioned, the process toward economic monetary union in Europe eventually conferred on the ECB an unprecedented "role and surveillance capacity over the management of the WAEMU (UEMOA) central Bank (BCEAO)," as a result of which the "BCEAO should be less influenced by clientelism and political considerations, than under the sole supervision of the French authorities."[47]

Were the current arrangements to fall apart, there is no evidence that ECOWAS's capacity to achieve its regional integration objectives would be enhanced given its lack of empowerment by member states and their limited internalization of macroeconomic reforms. UEMOA remains dependent on France's continuing commitment to act as an embedded guarantor and an agency of restraint. Options for the future could include the preservation of the status quo, or more likely, the adjustment of existing agreements to ensure a direct or indirect link with the euro zone.

Whatever solution prevails, the depth and sustainability of the drive toward integration within UEMOA raise more fundamental questions. Past expectations that the organization would promote the emergence of "a sub-regional hub comprising the Côte d'Ivoire and Senegal, with a rim comprising the other African members" of the union, have been severely damaged by the instrumentalization of xenophobia in Côte d'Ivoire and the increasing instability in the subregion, with conflicts raging in Côte d'Ivoire, Liberia, and Senegal's Casamance region.[48] There are three possible future scenarios for members of UEMOA: first, the progressive transformation of existing arrangements into empty shells through loss of territorial control and policy credibility; second, their formal or de facto reorganization within new sub-regional groupings; and third, their possible reorganization along lines of a Nigerian bid for regional hegemony (see Chapters 2, 13, and 14). It is important to note that these options are not necessarily mutually exclusive. Nor should Nigerian hegemony be automatically interpreted as a path toward enhanced regional stability.[49]

Intergovernmentalism: Mirage and Mirror

The ability to promote regionalism on an intergovernmental or supra-national basis mirrors the degree of internalization and enforcement of commonly agreed decisions by member states. Supranationalism, whether based on common institutions or organized around core states, is neither a universal panacea nor the deus ex machina of successful regional policies. The European construction process is worth recalling in this respect. The concept and implementation of Europe's *Sonderweg* (specific approach) toward "constitutionalism and federalism" are deeply rooted in the behavior of member states: domestic "constitutional actors . . . accept the European constitutional discipline . . . as an autonomous voluntary act . . . of subordination, in the discrete areas governed by Europe, to a norm which is the aggregate expression of other wills, other political identities, other political communities."[50] Herein lies the basis for policy credibility and sustainability.

Efficient regional integration schemes consistently point to the key contribution of "participatory supranational agencies." These agencies "are more functional than alien ones. Permanently credible reciprocal threats are more effective than temporary rewards."[51] The ECOWAS treaty of 1993 represents a curious succession of shortcuts, since it endorses a pattern of decisionmaking typical of authoritarian rule. Article 9 of the treaty stipulates that the powers of the Authority of Heads of State should "automatically enter into force . . . 90 days after their signature."[52] This disposition proceeds from the assumption that ECOWAS leaders are such omnipotent rulers that they can commit their countries to agreements without a ratification process. Not surprisingly, such bypassing of domestic decisionmaking structures and agencies of restraint like national parliaments and domestic courts has failed to promote faster implementation of ECOWAS decisions.

Whenever they refuse to implement common policies or agree to transfers of sovereignty in discrete areas, ECOWAS member states condone and consolidate by default the definition of national and subregional policies. The weak institutionalization of domestic agencies of restraint contrasts sharply with the depth of the nonreciprocal bilateral policy commitments

made by ECOWAS members. Over the past two decades, trade liberalization has progressed most significantly through adjustment and macroeconomic reforms negotiated with and supervised by the Bretton Woods
institutions—the World Bank and the IMF. Jeffrey Fine and Stephen Yeo
have argued that "since structural adjustment policies in sub-Saharan Africa
invariably entail trade liberalization on a multilateral basis, deeper integration is more likely to occur as a consequence of these policies rather than
through the efforts of regional and sub-regional entities especially established for this purpose."[53] It is primarily through these structural adjustment
programs, and not as a result of implementing initiatives specifically prescribed by ECOWAS, that tariff and nontariff barriers have been reduced in
West Africa. Heavy reliance on external as opposed to indigenous restraints
has undermined the effectiveness and legitimacy of these processes, since
they are usually adopted as a result of pressure from "deeply alien and non
participatory" external agencies.[54]

Supranationalism, hegemonic integration, and intergovernmentalism
can equally contribute to the promotion of regional integration, provided
that they underscore a genuine sense of "ownership" of the integration
process within member states. Two positive steps in this direction should be
noted: the progressive reconciliation between the actual macroeconomic
policies of member states and the objectives assigned to ECOWAS, and the
changing interactions between ECOWAS and UEMOA. A more enabling
environment for the implementation of the trade liberalization objectives of
ECOWAS and the CEAO/UEMOA has progressively emerged in conjunction with radical shifts in the macroeconomic policies of member states.
Within the former CEAO, the modus operandi of the Taxe de Coopération
Régionale (TCR) system—negotiations on a product-by-product basis—and
the existence of a common currency initially encouraged the rapid growth
of trade among member states. However, from the early 1980s onward,
trade stagnated, underlining the limited complementarity among these
economies. To overcome these limitations would have required macroeconomic reforms, which member states were unwilling to consider within
their respective countries. Within the broader ECOWAS context, the debate
did not even reach this stage. Obstacles arose right from the start, due to the
organization's adoption of a global approach to trade liberalization at a time
when most of its members "were pursuing import-substitution industrialization strategies behind high protective walls."[55] This approach generated
a "negative neighborhood effect" and no significant bloc of countries
emerged to support ECOWAS's integration goals (see Chapter 3).[56]

The heterogeneity of monetary regimes further undermined any possibility of enhancing official trade within West Africa. The coexistence of
inconvertible currencies with convertible ones complicated the dismantling
of tariff and nontariff barriers, since this goal challenged neopatrimonial

strategies and rent-seeking based on the exploitation of trade disparities across borders.[57] The first sign of a collective departure from this trend occurred in 1994, when the devaluation of the CFA franc and the dissolution of the CEAO signified an endorsement of macroeconomic surveillance by the seven francophone ECOWAS member states that signed the UEMOA treaty. Implementation of ECOWAS's larger trade liberalization agenda remained in the doldrums since Nigeria's military ruler between 1993 and 1998, General Sani Abacha, decided to break away from Nigeria's structural adjustment program. The devaluation of the CFA franc and the subsequent revival of trade liberalization within UEMOA coincided with the reevaluation of the naira. Abacha, who had seized control of the Nigerian state in November 1993, quickly sidelined Nigeria's finance minister, Kalu Y. Kalu, who was known to be a supporter of trade liberalization.[58] Nigeria's January 1994 budget reasserted strict controls on finance, trade, and foreign exchange. As Peter Lewis noted, emphasis was put on a "nationalist and statist agenda" that rapidly came to be little more than a convenient cover for massive diversion of state resources, corrupt transactions on the foreign exchange market, and "predatory rule."[59]

The significance of ECOWAS's program of trade and monetary integration adopted in 1999 may well lie in its promotion of a bottom-up approach to integration, based on domestic macroeconomic adjustment and regional convergence,[60] and not so much in its commitment to a "fast-track" process that rapidly encountered difficulties. On 27 July 2001, the Convergence Council for non-UEMOA ECOWAS countries requested them "to ensure stricter compliance with the convergence criteria," while expressing the need for "an enforcement mechanism including penalties."[61] In January 2003 the deadline for the establishment of the WAMZ could not be met and this timeline was extended to 1 July 2005. In May 2003, however, the implementation of the convergence criteria was criticized by the Convergence Council of Ministers and Governors of the WAMZ that met in Banjul, Gambia.[62]

The "fast-track" program has endorsed what should be viewed as a positive tactical shift toward the improvement of interactions between ECOWAS and UEMOA/BCEAO. After years of stillborn resolutions reiterating that ECOWAS should become the sole regional entity in West Africa, ECOWAS leaders agreed in Lomé in 1999 to the "relevance of a differentiated approach in the march towards integration," thus allowing "any group of states within the Community to adopt concrete and pragmatic measures so as to accelerate their integration."[63] This flexible approach opened the way for the Nigeria-Ghana initiative toward the WAMZ. Most important, it also moved away from past attempts to stigmatize UEMOA as a stumbling block and blame it for the failures of ECOWAS to achieve its integration objectives. As Michael Davenport noted:

The fact that the UEMOA countries have made such progress to a large extent will facilitate integration among the ECOWAS member-states as a whole. The first stage of ECOWAS trade liberalization will be largely an extension of the existing UEMOA preferential regime. UEMOA has pioneered the establishment of a CET [common external tariff] that, with minor modifications, is appropriate for the region as a whole. The UEMOA monitoring mechanism can serve as a template for the region.[64]

The WAMZ program bears testimony to changing perceptions of what West African integration should entail: UEMOA, with its monitoring and convergence mechanisms, is treated as a model to emulate and compete with, a welcome departure from the past. Decades-old allegations of CEAO/UEMOA procrastination in implementing ECOWAS integration schemes, however, were often justified. But simultaneous allegations that this was responsible for the poor performance of ECOWAS programs would have been more credible if non-UEMOA ECOWAS member states had themselves proved genuinely committed to the implementation of the same commonly agreed policies, which was often not the case.[65]

The Challenge of de Facto Regionalization Through Transstate Networks

De facto integration relates to processes that do not proceed from formal transfers of sovereignty, but from the role of microagents and corporate actors. West Africa hosts no equivalent to the dynamism of conglomerates in Southeast Asia or South African firms in southern Africa. Nor has intraregional trade based on economic complementarities developed significantly, as noted above. De facto regionalization in West Africa essentially proceeds from the dynamism of transstate networks.

The notions of transstate networks and integration have been suggested in order to account for processes that combine *trans*national features—through the involvement of nonstate actors—with inter*state* relations and state policies—due to treatment of public functions as opportunities for patronage or enrichment.[66] The capacity to penetrate and permeate the state is central to the scope for, and contents of, transstate interactions.

Transstate flows are underscored by the capacity of microagents (traders, farmers, but also agents of authority acting in their private capacity) to take advantage of opportunities created by porous borders, weak state territorial controls, and disparities in fiscal, tariff, and monetary policies. Depending on circumstances, cross-border transactions are described as informal, unrecorded, underground trade; smuggling; transit or reexport trade; bottom-up regionalism; or even grassroots regionalization. These expressions encompass, each in its own way, key features associated with transstate networks. They share in common an emphasis on the significance of borderlands and frontiers. This overlooks the more fundamental role of interactions with the state in the definition of the interactions being monitored. It is the pattern of relationships to the state that first and foremost shapes and defines the nature of the interactions across the boundary, hence the reference to trans*state* as opposed to such related notions as trans*border* or trans*frontier* interactions.

The literature on African borders often emphasizes how frontiers delineate and separate communities, without acknowledging that their porous nature and the disparities that they delineate simultaneously create opportunities for transactions.[67] In West Africa, transstate regionalization has been stimulated since the colonial period by the exploitation of tariff, fiscal, and monetary discrepancies between neighboring states. Trade networks have expanded in conjunction with transactions on basic products (petroleum, staple food, cash crops) as much as on more sophisticated or high value-added goods (arms, hi-fi equipment, medicine, diamonds, ivory, drugs). In all cases, the rapport to legality has been key to the process: plugging official circuits into transstate networks, as witnessed in the coastal "warehouse states" of West Africa (Gambia, Togo, and Benin) in the 1970s and 1980s, did contribute to legalizing some of the transactions concerned, but this never translated into open and public endorsement of the transactions, since the profits were usually realized at the expense of the state on the other side of the border.

Transstate regionalization draws its strength from its combination of elements of responsiveness to situations of dispossession and hardship with accumulation strategies of the more powerful participants. In their pioneering study of the Beninois warehouse state in 1992, John Igué and Bio Soulé emphasized the capacity of transstate networks to "somewhat alleviate" the difficulties of the population.[68] Even when the state has not dramatically collapsed, transstate flows contribute to a vital diversification of rural and urban income sources. Farmers living in areas where the state circuits are no longer operational can also derive vital markets for their production from this "second economy," which has increasingly spread to the extent that it is now being perceived as the "real" economy. Farmers can use the incomes from these networks to secure preharvest cash advances essential for the maintenance of their families, and they can also employ such income to purchase tools, seeds, and other inputs. In urban centers, this second economy provides a supplementary financial buffer for declining and unpaid public sector salaries. It also supplies consumers with food, fuel, and manufactured goods, while creating earning opportunities for women. Access to these networks still remains extremely uneven and intensely competitive, and participation in them is usually motivated by desperation rather than by choice.[69] Far from being an epitome of conviviality, transstate regionalization tends to promote the dispossession of the weak and poor to the benefit of the strong and rich, with domestic actors also benefiting less from these transactions than international networks.

In several regions of the world, this regionalization goes hand in hand with institutional strategies that constitute a political response by member states to the globalization of national economies. In West Africa, transstate regionalization challenges states that are unable or unwilling to assert their sovereignty. Transstate regionalization also acts as a powerful incentive for the deinstitutionalization and accelerated privatization of state agencies, since the prosperity of transstate networks depends on their capacity to evade state control and regulations. The internationalization and at times criminalization of Africa's transstate flows and the tremendous profits generated by these transactions greatly facilitate the tailoring of the activity of impoverished state agencies to their requirements.

Toward Effective Regionalization in West Africa

Discussing current patterns of regional cooperation and integration in West Africa through the prisms of supranationalism, hegemony, and intergovernmentalism leads one to conclude that the efficiency of these patterns of regional governance depends *in fine* on the degree of internalization of domestic and subregional policies by member states. Whatever progress has so far been achieved by ECOWAS and UEMOA remains largely externally driven due to the predominant role ascribed to external donors and foreign agencies of restraint in the field of development cooperation and integration. Current attempts to establish an effective state and a citizen-friendly Pax West Africana point to the urgent need for the empowerment of domestic agencies of restraint.

West Africa's regionalization process all too often exposes the inability of African states to seek proper mandates or secure the implementation of policies within their own countries. When states do not have full control over their territories or when their bureaucrats and officials are inclined to draw revenues from a "variable geometry," the treatment of regulations, whether these are of national or subregional origin, becomes irrelevant. The frequently denounced lack of commitment of states to subregional integration is often a replication of patterns prevailing within their own borders. The discriminatory treatment accorded to ECOWAS citizens from other countries often does not differ that much from the insecurity that ECOWAS nationals may encounter within their own states on grounds of nonindigeneity, political affiliation, or social status. This situation has been most glaringly demonstrated by the recent instability in Côte d'Ivoire over the implementation of the exclusionary policy of *Ivoirité,* discrimination against naturalized Ivorians.

Decades of purely symbolic state commitments to the promotion of institutionalized processes of regionalization have provided fertile ground for the growth of criminalized transactions and the exploitation of the "dividends of violence." This has translated into a formatting "by default" of what regionalization means to states and citizens: the persistence of transborder disparities and their exploitation on a rent-seeking basis, but also, and increasingly, the persistence of violence due to the regionalization of domestic conflicts. Herein lies the real challenge, one that must be confronted by politicians and policymakers before regionalization can become consonant with security for ECOWAS nationals.

Notes

1. Ernst B. Haas, *The Uniting of Europe* (Stanford: Stanford University Press, 1970), p. 607.

2. Helge Hveem, "Political Regionalism: Master or Servant of Economic Internationalization?" in Björn Hettne, Andreas Inotai, and Osvaldo Sunkel, eds., *Globalism and the New Regionalism,* vol. 1 (London: Macmillan, 2000), pp. 85–115.

3. Björn Hettne, "The New Regionalism: A Prologue," in Björn Hettne, Andreas Inotai, and Osvaldo Sunkel, eds., *The New Regionalism and the Frontiers of Security and Development,* vol. 4 (London: Macmillan, 2000), p. xix.

4. Charles Oman, *Globalization and Regionalization: The Challenge for Developing Countries* (Paris: Organization for Economic Cooperation and Development, 1994).

5. This distinction draws from the dichotomy between state construction and state formation in B. Berman and John Lonsdale, *Unhappy Valley: Conflict in Kenya and Africa* (London: James Currey, 1992).

6. For a comprehensive analysis of this point, see Walter Kennes, *Competing in the Big League: Small Developing Countries and Global Markets* (London: Macmillan, 2000), pp. 104–127. With respect to Africa, the most comprehensive schemes are the U.S. Growth and Opportunity Act, and the EU-ACP Economic Partnership Agreements.

7. Jeffrey Fine and Stephen Yeo, "Regional Integration in Sub-Saharan Africa: Dead End or Fresh Start?" in Ademola Oyejide, Ibrahim Elbadawi, and Paul Collier, eds., *Regional Integration and Trade Liberalization in Sub-Saharan Africa,* vol. 1, *Framework, Issues, and Methodological Perspectives* (New York: St. Martin's, 1997), p. 428.

8. On the Nigerian expulsions of West Africans, see A. A. Afolayan, "Immigration and Expulsion of ECOWAS Aliens in Nigeria," *International Migration Review* 22, no. 1 (1988): 4–27; and M. Leann Brown, "Nigeria and the ECOWAS Protocol on Free Movement and Residence," *Journal of Modern African Studies* 27, no. 2 (1989): 251–273.

9. ECOWAS, *Le progrès continu dépend d'un effort soutenu: Rapport intérimaire du Secrétaire Exécutif M. A. Bundu* (Lagos: Executive Secretariat, November 1992), p. 18.

10. ECOWAS, *Executive Secretary's Reports: Twenty-fifth Anniversary Report* (Abuja: ECOWAS, 2000), available at www.ecowas.int/sitecedeao/english/regional.htm.

11. Ibid.

12. Ibid.

13. Introduction to ECOWAS, *Executive Secretary's Report for 2000* (Abuja: ECOWAS, 2000), available at www.ecowas.int/sitecedeao/english/regional.htm.

14. UEMOA includes Benin, Burkina Faso, Côte d'Ivoire, Guinea-Bissau, Mali, Niger, Togo, and Senegal.

15. ECOWAS, *Executive Secretary's Reports: Twenty-fifth Anniversary Report.*

16. Other attempts to emulate the EU's macroeconomic convergence process exist within UEMOA and the Southern Cone Common Market (Mercosur).

17. Kevin Featherstone, "The Political Dynamics of Economic and Monetary Union," in Laura Cram, Desmond Dinan, and Neill Nugent, eds., *Developments in the European Union* (New York: St. Martin's, 2000), pp. 311–329.

18. Ratification, initially rejected by the Danish electorate in May 1992, was secured through a second referendum, held in 1993. In France, the referendum of September 1992 produced a slight majority of *yes* votes. In the UK, the British parliament reluctantly ratified the treaty, while in Germany the TEU was challenged before the constitutional court in Karlsruhe, which eventually ruled it compatible with German federalism.

19. By then, three member states (the UK, Sweden, and Denmark) had opted out of the final stage of the process. Greece, whose admission was postponed, eventually became a member of the euro zone on 1 January 2001.

20. Lansana Kouyaté, introduction, sec. 7, to ECOWAS, *Executive Secretary's Report for 2000.*

21. Paul Taylor, "Supranationalism: The Power and Authority of International Institutions," in A. J. R. Groom and Paul Taylor, eds., *Frameworks for International Co-operation* (New York: St. Martin's, 1990), p. 109.

22. Ibid., pp. 110–111.

23. Ibid., p. 112.

24. *Treaty of ECOWAS* (Abuja: ECOWAS Secretariat, 1993), available at www.xecowas.int/sitecedeao/english/stat-1.htm.

25. Ibid., preamble.

26. Ibid., art. 7, sec. 1.

27. ECOWAS, *Executive Secretary's Reports: Twenty-fifth Anniversary Report.*

28. The adoption of internal rules of procedure of the ECOWAS Court of Justice by its seven judges was widely publicized after its establishment. See *The Guardian* (Lagos), 9 August 2001.

29. *Treaty of ECOWAS,* art. 15, sec. 3.

30. Ibid., art. 15, sec. 4.

31. See Colin McCarthy, "SACU and the Rand Zone," in Daniel Bach, ed., *Regionalization in Africa: Integration and Disintegration* (Oxford: James Currey, 1999), pp. 159–168.

32. Robert W. Cox, *Production, Power, and World Order: Social Forces in the Making of History* (New York: Columbia University Press, 1987), p. 164.

33. Ibid.

34. James H. Mittelman and Richard Falk, "Global Hegemony and Regionalism," in James H. Mittelman, ed., *The Globalization Syndrome: Transformation and Resistance* (Princeton: Princeton University Press, 2000), p. 131.

35. The Greek historian recounts how, during the fourth century B.C., Athens's initial hegemonic status progressively evolved toward imperial domination. See John Wickersham, *Hegemony and Greek Historians* (Lanham, Md.: Rowman and Littlefield, 1994), p. 74.

36. Daniel C. Bach, "Regional Domination and Power Conversion in Africa: Soft and Hard Hegemony," paper presented at the annual meeting of the African Studies Association, Nashville, 2000, mimeo; and Adekeye Adebajo and Christopher Landsberg, "South Africa and Nigeria as Regional Hegemons," in Mwesiga Baregu and Christopher Landsberg, eds., *From Cape to Congo: Southern Africa's Evolving Security Challenges* (Boulder: Lynne Rienner, 2003), pp. 171–203.

37. Michel Lelart, "The Franc Zone and European Monetary Integration," in Bach, *Regionalization in Africa,* pp. 139–150.

38. Paul Collier, "Africa's External Economic Relations, 1960–1990," *African Affairs* 13, no. 3 (July 1991): 348.

39. Ibid.

40. According to Collier, agencies of restraint "(a) protect public assets from depletion, (b) prevent inflationary money printing, (c) prevent corruption, (d) protect socially productive groups from exploitation, and (e) enforce contracts." See Collier, "Africa's External Economic Relations," p. 339.

41. In September 1993, French prime minister Edouard Balladur personally wrote to each of the heads of state of the CFA franc zone informing them that, from January 1994, French budgetary aid would be tied to the existence of standing structural adjustment agreements with the two Bretton Woods institutions. French monetary authorities also suspended, from 2 August 1993, the repurchase of CFA francs originating from outside the interbanking system of the franc zone, thus restricting the convertibility of the CFA up to the present day. This measure was adopted to curtail an inflation of money laundering—a 40 percent increase in capital transfers was monitored over the first semester of 1993. See *Libération* (Paris), 21 September 1993.

42. Paul Masson and Catherine Pattillo, *Monetary Union in West Africa (ECOWAS): Is It Desirable and How Could It Be Achieved?* International Monetary Fund (IMF) Occasional Paper no. 204 (Washington, D.C.: IMF, 2001), p 58.

43. Fine and Yeo, "Regional Integration in Sub-Saharan Africa," p. 451.

44. Masson and Pattillo, *Monetary Union in West Africa,* p. 14. The penalty mechanism designed to ensure proper implementation of the convergence (2000–2002) and stability (2003–) phases of the CSGSP involves the possibility of a suspension of central bank financing.

45. Masson and Pattillo, *Monetary Union in West Africa,* p. 14.

46. Ibid.

47. Anne-Sophie Claeys and Alice Sindzingre, "The Impact of the Monetary Union on Developing Countries: The Case of the Franc Zone," in Franck Amalric and Marikki Stocchetti, eds., *The European Union Facing Global Responsibility: Past Records, Future Challenges* (Rome: Society for International Development, 2001), pp. 136–137.

48. Fine and Yeo, "Regional Integration in Sub-Saharan Africa," p. 452. Violence and discriminatory policies based on *Ivoirité* carry a strong regional dimension since migrancy traditionally "locked in" the economy of Côte d'Ivoire with the economies of neighboring Sahelian states. See Human Rights Watch, *The New Racism: The Political Manipulation of Ethnicity in Côte d'Ivoire* (New York: Human Rights Watch, August 2001). The late Ivorian president Félix Houphouët-Boigny was so acutely aware of the importance of these interactions that he once suggested the establishment of a "dual nationality." It is currently estimated that over 40 percent of the Ivorian population was born abroad or is descended from immigrants.

49. Daniel C. Bach, "Regionalization in a Comparative Perspective: Soft Structural Hegemony, Transstate Regionalization, and Deterritorialization in Africa,"

paper presented at the forty-third annual convention of the International Studies Association, New Orleans, La., 2002; see also Douglas Rimmer, "Le Nigeria ne sera pas, dans l'Afrique de demain, une puissance économique et politique significative," *Marchés Tropicaux et Méditerranéens* no. 3000 (9 May 2003): 961–963.

50. J. H. H. Weiler, "Federalism and Constitutionalism: Europe's Sonderweg," in Kalypso Nicolaidis and Robert Howse, eds., *The Federal Vision: Legitimacy and Levels of Government in the U.S. and the EU* (Oxford: Oxford University Press, 2001), p. 68.

51. Collier, "Africa's External Economic Relations," p. 347.

52. *Treaty of ECOWAS*, art. 9, para. 5.

53. Fine and Yeo, "Regional Integration in Sub-Saharan Africa," p. 428.

54. Collier, "Africa's External Economic Relations," p. 347.

55. Charles D. Jebuni, Olawale Ogunkola, and Charles C. Soludo, "A Case-Study of the Economic Community of West African States," in Ademola Oyejide, Ibrahim Elbadawi, and Stephen Yeo, eds., *Regional Integration and Trade Liberalization in Sub-Saharan Africa,* vol. 3, *Regional Case Studies* (London: Macmillan, 1999), pp. 26, 28.

56. Ibid.

57. Daniel C. Bach, "Institutional Crisis and the Search for New Models," in Réal Lavergne, ed., *Regional Integration and Cooperation in West Africa: A Multidimensional Perspective* (Ottawa: International Development Research Centre, 1997), pp. 77–102.

58. Peter Lewis, "From Prebendalism to Predation: The Political Economy of Decline in Nigeria," *Journal of Modern African Studies* 34, no. 1 (1996): 96.

59. Ibid. See also Fine and Yeo, "Regional Integration in Sub-Saharan Africa," p. 451.

60. The four mandatory (also known as "primary") convergence criteria are the limitation of budget deficits, excluding grants; inflation rates of no more than 5 percent by 2001 and 3 percent by 2003; central bank financing of budget deficits of no higher than 10 percent of tax revenues for the previous year; and gross official reserves equal to no more than six months of imports of goods and services.

61. A few weeks later, Ghana's finance minister, Yaw Osafo-Maafo, expressed concern that the five countries committed to the WAMZ could not "meet them fully despite the fact they will make some inroads." *Accra Mail,* 17 August 2001, available at www.allafrica.com.

62. Jide Olatuyi, "ECOWAS, IMF Score Nigeria [and] Others Low on EC Currency," *The Guardian* (Lagos), 20 May 2003.

63. CEDEAO, *Rapport intérimaire du Secrétaire Exécutif M. Lansana Kouyaté* (Abuja: Executive Secretariat, April 2000), CEDEAO mimeo, p. 2.

64. Michael Davenport, *Identification Study for Reinforcing the Capacity of the ECOWAS Secretariat* (London, March 2000), mimeo, p. 13.

65. Whether one consults the list of states in arrears of payment of their contributions to ECOWAS institutions or the state of ratification and implementation of its protocols and common policies, the cleavage between anglophone and francophone states is irrelevant. See Daniel C. Bach, "Régionalisme francophone ou régionalisme franco-africain," in Daniel C. Bach and Anthony M. Kirk-Greene, eds., *Etats et sociétés en Afrique francophone* (Paris: Economica, 1993), p. 224.

66. Daniel C. Bach, "Revisiting a Paradigm," in Bach, *Regionalization in Africa*, pp. 1–14. See also Daniel C. Bach, "Régionalisme et régionalisation à travers le prisme de l'aire Saharo-Sahélienne," in Laurence Marfaing and Steffen Wippel, dirs., *Relations transsahariennes aux XXème et XXIème siècles: Réorganisations et revitalisations d'un espace transrégional* (Paris: Karthala, forthcoming).

67. Paul Nugent and Anthony I. Asiwaju, "Introduction: The Paradox of African Boundaries," in Paul Nugent and Anthony I. Asiwaju, eds., *African Boundaries* (London: Pinter, 1996), pp. 1–17.

68. John O. Igué and Bio Soulé, *L'état-entrepôt au bénin: Commerce informel ou solution à la crise?* (Paris: Karthala, 1992), pp. 45–46.

69. Kate Meagher, "Informal Integration or Economic Subvention: The Development and Organization of Parallel Trade in Sub-Saharan Africa," in Lavergne, *Regional Integration and Cooperation in West Africa,* pp. 165–188.

PART 2

Challenges

5

Governance
and Democratization

Amos Sawyer

In West Africa, as in some other parts of the world, the end of the bipolar Cold War system has exposed the true nature of state failure with its attendant human tragedies. These developments have demonstrated the urgent need for a clear understanding of how governance institutions are constructed and how they interact with their environment. The magnitude of human tragedy, as manifested in massive killings, internal displacement, refugee flows, plunder and pillage in countries like Liberia and Sierra Leone, persistent sectarian violence in Nigeria, coups and attempted coups in Côte d'Ivoire, Guinea-Bissau, and Niger serves as a vivid reminder that the rudimentary requirements of human security have yet to be fully met in most West African societies. These problems underscore the need for a clear understanding of the link between governance and human security. I argue in this chapter not only that governance is linked to security, but that it is the central element in the attainment of human security. I further argue that the only viable form of governance is one that is rooted in its citizens; only through democratic governance can human security be effectively protected. I begin with a brief overview of Africa's governance experience and the place of security and democracy in that experience during the Cold War—a period that constitutes about three-quarters of Africa's post-independence existence. I then discuss critical post–Cold War governance challenges and initiatives in West Africa, before offering suggestions on how current African governance initiatives can be strengthened to produce durable democratic governance.

Governance, Security, and
Democracy During the Cold War

Governance Experience

West Africa's experience with governance during the Cold War cannot be comprehensively reviewed within the confines of this chapter. Yet a brief summary of this experience is important for an understanding of today's governance challenges. Governance institutions in West Africa have drawn from the legacies of colonialism and the anticolonial struggle and have been influenced by the imperatives of the Cold War's bipolar system. Like their colonial antecedents, African governance institutions have been characterized by overcentralization. For Africa's colonial rulers, overcentralization was an instrument for extraction. Regardless of their governance orientation within the global context of the Cold War, all postindependence African governments pronounced a commitment to development. On that basis, overcentralized governance institutions became a mobilizing tool. Africa's masses supported those governance institutions because the general preoccupation with development overwhelmed all other governance considerations, including concerns about democratization.[1]

The pursuit of development by African governments within the context of the Cold War, however, was fraught with pitfalls. Some leaders opted to assume a competitive posture in global bipolar politics; others remained in close relationships with their former colonial powers. This was particularly true in francophone Africa, where France established close political, economic, and military ties with its former colonies (see Chapter 15). Regardless of the ideological posture of African governments, Cold War machinations by external powers combined with unequal international exchange, high oil prices, rampant corruption, rent-seeking activities, and failed economic policies (brought about by inappropriate prescriptions, including some from the Bretton Woods institutions, the World Bank, and the International Monetary Fund) to pose insurmountable challenges to governance institutions in Africa. These policies brought enormous hardships to African populations who had expressed such high expectations at independence. Centralized governance became an extractive, repressive machine, particularly in rural Africa, where postcolonial modes of governance resembled the native authority structures of the colonial era.[2]

At the continental and subregional levels, governance initiatives designed to promote development yielded feeble results. The Lagos Plan of Action of 1980, whose intellectual father was Adebayo Adedeji, the executive secretary of the UN's Economic Commission for Africa (ECA) at the time, was adopted as Africa's economic development strategy by the Organization of African Unity (OAU). The Lagos Plan, however, was pitted against a

World Bank alternative whose intellectual father was World Bank economist Elliot Berg, and the African initiative became moribund.[3] A similar
fate befell an African alternative to World Bank–inspired structural adjustment programs (SAPs). The African plan was designed by the ECA in close
collaboration with the OAU and other African governance institutions.[4] At
the subregional level, the creation of the Economic Community of West
African States (ECOWAS) in 1975 as an organization not linked to any former colonial power or Cold War power bloc was a major achievement in
subregional governance designed to promote economic development (see
Chapters 2 and 3).

The Place of Security in Africa's Governance Experience

As the promise of development receded with the onset of the Cold War, the
legitimacy of African governance institutions and practices seemed to be
called into question. African societies struggled to develop coping mechanisms, and in some cases alternative (informal) governance institutions, as
African states struggled to exert their relevance and control.[5] Human security became the key challenge for African societies while, for African states
and leaders, regime security became the major preoccupation.[6] Repressive
laws such as "preventive detention" acts and all-embracing laws against
sedition and treason restricted the legal and political rights of citizens. Problems of food security, rising unemployment, and limited and diminishing
access to the basic essentials of life confronted most African populations.

Regime insecurity became manifest in the numerous coups and attempted
coups, civil wars, secessionist and rebel movements, and SAP-induced riots
that plagued many parts of Africa. Repression was buttressed at the continental level by the OAU's articulation of the principles of sovereignty and
territorial integrity as sacred and immutable. Yet these principles did not
inoculate regimes from instability. Nor did the OAU take any action to curb
the most egregious acts of brutal repression perpetrated by leaders such as
Idi Amin of Uganda, Macias Nguema of Equatorial Guinea, and Jean Bédél
Bokassa of the Central African Republic. There are several cases in which
African states made significant efforts to ensure regime security and to protect state sovereignty. Prominent among these are the role of African troop-
contributing states to the UN mission during the Congo crisis between 1960
and 1964; the role of the OAU and the Frontline States in the antiapartheid
struggle; the struggle against Portuguese colonialism; and the OAU peacekeeping interventions in Chad from 1979 to 1982. Important as these and
other such initiatives were, however, regime stability in Africa seemed
essentially to be excessively dependent on patterns of alignment within the
global bipolar structure, former colonial links, and the resourcefulness of
individual African leaders.

The Agenda for African Democracy and Development

The pursuit of development after independence in the 1960s determined the context and nature of democracy as conceived and practiced within African states. As development strategies were framed from outside the continent, largely by the two Bretton Woods institutions, so also were ideas related to democracy. Conceived as a precondition to development, democracy was conceptualized and practiced as political mobilization undertaken to help centralized governments to penetrate society and to harness society's resources in support of development goals determined by the state.[7] Questions of distribution, especially in relation to the urban-rural divide (rural development), dominated the development agenda and democracy was recast as decentralization[8] and implemented more as deconcentration of central authority than as devolution of power.[9] But these approaches to democracy, implemented within the context of the Cold War and growing centralization and personalization of power, only served to nurture the African state as a "Leviathan," often autocratic and sometimes predatory and despotic. The struggles of African peoples against postindependence autocracy and repression have been well documented.[10] Occurring in the crucible of "crypto-imperialism," many such struggles were unheralded or disguised by Cold War machinations.[11] In reality, these struggles signaled increasing governance failures and the crisis of the state that was beginning to unfold with tragic consequences in many parts of Africa.[12]

Although Africa's democracy agenda seemed to have been shaped by its development agenda and the vicissitudes of the Cold War, some progress was made in the area of governance during this period in promoting the human rights of African peoples at the continental level. For example, by the mid-1970s the OAU and African governments came under increasing criticism for their perceived indifference to gross abuses of human rights. In the United States, the Jimmy Carter administration (1976–1980) pronounced human rights to be the centerpiece of U.S. foreign policy, though it was inconsistently applied in practice. Many European countries also linked international assistance to human rights, though this was also applied selectively. It was during this period that the OAU began the preparation of the African Charter on Human and People's Rights of 1981 and the establishment of the African Commission on Human and People's Rights in Banjul, Gambia. Some analysts have argued that, as it is presently constructed, the commission cannot be effective in protecting individual and group rights because its investigative powers are weak and its implementation prerogatives are circumscribed.[13] Nonetheless, it is anticipated that current efforts to strengthen the commission could improve its effectiveness.

Asymmetries

In summary, governance, security, democracy, and development have been linked in asymmetrical relationships in Africa since independence. Characterized by scarcely reformed, centralized, colonially inherited structures and institutions, postindependence African governance systems tried to adapt to the continuing quest for development. These mostly weak states struggled to penetrate and control African societies. Failing to deliver development within the framework of an international system of unequal exchange and the Cold War, many African regimes turned autocratic and repressive and began to lose the support of African societies. Some of these regimes remained under the protection of Cold War patrons. Regime security was intertwined with former colonial alliances and nested in the security architecture of the Cold War. The absence of a significant indigenous African agenda for democratization, however, undermined the legitimacy of the African state and exposed the security needs of both African societies and states. The end of the Cold War truly exposed African governance failures and the vulnerability of African autocrats. This era also opened up opportunities for rethinking governance institutional arrangements and Africa's post–Cold War security and democratization agendas.

Governance, Security, and Democratization After the Cold War

The end of the Cold War has produced a unipolar world order dominated by the United States with globalization as its dominant characteristic. While increasing the concentration of capital, globalization has fostered a greater diffusion of transactions in ways that create new challenges for governance at the regional, national, and subnational levels.[14] These trends are forcing a redefinition of sovereignty, limiting policy arenas in which national actors can operate, and making regional cooperation imperative.[15] Economic globalization, for example, has heightened competition for investment capital and requires higher levels of productivity. These trends have serious implications for governance, security, and democratization in Africa. Economic competition within a global market operating under neoclassical economic principles is fierce and rife with conflict. To compete successfully in such a global marketplace, appropriate strategies in political and economic management are needed. Achieving these goals quite often requires processes of political and economic reordering (including greater regionalism), which in turn can engender further conflict. Ironically, democracy, with its own conflict-inherent character, has proved to be the best system for sustainable conflict management and sustainable development. Thus, democratic governance and regional cooperation, pursued in tandem, constitute Africa's best strategy for achieving durable peace and sustainable development in this era of globalization. This is the logic that underpins current ideas about Africa's governance, security, and democracy agendas in the post–Cold War era.

West Africa's emerging framework for human security, of which agendas for governance and democracy are a critical part, is nested in a larger African regional framework known as the Conference on Security, Stability, Development, and Cooperation in Africa (CSSDCA). The CSSDCA is a direct response to the challenges of globalization. Its conceptualization can be found in the Kampala Document of 1991, which successfully demonstrated the links between security, stability, and development in Africa and proposed an institutional framework for cooperation and coordination in advancing Africa's development in the evolving post–Cold War order.[16]

The principles and mechanisms stipulated by the CSSDCA process to underpin Africa's agenda for security and stability are comprehensive, mutually reinforcing, and stress the centrality of democratization. For example, regarding security, the CSSDCA process anchors national security on "the security of the individual citizen to live in peace and to satisfy basic needs while being able to participate fully in societal affairs and enjoying freedoms and fundamental human rights."[17] The CSSDCA identifies poor governance practices such as "lack of democracy, denial of personal liberties, abuse of religion, imbalance in public resource allocation favoring military expenditures over other sectors of national life, and the absence of proper machinery for the control and management of public funds" among the deep-rooted causes of insecurity.[18] With respect to stability, the CSSDCA notes that constitutionalism and principles of rule of law; respect for human and fundamental rights; political pluralism; participatory, accountable, and transparent governance; and gender equity and equality are among the most important requirements for entrenching democratic governance. The adoption of the CSSDCA by the OAU in 2000 marked a significant step toward advancing regional cooperation in Africa. The CSSDCA also strengthened the basis for effective subregional cooperation in West Africa. There are current attempts to institutionalize the CSSDCA under the governance and security organs of the new African Union (AU) (see Chapter 6).

Good Governance and Democratization Processes in West Africa: Some Proposals for Reform

Current efforts to improve governance in Africa have been conceptualized as the quest for *good governance*. Central to the concept of good governance is the idea that accountable, transparent, and inclusive governance is both the best promoter and the best producer of development. Good governance acknowledges three domains of governance: the government, the private sector, and civil society. It strives to ensure collaboration among them. Prominent among the concerns of good governance, in addition to issues related to the promotion of fundamental human rights and the rule of law, are issues of decentralization; the empowerment of women; civil service reforms; accountable executives; competent, credible, and independent judiciaries; independent legislative bodies; and knowledgeable, effective, and independent mass media. "Civil society" is defined as a range of groupings seen as embodying the aspirations and activities of citizens. Good governance strives to promote the empowerment of civil society and to enhance its consultative voice with governments. The concept also views the private sector as a partner in dialogue with civil society and governments in pursuit of the common good.[19]

The quest for good governance is essentially an initiative to create a *capable state* with the requisite institutional, technical, administrative, and political capabilities to be autonomous of special interests while enjoying their support. Such a state must also be responsive to societal needs by processing the demands of civil society.[20] Good governance initiatives designed to improve governance competence are essential, and measures should be taken to strengthen all aspects of governance that promote good governance. However, it is important to remember that competent governance is not the same as democratic governance. Unless capable states develop their democratic potential, they can easily slide into autocracy. This is precisely the challenge now faced by the so-called Asian Tigers. To sustain democracy and to continue to address the political and socioeconomic demands of their populations, Taiwan, South Korea, Singapore, and other newly industrialized Asian countries have been forced to deepen their democratization processes.

Learning from these experiences, Africa's governance agenda must strive from the start not only to install *good governance* but also to develop *democratic governance*. Therefore, in addition to strengthening capabilities essential for the competent governance of West African societies, ECOWAS's governance initiatives—and for that matter those of other subregions—should seek to deepen processes of democratization. Democratic governance requires that "governed" citizens themselves become "governors" determining their own future and not simply be beneficiaries of the goods and services provided by governments. The preparation of citizens for democratic decisionmaking and the crafting of governance institutions that repose governance authority in a knowledgeable citizenry are the hallmarks of a democratic society. This requires going beyond the strengthening of parliaments and electoral processes and other democratic institutions at the

level of the central government—as important as these are. It also requires
going beyond creating structures for dialogue between civil society and
governments—important as these also are. Democratic governance requires
removing governance constraints that create subcitizen jurisdictions for
rural people, women, and "minorities." It requires creating governance
structures, rooted in constitutional law, that truly devolve governance authority, including the authority to mobilize and dispense resources to local
communities. Above all, democratic governance requires the creation of an
enlightened citizenry, and in this regard the importance of literacy and education cannot be overemphasized.

West Africa's historical experience with centralized autocracies suggests a need to avoid a strategy that strengthens the state's capacity without
a corresponding counterbalancing strategy of strengthening the capacity of
citizens to resist the abuses of the state and to hold governments accountable. For example, the appointment by ECOWAS of eminent West Africans
in July 2001 to the Council of Elders as part of the ECOWAS security
mechanism of 1999 (see Chapter 13) could have constituted a good beginning in strengthening the role of citizens in conflict resolution. Unfortunately, West African governments, not West African peoples, were the
source of such appointments. The designation of "eminent elders" should
be the prerogative of the citizens of a country and not of their government.
So, while ECOWAS seeks to strengthen governance capabilities for good
governance, it must simultaneously deepen their foundations so as to
achieve democratic governance. ECOWAS's agenda for governance and
democracy should be strengthened to achieve this objective, and in order to
do so, the following suggestions are offered to reinforce current governance
initiatives and to deepen the democratization process in West Africa.

Among the key issues in current initiatives to promote good governance in Africa are the following: first, commitment to the rule of law and
the protection and promotion of human rights; second, establishment of
multiparty political systems and credible electoral systems; third, democratic executives and effective parliaments; fourth, the empowerment of
women; fifth, the empowerment of civil society; and finally, the establishment of independent and credible mass media.

Rule of Law and Protection of Human Rights

Under the rubric of the rule of law and the protection of human rights, one
can evaluate the full range of issues, from security for all to failed human
rights commissions. Measures are needed to strengthen the protection of individual rights at subnational, national, and subregional levels of governance.
At subnational and national levels, customary laws that discriminate against
women and "minorities" and consolidate arbitrary rule—often disguised as

"tradition"—need to be revisited with a view to establishing and protecting the legal standing of individuals in African systems of governance.[21]
National human rights commissions also need to be revitalized in ways that
involve greater civil society participation, ensure financial independence,
improve the credibility of such bodies within society, and enhance the
investigative powers of these commissions. The independence and integrity
of national judiciaries have to be ensured. With bilateral and multilateral
assistance, judiciaries in West Africa and elsewhere in Africa have been
refurbished with libraries, trained personnel, computers, and other logistical support. These are all useful additions to a branch of government that
has been by far the least effective of the three branches of government—
legislative, executive, and judiciary—in postindependence Africa. However, experience has shown that the true measure of progress in the judiciary's capacity to dispense justice and to protect the rights of African
peoples is the degree of autonomy it enjoys from executive manipulation.
Failure to ensure the independence of the judiciary from executive control
has meant that a fully equipped and well-trained judiciary has often become
an efficient machinery disingenuously employed for the perpetration of
injustice and repression. Finally, at the subregional level, there is a need to
strengthen the protection of the rights of ordinary people by establishing, or
in some cases strengthening, the legal standing of ordinary people in the
appropriate bodies of ECOWAS, such as the Council of Elders, the West
African Community Court of Justice, and the West African Parliament.[22]

Strengthening Multiparty Political Systems

Over the last decade, the establishment of multiparty political systems has
come to be seen as the strongest evidence of the growing success of the
democratization process in Africa. Pressure from the international community, especially external donors, and pressure from the opening of political
space as a result of the changed circumstances of the post–Cold War era,
have combined to make multipartyism the political system of choice in
West Africa and other parts of the continent. The one-party systems that
were so common in postindependence Africa have now become anachronistic. Needless to say, not all manifestations of multiparty systems are genuine. In some cases, autocracies have created "oppositions" in countries
like Burkina Faso, Gambia, and Guinea to satisfy donor conditionality. In
other cases, elections have produced regimes with questionable records of
democratic governance in countries like Côte d'Ivoire, Guinea-Bissau, and
Liberia. There are many cases, however, in which genuine multiparty systems appear to be taking root. These include Benin, Ghana, Mali, Senegal,
and perhaps Nigeria. In such cases, multipartyism seems to be the product of
an emerging political culture characterized by greater political tolerance,

especially among political elites. This process has also been facilitated by a greater focus on issues rather than personalities in the political process, and a growing sense among voters and civil society actors of their increasing strength in influencing the political system. This trend augurs well for the democratization of political processes at the national level. Although insufficient to develop and sustain democracy, the strengthening of multiparty political systems in West Africa must be encouraged. The democratization of rural society is an indispensable precondition to strengthening multipartyism in West Africa and other parts of Africa.[23] There is also a need for capacity-building initiatives that are relevant to strengthening party organizations, accountability, interparty cooperation, and civic education in order to entrench norms and practices that support pluralism instead of those that promote zero-sum politics. African-based foundations, research institutions, and other bodies are needed to assist with such capacity building. ECOWAS also needs to cooperate more closely with the African Union and academic institutions and research entities within and outside African countries in efforts to build a democratic culture.

African Electoral Systems and Political Leadership

Although pluralism is rapidly gaining ground, politics remains a zero-sum game in some parts of West Africa. In such places, centralized political institutions and autocracies are holding on tenaciously, stakes are high, and an electoral loss is regarded as a threat to personal and group interests. In such cases, elections are literally a rousing call to battle. After elections, losing candidates are forced to flee the country or find themselves arrested and detained largely on trumped-up charges. Their release becomes a bargaining chip. In virtually every West African country, the cost of losing elections is unacceptably high even for incumbents. This cost will remain high until the prerogatives of power in centralized institutions are reduced and monopolistic control of resources by a single power center is ended. These changes require democratization through devolution of government. In the short term, measures designed to improve electoral systems can help to reduce conflicts arising from elections.

Reforming electoral laws. For many countries, improving electoral systems must begin with a review of electoral laws. Electoral laws that are crafted solely by executives and enacted by executive-dominated parliaments are frequently viewed with suspicion by opposition parties and civil society actors. Quite often, such systems give an edge to ruling parties. The process of formulating and reviewing electoral laws must necessarily involve the participation of political parties, civil society—especially national bar associations—and other relevant and knowledgeable elements of society. Such reforms must be undertaken in an open and transparent manner that promotes learning and credibility.

Autonomous electoral commissions. It is important that electoral commissions in Africa be seen as independent, especially from the control of executive authority. Members of these commissions must be individuals of high integrity appointed either on the basis of consensus or by other methods that ensure broad-based representation and acceptance. Such individuals must be protected from political manipulation. Defraying the financial cost of elections is also a tool that can be used to manipulate electoral processes. Because democratization has become a conditionality of external donors in the post–Cold War era, many African governments have begun to rely on external sources of funding to hold elections, sometimes even to provide the bare essentials for electoral commissions. This tendency betrays a lack of commitment by such governments to the electoral process. Not only must the financing of elections be seen as a national responsibility, but the financial autonomy of electoral commissions must also be guaranteed in order to shield electoral processes from undue interference by external actors. The establishment of escrow accounts available only to electoral commissions has been one way of enhancing the financial autonomy of these bodies.

Creating a level playing field. In addition to credible electoral laws and autonomous, well-funded electoral commissions, there are other areas of electoral processes in Africa that require improvement. The lack of a level playing field during the conduct of elections is usually a major problem. While it is true that incumbency offers an advantage in elections everywhere, in many African elections these advantages can be so overwhelming that they undermine the credibility of elections, making it impossible to consider such elections "free and fair." Denial of equal access to the media, restrictions on campaigning by opposition parties, harassment and intimidation of their supporters by government security agents, and even murder of campaign workers and opposition party supporters have all been part of the tragic folklore of many African elections. These problems are related to the high stakes of elections, which can only be mitigated in the short run by improved electoral practices and effective elections monitoring, and in the long run by the reconstitution of political order to reduce the dominance of centralized authority and its monopoly over resources.

Elections monitoring. Elections monitoring by domestic and external actors is now widely accepted as essential for enhancing the transparency and credibility of elections and for undertaking appropriate reforms. Internal monitoring is also an important form of civic education. External monitoring often constitutes the basis for donor support not only to strengthen electoral systems, but also to enhance development programs. In this way, processes of democratization and development can be simultaneously strengthened. Elections monitoring is less useful for purposes of certifying the credibility of elections or assisting future reforms if organized simply to monitor the casting and counting of ballots on the day of the elections and for the subsequent declaration of returns. There have been many near-perfect voting processes in notoriously flawed elections, such as those in Liberia in 1997 and Gambia in 2001. Quite often, by the time voting occurs, the damage will already have been done. Elections monitoring must begin early, sometimes as early as during the consideration of electoral laws. Such monitoring must cover all aspects of elections, including the recruitment, training, and deployment of poll workers, security personnel, and others involved in electoral processes. In this respect, such monitoring must be sensitive to all the problems associated with agency relationships. Finally, elections monitoring must be done in a way that seeks to reduce conflicts and increase cooperation among contending political forces so as to strengthen electoral systems as instruments of sustainable multiparty democracy. This requires of election monitors an approach that encourages the reduction of political tension, the search for compromise among parties, and the building of consensus around areas that are critical for the preservation and strengthening of peaceful democratic competition. At the end of the day, societies must survive elections and elections must, over time, strengthen other social and political processes of society rather than pose a persistent danger to social peace and progress. Working in collaboration with relevant international and national entities, including civil society organizations and political parties, there is much that ECOWAS can do to address these and related issues in order to improve electoral processes in West Africa.

Enforcing constitutionalism. A fundamental problem of governance in Africa is the manipulation of constitutional rules to suit the circumstance of political leaders. For example, despite clear constitutional rules to the contrary, there is still a lingering tendency of elected leaders to act autonomously as autocratic rulers with all the prerogatives of power centralized in their hands. Addressing this problem requires a multifaceted approach involving action at the national, regional, and international levels. In the area of national politics, strengthening parliaments and judiciaries to counterbalance presidential powers, empowering civil society, and enshrining term limits as a constitutional provision are all important strategies, and are already under way in several countries. For example, citizens are increasingly finding the flouting of term limits unacceptable. Subregional, regional, and international actors should support such resistance of unconstitutional measures by citizens. In other cases, civil society–led efforts have helped to impose term limits on long-serving leaders.

The OAU's Algiers declaration of 1999 explicitly prohibits the recognition of governments that come to power through unconstitutional means. In an unprecedented action by subregional actors in Africa, the ECOWAS Cease-Fire Monitoring Group (ECOMOG) used force to restore the democratically elected government of Ahmed Tejan Kabbah to power in Sierra Leone in March 1998 following a military coup ten months earlier. However, the fact that Nigeria's military government, under General Sani Abacha, led this intervention produced the twin paradoxes of a military junta promoting democracy abroad while suppressing it at home, and a government that came to power through a coup at home reversing a putsch abroad. The ECOWAS security mechanism of 1999 allows external military intervention in cases of unconstitutional changes of government. However, in order for this principle to have any credibility, such interveners must themselves enjoy domestic and international democratic legitimacy. A counterbalancing principle should be laid down by the African Union, ECOWAS, and other subregional bodies to withdraw recognition from leaders who amend their state constitutions to extend their stay in office or to assume powers not previously constitutionally allotted. These and other disincentives must be created to break the stranglehold of some leaders on the political life of their countries.

Relevance in retirement. A corollary of disincentives to prevent unconstitutional acts should be the offering of appropriate incentives to encourage retirement of leaders who have served their constitutionally allotted terms. One possible incentive could be the provision of high-profile opportunities for "statesmanlike" service and continuing relevance and recognition for such leaders after retirement from office. ECOWAS should consider relevant initiatives and consult with African research and policy entities to find ways to design such activities to suit the skills and predispositions of retiring leaders.[24] One specific idea could be to incorporate such former leaders as Ghana's Jerry Rawlings, Gambia's Sir Dawda Jawara, and Benin's Nicéphore Soglo into the Council of Elders of ECOWAS's security mechanism. Nigeria's former military ruler from 1998 to 1999, General Abdulsalaam Abubakar, has already undertaken mediation and electoral initiatives in the Democratic Republic of Congo, Zimbabwe, and Liberia. Senegal's former president, Abdou Diouf, is currently head of the Francophonie, a Paris-based international organization of francophone states. Mali's Alpha Konaré was appointed chair of the African Union Commission in July 2003.

Ineffective parliaments. Another important issue in strengthening democratic governance is the problem of ineffective parliaments. This problem stems largely from two sources: first, the nature of recruitment to parliaments in Africa, and second, the lack of the skilled personnel needed to enhance the autonomy and integrity of parliaments. Majoritarian politics in Africa has required ruling-party domination of parliaments, while presidential control over ruling parties has often influenced the selection of parliamentarians. Due to these factors, many African parliaments remain rubber-stamping agencies of the president. A further problem is the lack of resources. Executives still control the purse strings in many African countries, including those now going through democratization processes. Inadequate research resources and logistical support and shortage of competent support staff are among the major problems limiting the effectiveness of even the most independent parliamentary bodies in carrying out their constitutional functions. Redressing these problems will require considerable public education and pressure on executives as a way of building constituencies for democratic reforms and enhancing parliamentary autonomy and integrity.

The Empowerment of Women

A genuine commitment to gender equality and equity is critical to processes of democratization in West Africa. The empowerment of women is not only a gender issue, but also an issue related to fundamental rights, and as such it should be implanted into national value systems. Women typically constitute about half of the population in African countries, and democratic systems are seriously compromised without their full and substantive participation in political systems. The empowerment of women is needed to redress historical structural imbalances in African societies and to reduce poverty. Fortunately, there are several comprehensive and closely coordinated frameworks for addressing issues related to the empowerment of women. The Beijing Platform, the Convention to Eliminate All Forms of Discrimination Against Women (CEDAW), and their associated protocols have elaborated all the principal aspects of this task. However, the implementation of a widely agreed agenda for the empowerment of women is hampered by several factors, principal among which is culture. Even where legal constraints are removed, the stubborn effects of culture continue to pose major obstacles to reform. Cultural obstacles to the empowerment of women are pervasive and are evident in every endeavor, from village microcredit schemes to recruitment into national politics. Multifaceted strategies are needed to overcome this problem. Male sensitization needs to be a major part of any successful strategy. Cultural impediments to the empowerment of African women are often manifested in forms of male resistance to what is perceived to be a "feminist" agenda. Changing this perception is vital to attaining progress in this important area. ECOWAS needs to encourage African research centers to probe more deeply into the connection between culture, gender, and power in West African societies as a basis for enhanced understanding and the formulation of policies and strategies for advancing gender equity and equality. Encouragingly, the

Council of Elders of the ECOWAS security mechanism has strong female representation.

The Empowerment of Civil Society

Civil society organizations manifest the complex patterns of relationships that exist in West African societies (see Chapter 12). To some people, this complexity is troubling, which explains the frequent calls by African governments for the rationalization of civil society organizations and their exclusion from governmental decisionmaking. Excessive regulation and exclusion of civil society groups, however, do not advance democratization. The proper course for African governments would be the provision of an *open public realm*. Open and informed dialogue and productive contestations among civil society organizations, governments, and the private sector are what constitute *civic education*. This requires an ongoing learning experience among citizens designed to enable each individual better to understand his or her own circumstances and acquire a sympathetic understanding of the circumstances of others. By acquiring such understanding, problem solving is facilitated. This is the essence of democratic empowerment.

The empowerment of civil society is critical to the advancement of democratization processes in West Africa. Empowerment cannot be conferred by external actors, though their help is often required. The success of democratic empowerment lies primarily with homegrown civil society organizations.[25] This calls into question the role of international nongovernmental organizations (NGOs) operating in African countries. Unless the work of such NGOs is organized in ways that enhance the empowerment of their local counterparts, their operations could very well create a dependency syndrome that will be unhelpful to sustaining indigenous civil society efforts in the long run. Democratization requires the nurturing of homegrown civil society organizations that can become an integral part of the democratic fabric of their societies. An open public realm is indispensable to nurturing such organizations. Nurturing indigenous civil society organizations also requires an orientation of self-reliance, meaning that civil society organizations should be driven by a commitment to their own agendas and not switch focus and objectives at the inducement of external donors. These organizations must strive to depend more on their own resources, especially their ingenuity, local knowledge, and other indigenous assets, in order to achieve sustainability and to avoid undue external influence. A good strategy is to use donor support to develop self-sustaining, indigenous capabilities. Another requirement for nurturing homegrown civil society organizations is the establishment of relations of cooperation among themselves—*networking*. Civil society organizations in Africa often maintain stronger vertical links with donor agencies abroad, rather than horizontal links with internal organizations at home that have complementary objectives and activities. Reliance on external funding often pits these groups against each other in a competition for scarce resources. Donors should be encouraged to support civil society organizations that are committed to networking and collaborating with others. ECOWAS and the African Union are both late starters in building their relationships with civil society. Their commitment to democratization will in large part be measured by their evolving relationships with civil society. For ECOWAS, a special initiative needs to be undertaken to ensure that this relationship is developed rapidly and productively. Encouragingly, ECOWAS agreed in 2003 to create a forum within its secretariat in Abuja to interact with, and obtain suggestions from, civil society groups in the subregion.

Independent and Credible Mass Media

The availability of informative media resources and accurate reporting of all shades of opinion are vital to enhancing public information and enlightenment within African societies. There is nothing wrong with the availability of government-controlled media; there is everything wrong with government-controlled media being the only media available. At this stage of West Africa's democratization efforts, there are still many West African governments that are resisting the establishment and operation of independent newspapers and radio and television stations. ECOWAS leaders should declare such resistance unacceptable and take steps to restrain member states from the suppression of mass media. Countries that enjoy press freedom still need strengthened capacity, including training and logistical support. There is also a continuing need for open communication channels between the media and governments. The establishment of media adjudication boards has been effective in improving the flow of communication between government and the mass media in a country like Ghana, for example, and should be constantly strengthened.

Establishing or strengthening indigenous language presses and radio and television stations at the village, town, and provincial levels will be critical to advancing democratization processes in West Africa. The enlightenment of individuals in villages and towns constitutes the foundation of civil society's empowerment, which in turn is the most critical element in democratization processes. ECOWAS would do well to cooperate with such organizations as the West African Journalists Association and the Media Foundation of West Africa on these issues.

Strengthening the Normative Foundations of Democracy in Africa

Establishing sustainable democracy in Africa requires more than creating structures such as executives, parliaments, courts, and other institutions to oversee the rule of law and elections. Democracy must be grounded in certain values, among them acceptance of the common humanity of all citizens, acceptance of diversity as an asset indicative of the richness of human endowments, tolerance, and the building of social trust guided by accepted rules. When grounded in these values, democratic institutions in Africa have a chance not only to survive, but also to thrive. Moreover, these values reinforce democracy's intrinsic qualities. Though they may not be dominant, these values are present in some form in most cultures of the world. The task is to identify these values within the configuration of values that are constitutive of a society's culture and to devise ways of making them dominant cultural values. Achieving this requires a much deeper understanding of culture and a greater reliance on *language*.[26] Norms that underpin democracy cannot be woven into systems of values that are constitutive of a community of shared understanding without a deeper appreciation of the links among culture, language, and democracy. African scholars and practitioners who are concerned with democratization in Africa have not paid sufficient attention to this relationship. One of the few exceptions involves the efforts of Kwesi Prah and his colleagues at the Centre for the Advanced Study of African Societies in Cape Town, South Africa, which deserves strong support.[27] African political elites speak and write English, French, Portuguese, and Arabic, and by and large conduct political business in these languages. Most Africans, however, do not speak or write any of these languages with the fluency required to participate in democratic governance. If democracy is to take root on the continent, the issue of rooting democracy's normative foundations in African cultures must be properly addressed. ECOWAS, in collaboration with the African Union, will have to make this issue a major item on the democratization agenda.

Drawing on African Democratic Principles

Related to the challenge of entrenching democratic norms is the challenge of crafting democratic institutions in ways in which they can find sustenance in African cultures. These are two sides of the same coin. Most of Africa's political institutions are not an outgrowth of the African experience in the way that European institutions emerged from European history and culture.[28] In Britain, for example, parliament evolved as an integral part of a complex set of institutions rooted in British history, culture, and systems of governance. Africans have adopted such institutions out of their own specific historical context. The challenge is to *adapt* these institutions to the African context so that they retain their democratic meaning and substance for Africans and become part of the African experience. For example, while consensus building has been the most widely employed strategy of political decisionmaking in most African societies, majoritarian democracy now dominates Africa's political landscape. Worse still, in some African countries,

majoritarian principles have become a democratic cloak to disguise intoler-
ance, arbitrariness, and repression—far beyond James Madison's warnings
about the "tyranny of the majority."[29] Thus, as the dominant principle shaping African political institutions, majoritarianism is fast becoming a per-
version of democracy and a potential source of violent conflict. The system
is not promoting learning due to its singular emphasis on the process of leg-
islating, nor is it identifying the *common good,* since it often excludes a
substantial number of people from decisionmaking processes. Majoritarianism, as employed in Africa, is at best preoccupied with the building of
winning coalitions and outsmarting others.

In stark contrast, consensus building, as employed in African societies,
requires considerable deliberations that foster learning and deepen legitimacy. Unfortunately, the preoccupation with majoritarian politics, with its
emphasis on building winning coalitions and passing laws, has reduced the
importance of public education and enlightenment and the need for acquiring a sympathetic understanding of other people's views, which are the true
hallmarks of consensus building and an essential attribute of democracy.
Deliberative structures designed to clarify, educate, and promote the empowerment of civic publics are in short supply in Africa. That is partly why ethnicity, religion, and related factors are more frequently mobilized as weapons
in political battles than as resources on which societies can draw for conflict
prevention, management, and resolution, as well as for development.

Africa's intergovernmental organizations, like ECOWAS and the AU,
would do well to pose the problem of the relationship between political
structure and culture in African governance as a challenge to African scholars, and should fund research in this area. I should emphasize that these
suggestions are not a call for a return to, or retention of, retrograde elements of culture and African institutions that promote despotism under the
guise of an African "authenticity." This is a call for the employment of a
rare and unprecedented level of ingenuity and adaptivity on the part of
African scholars and practitioners in the crafting of democratic institutions
for African societies. Much social scientific investigation is still required in
this vital area.

Reconceptualizing Decentralization

A reconceptualization of decentralization is crucial to putting current good
governance initiatives in Africa on a course that can yield democratic governance. At best, as currently conceptualized, decentralization initiatives in
Africa can yield deconcentration of powers but not democratic governance.
It is true that deconcentration can diffuse structures of centralized authority
throughout society and perhaps ensure a better delivery of social goods. However, such an approach does not necessarily offer citizens the opportunity to

make their own decisions, learn from their own mistakes and those of others, and develop the capabilities to be the arbiters of their own fate. These are the essentials of democracy and the ingredients for its sustainability. Africa needs a new approach to designing governance institutions that will build on the self-organizing potential of people at the grassroots and community levels, harness their creativity and ingenuity, and make them decisionmakers.[30] Systems of decentralization that have relied on principles of indirect rule such as the Native Authority systems of the colonial era or the postcolonial variant of chieftaincies have not been terribly successful at unleashing the civic energies of the vast majority of African people.

The Challenge of Youth and Children

In every African country, children and youth constitute the majority of the population. Yet issues surrounding this important constituency are seldom given priority in discussions about constituting order. Concerns about democracy and development are meaningless unless human development is seen as central to achieving these goals. The link between children and youth on the one hand, and development and democracy on the other, is direct and strong. One only has to examine Africa's high rates of infant mortality and malnutrition, the stubborn persistence of preventable diseases among children, deteriorating educational systems, and increased unemployment and criminality among youth to find both evidence and causes of underdevelopment and the crisis of governance in Africa. The scourge of HIV/AIDS has added to this condition of growing misery. What is most striking is that the crisis facing children and youth is virtually uniformly common to all African countries. Differences created as a result of violent conflicts are marginal.[31] Development strategies that prioritize the needs of children will enhance people-centered development in every area. Children-centered town planning, healthcare systems, and environmental policies, among others, can do much to advance general welfare. Similarly, children-centered governance practices can promote rights and security, enhance participation, and increase livelihood and self-actualization opportunities. In recent years, the United Nations Children's Fund (UNICEF) has endeavored to elevate children's issues on the international agenda, but the response among many Africans has been less than enthusiastic. More recently, ECOWAS has taken up these issues as a means of addressing the plight of war-affected children (see Chapter 11). The exploitation of children remains a growing problem, and youth hopelessness is on the rise. The failure to link these issues closely to democratization efforts has opened a dangerous void that must be filled if West Africa's democratization agenda is to yield sustainable democratic governance. ECOWAS must strengthen its efforts in addressing this challenge through research, advocacy, and other appropriate action.

Conclusion

Africa's current agenda for good governance represents post–Cold War responses to the crisis of governance in the wake of state failure and its attendant tragedies. Strengthening this agenda to deepen the democratization process is critical and indispensable to ensuring durable peace and sustainable democratic development in Africa. The task of nurturing democracy in West Africa, as in other subregions of Africa, requires sustained initiatives that should involve every West African society and government. West Africa's civil societies must play a vital role in this area. Democracy cannot be handed down from centralized state structures, nor can it be transplanted from abroad. Though they can be conflict-inherent, processes of democratization can also be conflict-preventing and conflict-resolving since they have the ability to turn disputes and potentially destructive conflicts into productive discourses that can enhance enlightenment and problem-solving capabilities. Economic development and other forms of human advancement become more difficult to sustain in the long run without democratic institutions. That is why the task of building democratic institutions has to be given priority by Africans. While this challenge is huge and demanding, it does not surpass the human ingenuity of Africans. Strengthening the democratization agenda in West Africa is a sine qua non for economic development and political stability.

Notes

1. See Claude Ake, *Democracy and Development in Africa* (Washington, D.C.: Brookings Institution, 1996).
2. See Mahmood Mamdani, *Citizen and Subject: Contemporary Africa and the Legacy of Late Colonialism* (Princeton: Princeton University Press, 1996).
3. Claude Ake has argued that African leaders lacked the political will to launch their own development initiative within the context of the ideological struggles of the Cold War and the unequal international economic exchange between North and South. African leaders therefore did not implement the Lagos Plan of Action, preferring instead to choose individually other forms of cooperation, mainly with former colonial powers.
4. See UNECA, *African Alternative Framework for Structural Adjustment Programmes for Socio-Economic Recovery and Transformation* (Addis Ababa: UNECA, 1989).
5. Studies of Africa's thriving parallel markets and black markets attest to this. See, for example, Detlev Puetz and Joachim von Braun, "Parallel Markets and the Rural Poor in a West African Setting," in Michael Roemer and Christine Jones, eds., *Markets in Developing Countries: Parallel, Fragmented, and Black* (San Francisco: Institute for Contemporary Studies Press, 1991).
6. Human security is concerned with the security of the individual and his or her relationship with the society and the state. The concept involves the protection

of life as lived in personal surroundings, communities, and one's environment. It involves protection from a full range of abuses: unstructured violence, state or other sources of repression and harm, pandemic diseases, violations based on gender, denial of access to basic essentials of life and of opportunities for political, economic, and cultural development, among others. There is a growing body of literature on human security. See, for example, Mahbub ul Haq, *Reflections on Human Development* (Oxford: Oxford University Press, 1999); Rob McRae, ed., *Human Security and the New Diplomacy: Protecting People, Promoting Peace* (Montreal: McGill-Queen's University Press, 2001); and Adamantia Pollis and Peter Schwab, eds., *Human Rights: New Perspectives, New Realities* (Boulder: Lynne Rienner, 2000). Regime rights, as used in this chapter, are concerned with issues associated with the protection, survival, and integrity of political regimes.

7. See Warren Ilchman and Ravindra C. Bhargava, "Balanced Thought and Economic Growth," in Fred W. Riggs, ed., *Frontiers of Development Administration* (Durham, N.C.: Duke University Press, 1971), pp. 227–246; and J. P. Nettl, *Political Mobilization: A Sociological Analysis of Methods and Concepts* (London: Faber, 1967).

8. See Dennis A. Rondinelli and G. Shabbir Cheema, "Implementing Decentralization Policies: An Introduction," in G. Shabbir Cheema and Dennis A. Rondinelli, eds., *Decentralization and Development: Policy Implication in Developing Countries* (Beverly Hills, Calif.: Sage, 1983), pp. 9–34; and Dennis A. Rondinelli, John R. Nellis, and G. Shabbir Cheema, *Decentralization in Developing Countries: A Review of Recent Experience,* World Bank Staff Working Paper no. 581 (Washington, D.C.: World Bank, 1983).

9. Rondinelli and Cheema, "Implementing Decentralization Policies"; Joel Barkan, ed., *Five Monographs on Decentralization and Democratization in Sub-Saharan Africa* (Iowa City: Center for International and Comparative Studies, 1998); A. C. Mondjanagni, ed., *People's Participation in Development in Black Africa* (Douala, Cameroon: Pan-African Institute for Development, 1984); and Judith Heyer, Pepe Roberts, and Gavin Williams, eds., *Rural Development in Tropical Africa* (New York: St. Martin's, 1980) are excellent studies of decentralization as applied to rural development in the 1970s and 1980s.

10. See Peter Anyang' Nyong'o, ed., *Popular Struggles for Democracy in Africa* (London: Zed Books, 1987); and Mahmood Mamdani and Ernest Wamba-dia-Wamba, eds., *African Studies in Social Movements and Democracy* (Dakar: CODESRIA, 1995).

11. Using Miles Copeland's depiction of manipulations that constituted the "games of nations" as a point of departure, Vincent Ostrom has observed that such manipulations also characterized relationships involving the Bretton Woods institutions and the former Soviet Union. "Cryptoimperialism," as he called it, contributed to the creation of autocratic and predatory states, as a result of which "the conditions of many of the peoples of the Third World have not been marked by progressive patterns of development but by seriously degenerative tendencies." Vincent Ostrom, "Cryptoimperialism, Predatory State, and Self-Governance," in Vincent Ostrom, David Feeny, and Harttmut Picht, eds., *Rethinking Institutional Analysis and Development: Issues, Alternatives, and Choices* (San Francisco: Institute for Contemporary Studies Press, 1988), pp. 43–68, quote at p. 43.

12. The enormous human tragedies that have unfolded in Liberia, Sierra Leone, Somalia, and the Democratic Republic of Congo, for example, can be attributed to many factors, but the fundamental causes of such tragedies can be found in governance failures associated with centralized states that turned autocratic, predatory,

and repressive. The continued and inappropriate mobilization and utilization of political, military, ethnic-based, economic, and other resources through flawed governance structures and institutions eventually led to state collapse, often accompanied by violence. Several studies have supported this view. See, for example, the mammoth study undertaken by the Clingendael Institute in the Netherlands: Luc Van de Goor, Kumar Rupesinghe, and Paul Sciarone, eds., *Between Development and Destruction: An Enquiry into the Causes of Conflict in Post-Colonial States* (London: Macmillan, 1996). In the case of Liberia, Amos Sawyer, *The Emergence of Autocracy in Liberia: Tragedy and Challenge* (San Francisco: Institute for Contemporary Studies Press, 1992) substantiates this view. Bill Berkeley, *The Graves Are Not Yet Full: Race, Tribe, and Power in the Heart of Africa* (New York: Basic Books, 2001), an analysis of the use of anarchy to perpetrate tyranny, provides an interesting insight into the dynamics of warlordism and persistent repression in Africa following governance failures.

13. See Gino J. Naldi, *The Organization of African Unity: An Analysis of Its Role*, 2nd ed. (London: Mansell, 1999); and Amadu Sesay, Olusola Ojo, and Orobola Fasehun, *The OAU After Twenty Years* (Boulder: Westview Press, 1984).

14. News reports from the global food security conference held in Bonn in 2001, titled "Sustainable Food Security for All by 2020," are particularly relevant in this respect. The Southern African Research and Documentation Center reports that at the conference, "the issue of seed availability to the small-holder farmers around the world was revisited. Participants agreed that the food security situation in most developing countries is worsened by the arrival of multinational seed companies armed with patenting rights on genetically-modified seeds that cannot be reused. This technology compels the small-holder farmer to buy seed every season and spray particular types of chemicals. The shift from the traditional practice of farming to new methods has left farmers in developing countries vulnerable. It has also exacerbated food insecurity in most developing countries that are then forced to import food." See www.sardc.net/sanf/2001.

15. See Thandika Mkandawire, "Crisis Management and the Making of Choiceless Democracies," in Richard Joseph, ed., *State, Conflict, and Democracy in Africa* (Boulder: Lynne Rienner, 1999).

16. The emerging CSSDCA initiative has its origins in the work of the African Leadership Forum, founded in 1988 by General Olusegun Obasanjo, current president of Nigeria. The Kampala Document was prepared by a conference organized by the African Leadership Forum and the OAU and ECA secretariats and held in Kampala, Uganda, in 1991. See Olusegun Obasanjo and Felix Mosha, eds., *Africa: Rise to Challenge* (New York: African Leadership Forum, 1993); and I. William Zartman, "African Regional Security and Changing Patterns of Relations," in Edmond J. Keller and Donald Rothchild, eds., *Africa in the New International Order* (Boulder: Lynne Rienner, 1996).

17. Kampala Document, p. 7.

18. Ibid.

19. The World Bank and the United Nations Development Programme (UNDP), the leading proponents of "good governance," are producing a growing body of literature covering all aspects of the concept. For a good summary account of their thinking, see UNDP, *UNDP and Governance: Experiences and Lessons Learned* (New York: UNDP Management Development and Governance Division, 1998); and World Bank, *Governance: The World Bank's Experience* (Washington, D.C.: World Bank, 1994).

20. The concept of the capable state has been extensively discussed in the literature. See for example, Peter Evans, Dietrich Rueschemeyer, and Theda Skocpol, eds., *Bringing the State Back In* (Cambridge: Cambridge University Press, 1985); and Merilee S. Grindle, *Challenging the State: Crisis and Innovation in Latin America and Africa* (Cambridge: Cambridge University Press, 1996).

21. I am aware that this is a contentious issue, since Africa struggles with a dual system of governance that seeks to preserve the traditional while embracing the so-called modern. But this issue need not be cast as a question of preference between monolithic opposites. Studies have shown that particularism and universalism are not always in contradiction. See, for example, Joseph Gusfield, "Tradition and Modernity: Misplaced Polarities in the Study of Social Change," *American Journal of Sociology* 72 (January 1967): 351–362; and Robert E. Ward, "Political Modernization and Political Culture in Japan," *World Politics* 15 (July 1963): 569–596. The main task is to use the particular when it reinforces the universal, or to seek a synthesis that enhances norms and values compatible with the advancement of human dignity. This is a substantial challenge that requires careful scientific study, intensive consultation, and informed debate in every African society.

22. With regard to parliaments, a starting point could be to have a designated quota of members elected directly by national electoral constituencies of citizens with electoral disputes adjudicated by ECOWAS. The implication of this proposal for improved national electoral processes is obvious: granting legal standing to ordinary individuals who seek redress from abuses perpetrated by governments is a significant step toward improved rule of law and systems of justice at the national and subnational levels.

23. The challenge here is, among other things, to give equal legal and political standing to associational life in rural communities as exists in urban settings. Mahmood Mamdani in his study *Citizen and Subject* has convincingly made this point.

24. Of West Africa's fifteen heads of state in 2001, three had been in office without interruption for fourteen years or more; another had already served more than fourteen years when returned to office after having lost a previous election. At least six West African presidents ended their terms of office in 2003.

25. See, for example, IPA, *The Infrastructure of Peace in Africa: Assessing the Peacebuilding Capacity of African Institutions* (New York: International Peace Academy, September 2002).

26. See Vincent Ostrom, *The Meaning of Democracy and the Vulnerability of Democracies: A Response to Tocqueville's Challenge* (Ann Arbor: University of Michigan Press, 1997).

27. See, for example, Kwesi Prah, ed., *Between Distinction and Extinction: The Harmonisation and Standardisation of African Languages* (Cape Town: Centre for Advanced Studies of African Society, 1998); Kwesi Prah, ed., *African Languages for the Mass Education of Africans* (Cape Town: Centre for Advanced Studies of African Society, 1995); and Kwesi Prah, ed., *Mother Tongue for Scientific and Technological Development in Africa* (Cape Town: Centre for Advanced Studies of African Society, 1993).

28. See Harold Berman, *Law and Revolution: The Formation of the Western Legal Tradition* (Cambridge: Harvard University Press, 1983).

29. See Alexander Hamilton, John Jay, and James Madison in Edward M. Earle, ed., *The Federalist* (1788) (New York: Modern Library, n.d.).

30. See Adebayo Adedeji and Bamidele Ayo, eds., *People-Centred Democracy in Nigeria? The Search for Alternative Systems of Governance at the Grassroots*

(Ibadan, Nigeria: Heinemann Educational Books and African Centre for Development and Strategic Studies, 2000); and Ostrom, *Meaning of Democracy.*

31. See Amos Sawyer, "Children, Governance, and Development: Toward a Framework for Protecting the Rights of West Africa's Children," paper presented at the conference "War-Affected Children in West Africa," sponsored by UNICEF and the governments of Ghana and Canada, Accra, 27–28 April 2000. See also UNICEF's annual *The State of the World's Children* (New York: UNICEF), from 1990 to 1999.

6

The Fifth Wave of Pan-Africanism

Christopher Landsberg

Pan-Africanism embodies a number of properties and features.[1] It is at once a political movement and a sociocultural phenomenon as well as an ideology and set of political ideas, norms, and values that seek to bring about the unity of African people. This chapter deals with pan-Africanism as politics, and assesses its contribution to African political development over the course of the past century, with special reference to the role that prominent West African leaders such as Ghana's Kwame Nkrumah and Senegal's Léopold Senghor, and more recently, Nigeria's Olusegun Obasanjo and Senegal's Abdoulaye Wade, have played in these efforts. Specifically, the chapter analyzes politics as a means of bolstering the liberation and emancipation of African people and of putting the African continent on the road to prosperity, peace, and security through promoting democratic governance. Africa appears to be experiencing a new wave of pan-Africanism that differs markedly from the four waves of pan-Africanism of the preceding century. This fifth wave is pitting the values of unity and solidarity against those of democracy, accountability, democratic governance, and transparent politics. At the very least, the new pan-Africanism seeks to find a balance between solidarity and continental unity on the one hand, and the politics of democratic governance on the other.

For most of the twentieth century, political pan-Africanism was embedded in an emancipatory project to rid the continent and its people of racism, colonialism, and foreign subjugation. During each wave, the pan-African movement has sought to achieve self-definition and self-rule by Africans. But no sooner had liberation from alien rule been attained than some power-hungry and selfish elites decided to define self-rule in rather narrow terms. These elites typically believed that they could rule over societies on their own terms without having to consult and include their citizens in political governance. Some of the continent's postindependence leaders even turned the presidency into a lifetime position, while one-party political systems flourished on the continent. By the late 1980s, most African states found themselves caught in the grips of a crisis of political legitimacy and governance. This crisis in turn triggered regime insecurity as many governments faced internal and external threats to their survival. Many states in Africa were weakened by a lack of political legitimacy.[2]

By the mid-1990s, the need for a new governance regime in Africa to address these challenges of political legitimacy on the one hand, and the link between peace, security, and governance on the other, were becoming clear. This realization led to a number of continental initiatives in the areas of security, governance, and democracy that signified the advent of a new wave of pan-Africanism. This pan-Africanism advocates a new interventionism that seeks to achieve a new form of good governance—democratic governance—in Africa. These new initiatives have already begun to challenge Africa's postindependence, elite-driven governing consensus, which was underpinned by a regime of nonintervention, national sovereignty, and the sanctity of borders, as enshrined in the charter of the Organization of African Unity (OAU) in 1963. The emphasis of this fifth wave of pan-Africanism is on the promotion of democracy, human rights, conflict management, participatory governance, transparency, and accountability. But just as pan-Africanist initiatives in the past were marked by many power struggles and pitted different political groupings against each other, this new "prodemocracy" wave of pan-Africanism is already unearthing power struggles among African states. Prodemocracy and democratic governance elites are squaring up against others who would like to cling to the old taboos of the inviolability of state sovereignty. The struggle for Africa's new interventionism involves the creation of alliances among like-minded leaders—what Jimmy Kandeh has described as "dominions of democracies"[3]—against leaders who oppose the notion of "sovereignty as responsibility."[4]

Whereas pan-Africanist waves of the past were concerned primarily with fostering solidarity and unity among African states and ending colonial rule in Africa, the fifth wave of pan-Africanism—also referred to here as the post–Cold War, postapartheid wave—poses and seeks to grapple with a fundamental question: How do Africans establish norms, values, institutions, and mechanisms to protect and guarantee the security of their citizens through democracy and accountable governance, without undermining security and engendering conflict among states? Put differently, how should Africans balance the rights of states with the rights of citizens? How can a more people-centered pan-Africanism be fostered based on a post–Cold War African governance regime in which governing elites agree to certain fundamental rights, norms, and values to guide their behavior?

This chapter attempts to answer these questions. After a brief assessment of the five waves of pan-Africanism, I analyze in more depth the current wave of pan-Africanism centered on five key initiatives: the Conference on Security, Stability, Development, and Cooperation in Africa (CSSDCA), the Millennium Africa Recovery Program (MAP), the Omega Plan, the New African Initiative (NAI), the New Partnership for Africa's Development (NEPAD), and the African Union (AU). The chapter then explains the implications of these processes for West Africa, before concluding with a brief review of Africa's evolving security and governance architectures.

The Five Waves of Pan-Africanism

This current post–Cold War wave of pan-Africanism has been preceded by at least four waves of pan-Africanism since 1880. The first wave was the one against European expansionism between 1880 and 1945; the second was the wave of decolonization between 1945 and 1962; the third was the wave of African unity between 1963 and 1975; and the fourth was the wave of devolution between 1975 and 1989. This fourth wave resulted in the creation of subcontinental bodies like the Economic Community of West African States (ECOWAS) and sought to promote regional political and economic integration. The current post–Cold War wave of pan-Africanism is the wave of the African Renaissance, a concept that will be explained in more detail below.

The Wave Against European Expansionism

The first wave of pan-Africanism can be described as the wave against European expansionism. This wave was born against the backdrop of the "scramble for Africa" and the partitioning of the continent by European powers. This process involved two phases.[5] The scramble for Africa occurred between 1880 and 1914 and was rapid and explosive. European powers acted out of mistrust of each other inside Europe and decided to play out their strategic games in Africa. They created the conditions for much of the divisions of postcolonial Africa.

The second phase of this wave lasted until the end of Europe's civil war in 1945—commonly dubbed World War II. The emphasis of pan-Africanism during this phase was on racial dignity and the liberation of Africa from the brutal colonial demarcation process that established boundaries and lumped people together without regard for their ethnic and cultural origins. This cynical cartographic exercise broke up many African communities and societies. For example, Ewes can now be found in Ghana and Togo, Yorubas in Benin and Nigeria, and Mandingos in Guinea and Liberia. At the end of the first phase of this pioneering wave, pan-Africanists such as Marcus Garvey, W. E. B. DuBois, C. L. R. James, George Padmore, Aimé Césaire, and Léopold Senghor spearheaded campaigns, both political and cultural, against the destructive legacies of the Berlin conference of 1884–1885, at which the leaders of Germany, Britain, France, Spain, Portugal, and Belgium agreed to:

1. utilize the principle that title to colonial territory rested on "effective occupation and management";
2. recognize the claims of Britain and France to areas of West Africa inland from their coastal possessions; and
3. acknowledge the Congo free state as a private estate "belonging" to King Leopold II of Belgium.[6]

These foreign powers practiced both "direct rule" and "indirect rule," as if they were performing some sort of favor for Africans.[7]

The Wave of Decolonization

The second wave of pan-Africanism, between 1945 and 1962, was the period of anticolonial revolts. Nationalist movements, both in Africa and in the Diaspora, embraced the idea of developing well-organized movements to fight for the independence of subjugated peoples and territories.[8] It was during this phase that the idea was espoused that the independence of one country would be meaningless until the entire continent was totally free of colonial rule. This notion was articulated most forcefully by Ghana's Kwame Nkrumah and Tanzania's Julius Nyerere.

West Africa was in the forefront of the pan-Africanist struggle for independence. There was, for example, the Ashanti resistance movement to British colonial rule in Ghana, and the Fulani resistance to the British subjugation of northern Nigeria.[9] Both of these West African examples aptly dispel the widespread myth that Africans welcomed colonial domination. Outside West Africa, a number of resistance movements emerged. For example, the Maji Maji rebellion against colonial policies in Tanganyika (now Tanzania) demonstrated that some African civil society groups were as organized as traditional authorities to resist foreign domination.[10] In Kenya, white European settlers dubbed a secretive, anticolonial guerrilla organization of poor Kikuyu in the 1950s the "Mau Mau," whose major objective, like that of other resistance movements, was to regain Kikuyu land from white settlers and rid the country of foreign domination.

The Wave of African Unity

By 1960, pan-Africanism had become an instrument of African nationalism and the stage was set for the third wave, which culminated in the official establishment of the OAU in Addis Ababa, Ethiopia, in May 1963. But divisions in African ranks, and even between African states, characterized the birth of the OAU, a trend that would later come to characterize the fifth wave of pan-Africanism. In 1961 a conference was held in Casablanca that was attended by the heads of state of Ghana, Guinea, Mali, Morocco, and the United Arab Republic.[11] This group became known as the Casablanca group and advocated a political union with, inter alia, a joint African high command to keep the continental peace. The Casablanca group also appealed to all African states to associate themselves with "our common action for the consolidation of liberty in Africa and the building up of its unity and security."[12]

A number of states, including Ethiopia, Liberia, Nigeria, Sierra Leone, Somalia, Sudan, Togo, and Tunisia, did not agree with this position. They instead held a conference to which all African states were invited. This conference took place in Monrovia in May 1961 and was opened by President William Tubman of Liberia, who emphasized the need for economic cooperation among states as a first step toward "unity in Africa."[13] These states came to be known as the Monrovia group. The views of its members were eloquently expressed by Senegal's poet-president Léopold Senghor, who declared: "If we wish to succeed, we must put the stress on cultural, technical and economic co-operation, rather than on the co-operation of political parties."[14]

The visionary Kwame Nkrumah led the Casablanca group. He associated himself closely with the view that "regionalism within Africa could retard progress towards political union in Africa."[15] Instead, Ghana's president advocated a committee of foreign affairs officials and experts empowered to establish

- a commission to frame a constitution for a union government of African states;
- a commission to work out a continentwide plan for a unified or common economic and industrial program including a common market for Africa, an African currency, an African monetary zone, an African central bank, and a continental communications system;
- a commission to draw up details for a common foreign policy and diplomacy;
- a commission to produce plans for a common system of defense; and
- a commission to plan for a common African citizenship.

When African heads of state and government met in Addis Ababa on 25 May 1963, the battle lines were clearly drawn between those who favored a modest organization that focused on unity and solidarity and those who sided with Nkrumah and his call to "agree here and now to the establishment of a Union of African States."[16] The vast majority of members voted against Nkrumah. Nigeria's premier, Sir Abubakar Tafawa Balewa, for example, maintained that the establishment of a "United States of Africa" would create too many problems. In favor of the territorial integrity of states and the Westphalian model, Balewa declared: "Our problems are here (in Nigeria) and only here."[17] African leaders voted against a supranational organization and in favor of the following guiding principles, which were enshrined in the OAU charter:

- the sovereign equality of all member states;
- noninterference in the internal affairs of states;
- respect for the sovereignty and territorial integrity of each state and its inalienable right to independent existence;
- peaceful settlement of disputes by negotiation, mediation, conciliation, and arbitration;
- unreserved condemnation, in all its forms, of political assassination as well as subversive activities on the part of neighboring or any other states;
- absolute dedication to the total emancipation of the still-dependent African territories; and
- affirmation of a policy of nonalignment with regard to all blocs.

Being the institutional embodiment of pan-Africanism, the OAU emphasized unity and emancipation. The organization set out to

- promote the unity and solidarity of African states;
- coordinate and intensify cooperation and efforts to achieve a better life for the peoples of Africa;
- eradicate all forms of colonialism from Africa; and
- promote international cooperation, having due regard to the Charter of the United Nations and the Universal Declaration of Human Rights.

Thus, from the outset, the OAU committed its members to the idea of continental unity. The OAU charter advocated the promotion of solidarity and cooperation among African states, as well as the defense of their sovereignty and territorial integrity. So, a close scrutiny of the OAU's founding principles reveals that the organization placed great emphasis on both unity and emancipation, while at the same time enshrining the strictures of state sovereignty into African politics and inter-African relations.

The Wave of Devolution

The fourth wave of pan-Africanism involved the establishment of subregional organizations in Africa, and attempts by these organizations to create communities and regional societies characterized by shared norms, values, institutions, and mechanisms (see Chapters 3 and 4). If this regional devolution and creation of subregional organizations were not a proper wave in their own right, then this certainly was a wave within a wave, a sort of "miniwave." This phase, which started in 1975, again saw West Africa playing the vanguard role in Africa with the establishment of ECOWAS (see Chapter 2). Though regional organizations had been created in Africa since the 1960s, ECOWAS represented one of the most ambitious efforts to build a subregional grouping that cut across colonial anglophone, francophone, and lusophone divisions in an effort to create a common market of sixteen states. ECOWAS was established to promote subregional integration, but soon came to appreciate the crucial link between economic integration and peace and security. West African leaders eventually understood that economic integration could only succeed under conditions of peace and security. While ECOWAS was established in 1975 primarily to promote economic integration, the organization later adapted its institutions to play a conflict management role in West Africa.[18]

Another defining moment for the fourth wave of pan-Africanism was the establishment of the Southern African Development Coordination Conference (SADCC) in 1980. Created in Tanzania by nine regional states, the SADCC's two objectives were to promote cooperation among its member states and to reduce their dependence on apartheid South Africa.[19] A major priority of the organization was to reorient regional transportation patterns to reduce dependence on routes through South Africa. The Frontline States— Angola, Tanzania, Mozambique, Zambia, and Zimbabwe—set for themselves the political objective of completing the anticolonial, antiapartheid revolution without sacrificing domestic and regional growth and development.

In 1992 the SADCC was transformed into the Southern African Development Community (SADC). The new organization set out to promote peace and security, human rights and democracy, the rule of law, and the peaceful settlement of disputes.[20] After the dismantling of apartheid in South Africa by 1994, it was widely assumed that southern Africa would automatically transform itself from a region characterized by liberation wars and antiapartheid struggles to one that was marked by cooperation, integration, and development. That assumption naturally proved ill-conceived and premature and this region, like West Africa, started to appreciate the crucial relationship between security, democratic governance, and economic integration.

The Wave of the African Renaissance

The fifth wave of pan-Africanism is the wave of the African Renaissance. Just as the third wave can be most closely associated with Ghana's Kwame

Nkrumah, this fifth wave has been most closely associated with South
Africa's Thabo Mbeki. It involves a series of initiatives that are already
having an impact on Africa's governing consensus, which was underpinned
for three decades by a regime of noninterference, nonintervention, and
national sovereignty. This African Renaissance seeks to set the parameters
for a new interventionism in favor of democratization, accountable governance, and human rights. Indeed, between 1994 and 1999 many African
scholars and politicians put interventionism firmly on the continental
agenda. Francis Deng argued that "the logic of the transcendent importance
of human rights as a legitimate area of concern for the international community, especially where order has broken down or the state is incapable
or unwilling to act responsibly to protect the masses of citizens, would tend
to make international inaction indefensible."[21] Former OAU secretary-
general Salim Ahmed Salim similarly stated in 1996: "We should talk about
the need for accountability of governments and of their national and international responsibilities. In the process, we shall be redefining sovereignty."[22] At the OAU summit in Ouagadougou in 1998, Nelson Mandela
coined what some have dubbed the "Mandela doctrine," when he told his
fellow leaders: "Africa has the right and the duty to intervene to root out
tyranny . . . we must all accept that we cannot abuse the concept of national
sovereignty to deny the rest of the continent the right and duty to intervene
when behind those sovereign boundaries people are being slaughtered to
protect tyranny."[23]

While some leaders clearly preferred the status quo, other African leaders felt compelled to censure putschists and warlords who were fueling
regional instability.[24] At the OAU summit in Algiers in July 1999, President
Thabo Mbeki and his Nigerian counterpart, Olusegun Obasanjo, emerged as
central actors seeking to put in place punitive measures against unconstitutional changes of government in Africa—notably coups d'état—in a bid to
entrench democratic norms of governance.[25] The OAU's leaders borrowed
a soccer analogy and invoked a "yellow" and a "red" card through which,
in the event of a coup, putschists would first be warned and urged to return
to democratic rule—the yellow card. In the event of a failure to comply,
such regimes would then be expelled from the OAU and face other punitive
sanctions—the red card. The OAU subsequently barred the military
regimes of Côte d'Ivoire and Comoros from attending its summit in Lomé
in 2000 as the idea of "sovereignty as responsibility" increasingly took root
in African diplomacy.

During the period of 2000 to 2001, the process of restructuring
Africa's governance architecture was further crystallized, when four leading African states—South Africa, Nigeria, Senegal, and Algeria—undertook five initiatives:

1. The formal incorporation of the 1991 Conference on Security, Stability, Development, and Cooperation in Africa into the OAU's conflict prevention, management, and resolution machinery of 1993.
2. The decision taken in Lomé in 2000 by the OAU to transform itself into the African Union.
3. The acceleration of the OAU-mandated drafting of the Millennium Africa Recovery Plan under the leadership of Mbeki, Obasanjo, and Algerian leader Abdelaziz Bouteflika.
4. The merger of MAP and the Omega Plan—the initiative spearheaded by Senegalese president Abdoulaye Wade—to create the New Africa Initiative.
5. The launch of the New Partnership for Africa's Development.

Thus, nothing short of a major restructuring of Africa's governance ethos and intervention in defense thereof may well be under way in these early years of the twenty-first century. This revolution can only succeed, however, if a condominium of African democracies can muster the will to achieve these goals. Whatever the outcome of this great battle for Africa's democratic soul, the once sacrosanct legal principle of the sovereignty of, and noninterference in, the domestic affairs of states has been eroded and is now being balanced by greater emphasis on the rights of peoples and the responsibility of governments to their citizens (see Chapter 5).

The CSSDCA:
The Born-Again African "Helsinki" Initiative

Modeled on Europe's 1975 Helsinki process, the Conference on Security, Stability, Development, and Cooperation in Africa has had two incarnations. The first CSSDCA initiative was launched in Kampala, Uganda, in 1991 under the sponsorship of the African Leadership Forum (ALF), the OAU, and the UN's Economic Commission for Africa (ECA). The goal of the CSSDCA at the time was to have the initiative adopted by the OAU heads-of-state summit in Abuja in 1991 under the chairmanship of Nigeria's General Ibrahim Babangida. The principal motivation of the CSSDCA concept was the urgent need for a redefinition of security and sovereignty. As Olusegun Obasanjo noted in 1991: "We must ask why does sovereignty seem to confer absolute immunity on any government who [sic] commits genocide and monumental crimes."[26]

In a similar vein, Uganda's Yoweri Museveni noted at the same Kampala meeting in 1991: "Sovereignty became a sacred cow and many crimes have been committed in its name. . . . If the Europeans can surrender some of their sovereignty for greater development, African states can similarly surrender some of their sovereignty for greater security, both at the intra and interstate levels."[27]

These decade-old ideas were revolutionary in the context of the non-intervention and prostate security context of postindependence Africa. But they were not initially implemented. These concepts were enshrined in the Kampala Document, which incorporated both the 1990 OAU heads-of-state Declaration on the Political and Socioeconomic Situation in Africa and the Fundamental Changes Taking Place in the World, and the 1990 African Charter for Popular Participation in Development. Essentially the Kampala Document contained four interrelated calabashes (baskets):

- The security calabash was to focus on principles and modalities for ensuring peaceful interstate relations.
- The stability calabash was to focus on the need for democratization, good governance, and popular participation within member states.
- The development calabash was to focus on strategies to raise and improve general standards of living.
- The cooperation calabash was to focus on the modalities for accelerating regional integration processes and harmonizing the development of vital sectors of African economies.

Although the CSSDCA had some influence on the evolution of the sixteen-member central organ of the OAU's security mechanism—a sort of African security council modeled on the UN's fifteen-member body—of 1993,[28] Obasanjo's plan for the integration of the CSSDCA into the OAU to promote institutional reform was derailed, and had to be postponed until a decade later. After Obasanjo was elected president of Nigeria in 1999, he reintroduced the idea of the CSSDCA to the OAU at the Algiers summit in the same year. Hence the "second coming" of the CSSDCA saw its adoption as a proposal for establishing a permanent machinery covering continental peacekeeping, promoting conflict prevention and military self-reliance in Africa, establishing an African peace council of elder statesmen to mediate conflicts, and promoting a drastic reduction in military expenditure. Some of these ideas are currently being incorporated into the nascent African Union project.[29]

The thirty-sixth ordinary session of the OAU/African Economic Community (AEC) assembly of heads of state and government, which took place in Lomé, Togo, in July 2000, adopted the report of the first ministerial meeting of the CSSDCA, which had been held in Abuja two months earlier. The Lomé summit acknowledged the need for the CSSDCA process to create synergy between the various initiatives undertaken by the OAU and the AEC,[30] and stressed the need to consolidate the work of both bodies in the areas of peace, security, stability, development, and cooperation.[31] In this regard, it was suggested that the CSSDCA should provide a policy development forum for the elaboration and advancement of common values within the main policy organs of the OAU.[32] The Lomé meeting agreed that detailed discussions should be undertaken on the four CSSDCA calabashes in order to incorporate the conference's goals into the work of the OAU.

The CSSDCA's operational terms of reference for breathing life into its calabashes are still unclear. There is, as yet, no indication of how the CSSDCA process will be implemented at the regional and subregional levels, or of how its machinery will relate to specific conflicts and peace-building initiatives in Africa. It is also unclear how and whether this process can be nationalized as an operational process within each AU state. In the case of South Africa, the calabash system has informed an innovative computerized scenario planning process within the Department of Foreign Affairs to track developments and make projections within specific African subregions and countries. Thus the CSSDCA can serve as a tool for policy planning as well as a machine for driving a conflict prevention, management, and resolution process.

After the launch of the African Union in Durban, South Africa, in July 2002, it was agreed that the CSSDCA would temporarily form part of the AU until greater clarity emerged about its place within Africa's evolving security architecture. As soon as the CSSDCA was given a new lease on life, a CSSDCA unit was set up within the AU secretariat in Addis Ababa. The CSSDCA initiative has slowly started to generate consensus around a set of governance and democratization benchmarks and indicators.[33] The initiative aims to be an inclusive pan-African project. The CSSDCA has now developed over fifty emerging security, governance, cooperation, and development indicators, underpinned by the idea that the security and development of every African country are inseparable from those of other countries. Recognizing that instability in one country affects the stability of neighboring countries and can have serious implications for continental peace and development, the CSSDCA argues that the interdependence of African states and the link between their security, stability, and development make it imperative to develop a common agenda for Africa.

Other ideas in the CSSDCA's evolving principles include a plea that Africa's resources be used more effectively to meet the needs of African people and to improve their well-being. Peace, security, and development require the strengthening of Africa's solidarity and cooperation with external actors so as to meet the challenges of globalization and to avoid the continent's marginalization. Furthermore, HIV/AIDS and other pandemics on the continent constitute a threat to human security, as well as to short- and long-term sustainable growth in Africa. According to the CSSDCA vision, the concept of security must therefore embrace all aspects of society, including economic, political, social, and environmental dimensions of individual, family, community, and national life.

The emerging peace and security norms and values encompassed in the CSSDCA stress the peaceful resolution of disputes with an emphasis on seeking "African solutions to African problems." This is based on the belief that the prevention, management, and resolution of conflicts provide the enabling environment for security and development to flourish. The responsibility for the continent's future lies primarily with African states, and the African Union remains the premier organization on the continent for promoting security, stability, development, and cooperation. The CSSDCA further notes that there is an imperative need to build and enhance Africa's capacity for peace support operations, emergency relief preparedness, and natural disaster response at the subregional and continental levels, including the strengthening of regional efforts and initiatives. According to this initiative, the problem of refugees and internally displaced persons constitutes a threat to peace and security and its root causes must be urgently addressed. Uncontrolled spread of small arms and light weapons, as well as the problem of land mines, is also recognized by the CSSDCA as a threat to peace and security in Africa.

Finally, the CSSDCA makes a strong case for political stability, arguing that security requires strict adherence to the rule of law, good governance, the participation of citizens in public affairs, respect for human rights and fundamental freedoms, and the establishment of political organizations devoid of sectarian, religious, ethnic, regional, and racial extremism. The executive, legislative, and judicial branches of government must therefore respect their national constitutions and adhere to the provisions of law and other legislative enactments. No one should be exempted from accountability. These principles are now playing an important role in the AU's evolving African Peer Review Mechanism (APRM).

MAP and the "New" African Conditionalities

Out of South African president Thabo Mbeki's idea of the African Renaissance[34] was born the Millennium Africa Recovery Program, a "comprehensive and far-reaching global plan of action" to tackle poverty and Africa's development needs.[35] MAP was premised on the idea of Africa leading its own recovery with the support of key donor partners who would provide crucial assistance in overcoming the challenges posed by globalization. The eradication of poverty lay at the heart of the MAP initiative. The MAP document noted that it is essential that conditions conducive to social and economic development be created in Africa, and argues that conflict and instability continue to inhibit development on the continent. Therefore, principles of democracy, good governance, and the respect for human rights need to be entrenched in Africa's political life.

The plan recognized that there had been attempts in the past to set out continentwide development programs. It noted, however, that "for a variety of reasons, both internal and external, including questionable leadership and ownership by Africans themselves, these have been less than successful. However, there is today a new set of circumstances, which lend themselves to integrated practical implementation."[36] MAP took for granted that the benefits for countries engaging in the project would be self-evident. The plan acknowledged the interrelationship between socioeconomic development, security, and good governance, and sought to create the conditions for sustainable development in Africa. The MAP document singled out the need for "a new corps of progressive African leaders" committed to the renaissance vision and to tackling the twin evils of poverty and underdevelopment.[37] The plan envisages that these endeavors by African leaders would be supported by multilateral institutions and industrialized countries that would provide debt relief, open foreign markets to African products, invest in Africa's future, share their technologies and medicines, and contribute to international peacekeeping missions in Africa.

For their part, African leaders who signed up to MAP pledged themselves to the ideals of nurturing peace, democracy, good governance, and respect for human rights. One of MAP's main goals is "the expansion of democratic frontiers and the deepening of a culture of human rights and tolerance."[38] The program offered a "strategy for achieving sustainable development in the 21st century" by mapping out preconditions and sectoral priorities. MAP's preconditions for development included: peace, security, democracy, and political governance; economic and corporate governance, with a focus on financial management; and regional cooperation and integration. The program's priority sectors included information and communications technology; human development, with a focus on health, education, and skills development; agriculture; and the promotion of diversified production and exports.

The Omega Plan for Africa

The Omega Plan for Africa was initiated by Senegalese president Abdoulaye Wade in 2001. The plan was informed by the belief that "Africa must, in order to keep pace with globalization, pursue a new strategic development vision based on a comprehensive and realistic program which clearly sets out the priorities and resources to be mobilized for strong and sustainable growth which benefits all strata of its population and the rest of the world."[39] Omega was presented as an attempt to find an original approach, drawing inspiration from the relevant principles of self-sustaining growth, to formulate economic policies that would eradicate poverty and improve the well-being of Africans. To do this, Africa would, according to the plan, have to attain and maintain a mean annual growth rate of 7 percent.[40]

The Omega Plan was based on "a clean break with the vision of self-sustaining national development conducted by a developing state, and relies principally on an economic construct built within the framework of regional integration."[41] Put in concrete terms, regional integration logically became the basis of the Omega Plan and required the development of subregional plans by each of Africa's five subregions (central, East, West, southern, and North Africa) under the joint secretariat of the OAU, the UN's ECA, and the African Development Bank.

Omega's basic assumption was that "all investment needs in the priority sectors of basic infrastructural, educational, health and agricultural facilities would be evaluated and brought under the purview of a single national authority. The financing mobilized would boost the growth of Africa and the world economy."[42]

The four priority sectors of the Omega Plan were basic infrastructure, education, health delivery, and agricultural extension facilities. Like MAP, Omega argued that Africa should no longer rely exclusively on foreign assistance and lending to finance major infrastructural investment. Instead, investment should depend on the mobilization of every source of domestic and external financing as well as the creation of special funds.[43] With regard to external funding, the plan envisaged official borrowing, resources being allocated to infrastructural and educational development in Africa and new funds being created or mobilized for these sectors (with a clear understanding that these funds would be the most substantial means of external funding), foreign direct investment, and the creation of special drawing rights for Africa.

Omega envisaged two stages to the plan's financing. The first stage would entail the coherence and practicability of the plan being tested by economists and other financial experts. The second stage would entail selling the Omega Plan to funding agencies, including the World Bank and the International Monetary Fund, the European Union (EU), the United States, Japan, Canada, and other external donors.

The New African Initiative

Many observers saw the Omega Plan as a rival to MAP and vice versa. These perceptions led to talk of an anglophone-francophone divide in the quest for a vision to define Africa's future.[44] This development threatened to revive the divisions and rival blocs of the 1960s during the third wave of pan-Africanism. To avoid such an outcome, the leaders of MAP and Omega decided that the two plans should be merged, from which the New African Initiative resulted in July 2001.[45] The OAU summit that took place in Lusaka, Zambia, in July 2001 adopted the NAI as its final working document after much horse-trading and difficult diplomacy. But it is clear from a reading of both MAP and the Omega Plan that the NAI is based more liberally and substantially on MAP's elements, although the merger largely employs Omega's references to infrastructural development and adopts some of its investment targets.

The NAI noted that "the resources, including capital, technology and human skills, that are required to launch a global war on poverty and underdevelopment exist in abundance, and are within our grasp. . . . [W]hat is required to mobilize these resources and to use them properly, is bold and imaginative leadership that is genuinely committed to a sustained effort of human upliftment and poverty eradication, as well as a new global partnership based on shared responsibility and mutual interest."[46] The danger with these ideas is that the NAI and Africa's recovery initiatives might come to depend heavily on tutelage and buy-in from the industrialized countries, rather than on Africa's own resources.[47] The initiative does not, however, shy away from addressing the issue of undemocratic and unaccountable governance on the continent, noting that postcolonial Africa inherited weak states and dysfunctional economies that were further aggravated by poor leadership, corruption, and bad governance in many countries. These factors, together with the divisions created by the Cold War, hampered the spread of accountable governments across the continent.[48]

The NAI argued, however, that these obstacles could be overcome, since this African initiative was focused on African "ownership" and management. Thus, African leaders were determined to set the agenda for the renewal of the continent. This agenda was based on their conceptualization of national and regional priorities and development plans, and was viewed as a new framework for interaction with the rest of the world, including industrialized countries and multilateral institutions. Significantly, the initiative asserted that in exchange for buy-in from external actors, African leaders would take responsibility for, and commit themselves to, promoting new norms and values that break with postindependence taboos such as nonintervention in the internal affairs of member states. This initiative represented an unprecedented attempt by African leaders at self-imposed conditionalities. The principal goals of the NAI included:

- strengthening mechanisms for conflict prevention, management, and resolution at the regional and continental levels, and ensuring that these mechanisms are used to restore and maintain peace;

- promoting and protecting democracy and human rights in African countries and regions by developing clear standards of accountability, transparency, and participatory governance;
- restoring and maintaining macroeconomic stability, especially through the development of appropriate standards and targets for fiscal and monetary policies and the introduction of appropriate institutional frameworks to achieve these standards;
- institutionalizing transparent legal and regulatory frameworks for financial markets, including the auditing of both private companies and the public sector;
- revitalizing and extending the provision of education, technical training, and health services, with a high priority on tackling HIV/AIDS, malaria, and other communicable diseases;
- promoting the role of women in social and economic development by reinforcing their capacity in education and training, by developing revenue-generating activities for them through the facilitation of access to credit, and by ensuring their participation in the political and economic life of African countries;
- building the capacity of African states to set and enforce legal frameworks, as well as to maintain law and order; and
- promoting the development of infrastructure and agriculture and the diversification of farming into agroindustries and manufacturing in order to serve both domestic and export markets.[49]

These commitments suggest that African leaders involved in the NAI project were engaging in a self-imposed structural adjustment program that they would "own." This grouping of African leaders sought to attract Western and other external partners to invest in the initiative by demonstrating their commitment to these self-imposed obligations. The five priority sectors of NAI that African leaders wanted external partners to support were infrastructure; information and communications technology; human development, with a focus on health, education, and skills development; agriculture; and the diversification of production and exports, with a focus on market access for African exports to industrialized countries.[50]

Finally, on the issue of mobilizing resources, NAI urged Africa's external partners to recognize that resources would accrue from increased savings and capital inflows through debt relief, increased overseas development aid, and private capital, as well as through better management of public revenue and expenditure. The initiative stressed, however, that African leaders were interested in forging a genuine partnership with external actors and not in continuing foreign tutelage. Industrialized countries should therefore treat Africans as genuine partners, not as dependent recipients of Western aid.

The New Partnership for Africa's Development

On 23 October 2001, African leaders renamed NAI and launched the initiative as the New Partnership for Africa's Development at an implementation meeting in Abuja, Nigeria.[51] At this meeting, it was decided that a coordinating NEPAD secretariat would be established in Pretoria, South Africa—a sign of the adroit diplomacy played by Thabo Mbeki. Obasanjo was elected as chairperson of NEPAD's implementation committee, and Abdoulaye Wade was elected as deputy chairperson of this committee. It was decided that the implementation committee would meet once every four months. The Abuja meeting also created task agencies that would implement NEPAD's projects. These task forces were established in five areas: capacity building on peace and security, economic and corporate governance, infrastructure, central bank and financial standards, and agriculture and market access.

A subcommittee on peace and security was established to focus on conflict management, prevention, and resolution, with South Africa as its chair, and Algeria, Gabon, Mali, and Mauritius as the other members. NEPAD then adopted a declaration on democracy and political, economic, and corporate governance,[52] through which participating African states committed themselves to demonstrate and exercise the necessary political will for achieving NEPAD's core values and obligations. Two of these values are empowering citizens and institutions within civil society, and fostering an active and independent civil society that can hold governments accountable to their people. These are profound commitments, since they speak to one of the most fundamental challenges faced by democratization processes in Africa: public participation. NEPAD also commits African leaders to adhere to the principles of constitutional democracy, the rule of law, and the strict separation of powers, including the protection of the independence of the judiciary. The plan further commits members to promote political representativity, thus providing opportunities for all citizens to participate in the political process in a free and fair political environment.

NEPAD's leaders pledged to ensure the periodic democratic renewal of leadership in line with the principle that heads of state should be subjected to fixed terms in office. Freedom of expression, including an independent media, as well as commitments to ensuring the effective participation of women, "minorities," and disadvantaged groups in political and economic processes, is also part of NEPAD's emerging norms. NEPAD's members have further committed themselves to ensuring impartial, transparent, and credible electoral oversight and administration; to combating and eradicating corruption; to ensuring a dedicated, honest, and efficient civil society; and to promoting transparent and accountable governance. African leaders who sign up to this plan are seeking to commit themselves to respecting and protecting universal human rights and to strengthening their institutional capacity to ensure the proper functioning of democratic institutions.

NEPAD has drawn up plans for its African Peer Review Mechanism, the purposes of which will be to:

- enhance African ownership of its development agenda;
- identify, evaluate, and disseminate best practices;
- monitor progress toward agreed goals;
- use peer review to enhance the adoption and implementation of best practices;
- ensure that policy is based on best current knowledge and practice; and
- identify deficiencies and capacity gaps and then recommend suitable approaches to addressing these issues.

During the seventh summit of the NEPAD Heads of State and Government Implementation Committee (HSGIC) in Abuja in May 2003, the committee approved the proposed initial membership of the panel of eminent persons for the APRM:[53] Adebayo Adedeji, Bethuel Kiplagat, Graca Machel, Dorothy Njeuma, Marie-Angelique Savane, and Chris Stals.[54]

The Group of Eight (G8) industrialized countries has outlined clear conditions for African leaders to fulfill before they can support NEPAD. Donors have made their support for NEPAD contingent on the adherence of African leaders to NEPAD's principles, as determined by G8 leaders. Many Africans, however, remain skeptical about the ability of the G8 to fulfill its pledges to NEPAD, given competing demands on resources and the generally low priority accorded to Africa. Widespread fears have been expressed in Africa that the NEPAD peer review mechanism will simply become a stick for the West to punish selective African leaders like Zimbabwe's Robert Mugabe. It is also unclear whether African leaders, many of whom have supported each other in the past, can monitor each other's behavior effectively without the participation of their civil societies in any review process.

The African Union:
Legislating African Governance, Peace, and Security?

The African Union inherited the OAU's existing conflict prevention, management, and resolution machinery. The AU, through its Constitutive Act of Union, has a political mandate to intervene against members who violate principles of good governance and the rule of law—an element that clearly sets the organization apart from its predecessor, the OAU. The Constitutive

Act automatically becomes law in all African countries that have signed and ratified it.[55] But tensions remain between the principles and objectives outlined in the AU's Constitutive Act, such as intervention in the internal affairs of member states.

The African Union explicitly recognizes the right of intervention in three specific cases: first, if a regime has been toppled through unconstitutional means, notably through a military coup; second, in cases of genocide; and third, if instability in one country threatens broader stability in any African subregion.[56] Based on the principles of the Constitutive Act, an unconstitutional interruption of the democratic order or an unconstitutional alteration of the constitutional regime that seriously impairs the democratic order in a member state would jeopardize the erring government's participation in AU meetings.

Under the AU's Constitutive Act, four changes of government are defined as unconstitutional:

1. A military coup d'état against a democratically elected government.
2. Intervention by mercenaries to replace a democratically elected government.
3. The replacement of a democratically elected government by armed dissidents and rebels.
4. The refusal of an incumbent government to relinquish power to the winning party after a free and fair election.[57]

In the event of an unconstitutional change of regime, any member state, the AU Assembly, and/or the AU Peace and Security Council may request the immediate convocation of the assembly to undertake a collective assessment of the situation and to take such decisions as they deem appropriate. The Peace and Security Council may then adopt decisions for the restoration of constitutional order as defined under the security and stability pillars of the CSSDCA's Solemn Declaration. These decisions may include, but are not limited to, the deployment of diplomatic missions and good offices, mediators, peace monitors, peacekeepers, peacemakers, and peace enforcers.

If such initiatives prove unsuccessful, or if the urgency of the situation so warrants, the AU Peace and Security Council would immediately convene a special session of the AU Assembly, which would then take appropriate action, including diplomatic initiatives, in accordance with the AU's Constitutive Act and the provisions of the UN Charter. The idea behind these clauses is clearly to build into the AU's evolving governance system the notion of multilateral legitimacy. If the special session of the AU Assembly determines that there has been an unconstitutional change of regime and that diplomatic initiatives have failed, the special session has the power to suspend the errant member state from participating in the

AU's institutions by an affirmative vote of two-thirds of its member states. Such a suspension would take effect immediately. As the centerpiece of this emerging system of continental governance, the AU is in a unique position to promote a new set of norms and values in Africa based on democratic principles and human rights, and to demonstrate that the old principles of absolute sovereignty and noninterference are no longer sacrosanct in the post–Cold War era.

Implications for West Africa

Before concluding this chapter, we must examine how synergies can be built between the CSSDCA, the AU, and NEPAD. It is also important that the CSSDCA and NEPAD are linked to the conflict management efforts of Africa's subregional organizations like ECOWAS. Attempts at promoting the CSSDCA, the AU, and NEPAD in West Africa will have to take into account the commonalities and complementarities between each of these governing components, as well as the specificities of West Africa's security architecture. Compared to other subregional and regional organizations, ECOWAS appears to have articulated the most advanced security architecture in Africa (see Chapter 13). Nevertheless, the same questions about strategic synergies, complementarities, and niches between the different elements of this architecture apply in West Africa as elsewhere, especially in terms of how the CSSDCA, the AU, and NEPAD will relate to each other and to existing subregional mechanisms and initiatives.

Unlike the cases of SADC, the Intergovernmental Authority on Development (IGAD), and the Economic Community of Central African States (ECCAS) so far, the ECOWAS Mechanism for Conflict Prevention, Management, Resolution, Peacekeeping, and Security of 1999 presents a well-elaborated infrastructure with which the CSSDCA, the AU, and NEPAD can productively interact. The ECOWAS mechanism has already incorporated aspects of the CSSDCA such as a Council of Elders. ECOWAS's Council of Elders, together with other organs such as its Mediation and Security Council and a Defense and Security Commission, should complement the AU and NEPAD's peacemaking and democratization efforts. The ECOWAS mechanism presents an instrument that NEPAD's peer review mechanism can use in addition to ECOWAS's outreach to civil society (see Chapter 12). But now that plans have been elaborated, there is an urgent need to move beyond models and toward implementation.

Working together, ECOWAS and NEPAD could play a key role in the AU's decision of whether to intervene and/or to endorse interventions in subregional conflicts involving West African states. The processes through which the AU will incorporate the CSSDCA machinery into its Peace and

Security Council remain undefined. Just as unclear is the question of whether the CSSDCA could itself become subregionalized and integrated more fully into organizations such as ECOWAS. What is clearly required is a process of strategic planning in three key areas: first, an audit of the existing subregional peace and security mechanisms, including an evaluation of the performance of each component within the overall context of the ECOWAS security mechanism; second, an assessment of how the ECOWAS security mechanism can accommodate the CSSDCA/AU/NEPAD governance initiatives in a manner that clearly delineates niches, complementarities, and divisions of labor within an integrated operational framework; and, third, an assessment of how this architecture can interact with external actors such as the UN (see Chapter 14).

Africa's Emerging Peace, Security, and Governance Architecture

The fifth wave of pan-Africanism covers the areas of peace, security, and governance. But this emerging architecture did not fall out of the sky. It came about as a result of persistent, sometimes protracted African diplomacy and infighting. At times, this diplomacy drove wedges between different camps: those in favor of a supranational AU and/or NEPAD process and those against; those who saw the projects as all about governance and those who saw other rationales behind them. Some states saw the AU as a Libyan plot,[58] while others regarded NEPAD as a Western plot promoted by African leaders considered close to the West.

Clearly, in order to be successfully implemented, these diplomatic projects have to win the support and approval of as many African governments as possible, and have often relied on compromises and horse-trading. For example, in early 2001 the OAU endorsed MAP at a special summit in Sirte, Libya, to the visible chagrin of the host government. This endorsement appeared to have been the outcome of considerable inter-African horse-trading strongly led by Mbeki and Obasanjo, who supported the establishment of a new AU in exchange for the OAU's endorsement of MAP. This strategy also reflected Pretoria and Abuja's success in altering Tripoli's utopian vision of a "United States of Africa," a plan, according to some, devised by Muammar Qaddafi to propel Libya back into international respectability in the aftermath of his country's isolation. Another example of political compromise was when MAP and Omega were merged into NAI. NAI was thereafter adopted by the outgoing OAU, and subsequently endorsed by the G8 at its Genoa summit in July 2001. Yet another example of political compromise between African political actors was the incorporation of the CSSDCA into the AU. This initiative came about as a result of many strategic meetings between key African states in 2001 and 2002.

Africans have proved far less successful at negotiating with the outside world than they have been among themselves. For example, while the G8, the EU, and other donors have formally endorsed NEPAD, endorsement is clearly not the same as delivering on pledges. Rich countries will still have to demonstrate their commitment to NEPAD through actual disbursement of their pledges. Indeed, one of the implications of the reticence of G8 members to deliver on their pledges is that the partnership between Africa and the industrialized world might be crippled at birth. Whereas NEPAD leaders are in favor of the G8 establishing a structure to thrash out issues of mutual accountability, the G8 tends to view NEPAD as a vehicle through which it can play the role of "gatekeeper" in extending aid, trade, and foreign investment to AU member states on the basis of their compliance or noncompliance with NEPAD.

There can be no doubt that Africa's emerging peace, security, and governance architecture is an ambitious one. It is also a process that will be strewn with difficulties. But there are some positive dimensions to this. The past decade has seen the most far-reaching attempt by African leaders to institutionalize an inter-African system of accountability for democratic governance. Collectively, these developments could have major implications for conflict management and good governance efforts in Africa. A major reason for optimism is that each of these initiatives has as its common denominator the idea of Africans taking responsibility for their own destiny. These initiatives are all concerned with enshrining new norms of peace, security, and governance on the continent. They reflect a recognition by committed African leaders that peace, security, and governance are interconnected, and should become more mutually accountable processes between Africa's governing elites and citizens, as well between member states. This fifth wave of pan-Africanism has led to the dilution of the principle of noninterference in the internal affairs of member states, the cornerstone of the OAU charter for three decades. At the core of this attempt at redefining the responsibilities of African leaders to their citizens is a clear recognition that peace and security must become a precondition for continental renewal. The key challenge is finding a balance between the rights of states and the rights of citizens. But again, how will these norms be enforced? Will there be a condominium of African democracies that can take the lead in ensuring that other states comply with them?

The CSSDCA, NEPAD, and AU initiatives are attempting to forge a new holy trinity of African governance in general and an evolving pan-African peace and security regime in particular. These initiatives will be strongly supported by a few core countries such as Nigeria and South Africa as strategic allies, as well as by Senegal, Ghana, Tanzania, Botswana, and

Mozambique. But how do all these initiatives translate into a system of strategic synergies that can interact effectively with evolving security mechanisms at the subregional level?[59] The answer to this question is important due to the dangers of duplication and overlap. Are there not too many unimplemented initiatives gathering dust on the shelves and in the drawers of Africa's ministries?

African leaders have done well in creating norms, values, and mechanisms for peace, security, and governance. Urgent attention must now be given to the challenges of implementing these initiatives. There is a pressing need to build synergies and coherence between these various initiatives in order to ensure the emergence of a new, coherent pan-Africanism. How such a strategic process unfolds will have a major bearing on whether the current changes under way in African governance structures are perceived merely as cosmetic dabbling or substantive departures from the past.

At the time of writing, there are already indications that AU and NEPAD leaders have impressed upon their respective secretariats the need to cooperate more effectively and to iron out their differences to avoid damaging divisions. A good starting point is that NEPAD can only gain its legitimacy within Africa from the AU, and must therefore be seen as a program of the AU. Subregional organizations have been asked to reorganize and restructure themselves to conform with the programs of the AU and NEPAD. For example, some of the CSSDCA's ideas have been incorporated into the 1999 ECOWAS security mechanism, while in southern Africa, South Africa, Botswana, and Mozambique have been pushing for the SADC to be reorganized to conform to the structures and principles of NEPAD and the AU. In February 2003 the AU and NEPAD were pushed into closer cooperation due to tensions between their respective secretariats from 2002 to early 2003. In November 2002, African leaders directed that "the relationship between the AU Commission [in Addis Ababa] and the NEPAD Secretariat [in Pretoria] should henceforth be characterized by closer coordination, cooperation and collaboration."[60] A decision was later taken to subsume NEPAD into the AU as one of its programs by 2006.

African leaders confirmed that the AU is the continental body with primary responsibility for implementing the African agenda on peace and security in general, and that NEPAD complements these efforts by strengthening the AU's role in the areas of advocacy and mobilizing support for the implementation of national, regional, and continental peace and security initiatives, including in the critical areas of postconflict reconstruction and development. The AU/NEPAD peace and security agenda is now seen as a "single and indivisible agenda for addressing issues and challenges relating to peace and security in Africa."[61] But confident though African leaders may be about bridging the divisions between the AU and NEPAD, questions will almost certainly still linger about the relationship between the two bodies.

NEPAD, in particular, will have to earn its legitimacy by showing that it respects the authority of the AU.

To conclude, the period from 2001 to 2003 was indeed eventful for the African continent. The year 2001 saw the launch of NEPAD, 2002 saw the birth of the African Union, and at the AU summit in Maputo in July 2003, Mbeki handed over the baton of AU chairmanship to his close ally Joaquim Chissano, president of Mozambique. In Maputo, a prominent West African, former Malian president Alpha Konaré, replaced another West African, former Ivorian foreign minister Amara Essy, as chairperson of the AU commission. These developments have symbolized the fifth wave of pan-Africanism, the emphasis of which has been on attempting to break with the past by establishing and defining a new African agenda based on new norms, values, principles, and mechanisms in the areas of democratic governance, peace, and security. A new generation of African leaders has finally started to address the postindependence taboos of nonintervention and to articulate new norms of intervention and democratic governance. These leaders have established new institutions such as the AU and NEPAD and adopted protocols for the AU Peace and Security Council and its Pan-African Parliament. So the African calabash is half full as far as new norms and principles are concerned. Over the next decade and beyond, the major challenge will be to implement these plans and to operationalize these new institutions. African leaders will have to muster the political will to encourage and cajole each other to live by new norms, values, and principles that they have themselves articulated and agreed to.

Notes

1. On pan-Africanism, see P. Olisanwuche Esedebe, *Pan-Africanism: The Idea and Movement, 1776–1963* (Washington, D.C.: Howard University Press, 1982); Joseph E. Harris (in collaboration with Slimane Zeghidour), "Africa and Its Diaspora Since 1935," in Ali A. Mazrui, ed., *Africa Since 1935,* General History of Africa, vol. 8 (Berkeley: University of California Press, 1993), pp. 705–723; Hollis R. Lynch, "Pan-African Responses in the United States to British Colonial Rule in Africa in the 1940s," in Prosse Gifford and W. M. Roger Louis, *The Transfer of Power in Africa: Decolonization, 1940–1960* (New Haven, Conn.: Yale University Press, 1982), pp. 57–86; Ali Mazrui, *Towards a Pax Africana: A Study in Ideology and Ambition* (Chicago: University of Chicago Press, 1967); Kwame Nkrumah, *Africa Must Unite* (London: Heinemann, 1963); and Immanuel Wallerstein, *The Politics of Unity* (New York: Vintage Books, 1967).

2. See, for example, Richard Joseph, "The Reconfiguration of Power in Late Twentieth-Century Africa," in Richard Joseph, ed., *State, Conflict, and Democracy in Africa* (Boulder: Lynne Rienner Publishers, 1999), pp. 57–80; and Adebayo Olukoshi, "State, Conflict, and Democracy in Africa: The Complex Process of Renewal," in Joseph, *State, Conflict, and Democracy in Africa,* pp. 451–465.

3. A point made by Jimmy Kandeh during a policy seminar in Abuja in September 2001.

4. Adekeye Adebajo and Chris Landsberg, "The Heirs of Nkrumah: Africa's New Interventionists," *Pugwash Occasional Papers* 2, no. 1 (January 2001): 75.

5. See Ali A. Mazrui, *The African Condition* (New York: Cambridge University Press, 1980).

6. Claude S. Phillips, *The African Political Dictionary* (Oxford: Clio Press, 1982).

7. Direct rule was applied with little regard for local traditions or interests and was typically associated with French and Belgian rule. Indirect rule utilized traditional authorities. The British first employed this method in northern Nigeria and then sought to replicate it in other African countries.

8. For a discussion of decolonization, see Tony Smith, ed., *The End of European Empire: Decolonization After the Second World War* (Lexington, Mass.: D. C. Heath, 1975). See also Miles Kahler, *Decolonization in Britain and France: The Domestic Consequences of International Relations* (Princeton: Princeton University Press, 1984).

9. Smith, *End of European Empire,* p. 10.

10. Ibid.

11. Adekunle Ajala, "Background to the Establishment, Nature, and Structure of the Organisation of African Unity," *Nigerian Journal of International Affairs* 14, no. 1 (1988): 50. See also Z. Cervenka, *The Organization of African Unity* (London: Julien Friedman Press, 1977); Yassin El-Ayouty and I William Zartman, eds., *The OAU After Twenty Years* (New York: Praeger, 1984); and Amadou Sesay, ed., *The OAU After Twenty-five Years* (Cambridge: St. Martin's, 1990).

12. Cited in Ajala, "Background," p. 51.

13. Cited in ibid., p. 52.

14. The prime minister of Sierra Leone, Sir Milton Margai, reiterated "the principle of African unity which respects the territorial integrity of each state, the free choice of political ideology and form of government" before pledging "co-operation in the defense of the territorial integrity and sovereignty of all freedom loving states in Africa, particularly with a view to curbing any internal subversion against the lawfully constituted government of any friendly state." Ajala, "Background," p. 52.

15. R. A. Akindele, "The Organisation of African Unity, 1963–1988: An Introductory Overview," *Nigerian Journal of International Affairs* 14, no. 1 (1988): 6. When the foreign ministers met in Addis Ababa on 15 May 1961, prior to the heads of state and government meeting, there were two divergent proposals on the table for the establishment of a formal pan-African structure. Ethiopia proposed its own draft Charter of African Unity, while Ghana proposed a Union of African States. When agreement could not be reached, the majority of foreign ministers recommended that the summit conference accept the Ethiopian document as a basis for discussion, with a view to drawing up a charter for an all-African organization.

16. Akindele, "Organisation of African Unity," pp. 6–7.

17. Ibid., p. 7.

18. See IPA and ECOWAS, *Toward a Pax West Africana: Building Peace in a Troubled Sub-Region,* seminar report, Abuja, September 2001.

19. *Southern Africa's Evolving Security Architecture: Problems and Prospects,* report of a seminar by the International Peace Academy, in partnership with the African Renaissance Institute, the Southern African Regional Institute for Policy Studies, and the University of the Witwatersrand, Gaborone, Botswana, December 2000.

20. Mwesiga Baregu and Christopher Landsberg, eds., *From Cape to Congo: Southern Africa's Evolving Security Challenges* (Boulder: Lynne Rienner, 2003).

21. Francis Mading Deng, "State Collapse: The Humanitarian Challenge to the United Nations," in I. William Zartman, ed., *Collapsed States: The Disintegration and Restoration of Legitimate Authority* (Boulder: Lynne Rienner, 1995), p. 213.

22. Cited in Solomon Gomes, "The OAU, State Sovereignty, and Regional Security," in Edmond Keller and Donald Rothchild, eds., *Africa in the New International Order: Rethinking State Sovereignty* (Boulder: Lynne Rienner, 1996), p. 41.

23. Cited in Eboe Hutchful, "Understanding the African Security Crisis," in Abdel-Fatau Musah and J. Kayode Fayemi, eds., *Mercenaries: An African Security Dilemma* (New York: Pluto Press, 2000), p. 218.

24. Adebajo and Landsberg, "Heirs of Nkrumah," p. 69.

25. Adekeye Adebajo and Christopher Landsberg, "South Africa and Nigeria as Regional Hegemons," in Baregu and Landsberg, *From Cape to Congo*, pp. 171–203.

26. Olusegun Obasanjo, "Africa's Rendezvous with History," in Olusegun Obasanjo and Felix Mosha, eds., *Africa: Rise to Challenge* (Abuja: African Leadership Forum, 1993), p. 260.

27. Statement by H. E. Yoweri Kaguta Museveni to the Kampala Forum, 19 May 1991, in Obasanjo and Mosha, *Africa*, p. 266.

28. See International Peace Academy (IPA), *Report of the Joint OAU/IPA Task Force on Peacemaking and Peacekeeping in Africa*, New York, March 1998; IPA, *OAU-IPA Seminar on Peacemaking and Peacekeeping*, Addis Ababa, November–December 1998; and Monde Muyangwa and Margaret A. Vogt, *An Assessment of the OAU Mechanism for Conflict Prevention, Management, and Resolution* (New York: IPA, 2000).

29. See Musifiky Mwanasali, "From the Organization of African Unity to the African Union," in Baregu and Landsberg, *From Cape to Congo*, pp. 205–223.

30. See South African Department of Foreign Affairs, *The Conference on Security, Stability, Development, and Co-operation in Africa (CSSDCA), Documentation*, 21 June 2001.

31. Ibid.

32. Ibid.

33. "The NEPAD African Peer Review Mechanism: Prospects and Challenges," *African Security Review* 11, no. 4 (2003): ii.

34. See Thabo Mbeki, prologue to Malegapuru William Makgoba, ed., *African Renaissance* (Cape Town: Mafube and Tafelberg, 1999), pp. xiii–xxi.

35. See *The Millennium Partnership for Africa Recovery Programme, Draft 3A*, South African Department of Foreign Affairs, Pretoria, July 2001.

36. Ibid.

37. Ibid., p. 6.

38. Ibid.

39. *The OMEGA Plan*, Dakar, Senegal, February 2001.

40. Ibid., p. 4.

41. Ibid.

42. Ibid., p. 5.

43. Ibid., pp. 20–21.

44. Chris Landsberg, "From African Renaissance to NEPAD . . . and Back to the Renaissance," *Journal of African Elections* 1, no. 2 (September 2002): 91.

45. Ibid.

46. *A New African Initiative: Merger of the Millennium Partnership for Africa Recovery Programme (MAP) and Omega Plan,* Pretoria, July 2001, p. 2.

47. See Adebayo Adedeji, "From Lagos to NEPAD," *New Agenda* no. 8 (Fourth Quarter 2002): 32–47; and Landsberg, "From African Renaissance to NEPAD," pp. 87–98.

48. *New African Initiative,* p. 5.

49. Ibid., pp. 23–48.

50. Ibid., pp. 26–45.

51. See communiqué issued at the end of the meeting of the Implementation Committee of Heads of State and Government on the New Partnership for Africa's Development, Abuja, 23 October 2001.

52. For the elements making up the democracy and governance elements of NEPAD, see NEPAD, "Declaration on Democracy, Political, Economic, and Corporate Governance," 18 June 2002, available at www.nepad.org/doc004.pdf.paragraphs, paras. 7–15.

53. Communiqué issued at the end of the NEPAD seventh summit of the Implementation Committee of Heads of State and Government, Abuja, 28 May 2003.

54. Ibid.

55. K. Mamila, "Mbeki MAPs out Africa's Fresh Beginning," *The Star,* 20 July 2001, p. 7.

56. See Chris Landsberg and Shaun Mackay, "Political Will Needed for New Doctrine," *Synopsis* 7, no. 1 (April 2003): 4.

57. The AU is in the process of drafting a Charter on Elections, Democracy, and Governance. The information pertaining to unconstitutional changes of government is contained in the draft. The author was part of a team of policy researchers who helped to draft the charter.

58. See Francis Kornegay, "Should SA Lead a Split in Africa?" *Global Dialogue* 6, no. 2 (July 2001): 1–2.

59. See Francis Kornegay, *Reflections on African Peace-Building: A Background Paper Exploring a Regional Role for a Strategic Recovery Facility,* Johannesburg, 2001, p. 30. This unpublished discussion paper of the Centre for Africa's International Relations, University of the Witwatersrand, explores options and possibilities for integrating the AU, MAP, and the CSSDCA mechanisms.

60. African Union, *Report of the AU-NEPAD Consultations on Peace and Security,* Addis Ababa, 17–18 February 2003, pp. 1–10.

61. Ibid.

7

Civil-Military Relations

Jimmy D. Kandeh

While the incidence of military coups d'état appears to be on the wane in West Africa, the conditions that give rise to military interventions persist and may yet obstruct and derail the subregion's fragile democratic experiments. Political classes and military establishments in many West African countries remain opposed to democratization. The military, wrote Eboe Hutchful in 1998, remains "uncaptured" by democracy movements that "may . . . have won the battle for civil society but lost the battle for the military."[1] Aligning, or in some cases realigning, the military with democratic forces is indispensable to democratic maturation and consolidation in West Africa. This would require incorporating the legitimate demands and concerns of military personnel, especially the lower ranks, into the overall agenda of democratic forces. It would also entail reaching out to the military in an effort to change attitudes and convince soldiers that they are better off under a democracy than under an autocracy. Such an effort can only succeed if elected governments perform creditably. Democratic forces and elected governments must, in other words, seek to "surround" the military—as Antonio Gramsci advocated—before attempting its capture and democratic subordination.

This chapter outlines the changing patterns of military interventions and political dictatorships in West Africa. After providing a brief historical overview of military coups in West Africa, I call for a radical rethinking of national security that prioritizes domestic legitimacy and economic development. The chapter then advocates a redefinition of the role and mission of West Africa's militaries, urges greater care in the recruitment and training of military personnel, and suggests more skillful political management of issues relating to military budgets and privileges. Before concluding the chapter, I propose several options for reforming and subordinating West African militaries under civilian control, specifically arguing that forging a consensus between military and civilian leaders on such issues as force levels, military missions, and the overall direction of security sector reform, as well as seeking accommodation between military forces and civilian populations, can help to reduce tensions between armies and civilians and facilitate democratic consolidation. The success of this approach would require a radical rethinking of civil-military relations along lines suggested by Rebecca Schiff, who proposes a "concordance theory" of civil-military relations. Concordance theory

>
> highlights dialogue, accommodation, and shared values or objectives among the military, the political elites and society. . . . In contrast to the prevailing theory, which emphasizes the separation of civil and military institutions, concordance encourages cooperation and involvement among the military, the political institutions, and the society at large. In other words, concordance does not assume that separate civil and military spheres are required to prevent domestic military intervention. Rather, it may be avoided if the military cooperates with the political elites and citizenry. . . . Concordance theory views the military, the political leadership, and the citizenry as partners and predicts that when they agree about the role of the armed forces by achieving a mutual accommodation, domestic military intervention is less likely to occur in a particular state.[2]

"Constructive engagement" of the military by the political establishment and popular sectors may not conform to orthodox methods of subordinating the military under civilian rule, but such an approach can help deter coups, improve the image of soldiers among the citizenry, and strengthen fragile democracies in West Africa.

Historical Review

Two waves of military intervention can be identified in West Africa. The first coincided with the first two decades of independence, in the 1960s and 1970s, when senior officers mostly masterminded coups. Coups of the second wave, in the 1980s and 1990s, in contrast, were in many cases instigated and led by junior officers or the rank and file. Differences with respect to social class, rationalizations for military interventions, the targets of grievances, and the consequences of the coups distinguish these two waves of military intervention. While intraclass tensions and intrigues most frequently prompted senior officers to stage coups, subaltern interventions by more junior officers were invariably expressive of class polarization within national armies and the broader society. "Coups from below" have often started as pay strikes and mutinies directed at senior military officers and/or civilian political incumbents. Unlike subaltern coups, whose leaders may initially espouse some variant of populist ideology—with the usual emphasis on fighting corruption, alleviating poverty, and returning power to the people—interventions by senior officers have tended to be conservative affairs devoid of any transformative agenda. What is perhaps most unique about coups staged by West Africa's lumpen militariat is the duality of such usurpations—both the command structure of the army and the broader leadership patterns of society are inverted when armed marginals capture state power.[3]

Senior officers did not, however, always lead first-wave coups, nor were junior or noncommissioned officers the only architects of second-wave coups. Emmanuel Bodjolle, a former master-sergeant in the French army, led the first successful coup in West Africa, which occurred in Togo in 1963. The proximate cause of this intervention was the refusal by the government of Sylvanus Olympio to absorb 626 former servicemen from the French army into the new Togolese army. The coup leaders installed a civilian government led by Nicholas Grunitzky, an opponent of Olympio, but four years later, Etienne (now Gnassingbé) Eyadéma, also a former sergeant in the French army, wrested control of the army from Bodjolle, promoted himself to colonel, and removed Grunitzky from power. After the Togolese usurpation, there were three other successful coups (Benin in 1963, Sierra Leone in 1968, and Ghana in 1979) by the military underclass in West Africa during the first two decades of independence. The 1968 and 1979 interventions in Sierra Leone and Ghana respectively targeted senior officers—eight of whom were executed in the Ghanaian case—and paved the way for the restoration of constitutional democratic authority, albeit temporarily.

At last count, there have been at least seventy-five successful coups in sub-Saharan Africa since 1956.[4] There were an average of two successful coups a year between 1956 and 1985, but this figure has declined to about one a year since then. The majority of these coups have occurred in West Africa, with five countries—Nigeria, Benin, Ghana, Burkina Faso, and Sierra Leone—accounting for a third of them. The Nigerian army has been responsible for more changes in government than any other military establishment in West Africa (see Table 7.1). Benin is the only country in West Africa where a successful civilian "coup d'etat"—the national conference—forced a military dictatorship to transfer power to an interim civilian government in 1990. Burkina Faso, ruled by military brass hats for thirty-one years, ranks first in the longevity of military rule in the subregion, closely followed by Nigeria (twenty-nine), Mali and Togo (twenty-three each), Ghana (twenty), Niger (eighteen), and Benin (seventeen).

Sierra Leone leads the pack in West Africa in terms of the number of successful coups "from below." Junior and noncommissioned officers

Table 7.1 Successful Coups in West Africa, 1963–1999

	Number of Coups	Coup Years	Number of Years of Military Rule
Benin	6	1963, 1967, 1969, 1970, 1972, 1990	17
Burkina Faso	5	1966, 1980, 1982, 1983, 1987	31
Cape Verde	—	—	—
Côte d'Ivoire	1	1999	1
Gambia	1	1994	2
Ghana	5	1966, 1972, 1978, 1979, 1981	20
Guinea	1	1984	10
Guinea-Bissau	2	1980, 1999	14
Liberia	1	1980	5
Mali	2	1980, 1999	23
Niger	3	1974, 1996, 1998	18
Nigeria	6	1966 (2), 1975, 1983, 1985, 1993	29
Senegal	—	—	—
Sierra Leone	5	1967 (2), 1968, 1992, 1997	6
Togo	2	1963, 1967	23

Source: Compiled by author.

orchestrated three (1968, 1992, 1997) of Sierra Leone's five successful coups. Ghana has had two military putsches (1979, 1981) by the ranks or elements associated with them, while Liberia (1980), Burkina Faso (1983), and Gambia (1994) have each had one coup by low-ranking soldiers. With the two notable exceptions of Ghana (under Jerry Rawlings) and Burkina Faso (under Thomas Sankara), subaltern military dictatorships in West Africa have been unmitigated governance disasters. In Liberia and Sierra Leone, rule by the military underclass expedited processes of state collapse. Samuel Doe may be gone from the Liberian political scene, but the reverberations of his dictatorship continue to be felt even today.

The military has twice toppled democratically elected governments in Nigeria, Ghana, and Sierra Leone. The first successful coup in Nigeria (January 1966) and Sierra Leone (March 1967) replaced democratically elected governments with military dictatorships; in Ghana, the military first removed a democratically elected government in 1972. All three countries, Ghana in 1979, Nigeria in 1983, and Sierra Leone in 1997, went through similar upheavals for a second time with negative consequences. One of the architects of the 1983 Nigerian coup, General Ibrahim Babangida, also presided, as head of state, over Nigeria's aborted transition to democracy in 1993. Democratically elected governments were also overthrown in Togo (1963), Gambia (1994), and Niger (1998).

Nine of the twenty African states that have escaped military dictatorships are in eastern Africa (Djibouti, Eritrea, Kenya, Madagascar, Malawi,

Mauritius, Mozambique, Tanzania, and Zambia), six are in southern Africa (Angola, Botswana, Namibia, South Africa, Swaziland, and Zimbabwe), two are in central Africa (Gabon and Cameroon), two are in West Africa (Cape Verde and Senegal), and one is in North Africa (Morocco). No former British colony in West Africa has been spared the scourge of military rule. This is in sharp contrast to eastern and southern Africa, where only two (Uganda and Lesotho) out of nine former British colonies in these subregions have experienced military rule. Senegal, the only francophone country in West Africa to have avoided military dictatorship, has had the luxury of neocolonial protection. Existing defense agreements between France and Senegal, and the presence of French troops in Dakar, have served to deter the army from staging coups. This was also the case, until recently, in Côte d'Ivoire, which hosts a French military base. A military coup in December 1999, however, toppled the elected regime of Henri Konan Bédié when France decided not to prop up his regime. About 6,500 French troops are currently deployed in Africa, and the French army intervened at least thirty times in Africa between 1963 and 1993 to prop up or replace client regimes (see also Chapter 15).[5]

A disturbing pattern in West Africa is the tendency of military leaders to civilianize their dictatorships rather than step down or disengage from politics. Self-succession started with Eyadéma's quasi-fraudulent elections in Togo (1979); it was continued by Doe's electoral charade in Liberia (1985), Blaise Compaoré's "unopposed" election in Burkina Faso (1991), Rawlings's first election in Ghana in 1992 (an election partly boycotted by the opposition), and Yaya Jammeh's controversial election in Gambia in 1996. Interestingly, some of these leaders—notably Doe, Jammeh, and Compaoré—became more despotic after shedding their military uniforms for civilian mufti. Other military dictators, notably Kutu Acheampong in Ghana, Valentine Strasser in Sierra Leone, and Robert Guei in Côte d'Ivoire, who had similar aspirations of "civilianizing" their regimes, tried and failed disastrously. Nigeria's General Sani Abacha was on the verge of contesting an election in which all five parties—famously described by former justice minister Bola Ige as "five fingers of a leprous hand"—had selected him as their presidential candidate. If he had not died under mysterious circumstances in June 1998, Abacha would almost certainly have accomplished what no other Nigerian military leader had been able to do: metamorphosing from serving military autocrat to civilian ruler.

Military coups in West Africa have reinforced the primacy of violent domination over popular legitimation. They have exacerbated tensions between state and society, and in some cases have led to the transformation of violence from a tool of domination to an instrument of criminal extraction. This utilization of violence as an instrument of criminal extraction has prompted comparisons by several analysts between seventeenth-century Europe, where war making, state making, and capital accumulation became intertwined as products of organized crime.[6] As Charles Tilly wrote, "In times of war . . . the managers of full-fledged states often commissioned privateers, hired sometime bandits to raid their enemies, and encouraged their regular troops to take booty. In royal service, soldiers and sailors were often expected to provide for themselves by preying on the civilian population: commandeering, raping, looting, taking prizes. When demobilized, they commonly continued the same practices, but without the same royal protection; demobilized ships became pirate vessels, demobilized troops bandits."[7]

Comparing contemporary Africa to seventeenth-century Europe, however, can be misleading, especially when the different historical conjuncture and global context of state formation in Africa are ignored or downplayed. William Reno's contention in 1995 that in Taylor's Liberia "a new kind of state, an alternative institutionalization of sovereign authority capable of defending itself and doing things without significant bureaucracies" was in the making, is typical of the overdrawn analogization of medieval Europe to the African experience.[8] How debureaucratization of the state, militarization of commerce, and privatization of violence can possibly form the basis of an "alternative institutionalization" in Liberia or any other state in West Africa is difficult to fathom. Taylor's ascent to political power through elections in July 1997 also raised serious questions about this analysis, which seemed to suggest that the Liberian warlord was more interested in economic extraction than political power. The former warlord's acquisition of political power in fact provided him with the means—including a bureau-cracy and army—for more effective economic extraction.

Rethinking National Security

The role of the military in Africa is not simply "to fight and win wars."[9] Most armies on the continent are, in fact, too ill equipped and poorly paid to fight and win wars. With a few exceptions, African armies were historically created not with a view to responding effectively to external threats, but with the explicit goal of subjugating local communities. Colonial armies were alien in both conception and vocation, and little has changed since independence. Threats to the state now, as were threats to the colonial state, are more likely to come from domestic groups than from foreign enemies. Local opposition to an incumbent government should not, however—contrary to the view of several African autocrats—qualify as a threat to state security unless such opposition embraces and promotes violence in furtherance of its agenda. Resorting to violence becomes a threat to state security only to the degree that an incumbent government is seen to be legitimate and mechanisms exist for its replacement by peaceful means. In the absence of a legitimate political order, while domestic conflict involving the use of violence may threaten incumbents, it does not necessarily threaten the state. Governments, in many instances, constitute the most serious threat to state security. That is why it is essential to decouple state security and regime survival.[10]

Traditional approaches to "national security" equate this concept with the defense of a state's territorial boundaries and the protection of its basic values. In this definition, security is the preeminent national interest of states. The "national interest" encompasses what a state needs—security, economic well-being, and so forth—and what it aspires to become—a developed country, a regional power, the promoter of ideological preferences, and so forth. The needs and aspirations of the national interest are closely intertwined. For example, by promoting capitalism and liberal-pluralist democracy, Western countries have historically sought to bolster their own security and to enhance the economic well-being of their peoples. Similarly, by promoting welfare and development, West African states would not only be improving the quality of life of their populations, they would also be enhancing their security. Development affords people the opportunity of defending a system that is worth having. As Sunday Ochoche noted, "Where people have difficulty knowing what benefits they derive from belonging to a system, they will have little incentive to fight for its survival."[11]

The unmistakable link between Africa's insecurity and underdevelopment was aptly summed up by Robert McNamara, a former World Bank president and former U.S. secretary of defense, during the administration of John F. Kennedy: "In a modernizing society, security means development. Security is not military hardware, though it may include it; security is not traditional military activity, though it may encompass it. Security is development, and without development there can be no security. A developing nation that does not, in fact, develop simply cannot remain secure for the intractable reason that its citizenry cannot shed its human nature."[12]

Underdevelopment is thus the greatest threat to security and it is a threat against which guns are impotent. Armaments have failed to make African societies more secure not because of the classic security dilemma—according to which states become less secure as they strive to become more secure—but because the military approach to security in Africa is usually geared toward regime survival rather than national security.

Any serious rethinking of national security in West Africa must first specify the nature and types of security threats that states have to deal with in this subregion. In terms of military security, three main types of threats can be identified: first, those originating from outside Africa; second, those emanating from within Africa; and third, those rooted in domestic causes. With the end of the Cold War, military threats from outside Africa, with the exception of mercenary forces, are the least troubling threats to most governments.

The same, however, cannot be said about intra-African and domestic conflicts. The emergence of "rogue leaders" has transformed West Africa into an insecure neighborhood, with leaders like Liberia's Charles Taylor and Burkina Faso's Blaise Compaoré jointly sponsoring mayhem in Liberia, Sierra Leone, and Guinea. By far the most significant threat to military security, however, resides within states. Excluding South Africa, African states have fought at least eighteen full-scale civil wars since 1960. Sunday Ochoche maintains that, "in terms of number, disruption of national life, total cost in lives and property, production of refugees, and other indications of insecurity, domestic conflicts have been the worst type of conflict in Africa."[13]

Since the most serious threats to state security in West Africa are internal, it is important to identify their sources before considering how to respond to them. While some domestic armed conflicts in the subregion have been secessionist—as in the cases of Biafra in Nigeria and Casamance in Senegal—the vast majority of conflicts have been struggles to capture state power. Whether secessionist or not, domestic military threats to national security share the common characteristic of exposing the absence of internal legitimacy and a low level of political institutionalization. Internal challenges to political authority and attempts to reconfigure the boundaries of the state have bedeviled all countries in West Africa, including apparently coup-proof Senegal.

It must be noted, however, that the most important domestic threats to national security in West Africa are not always a result of military or civilian autocracy. The sources of nonmilitary threats to domestic security include poverty, population growth, disease, lack of social services, foreign debt, structural adjustment programs, environmental degradation, and narcotic drugs. Although debt and environmental degradation lend a global dimension to some of West Africa's security problems, the debt burden remains not only a crisis for banks and creditor nations, but a disaster for debtor states. After the continent's political classes, the International Monetary Fund (IMF) has become the second major producer of human misery in Africa. To paraphrase Thandika Mkandawire, IMF conditionalities are undemocratic to the extent that they undermine national sovereignty, weaken state capacity, exacerbate social conflict, and fail to respond to popular currents.[14] Without an "effective state," Adam Przeworski has warned, "there can be no democracy and no markets."[15]

Demilitarizing security and harnessing security to development should be among the priorities of military reform in West Africa. Underdevelopment and the lack of political legitimacy are the greatest threats to national security, and neither is amenable to military solutions. For any meaningful reform of the military to take place in West Africa, there must be a concerted and sustained effort radically to alter the nature of political systems and regimes in the subregion. A predatory regime cannot reform its security sector, because to do so would be to undermine the interests of its leaders and supplicants. There have been many changes of government in West Africa, but hardly any of these transitions have produced regime transformation. Unless political power is legitimized and the burdens of underdevelopment are reduced, it would be unrealistic and naive to expect any significant reform of military establishments in West Africa.

Redefining Role and Mission

Neither public order nor political order should fall within the jurisdictional competence of military establishments. The involvement of the military in these two areas has spelled disaster in many West African countries. Individual security is threatened when the military resorts to violence to settle political disputes and, in some cases, when embattled civilian regimes call on the army to quell social unrest, actions that have often backfired. This happened in Liberia during the April 1979 "rice riots" when soldiers refused to shoot at demonstrators. This incident precipitated the downfall of William Tolbert and the True Whig Party a year later. In many cases, "police-type operations" and "commitment to internal security" have "destroyed the army's impartial image."[16] The involvement of the Nigerian army in policing activities by the civilian government of Abubakar Tafawa Balewa in 1965 was thought to have politicized the army, culminating in the two military coups of 1966. Defining the appropriate role of the army and limiting its involvement in internal security matters to the barest minimum are critical to reforming West African armies.

Legitimation of political institutions is the surest way of creating political order, but this is a task for which the military is fundamentally unsuited. As Roger Murray noted in 1966, West African armies are "endowed neither with great popular affection nor exceptional skills and resources."[17] James Coleman and Belmont Brice had also observed four years earlier that "except for the Sudan and Senegal, African armies are perhaps the least developed in the contemporary world."[18] There is hardly any country in West Africa where the army has played a positive role in institution building. Military regimes have been chronically unresponsive to popular currents, and their very existence obviates the legitimation of political authority. With the possible exception of Jerry Rawlings, who reversed processes of state decomposition in Ghana, no other military leader or regime has rescued a state from collapse or laid the foundations for the construction of legitimate political institutions.

If the military is unsuited to the tasks of maintaining public order and creating political order, what then must be its role and mission? Defending the state against external aggression is the primary role of military establishments, but this has not been an area in which West African armies have distinguished themselves. As noted earlier, very few states in the subregion face serious external threats, and where these threats have arisen, armies have often been unequal to the task of protecting their states. Libya has posed the greatest military threat to the security of states in West Africa. The Libyans trained and financed rebels in Liberia and Sierra Leone and used former Liberian president Charles Taylor and Burkinabè leader Blaise Compaoré as conduits of destabilization in the subregion. Côte d'Ivoire also supported National Patriotic Front of Liberia (NPFL) rebels in Liberia and Revolutionary United Front (RUF) rebels in Sierra Leone, while Guinea and Liberia have accused each other of supporting armed dissidents in their respective countries. The main sources of aggression in West Africa have been Liberia under Taylor and Burkina Faso under Compaoré. Guinea, unlike Sierra Leone, was able militarily to repel insurgents supported by Taylor and Compaoré. (Taylor was forced into exile in Nigeria in August 2003.) Nigeria in the 1980s was also concerned that Muammar Qaddafi could stir up secular and religious disaffection among Nigeria's youth, and led three peacekeeping missions into Chad from 1979 to 1982 in a bid to stem Libyan influence on its borders. More recently, however, this concern seems to have abated.[19]

In addition to defending states against external aggression, standing armies are responsible for protecting the borders, territorial integrity, and economic assets of states. There are many unresolved border disputes in West Africa, but it is unlikely that any of them will be settled militarily. One such dispute is over the Bakassi peninsula, which has been claimed by both Nigeria and Cameroon. This 400-square-mile border area is believed to contain rich oil reserves that both countries would like to exploit. Although the International Court of Justice ruled largely in favor of Cameroon's claims to most of the territory in 2002, the Nigerian government has not unambiguously accepted this decision.

There are certainly domestic security problems of a nonpartisan nature that may require the involvement of military forces, especially in situations where police forces are overwhelmed or prove inadequate to the task at hand. Ethnic chauvinists, religious zealots, and criminal adventurers represent some of the most serious domestic threats to state security in West Africa. In Nigeria, for example, ethnic groupings like the Oodua People's Congress, the Ijaw Youth Movement, the Arewa People's Congress, and the Bakassi Boys have clashed repeatedly with opponents and security forces. Nigeria has also had its share of religious riots, not all of which have been between members of different faiths. The Nigerian police force was unable to deal with the 1980 Maitatsine riots in Kano, which resulted in the deaths of over 5,000 people. The rioting only ended after the army was deployed to restore law and order. The recent upsurge in religious extremism in Nigeria, with a dozen states adopting *sharia* criminal law, also poses a threat to the secularity and continued existence of the Nigerian state.

Not all armed internal threats to national security, however, are related to ethnicity or religion. Criminal elements in West Africa have also sought to capitalize on the protective retreat of states to launch insurgencies in Liberia and Sierra Leone, where armed factions have used terror, rape, and mutilations to prosecute wars of aggrandizement (see Chapter 8). Such insurrections are often supported by external patrons, and national police forces have been overwhelmed by these insurgents. In such instances, the military is the most appropriate counterinsurgency force. As a general rule, however, military interventions to counter domestic threats must be limited to armed insurrections, be they ethnic, religious, or criminal. The military should never be used to restrict or suppress the peaceful and lawful exercise of basic rights and freedoms by citizens.

Recruitment and Training

Colonialism had a profound impact on the recruitment practices of armies in West Africa. Rural men who were categorized by colonial powers as belonging to "martial tribes" and possessing "unique" fighting abilities dominated the lower ranks of colonial armies. Rural men were preferred because, as Garnet Wolseley, a nineteenth-century colonial apologist reasoned:

> The wild tribes dependent upon hunting for their daily food possess a sort of intuitive knowledge of wild animals, of their ways and habits, which gives them in war an immense advantage over the ordinary town-bred soldier. The trapper's rude life of daily hardship and privation fits him physically for the ups and downs and rough usage which war brings with it. The hunter is already half a soldier, and not only accepts the miseries of war in an uncomplaining spirit, but regards them as the natural and ordinary incidents of everyday life.[20]

Army recruits throughout West Africa were sought from remote, peripheral areas with the least exposure to Western influences and institutions. In the case of the British, this meant northern Nigeria, northern Ghana, and northern Sierra Leone where "martial" *ethnies* included Hausas, Idomas, Tivs, Mossi, Grunshis, Mamprusis, Korankos, and Yalunkas. One ethnic group that earned the grudging admiration of the British, but was largely excluded from the colonial army in Ghana, was the Ashanti.

Colonial-era recruitment based on ethnicity and a preference for rural subalterns continue to shape current practices in many West African states. Ethnic identity, patronage, and loyalty to political superiors are key factors that continue to determine recruitment and promotion in West African armies. Until the advent of the civilian regime of Olusegun Obasanjo in 1999, Hausa-Fulani and other northern groups dominated the most senior and strategic positions in the Nigerian army. Liberia's Samuel Doe relied almost exclusively on Krahns within his army to defend his dictatorship. In the Togolese army, an estimated 90 percent of the officers and 70 percent of soldiers belong to Gnassingbé Eyadéma's Kabre ethnic group. [21] Former Ivorian leader Félix Houphouët-Boigny's army was often referred to as the "Baoulé warriors" due to the dominance of his ethnic group in the military. In Sierra Leone, successive governments politicized the army along ethnic lines and in the process created one of the most disloyal military establishments in West Africa. Invariably, the ethnic selectivity of army recruitment and promotions, as well as the preference for rural drifters and peasants, has reinforced the disconnection between soldiers and civilians.

Sierra Leone is particularly illustrative of how parochial recruitment practices can rapidly deprofessionalize armies. As President Ahmed Tejan Kabbah noted in 1997 about the army he inherited:

> The government of the day regarded the army as an instrument of the ruling party and not as a national institution. Its role was relegated to that of protecting the ruling party, insulating it from the people and ensuring that however unpopular the party in power became, it remained in office indefinitely. To give practical effect to its newfound role, the mode of recruitment into the army was altered from that based on qualification to one based on the card system—that is, one based on political, tribal or regional affiliation. In the course of time, the army came to be composed almost entirely of men and women loyal only to the ruling party. The result of this mode of recruitment was that every soldier had a political patron and collectively those patrons belonged to the ruling party, to which the army owed its loyalty and allegiance, and not to the nation.[22]

Recruitment of soldiers in West Africa should be taken out of the hands of politicians and entrusted to an impartial body that relies on objective criteria in determining the qualifications and fitness of recruits. All recruits must be able to read and write, and officers must possess at least a college degree or its equivalent. Legislatures and defense ministries are responsible for establishing recruitment guidelines and procedures, but they should not be in charge of the actual selection process. A concerted effort is urgently required to de-ethnicize both the officer corps and the rank and file of military establishments in West Africa with the goal of making their composition broadly reflective of society. This does not suggest a consociational approach to recruitment, but it does call for avoiding overrepresentation in the army by any single group. The military must not be so desperate for recruits that it opens its doors to criminal elements, as happened in Liberia and Sierra Leone. The need to ensure that no single group is overrepresented in the army, however, must be balanced with the goal of developing a professional, meritocratic army.

How soldiers are trained is just as important as who qualifies for such training. The goal of any training regimen for officers is to produce professional soldiers. Military professionalism is a composite of professional expertise, organizational discipline, political neutrality, and client (state) protection. Currently, there are several training and retraining programs under way in West Africa. Most of these programs involve expatriate funding, training, and control. One such effort is the British retraining program in Sierra Leone, which has involved a series of six-week training programs for an assortment of former renegade soldiers, loyal soldiers, new recruits, and former RUF rebels.[23] The goal of British involvement in Sierra Leone is to "ensure that the Sierra Leone army continues on course to becoming a democratically accountable, self-sustaining force."[24] According to Geoff Hoon, the British defense secretary:

> Training the Sierra Leone army is an important contribution to stability in Sierra Leone. British units have done splendid work building up the Sierra Leone army. We now need to complete this job by making them self-sufficient and by "training the trainers," before handing [them] over to the International Military Advisory and Training Team. Our rapid reaction capability remains available to the United Nations, and we expect to exercise periodically in Sierra Leone to demonstrate how we can deploy quickly if necessary.[25]

In addition to training new recruits and former soldiers, the British have provided a package of equipment support for both the Sierra Leone Army (SLA) and police force. They have also set up an operational-level headquarters to command British efforts and provide high-level technical advice to the SLA. In an announcement that may have deterred any further attempts by the RUF to attack Freetown in May 2000, the British pledged to deploy, if necessary, a rapid reaction force of 5,000 soldiers to support UN peacekeeping efforts and to defend the democratically elected government of Ahmed Tejan Kabbah (see Chapters 14 and 15).

British training, equipment, and advice to the SLA put the RUF on the defensive and helped stabilize the security situation in the country. Many Sierra Leoneans are convinced that the RUF would not have disarmed were it not for the robust presence of the British forces and the commitment of the administration of Tony Blair to defending the democratically elected government in Sierra Leone. While the British military intervention and presence have won praise from Sierra Leoneans, there are still doubts about the reliability of the new army being assembled. Many of the retrained soldiers in the new army are former *sobels* (renegade soldiers) and rebels who committed horrendous atrocities during the decade-long civil war. Also, some of the officers reabsorbed into the army were serving long jail sentences for their role in the Armed Forces Ruling Council (AFRC) junta between May 1997 and February 1998. One such officer, Colonel Gabriel Mani, was arrested in 2001 after the discovery of a large cache of weapons at his residence. Many Sierra Leoneans still harbor serious misgivings about the loyalty of a force that was largely responsible for the January 1999 carnage in Freetown, which resulted in at least 3,000 civilian deaths.

Another country that is attempting to reform its security sector, though with less external assistance, is Nigeria.[26] These efforts, since 1999, have included the retirement of officers who held political offices in the past, the appointment of new service chiefs, legislative oversight over the military, the use of foreign military consultants—mainly retired American army officers—and the prosecution of former cronies of General Sani Abacha. Among the Abacha cronies facing prosecution are the former chief of army staff, General Ishaya Bamaiyi, and Abacha's former chief security officer, Major Hamza El-Mustapha. Commenting on efforts to prosecute these individuals, Abiodun Alao noted: "The prosecutions have a number of consequences for security sector reform. They have further demystified the military . . . and taken accountability in Nigeria to a new level. In the past, successive governments have been selective in the way that they have tried their predecessors. There were often probes into financial mismanagement, but this is the first time that former office holders have been charged with misusing power and abusing human rights."[27]

But the security sector reforms of Olusegun Obasanjo's civilian regime have been just as "selective" as those of previous governments in Nigeria. The failure to investigate the finances of General Ibrahim Babangida, who was in power between 1985 and 1993, calls into question the sincerity of the government's reform efforts. Babangida is reported to have contributed large sums of money to the 1999 presidential campaign of Obasanjo, which, among other things, may help explain why the government now thinks an investigation of Babangida amounts to an unnecessary witch hunt. Obasanjo's current views on Babangida are at odds with statements he made prior to the current Nigerian president's arrest and imprisonment by Abacha in 1995. A year earlier, Obasanjo had said: "Babangida came out in his true colors, demonstrating again and again that he is a great master of intrigue, mismanagement, corruption, manipulation, deceit, settlement, cover up and self-promotion at the expense of almost everybody else. . . . I need only to add at this juncture that General Babangida is the main architect of the state in which the nation finds itself today, and that General Abacha was his eminent disciple, faithful supporter and beneficiary."[28]

If Abacha, whose family was forced to return $2 billion of stolen funds to the Nigerian government in April 2002, was a disciple of Babangida, why are the relatives and cronies of the "disciple" being hounded while the "prophet"—Babangida—is allowed to roam free? Making all military officers, past and present, accountable is a tall order in Nigeria, and nothing Obasanjo has done so far suggests that he is up to the challenge. Many former military officers in fact continue to occupy senior positions in Nigeria's legislature, Obasanjo's ruling People's Democratic Party, and the private sector.[29] Three of the strongest presidential candidates in the April 2003 elections—Obasanjo (the incumbent), Muhammadu Buhari (head of state between 1983 and 1985), and Ike Nwachukwu (a former foreign minister)—were themselves retired generals.

Military Budgets and Privileges

Reducing military budgets and improving the operational capabilities of military establishments represent two of the major challenges confronting military reform in West Africa. It is unwise, on the one hand, to continue spending large sums of money on an institution that cannot perform its basic functions; on the other hand, it is dangerous to downsize national armies without adequate consultation and preparation to reabsorb demobilized soldiers into other areas of work. The words of Britain's former development secretary, Clare Short, are noteworthy in this regard: "While governments must lead the reform effort in their country, for reform to be successful it needs a healthy and vigorous civil society able to hold governments to account and to push for faster progress. . . . Donor efforts to impose cuts to levels of military expenditure—without regard to the security and political context—will fail."[30]

The risks of military resistance or rebellion against reform measures by governments, however, could be eventually minimized if elected leaders are able to reduce the perceived costs to the military of according it a position of high status, honor, and income.[31] Military privileges constitute an area in dire need of reform. Incumbents have often used privileges and payoffs to secure the loyalty of soldiers. Some of these perks create the feeling among soldiers that they constitute a privileged class whose interests supersede those of the rest of society. In Sierra Leone, every soldier was entitled to three bags of rice a month and senior officers were known to take home in excess of five hundred bags of rice a month, the bulk of which was sold for personal profit. When the current government announced its intention of slashing this ration by half, the entire army strongly resisted this measure. Special privileges can be counterproductive because the more they "are offered, the less effective each becomes in purchasing support; while, at the same time, it also becomes more necessary to offer them and the cumulative consequences become more unbearable for everyone."[32] It is far better for soldiers to be well paid—at least they can then feed themselves—than to be fed and not paid well or regularly. Nigeria's civilian government, which had announced plans to reduce Nigeria's army from 78,500 to 50,000, reversed itself as a result of the destabilizing effects of such a drastic cut. Since militaries in West Africa wield so much power and can cause tremendous havoc, any "reduction of military prerogatives must be a gradual process that relies on bargaining, engagement, dialogue, and consensus building rather than blunt confrontation."[33]

Most West African states have been forced by declining revenue and external pressure to scale back their military budgets. Official military expenditure in Nigeria was reduced by two-thirds between 1979 and 1989, and military expenditure as a percentage of gross national product dropped by nearly 80 percent, from 2.4 percent to 0.5 percent, during the same period. While the rest of sub-Saharan Africa spent 3.2 percent of their gross domestic product on their armed forces, Nigeria spent only 1.1 percent.[34] These figures do not obviously reflect the costs of Nigeria's involvement in Liberia and Sierra Leone, which dramatically reversed some of the earlier gains in spending cutbacks.

Reducing military budgets need not result in sacrificing military preparedness, training, equipment, and effectiveness. The military requires proper

Table 7.2 Military Forces and Expenditure in West Africa, 1999–2000

	Total Armed Forces	Military Expenditure (in U.S.$ millions)	GDP (in U.S.$ millions)
Benin	4,750	37	2,400
Burkina Faso	10,000	69	3,500
Cape Verde	1,200	7.6	257
Côte d'Ivoire	13,900	134	13,100
Gambia	800	15	446
Ghana	7,000	96	10,100
Guinea	9,700	58	3,600
Guinea-Bissau	9,250	6	303
Liberia	15,000	25	450
Mali	7,350	30	2,900
Niger	5,300	27	1,700
Nigeria	78,500	2,400	50,000
Senegal	9,400–10,000	69	5,200
Sierra Leone	6,000+	9	724
Togo	9,450	31	1,500

Source: International Institute for Strategic Studies, *The Military Balance 2000/2001* (Oxford: Oxford University Press, 2000).

training and the acquisition of skills that are commensurate to the threats faced by states in West Africa. Budget reductions should not result in pay cuts or drastic reductions in military privileges. Savings from reducing the size of armies should, however, be spent on better pay, improved working conditions, and superior equipment for soldiers.

Democratic Subordination of the Military

Civil-military relations can be analyzed in terms of three sets of relationships: first, between political leaders and senior military officers; second, between civilian elites and the military's officer corps; and third, between civil society and the army.[35] By far the most critical of these relationships is that between civil society and the military. The perennial role of the military as an instrument of oppression and the frequent hostility of officers and the lower ranks to democratization have in many cases solidified the distrust and animosity that texture societal attitudes toward the military.

But why are many armies in West Africa opposed to democratization, and how can democracy movements establish ties with the military and undertake joint endeavors without politicizing soldiers along partisan lines? Part of the problem lies with the military itself, but democratic forces must also accept a share of the blame for not reaching out to soldiers. Undifferentiated attacks against the military by civil society groups have alienated many soldiers, and self-appointed "democracy activists" have often failed to distinguish themselves from authoritarian rulers. Reflecting on General Babangida's annulment of the results of Nigeria's June 1993 elections, Julius Ihonvbere wrote:

> One reason why the military has always found it easy to hijack popular contestations for political power, aside from its legal control over the means of coercion, is the weakness and fragmentation of civil society. Although labor and student unions voiced grievances and pursued popular agendas, most self-help and community-based associations were largely individualistic and narrow in focus. There were few points of convergence at which to articulate a national project. Though they often sponsored candidates for office, the vast majority of associations had no political agenda whatsoever. In fact, many were set up in the context of state failures to meet the basic needs of the people and their communities.[36]

Many ostensible democracy activists, including Baba Gana Kingibe, the running mate of Moshood Abiola, presumed winner of the 1993 presidential election in Nigeria, and Iyorchia Ayu, president of the senate at the time and a stalwart of Abiola's Social Democratic Party, abandoned Nigeria's democracy movement to join forces with the military leaders who had aborted the 1993 transition. Abiola himself is widely reported to have encouraged Abacha to seize power on the understanding that the latter would then hand over power to him. The divisive fragmentation and rank opportunism displayed by Nigeria's political class underscore the vulnerability of prodemocracy activists to co-optation by antidemocratic forces. Human rights lawyer and political activist Gani Fawehinmi stands out as a shining exception to this general rule in Nigeria.

Democratic subordination of the military assumes governmental legitimacy. "The chief condition of civilian control," observed David Goldsworthy in 1981, "is the existence of civil institutions which are both legitimate and effective."[37] Governments that lack legitimacy and are ineffective in the performance of their basic governance tasks will always provide a pretext for military interventions. Popular legitimation of civilian political authority and effective governance are the best safeguards against military coups (see Chapters 5 and 6). "Good governance" engenders public support for political institutions and can serve as an objective deterrent against coups. On the other hand, as Robin Luckham has noted: "If civilian governments cannot create a genuine base of popular support, govern effectively, produce development within constraints imposed by external donors, and find some way of resolving the inevitable conflicts between these goals, they will face large constituencies of discontent. Moreover, they will be tempted to use their military and security forces to repress the latter, providing soldiers with pretexts for reintervention."[38]

Constitutional and legal provisions are among the most objective but least effective instruments for keeping soldiers out of politics. Nigeria's 1999 constitution stipulates that "the Federal Republic of Nigeria shall not be governed nor shall any person or group of persons take control of the government of Nigeria or any part thereof, except in accordance with the provisions of this constitution."[39] A similar provision in the 1979 constitution did not prevent the 1983 coup, and there is no reason to believe that the 1999 constitution will be any different. Ghana's 1992 constitution not only classifies any armed seizure of power as a treasonable offense punishable by death, but it also provides for compensation to be paid to those who suffer bodily harm and loss of possession while resisting armed takeovers of government. These provisions, however, amount to very little unless soldiers are convinced that democracy is in their interest and citizens are prepared to defend democratic rule. Despite their obvious limitations, however, constitutional provisions are indispensable to the success of military reforms insofar as they increase the political costs of coups for putschists and provide a source of "confidence for citizens willing to resist violent overthrow of elected governments."[40]

An important institutional mechanism for subordinating the military to democratic control is the legislature. The problem, however, is that most legislatures in West Africa are appendages of their respective executives and are seldom in a position to perform the oversight functions necessary to keep the military in check. Parliamentary approval of military budgets and key appointments, scrutiny of military operations, especially those that go wrong, and making service heads accountable to parliament can help strengthen the hand of legislatures in dealing with their respective national armies. Legislatures must also develop effective committees with independent research and investigative capabilities. National parliaments, however, must first overcome their marginalization by incumbent executives before they can be expected to play a significant role in the democratic subordination of military establishments.

It is impossible to depoliticize the military in West Africa unless politics itself is demilitarized. Demilitarization, which involves limiting the influence of the military in the political process to the barest minimum, starts with the executive. It is the responsibility of the executive branch to formulate military policy, define goals, shape the curricula of military academies, and respond to the legitimate demands of servicemen and servicewomen. How governments respond to the internal problems that beset national armies can go a long way in determining the posture of soldiers vis-à-vis the political process. A government that is sympathetic and responsive to military needs and concerns reduces the probability of military intervention by rendering obsolete the perennial grievances of mutineers and putschists. All of this, however, assumes that civilian incumbents have an interest in depoliticizing the military; politics can be demilitarized without depoliticizing the army, and in many cases depoliticization has not been accompanied by formal military disengagement from politics.

The purest form of democratic subordination of a standing army is civic defense. If properly conceived and instituted, especially in war-torn and collapsed states, civic defense can serve as an effective counterweight to the military and a deterrent to adventurist soldiers. Civic defense does not establish a right to bear arms during peacetime; what it does provide is a mechanism for mobilizing society against armed insurgents in the event of a breakdown of national security. Yusuf Bangura makes the compelling argument that "the setting up of professional armies under conditions of widespread poverty and undeveloped civic institutions is likely further to enhance the power of armies . . . to make coups." Bangura calls for the "democratization of defense," which requires "much more than the training of a few civil defense forces. Neighborhoods and individuals need to be able to defend themselves if they are confronted with a breakdown of security. This would involve a proper program of military and security education, methods of arms use, ways of guarding homes, securing food and medical supplies, and creative methods of self-defense."[41] Restructuring security along the lines suggested by Bangura constitutes a bold and unprecedented step that can only be contemplated by a transformative regime that embodies the interests and promotes the aspirations of society.

Given the fragility of democratic experiments in West Africa, the international donor community has an important role to play in preventing authoritarian reversals. This does not have to involve the use of force by external patrons to protect democratically elected governments, since coercive diplomacy could be all that is needed in some situations to deter potential troublemakers. It is becoming increasingly obvious, as Samuel Decalo has noted, that "only the credible threat of foreign force might deter the emergence of dictatorship and/or military rule as the inevitable democratic dropouts of the future slowly emerge."[42] Britain's involvement in Sierra Leone has made all the difference in terms of giving that country a chance to restructure its armed forces, while protecting its government from armed insurrections. But while such an external bulwark may have worked in Sierra Leone, it is doubtful whether this approach can be effective in a country like Nigeria. A proposal by the Nigerian senate in 1999 to negotiate an anticoup defense pact with the United States that would have committed Washington to preventing coups in Nigeria did not go over well with the Nigerian public and was eventually dropped.[43] It was also clear that the U.S. government was itself unwilling to underwrite such a pact.

Another approach to protecting democratic governments in West Africa is the creation of a condominium of states with democratic governments whose principal task would be to prevent armed usurpations among its members. Such an arrangement would exclude "rogue regimes" like Taylor's Liberia and Burkina Faso and those states where elections have been certified as fraudulent. Potential members of such a democratic security alliance would include Senegal, Ghana, Nigeria, Mali, Benin, Sierra Leone, Côte d'Ivoire, and Niger. Although the performance of the Economic Community of West African States Cease-Fire Monitoring Group (ECOMOG) in Liberia and Sierra Leone does not inspire much hope for such a proposal (see Chapters 2, 13, and 14 for alternative perspectives on ECOMOG), it is an idea worth exploring, especially if a relationship can be worked out with the UN through which the international body can assist West African states in their collective efforts to resist military coups and institutionalize democratic governance.

Subordinating the military under democratic control will remain an elusive goal in cases in which such an approach is incompatible with the interests of the political class. "Democratization," as Samuel Decalo has noted, "disinherits, disadvantages or threatens some groups."[44] Incumbent politicians and senior officers are two groups who continue to feel threatened by democracy. As an integral fraction of a predatory, unproductive, and nonhegemonic political class, senior military officers may be less receptive to democratic governance than the lower ranks. It would be comparatively less difficult, for example, to incorporate the grievances of the military rank and file into the overall agenda of democratic forces than it would be to forge some kind of political accommodation between popular sectors and the political class. Popular sectors aligned with the lower ranks of the military can provide a powerful safeguard against internal threats to democratic rule.

Toward Democratic Control of the Military

The task of establishing stable civil-military relations in West Africa must of necessity involve the political class, the military, and civil society. Civil society, in alliance with the lower ranks of the military, can force politicians either to embrace democratic tenets and procedures or to wither on the vine. Such an alliance is possible if popular sectors and the military can overcome their mutual antagonism. There are already signs of this occurring in Mali, where the former ranks of the Malian army played a critical role in that country's transition to constitutional democracy in 1992. Even in Sierra Leone, the public seems poised to forgive renegade soldiers for past abuses and atrocities through the country's Truth and Reconciliation Commission. But unless these soldiers, many of whom have been retrained by the British, are weaned from their retrograde proclivities, they will continue to pose a threat to democratic governments in Freetown.

If democratic governments succeed in promoting economic development in West Africa, and the benefits of development are not concentrated in a way that excludes the vast majority of society, then it will be much easier to sell democracy to the lower ranks of the army. Democracy, development, and security are closely intertwined, and the absence of both democracy and development is the most formidable systemic threat to national security. By stifling democracy and development, political classes in West Africa have made states more insecure, even as they have acquired increasingly sophisticated military hardware. Ultimately, the success or failure of democratization rests on its impact on development and security. Provided that "they succeed in generating development, democracies can survive even in the poorest nations."[45] Butter, not guns, is needed to protect democracy in West Africa.

There can be no meaningful reform of the military in West Africa unless there is a conscious attempt to break away from the discredited governance practices of the postindependence era. Institutional reconstruction requires the decoupling of the state and the government, and the legitimation of political power. Unless the organization and exercise of political power is legitimized, unless government is subordinated to the state, and unless private wealth and public power are delinked, democratic subordination of the military will remain elusive. Securing "entrance legitimacy" through democratic elections is a beginning, but this can be quickly undone by the performance of elected governments that find it congenitally impossible to disavow the prevalent "spoils" logic of governance in West Africa.

Notes

1. Eboe Hutchful, "Military Issues in the Transition to Democracy," in Eboe Hutchful and Abdoulaye Bathily, eds., *The Military and Militarism in Africa* (Dakar: CODESRIA, 1998), p. 608.

2. Rebecca Schiff, "Civil-Military Relations Reconsidered: A Theory of Concordance," *Armed Forces and Society* 22, no. 1 (1995): 12–13.

3. For an elaboration of the term *lumpen militariat,* see Ali Mazrui, *Soldiers and Kinsmen in Uganda: The Making of a Military Ethnocracy* (London: Sage, 1975).

4. A study by Pat McGowan and Thomas Johnson records sixty coups in sub-Saharan Africa from January 1956 to December 1985. For details, see Pat McGowan and Thomas Johnson, "Sixty Coups in Thirty Years: Further Evidence Regarding African Military Coups d'Etat," *Journal of Modern African Studies* 24, no. 3 (1986): 539–546. Since this study, at least fifteen more successful coups have been staged, bringing the estimated total number of successful coups since independence to seventy-five.

5. Guy Martin, "Francophone Africa in the Context of Franco-American Relations," in John W. Harbeson and Donald Rothchild, eds., *Africa in World Politics: Post–Cold War Challenges,* 2nd ed. (Boulder: Westview Press, 1995), p. 176.

6. Charles Tilly, "War Making and State Making as Organized Crime," in Peter Evans, Dietrich Rueschemeyer, and Theda Skocpol, eds., *Bringing the State Back In* (Cambridge: Cambridge University Press, 1985), p. 173.

7. Ibid.

8. William Reno, "Reinvention of an African Patrimonial State: Charles Taylor's Liberia," *Third World Quarterly* 16, no. 1 (1995): 109.

9. Samuel Huntington, *The Soldier and the State: The Theory and Practice of Civil-Military Relations* (Cambridge: Harvard University Press, 1957), p. 7.

10. See, for example, Eboe Hutchful, "Understanding the African Security Crisis," in Abdel-Fatau Musah and J. Kayode Fayemi, eds., *Mercenaries: An African Security Dilemma* (London: Pluto Press, 2000), pp. 210–232.

11. Sunday Ochoche, "The Military and National Security in Africa," in Hutchful and Bathily, *Military and Militarism in Africa,* p. 123.

12. Robert McNamara, *The Essence of Security: Reflections in Office* (New York: Harper and Row, 1968), p. 149.

13. Ochoche, "Military and National Security in Africa," p. 111.

14. Thandika Mkandawire, "Crisis Management and the Making of Choiceless Democracies," in Richard Joseph, ed., *State, Conflict, and Democracy in Africa* (Boulder: Lynne Rienner, 1999), pp. 119–136.

15. Adam Przeworski, *Sustainable Democracy* (Cambridge: Cambridge University Press, 1995), p. 12.

16. Robin Luckham, *The Nigerian Military: A Sociological Analysis of Authority and Revolt, 1960–1967* (Cambridge: Cambridge University Press, 1971), pp. 248–249.

17. Roger Murray, "Militarism in Africa," *New Left Review* 38 (July–August 1966): 36.

18. James Coleman and Belmont Brice, "The Role of the Military in Sub-Saharan Africa," in John Johnson, ed., *The Role of the Military in Underdeveloped Countries* (Princeton: Princeton University Press, 1962), p. 403.

19. Abiodun Alao, *Security Reform in Democratic Nigeria.* Conflict, Security, and Development Group Working Paper no. 2 (London: Centre for Defence Studies, King's College, February 2000), p. 38.

20. Garnet Wolseley, "The Negro as Soldier," *Fortnightly Review* (London), December 1888, p. 86.

21. See "In Togo, the Big Man Looms Large," *Washington Post,* 7 September 2001, p. A22. Kabres make up no more than 25 percent of the population and are thus heavily overrepresented in both the rank and file and the officer corps of the Togolese army. The Ewes, in contrast, have been largely purged from the army since the overthrow of Sylvanus Olympio (an Ewe) in 1963, even though they are the largest ethnic group in Togo, accounting for almost half of the population.

22. See speech given by Ahmed Tejan Kabbah at the London conference on restoring democracy in Sierra Leone, in "A Recipe for Anarchy," *West Africa,* 20–26 October 1997, p. 1672.

23. For an overview of security reform in Sierra Leone and the role of the British, see Comfort Ero, *Sierra Leone's Security Complex.* Conflict, Security, and Development Group Working Paper no. 3 (London: Centre for Defence Studies, June 2000).

24. See United Kingdom Government, "Military Assistance to Sierra Leone," available at www.mod.uk/index.php3?.

25. See United Kingdom Government, "Sierra Leone Army to Receive More Military Training," available at www.mod.uk/index.php3?.

26. For an overview of these efforts, see Alao, "Security Reform in Democratic Nigeria," p. 38.

27. Ibid., p. 26.

28. Keynote address delivered by Olusegun Obasanjo at the Arewa House Conference, Kaduna, Nigeria, 2 February 1994. Cited in Claude Welch, "Civil-Military Agonies in Nigeria: Pains of an Unaccomplished Transition," *Armed Forces and Society* 21, no. 4 (1995): 610.

29. See, for example, J. 'Bayo Adekanye, *The Retired Military as an Emergent Power Factor in Nigeria* (Ibadan, Nigeria: Heinemann Educational Books, 1999).

30. Clare Short, keynote address at the symposium "Security Sector Reform and Military Expenditure," London, 17 February 2000, available at www.dfid.gov.uk.

31. Larry Diamond, Juan Linz, and Seymour Martin Lipset, "What Makes for Democracy," in Larry Diamond et al., eds., *Politics in Developing Nations: Comparing Experiences with Democracy* (Boulder: Lynne Rienner, 1995), p. 48.

32. Simon Baynham, "The Subordination of African Armies to Civilian Control: Theory and Praxis," *Africa Insight* 22, no. 4 (1992): 260.

33. Diamond, Linz, and Lipset, "What Makes for Democracy," p. 48.

34. Welch, "Civil-Military Agonies in Nigeria," p. 605.

35. David Goldsworthy, "Civilian Control of the Military in Black Africa," *African Affairs* 80, no. 318 (1981): 54.

36. See Julius Ihonvbere, "Are Things Falling Apart? The Military and the Crisis of Democratization in Nigeria," *Journal of Modern African Studies* 34, no. 2 (1996): 201.

37. Goldsworthy, "Civilian Control of the Military in Black Africa," p. 55.

38. Robin Luckham, "Taming the Monster," in Hutchful and Bathily, *The Military and Militarism in Africa,* p. 594.

39. *1999 Constitution of the Federal Republic of Nigeria* (Lagos: Federal Government Press, 1999), chap. 1, sec. 1(2).

40. Pita Agbese, "Options for Democratic Control of the Military," paper presented at the workshop "The Military Question in West Africa," Hill Station Hotel, Jos, Nigeria, 15 July 2000, p. 18.

41. Yusuf Bangura, "Strategic Policy Failure and Governance in Sierra Leone," *Journal of Modern African Studies* 38, no. 4 (2000): 570–571.

42. Samuel Decalo, "Not by Democracy Alone," *Journal of African Policy Studies* 1, no. 3 (1995): 105.

43. Alao, "Security Reform in Democratic Nigeria," p. 25.

44. Decalo, "Not by Democracy Alone," p. 102.

45. Adam Przeworski and Fernando Limongi, "Modernization: Theories and Facts," *World Politics* 49, no. 2 (1997): 177.

8

Rebel Movements

Ibrahim Abdullah and Ismail Rashid

West Africa presents us with a looming political paradox. With the exception of Guinea-Bissau, this subregion was the only one in Africa that did not experience armed insurrection to end colonial rule. Yet from the first decade of independence, West Africa became the theater of numerous armed conflicts. Whether it was bloody coups d'état, rebellions, violent separatist projects, or the more recent nihilistic movements of the *sans-culottes,* no single West African country has escaped armed intervention in its politics. Originating from Togo and Benin in 1963, coups d'état have been the most ubiquitous and recurrent type of armed intervention in West Africa.[1] After the military takeover by General Robert Gueï in Côte d'Ivoire in December 1999, Senegal and Cape Verde remain the only countries in West Africa to have avoided the scourge of military coups. The reasons most often cited for the recurrence of coups in West Africa include political instability, economic mismanagement, and corruption (see Chapter 7).

In the 1960s and 1970s, some coups were transformed into another type of prolonged armed intervention: violent secession. West Africa's secessionists backed their claims for the independence of certain ethnic groups or regions through the barrels of guns. Nigeria and Chad, with their rival generals and ethnic warlords, represented the most glaring examples of this tendency in the 1960s. In the 1980s and 1990s, new secessionist movements emerged in Niger, Mali, and Senegal. The Malian and Nigerian movements emerged mainly out of Tuareg disaffection with political and economic marginalization in the two countries. Changes of regime and broader political representation and accommodation of Tuareg interests have since led to the diffusion of secessionist violence in both countries. In Senegal, the Mouvement des Forces Démocratiques de Casamance (MFDC), which had agitated for regional autonomy since 1947, chose the path of violent secession only in 1982. Like other secessionist groups, the MFDC has framed its struggle around regional particularism and historical autonomy.[2]

Despite their divergent and sometimes dubious political agendas, the putschists of the postindependence era concentrated largely on purely military and visible political targets. The *sans-culottes* wars of the 1990s, however, present us with a different problematic: these movements have combined the conventional and unconventional to turn the region upside down in a seemingly incomprehensible manner. Between the Chadian disaster of the 1960s and the carnage in Sierra Leone and Liberia in the 1990s, there seems to have been a qualitative leap from the narrow Clausewitzian conception of war as an extension of politics by other means to the unbridled deployment of violence as an instrument of terror to achieve political objectives. The armed interventions in Liberia and Sierra Leone have been characterized by the targeting of defenseless civilians—particularly women and children—by the different military factions.[3]

What are the factors responsible for the postindependence upsurge of armed conflicts in West Africa? How do we explain the paradox of a supposedly peaceful region becoming awash with all types of light weapons and bloody conflicts? Who are the main protagonists in these conflicts? What do these new rebel movements teach us about governance, politics, economics, and the condition of the state in West Africa? Is there any new logic to these conflicts that could help untangle the corridor of violence stretching from the turbulent coast of southern Senegal to the once serene shores of Côte d'Ivoire?

The search for answers to some of these questions has produced some problematic journalistic and academic writings. The journalistic writing that is usually directed at Western audiences and the donor community tends to be sensationalist, condescending, and anecdotal. Despite purporting to provide explanations to the contrary, it often perpetuates Africa's image as a cesspool of "evil," savagery, and barbarism. Robert Kaplan, for example, attributes West Africa's conflicts to social atavism, youth delinquency, and environmental depletion.[4] Bill Berkeley sees "a method in the madness," and ascribes Africa's conflicts to the "calculated tyranny" and "organized crime" of the continent's politicians.[5] An interesting characteristic of these journalistic exposés is their self-recriminatory acknowledgment of the culpability of the U.S. government in Africa's incessant conflicts.

Academics tend to be more sophisticated than journalists in their rehashing of Eurocentric paradigms and their creation of static models and "novel" theories to explain Africa's conflicts. But as with journalistic writing, the "theories" and models of these academics usually rest on weak empirical foundations. Thus for William Reno and David Keen, Africa's conflicts can be understood through rational choice theory and market-centered analyses in which struggles for personal control, appropriation and exchange of resources, and commercial networks, rather than state power and institutions, provide the primary motivations for rebels (see Chapter 9). Reno, for example, maintains that, for warlords in weak states, "jettisoning bureaucracy, abjuring the pursuit of broad public interest, and militarizing conflict are rational responses."[6]

For social anthropologists, Africa's wars invoke another dimension of the "crisis of modernity," a dimension that cannot be understood without first understanding some of the esoteric, psychological, and religious foundations of different cultures. Thus, according to Stephen Ellis, in order to understand the Liberian civil war of 1989 to 1996 "rationally," a mere chronicling of the historical fortunes of Liberia is insufficient. It is important for outsiders to understand how Liberians have manipulated the traditional secret societies, ritualistic cannibalism, and beliefs in spirits and evil to engage political problems and to mobilize support to fight the war.[7] Even Ellis's friendliest critics have accused him of relying on "shaky evidence" and selective use of sources to bolster his exotic theories.[8]

In exploring some of the troubling questions raised above, we believe that an investigation of the history and sociology of Liberia and Sierra Leone can yield more profound insights than the economistic and culturally stereotypical accounts we have just described.[9] Our approach seeks to provide more credible explanations of these two civil wars, which will be the focus of this chapter.[10] We argue that in order to understand the phenomenon of rebel movements in Liberia and Sierra Leone, special attention must be paid to the roles of the intelligentsia, the urban youth, and popular culture in the postcolonial period. Particular attention must be paid to the issue of how these groups shaped national political discourses, the character of armed movements, and the dynamics of the two conflicts under examination. Our main arguments thus hinge on the centrality of *politics* in understanding the character and objectives of rebel movements, not only in Africa but also, we dare say, in the rest of the "Third World." The history, character, and dynamics of armed rebel movements in Africa suggest that they are initially propelled by political considerations. By this, we mean the often popular but sometimes not clearly articulated call for inclusivity, openness, and democracy in the determination of how decisions are made and resources allocated. The formulation of political objectives and strategies by these movements are neither linear nor static, but are instead part of a process that includes the dynamic interplay between local and international politics, changes in the configurations of power and alliances, and shifts in the relationships of the different protagonists. Conceived in this way, it becomes possible to investigate the complexities and dynamics of the conflicts, particularly the numerous failed peace initiatives, the realignment and proliferation of groups in Liberia, and the different fortunes of Sierra Leone's Revolutionary United Front (RUF) and the National Patriotic Front of Liberia (NPFL).

The chapter is divided into four sections. The first section provides a historical background to the conflicts in Liberia and Sierra Leone, including the evolution of formal and informal opposition movements to the hegemony of the True Whig Party (TWP) in Liberia and the one-party dictatorship of the ruling All People's Congress (APC) in Sierra Leone. The second section describes the tussle between military dictatorships and subaltern revolts in both countries. Sections three and four discuss the struggles by the NPFL and the RUF for power in Liberia and Sierra Leone. The conclusion briefly summarizes the main arguments of the chapter.

State Autocracy and Its Discontents

The conflicts of the 1990s in Liberia and Sierra Leone should be set against the background of the extreme socioeconomic and political polarization in both countries. The historical roots of this polarization lay in the settlement of both countries by minority populations of repatriated former slaves from the Americas, Europe, the Caribbean, and other parts of Africa. These new minorities, imbued with Euro-Christian ideas, values, and culture, arrived in Liberia and Sierra Leone with an innate sense of cultural and religious superiority over the majority indigenous population. Both groups became part of a colonial system that discriminated against and exploited the indigenous population. Settler elites in both countries had privileged access to educational institutions, the legal profession, churches, and bureaucratic positions. This access was to create a large social and economic gulf between the newcomers and indigenes in both countries. The crucial point of divergence, however, was that the minority in Liberia (Americo-Liberians, as they called themselves) were "independent" and ran the "colonial" state, while the minority in Sierra Leone (the Creoles, as they became known) had to play second fiddle to British imperial administrators who had taken over their nascent colony in 1808.[11]

The political economies of both countries were similar in the late nineteenth and early twentieth centuries. From the 1880s, the state structure in Liberia became more autocratic, hegemonic, and exploitative as competitive politics among the Americo-Liberian elite gave way to the dictatorship of the True Whig Party and the "imperial" presidency. The Liberian state increasingly became a mirror of the British state in Sierra Leone. State autocracy and hegemony in both countries rested on similar economic foundations: the extraction of rents and duties from predominantly agricultural societies whose formal economies were predicated on revenue from the mercantile trade, and the export of agricultural and forestry products and minerals. In the twentieth century, rubber and iron ore became Liberia's dominant exports, while iron ore, rutile, diamonds, and palm products became Sierra Leone's. Both countries had very rudimentary manufacturing sectors and were heavily dependent on the import of manufactured goods and petroleum fuel.[12] The lack of indigenous capitalist entrepreneurs meant that the investment in the large-scale production of forest and mineral resources in both countries had to come from external sources.[13]

In the era after World War II, autocratic leaderships in Liberia and Sierra Leone had to respond to the popular continental call for decolonization and self-government. In Sierra Leone, the British response was the creation of a liberal democratic framework within which local elites were expected to organize political parties and to compete for the leadership of the colonial state. Using the language of majority rule, an alliance of the "indigenous" elite edged out the Creole elite in the race to inherit the state from the British.[14] The "indigenous" elite subsequently fragmented into the Sierra Leone People's Party (SLPP), a coalition of chiefs and middle-class professionals that came to represent the predominantly Mende southeast, and the All People's Congress, which garnered support from the Temne and Limba in the north, the Kono in the east, and the Creoles in the west. The SLPP won the first round of this struggle in 1957 and 1962. Like Nigeria on the eve of independence, the contest for political power became a north-south struggle between regions and ethnic coalitions. In Liberia, the Americo-Liberian elite responded to the continental call for decolonization by ameliorating the "colonial" aspects of the relationship between the ruling oligarchy and indigenous Liberians. Through a series of social and bureaucratic reforms, President William Tubman (1944–1971) brought sections of the indigenous majority into the mainstream of Liberia's society and state. But Tubman undertook these reforms without conceding the autocratic position of the TWP and the hegemony of the Americo-Liberian minority.[15]

In the 1960s, while presidential autocracy held sway in Liberia, postcolonial Sierra Leone continued its uncertain experiment with liberal democracy. Political parties and civil groups operated unhampered. The liberal democratic experiment, however, ran aground in 1967 following the defeat of the SLPP government by the opposition APC. During the tussle over the electoral results, the military intervened. The soldiers held state power for a year before turning it over to the APC. While the transfer of power seemed, at the time, to signal the strength of the country's postcolonial liberal democratic culture, in retrospect it marked the beginning of the return to autocracy. After assuming power in 1968, the APC, under the leadership of Siaka Stevens, who remained president until 1985, turned the state into a one-party dictatorship within a decade. Through a series of fraudulent elections

in 1973 and 1977 and a one-party referendum in 1978, the APC criminalized all forms of political opposition. The ruling party centralized state
power and access to resources, and "made membership of the party a *sine
qua non* to get by; exclusion meant death by attrition."[16]

The socioeconomic foundations of the political autocracy in Liberia
and Sierra Leone were, however, less secure in the late 1970s and 1980s
than they had been in previous decades. The economies and societies of
both countries, like those of many other states in Africa, were unraveling.
Following the price hike of the Organization of Petroleum-Exporting Countries (OPEC) that trebled international oil prices in 1973, the decline in
export receipts led to spiraling budget deficits, currency devaluations, mass
unemployment, and the virtual collapse of state-financed social services.
The expansion of the youth population and the increased urbanization of
the capitals of Freetown and Monrovia compounded these problems.

The initial struggles against autocracy in Liberia and Sierra Leone in the
1970s and 1980s had been centered on the same social groups: the intelligentsia and the urban youth. Imbued with aspirations that were increasingly
difficult to attain within the narrow confines of the decrepit neocolonial political economies of the two states, this new generation of Liberian and Sierra
Leonean actors—radical, populist, and antiestablishmentarian—initiated
processes and actions that would destabilize and lead to the collapse of the
old entrenched regimes in Liberia and Sierra Leone. By failing to accept fully
the existence of a plurality of political voices and organizations or a change
of political power through peaceful means, the ancien régimes in Liberia and
Sierra Leone placed their countries on the path of violence.

In Liberia, one of the groups that embodied the political tendencies of
this new generation was the Movement for Justice in Africa (MOJA), established by lecturers (Togba-Nah Tipoteh, Henry Boima Fahnbulleh Jr., Amos
Sawyer, and Dew Mayson) and students at the University of Liberia in
1973.[17] Inspired by the struggle for liberation in southern Africa, MOJA
transcended the old divide between Americo-Liberians and indigenes. The
group sought to raise national consciousness, mobilize the masses, and promote national development and social justice. Its popularity rapidly extended from the university to the wider populace.[18] The Progressive
Alliance of Liberia (PAL), a product of political discontent among Liberian
students in the United States, was the other main opposition group. Led by
Bacchus Matthews, PAL portrayed itself as more radical than MOJA, with
quasi-Marxist inclinations.[19] While MOJA was initially anchored among
university students, PAL's popularity rested on unemployed urban youth
and lower classes.[20]

William Tolbert, who came to power in Liberia in 1971, initially tolerated MOJA and PAL. But he eventually fell out with both groups. MOJA
challenged the True Whig regime over press freedom, the legalization of

gambling, and the mayoralty of Monrovia.[21] PAL directly confronted the government in 1979 over continued nepotism by the ruling party and the removal of subsidies on rice. PAL, supported mainly by hundreds of urban youth and students, demonstrated against the 50 percent hike in the price of rice—the national staple food—on 14 April 1979, triggering the "rice riots" and the "year of ferment" that would eventually topple Tolbert's regime. An estimated 140 people died in the looting and rioting that followed the attempt by security forces to break up the demonstration. Tolbert panicked and called in Guinean troops to help stabilize his tottering regime. The government briefly detained the leaders of MOJA and PAL. Even though they were subsequently released, the government's repressive tactics effectively ended the myth of political stability in Liberia as well as the regime's tolerance of formal opposition.[22] Tolbert's subsequent attempt to eliminate this organized opposition to his rule removed his last veneer of legitimacy. PAL members had decided to press home their moral advantage by registering the Progressive People's Party (PPP), the first such opposition party in Liberia in a quarter of a century to compete in the electoral process. The PPP then amateurishly attempted to force Tolbert to resign by calling a nationwide strike in 1980.[23] The government reacted by arresting and charging the PPP leadership with treason. The death knell of the TWP regime came after wild rumors spread that the government intended to try and summarily execute the PPP leadership.

In Sierra Leone, where the opposition to autocracy rested on a less solid organizational foundation, the confrontation between a new generation of political actors and the government took a dramatic turn in 1977. As in Liberia, the inspiration for political action was the southern African liberation struggles.[24] Influenced by exiled students from southern Africa as well as the deteriorating conditions in the country, students of Fourah Bay College staged a major protest. The 1977 demonstration—popularly dubbed a "revolution" among students and their allies—was the first nationwide uprising against the APC dictatorship. Schoolchildren and unemployed urban youths joined the protest, which rapidly spread throughout the country. Through the National Union of Sierra Leone Students (NUSS), the protesters demanded electoral reform, "free and fair" national elections, the reduction of the bloated cabinet, and the curtailment of foreign interference in the economy.[25] The government held national elections in 1977, which were rigged. The following year, Stevens instituted a one-party system. In 1980 and 1981 the government repressed the independent press and trade unions. Optimists who had predicted the 1977 elections would be a replay of the events of 1967 were shocked to discover that the APC was determined to use violence to maintain its grip on power.

Like the True Whigs in Liberia, the APC government in Sierra Leone had made nonviolent political discourse impossible. The arrest of Bacchus

Matthews was the principal event in Liberia that symbolized this fact. In Sierra Leone, the elections of 1977 and the one-party referendum of 1978 were the key events that shaped the evolution of a subaltern discourse centered on the use of violence. In both Liberia and Sierra Leone, youths, students, and other subaltern forces learned that a change of government was impossible through the ballot box. The deepening economic crisis of the late 1970s, amid spiraling oil prices and lower export revenues, merely provided the material basis for this discourse to flourish in both countries. The first violent salvo against autocracy in West Africa during this period had been fired by the youths of Liberia.

Subalternity Versus Dictatorship

Liberia

Led by Master-Sergeant Samuel Kanyon Doe, seventeen low-ranking soldiers stormed the executive mansion and killed Tolbert on 12 April 1980. Many of these soldiers had been politicized by MOJA and PAL. Calling themselves the People's Redemption Council (PRC), the junior officers claimed power in the name of the Liberian people and pledged to pursue the political agenda of the progressive movement (MOJA and PAL). Their refrain became: "In the cause of the people, the struggle continues"—a PAL slogan. The PRC symbolically tried to destroy the 133-year Americo-Liberian rule by publicly executing thirteen former cabinet ministers,[26] banning the TWP, and outlawing the powerful Masonic lodge through which the Americo-Liberian elite had maintained its dominance over society.

Behind the PRC's progressive pretensions, three crucial social characteristics stood out. First, all seventeen soldiers came from the lower ranks of the army and none was educated beyond the eleventh grade. The soldiers were poorly paid, deficient in military discipline, and lacked much command experience.[27] Second, these soldiers were from indigenous groups— Krahn, Dan, Gio, and Kru—which had been historically marginalized from the mainstream of Liberian politics. The leader of the coup by default of rank, Doe, and his deputy, Weh Syen, were Krahn from Grand Gedeh county, the most impoverished and underdeveloped part of the country. Thomas Quiwonkpa, a Gio from Nimba county, headed the army. Third, in spite of their indigenous background, many PRC members had been partly socialized within the delinquent youth subculture of Monrovia. Their politics and behavior in power would be marked by the "greed," "suspicion," and "opportunism" characteristic of the capital's urban youth subculture.[28]

Since they lacked the requisite political and administrative skills, popular support base, and political legitimacy, Liberia's putschists reached out to members of the progressive movement, the deposed government, and Liberian exiles. PAL and MOJA leaders, namely Bacchus Matthews (foreign affairs), Boima Fahnbulleh (education), and Togba-Nah Tipoteh (planning and economic affairs), received ministerial appointments. The PRC retained three former TWP ministers, and incorporated into its regime student leaders, such as Charles Taylor and Gbai Bala, who had been based in the United States.

The broad spectrum of political appointees, however, including those from MOJA and PAL, failed to provide clear direction for the regime. Without a program, common agenda, or political discipline, the PRC became mired in halfhearted populist schemes, bad financial and economic policies, and the pursuit of personal wealth and state power.[29] The regime's politics became a struggle to control, rather than to transform, the decrepit autocratic state. Without solid political constituencies, the protagonists in the intra-PRC struggle resorted to the manipulation of their crude ideological and ethnic differences. Even the "progressives" became "bounty hunters, fortune seekers and ethnicists" in the struggle for power.[30] The different factions within the PRC soon resorted to violence as the main instrument for resolving their differences.[31] In 1981 the Doe faction executed Syen, the first PRC vice chairman, and four other PRC members for "treason." Though a fellow Krahn, Doe perceived Syen as disloyal. Syen was also the PRC member who had been most influenced by the ideas of MOJA and PAL. Employing similar tactics, the Doe faction expelled Quiwonkpa (a Gio) and his allies from the government.[32] By 1984, nearly all the radicals and non-Krahns had been purged from the PRC, a fact underlined by the regime's brutal repression of a student protest in the same year.

Liberia's foreign policy came to reflect the orientation of the winning faction. The Doe faction reversed the earlier policy of making overtures to "radical" socialist states such as Ethiopia, Libya, Cuba, and the Soviet Union, and adopted strong pro-Western policies. Doe's regime became staunchly pro-U.S., recognized Israel, expelled Soviet diplomats, and committed itself to free market capitalism.[33] U.S. president Ronald Reagan rewarded Doe with half a billion dollars of aid during the decade of the 1980s, and Washington continued to support Doe as a Cold War ally in Africa even after he blatantly rigged elections in 1985.

Doe refused to concede to popular demands for the democratization of Liberian politics. He did establish a constitutional commission involving Amos Sawyer, Albert Porte, Tuan Wreh, and Boima Fahnbulleh. But Doe perverted the work of the commission by altering its final draft to suit his presidential ambitions. In 1985 he banned, bullied, and brutalized his opponents to steal presidential and parliamentary elections and usher in Liberia's flawed second republic.[34] In the short run, Doe got away with a stolen election mainly because of U.S. support, elite opportunism, opposition disunity, and state violence. Like his predecessor, the hapless William Tolbert, Doe made peaceful change through the ballot box impossible. The losers, both in the PRC's internal struggle and in the 1985 national elections, could continue the political fight only through violent means.

Sierra Leone

The subaltern project in Sierra Leone took a decade longer to unfold than the one in Liberia. President Siaka Stevens held on tighter than Tolbert to the reins of power with a mixture of repression and co-optation. However, in 1985, buffeted by old age, an ailing economy, and rumblings within his APC, Stevens transferred power to Major-General Joseph Momoh, the loyal head of his army. Like Tolbert in Liberia, Momoh lacked the Machiavellian political survival skills that Stevens and William Tubman had frequently demonstrated. Momoh was unable to break the stranglehold on Sierra Leone's economy of the Lebanese business class and their political allies. Nor was he able to establish an alternative economic network that would guarantee his regime much-needed economic resources.[35] The "new order" that Momoh's regime promised never materialized. The election of 1986 that might have reenergized the APC turned out to be a sham. The economic emergency laws of 1987 stopped neither smuggling nor illegal currency speculation. Momoh was unable to eliminate the graft and corruption that had become the hallmark of Sierra Leonean politics under Stevens's rule.[36] Isolated, Momoh surrounded himself with his Limba kinsmen and proudly informed the nation that others should follow his example.[37]

Amid Momoh's inept rule and the absence of a credible political alternative, a subaltern political project was already taking shape. The main architects of this project were radical students who had been expelled from Fourah Bay College in the wake of Stevens's transfer of power in 1985. Interestingly, the project began with Sierra Leone's intelligentsia attempting to do what their counterparts in Liberia had done in the 1970s: to construct organizational vehicles for their radical ideas. Unfortunately, Sierra Leone's intellectuals had neither studied nor learned lessons from MOJA's experience in Liberia.

Like MOJA, Sierra Leone's intelligentsia drew on the language of pan-Africanism and the antiapartheid struggle to build an informal university-based opposition against the APC dictatorship. In 1982, lecturers and students set up the Pan-African Union (PANAFU), a group dedicated to campaigning against apartheid in South Africa as well as fighting neocolonialism in Africa. PANAFU became one of several "leftist" and "progressive" groups, including the Green Book Study Group, the Juche Idea Study Group, and the Socialist Club, that were emerging on the Fourah Bay College campus. Sharing overlapping memberships and ties of camaraderie, these groups rallied to support the Mass Awareness and Participation (MAP) student government led by Allie Kabba. MAP, a loose coalition of radical nonconformist students employing populist antigovernment rhetoric, made no secret of its intention to put into practice the "leftist" and "populist" ideas emanating from the ivory tower.[38]

What made this new student project explosive was the sociological and historical context within which it was born. In the 1970s and 1980s, radical and nonconformist students and urban unemployed youth had increasingly converged around a number of cultural sites and trends—the *pote* (a place for alienated and marginal youth to congregate, smoke, gamble, and talk), reggae music, odelay festivals, drugs, a new Krio language, and the neighborhood—which had hitherto separated respectable middle-class youth from the lumpen "riffraffs." Through these sites, radical college students "conscientized" their less fortunate brethren with ideas from *The Green Book* and Pan-Africanism. The lyrics of Bob Marley, Peter Tosh, Fela Anikulapo-Kuti, and other politically conscious musicians contributed to this emerging "conversation from below."[39] In the eclectic political discourse that emerged, and in the wake of the repressive and violent elections of the 1970s and 1980s, both students and youth came to believe that "*de system*" could only be changed through violence. In the process, the idea of the lumpen proletariat as antisocial was shattered, and the *pote* became a training ground for a new breed of "revolutionaries" in Freetown. During the 1980s, the alliance between youths and students was regularly manifested in the intermittent street battles they fought against state security forces during student-led demonstrations.

When the university authorities at Fourah Bay disbanded the "MAP government" and rusticated forty-one "radical" students in 1985, the student-urban youth alliance entered a new phase. A good number of the expelled student leaders were members of PANAFU and the Green Book Study Club. Some of these expelled students would undertake three crucial activities that led directly to Sierra Leone's civil war and the Sierra Leone–Liberian conflict of the 1990s. First, throughout the late 1980s, while the Momoh regime continued on its downward spiral, former Fourah Bay College students disseminated their radical ideas among the urban youth in Freetown and other urban centers. Second, the exiled Sierra Leonean student leadership in Ghana began recruiting urban youths for military training in Libya. Third, this exiled group of self-styled revolutionaries recruited other Sierra Leoneans as well as anti-Doe dissidents from Liberia. In short, 1985 was a significant year in the buildup to, and convergence of, the civil wars in Liberia and Sierra Leone. This was the year in which the forces that ignited the wars in both countries began coalescing.

The NPFL and the Struggle for Power in Liberia

The coalescing of anti-Doe forces in Liberia began in November 1985. In a bid to settle old scores and to stop Doe from benefiting from stolen elections, Thomas Quiwonkpa, the former commander of Doe's army, and a group of dissidents calling themselves the National Patriotic Forces of Liberia crossed the Sierra Leone border in a bid to overthrow the Doe regime.[40] Quiwonkpa had the support of some MOJA members as well as Siaka Stevens, who intensely disliked Doe. Despite early successes including control of strategic buildings and the announcing of Doe's ouster over the radio, bad planning and miscommunication between the coup plotters eventually doomed the invasion. Doe trapped and killed Quiwonkpa along with his fellow putschists.[41] The Liberian autocrat then undertook extensive reprisals against suspected supporters of Quiwonkpa, especially the Gio and Mano of Nimba county, 3,000 of whose citizens were estimated to have been killed by Doe's Krahn-dominated military. Despite the failure of his coup, Quiwonkpa had fired the first shot in Liberia's coming civil war.[42]

Quiwonkpa's associates regrouped and, with a slight amendment of the *F* in *NPFL* from "Forces" to "Front," resumed the war against Doe on 24 December 1989. One hundred and sixty-eight NPFL fighters entered Nimba county through Côte d'Ivoire to exploit the reservoir of popular hostility against the Doe regime.[43] Though disorganized at first, they quickly acquired weapons from government garrisons. Thousands of new recruits soon joined NPFL ranks, as the Armed Forces of Liberia (AFL) created more animosity by terrorizing and massacring civilians. Within six months, the NPFL had overrun most of Liberia and besieged the embattled remnants of the Doe regime in Monrovia.

Horrified by the atrocities, the flood of hundreds of thousands of refugees into neighboring countries, and the regional implications of Taylor's violent takeover of Monrovia, the Economic Community of West African States (ECOWAS) embarked on mediation efforts with the parties in Freetown in July 1990. Despite the refusal of the Liberian factions to agree to a cease-fire and amid threats from Taylor to attack any regional peacekeeping force that entered Liberia, ECOWAS deployed a cease-fire monitoring group (ECOMOG) consisting of Nigerian, Ghanaian, Sierra Leonean, Guinean, and Gambian troops in Monrovia on 24 August 1990.[44] Two weeks later, a breakaway NPFL unit headed by Prince Yormie Johnson, which had successfully infiltrated Monrovia, trapped and executed Samuel Doe. After halfhearted attempts to shore up the Doe regime, the United States abandoned him to his fate. The Cold War was over and U.S. assets in Liberia—the Omega Navigational System, the Voice of America (VOA) relay station, and an intelligence network system—had lost their strategic value.[45] Following Doe's death, Taylor, Johnson, and David Nimley—the deputy commander of the AFL—all declared themselves "president" of Liberia. A military and political stalemate ensued.

For the next six years, ECOWAS and ECOMOG, led by Nigeria, tried to rein in the factions, bring peace to Liberia, and reconstitute the shattered state (see Chapters 13 and 14).[46] ECOMOG supported an Interim Government of National Unity (IGNU) under the leadership of Amos Sawyer, but IGNU never established its authority much beyond Monrovia. Meanwhile at least five new factions emerged: the United Liberation Movement of Liberia for Democracy (ULIMO), which split into two factions by 1993 under the leadership of Alhaji Koromah (ULIMO-K) and Roosevelt Johnson (ULIMO-J). George Boley led the Liberia Peace Council (LPC), François Massaquoi led the Lofa Defense Force (LDF), and Tom Woewiyu and Laveli Supowood led a breakaway NPFL faction calling itself the Central Revolutionary Council (CRC). These factions splintered due to leadership struggles, ethnic fragmentation, and the creation of proxies, to wreck numerous peace agreements. After twelve peace agreements that were never implemented, ECOWAS leaders included the warlords on an executive council of state in 1995 in a bid to ensure the disarmament of their factions. Throughout the peacemaking process, Charles Taylor and the NPFL held the key. He had the most military and financial resources, controlled the largest territory, had the most international connections, and perhaps had the largest local and overseas support network.[47]

Taylor's ascendance from a U.S.-based student leader in 1980 to the leader of the largest armed faction in Liberia by 1989 was due to his personal machinations, the dynamics of exile politics, and strong support from Libya and Burkina Faso. As chair of the Union of Liberian Associations in the Americas (ULAA), he had led a protest against William Tolbert's regime in New York. As a placatory gesture, Tolbert had flown the leadership of the ULAA to Monrovia.[48] The gesture swept them into the maelstrom of the Doe-led coup. Taylor hitched his fortunes with his in-law Quiwonkpa, who appointed him director of Liberia's General Services Agency, a government procurement body. The future NPFL leader fled to the United States in 1983 before Quiwonkpa's failed coup, whereupon Doe invoked a bilateral extradition treaty after accusing Taylor of embezzling $900,000 from the General Services Agency. While awaiting trial, Taylor managed to escape from jail and made his way from the United States back to West Africa.

Using his ULAA connections and association with Quiwonkpa, Taylor established contacts with the important network of financial and military support for Liberian political exiles. He convinced Blaise Compaoré, president of Burkina Faso, and Muammar Qaddafi, leader of Libya, that he was more credible than anti-Doe veterans like Boima Fahnbulleh, Amos Sawyer, and Moses Duopu. In Libya and Burkina Faso, Taylor met and forged links with other African dissident leaders and groups, including Foday Sankoh, leader of Sierra Leone's rebel movement, the RUF.[49] Though other NPFL personalities would attribute Taylor's ascendance to a series of contingencies, it was clear that his control of the connections to NPFL lifelines gave him a decisive edge over his rivals.

Taylor subsequently used the war to eliminate potential leadership contenders. Duopu, who had publicly declared his ambition to lead the NPFL and had suggested the need for a political process to decide the leadership, was killed while in NPFL-occupied territory during the civil war. Elmer Johnson, the NPFL's chief military strategist, and Cooper Teah, a participant in Quiwonkpa's abortive coup attempt in 1985, also died under suspicious circumstances. Popular politicians like Jackson Doe and Gabriel Kpolleh who hurriedly crossed over.to the NPFL in 1990 also died mysteriously.[50] After Tom Woewiyu broke away from the NPFL in 1994, he publicly accused Taylor of having ordered these killings. By the end of 1990, Taylor was the undisputed leader of the NPFL. Only Prince Johnson and Samuel Varney managed to break free of Taylor, having secured sufficient military supplies from the initial raid on the Liberian town of Butuo to form their own independent NPFL (the INPFL).

The NPFL changed in size, character, and organization over the course of the six-year conflict. It began the war as a loose coalition of former soldiers, "radical" intellectuals, politicians, exiles, and refugees hostile to Doe's dictatorship.[51] Most of the original leaders and members of the NPFL had some association with the original Quiwonkpa faction of the PRC. By 1996 the NPFL's original fighting core of 168 (former AFL soldiers, Gio-Mano "peasants," and Burkinabè, Sierra Leonean, and Gambian exiles) had increased to over 15,000 fighters of widely differing ages and levels of training, skills, and discipline. Many of the initial fighters came from Nimba county but recruits from other regions and defections from the INPFL and AFL soon gave the NPFL a more "national" character. At the height of the war, over 33,000 fighters (figure revised downward from 60,000 by the UN in 1996) were involved on different sides of the war.

The rapid expansion of the membership of the NPFL and the other armed factions defined the nature of Liberia's civil war. About 80 percent of the fighters were rural and urban youth, as well as abducted and orphaned children; 15 percent of these fighters were women and 10 percent were child soldiers.[52] The most notorious child soldiers were the "Small Boys Unit." Taylor had put the unit together after Johnson defected with the better-trained NPFL Special Forces. Impoverished, poorly socialized, and without sufficient military training or political education, these youth and children were notoriously brutal and rapacious (see Chapter 11).[53] If the political elite gave the war its ethnic character, the rural and urban subalterns gave it its homicidal stamp.

These subalterns killed with impunity and saw the possession of firearms as an opportunity for settling regional, ethnic, or personal scores and for pursuing crude appropriation and self-enrichment. The plight of Monrovia after the two abortive attempts by the NPFL to capture the capital in 1990 and 1992, and brutal factional fighting in 1996 that left 3,000 people dead, are demonstrative of this trend. The different factions looted Monrovia of cars, furniture, and moveable items, and basically lived off the communities that they overran. They appropriated labor, food, shelter, commodities, and cash. Young women in these communities were targets of sexual assault.[54] Drug use, especially cannabis, cane-juice, and amphetamines—long a feature of urban subculture—escalated during the war. The combatants wore frightening costumes, awarded themselves high-sounding military titles, and adopted terrifying *noms de guerre* depending on their deeds, self-perception, and images derived from the popular media and movies.

In seeking to explain the war and the behavior of Liberia's fighters, several analysts have produced social anthropology of poor quality. Stephen Ellis, for example, has amplified the atrocities, the paraphernalia of the combatants, the use of indigenous rituals as instruments of terror and coercion, and the proliferation of rumors during the war, as if these were the main essence of the fighting, rather than products of the material, social, and political conditions under which the war was fought.[55] The behavior of Liberia's fighters actually has a much simpler explanation. The factions lacked resources to provide uniforms to their fighters, as evidenced in their ghoulish attire and the crude weapons of some of the fighters. Furthermore, while the personal paraphernalia of the fighters may have been influenced by its ritual and protective value, its meaning should not be exaggerated. For many fighters, the ghoulish outfits merely highlighted the strange bounties of indiscriminate looting and the desire of these combatants to terrorize others.

The lack of social, military, and political discipline among the factions heightened their propensity toward atrocities. The administration of justice in the different factions was summary: treason, dereliction of duty, betrayal, or suspicion of disloyalty, and many petty crimes frequently carried the death penalty. In the absence of strong political ideologies or military discipline, the combatants searched for alternative or complementary resources to tip the balance in their favor. Yet the resort to "religious" or "cultural" strategies should not be exaggerated, as Ellis has done. The factions recognized that the difference between success and defeat on the battlefield lay in solid military training and organization, machine guns, rocket-propelled grenades, and other instruments of contemporary warfare. As the war progressed, all the armed militias endeavored to regularize and organize their fighting forces along conventional lines with general staffs, brigades, battalions, platoons, and the supporting cast of porters, laborers, and hangers-on.

In fact it was the NPFL's ability to reorganize its forces after its early split in 1990 that gave it a decisive edge over other factions during the Liberian conflict. After ECOMOG prevented Taylor's attempt to capture Monrovia in October 1990, the warlord tried to reconstitute an alternative political center at Gbarnga, the capital of what he labeled "Greater Liberia" (as opposed to the smaller enclaves being administered by the ECOMOG-backed government led by Amos Sawyer). "Greater Liberia" had a dual command structure—military and civilian—both under Taylor's authority. The NPFL remained the military structure, responsible for prosecuting the war and for formulating policy in areas under Taylor's control. The civilian administration took the form of the National Patriotic Reconstruction Assembly Government (NPRAG), which was mainly staffed by some of Taylor's previously exiled political allies, Liberian technocrats and administrators, as well as political leaders who had fled the Doe regime or were displaced by the war or trapped behind NPFL lines. District commissioners, superintendents, and mayors in "Greater Liberia" were under the authority of the NPRAG. As president of "Greater Liberia," Taylor headed the NPRAG, assisted by Enoch Dogolea, a politician from Nimba county. Tom Woewiyu, Sam Dokie, and Laveli Supuwood—all among Liberia's most experienced politicians—were given "ministerial" or other government responsibilities.[56]

The existence of the NPRAG gave the NPFL rudimentary experience in government administration.[57] The body also enabled Taylor to maintain his leverage over political rivals in the tortuous diplomacy and transitional political arrangements that eventually led to peace in Liberia between 1990 and 1997. This arrangement further allowed Taylor to systematize the NPFL's extraction and sale of resources, with the help of shady French, Ivorian, and eastern European businessmen, and to demonstrate his administrative skills to his external supporters in West Africa and the United States. Most important, perhaps, "Greater Liberia" permitted Taylor to generate independent sources of economic support beyond those being provided by Libya and Burkina Faso. The collusion of foreign and local businessmen in the economic strategies of "Greater Liberia," however, should not be overstated. First, for its protagonists and its bootleggers, war is highly profitable, and unless compelled otherwise, businessmen have little ethical compulsion not to profit from African conflicts. Second, the ultimate objective of the faction leaders in Liberia was not, as scholars like William Reno have argued, to create these criminal economic networks as alternatives to the substantive Liberian state, or to capture existing markets in order to reproduce political patronage networks.[58] Their ultimate aim was to capture the contested state, as Taylor demonstrated through his election in

July 1997. The leaders of Liberia's factions knew that, despite the presence in their fiefdoms of local and international actors, they could not inherit the historical memory of the entire Liberian state, its juridical and moral legitimacy, or its sources of citizenship, without capturing Monrovia. This the NPFL did in 1997, albeit through the ballot box.[59]

The RUF and the Struggle for Power in Sierra Leone

Exiled radical West African students in Ghana had provided the opportunity for the Liberian and Sierra Leonean rebellions to converge, but these students were unaware of the magnitude of the catastrophe that they had set in motion. Lacking a clear-cut agenda about the aftermath of military training, Sierra Leone's radical student groups eventually split up and completely abandoned their "revolutionary" project. From the ashes of the abandoned project rose the Revolutionary United Front, a creation of Foday Sankoh, a cashiered army officer, and a motley collection of unemployed youth recruits. Sankoh, the future leader of the RUF, and two other leading lights, Abu Kanu and Rashid Mansaray, worked closely with Charles Taylor, whom they had first met in Libya in the late 1980s. Other Sierra Leoneans were later recruited in Liberia, Côte d'Ivoire, Ghana, and Nigeria for training at Po in Burkina Faso. The Burkinabè and Libyan-trained Sierra Leoneans took part in the initial NPFL campaign against Doe in December 1989. In return, Taylor provided a base in Liberia for the RUF to launch its "revolution" with the help of 200 Burkinabè regular soldiers and NPFL veterans on 23 March 1991. It must be underlined that Taylor neither put the RUF force together nor did he consider the rebels to be a rearguard action against ECOMOG. Similarly, the initial NPFL push into Liberia, though aided by regular Burkinabè soldiers, was not a Burkinabè project but Taylor's own brainchild.

Lacking clear methods of how to convey their message, the RUF and its allies took control of Sierra Leone's border region with Liberia, killing traders, religious leaders, chiefs, and state officials. This indiscriminate killing alienated potential sympathizers in eastern Sierra Leone and the RUF's "revolutionary" message fell on deaf ears. The local population rejected the invaders.[60] The RUF had no concrete program or systematic explanation of its objectives except the vague and generalized pronouncements of its leader, Foday Sankoh, to terrified residents in Kailahun. The only document that was distributed in the border area was the one originally written by exiled students in Accra. The populist refrain, "power to the people, arms to the people, and wealth to the people," appropriated from student politics, failed to attract the youth. The RUF started to abduct children. It would later conscript youths and teenagers to serve as carriers and porters, and eventually as combatants. It would take the RUF another five years to produce a propaganda booklet—*Foot Path to Democracy*—explaining its goals and supposed ideology.

In stark contrast to the NPFL invasion of Nimba county in 1989, which had been able to rally popular support, the RUF failed in its attempts to garner support among the local population in eastern Sierra Leone, and all sections of the embattled political class and the masses denounced the rebellion. The rebels eventually found a kindred constituency among the lumpen proletariat in the rural areas of southeastern Sierra Leone, particularly the young illicit miners in the diamond-producing areas. Living mostly by their wits, this group welcomed the RUF because it gave them access to lucrative mining sites and protection for their illegal activities. Their everyday work culture as gangs under the control of a headman perfectly fit the RUF's modus operandi. Sam Bockarie, the former field commander and later interim head of the RUF, was one of these illicit miners. Before that, he had worked as a disco dancer, a barber, and a security officer at the diamond mines. The antisocial culture of the illicit miners resonated with that of the urban riffraffs so that drunkenness, theft, drug addiction, rape, and abuse of women became the key markers of the RUF. The RUF's urban marginals, its original recruits, and the illicit miners found an ally in another group in the south: the *njiahungbia gorngesia,* or unruly youths. It was this unholy alliance of marginals, criminals, and social misfits—the lumpen proletariat—that became the key to the RUF's survival as a military outfit.[61]

Unburdened by primordial or regional sentiments, these "loose molecules" and their growing army of abducted children and teenagers became doggedly loyal to their "commandos," as they called their commanders.[62] Membership of the RUF "family" empowered them: it provided the weapon that made it possible for them to mine diamonds and live off the captive population. These rebels were only accountable to their battle-front commanders, who were in turn accountable to their battle-group commanders. The latter were only answerable to "Papay," Foday Sankoh, the "head of the ideology." This was the organizational structure that emerged in what could be called the first phase of the war, from 1991 to 1993, after which the government in Freetown, with the help of Guinean and Nigerian troops, was able to push the rebels back into Liberia and the heavily forested areas of Pujehun and Kailahun districts.

The RUF invasion of the border areas in 1991 caught the APC regime off guard. The paramilitary State Security Defense (SSD) deployed to counter the rebels was poorly armed. It was quickly pushed back, having suffered heavy losses. By the time the Sierra Leone army was deployed, the regime did not trust its army, and the rebels had spread out from Pujehun and Kailahun and were poised to attack Bo, Kenema, and Kono. The Sierra Leone Army (SLA) held back the RUF, but could not defeat the rebels due to lack of morale and equipment. The military stalemate created the window of opportunity for a coup that had been planned well in advance. When young officers in the army went to Freetown, ostensibly to agitate for more pay and better conditions to enable them to prosecute the war more effectively, they met Momoh, a panic-stricken head of state who was only too willing to cede power to them. Calling itself the National Provisional Ruling Council (NPRC), the new youthful administration, led by the twenty-seven-year-old Captain Valentine Strasser, declared a "revolution" and pledged a speedy end to the war and a return to multiparty democracy.

Before long, the NPRC became mired in the very corruption that had characterized the previous regime. Inexperienced and consisting mostly of high school graduates, the NPRC's leaders became surrounded by the same group of people who had ruined the country: discredited politicians and senior civil servants. Their preferred solution to ending the war was to increase the size of the army from 3,000 to almost 15,000. The new recruits were mostly the urban riffraff, the very social group that was in the RUF.[63] The enrollment of these individuals into the army created a lumpen militariat and tipped the balance of the war in favor of the RUF.

Arthur Abraham has persuasively argued that Sierra Leone's civil war was prolonged due to elite and state conspiracy. Abraham noted that the NPRC prolonged the war because it did not want to cede power to an elected civilian government.[64] The senior army officers, who were mired in corruption and diamond mining, abandoned the war to the junior officers and lower ranks. Many senior officers were busy living lavish lifestyles in Freetown while the war dragged on in the countryside. Some senior officers collaborated with the RUF, and were tried for such offenses.[65] Realizing that their senior officers had abandoned them to enrich themselves, the rank and file refused to fight and chose instead to engage in looting to augment their meager salaries.

Abraham has wondered how the RUF was able to regroup and launch further attacks after the NPRC had declared the war over and won in 1993. The answer to this seeming puzzle can be found in the common cause that the army rank and file made with the RUF. Through this arrangement, the RUF obtained intelligence on imminent military offensives. This phenomenon, popularly referred to as *sobel*—soldier by day, rebel by night—was the principal reason why civil militias, most prominently the Kamajors, emerged in communities in the southeast. With this background, the alleged military superiority of the RUF begins to wear thin. It is this collaboration—which Sierra Leoneans have dubbed "sell game"—that is key to understanding why the war took so long and why an estimated 80 percent of the Sierra Leonean army defected to the rebels in 1997.

The popular belief about the military superiority of the RUF is a myth invented to explain away the *sobel* phenomenon. This phenomenon emerged during the second phase of the war (from 1994 to 1997) when the RUF had changed its military strategy from the conventional mode of the early NPFL to one of classical guerrilla tactics using bypass routes to hit strategic targets. It was during this period that the RUF captured the rutile mines, threatened Bo—Sierra Leone's second largest city—and fought a major battle twenty miles outside Freetown. It is important to keep in mind that, on both occasions that the RUF entered Freetown (in 1997 and 1999), the national army brought the rebels into the capital. This collaboration between the rebels and the army underlines the grave security implications of recruiting lower-class "riffraffs" into security organizations.

To argue that, if not for internal sabotage within the SLA, the RUF would not have been a military match for the army and ECOMOG, only begins to explain why the war continued for as long as it did. What also needs to be emphasized is the nature of the war that the RUF was waging. After 1991, when the RUF entered Bomaru, the rebels employed terror tactics that belied the RUF's rhetoric of "power to the people." These tactics led to some internal wrangling that resulted in the execution of two of the RUF's original founders and commanders, Abu Kanu and Rashid Mansary. Sankoh, who became the omnipotent patriarch of a band of marginal youths, did not restrain his commanders from committing atrocities. He is reported to have promised to apologize to the people at the appropriate time.[66] Thus civilians were constantly targeted because RUF fighters accused them of opposing the rebellion. Rape was common among RUF combatants, and Sankoh himself reportedly told NPFL combatants to help themselves to the "sisters."[67] Looting and maiming of children and women became the defining feature of the RUF's presence in areas under its control. The gruesome amputation of limbs that became synonymous with RUF terror surfaced on the eve of the February 1996 election, when Sankoh issued a statement justifying the amputations as a way of stopping people from voting. Incidents of terror by the RUF arguably decreased during the second phase of the war, when the organization had established some modicum of civil and military administration in areas under its control. But once the RUF and its Armed Forces Ruling Council (AFRC) allies were expelled from Freetown by Nigerian soldiers in February 1998, their mode of operation became thoroughly criminal. This stage of the war coincided with the leadership of Sam "Maskita" Bockarie.

Sam Bockarie was the sole leader of the RUF between March 1997—when Foday Sankoh was under detention in Nigeria—and January 1999, when renegade elements of the Sierra Leonean army invaded Freetown with the RUF's support. The short-lived alliance between the RUF and the AFRC under Captain Johnny Paul Koromah momentarily united the different strands of the lumpen rebellion against the country's political establishment. All through this period, the makeshift RUF war council, active and functional under Sankoh, never met. Bockarie did not consult or involve the battle commanders in the planning of military operations. He acquired the fearful reputation of "Attila the Hun," and all the commanders, without exception, were afraid of him. He ran the RUF single-handedly, doling out instructions to all combatants and communicating with the outside world as the sole voice of the movement. Bockarie would later completely dominate, and even incarcerate, his erstwhile ally Johnny Paul Koromah after ECOMOG expelled the AFRC from Freetown. Following the rebel invasion of Freetown in January 1999, the RUF strongman reportedly gave orders for the mass slaughter of civilians when he proclaimed "Operation No Living Thing" and instructed his men to loot indiscriminately during his "Operation Pay Yourself." At least 3,000 people were killed in Freetown during this invasion.

Under Bockarie, a man who publicly announced that he wanted to be heard and recognized as an important individual, the RUF was transformed into a largely criminal enterprise with connections to international crime syndicates in Monrovia. Recruited by Taylor in Abidjan in early 1989, Maskita was responsible to no one but Taylor, who now became the principal spokesperson of the RUF in the absence of Sankoh. It was during this period, from 1997 to 1999, that the diamond-for-arms trade between the RUF and Taylor's Liberia became most widespread. Maskita's command of the RUF gave the erroneous impression that the RUF was a creation of Charles Taylor.

In spite of Bockarie's criminal depredations, the RUF, like the NPFL, never abandoned its political objective. Contrary to the market-centered analysis advanced by scholars like William Reno and David Keen that the war was primarily a function of economics and that the RUF was more interested in mining than in capturing political power, the RUF's strategy, as demonstrated by its participation in the 1999 invasion of Freetown and in the AFRC regime from 1997 to 1998, was to seize political power by any possible means.[68] What analysts like Keen and Reno have failed to grasp is that the RUF and the NPFL are *military* outfits with *political* agendas. How could one otherwise explain the numerous attempts to capture Freetown and Monrovia?

Conclusion

The murderous factions in the Sierra Leonean and Liberian civil wars partly reflect the nature of the new volatile social forces thrown up by the deteriorating postcolonial economic and political conditions in many parts of Africa. By doggedly defending their fiefdoms, by refusing to acknowledge the existence of these forces and the demands they made on the state, and by repressing nonviolent means of political discourse, ruling classes in both countries—the True Whigs and the APC—sat on military powderkegs of their own making. What was distinct about the toxic mélange of forces—students, urban youths, soldiers, and politicians—that finally ignited this powderkeg was the nature of the counterhegemonic projects that they had conceived. In the 1990s these counterhegemonic projects combined traditional forms of armed intervention, coups, and untraditional means such as subaltern insurrections to destabilize ancien régimes in Sierra Leone and Liberia. Though the two projects intersected, their courses and fortunes were different. The dissimilarities in the development of political culture, the differences in the leadership of the rebel movements, the dynamics of the two civil wars, the choices made by the old political elite, and the timing of regional interventions all affected the outcomes of the conflicts. In Liberia, the changing dynamics ultimately allowed Taylor to capture power through elections in 1997 and continue to destabilize Sierra Leone through his support of the RUF until he was forced into exile in Nigeria by an armed rebellion in August 2003. The changing dynamics in Sierra Leone, however, denied the RUF political power in a crushing and humiliating electoral defeat in May 2002, and provided the opportunity for the construction of a more durable peace.

Notes

1. See Samuel Decalo, *Coups and Army Rule in Africa,* 2nd ed. (New Haven: Yale University Press, 1990); and Eboe Hutchful and Abdoulaye Bathily, eds., *The Military and Militarism in Africa* (Dakar: CODESRIA, 1998).

2. Michael C. Lambert, "Violence and the War of Words: Ethnicity vs. Nationalism in the Casamance (Senegal)," *Africa* 68 (Fall 1998).

3. Yusuf Bangura, "Understanding the Political and Cultural Dynamics of the Sierra Leone War: A Critique of Paul Richards's *Fighting for the Rainforest,*" in Ibrahim Abdullah and Yusuf Bangura, eds., *African Development* 22, nos. 2–3 (1997): 117–148 (Special Issue: "Youth Culture and Political Violence: The Sierra Leone Civil War").

4. Robert. D. Kaplan, "The Coming Anarchy," *Atlantic Monthly* 271, no. 2 (February 1992): 32–69; and Robert. D. Kaplan, *Ends of the Earth: A Journey at the End of the Twenty-First Century* (New York: Random House, 1996), pp. 401–409.

5. Bill Berkeley, *The Graves Are Not Yet Full: Race, Tribe, and Power in the Heart of Africa* (New York: Basic Books, 2001), pp. 5–19.

6. William Reno, *Warlord Politics and African States* (Boulder: Lynne Rienner, 1998); and David Keen, *The Economic Functions of Violence in Civil Wars,* Adelphi Paper no. 320 (Oxford: Oxford University Press, 1996).

7. Stephen Ellis, "Liberia 1989–1994: A Study of Ethnic and Spiritual Violence," *African Affairs* 94, no. 375 (April 1995): 165–197; and Stephen Ellis, *The Mask of Anarchy: The Destruction of Liberia and the Religious Dimension of an African Civil War* (London: Hurst, 1999).

8. Paul Richards, "'Witches,' 'Cannibals,' and War in Liberia," (book review), *Journal of African History* 42 (January 2001): 167.

9. For an intelligent critique of these approaches, see Thandika Mkandawire, "The Terrible Toll of Post-Colonial 'Rebel Movements' in Africa: Towards an Explanation of the Violence Against the Peasantry," *Journal of Modern African Studies* 40, no. 2 (June 2002): 181–215.

10. Ibrahim Abdullah, "Youth Culture and Rebellion: Understanding Sierra Leone's Wasted Decade," *Critical Arts* 16, no. 2 (2002): 19–37.

11. J. Gus Liebenow, *Liberia: The Quest for Democracy* (Bloomington: Indiana University Press, 1987), pp. 24–29; Stephen S. Hlope, *Class, Ethnicity, and Politics in Liberia: A Class Analysis of Power Struggles in the Tolbert and Tubman Administrations from 1944–1975* (Washington, D.C.: University Press of America, 1979); John Cartwright, *Politics in Sierra Leone* (Toronto: University of Toronto Press, 1971); and Martin Kilson, *Political Change in a West African State* (Cambridge: Harvard University Press, 1966).

12. Cartwright, *Politics in Sierra Leone;* Fred Hayward, "Sierra Leone: State Consolidation, Fragmentation, and Decay," in Donal B. Cruise O'Brien et al., eds., *Contemporary West African States* (Cambridge: Cambridge University Press, 1991); and Eliphas Mukonoweshuro, *Colonialism, Class Formation, and Underdevelopment in Sierra Leone* (Lanham, Md.: University Press of America, 1993).

13. A. B. Zack-Williams, *Tributors, Supporters, and Merchant Capital: Mining and Underdevelopment in Sierra Leone* (Aldershot, England: Avebury, 1995).

14. Cartwright, *Politics in Sierra Leone;* and Kilson, *Political Change in a West African State.*

15. Amos Sawyer, *The Emergence of Autocracy in Liberia: Tragedy and Challenge* (San Francisco: Institute for Contemporary Studies Press, 1992); Tukumbi Lumumba-Kasongo, "Social Movements and the Quest for Democracy in Liberia: MOJA and Its Transition into a Political Party," in M. Mamdani and Ernest Wambadia-Wamba, eds., *African Studies in Social Movements and Democracy* (Dakar: CODESRIA, 1995), p. 420; and Amadu Sesay, "Historical Background to the Liberian Crisis," in Margaret Vogt, ed., *Liberian Crisis and ECOMOG: A Bold Attempt at Regional Peacekeeping* (Lagos: Gabumo Press, 1992), pp. 32–33.

16. Ibrahim Abdullah, "Bush Path to Destruction: The Origin and Character of the Revolutionary United Front/Sierra Leone," *Journal of Modern African Studies* 36, no. 2 (1998): 206.

17. Hlope, *Class, Ethnicity, and Politics in Liberia;* and Christopher Clapham, "Liberia," in O'Brien et al., *Contemporary West African States,* p. 123.

18. Sawyer, *Emergence of Autocracy in Liberia,* pp. 289–290; Lumumba-Kasongo, "Social Movements," pp. 409–410; and Sesay, "Historical Background to the Liberian Crisis," p. 26.

19. Ellis, *Mask of Anarchy,* p. 50. Another group was the Union of Liberian Associations in the Americas, whose leadership included Charles Taylor, Moses Duopu, Blamo Nelson, and Tom Woewiyu—all destined to play prominent roles in Liberian politics in the 1980s and 1990s. See also Mark Huband, *The Liberian Civil War* (London: Frank Cass, 1998), pp. 16–17.

20. Clapham, "Liberia," p 101.

21. Lumumba-Kasongo, "Social Movements," p. 435.

22. Ibid., p. 437.

23. Clapham, "Liberia," p. 102.

24. Ismail Rashid, "Subaltern Reactions: Lumpens, Students, and the Left," *African Development* 22, nos. 2–3 (1997): 19–43.

25. Ibid.

26. Adolphus Tolbert, the son of the deposed ruler and son-in-law of President Houphouët-Boigny of Côte d'Ivoire, who had taken refuge in the French embassy, was also later killed, an act that was to haunt the Doe regime a decade later. Côte d'Ivoire would become a launching pad for Doe's enemies in 1989, and the Ivorian government, when it was not complicit, would turn a blind eye to the activities of Liberian dissidents.

27. Clapham, "Liberia," p. 101.

28. Sawyer, *Emergence of Autocracy in Liberia,* p. 293.

29. Fahnbulleh, for his part, suggested that the "revolution" was not "thorough enough." See H. Boima Fahnbulleh, *Disarmament and the International Community in the Resolution of the Liberian Civil War* (Monrovia: Yandia Press, 1994).

30. Amos Sawyer, *Effective Immediately: Dictatorship in Liberia, 1980–1986: A Personal Perspective* (Bremen, Germany: Liberian Working Group, 1987), p. 16.

31. Sawyer, *Emergence of Autocracy in Liberia,* p. 293.

32. Quiwonkpa had eschewed the flamboyant lifestyle of the other PRC members and had remained close to the rank and file of the army, and Liberia's masses.

33. See the memorandum by John G. Rancey in Huband, *Liberian Civil War,* Xp. 35. See also Herman Cohen, *Intervening in Africa: Superpower Peacemaking in a Troubled Continent* (New York: St. Martin's, 2000); Katherine Harris, *African and American Values: Liberia and West Africa* (Lanham, Md.: University Press of America, 1985); and Reed Kramer, "Liberia: A Casualty of the Cold War's End?" *CSIS Africa Notes* no. 174 (July 1995).

34. Lumumba-Kasongo, "Social Movements," p. 451; and Sawyer, *Emergence of Autocracy in Liberia,* p. 297.

35. William Reno, *Corruption and State Politics in Sierra Leone* (Cambridge: Cambridge University Press, 1995), p. 157.

36. Hayward, "Sierra Leone."

37. Jimmy D. Kandeh, "Politicization of Ethnic Identities in Sierra Leone," *African Studies Review* 35, no. 1 (April 1992): 81–99.

38. Rashid, "Subaltern Reactions."

39. Abdullah, "Bush Path to Destruction."

40. Ellis, *Mask of Anarchy,* p. 59.

41. Huband, *Liberian Civil War,* p. 92.

42. Ibid., pp. 38–40.

43. Ellis, *Mask of Anarchy,* p. 113.

44. Colonel Festus Aboagye, *ECOMOG: A Subregional Experience in Conflict Resolution, Management, and Peacekeeping in Liberia* (Accra: Sedco Enterprise, 1999); Adekeye Adebajo, *Liberia's Civil War: Nigeria, ECOMOG, and Regional Security in West Africa* (Boulder: Lynne Rienner, 2002); Ademola Adeleke, "The Politics and Diplomacy of Peacekeeping in West Africa: The ECOWAS Operation in Liberia," *Journal of Modern African Studies* 33, no. 4 (1995): 569–593; Abiodun Alao, John Mackinlay, and 'Funmi Olonisakin, *Peacekeepers, Politicians, and Warlords: The Liberian Peace Process* (Tokyo: United Nations University Press, 1999); Ellis, *Mask of Anarchy;* Karl Magyar and Earl Conteh-Morgan, eds., *Peacekeeping in Africa: ECOMOG in Liberia* (London: Macmillan, 1998); Klaas Van Walraven, *The Pretence of Peace-Keeping: ECOMOG, West Africa, and Liberia (1990–1998)* (The Hague: Netherlands Institute of International Relations, 1999); and Margaret Vogt, ed., *The Liberian Crisis and ECOMOG: A Bold Attempt at Regional Peacekeeping* (Lagos: Gabumo Press, 1992).

45. See Cohen, *Intervening in Africa;* and Yerkutiel Gershoni, "From ECOWAS to ECOMOG: The Liberian Crisis and the Struggle for Political Hegemony in West Africa," *Liberian Studies Journal* 18, no. 1 (1993): 33.

46. See Alao, Mackinlay, and Olonisakin, *Peacekeepers, Politicians, and Warlords;* and Yerkutiel Gershoni, "Military and Diplomatic Strategies in the Liberian War," *Liberian Studies Journal* 22, no. 2 (1997): 199–239.

47. Gershoni, "From ECOWAS to ECOMOG."

48. Huband, *Liberian Civil War,* pp. 15–17.

49. Abdullah, "Bush Path to Destruction."

50. Ellis, *Mask of Anarchy,* p. 87.

51. Ibid., p. 74.

52. Lois Whitman and Janet Fleischman, "The Child Soldiers: Liberia's Civil War," *Africa Report* 39, no. 4 (July–August 1994): 65–66; and Ellis, *Mask of Anarchy,* pp. 113, 132.

53. Kenneth L. Cain, "The Rape of Dinah: Human Rights, Civil War in Liberia, and Evil Triumphant," *Human Rights Quarterly* 21 (May 1999): 265–307.

54. Emma T. Lucas, "Sexual Abuses as Wartime Crimes Against Women and Children: The Case of Liberia," *Liberian Studies Journal* 22, no. 2 (1997): 240–260; Shana Swiss, Peggy J. Jennings, Gladys V. Aryee, Grace H. Brown, Ruth M. Jappah-Samukai, Mary S. Kamara, Rosana D. H. Schaack, and Rojatu S. Turay-Kanneh, "Violence Against Women During the Liberian Civil Conflict (Letter from Monrovia)," *JAMA: Journal of the American Medical Association* 279, no. 8 (25 February 1998): 625–629; and Shana Swiss and Binaifer Nowrojee, "Women Are the Silent Victims in Liberia," *Africa News* 37, no. 5 (23 November 1992): 5.

55. Ellis, *Mask of Anarchy.*

56. C. E. Zamba Liberty, "Butuo: A Lilliputian Testament to a Struggle," *Liberian Studies Journal* 23, no. 1 (1998): 135–198.

57. Ibid., pp. 162–163.

58. See Reno, *Warlord Politics.*

59. David Harris, "From 'Warlord' to 'Democratic' President: How Charles Taylor Won the 1997 Liberian Elections," *Journal of Modern African Studies* 37, no. 3 (1999): 431–455.

60. Paul Richards, *Fighting for the Rainforest* (London: James Currey, 1996).

61. Ibrahim Abdullah and Patrick Mauna, "The Revolutionary United Front: A Revolt of the Lumpenproletariat," in Christopher Clapham, ed., *African Guerrillas* (London: James Currey, 1998).

62. Kaplan, "The Coming Anarchy."

63. Abdul Karim Koroma, *Sierra Leone: The Agony of a Nation* (Freetown: Andromeda, 1996).

64. Arthur Abraham, "War and Transition to Peace: A Study of State Conspiracy in Perpetuating Armed Conflict," in Abdullah and Bangura, *African Development,* pp. 101–116.

65. See Koroma, *Sierra Leone,* for details.

66. Abdullah, "Bush Path to Destruction."

67. Interviews with former combatants, April–July 2000.

68. Reno, *Warlord Politics;* and David Keen, "Incentives and Disincentives for Violence," in Mats Berdal and David M. Malone, eds., *Greed and Grievance: Economic Agendas in Civil Wars* (Boulder: Lynne Rienner, 2000), pp. 19–41.

9

The Political Economy of Conflict

Eboe Hutchful and Kwesi Aning

During the 1990s, West African conflicts in places like Liberia, Sierra Leone, and Nigeria's oil-rich Niger Delta contributed to an increasingly heated debate concerning "new" forms of warfare and violence. While these different perspectives provide interesting insights into the proximate and long-term causes of conflicts, this literature is uneven in explaining the driving forces behind such conflicts. Recent attempts at interpreting the dynamics of some of these conflicts have been presented in the context of either "greed" and/or "grievance." This particular framework seeks to explore the real or imagined "economic agendas in . . . these civil wars."[1] Until recently, these crises were perceived to be totally unconnected processes, and often attributed simply to Africans having "the habit of conflict."[2]

Such processes were also often seen as part of a complex series of occurrences that simply saw the state in Africa as being "criminalized,"[3] resulting in a distinctive "politics of the belly."[4] The persistence of wars in certain parts of Africa has made pseudo-academic Afro-pessimism fashionable and acceptable in some circles in the West.[5] In academic circles, it is becoming trendy and acceptable to argue that historical anthropology can provide answers to questions related to some of Africa's civil wars. This has resulted in the dubious suggestion by Stephen Ellis that "there is an echo of this [African] historical tradition in the practice of present-day warlords."[6] Thus these conflicts are interpreted as decidedly "African" civil wars, reflective of "an instrumentally plausible re-traditionalisation of society," and the excesses that routinely occur in these conflicts are presented as the way in which "Africa works." Such conflicts have thus become "part of [the] everyday calculus of power in contemporary Africa."[7] Western journalists have also joined the fray in "interpreting" African conflicts. In

May 2000 the *Economist* simply declared Africa "The Hopeless Continent,"[8] with a depiction of a gun-toting youth from a random African civil war on its front cover.

This chapter attempts to untangle the different conceptual frameworks and explanations for Africa's conflicts. We focus, in particular, on the extent to which discourses around greed, grievance, and economic agendas in these wars are tenable. The chapter then proceeds to suggest alternative frameworks for explaining the multiple relationships and trajectories between political economy and conflict in West Africa, focusing particularly on the cases of Liberia, Sierra Leone, and Nigeria's oil-rich Niger Delta. We offer a brief "counterfactual" of conflict avoidance based on the Ghana case, before concluding the chapter with five key lessons from our analysis and the four case studies.

Understanding Contemporary Warfare

Violence appears to have become a significant feature of the political discourse in many parts of West Africa. The classic representation of this phenomenon is the so-called internal or civil wars that now blight the landscape of this subregion. Although observers of the West African scene have long been aware of a "crisis of the state,"[9] most were unprepared for the nature of civil conflicts that have occurred in the subregion. These civil wars, also known as "wars of the third kind," have certain general characteristics.[10] According to Yusuf Bangura:

> Combatants deliberately target civilians rather than armed opponents in prosecuting goals, and atrocities are freely committed as part of strategies aimed at publicising political statements. In countries rich in natural resources, . . . the political goals of wars often interact with the multiple logics of resource appropriation . . . the looting of private property, and vandalism. Such complicated outcomes have led many commentators to portray contemporary wars as being basically anarchical.[11]

Donald Snow concurs, noting:

> Somehow different from the wars we have traditionally thought of as civil conflicts they [these "new" wars] seem, for instance, less principled in political terms, less focused upon the attainment of some political ideal. They seem more vicious and uncontrolled, one cannot find the restraining influence of . . . political philosophies. Instead, these wars appear to be little more than rampages by groups within states against one another with little or no apparent ennobling purpose or outcome, they are indeed uncivil wars.[12]

Consequently, in such wars, the distinction between combatants and civilians is unclear. There are no "fronts," no "lines," no "uniforms," and no "formal hierarchies." Where such command structures are present, they are weak and are unable to exert disciplined control over troops. Another characteristic of these wars is the new prominence demanded by, and given to, subnational actors and groups like rebel movements and mercenaries who have functioned as though they were recognized members of the international community. The actions of these actors and the nature of these crises have undermined perceptions of the state in Africa as the dominant and significant actor in the international system. These groups have succeeded in introducing new practices into the conduct of armed conflicts, effectively contesting some archetypal conceptions of modern warfare. Subsequently, the dynamics of these conflicts have also influenced, and indeed transformed, the patterns of subregional and external involvement in, and responses to, such internal crises.

Interpreting African Conflict: Which Framework and for Whom?

Attempts at theorizing African politics and conflicts have spawned different approaches and frameworks. One of the most enduring paradigms is the concept of neopatrimonialism, which has been presented by some analysts as the "distinctive institutional hallmark of African regimes."[13] A core tenet of this concept is that processes of rule and leadership are personalized and operate through patronage rather than through ideology or law. The effect of such personalization of power is that violence becomes part of everyday life.[14] As a result, the current rebellions in Africa are a reflection of state-related violence.[15] Chris Allen, for example, has argued that the violence found in African societies can be explained by the internal dynamics of what he terms as "spoils politics," in which self-enrichment is a key issue.[16] Though this framework has its utility, it does not fully explain *why* other states in similar situations do not disintegrate or experience similar violence.

A second popular framework employs "rational choice" analysis to explain the seemingly senseless violence and brutalities that occur in some of Africa's conflicts. The basic argument of this school of thought is that social action and reaction are closely related to either group or individual calculus based on self-interest and the expectation of gain. This approach claims to perceive an underlying rationality to the actions of rebel factions. Aside from West Africa, this concept has also been applied to conflicts in Angola, Mozambique, and more recently, the Democratic Republic of Congo (DRC). Although rational choice proponents tend to be cognizant of the "mindless violence" employed by insurgent groups, some of its leading apostles, like David Keen, characterize the actions of rebel groups as a "particularly organised kind of chaos, [a] rational kind of madness."[17] Adam Hochschild offered a journalistic version of this argument when he suggested that "the Congo's current situation—Balkanized, occupied by rival armies, with no functioning central government—suits many people just fine. Some are heads of Congo's warring factions, some are political and military leaders of neighboring countries, and some are corporations dependent upon the country's resources. The combination is deadly."[18]

The third framework for analyzing African conflicts is in fact a variant of the rational choice approach. The arguments about the economistic rationales for civil war that have been put forward by Paul Collier and Anke Hoeffler—two Western economists, with the former based at the World Bank—have generated some of the most heated debates in the recent study of the political economy of Africa's civil wars.[19] This work deserves particular attention because of the importance that it has been given in influential policy circles in which a nuanced understanding of African issues is important to informing policy debates and decisions.

In a volume published in 2000, Collier argues in a chapter titled "Doing Well out of War: An Economic Perspective" that "economic agendas appear to be central to understanding why civil wars start." He posits that "conflicts are far more likely to be caused by *economic opportunities* than by *grievance*" (emphasis added).[20] Collier uses the idea of *proxies* to "capture the notion of an economic agenda."[21] He argues that, "since both greed-motivated and grievance-motivated rebel organizations will embed their behavior in a narrative of grievance, the observation of that narrative provides no *informational* content . . . as to the true motivation for rebellion" (emphasis added).[22] To circumvent such an a priori approach, Collier then chooses to "infer the motivation from patterns of observed behaviour." To achieve this purpose, he determines patterns in the *origins* of civil war, distinguishing between those causal factors that are broadly consistent with an "economic motivation and those that are more consistent with grievance." He uses two proxies to predict whether states are prone to civil war. The first is the existence of primary commodity exports that are likely to be lootable—that is, commodities that are "based on the exploitation of idiosyncratic natural endowments" such as alluvial diamonds.

Collier's second proxy is the proportion of young men in a society, especially those between fifteen and twenty-four years old. In his view, the greater the proportion of young men in a country, the easier it is to recruit rebels. The argument here is that due to poverty and lack of income-earning opportunities, young men might be more willing to join rebellions. A related point is educational opportunities: the fewer the young men enrolled in high school, the greater the prospect that there will be male youths available for recruitment into rebel movements. Collier summarizes his own argument: "a country with large natural resources, many young men, and little education is very much at risk of conflict."[23]

Unfortunately, the picture painted by Collier is done in rather broad-brushed strokes. These ideas can, in fact, be applied to various degrees to many postcolonial African countries. His argument fails to explain why and how some of the countries with the proxies he identifies manage to avoid conflict while others fall victim to war. Collier's picture is also static, and lacks any sense of the underlying political dynamics that actually drive countries possessing these proxies toward conflict. What emerges in this formulation is an eclectic assemblage of "causal factors," often with little obvious or rational linkage between them and little grasp of the processes that actually work to produce (or avert) conflict. This is surely the result of relying excessively on formal statistical tools uninformed by a sense of political analysis.

It is probably unnecessary to repeat the incisive and devastating critiques that have been leveled against the conceptual basis of rational choice arguments in general and the Collier variant in particular.[24] Thandika Mkandawire has criticized the approach for its lack of "process," in other words, its elementary failure to undertake the empirical research necessary to determine if participants in rebellions made choices in the way depicted by the model. Mkandawire is critical of what he calls "stylized facts" that are marshaled selectively to fit these arguments. He cites two reasons for the methodological flaws inherent in the way such arguments are presented. First, most of the "evidence" used to support such arguments is obviously anecdotal, and is often employed to support predetermined aims or conclusions. Second, such analysts lack independent evidence of the preferences of the individuals and groups in question. Where terrible crimes have been committed, it often serves specific purposes to rationalize such actions at a certain point in time, since self-serving ex post facto explanations of rebel groups can rarely be taken at face value. Mkandawire suggests that even if "income derivation" is the driving motive for insurgencies, the "reward" for participating in acts of violence cannot be seen narrowly in financial or material terms, but may also be psychic in character.

On a more empirical level, one can also raise the objection that "resources" (as this literature has defined them) have featured in only a minority of African conflicts. There have been conflicts where such resources have played little role, for example in Chad and Ethiopia, or where resources were not a key factor in generating the conflict, but became more important as the conflict progressed, for example in Angola, Sudan, and Afghanistan. In other words, resources did not necessarily *cause* conflicts in these situations, but almost certainly contributed to their intensification and sustenance. Situations in which resources have been salient to conflict—for example in Rwanda and Somalia—are of a different order than the types postulated in this literature. The only conflicts in which resources appear to have featured from the start are those that erupted in the post–Cold War era, namely in Liberia, Sierra Leone, and in some respects the DRC. But even in these cases, there is scope for legitimate argument about the actual role of resources vis-à-vis other factors. This may not completely undermine rational choice frameworks, but it does suggest that these concepts, at best, fit some conflicts better than others.

As even a casual acquaintance with these conflicts suggests, "resources" are only a part—even if a crucial part—of a much more complex structure of causation. These conflicts are often intertwined with issues of political and economic marginalization, as well as social exclusion, identity, and citizenship. Nor is there any reason why greed and grievance cannot both be key factors in explaining these conflicts. To dismiss grievance as blithely as Collier does requires an almost breathtaking insensitivity to, or ignorance of, the existential pressures to which Africans have been subjected in the last four decades of independent statehood. The result is a thesis that is crudely and unnecessarily reductionist and ahistorical.[25] In protracted conflicts, it becomes increasingly difficult to disentangle the complex and shifting motivations that become embedded in them. In a similar vein, it is not easy to attribute a single or consistent set of motivations to the various actors at different stages of conflicts. As conflicts unfold and mutate, so do the motivations and relationships underpinning them. Monocausal explanations of conflicts may be deceptively attractive or persuasive due to their apparent simplicity, but they are ultimately unhelpful. Conflicts must be understood on the basis of multiple and complex causes. Each conflict is unique, varying in its specific dynamics and trajectory. Analyzing conflicts therefore demands a more nuanced, multidisciplinary, and dynamic approach.

The growing role of resources in conflicts—surely a global rather than simply "African" problem—and in the politics of rebel movements does not stem simply from greed. Though greed cannot be discounted, strategic necessity—relating to the shifting geopolitical environment after the Cold War and the subsequent transformation of war—can also be a critical factor. War demands resources that in the past could largely be secured from external patrons with their own geopolitical agendas. As foreign powers redefined their strategic agendas in the post–Cold War era, and as African governments and rebels could no longer play off East against West following the disintegration of the Soviet Union by 1991, such external support dried up. Rebel movements, irrespective of their political orientation and methodology, have had no choice but to fall back on their own devices. They have resorted to the exploitation of local resources including illicit taxes, drugs, mining, and lumber exports. Not only has this logic driven more recent conflicts, but it is also evident in the mutation of "old" into "new" conflicts. It is not rare for illicit resource extraction (and even criminal activity)—initially rationalized in terms of its service to the "struggle"— to become an end in itself, as appears to be the case in Afghanistan, Colombia, and Yugoslavia. In some instances, movements have progressed from offering "protection" to the drug trade to becoming drug dealers themselves.

Privileging the struggle over resources in explaining conflicts serves a number of useful functions. First, it allows conflict theories to be aligned with an existing rational choice–driven paradigm of human and economic behavior favored by the World Bank and many neoliberal Western economists. Second, it provides comfort that some "rationality"—in a very Western idiom—can be discerned beneath the otherwise baffling violence witnessed in many of these wars. Third, this approach furnishes a tangible basis for international actions such as initiatives against "conflict diamonds" that admittedly would not be possible if conflicts were simply ascribed to some "primordial African culture." As David Keen, probably one of the most prolific writers in this genre, has put it:

> The task of reviving the analysis of war from a political and economic perspective is all the more urgent since the portrayal of war as chaos and "sheer madness" seems to play a part in paralysing international response. If the portrayal of war as chaos suggests that "nothing can be done," then it could follow that no structured intervention can be made. This may sometimes serve as a convenient excuse for international inaction.[26]

This is a good example of how policy-interested outcomes may shape the intellectual agenda and the way and manner in which conflict is understood. Alex de Waal has drawn attention to this problem, pointing in particular to the fact that

> the debates on conflict and humanitarianism in Africa have been dominated by concepts and discourses that originate in Europe and North America. It is not too strong to speak of an "ideology" of conflict resolution, humanitarianism, and governance that is "owned" by international institutions, western governments, and their associated think-tanks and universities. Despite lip-service to the need for African "partnership," and even "ownership" of these discourses, the reality remains that the African input has been disappointingly modest.[27]

In de Waal's opinion, "the challenge for an African input into international doctrines and practices of peace and security, and humanitarian action, has never been greater."[28] To understand the basis and origins of conflict, however, one has to go beyond the fixation with "resources" and the rationalization of violence to fit current Western paradigms. A proper analysis of conflict must surely begin with the dramatically increased fragility of states in West Africa *as a whole,* their vulnerability to conflicts during the 1980s and 1990s, and the growing inclination or willingness of citizens to challenge power holders, if necessary by resort to arms. In essence, there has been a convergence of two negative developments at the level of both "high" and "low" politics. From above, African states and peoples were subjected to much structural violence by national regimes as well as market conditions and international financial institutions. From below, these states and regimes increasingly came unstuck, and with the end of the Cold War became more open to "radical" challenges. To explain conflicts in Africa then, a framework that simultaneously captures the "top" and "bottom" elements in the conflict nexus is required.

The 1980s laid the silent basis for the complex humanitarian emergencies of the 1990s in several key respects.[29] Severe economic and fiscal compression and adjustment shocks eroded the political legitimacy and institutional capacity of states, destroying the social safety nets and survival mechanisms of many populations. African states were subjected to multiple sources of pressure that eroded their sovereignty. From above, international financial institutions and a variety of donor agencies co-opted crucial areas of policy initiatives. From below, civil society activists became more activist and nongovernmental organizations came increasingly to command more power and resources (see Chapter 12). The state also lost some of its centrality and credibility as its resources and capacity to deliver essential services contracted. This impaired the ability of many governments to act as centers of social cohesion, and negatively affected their legitimacy and inclusiveness. Finally, state militarism, so widespread in certain regions of Africa in the 1980s, laid the foundation for the more deadly new "militarisms" and conflicts of the 1990s. This phenomenon dislocated fragile economies, inhibited accountable governance, hollowed out state institutions—particularly in the security sector itself—implanted a culture of violence, and discouraged peaceful conflict resolution and reform processes. Hence, by the end of the 1980s, states and political authorities in West Africa and much of the rest of Africa faced a pervasive crisis of "hegemony" and "stateness." The hallmarks of this crisis were sharply diminished control over resources, institutional debilitation, and loss of legitimacy, precipitated in part by prolonged mismanagement and in part by cutbacks and deficit reduction and liberalization. This reduced the capacity of the state to respond to grievances (particularly socioeconomic ones) and to pursue traditional incorporative strategies.[30]

The 1990s further redefined the nature of both politics and conflicts in Africa, introducing an essentially new equation. There are three salient dimensions to this new equation. First, shifts in global and regional geopolitical power relations, in particular the end of the Cold War and the withdrawal of superpower support to local proxies, allowed former client regimes to be challenged in ways that were unimaginable in the past. Second, the increased availability and privatization of the instruments of violence transformed the military balance between state and society.[31] This trend was due to two main factors: massive retrenchment and a growing surplus of military assets occurring simultaneously with a breakdown in supply-side and demand-side controls on global arms markets; and local recycling of decommissioned weapons as most of the wars of the 1980s wound down. The third dimension of the post–Cold War environment is the particularistic new forms of consciousness and identity, often structured around religion and ethnicity, that replaced the extant "universalistic" debates between capitalism and socialism that had underpinned the Cold War era. This development reinforced the erosion of a sense of common citizenship fostered by state contraction and popular disillusionment with politics. These trends conspired to fuel the shift from the coups d'état that had characterized West African politics up to the 1980s to the broad-based and increasingly common conflicts of the 1990s in which states and nonstate formations became the main antagonists.

If the 1960s and 1970s marked the consolidation of authoritarian dispensations in Africa, the 1980s marked their unraveling, while the 1990s was the decade of subaltern revolt. However, this analysis still does not answer the question posed earlier: Why did conflicts break out in some countries but not in others? The key to explaining violent conflicts must be sought primarily (though by no means exclusively) in specific local dynamics and responses on the part of communities and states to the crisis conditions that emerged in Africa in the 1980s and 1990s. The common element in the "new" conflicts is that they have manifested themselves primarily in African countries that are undergoing rapid political transitions and/or experiencing deep-seated political challenges to entrenched regimes, having been hollowed out by a previous history of militarization and authoritarianism. The emergence of violent conflicts in Africa has often been tied to contestations over political power and struggles to redefine political space and the associated breakdown—even deliberate erosion—of political institutions and conflict management structures and processes.[32]

The first key to understanding conflict in Africa may lie in identifying the particular patterns and processes of politicization of subaltern and oppositional groups that tend to differ from country to country (see Chapter 8). Conflict is contextual and process-driven. A "process approach" to understanding conflict privileges the conscious political choices that people and groups make and derive its rationality from a particular context. These choices, far from being random, reflect the particular social realities and psychological disposition of these actors, including a previous history of violence, collective memories, the nature of power relations, the strength of civil societies, and the depth of political cultures. A precursor to violent conflict is often the development—if not an embedded history—of exclusionary and antagonistic forms of consciousness, interlocking in a variety of ways with state repression.[33]

Africa's experience in the 1970 and 1980s with the authoritarian closure of political space and debate, the contraction of the state, the erosion of social safety nets, and the disillusionment with the postcolonial state and citizenship favored the emergence of localized and particularistic identities. The forms of opposition ("civil society" as well as political parties) that arose from this situation were, as a rule, fragmented and particularistic in outlook, with shallow roots and limited democratic and coalition-building experience. In addition, democracy movements were primarily urban and elite-driven, with limited appeal to the rural masses.[34] Nevertheless, there were crucial differences in the way in which these forces played themselves out in individual countries, giving specificity and situational rationality to the politics and choices of oppositional groups, including rebel factions. An example of sensitivity to the role of such localized microprocesses in generating conflict is the fascinating analysis by Ibrahim Abdullah and his colleagues of youth politics in Sierra Leone. This analysis sought to explain the cultural and political dynamics that not only conditioned the response of Sierra Leonean youth to the unfolding crisis in their country, but also differentiated their politics from those of youth in the somewhat similar conditions of Ghana and Nigeria.[35] According to Abdullah and his colleagues, in contrast to youth politics in Ghana and Nigeria, where various forms of Marxism were more in vogue, the ideological response of Sierra Leone's educated but unemployed youth took the form of a lumpen culture. This culture, reflecting a mixture of reggae and ganja, elements of Qaddafi's *Green Book,* and rather abstract pan-Africanist notions, led these youth ultimately in the direction of rebellion through the Revolutionary United Front (RUF).

Many of the alternative explanations of conflicts focusing on a bottom-up view, while not unmindful of the role of resources in fueling West Africa's wars, have placed much greater emphasis on the psychological, cultural, and ideological mechanisms that bind or alienate youth and other critical groups from the community and from authority figures. These mechanisms foreclose a sense of hope in the future. Hence, Jennifer Leaning and Sam Arie have suggested that, in explaining why conflicts erupt in some societies but not in others, we need to understand the sources of vulnerability or resilience in particular societies. For a society to be resilient, these authors argue that it need not be rich: "Instead, what is required is a core bundle of basic resources—material, psychological and social—which together ensure a minimum level of survival." The authors suggest that "individuals and communities have greater resilience when their core attachments to home, community and the future remain intact." When these attachments are undone, individuals may turn to other sources of participation, recognition, and empowerment, usually identity groups established around race, religion, geography, or age and characterized by an aggressive stance toward established institutions and practices. Leaning and Arie implicitly criticize the developmentalist thrust of many "human security" proponents, as well as the "resources" argument of the "political economy of violence" school. In their view, a narrow focus on material resources has prevented analysts from identifying the true sources of vulnerability or resilience in a society.[36]

In a similar vein, Angela McIntyre, Kwesi Aning, and Prosper Addo have proposed the concept of "constructive social incentives":

> those elements within a society that contribute to stability, and orderly, as opposed to violent, social change. They constitute the broad range of elements that shape people's choices, including those of youth. The erosion of incentives can be brought about by warfare, taking the form of disintegration of family and community cohesion, educational and economic opportunities; narrowing the available choices and survival strategies and ultimately, the protected social spaces afforded to young people for growth and development.[37]

And when this happens—as occurred in Sierra Leone—youth may be attracted to "destructive social incentives," which may include rebellion and violence against their own community.[38] These ideas locate conflict in deprivation from a wide range of valued goods, not only material, but also psychic, cultural, and so on. The second trigger mechanism of conflict—the top-down perspective—can be located in the pattern of state responses to these oppositional or subaltern challenges. Such responses have varied, as have the political systems to which demands for change have been directed. Some of these polities have been scarred by a history of violence and institutionalized discrimination, while others have been characterized (even within the context of a single-party or party-dominant system, such as in Senegal or Tanzania) by a tradition of accommodative politics. It is crucial to political outcomes whether leaders such as Mali's Alpha Konaré and South Africa's Nelson Mandela have responded with conciliatory gestures and encouragement of "good governance" and inclusiveness or, as is more often the case, with a strategy of state terror. Kalevi Holsti has identified state-sponsored terror—"politicide"—disbursed by a wide range of formal and informal instruments, as the trigger mechanism in many cases of catastrophic conflict.[39] The behavior of security forces has often been crucial in determining whether or not the struggle for a new political order degenerated into violent conflict.

However, brutal repression has not, by itself, necessarily triggered catastrophic conflict—as illustrated by the cases of Togo and the "dead cities" campaign in Cameroon—any more than a determined campaign by civil society has necessarily succeeded in dislodging recalcitrant regimes, as evidenced by the case of General Sani Abacha's Nigeria between 1993 and 1998. Where the state continues to be relatively strong or effectively repressive, as in the examples of Nigeria and Kenya in the 1990s, it may be possible for governments to escape the immediate consequences of such repression, possibly buying the regime more time to impose its own "settlement"—to coin a term popularized by the Nigerian opposition. While contested transitions have often led to violent conflicts, such crises have a real possibility of occurring in democratic transitions, even in more apparently stable countries, particularly under the conditions of profound state weakness that have characterized many parts of Africa.

The Genealogy of Conflict in West Africa

It is necessary to avoid exaggerating the role of resources in conflicts and the excessive generalization of the nature of "resource conflicts." Different types of resources and resource-extraction regimes are associated with different types of politics and patterns of conflict. Some types of local resource-driven conflicts, for example those involving "survival assets" such as grazing or farming land and water resources, have received less attention in the academic literature, presumably because they lack the glamour of diamonds and other internationally traded resources. However, as the recent case of Nigeria has demonstrated, such local resource conflicts coexist with the more celebrated conflicts over "precious resources," and many West African conflicts have as a result been transformed in scope and lethality.

The cases of Liberia, Sierra Leone, and Nigeria's oil-rich Niger Delta present different forms and settings of resource conflicts in West Africa. Though these three cases should be seen as representing particular trajectories of struggle and responses to state repression and decay, they nevertheless share certain common characteristics. While neither Liberia nor Sierra Leone may conform to the argument that current violent conflicts have a previous history of conflict, both countries do share with Nigeria a *political* history of bad governance, virtual one-party statism and/or military rule, and mismanagement of key resource industries. Furthermore, these conflicts were preceded by popular struggles that undermined sitting regimes that were subsequently preempted by a process of militarization. Samuel Doe's coup in Liberia in April 1980, Valentine Strasser's putsch in April 1992, and Sani Abacha's seizure of power in November 1993 all attest to this point (see Chapter 7). West Africa's new military "proconsuls" faced subaltern armed revolts, even as other actors increasingly stepped in to challenge the ability of the state to exercise its authority. Regime resistance to legitimate struggles for change by civil society opened the door to more radical and destructive attacks on the state by warlords, revolutionaries, as well as legitimately aggrieved movements. Civil-political struggles, however, persisted in the shadow of armed conflicts and provided a countertrend, challenging the culture of militarization and weaponization in West Africa. This dialectic also challenged fashionable depictions of conflicts in these countries as unrelieved cases of unedifying brutality that could be salvaged only by external intervention.

Another overarching theme is the extent to which these conflicts have seen the intertwining of youth, ethnicity, and resources. Paul Collier's thesis, and much recent writing, converge on the analysis of the politics of youth as a critical opposition group and key ingredient in these conflicts. "Youth politics," however, is seen in much of this literature as both homogeneous and debased. While Collier is right to identify the preeminent role of youth in driving conflicts, there is no hint in his analysis of the heterogeneity of this social stratum and of its politics. "Youth" is socially determined, and who or what constitutes it differs, to some degree, according to one's culture and society. While youth politics embodies certain universal traits or tendencies, they are also contextual. Though much emphasis is often placed on the agency and autonomy of youth as political actors, they are also open to manipulation by other groups in society (see Chapter 11).

All across West Africa, the marginalization of youth is painfully evident. Alienation caused by frustrated aspirations, collapsing mobility structures, and damaged family and community social safety nets has led the subregion's youth to seek radical alternatives. These radical alternatives have manifested themselves in the forms of new fundamentalist and revivalist religious movements (Christian and Muslim), cultural identities (Rastafari and "hip-hop"), and revolutionary and populist ideas. This phenomenon has spawned different types of religious sects, gangs, and "revolutionary" political factions. Both the National Patriotic Front of Liberia (NPFL) and the RUF were initially able to attract youth through populistic rhetoric, much of which was patterned on the language of "revolutionary regimes" in other parts of Africa like Ghana, Burkina Faso, and Libya. The globalization of Hollywood imagery, with its hypermasculine and ultra-violent "Rambo" culture, has also insidiously impacted West African youth and intersected with these "revolutionary" adventures, as clearly evidenced by the cases of Liberia and Sierra Leone.

Ultimately, the impact of different competing ideas and beliefs on youth depends on the strength and coherence of community ties at the social level; at the political level, it depends on the success of regimes such as those of Jerry Rawlings in Ghana and Thomas Sankara in Burkina Faso to invent new modes of political incorporation of youth. The critical factor to understanding this phenomenon is therefore not the abstract properties of youth, but the nature of the alternative oppositional discourse or organizational forms that arise to "interpellate" and incorporate this mobilized section of the population. "Ethnicity," though present in all three case studies—Liberia, Sierra Leone, and Nigeria—that we next examine, has played rather different roles in each case. However, in none of the cases can ethnicity be regarded as the primary cause of conflict. Ethnicity has been deployed instrumentally, mobilized by marginalized populations as a means of protesting conditions of deprivation (as in the Niger Delta); employed by leaders to try to rally and protect a shrinking power base, as well as to repress opposition (as in Samuel Doe's Liberia); or used as an instrument in interfactional conflicts. In Liberia, Taylor's efforts at building a "pan–West African" rebel force incorporating many non-Liberian fighters were belied by the ethnic polarization of Liberian politics and the organization of rebel movements during the civil war. In Sierra Leone's civil war, on the other hand, issues of ethnicity were relatively marginal.

Finally, these conflicts need to be related to emergent forms of post–Cold War interstate relations in West Africa, with the phenomenon of crisis-ridden states like Nigeria and Senegal attempting to salvage even more crisis-ridden neighbors. Many inescapable ironies are associated with this development—the supreme expression being General Abacha's Nigeria, with its internal conflicts and viciously authoritarian government under international sanctions for human rights abuses, intervening militarily to suppress civil conflicts in Liberia and Sierra Leone, and even restoring democratic rule to Sierra Leone in 1998 (see Chapters 13 and 14).

Our approach assumes that some level of rationality underlies and informs the actions of diverse groups, however reprehensible these actions may seem to distant observers. This rationality may not exclude economic motivations, but cannot be adequately understood within a solely economic prism. Grievance has been an undeniable and persistent feature in these conflicts, whether they remain precariously within the confines of the state (as in the case of the Niger Delta) or assume the status of a full-blown rebellion to contest the power of, and indeed to displace, the state (as in Liberia and Sierra Leone). A discussion of the specific characteristics and dynamics of these conflicts is thus essential in order to situate the rationales of the major protagonists in these conflicts within a specific nexus. Such an approach allows us to appreciate the interests of the diverse factions, their capabilities, and the motivations driving their actions. It also provides us with useful insights into the diversity of functions that violence serves, particularly in politically fragile, ethnically divided, and economically weak states like Liberia, Sierra Leone, and Nigeria. Through this analysis, we also hope to contribute to demystifying some perceptions of wars in Africa as intrinsically unjustified, irrational, and dysfunctional. We will briefly assess the political economy of the conflicts in Liberia, Sierra Leone, and

Nigeria's Niger Delta, before briefly examining the apparently exceptional case of Ghana.

The Political Economy of Civil War in Liberia and Sierra Leone

The struggle to control resources to sustain the state and state elites has a particularly long and poignant, if not tragic, history in Liberia, related to the peculiar origins of the state and the patterns of dependency woven into its fabric from the very beginning. Different Liberian administrations, from William Tubman (1944–1971) to William Tolbert (1971–1980) to Samuel Doe (1980–1989) to Charles Taylor (1997–2003), managed, or more appropriately, controlled "reforms" to acquire new resources. In Chapter 8, Ibrahim Abdullah and Ismail Rashid trace the roots of the Americo-Liberian oligarchy's use of the True Whig Party to maintain political hegemony over the indigenous majority population, culminating in Samuel Doe's 1980 coup and his own subsequent manipulation of the political system in favor of his ethnic Krahn and Mandingo allies. Taylor perpetuated this trend by using security forces dominated by Gio and Mano fighters to maintain a ruling clique in power. Abdullah and Rashid also trace the roots of state decay in Sierra Leone. Since these issues are covered in more detail elsewhere in this book, we will focus in this brief section on some of the economic agendas of Liberia's factions during the civil war of 1989 to 1997, and on the political economy of Sierra Leone's civil war between 1991 and 2000.

During Liberia's civil war, Charles Taylor's NPFL was able to exploit the country's resources, while simultaneously having access to strategic communication lines. Nimba county, the launching stage for the NPFL's march toward Monrovia, was rich in iron ore and shared a contiguous border with Côte d'Ivoire, which provided consistent political and military support to Taylor. Nimba was also linked by rail to Buchanan, Liberia's second major port for exports and arms transported from Côte d'Ivoire. Aside from the NPFL, seven other factions emerged by 1994 to prevent Taylor from taking over the country. The leaders of these factions claimed to have built their armies to defend their own ethnic groups against attacks from other armed factions. Ethnicity, however, was employed simply as a facade to camouflage political ambitions and aspirations to maintain power within a small circle of Liberia's elites. Control and access to natural resources and minerals contributed to the emergence of the different factions. Some of the heaviest fighting in Liberia occurred in areas rich in natural resources, such as Tubmanburg, Tapeta, and Bomi county.

Economic opportunities became an important factor in reproducing conflict and undermining prospects for peace in Liberia. Over time, such economic calculations came to determine the pattern of the war, and were a major factor in the failure of thirteen peace accords between 1990 and 1996. The NPFL was able to take advantage of this situation while aligning with conventional state-driven geopolitical agendas within the subregion. Large business firms domiciled in France—a historical regional rival of Nigeria—established temporary bases in Côte d'Ivoire and negotiated business deals with the NPFL in the timber trade without having to satisfy export controls and other demands.

Due to the relative success and innovativeness with which faction groups exploited natural resources and negotiated economic deals with European, North American, and Asian firms, there was a particularly opportunistic and instrumental edge to the manner in which Liberia's war was fought. By March 1991 the political economy of the war and war-related enterprises had expanded to such an extent that it involved several thousand people who had a stake in the continuation of the conflict. The unwillingness of the warlords to end the civil war thus mirrored a "rational choice" analysis of the costs and benefits of continuing the war. With control over vast territories rich in natural and mineral resources, the NPFL commenced the efficient and calculated exploitation of these abundant commodities. From this period, a lucrative export business based on diamonds, timber, iron ore, and gold was initiated with French, Belgian, Turkish, and Taiwanese firms. To circumvent the blockade that had been placed on the ports of Buchanan, Harper, and Greenville by the Economic Community of West African States (ECOWAS) Cease-Fire Monitoring Group (ECOMOG) in 1993, these products were shipped through the Ivorian port of San Pedro. Ivorian intermediaries and their French counterparts dealt directly with the NPFL in order to avoid the export controls and restrictions resulting from the embargo. The NPFL is estimated to have made $450 million from these illicit exports during the course of Liberia's war.

Like Liberia, Sierra Leone had abundant natural resources, principally diamond, gold, iron ore, rutile, and bauxite. Ethnic disputes were not unknown in the country: conflict between the Creole elite and interior "tribes" had driven colonial politics. Ethnoregional divisions had also shaped postindependence politics, and the two main parties—the Sierra Leone People's Party and the All People's Congress—derived their support primarily from the southeastern-based Mende and northern-based Temne respectively. Compared to other African countries, however, Sierra Leone was relatively free of sectarian strife. The seemingly tranquil Sierra Leonean polity, however, masked a history of militarization and consistent mismanagement of the country's mineral industry. Mineral resources were primarily exploited by foreigners, especially Lebanese, with little benefit to ordinary Sierra Leoneans. By the 1970s and 1980s the economy had plummeted as a result of unbridled corruption, centralization of power, and a variety of clientelistic practices under Siaka Stevens's regime between 1968 and 1985. The increasing privatization of state resources and the economy as a whole was graphically symbolized by the surrendering of the country's entire diamond and fishing industry to Jamil Mohammed, an Afro-Lebanese business partner and crony of Siaka Stevens.[40] Smuggling and corruption decimated the diamond industry: in 1970 the country produced 2 million carats of diamonds; by 1988 this figure had declined to 480,000 carats.

From 1992 to 1994, Valentine Strasser's regime earned praise from external donors for its rigor in pursuing a structural adjustment program, but this adulation proved to be short-lived. Before long, members of the military junta were openly involved in the diamond trade. Meanwhile the war with RUF rebels spiraled out of control, with government soldiers becoming *sobels:* soldiers by day and rebels by night. Both soldiers and rebels soon became involved in a $250 million annual diamond trade. This was the context of economic and political crisis that precipitated the increasing alienation of Sierra Leone's youth and helped to provide a fertile breeding ground for the RUF rebellion.

The Conflicts in Nigeria's Oil-Rich Niger Delta

The complex amalgam of resource politics, identity, youth, and violence has been most clearly played out in Nigeria's oil-rich Niger Delta. Like other conflicts on the continent, the one involving Niger Delta youth metamorphosed in the 1990s, graduating from the episodic, unstructured, and often unpredictable struggles of the 1970s and 1980s into one that was more broad-based and militant, political and violent, and paradoxically, more "ethnic" in its manifestations.[41] These struggles, as noted by Cyril Obi, have taken the form of "mass demonstrations, blockadings of oil installations, and national and international protests by the organized interest groups of the oil producing areas."[42] The basis of the conflict derives from the fact that, while oil from the Niger Delta provides over 80 percent of Nigeria's federal revenues and 95 percent of national exports, the states and communities that produce this oil are among the most destitute and marginalized in the entire federation. These communities have also suffered adverse effects on their livelihoods from widespread oil pollution and unregulated exploration and extraction activities. Production relations are organized in ways that disempower host communities. Legislation in 1978 and 1979 placed ownership of all land, as well as on- and offshore minerals in Nigeria, in the hands of the federal government, thus stripping local communities and states not only of access to their oil revenues, but also of any form of control over foreign oil companies and their operations. Oil and environmental matters continue to be treated as "national security" issues in Nigeria, enjoying little transparency and accountability.

An important catalyst in the troubles of the Niger Delta was the struggle of the Ogoni people under the leadership of the Movement for the Survival of the Ogoni People (MOSOP) and writer Ken Saro-Wiwa.[43] This struggle opened the door to further activism on the part of other communities in the area, and also introduced new dimensions to the struggle. MOSOP activists developed an international platform for their cause by tapping into international environmental concerns and the rights of "minority peoples." They linked these struggles with the broader national struggle for democracy and human rights against militarism and authoritarianism. However, the increase in the pace of the struggle in the late 1980s and 1990s also reflected the effects of shrinking oil revenues, the adoption of a structural adjustment program by the government of General Ibrahim Babangida in the mid-1980s, and increased economic hardships for the already marginalized Delta communities. While the activities of MOSOP brought unprecedented publicity and international attention to the suffering of these communities, they also provoked equally unprecedented repression by the state. This culminated in the hanging of Saro-Wiwa and eight of his colleagues by the regime of General Sani Abacha in November 1995. Large parts of the Niger Delta were also transformed into a militarized and heavily garrisoned area.

The Nigerian state's increasingly militaristic response to the Niger Delta crisis—a development that civilian rule under the administration of Olusegun Obasanjo since 1999 has done little to curb—has also raised serious questions over the governance and control of the country's security forces. Nigeria's security forces have shown a repeated tendency to act independently—and sometimes in clear defiance—of the civil authorities and to take extreme measures in "settling scores" with local populations whose youths have sometimes attacked or killed members of the security forces. The army massacres in Odi and Gbeji during the past four years of civilian rule are just two such examples of this trend. There have also been disturbing signs of "privatization" of security forces by oil companies like Shell, which have sometimes funded, armed, and deployed the state police, the notorious "kill and go" paramilitary mobile police, and the military to protect their operations against local militants. Youths in the Niger Delta have demonstrated an increasing willingness to resort to armed violence against these "security" agencies, using now widely available weaponry, some of which has been smuggled through the Delta's labyrinthine network of creeks and rivers. This has resulted in a succession of tit-for-tat killings. This growth of armed militancy in the Delta must be assessed against the background of the emergence of a more generalized phenomenon of private and community militia in Nigeria like the Oodua People's Congress and the Bakassi Boys, often through the sponsorship of powerful public figures and even state governors.

However, unlike the predatory images associated with RUF youth in Sierra Leone and Liberia's factions, the youth of the Niger Delta struggle as members of *communities*. They are a mix of educated and uneducated youth working together, not the "illiterates" of Paul Collier's colorful imagination. While Delta youth conform to Jennifer Learning and Sam Arie's paradigm in the sense that they are indeed alienated from the federal and local governments, they have shown much greater commitment to the cause of their local communities. At the same time, however, these youths have not hesitated to contest the meanings and traditional structures of community, often generating intense intracommunity rivalries and splits—particularly with elders—over leadership, tactics, and benefits from the area's oil wealth.[44]

These community aspirations have been articulated through declarations of self-determination and autonomous resource control, such as the Ogoni Bill of Rights, the Bill of Rights of Oron People, the Aklaka Declaration, the Urhobo Economic Summit, and the Kaiama Declaration. As Iyabo Olojede and her colleagues note: "All these declarations bear a striking similarity and signify lack of confidence in the existing federal system."[45] These groups are not yet openly "secessionist," but their declarations have begun to raise questions about the nature of Nigerian federalism and indeed of the continued existence of the nation-state itself. As Cyril Obi warns: "Within the context of Nigeria's federalism, oil has become immersed in the National Question. The oil minorities from under whose soils and waters the oil is mined and piped away are beginning to question the basis of Nigeria's federalism in a context in which they who produce oil and bear the brunt of its environmental costs are excluded from the allocation of the oil proceeds."[46]

Under a derivation principle, 13 percent of Nigeria's oil revenues should return to oil-producing areas, but these funds barely reach people on the ground. The "national question" is now being posed in other ways as well. While continuing to be overdetermined by the increasingly violent confrontations between oil communities, oil companies, and the federal government, the Niger Delta struggle has been conducted at multiple and complex levels. A key paradox of the Delta protest movements—particularly after the earlier Ogoni struggle and the murder of Ken Saro-Wiwa— is that they have attempted to transcend their local bases by building broader political platforms and constituencies through regional, national, and international alliances and campaigns. Simultaneously, the groups have generated even more intense local cleavages and increasingly violent struggles between and within the "minority" communities themselves. On the one hand, these groups have attempted to launch pan–Niger Delta movements and coalitions such as the Chikoko Movement and the Kaiama Declaration.[47] On the other, these areas have been wracked by unprecedented and protracted conflicts between "minority" communities, such as between the Ijaw, Itsekiri, and Urhobo; between the Kalabari and Okrika; and between the Ogoni and Andoni.[48] In a sense, the very success of these movements in attracting greater international and national attention may have helped to precipitate these local cleavages.

Not only is this fragmentation "rational" within these communities, but it is actually propelled by the rules of the national political game in Nigeria, in which control of the subsidiary levels of the state structure—especially the states and local government authorities—is seen as not only necessary to expressing and affirming "identity," but also critical to accessing and controlling resources at the local level. This development is also consistent with a political elite strategy that, far from seeking to build a coherent and united nation based on fair management and sharing of resources, instead replicates ethnic and community divisions in order to create "protected" fiefdoms for subelites and to demobilize and confuse subaltern interests. The politics of "state creation" (thirty-six states have now been created from Nigeria's initial three regions in 1960), whatever it may have done for broader national unity in Nigeria, has intensified cleavages between the minority communities themselves, with attacks on local oil companies and installations often going hand in hand with attacks on rival communities.

Ethnicism is also built into Nigerian oil politics at several levels. First, there is a perception that the three majority ethnic groups—the Hausa-Fulani, the Yoruba, and the Igbo—are benefiting from oil at the expense of the oil communities due to their control of, and greater representation within, the federal government, as well as their dominance of jobs within the oil industry. Such jobs are seen by many people within oil-producing communities as rightly belonging to "indigenes." For many members of these communities, "there appear[s] no justifiable reason why an area that produces so much wealth for the nation wallows in abject poverty or scarcity of resources while other parts of the country without oil resources are developed."[49] Second, the oil communities are in rivalry with each other for the perceived largesse of oil company development funds. Some have done conspicuously better than others in accessing these funds. The solution to these problems is seen by many Delta communities partly in greater political representation and "ownership" of their own state. This has been made possible through progressive rounds of state creation since 1967. "Statehood" has often led to greater political representation and increased access to federal resources. However, state creation has also often brought local communities directly into conflict with other "minority" communities with similar aspirations. The logic of state multiplication in Nigeria has thus produced increasingly unviable microstates and, far from facilitating national unity by bringing ethnicity into alignment with political representation, merely spurred further exclusionary and politicized microidentities.

In the final analysis, the grassroots movements of the Niger Delta seem to have had only limited success in breaking out of the regional confines of their struggle to create and sustain broader political alliances across Nigeria. This is perhaps not surprising given the fact that Nigeria's dominant regions have little incentive in reforming a fiscal system that benefits them so profitably vis-à-vis oil-producing communities. Ironically, the failure of Delta communities to align with wider national movements in Nigeria has been exacerbated by the multiplication of theaters of protest and struggle unleashed by the transition to democratic government in 1999, as well as the growing state of endemic disorder and ungovernability across Nigeria. This has shifted some of the focus from the grievances of the peoples of the Niger Delta.

Finally, the Delta case also suggests a need to interrogate and qualify dominant definitions of "internal war."[50] The case of Nigeria proves the existence of many forms of low-intensity conflicts across West Africa that, under a different set of indices, could well qualify as internal war. Such wars can be confined to a specific region, while the rest of the state continues to function normally and even enjoy a high degree of legitimacy, as is also the case with Senegal and its long-running Casamance crisis. These struggles may also take the form of conflicts that may simmer and erupt sporadically over several decades—such as the conflict in northern Ghana—or of high levels of open and endemic religious and criminal violence, such as armed robbery and religious riots in parts of Nigeria. These "wars" can also indicate the existence of "no go" areas such as northern Chad. In the case of Nigeria, one must consider the growing attraction of secret cults and militia among Nigerian youth, and the possibility that, in the context of the spiraling violence and multifaceted conflicts in the Niger Delta and elsewhere, these may emerge as functional parallels to the rebel movements in Liberia and Sierra Leone. However, conflicts such as those in the Delta differ from the formal definition of "internal war" and hence do not fall under the purview of the ECOWAS security mechanism in spite of the extensive human rights abuses often generated by them.

The Ghanaian Sphinx

Is conflict irreversible in the context of misgovernance, state decay, and economic implosion, as these case studies of Liberia, Sierra Leone, and the Niger Delta, as well as many other examples in the subregion, would seem to imply? The example of Ghana suggests that this is not necessarily the case.[51] Ghana has greatly influenced subregional conflicts at two very different levels. On the one hand, Jerry Rawlings's coup of 1981 inspired similar "radical" subaltern coups in Liberia (1980), Sierra Leone (1992), and Gambia (1994), and contributed to shaping the rhetoric of the NPFL and the RUF. On the other hand, Ghana was the second largest contributor to the two ECOMOG missions in Liberia and Sierra Leone, sent troops to the ECOWAS force in Côte d'Ivoire, and played a leading role in sub-regional mediation efforts. Yet remarkably, Ghana—once dubbed "the sick man of West Africa" during the inept military era of the 1970s—traveled on a different trajectory than most of its neighbors.

Between 1983 and 2000, far-reaching macroeconomic reforms were undertaken by a "patriotic" regime that was not afraid to cut deep into the political rot, combat corruption, and reorganize the public sector and security institutions. These reforms were largely successful in restoring order to the economy, regaining resource control, and breaking the recurring cycle of militarism. This eventually led to elections in 1992 and 1996, which Rawlings won, and then to a transition to formal democracy, authenticated by the victory of the opposition New Patriotic Party in December 2000. It has been argued that Ghana's transformation from the corruption of the 1970s requires explanation at not one but three levels. First, the state experienced improved governance and better management of resources. Second, the strength and resilience of community and social networks in Ghana meant that the progressive weakening of the state did not imply complete collapse, but was counterbalanced by the emergence of alternative centers of social cohesion.[52] Third, the quality and relative maturity of Ghanaian civil society meant that the struggle against militarism not only strengthened civil society, but also galvanized it around a largely ideological politics that counterposed liberal constitutionalism and Marxism, rather than ethnicity and religion.

However, a key part of this riddle also lay in the response of the Ghanaian state, in contrast to that of Sierra Leone and Nigeria, to the challenge of the economic and political marginalization of youths. Rawlings's initial support, particularly on the ideological "left," derived preponderantly from Ghanaian youth who were incorporated into his civil defense committees. Within these committees, youths challenged the power of rural chiefs and urban bureaucrats, and even after these bodies were de-emphasized the regime continued to reflect its youthful origins. While the state took aggressive and largely successful steps to recapture control over its resources, the attempt of youths to challenge the state for access to mineral resources through *galhamse* (illegal gold mining) was deflected by the 1989 Small-Scale Gold-Mining Law. The law legitimized *galhamse* operators, allowing them to work through the Precious Minerals Marketing Corporation, and provided marketing and other support to small-scale miners. During the first two years of the operation of this initiative, licenses were granted to organizations representing over 15,000 small-scale miners. Purchases from these small-scale miners went from zero in 1988 to $18.4 million in 1998 for gold and $11.2 million for diamonds.[53] The question was not whether these reforms were unambiguously successful—they were clearly not— but whether they were successful enough to make a crucial difference in creating jobs for youths and offering them alternatives to rebellion against the state.

Learning Lessons

This analysis suggests five key lessons, which we will briefly discuss in concluding this chapter. First, conflicts in West Africa tend to have multiple causes, but the most important single cause is poor governance over a sustained period coupled with frustrated aspirations for political change, often occurring in a context of profound state debilitation. In the longer view, violent struggles for control of resources in these weak economies should be seen to result from conflict at least as much as they cause it. To challenge the state is to challenge state control over resources, and vice versa. State mismanagement of resources, such as minerals in Sierra Leone and Liberia and oil in Nigeria, has given rise to persistent and long-term conflicts over distributional issues. While resource control has been central to postcolonial state formation and politics in Africa, it is important to note that "resource conflicts" were initially played out at the level of politics. The main intellectual and policy challenge today is to understand the violent turn of resource politics in the 1990s, a development that we associate preeminently not with resources themselves, but with the destruction of political institutions and processes on the continent. It is this degradation of politics, which mediates or should mediate the way that resources are distributed, that requires explanation, not resources themselves.

Second, we have learned again and again that continued repression in situations of state weakness is counterproductive. It is usually better to maneuver a political opening, change course, or yield power altogether. This may prove embarrassing and even traumatic in the short term, but can actually yield long-term benefits. The growing number of former West African military leaders who have stepped graciously aside and were subsequently elected to power in a free vote—Nigeria's Olusegun Obasanjo, Benin's Matthieu Kérékou, and Mali's Amadou Touré—are living testimony that such an outcome is possible. A fundamental tenet of international relations theory is that military weakness is an open invitation to attack by rival powers. Today, the idea that military weakness is equally an invitation to attack by domestic nonstate insurgents must be added. Third, analyses of the political economy of conflicts in Africa must stress the critical importance of proper security sector governance, in terms of both accountability and operational effectiveness and reform. The conduct of the security sector, including its repressive capability, has made a crucial difference to whether a country is plunged even further into conflict, or whether conflict is averted and controlled. The failure to reform Taylor's security forces after elections in Liberia in 1997 saw the country's subsequent descent into conflict within two years—perhaps the most obvious recent example. Fourth, as we have briefly tried to demonstrate with the case of Ghana, broader reforms through skillful political management can help to avert conflict, particularly if economic and political reforms can be successfully articulated and implemented.

Finally, ECOWAS's security mechanism of 1999 faces many challenges, including those of funding, capacity, and political will. However, its core problem is the conflicting geopolitical agendas of a variety of subregional actors, primarily West African leaders themselves. Unless West African states and leaders make their legitimate geopolitical objectives more transparent, and show greater candor in addressing this problem, ECOWAS members will continue to work at cross-purposes with each other.

Notes

1. Mats Berdal and David M. Malone, eds., *Greed and Grievance: Economic Agendas in Civil Wars* (Boulder: Lynne Rienner, 2000).

2. Oliver Furley, "Introduction: Africa—The Habit of Conflict," in Oliver Furley, ed., *Conflict in Africa* (London: I. B. Tauris, 1995), pp. 1–18.

3. Jean-François Bayart, Stephen Ellis, and Beatrice Hibou, *The Criminalization of the State in Africa* (Oxford: James Currey, 1998).

4. Jean-François Bayart, *The State in Africa: The Politics of the Belly* (London: Longman, 1993).

5. One of the most influential articles of this genre is Robert Kaplan, "The Coming Anarchy," *Atlantic Monthly* 271, no. 2 (February 1994): 44–76. For a similar perspective, see David Rieff, "In Defense of Afro-Pessimism," *World Policy Journal* 15, no. 4 (Winter 1998–1999): 10–22. Several books are now being published in rebuttal of these perspectives; see, for example, William Makgoba, ed., *African Renaissance* (Cape Town: Tafelberg, 1999).

6. Stephen Ellis, *The Mask of Anarchy: The Destruction of Liberia and the Religious Dimensions of an African Civil War* (London: Hurst, 1999). The term "warlordism" has been used variously to refer to all sorts of rebel activities. For more sophisticated analysis of this phenomenon, see J. A. G. Roberts, "Warlordism in China," *Review of African Political Economy* 16, nos. 45–46 (Summer 1989): 26–34; Roger Charlton and Roy May, "Warlords and Militarism in China," *Review of African Political Economy* 16, nos. 45–46 (Summer 1989): 12–26; and Colin Darch, "Are There Warlords in Mozambique?" *Review of African Political Economy* 16, nos. 45–46 (Summer 1989): 34–50. See also Edward McLord, "Warlords Against Warlordism: The Politics of Anti-Militarism in Early Twentieth-Century China," *Modern Asian Studies* 30, no. 4 (October 1996): 795–827; and Paul B.

Rich, "Warlords, State Fragmentation, and the Dilemma of Humanitarian Intervention," *Small Wars and Insurgencies* 10, no. 1 (Spring 1999): 78–96.

7. Patrick Chabal and Jean-Pascal Daloz, *Africa Works: Disorder as Political Instrument* (London: James Currey, 1999).

8. Richard Dowden, "The Heart of the Matter," *The Economist,* 13–19 May 2000, pp. 23–25.

9. Julius Ihonvbere and Terisa Turner, "Africa in the Post Communist Era: Constraints, Pressures, and Prospects for the Twenty-First Century," *Round Table* no. 328 (October 1993): 443–460.

10. Edward E. Rice, *Wars of the Third Kind: Conflict in Underdeveloped Countries* (Berkeley: University of California Press, 1988). See also Michael Ignatieff, *Blood and Belonging: Journeys into the New Nationalism* (Toronto: Penguin Books, 1993); Russell Hardin, *One for All: The Logic of Group Conflict* (Princeton: Princeton University Press, 1995); John Mackinlay, "War Lords," *RUSI Journal* 143, no. 2 (April 1998): 24 ff.; Kalevi K. Holsti, *The State, War, and the State of War* (Cambridge: Cambridge University Press 1996), pp. 123–140; and Donald M. Snow, *Uncivil Wars: International Security and the New Internal Conflicts* (Boulder: Lynne Rienner, 1996), pp. 1–2.

11. Yusuf Bangura, "Understanding the Political and Cultural Dimensions of the Sierra Leone War: A Critique of Paul Richards's *Fighting for the Rainforest,*" in Ibrahim Abdullah and Yusuf Bangura, eds., *African Development* 22, nos. 2–3 (1997): 117–148 (Special Issue: "Youth Culture and Political Violence: The Sierra Leone Civil War"). On economic agendas, see David Keen, *The Economic Functions of Violence in Civil Wars,* Adelphi Paper no. 320 (Oxford: Oxford University Press, 1998); and David Keen, "Crime and Access to Resources," in E. Wayne Nafziger, Frances Stewart, and Raimo Väyrynen, eds., *War, Hunger, and Displacement: The Origins of Humanitarian Emergencies* (Oxford: Oxford University Press, 2000), pp. 283–304.

12. Donald M. Snow, *Uncivil Wars* (Boulder: Lynne Rienner, 1996), p. 1.

13. Michael Bratton and N. van de Walle, "Neopatrimonial Regimes and Political Transitions in Africa," in Peter Lewis, ed., *Africa: The Dilemmas of Development and Change* (Boulder: Westview Press, 1998), pp. 273–309.

14. Chabal and Daloz, *Africa Works.*

15. In this respect, these arguments seem to amount to little more than an extension of the "neopatrimonialism" thesis to oppositional or rebel politics that are seen to share the amoral politics of the state. Like indiscriminate charges of "terrorism," these can have the effect, intended or not, of delegitimizing even struggles in pursuit of genuine causes.

16. Chris Allen, "Understanding African Politics," *Review of African Political Economy* 22, no. 65 (September 1995): 301–320.

17. David Keen, "A Rational Kind of Madness," *Oxford Development Studies* 25, no. 1 (1997): 67–75.

18. Adam Hochschild, "Chaos in Congo Suits Many Parties Just Fine," *New York Times,* 20 April 2003, p. A3.

19. Paul Collier, "Doing Well out of War: An Economic Perspective," in Berdal and Malone, *Greed and Grievance,* pp. 91–111; and Paul Collier and Anke Hoeffler, "Justice-Seeking and Loot-Seeking in Civil War" (Washington, D.C.: Development Economics Research Group, World Bank, February 1999), mimeo.

20. Collier, "Doing Well out of War," p. 91.

21. Ibid., p. 93.

22. Ibid., p. 92.

23. Ibid., p. 97.

24. See in particular Thandika Mkandawire, "The Terrible Toll of Post-Colonial 'Rebel Movements' in Africa: Towards an Explanation of the Violence Against the Peasantry," *Journal of Modern African Studies* 40, no. 2 (2002): 181–215; and Jodo Gomes Porto, "Contemporary Conflict Analysis in Perspective," in Jeremy Lind and Kathryn Sturman, eds., *Scarcity and Surfeit: The Ecology of Africa's Conflicts* (Pretoria: Institute for Security Studies, 2002).

25. It is notable that both Collier and Hoeffler have backed away from earlier crude versions of their "greed" thesis to a more nuanced position that allows the possibility of other motivations, including those associated with "grievance." However, this is not followed by empirical analysis to determine the nature of grievance in conflict societies, but by more use of statistical proxies (levels of poverty, levels of enrollment in high school, etc.). See Anke Hoeffler, "Economic Determinants of Conflict," *Bulletin of the Conflict, Security, and Development Group* (Centre for Defence Studies, King's College) no. 16 (2002): 1–2.

26. David Keen, "The Political Economy of War," Workshop on Economic and Social Consequences of Conflict, Queen Elizabeth House, University of Oxford.

27. Alex de Waal, ed., *Who Fights Also Cares? War and Humanitarian Action in Africa* (Asmara: Africa World Press, 2000), p. 6.

28. Ibid.

29. E. Wayne Nafziger and Juha Auvinen, "The Economic Causes of Humanitarian Emergencies," in Nafziger, Stewart, and Väyrynen, *War, Hunger, and Displacement*.

30. Thandika Mkandawire, "Shifting Commitments and National Cohesion in African Countries," in Lennart Wohlegemuth et al., eds., *Common Security and Civil Society in Africa* (Stockholm: Afrikainstitutet, 1999).

31. Peter Lock, "Africa, Military Downsizing, and the Growth of the Security Industry," in Jakkie Cilliers and Peggy Mason, eds., *Peace, Profit, or Plunder: The Privatization of Security in War-Torn African Countries* (Halfway House, South Africa: Institute of Security Studies, 1999).

32. Elizabeth M. Cousens and Chetan Kumar, *Peacebuilding as Politics: Cultivating Peace in Fragile Societies* (Boulder: Lynne Rienner, 2001).

33. The classic studies in this area—how "idiosyncratic" forms of historical consciousness shape conflicts—have been produced in the context of Rwanda and Burundi, attesting to the intensification of ethnicized and racist discourses that preceded (and rationalized) genocide in both countries. See René Lemarchand, *Burundi: Ethnocide as Discourse and Practice* (New York: Cambridge University Press, 1994); Lisa Malkki, *Purity and Exile* (Chicago: University of Chicago Press, 1995); Mahmood Mamdani, *When Victims Become Killers* (Princeton: Princeton University Press, 2001); and Peter Uvin, *Aiding Violence: The Development Enterprise in Rwanda* (West Hartford, Conn.: Kumarian Press, 1998).

34. Maxwell Owusu, "Tradition and Transformation: Democracy and Politics of Popular Power in Ghana," *Journal of Modern African Studies* 34, no. 2 (1996): 307–343.

35. Ibrahim Abdullah, "Bush Path to Destruction: The Origin and Character of the Revolutionary United Front (RUF/SL)," *Africa Development* 22, nos. 3–4 (1997): 45–76. For a critique of this thesis and a slightly different formulation of the problem, see Angela McIntrye, Kwesi Aning, and Prosper Addo, "Politics, War, and Youth Culture in Sierra Leone: An Alternative Interpretation," *African Security Review* 11, no. 3 (2002): 8.

36. Jennifer Leaning and Sam Arie, *Human Security: A Framework for Assessment in Conflict and Transition* (Washington, D.C.: U.S. Agency for International

Development/Complex Emergency Response and Transition Initiative, December 2000).

37. McIntyre, Aning, and Addo, "Politics, War, and Youth Culture," p. 8.

38. Ibid.

39. Kalevi Holsti, "Political Causes of Humanitarian Emergencies," in Nafziger, Stewart, and Väyrynen, War, Hunger, and Displacement, pp. 239–282.

40. McIntrye, Aning, and Addo, "Politics, War, and Youth Culture," p. 10.

41. Abubakr Momoh, "Popular Struggles in Nigeria," African Journal of Political Science 1, no. 2 (1996): 154–175; cited in Charles Ukeje, "Youths, Violence, and the Collapse of Public Order in the Niger Delta of Nigeria," Africa Development 26, nos. 1–2 (2001).

42. Cyril Obi, Structural Adjustment, Oil, and Popular Struggles: The Deepening Crisis of State Legitimacy in Nigeria, Monograph Series no. 1/97 (Dakar: CODESRIA, 1997). In reality these were not entirely new developments, as Eboe Hutchful showed for the period of the 1970s and 1980s. See Eboe Hutchful, "Oil Companies and Environmental Pollution in Nigeria," in Claude Ake, ed., The Political Economy of Nigeria (Ibadan, Nigeria: Longman, 1985). What changed, however, were the scope and methods of these protests.

43. See Ken Saro-Wiwa, A Month and a Day: A Detention Diary (London: Penguin Books, 1995).

44. Some elders see federal soldiers as providing protection against their own "wild youth." See Iyabo Olojede, Banji Fajonyomi, Ighodalo Akhape, and Suraju Mudashiru, Nigeria: Oil Pollution, Community Dissatisfaction, and Threats to National Peace and Security, Occasional Paper Series vol. 4, no. 3 (Harare: African Association of Political Science, 2000). A prominent example of these intracommunity cleavages was the split in MOSOP between conservative and militant factions in the 1990s, which led to the ascendancy of the "radicals" and the murder of four Ogoni chiefs. Many youth see the elders as having been "co-opted" by foreign oil companies.

45. Olojede et al., Nigeria, pp. 40–41.

46. Obi, Structural Adjustment, Oil, and Popular Struggles, p. 2.

47. The Chikoko Movement was a pan–Niger Delta movement launched in August 1997 in Bayelsa State by over 10,000 participants representing various Niger Delta communities, human and environmental rights organizations, and women's and youth groups. The movement saw itself as a "representative mass organization of the minority oil-producing areas," bringing new tactics of struggle to bear. The Kaiama Declaration was issued in December 1998 by the All-Ijaw Youth Conference, a meeting of over 5,000 Ijaw youth from over 500 communities.

48. See, for example, Karl Maier, This House Has Fallen: Midnight in Nigeria (New York: PublicAffairs, 2000); and Rotimi T. Suberu, "Can Nigeria's New Democracy Survive?" Current History, May 2001, pp. 207–212.

49. Olojede et al., Nigeria, p. 7.

50. One of the better known definitions of "internal war" is by Patrick Regan, who refers to "an armed combat between groups within state boundaries in which there are at least 200 fatalities." See Patrick Regan, Internal Wars and Foreign Powers: Outside Intervention in Interstate Conflicts (Ann Arbor: University of Michigan Press, 2000), p. 21.

51. This argument is presented more fully in Eboe Hutchful, "Pulling Back from the Brink: Ghana's Experiences," in Gavin Cawthra and Robin Luckham, eds., Security Structures and Democratic Governance in Conflict-Torn Societies (London: Zed Press, 2003).

52. See, for example, Kwame A. Ninsin, ed., *Ghana: Transition to Democracy* (Dakar: CODESRIA, 1998).

53. Eboe Hutchful, *Ghana's Adjustment Experience: The Paradox of Reform* (Oxford: James Currey, 2002), pp. 83–84.

10

Small Arms, Light Weapons

Comfort Ero and Angela Ndinga-Muvumba

International concern about the widespread availability and misuse of small arms and light weapons (SALWs) has grown dramatically in recent years. While small arms and light weapons do not, of course, cause conflicts, they soon become part of the conflict equation by fueling and exacerbating underlying tensions, generating more insecurity, deepening the sense of crisis, and adding to the number of casualities. Moreover, these weapons often contribute to exacerbating human rights violations and hampering peacebuilding efforts and sustainable development. The problems associated with the widespread availability of small arms can also be linked to bad governance in many societies.

Difficult conditions often exist within societies that are awash with small arms and light weapons. These societies suffer from poor socioeconomic development, unequal access to resources, low employment or underemployment, and high levels of poverty. The conditions of such states and their key institutions are important to understanding the complexities arising from the proliferation of small arms and light weapons within them. In such states, the institutions tasked with providing security for their citizens and maintaining law and order are weak or nonexistent. Their power to control or perform such functions has been seriously eroded. In fact, the state itself, in several instances, is a major source of insecurity. Many key actors who have access to small arms are nonmilitary groups that seek to protect themselves from the state and/or criminal and opportunistic groups who benefit from zones of crisis in which the state has lost its monopoly over the use of force. The result is an internal arms race between the police, the military, presidential security forces, rebel groups, criminal gangs, vigilantes, warlords, and criminal gangs.

Several international, regional, and subregional agreements and structures have emerged in the post–Cold War era to tackle the spread of small arms and light weapons. Significant among these agreements is a renewable three-year moratorium on the importation, exportation, and manufacture of light weapons signed on 31 October 1998 by member states of the Economic Community of West African States (ECOWAS). The moratorium was renewed for a further three years in 2001. Regional leaders in West Africa also approved a code of conduct in Lomé, Togo, in December 1999, spelling out the concrete steps to be taken by ECOWAS member states to implement the moratorium. The moratorium is a voluntary commitment: in essence, a confidence-building measure aimed at tackling widespread instability in West Africa.[1]

Technical assistance to support implementation of the moratorium is being provided through the Programme for the Coordination and Assistance for Security and Development (PCASED), directed by the United Nations Development Programme (UNDP). The project was set up in March 1999, four months after the moratorium came into effect, and will run for five years. Until 2001, PCASED was being managed through the UN regional disarmament center in Lomé, but it is currently based in Bamako, Mali. ECOWAS has received widespread praise for taking a decisive step in drawing up this important mechanism. The idea of a moratorium in a subregion as volatile as West Africa is widely seen to represent a critical step in efforts to reduce the spread and devastating effects of conflicts. Yet since the signing of the moratorium in 1998, progress in achieving concrete results has been patchy: ECOWAS and PCASED have found it difficult to effect change on the ground.

This chapter begins with a brief discussion of the threat posed to peace and security in West Africa by small arms and light weapons. It then critically sets out the constraints to achieving progress on the small arms moratorium, and considers the options available to ECOWAS and PCASED in influencing the implementation of the moratorium at a national and regional level. While the moratorium and PCASED should, in principle, contribute to conflict prevention and peacebuilding in West Africa, doubts remain about their capacity to fulfill this mandate. This chapter will also address the obstacles confronting both institutions, and offer policy options to make the ECOWAS moratorium a functioning reality.

Small Arms, Light Weapons, and Conflicts

A UN panel of experts had produced a clear and fairly comprehensive definition of small arms and light weapons in 1977. The panel categorized small arms as revolvers and self-loading pistols, rifles, carbines, submachine guns, assault rifles, and light machine guns. Small arms are designed for individual use. Light weapons are heavy machine guns, handheld underbarrel and mounted grenade launchers, portable antiaircraft guns, portable antitank guns, recoilless rifles, portable launchers of antitank missile and rocket systems, portable launchers of antiaircraft missile systems, and mortars of calibers of less than 100 millimeters. Light weapons are designed for carrying and use by a team or crew of two or more persons. Because SALWs are only effective when loaded with ammunition, their accessories are an essential part of the SALW problem. These include cartridges for small arms, shells and missiles for light weapons, antipersonnel grenades, antitank hand grenades, land mines, explosives, and mobile containers with missiles or shells for single-action antiaircraft and antitank systems.[2]

It is estimated that SALWs currently in circulation globally number more than 500 million, and that half of the world trade in small arms is represented by illicit trafficking. As a result of decades of procurement, an estimated 7 million weapons are circulating in West Africa.[3] The availability of small arms and light weapons is often linked to the changing nature or transformation of conflict since the end of the Cold War, from predominantly interstate to intrastate conflicts. During the Cold War, state arms transfers were primarily in heavy, high-maintenance equipment. This equipment included helicopters, jet fighters, and transport aircrafts. The superpowers—the United States and the Soviet Union—and their allies supplied these items. Because of the competitive nature of the bipolar Cold War system, arms transfers were motivated by ideological or geopolitical considerations. Grey (commercial) and black (illicit) arms trafficking in light weapons has increased during the post–Cold War era. These light weapons are primarily low-maintenance durables including AK-47s, rocket-propelled grenade launchers, mortars, and land mines. The primary motivation for suppliers in these transfers is economic gain.

The accumulation and uncontrolled proliferation of SALWs are also closely related to the high levels of crime and violence in many societies, even in times of peace. The popularity of such weapons can be attributed to their widespread availability, their durability (many weapons from the two world wars are still serviceable) and minimal maintenance requirements, their relative cheapness, and the ease with which most small arms can be carried, used, and concealed (even by young children). These characteristics make SALWs easy "currency" for smugglers, illegal traders, sanctions busters, and terrorists. As the conflicts in Sierra Leone and Angola have demonstrated, small arms and light weapons are widely traded for diamonds, and used to protect the illicit trade in diamonds, which itself fuels conflict.

There is a close link between legal and illegal flows of SALWs. In the supply chain, most transactions are legal. However, it is usually at the last stage, in a final transaction, that these weapons become illegal. Grey and illicit traffickers include government agencies operating with or within state agencies, African diaspora communities, private security firms, individual arms dealers, brokers from public and private transportation companies, businesspeople, and companies and countries selling or providing end-user certificates.[4] For example, in Africa's Great Lakes region, financing of arms has been arranged by banks in Asia, Europe, and the Middle East, as well as in North American financial institutions located in the British Virgin Islands, Hong Kong, the Seychelles, and Singapore. Public and private sector arms suppliers have operated out of Belgium, Britain, Bulgaria, France, Egypt, North Korea, Libya, Poland, Russia, South Africa, and Ukraine.[5]

The pathways for arms transfers provide complex yet important clues to understanding how the flow of illegal SALWs may be halted. Policymakers have highlighted various strategies that focus on controlling the use and supply of these weapons. It is important to note that supply-side initiatives complement strategies that target the use of SALWs. Supply-side initiatives that increase traceability and transparency include the use of permanent, unique serial numbers, keeping good records of transit, and placing trace chemicals in ammunition to track their origin. Improved transparency arrangements would allow governments to exchange information such as the identity of legitimate producers and lists of arms that have been recently confiscated or destroyed. Further, in terms of supporting traceability, efforts to coordinate regulatory regimes at borders and with customs officials would contribute to monitoring end-user certificates, and ensure that arms control measures, embargoes, and agreements are more effective.[6]

Small arms and light weapons have killed and injured the largest number of people—combatants and civilians alike—in conflicts since the end of the Cold War. While there are no official figures, an estimated 300,000 people have been killed by small arms and light weapons in conflicts each year since the end of the Cold War. In many cases, the victims of SALWs are noncombatants: children, women, and elderly people who have also often been displaced from their homes. Widespread availability of small arms is often coupled with the recruitment of children and teenagers into fighting units. The proliferation and reliance on light weaponry are correlated with the use of young children to bear and use arms (see Chapter 11).

Both during and after armed conflicts, the uncontrolled and easy access to, and use of, SALWs—mostly by unauthorized persons—endangers sustainable development and postwar recovery. Not only are these weapons recirculated from one conflict to another (passing, for example, between rebel forces fighting in support of other factions in Liberia, Sierra Leone, and Central Africa), but they are also becoming a persistent threat to fragile, postconflict societies that are struggling to establish peace and the rule of law.[7] Efforts at comprehensive disarmament and weapons collections, together with initiatives to reintegrate former combatants into local communities, can both be undermined by the ready availability of small arms and light weapons. Moreover, death rates in postconflict societies can remain high due to these weapons, while crime statistics often soar, as witnessed in the early stages of postwar reconstruction in Mozambique and El Salvador.

The Scourge of Small Arms and Light Weapons in West Africa

Many of the factors associated with the proliferation of small arms, namely the collapse of the rule of law and the proliferation of crime—in essence, bad governance, the intensity and impact of intrastate armed conflicts, underdevelopment, and the absence of an effective state and public welfare infrastructure—are rife in West Africa. Four points are important to highlight in this regard. First, West Africa's states and institutions were already generally inefficient and weak—a legacy of colonial "indirect rule," which established the state primarily for resource extraction. Second, during the immediate postcolonial era, West African leaders largely failed to create the enabling environment for their citizens to meet their economic and political needs, reproducing instead a predatory state where the rule of law was ineffective in managing the equitable distribution of rights and opportunities. Third, the end of the Cold War created a geopolitical vacuum,[8] while coinciding with an era of globalization in which trade and the transfer of technologies and resources have become more fluid, making it easier to conduct illicit and licit financial transactions and arms transfers. Finally, intrastate conflicts, often involving civilian populations as targets, have seen state and nonstate actors at times competing, and at other times collaborating, in resource exploitation and arms trafficking.

West African militaries have been politicized, its governments and bureaucracies have been primarily concerned with regime security, while local warlords have competed with the state for control of scarce resources. High-intensity and low-intensity armed conflicts in West Africa have placed arms and weaponry in the hands of nonstate and state, legitimate and illegitimate, democratic and nondemocratic forces. The proliferation of weapons used to fight these wars has flourished in part because of a lack of proper regulation and accountability. State institutions that would normally monitor the purchase and distribution of SALWs have either been sidelined or co-opted by national militaries. Executives preoccupied with defeating insurgencies have participated in illicit arms trafficking through corrupt bureaucrats, or have simply lacked the institutional capacity to control the flow of arms into criminal hands.

Civilians have been vulnerable to both a predatory state and ruthless nonstate actors, and thrust into the middle of a battle for power and, ultimately, more weapons.[9] As a result, civilians in conflict as well as nonconflict states have opted to arm themselves in order to ensure their own security from the threat posed by the proliferation of SALWs. Without a guarantee of security, the affluent and elite have hired private security firms, while the more impoverished masses have sometimes organized themselves into militias and civilian defense forces. Ostensibly established to provide security where the state has failed, these groups have often developed into politically motivated, murderous gangs engaged in urban guerrilla warfare. In Nigeria, groups like the Oodua People's Congress and the Bakassi Boys have become private armies of powerful individuals who often use them to settle personal scores.[10]

The present climate of criminalized and militarized activities in West Africa has been difficult to change. Despite broad movements toward democratization since the end of the Cold War, increased insecurity has pervaded the subregion. The Mano River Union states of Guinea, Liberia, and Sierra Leone erupted into intense armed conflicts, helping to cultivate a climate of criminality and political instability throughout the 1990s. The temporary conclusion of the Liberian civil war in 1997 following elections saw Charles Taylor establish autocratic rule that involved human rights abuses, illegal exploitation of mineral and natural resources, and support for rebel insurgencies in neighboring countries, thus prolonging the climate of insecurity in this area.[11] Simultaneously, Guinea's leader, Lansana Conté, provided military support to anti-Taylor rebels calling themselves Liberians United for Reconciliation and Democracy (LURD), who attacked Liberia in 1999 in a bid to topple Taylor's regime.

The Mali Experience

One of the first serious attempts to tackle the problem of SALWs in West Africa after the Cold War was launched in 1993 when the government of Mali sought to halt the continued instability posed by cross-border rebel activities and the flow of small arms into its country.[12] In partnership with the UN, peacemaking initiatives were undertaken by Bamako to address the problem of small arms in and around Mali. Recognizing the difficulties of dealing with the cross-border collaboration of rebel groups and the supply of weapons to Tuareg rebels in the north of the country, the Malian president at the time and the current chair of the African Union (AU) Commission, Alpha Oumar Konaré, proposed working with the UN on a subregional approach to disarmament. A UN advisory mission visited seven countries in the Sahara-Sahel region in 1994 and 1995, and concluded that the control of small arms and light weapons was essential to ensuring peace and stability, defined in terms of political progress and economic and social development.

Significant in this partnership with the UN on controlling the movement of small arms and light weapons was the March 1996 La Flamme de la Paix (The Flame of Peace), in which up to 3,000 weapons collected from rebels were burned in a public ceremony in Timbuktu. The "Flame of Peace" was both a symbolic display of disarmament as well as an affirming gesture— that the Malian "security first" approach to resolving the conflict between the government of Mali and Tuareg insurgents was working and would continue to work.[13] The success of Mali's disarmament process would seem to support arguments that approaches to disarmament in West Africa should integrate developmental goals and methods.[14] In fact, the Malian case suggests that the nexus between human security and human development is crucial for any successful demobilization and disarmament program.

Mali's approach emphasized integrated policies that were coordinated with local as well as external partners. There were three important dimensions to this approach. First, at the national level, the Malian government called for UN assistance, establishing the government's reputation as a credible and legitimate authority committed to disarmament and, more important, reintegration. Mali's disarmament process included efforts to institutionalize, through national legislation, procedures for establishing adequate internal security, border controls, and policing. These institutional mechanisms often complement supply-side approaches. By establishing functioning institutions and norms for both licit and illicit arms, this approach could help strengthen supplier initiatives in tracking and recording the manufacture and sale of weapons. The national capacity to monitor and track SALWs has the long-term potential of strengthening the legitimacy and authority of the state. Mali also established a commission on small arms. Second, at the external level, the UNDP coordinated these efforts, becoming the Malian government's main partner in organizing a roundtable conference at which donors and government authorities worked on the rehabilitation program in northern Mali.

Third, at the grassroots level, civil society actors led the way in encouraging Tuareg insurgents in the north to disarm. Following these initiatives, government authorities reentered the process in order to implement demobilization and the cantonment of former insurgents, as well as to facilitate their integration into the Malian army and society. The role of civil society actors in Mali is a useful illustration of the potential role of local nongovernmental organizations in disarmament and demobilization. Specifically, grassroots actors can serve as a legitimate supporting partner for disarmament because of their ability to incorporate local needs for human security into the process. As advocates for disarmament, these actors possess legitimacy at the local level that can influence combatants and noncombatants. The inclusion of local needs in Mali allowed for a more realistic and sustainable vision of peace to take root in local communities.

Stemming the flow of SALWs had an immense impact in Mali. According to the UNDP, Mali's disarmament process allowed the government to "sidestep civil war."[15] It is important to note that Bamako's partnership with the UNDP incorporated the development agenda at an early stage of the process, thus integrating development and security and enhancing investment in disarmament and demobilization. A relatively small investment by external donors in disarmament and demobilization can help avoid much larger investments in development during postconflict peacebuilding.

As an extension of its efforts to combat the proliferation of light weapons and small arms, and aware of the subregional impact of these weapons on its own internal stability, the government of Mali proposed a West African moratorium on the export, import, and manufacture of light weapons at a November 1996 conference in Bamako on conflict, prevention, disarmament, and development in West Africa. Conference participants recommended that a moratorium be consolidated with arms-manufacturing and arms-supplying states under the Wassenaar Arrangement, which came into force in July 1996.[16] On 31 October 1998, ECOWAS states declared a three-year renewable moratorium on the importation, exportation, and manufacture of light weapons. The moratorium came into force on 1 November 1998, coinciding with a second "Flame of Peace" in Mali. ECOWAS subsequently adopted a code of conduct to govern implementation of the moratorium. In December 1998 the thirty-three arms-producing and arms-exporting countries of the Wassenaar Arrangement declared their support for the ECOWAS moratorium.[17] Arms suppliers in Europe have started to inform ECOWAS of countries placing orders for weapons. However, arms can still be imported from unauthorized sources in countries such as Bulgaria and Ukraine. In March 1999, ECOWAS announced the creation of the UNDP-led PCASED, which started assisting in the implementation of the ECOWAS moratorium.

The ECOWAS Moratorium and PCASED

The ECOWAS small arms moratorium is the first such initiative to have been launched by a regional organization. As a voluntary, confidence-building mechanism, the moratorium has the potential of reducing the demand for new SALWs at the governmental level.[18] There were high expectations that implementation of the moratorium would proceed gradually under PCASED, but this has not yet occurred. When the moratorium was declared, it was seen as groundbreaking and visionary. But this early enthusiasm has waned, as difficulties and doubts developed about the capacity of PCASED and ECOWAS to implement the project, as well as about the political will of national governments. Three factors can be identified to explain why the moratorium and PCASED have not made the significant impact that their architects expected: West Africa's security environment, problems of governance and insecurity, and a lack of political will among governments.

The West African Security Environment

As noted above, a major problem impeding efforts to halt the proliferation of small arms and light weapons in West Africa is the widespread prevalence of conflict, criminality, and political violence. The scale and spread of conflicts, combined with the support of rebels by several ECOWAS governments since the beginning of the 1990s, remain a major obstacle for any successful implementation strategy to stem the flow of small arms and light weapons. West Africa has been plagued by the consequences of Liberia's first civil war (1989–1996) and later the civil war in Sierra Leone (1991–2002). Both conflicts triggered a series of regional security dilemmas, including the rapid increase in the proliferation of arms. The support of Charles Taylor by the leaders of Libya, Côte d'Ivoire (under Félix Houphouët-Boigny and the military junta of General Robert Gueï), and Burkina Faso gave him access to countries that supplied his rebel movement, the National Patriotic Front of Liberia (NPFL), and later his government, with arms. Taylor's alliance with the Revolutionary United Front (RUF) rebel group in Sierra Leone not only triggered conflict in that country, but was based on the principle that Taylor would supply arms in exchange for diamonds in the mining fields of Kono district and Tongo fields under RUF control.

One of the clearest indications of the deleterious effects of small arms and light weapons in West Africa was provided in the October 2002 UN panel-of-experts report on sanctions in Liberia. The report, which is discussed in further detail below, eloquently reveals how the persistent conflict in Liberia has made the country a haven for small arms. Despite the arms embargo that was reimposed on Liberia by the UN Security Council in May 2001 (first imposed in 1992), Charles Taylor, until he was forced into exile in Nigeria in August 2003, continued to benefit from the same supply lines as before the embargo. As the UN sanctions report of October 2002 noted, the renewal of conflict in Liberia between government forces and LURD rebels resulted in the continuation of the arms trade in the subregion, particularly in the Mano river basin. LURD not only received significant military assistance from a range of anti-Taylor forces in West Africa, including Guinean military forces, but it also benefited from using Guinea as a base from which to launch attacks into Liberia. The UN report further noted that "arms also continue[d] to reach LURD rebels through the neighbouring countries of Sierra Leone, Côte d'Ivoire or Guinea."[19] The report noted that a significant portion of LURD's arms, however, had been captured from Liberian government forces.[20]

Finally, the instability that has confronted Côte d'Ivoire since its first coup in December 1999 culminated in a civil conflict between the government of Laurent Gbagbo and at least three rebel groups by December 2002, raising further concerns about the spread of arms in West Africa.[21] While no evidence was available at the time of writing to explain the rebels' access to weapons, the rebels have gained some sympathy in the subregion due to the large-scale xenophobic sentiments directed at the large West African migrant populations in Côte d'Ivoire by Gbagbo's government.[22] The discrimination against naturalized Ivorians through policies of *Ivoirité* and the expulsion of northern Ivorian officers from the army further contributed to these problems.

Governance and Insecurity

Many of the conflicts affecting West Africa are associated with a history of bad governance and the poor administrative capacity of subregional governments over key institutions of state, namely security forces. In states where weak and fragmented security forces are unable to protect citizens, civilians have created alternative forms of security. One result has been that citizens have acquired arms to protect their communities. Such solutions have contributed considerably to the proliferation of small arms in West Africa. For example, in Nigeria, vigilante groups such as the Bakassi Boys emerged to provide security in place of weak and ineffective local police forces. Access to small arms has fueled criminal activities, banditry, and looting. Long porous borders have also contributed to the difficulty of monitoring and controlling the proliferation of arms in West Africa.

Lack of Political Will at the National Level

A number of West African states conducted symbolic arms reduction ceremonies to coincide with the UN Conference on the Illicit Trade in Small Arms and Light Weapons, which took place in New York from 9 to 20 July 2001 (a follow-up meeting was held in New York in July 2003 to assess progress after two years). In Mali, at least 500 small arms were burned in 2001 in a "weapons-for-development" program under the auspices of the "Malian National Commission Against the Proliferation of Small Arms" and PCASED. This program involved the exchange of arms for agricultural tools. Similarly, Nigeria also destroyed a stockpile of up to 2,421 firearms and weapons, including submachine guns, automatic and pump-action rifles, double-barreled shotguns, and pistols, in the northern city of Kaduna in 2001.[23] Finally, PCASED has been supporting the fragile peace process in Sierra Leone by conducting weapons destruction programs.

But despite these various initiatives, there remains a substantial lack of political will in disarmament efforts at the national level. Although ECOWAS members have consistently supported the small arms moratorium in their public statements, this support has not been followed by meaningful commitments. Not all states are complying with the moratorium, while others have been accused of openly fueling or sustaining conflicts. Burkina Faso and Charles Taylor's Liberia, for example, were named in various UN reports as states that supported RUF rebels during the civil war in Sierra Leone. Reports since August 2001 that arms were reaching Liberia from Côte d'Ivoire further reveal the difficulties of convincing governments that are under constant threat of rebel attacks to comply with the moratorium. In response to fighting in the northern Liberian county of Lofa, Charles Taylor reportedly received arms from General Robert Guëi, the former Ivorian military ruler and a close ally of Taylor, who was killed during a September 2002 military rebellion in Côte d'Ivoire.[24]

The lack of political will by West African governments was further illustrated by the slow progress toward creating the individual national commissions called for by the ECOWAS moratorium. Article 4 of the moratorium's code of conduct recommended that member states establish national commissions, consisting of government and civil society representatives, to promote and ensure the coordinated implementation of the moratorium. Subsequently, in the December 1999 "Decision Establishing National Commissions for the Control of the Proliferation and Illicit Circulation of Light Weapons" adopted by ECOWAS leaders in Lomé, member states were called upon to establish commissions for the "control of the proliferation and circulation of illicit light weapons." The commissions are seen as the backbone of PCASED's operations. They are the vital link between PCASED and ECOWAS member states. In essence, the commissions "serve as focal points for implementation of activities at the national level."[25]

The goal of the commissions is to create an environment for the successful implementation of the small arms moratorium, to assist in coordination between key ministries (defense, internal affairs and security, justice, and foreign affairs) and other stakeholders, notably the security sector and civil society actors. But this has yet to happen. One common criticism of the decision establishing the commissions is that it did not include civil society groups as partners in developing a meaningful framework for implementing the moratorium, as stipulated in Article 4 of the code of conduct. In its December 2001 presentation to the meeting of ECOWAS foreign ministers in Dakar, the ECOWAS executive secretariat noted that the commissions should include representatives of all significant actors within and outside government. Yet it remains unclear whether the composition of national commissions will follow the strictures of the code of conduct and the advice of the ECOWAS secretariat. Whatever the outcome of this important issue, the fact remains that very few functional national commissions have been established.

Some members of the PCASED advisory group who met in Bamako, Mali, from 26 to 27 June 2000 argued that ECOWAS member states did not need external funding to establish these commissions. Other appraisals suggest that national commissions need external funding to become operational and sustainable. Several member states have complained that PCASED has not supplied any financial or material resources to implement the moratorium.

Where national commissions have been established, this has often taken place in an ad hoc manner involving the passing of legislation and decrees, but has not necessarily led to the creation of active commissions. Several countries, however, have established national commissions or are in the process of establishing them. At the end of 2003, only three commissions had been established, in Guinea, Mali, and Niger. None of these commissions, however, have been fully operationalized. The commissions in Mali and Niger were established before PCASED came into existence. Financial and capacity constraints have resulted in weak national commissions. Other ECOWAS states are at different stages in the development of their national commissions. Benin and Senegal, for example, are the most advanced in their planning. Burkina Faso is working out the details of its own commission. Cape Verde, Côte d'Ivoire, Guinea-Bissau, and Sierra Leone are at a very early consultative stage. The early establishment of the commission in Togo is unlikely to occur, since the proposed building for the commission is dilapidated and in urgent need of rehabilitation and external funds. Togo, however, has a national small arms committee. Gambia and Ghana are in the process of developing institutions to tackle the spread of small arms in their countries, as the latter, like Togo, has set up a national small arms committee.

In Liberia, the process of establishing a national committee began on 18 October 1999, when thousands of weapons and rounds of ammunition used during the seven-year civil war (1989–1996) were destroyed in Tubmanburg. The destruction of these weapons was part of a three-month program initiated in Monrovia. ECOMOG troops and weapons experts worked with the UN to collect nearly 20,000 pistols, rifles, and machine guns, and over 3 million rounds of ammunition. The Liberian weapons destruction program mirrors the 1996 Malian "Flame of Peace." Recurrent instability in Liberia had stalled earlier efforts at disarmament and is likely to obstruct future efforts. Charles Taylor seemed to believe, before his departure into exile in Nigeria in August 2003, that his survival in power depended on a sufficient buildup of weapons to ward off a rebel assault on Monrovia. As the 2002 UN panel-of-experts report on sanctions in Liberia noted:

> On 31 May 2002, an Ilyushin 76 freighter aircraft left the airport of Belgrade with military equipment on board. After a fuel stop in Tripoli (Libyan Arab Jamahiriya), the plane flew to Roberts International Airport, Monrovia, and arrived early on 1 June 2002.
>
> This was the first flight of a series of six, conducted between May and the end of August 2002. An additional flight on 29 September 2002 was eventually canceled. The arms on board were delivered in Liberia on 1, 7 and 29 June, 5 July, and 23 and 25 August 2002 (initially by an Ilyushin and in August by a Lockheed).[26]

Finally, Nigeria only started the process of establishing a national small arms committee in 2000. Following an Organization of African Unity ministerial meeting in Bamako in December 2000, President Olusegun Obasanjo inaugurated the Nigerian committee on illegal proliferation, circulation, and trafficking in small arms and light weapons.

The slow progress in implementing the small arms moratorium, especially in regard to creating the national commissions, has been compounded by the lack of cooperation among states in harmonizing their policies on a bilateral and regional basis. In particular, progress to harmonize national legislation on the small arms issue has been very slow, though, as a preliminary step, documentation on this issue prepared by some member states has been submitted to the ECOWAS secretariat.

Articles 11 and 12 of the moratorium's code of conduct called for intra- and interstate cooperation in monitoring and controlling the flow of weapons and strengthening border controls. However, the results of such cooperation have been decidedly mixed. Some appraisals note that no such cooperation exists, while others claim that some level of cooperation exists, though it is dependent on bilateral relations between states—notably between Ghana and Nigeria, and more recently between Ghana and Togo. Major obstacles to cooperation also include the lack of training and equipment. A training curriculum has been developed by PCASED in collaboration with the ECOWAS secretariat, but training programs on weapons management techniques for law enforcement officers had yet to be held at the time of writing.

Institutional Problems
Confronting ECOWAS and PCASED

There are a number of weaknesses confronting ECOWAS, perhaps the most important of which is the need to strengthen ownership of the small arms moratorium by ECOWAS and its member states. The main stumbling block, however, remains the lack of political momentum both within member states and within the ECOWAS secretariat.

Also significant is the lack of capacity within the ECOWAS secretariat to play a stronger role in providing oversight for the implementation of the moratorium. This is reflected in the limited number of personnel working on small arms issues within the secretariat, making it difficult for ECOWAS to provide the necessary political leadership for implementing the moratorium. The recently established Department for Political Affairs, Defense, and Security under the ECOWAS security mechanism of 1999 (see Chapter 13) should take on primary responsibility for the implementation of the moratorium, but it is too soon to assess the mechanism's capacity to fulfull these tasks.

There is still great uncertainty about the viability of ECOWAS's restructuring plans in meeting the needs of the moratorium and other regional security concerns. A lingering impression remains that ECOWAS lacks the capacity to support PCASED's work and that PCASED has not secured ECOWAS's close participation and interest in its activities. At the time of writing, there was no PCASED liaison officer attached to the ECOWAS secretariat in Abuja. Moreover, in its present configuration, PCASED is seen as a Malian project, stemming directly from the "Flame of Peace" initiative.

While ECOWAS has been unable to make substantial progress in convincing its members about the benefits of the moratorium, its partner, PCASED, has also faced difficulties in enhancing subregional institutional capacity for controlling the spread of small arms and light weapons. Since its establishment in March 1999, PCASED has faced a number of obstacles and constraints, many of which were highlighted in a critical evaluation report conducted for the UNDP in November 2000.[27] The evaluation report noted that PCASED had ambitous objectives that would be difficult to achieve given its resource constraints. It also found that the project's institutional arrangements—in which the director of the UN regional center for peace and disarmament in Lomé also served as the director of PCASED— were obstacles to building an effective project focused on supporting implemention of the moratorium. Although PCASED is undergoing a review of its program with a view to implementing recommendations from its evaluation report of 2000, a number of issues still need to be resolved.

PCASED is a politically sensitive program, and all its operational and management decisions must be judged accordingly. ECOWAS, as the principal political body charged with implementing the small arms moratorium, should become more involved in all aspects of PCASED's activities. Both institutions, however, have yet to develop a constructive political and cooperative relationship. A major problem is the disconnect between PCASED and ECOWAS: the former was created to provide technical support for the moratorium, while the latter was charged with ensuring that its members implement the moratorium. However, relations between the two bodies have so far proved difficult and competitive. The absence of a meaningful working relationship between ECOWAS and PCASED is a major impediment to the long-term sustainability of the ECOWAS small arms moratorium.

Another significant problem that may have been resolved following recommendations made in the UNDP's 2000 evaluation report was establishing a proper chain of command between the UN's disarmament offices in Lomé and Bamako. As highlighted in the report, the most significant challenge to the effectiveness of PCASED emanated from the fact that the director of the UN regional disarmament center in Lomé held dual responsibilities in managing the Lomé center and the PCASED office in Bamako. Visits by the director to Bamako were often irregular and new initiatives were usually announced unilaterally without consultation with the staff in Bamako. According to the UNDP's tripartite review meeting in November 1999, the director's role is primarily political and also involves fundraising. More important, this role should have been transitional, with operational matters ultimately transferred to the deputy director. This, however, did not happen. Following the November 2000 independent evaluation, the UNDP convened a tripartite review meeting in April 2001. This meeting recommended the development of clearer, more functional linkages between the UN's disarmament center in Lomé and the PCASED headquarters in Bamako. Since the evaluation report was conducted, further attempts have been made to consolidate all PCASED management functions under a fulltime executive director based in Bamako.

The overly ambitious agenda set by PCASED at its creation also turned out to be problematic. PCASED's plan of action involved nine priority areas: establishing a culture of peace; conducting training programs for the military, security, and police forces; enhancing weapons controls at border posts; establishing a database and a regional arms register; collecting and destroying surplus or unauthorized weapons; facilitating a dialogue between producers and suppliers; reviewing and harmonizing national legislation and administration procedures; mobilizing resources for PCASED's objectives and activities; and enlarging membership of the small arms moratorium.

Largely because of its inability to deliver fully on any of these areas, PCASED's priority areas were significantly reduced at a meeting in Bamako in May 2000, to focus on the following five priority areas: establishing the national commissions and providing assistance to them; mobilizing resources; conducting information, communication, and enlightenment campaigns; training armed and security forces as well as border patrols; and establishing an arms register. These five priority areas will be used as future guides to assess progress within PCASED in implementing the ECOWAS small arms moratorium. Yet it is possible to argue that even this narrowed focus remains too ambitious. PCASED needs an overarching framework and policy direction from ECOWAS about how to implement its moratorium.

Other problems within PCASED involve administrative and financial deficiencies in its projects. There have been delays in recruiting staff and procuring equipment, but PCASED is now fully staffed. Some observers have noted that though PCASED has sufficient personnel with expertise in the regional security dynamics of West Africa, it remains understaffed in terms of personnel with expertise in the technical aspects of SALWs. Compounding PCASED's problems is its lack of communication, visibility, and information-sharing throughout West Africa. Its more active participation and involvement in weapons-burning ceremonies in the subregion could have enhanced its visibility. Moreover, PCASED is still struggling to build up ties with important subregional actors, most notably civil society groups. PCASED has no visibility, locally or regionally, and lacks an effective media and communications strategy. A weak financial base has also constrained PCASED's capacity to fulfill its mandate effectively.

Financial constraints are also a major obstacle for ECOWAS, although the organization received up to $1.9 million from the European Commission in Brussels in 2001 for the establishment of zonal observation bureaus for its security mechanism. The potential of the small arms moratorium to contribute to arms control efforts in West Africa certainly warrants an increased commitment of resources for its implementation. Significantly, one of PCASED's principal tasks is to mobilize support and resources for the ECOWAS moratorium, and to contribute its own resources to the moratorium's implementation. Unfortunately, funding for PCASED has been disappointing. Although more than $5 million had been contributed by September 2000, there remained, at the end of 2003, a shortfall of around $8 million in the funds required for its envisaged programming activities. Although the UNDP has committed itself to assisting in resource mobilization, PCASED still lacks a viable fundraising strategy.

According to a project document approved in February 1999, PCASED was budgeted to receive $13 million for the period 1999 to 2004. However, it had received only $5.4 million by 2002. The gap between estimated costs and donor contributions may be attributed to PCASED's poor performance and ad hoc approach to donor reporting and fundraising.

Despite these various obstacles and constraints, there have been a few small successes. PCASED initiated dialogue between some small supplier states under the Wassenaar Arrangement and the ECOWAS secretariat, after which applications for small arms acquisitions were received from West African states and channeled through accountable bodies. However, no progress has been made in developing PCASED's arms register and database, which are among its core objectives. An overly ambitious agenda, combined with structural and management problems, has undermined PCASED's ability to deliver tangible results.

Policy Recommendations

The greatest indictment against the credibility of the ECOWAS small arms moratorium and PCASED can perhaps best be seen in the various UN panel-of-experts reports that have been published since UN sanctions were imposed on Liberia on 6 May 2001. The violations of the UN's arms embargo with the assistance of arms dealers from eastern Europe, especially from Yugoslavia, proves the ineffectiveness of ECOWAS and PCASED in curbing the flow of these weapons. More troubling, however, is the fact that most of these violations are thought to have been committed by West African states exploiting loopholes in the way that the moratorium and PCASED have operated. Under current requirements, the ECOWAS secretariat is expected to receive notification about small arms exports to countries in West Africa. This would allow ECOWAS to decide which orders can be exempted from the moratorium. But member states are not obliged to supply copies of the end-user certificates that are issued by the ECOWAS secretariat once such exemptions have been granted. This has led to several ECOWAS states being accused of copying or forging a number of certificates. In Liberia, for example, a number of arms that were eventually received by the Taylor government were said to have been supplied through forgeries made by brokers. Moreover, the forgeries were said to have been made largely by West African states, most notably Côte d'Ivoire.

The October 2002 report of the UN panel of experts provides some of the most concrete recommendations for tackling the scourge of small arms in West Africa:

> The Panel strongly recommends that a requirement to also submit copies of the end-user certificates become part of the procedure to obtain waivers for the importation of arms into West Africa.
>
> The Panel reiterates its recommendation that the moratorium be broadened to an information exchange mechanism for all types of weapons procured by ECOWAS members.
>
> . . . The availability of arms in West Africa is a very serious problem that cannot be solved without the assistance of all parties concerned: law enforcement agencies in West Africa and regional institutions dealing with the issue such as the Interpol regional offices or PCASED, the ECOWAS/ PCASED Liaison Bureau and the various national commissions set up to oversee the implementation of the moratorium. The Panel has exchanged information with Interpol and PCASED and stresses the importance of this regional framework which already exists and might be used in a more effective way to come to grips with the problems posed by uncontrolled

flows of light weapons into the region, including the operations of arms-trafficking networks.

The Panel also recommends that more efforts be made, both by ECOWAS member states and by donor countries, to strengthen the national commissions and the secretariat in terms of staffing and equipment.[28]

The ECOWAS small arms moratorium can only be effective if West African states have sufficient technical, human, and financial resources to monitor borders, airfields, and seaports effectively. ECOWAS states must develop the political will to implement the moratorium. Donors must also support ECOWAS and PCASED's efforts in this important area. Since SALWs proliferate in a climate of political instability and conflict, the importance of halting the flow of these weapons cannot be overstated. Since the presence of SALWs also heightens the potential for violence and insecurity in West Africa, the problem must be linked to governance issues and the need to build effective, transparent, and accountable institutions (see Chapters 5 and 6). Such institutions are vital to monitoring and implementing the moratorium. ECOWAS members, in collaboration with civil society and multilateral agencies, must commit resources to peacebuilding and programs that enhance the capacity of state institutions such as customs and police, as well as national commissions. These institutions must be given the resources to monitor the flow of arms in the subregion more effectively.

In their collaboration, ECOWAS and PCASED have set out to contribute to peacebuilding efforts and an improved security environment that would create a climate for sustainable economic development in West Africa. But these lofty aspirations remain unfulfilled six years after the ECOWAS small arms moratorium was signed. High levels of insecurity, lack of institutional consensus, and limited human and financial resources have undermined the potential role that the ECOWAS moratorium and PCASED had hoped to play in curbing the spread of SALWs in West Africa. The UN panel-of-experts report of October 2002 offered a critical appraisal: "It seems that, so far, although (a regional framework) has been set up, there are few results in terms of combating arms trafficking. Some member states also seem to violate the moratorium by importing arms without requesting waivers and only about one half of the member states of ECOWAS have effectively set up national commissions."[29] This is a stinging indictment of the failure of the ECOWAS small arms moratorium to fulfill its mandate and implement its noble ideals.

Notes

This chapter draws on research conducted by Comfort Ero with Roxaneh Bazergan, former chief information officer at the Centre for Defence Studies, King's College

London. It is also based on visits conducted by Comfort Ero to the PCASED head-quarters in Bamako, Mali, in June 2000, as well as discussions with PCASED staff throughout 2000–2001. The authors are grateful for comments received from participants attending the IPA/ECOWAS seminar in September 2001, in particular Adrienne Yande Diop of the ECOWAS secretariat in Abuja.

1. Joseph P. Smaldone, "Mali and West African Small Arms Moratorium," in Jeffrey Boutwell and Michael T. Klare, eds., *Light Weapons and Civil Conflict: Controlling the Tools of Violence,* Carnegie Commission on Preventing Deadly Conflict (Lanham, Md.: Rowman and Littlefield, 1999), p. 135.

2. For a comprehensive survey of the small arms in use by militaries during World Wars I and II, the Cold War, and the 1980s that were dispersed into conflict zones, see Ian V. Hogg and John S. Weeks, *Military Small Arms of the Twentieth Century,* 4th ed. (Northfield, Ill.: DBI, 1981).

3. The United Nations Development Programme (UNDP) calculates these weapons to be SALWs acquired through both legal and illegal channels of supply, including weapons from the Cold War era. See www.undp.org/erd/archives/brochures/small.

4. On the mechanics of arms trafficking, see Kathi Austin, "Illicit Arms Brokers: Abiding and Abetting Atrocities," *Brown Journal of World Affairs* 9, no. 1 (Spring 2002): 203–216; and Brian Johnson-Thomas, "Anatomy of a Shady Deal," and Brian Wood and Johan Peleman, "Making the Deal and Moving the Goods: The Role of Brokers and Shippers," both in Lora Lumpe, ed., *Running Guns: The Global Black Market in Small Arms,* Norwegian Initiative on Small Arms Transfers (NISAT) and the International Peace Research Institute (London: Zed Books, 2000), pp. 13–26.

5. The World Policy Institute's report *Deadly Legacy: U.S. Arms to Africa and the Congo War,* written by William D. Hartung and Bridget Moix of the Arms Trade Resource Center in January 2000, focuses on arms transfers to the Congo, and also describes the methods of these arms transfers.

6. "Civil Society Support for the Program for Coordination and Assistance on Security and Development," report prepared by Lora Lumpe, Norwegian Initiative on Small Arms Transfers, Bamako, Mali, March 1999, available at www.nisat.org/west%20africa/civil_society_support_for_the.htm.

7. On 1 June 2000, the BBC reported that truckloads of small arms, including rocket-propelled grenades and AK-47 ammunition, were sent from Liberia for the Revolutionary United Front (RUF) rebel group in Sierra Leone. The RUF's links with Liberian president Charles Taylor have been well documented. A UN Security Council report in December 2000 noted that Taylor had routinely flown supplies of arms, ammunition, fuel, food, and medicines into RUF-controlled areas by helicopter. See United Nations, *Report of the Panel of Experts Appointed Pursuant to UN Security Council Resolution 1306 (2000), Paragraph 19, in Relation to Sierra Leone,* UN Doc. S/2000/1195, 20 December 2000.

8. On the negative and positive roles of external actors in West Africa before and after the Cold War, see Adekeye Adebajo, *Building Peace in West Africa: Liberia, Sierra Leone, and Guinea-Bissau* (Boulder: Lynne Rienner, 2002), pp. 141–142.

9. Abdel-Fatou Musah, "Small Arms: A Time Bomb Under West Africa's Democratization Process," *Brown Journal of World Affairs* 9, no. 1 (Spring 2002): 241–243.

10. Ibid., p. 246.

11. Ibid., p. 245; and Dena Montague, "The Business of War and the Prospects for Peace in Sierra Leone," *Brown Journal of World Affairs* 9, no. 1 (Spring 2002): p. 231.

12. The government of Mali and the Tuareg movements in northern Mali had been locked in years of conflict when General Moussa Traoré's twenty-three-year military dictatorship was overthrown in 1991. As part of a 1995 peace agreement, 3,000 fighters committed themselves to a process of cantonment and reintegration that built enough confidence for an additional 10,000 former combatants to come forward. The Malian government called for a large-scale rehabilitation program for northern Mali, with a focus on reestablishing security in the area. The government withdrew many of its military forces from the north and allowed civil society to take the lead in negotiating the disarming of rebels.

13. R. Poulton and I. Youssouf, eds., *A Peace of Timbuktu: Democratic Governance, Development, and African Peacekeeping* (New York: United Nations Institute for Disarmament Research, 1998).

14. This comprehensive development/disarmament approach may also be termed a "security first" approach. Components of such an approach include: (1) disarmament, demobilization, and reintegration of combatants; (2) repatriation and reintegration of refugees; (3) rule of law and respect for human rights; (4) democratization; and (5) socioeconomic development. See Sverre Lodgaard and Ivor Fung, "A Moratorium on Small Arms," in Sverre Lodgaard and Carsten F. Rønnfeldt, eds., *A Moratorium on Light Weapons in West Africa* (Oslo: Norwegian Initiative on Small Arms Transfers, May 1998), available at www.nisat.org/publications.

15. See UNDP, Emergency Response Division, small arms brochure section on Mali's "'Security First' Approach to Conflict Resolution and Development," available at www.undp.org/erd/archives/brochures/small_arms/sa3.htm.

16. The Vienna-based Wassenaar Arrangement on Export Controls for Conventional Arms and Dual-Use Goods and Technologies came into force on 12 July 1996. It is the successor regime to the Coordinating Committee on Multilateral Export Controls (COCOM), which limited arms exports and arms-related goods from the Organization for Economic Cooperation and Development (OECD) countries.

17. Participating states in the Wassenaar Arrangement include Australia, New Zealand, Japan, the Republic of Korea, Argentina, the United States, Canada, and all countries in Europe including the Russian Federation and Turkey. For a discussion on the response to the ECOWAS small arms moratorium by the Wassenaar states, see a speech made by Ambassador Staffan Sohlmans, chairman of the Wassenaar Arrangement, on 5 May 1999, published by the Henri Dunant Centre and titled "The Wassenaar Arrangement and the Moratorium for West Africa," available at www.nisat.org/west%20africa/wassenaar_arrangemetns_and_the_mo.htm.

18. For a discussion on the role of confidence- and security-building mechanisms and how they could help to ease demand for new armaments and complement supply-side initiatives and arms control agreements, see William Durch, *Constructing Regional Security: The Role of Arms Transfers, Arms Control, and Reassurance* (New York: Palgrave, 2000).

19. United Nations, *Report of the Panel of Experts Appointed Pursuant to Security Council Resolution 1408 (2002), Paragraph 16, Concerning Liberia*, UN Doc. S/2002/1115, 25 October 2002.

20. Ibid., paras. 104–108, pp. 25–26.

21. United Nations, *Report of the Secretary-General on Côte d'Ivoire*, UN Doc. S/2003/374, 26 March 2003.

22. The government of Burkina Faso has been the focus of much of the accusations about arms supply to the rebels, but there has been no substantial evidence to support this allegation. However, a number of exiled Ivorians, particularly those who fled from General Robert Gueï's military junta and later Gbagbo's regime,

lived in Burkina Faso, and a number of those soldiers are known to have been involved in the 19 September 2002 attempted coup.

23. See "West Africa: Weapons Burned Across the Region," *UN-IRIN Weekly West Africa Update,* 13 July 2001.

24. See D. Farah, "In West Africa's Borderlands, Wars Start to Flare Up Again," *International Herald Tribune,* 7 August 2001, p. 2.

25. *Report of the Third Advisory Group Meeting,* Programme for Coordination and Assistance for Security and Development, Bamako, Mali, 26–27 June 2000, p. 6.

26. United Nations, *Report of the Panel of Experts Appointed Pursuant to Security Council Resolution 1408 (2002), Paragraph 16, Concerning Liberia,* paras. 64–65, p. 18.

27. UNDP, *Independent External Evaluation of the PCASED Project* (New York: UNDP, November 2000).

28. United Nations, *Report of the Panel of Experts Appointed Pursuant to Security Council Resolution 1408 (2002), Paragraph 16, Concerning Liberia,* paras. 104–107, p. 26.

29. Ibid., para. 108, p. 26.

11

Children and Armed Conflict

'Funmi Olonisakin

When the subject of children is discussed in the context of West Africa's wars, the focus of attention tends to be on the phenomenon of child soldiers. An estimated 300,000 children are serving as members of armed groups around the world.[1] Like other regions of the world affected by armed conflicts, children in West Africa have been conscripted (some have volunteered), abducted, and coerced into joining different armed factions.[2] Under the influence of narcotic substances or pressure from older fighters, young people have committed horrendous atrocities against innocent civilians including, in some cases, members of their own families. However, victims of the physical and psychological consequences of violent conflict are not limited to impressionable young soldiers. Conflicts have also had a negative impact on noncombatant children in war-torn areas. Children constitute about half of refugee and displaced populations in these wars, and many of them are orphaned and lack the opportunities for personal development.[3] Youths sometimes suffer massive abuse at the hands of members of armed groups, including rape, sexual slavery, forced labor, and exposure to sexually transmitted diseases like HIV/AIDS. The proliferation of arms and violent conflicts in West Africa, coupled with the illicit trafficking and trading in valuable mineral resources and commodities, has compounded the plight of children in this subregion, particularly in the last decade.

This chapter examines the impact of armed conflicts on children. The focus will mainly be on Sierra Leone and Liberia, though I will assess the larger implications of these wars on children in West Africa as a whole. The chapter examines the different strategies that are currently being adopted to rehabilitate children affected by armed conflict. Given the different developmental and security dimensions of this challenge, I argue that

concerted regional approaches offer the best chance for success in ameliorating the plight of children in armed conflicts.

The Plight of Children Affected by Armed Conflict

Neither the involvement of children in warfare nor the devastating consequences that such conflicts have had on children are new. Wars have taken
their deadly toll not only on adults but also on minors. Children have been
used as military auxiliaries for centuries. However, norms and conventions
of contemporary warfare have helped to curtail the use of children in armed
conflicts.[4] Yet in Africa, Asia, and Latin America, the use of children in
warfare still represents a chronic and sordid contemporary problem. Even
though there have been concerns raised about the plight of children in conflict zones and these activities have been documented, it took an influential report prepared for the United Nations General Assembly by Mozambique's former education minister, Graca Machel, in 1996, to draw attention
to the fact that this is not a localized phenomenon but an issue of truly
global proportions. The Machel report of 1996 called for "an end to the
cynical exploitation of children as soldiers."[5] The document became a crucial watershed in galvanizing global concern as well as academic interest in
the issue of child soldiers. Several other reports and studies by the United
Nations Children's Fund (UNICEF), the office of the Special Representative of the UN Secretary-General for Children and Armed Conflict, international human rights groups, and other nongovernmental organizations
(NGOs) have been subsequently published. These reports have focused
largely on the phenomenon of child soldiers in Africa, Asia, and Latin
America and provide vivid descriptions of the abysmal conditions of the
majority of these children, as well as the negative impact of their activities
on their families and the larger society. Most important, these reports have
also conveyed images, views, and heart-wrenching personal experiences of
these war-affected children to a wider audience.[6]

   These studies have made a significant contribution to explaining the
political, military, psychological, and sociocultural dimensions of this phenomenon.[7] The issue of children in armed conflict has been examined from
the vantage point of the main protagonists of conflicts as well as from the
vantage point of children affected by war. These reports have suggested two
broad and plausible explanations as to why armed factions and their commanders target children. First, in many impoverished African, Asian, and
Latin American conflicts, children simply are cheaper and more pliable soldiers. Adults are more difficult to control because they can migrate, hide,
refuse, or resist the pressures of armed factions (which they have done in
many cases). Adults are also more expensive to support, more difficult to

discipline and command, and most important, can switch allegiances at critical moments. Second, children are easier to indoctrinate and can more easily become emotionally attached to adult soldiers.[8] Both Charles Taylor, the leader of the National Patriotic Front of Liberia (NPFL), and Foday Sankoh, the head of the Revolutionary United Front (RUF) in Sierra Leone, were fondly called "Papay" by their juvenile followers. Based on this nefarious adult influence—bolstered sometimes with additional narcotic inducement—children can be made to perform military tasks and fight in situations or commit atrocities that would make their adult counterparts more hesitant.

Several scholars and policymakers have cautioned against viewing children in conflict situations as merely passive victims. Five reasons have been suggested to explain why children join armed factions. First, for some children, enrollment in a military faction is a survival strategy; in conflict zones, this is sometimes the surest means through which youths can get access to food and resources for themselves and their families.[9] Second, in some cases, children and young people have an astute sense of the economic deprivation, political corruption, and social injustice around them, and sometimes believe these societal problems can be redressed through violence.[10] Third, children might join rebel groups because of the loss of family members and the need to rediscover some sense of community or to avenge the killing of relatives. Fourth, the ownership and operation of a lethal weapon, imparting the capacity to inflict harm on others (especially people who are older and more socially powerful than youths), actually provide some children with a sense of empowerment. Finally, some analysts have argued that the participation of children in violent conflicts may represent an effort to enact heroic fantasies, especially those derived from the global media culture of violence (such as the "Rambo" movies) or the propaganda of different factions.[11] Nonetheless, the extent to which children's choices and actions in conflict situations are actually voluntary is debatable, given the often chaotic environments within which such decisions are being made. Conflict situations rarely present many vulnerable young people with meaningful alternatives to joining armed groups.

Whether children are forcibly recruited, "choose" to fight, or are trapped in conflict zones, many studies have shown that the impact of violence on their lives can be equally devastating. As "combatants," children are frequently killed or maimed in action. Captured as prisoners of war, they are often brutalized, detained, and badly treated. As abductees, they are used as drudges and sexual objects in the criminalized economies and perverted social landscapes spawned by conflicts. As refugees, children experience extensive disruption of their lives—they are frequently uprooted, displaced from their homes, and deprived of their parents and friends. In refugee camps, these children usually have limited access to educational opportunities, recreation, or leisure. In all of its multiple dimensions, war exposes children to tremendous brutality and adversity, traumatizes them emotionally and mentally, and exposes them to diseases. The situation of children is all the more pathetic given their lack of skills, resources, and maturity to cope with the negative consequences of conflicts. War has the potential of stunting the development and growth of children.[12]

The Liberia Contagion

The situation of children affected by war in West Africa has to be placed within the larger context of the socioeconomic and political breakdown of states in this subregion, the ensuing violent struggle over power and resources, and the spillover effects of conflicts into neighboring states over the past decade. Years of political exclusion and mismanagement, coupled with economic stagnation, have produced widespread poverty, unemployment, and the breakdown of both state and social structures in West Africa. Many states have lost their capacity to generate employment, to provide welfare support, and most important, to control, discipline, or rehabilitate juveniles.[13] Similarly, with diminished access to resources, many parents have struggled to meet the needs of their children and consequently faced tremendous challenges in monitoring them. A significant number of these children have ended up as petty hawkers, vehicle apprentices, laborers, beggars, vagrants, or petty criminals.[14] With limited access to education, employment, and political power, many young people and children became alienated from the state and mainstream society (see Chapter 8). Thus, a vulnerable pool of children and young people already existed before the outbreak of widespread conflicts in West Africa, and these children became the cannon fodder of the subregion's ruthless warlords.[15]

Children first became a reported feature of war in West Africa following the outbreak of the Liberian conflict in December 1989. The Liberian experience revealed several dimensions of the systematic use and targeting of children as soldiers by armed groups that had not been previously well understood. It is estimated that between 15,000 and 20,000 children, including young women and girls, were eventually used in various capacities by the different armed factions.[16] Within a few months of the outbreak of armed violence in Liberia in 1989, children became a conspicuous presence among rebel groups. The NPFL was the first faction to use children. There were several reasons for this strategy. Taylor's initial invasion of Liberia was met with skepticism, and his NPFL did not have widespread support, though it did eventually garner support among Gios and Manos in Nimba county. Second, within the first six months of the war, the NPFL had split into two factions. Prince Yormie Johnson, leading the breakaway faction the Independent National Patriotic Front of Liberia (INPFL), took away some of Taylor's best-trained rebel combatants. Third, the vicious reprisals by Samuel Doe's Armed Forces of Liberia (AFL) against perceived rebel sympathizers in Nimba and Lofa counties left many children without families.[17] These orphaned children became easy prey for rebels, who convinced them to join the opposing side if only to avenge the death of their family members.[18] Fourth, Liberia's predatory armed groups provided access to food and a measure of security as the state and society disintegrated.

As the death toll from Liberia's war rose, adult populations fled war zones and the NPFL and the AFL fragmented into multiple armed factions (there were at least seven such groups by 1994). The competition for new recruits intensified. Recruitment by rebel groups assumed more sinister proportions as young men and boys were forced to join the war. Charles Taylor organized what became known as the notorious "Small Boys Unit," a lethal and viciously loyal Lilliputian gang.[19] Press-ganged, psychologically primed, and dosed with cane-juice, marijuana, and other narcotic substances, many of these children committed cruel atrocities against innocent civilians, as did the child soldiers of Liberia's other factions.

Many of Liberia's children who had inhabited conflict zones and displaced camps emerged from the seven-year war (1989–1996) profoundly traumatized. Those who had fought with armed factions later described how they were made to commit horrific atrocities against innocent civilians. Women were disemboweled, limbs of people hacked, and innocent people summarily executed. Young boys were not the only ones involved in these atrocities. Many young girls performed acts of brutality that exceeded those of their male counterparts, a situation that shocked many observers since this behavior was seen to be at odds with the role that girls and women had been socialized to perform. These young fighters were ordered to commit the most gruesome atrocities against innocent civilians, often members of their own families and communities. These acts in turn strengthened the ties of these youths to armed groups and reduced the prospect of the children returning to their communities after the end of hostilities. Fighters of the NPFL, the AFL, and other factions used children as spies, laborers, and sex slaves. Children who were recalcitrant or disobeyed orders were severely punished and brutalized.[20]

As the first Liberian war reached its denouement in 1996, it was evident that Liberia's war-affected children represented a serious problem for the future of the country and the entire subregion. Yet Liberians, West Africans, and external actors involved in peacemaking efforts clearly failed to address fundamentally the situation of children affected by the war. None of the Liberian factions were held to account for their extensive violations of international laws and conventions or their crimes against children. No systematic attempt was made to redress the needs of these children after the war was over. When the opportunity arose for a comprehensive peace accord in Cotonou in July 1993, a blanket amnesty was granted to all the combatants from the different factions, even those who had committed gross violations of human rights and crimes against humanity.[21] Throughout Liberia's unsuccessful peace conferences and thirteen failed peace agreements, the insistence on a blanket amnesty for fighters became a cornerstone of peacemaking until the final accord was signed in Abuja in August 1996. In trying to provide "incentives" to the warring parties, peacemakers inadvertently rewarded impunity.[22] This was a concession that would later come back to haunt the international community, as evidenced by events in neighboring Sierra Leone and renewed fighting in Liberia by 1999.

Liberia's flawed and incomplete disarmament, demobilization, and reintegration (DDR) program was equally disappointing, not only for its failure to address the country's long-term security situation, but also for its inability to do anything significant to improve the conditions of war-affected children. Liberia's DDR program was completed hastily and haphazardly between the Abuja II Agreement in August 1996 and the period leading up to elections in July 1997. During renewed violence in Monrovia in April and May 1996, armed groups looted the materials intended for DDR use, and external donors refused further substantial support to the program. These projects thus had to be drastically scaled down.[23] In the end, demobilization programs that were initially planned to last for months, and later weeks, took place in a matter of hours. In exchange for their guns, many young fighters walked away with worthless education or vocation vouchers, since the services for which they were to be redeemed were practically nonexistent. Unsurprisingly, some of these former combatants drifted into the alternative security structures that were then being created by warlord-turned-president Charles Taylor, who had won the July 1997 elections by a landslide. Others joined the RUF's rebellion in Sierra Leone.

The Sierra Leone Infection

One can argue that the extension of child soldiering into Sierra Leone, which experienced its own civil war between 1991 and 2002, was in part the result of the failure to deal swiftly with this phenomenon in Liberia. The conflict in Sierra Leone took on some of the features of Liberia, a development that was not surprising given the links between the RUF and the NPFL leaderships. The initial members of the RUF actually had their first combat experience in Liberia. The RUF had difficulty recruiting adults after its initial campaigns in Kailahun and Pujehun in 1991. After reaching

Kono, where it found a ready pool of adolescent and young illicit miners, child soldiers became a systematic part of the RUF's recruitment strategy.[24] Boy soldiers had long been members of the Sierra Leone Army (SLA), and after the outbreak of the conflict in March 1991 the government in Freetown used many underage fighters. The irregular Civil Defense Force (CDF), which provided defense for local communities, also recruited young people into its ranks. In all, an estimated 8,000 Sierra Leonean children were separated from their families, and about 7,000 of these were forced to fight on the sides of the RUF, the SLA, and the Kamajors.

The war in Sierra Leone produced its own share of horrifying headlines, highlighting widespread violence and atrocities between the different factions and against civilians. As in Liberia, there were large-scale killings and torture of civilians, as well as looting and destruction of property that culminated in the systematic mutilation and maiming of innocent civilians, both young and old. The youngest known victim of these terrible atrocities was a two-month-old baby whose foot was amputated by one of the rebel fighters in the attack on Freetown by the RUF and former SLA soldiers in January 1999. Children were an integral part of Sierra Leone's sordid reality of violence. Those who did not serve on the war front directly as soldiers served the war efforts of the rebels in other ways: as sex slaves or "wives" of the commanders (some of whom were themselves children), as laborers, and as cooks.[25] Many of these children were reportedly drugged on a daily basis. At the end of the formal disarmament phase in Sierra Leone in January 2002, the United Nations Mission in Sierra Leone (UNAMSIL) had disarmed about 7,000 children.

The Regional Conundrum

The conflicts in Liberia and Sierra Leone led to the internal displacement of millions of people and the spilling of 1.2 million refugees into neighboring countries. Children and women constituted the largest part of this refugee population. The more fortunate migrants found shelter among local communities in the true spirit of African hospitality.[26] The movement of refugees into neighboring states has several implications. First, the sheer number of refugees that communities must accommodate often has an adverse impact on a country's economy. Second, hosting a foreign population often creates social problems of integration, which sometimes in turn generates its own conflict. Third, the potential for insecurity is often high in situations in which armed elements can mingle freely with refugee communities. For children, refugee and displacement camps mean potential exposure to malnutrition, disease, violence, sexual violation, and absence of regular education. The situation in Guinean refugee camps typifies this problem in

West Africa. At one stage, Guinea was hosting about 500,000 refugees from neighboring Liberia and Sierra Leone, a figure that constituted nearly 10 percent of Guinea's population. Guinea has suffered several incursions by armed groups from across its borders, and only decisive action by its government has saved it from the fate of its southern neighbors. Ultimately, this created other security threats, which in turn aggravated the country's internal security problems.

Children, especially former combatants, emerged from these conflicts not only with bullet wounds and malnutrition, but also with sexually transmitted diseases (STDs) and respiratory illnesses that traveled the region through conduits that emerged between the combat zones, refugee camps, and home communities.[27] There is increasing evidence of HIV/AIDS traveling along the paths of West Africa's armed conflicts. The main perpetrators of sexual abuse and exploitation during wars are members of armed forces or groups whose infection rates for STDs—according to the UN Joint Program on HIV/AIDS (UNAIDS)—may be up to fifty times those of peacetime civilians. This increase in infection rates presents two major dangers. First, the environment of rape, early and unprotected sex, and often forcible intravenous drug use places the youngest members of armed factions—and the people they oppress—at particularly high risk. Second, the broader social impact of war—increased levels of poverty, homelessness, separation from, or loss of, family—increases the vulnerability of a wider section of a country's children to activities that carry a high risk of HIV/AIDS infection (sexual abuse, child prostitution, enlistment in an armed faction). There is clearly a need for a systematic subregional campaign on the impact of HIV/AIDS. However, perhaps the greatest security threat that HIV/AIDS poses to the entire subregion is its potential to decimate populations, productivity, and economic growth in the medium to long term.[28] The impact of this epidemic on children will soon become apparent in the number of children who are orphaned by the disease and the loss of their teachers and health workers.

The war in Sierra Leone also impacted considerably on the emotional and mental health of children. The depth of the problem has yet to be fully revealed, but from the few reports and studies that have been undertaken so far, it is clear that many war-affected victims have suffered deep emotional and mental trauma. Many of these children participated in gruesome acts, often against innocent people. Some of them participated in rapes, while others witnessed the rape of family members. Many lost or witnessed the killings of loved ones, including relatives and friends. In Sierra Leone and Liberia, counselors have indicated that many children suffer from the classic symptoms of posttraumatic stress disorder (PTSD): anxiety, nightmares, flashbacks, depression, and sleeplessness.[29] Some of these children, after years in the "bush," have had difficulty readjusting to mainstream society, and are quick to resort to threatening and violent behavior, a plight that for some of these children has been compounded by stigmatization and alienation. Many communities in Sierra Leone and Liberia have made concerted efforts to reintegrate war-affected children back to society, and have mobilized indigenous cultural and medical practices to try to "heal" these youths. Cleansing ceremonies and reconciliation ceremonies took place in many villages simultaneously with the DDR process in Sierra Leone in 2000 and 2001. However, many children still need long-term medical help and support, as emotional traumas are often repressed for long periods.

The issue of children affected by armed conflict is not just a national problem within countries afflicted by wars. Children were reportedly used in large numbers in Guinea-Bissau during its civil conflict from 1998 to 1999. For West Africa, the problem of children raises a plethora of interrelated issues, including arms flows, violence, illicit trafficking of resources and drugs, population displacement and resettlement, the outbreak and spread of diseases, and child labor exploitation. All of these problems have major security implications and necessitate regional approaches to resolving them. The persistence of high- and low-level conflicts in West Africa, from Casamance to Nigeria's oil-rich Niger Delta, means that arms will continue to flow into this subregion and compound the already high level of insecurity. Different factions and armed gangs continue to draw children into zones of violence as victims.

As indicated earlier, the social problems affecting children in countries wracked by conflicts are present in nearly all countries in West Africa. Huge numbers of street children exist throughout the subregion, many of them victims of the recent decade of political turmoil, economic decline, and social conflicts. It is clear that the challenge of how to engage the time and talents of young people will intensify as more children and young adults are disarmed and demobilized. Without long-term programs and adequate resources, the situation of youth and children in postconflict societies like Sierra Leone will be volatile and potentially explosive. The prewar destitution of youth and children has been exacerbated by these conflicts, and the streets of Freetown and Monrovia are now more crowded with underage peddlers and beggars. The relapse of Liberia into violent conflict in 1999 and a battle for control of Monrovia in July 2003, as well as the unexpected outbreak of civil war in Côte d'Ivoire in September 2002, are an ominous warning not only to the governments of these three countries, but also to all of West Africa's rulers. Young people in the subregion's war zones feel alienated, abused, discouraged, and abandoned. Often illiterate and unemployed, with little hope of finding gainful work, children are susceptible to drug and alcohol abuse and lingering bitterness and anger. These problems need to be properly addressed by regional governments to avoid the fomenting of further rebellions by a lost generation of alienated youth.

Regional Solutions

In the years after the 1996 report by Graca Machel, and following the lessons of the flawed Abuja and Lomé peace accords for Liberia and Sierra Leone (1995 and 1999 respectively), there seems to be greater awareness among regional and external policymakers that more comprehensive approaches are needed to tackle the situation of children affected by war in West Africa. A possible blueprint for a regional approach emerged in April 2000 at the Accra Conference on War-Affected Children, which was co-sponsored by the governments of Ghana and Canada. This initiative aimed at launching a dialogue among West African states on the problems of war-affected children with a view to promoting efforts at the subregional level to protect such children. During the conference in Ghana, members and representatives of the Economic Community of West African States (ECOWAS) adopted the Accra Declaration and the Accra Plan of Action. Both of these documents built on the Declaration of ECOWAS Foreign Ministers on Child Soldiers, signed in Bamako in March 1999, as well as the African Charter on the Rights and Welfare of the Child. They add further impetus to the ECOWAS Protocol Relating to the Mechanism for Conflict Prevention, Management, Resolution, Peacekeeping, and Security, signed in Lomé in December 1999 (see Chapter 13).

The Accra Declaration and the Accra Plan of Action of 2000 called on ECOWAS member states, civil society representatives, and international organizations to undertake actions designed to address the multiple crises of children affected by conflicts. The Accra meeting set broad principles for the protection of war-affected children in West Africa, and the action plan has several elements aimed at addressing many of the problems highlighted above:

- Implementing international conventions and legal instruments for the protection of children, including UN Security Council Resolutions 1261 (1999) and 1265 (1999), the four Geneva Conventions and their Additional Protocols, the African Charter on the Rights and Welfare of the Child, the Convention on the Rights of the Child, and the Optional Protocol on the Involvement of Children in Armed Conflict, among others.
- Working closely with civil society groups and other actors to ensure the successful DDR of child combatants and the rehabilitation of all war-affected children.
- Working with donors to ensure that children have access to quality education.
- Taking political, social, and economic measures to address the factors that contribute to the occurrence or recurrence of armed conflicts— including good governance and democratic practice.

- Incorporating child rights and the protection of children into training programs for the military and other security services.
- Ensuring the awareness of the media of all aspects of child rights and protection.
- Implementing early warning systems to forestall armed conflicts and the victimization of children, as well as their involvement in armed conflicts.
- Integrating child protection into ECOWAS's peacemaking and peace-keeping initiatives and its security mechanism.
- Promoting subregional cross-border activities to reduce the flow of arms.
- Implementing the ECOWAS small arms moratorium of 1998 in order to halt the proliferation of small arms and light weapons in the subregion (see Chapter 10).
- Institutionalizing child protection within ECOWAS and establishing an office within the ECOWAS secretariat in Abuja for the protection of war-affected children.
- Taking measures to involve young people as participants and advocates in the movement for the protection of war-affected children.

Ensuring that these principles are translated into policies that can be harmonized throughout the subregion will be a major challenge. The Accra Plan of Action's call for the establishment, within the ECOWAS secretariat, of a focal point dedicated to the protection of war-affected children in West Africa could prove to be an important tool for harmonizing child protection policies in the subregion. The ECOWAS Child Protection Unit, which has now been established, will be responsible for monitoring the conditions of children in situations of conflict and promoting preventive mechanisms for protecting children.

Specific policies being implemented at the country level might also prove to be useful at the subregional level. ECOWAS could learn from processes that are being developed by individual states in response to child protection needs and apply them subregionally. This seems to be the case in the area of building local capacity to address the problem of war-affected children in select countries. For example, the creation of national commissions has been identified as an area of priority that would ensure that the interests and needs of children and young people are a key part of national priority-setting and resource allocation. The commissions would also be responsible for ensuring that norms and policies set at regional and international levels are implemented at the country level. For example, national commissions could monitor the implementation of the Convention on the Rights of the Child. Ghana was the first country to ratify this convention, and it has established a national commission for children. Similar commissions are regarded as especially important in the rehabilitation and reintegration of children affected by armed conflicts.

At the country level, developments and experiences in postwar Sierra Leone can serve as an instructive guide for the entire subregion, especially for governments, in the areas of paying sufficient attention to war-affected children, devoting the necessary resources to this problem, and forging the strategic local and international partnerships to prevent a culture of impunity. As part of efforts to contribute to child protection in Sierra Leone, Olara Otunnu, the Special Representative of the UN Secretary-General for Children and Armed Conflict, proposed a national commission for war-affected children in 1999. In April 2000, Sierra Leone's president, Ahmed Tejan Kabbah, announced and subsequently established the commission within the framework of promoting the consolidation of peace and postwar reconstruction. This example offers useful lessons for the subregion. The commission's primary task is to prioritize and ensure that issues concerning children affected by war are translated into policies and become part of the national resource allocation process. The commission is also expected to advocate and coordinate national efforts, and to develop "best practices" to meet the needs of war-affected children. Finally, Sierra Leone's commission will pay close attention to, and take into consideration, issues facing adolescents and youth that impact on the rehabilitation and development of such children.[30]

Following earlier experiences in which the international community failed to address impunity by armed groups in Liberia and Sierra Leone, President Kabbah asked the UN for assistance in establishing a Special Court for Sierra Leone. Unlike the international criminal tribunals for Rwanda and Yugoslavia, which are subsidiary organs of the UN, the Special Court for Sierra Leone is a treaty-based court of mixed composition and mixed jurisdiction. In line with UN Security Council Resolution 1315 (2000), Kofi Annan, the UN Secretary-General, proposed a statute for the court following negotiations with the government in Freetown. As proposed by the UN Secretary-General in his report to the Security Council of 4 October 2000, the court will try crimes committed in Sierra Leone after 30 November 1996—when the first comprehensive peace agreement between the government and the RUF was concluded in Abidjan. The court is mandated to investigate mass killings, mutilations and amputations, extrajudicial executions, torture, rape and sexual slavery, intentional attacks on civilian populations, abduction, hostage-taking, forced recruitment of children under the age of fifteen into military or militia forces, and widespread arson. The primary targets will be those persons most responsible for these crimes.[31]

The creation of the court triggered a debate about whether children or young people between the ages of fifteen and eighteen should be tried for crimes against humanity. This issue was hotly debated by a cross section of actors within and outside Sierra Leone. Key UN and NGO actors presented conflicting views. Those opposed to the possible prosecution of juvenile offenders argued that many children could not have understood the full implication of what they were forced to do, that children who are tried for war crimes will be stigmatized and find it difficult to be reintegrated into local communities, and that many children still living behind former rebel lines will be reluctant to surrender their weapons for fear of being arrested. Those opposed to the prosecution of child soldiers also suggested that, instead, Sierra Leone's Truth and Reconciliation Commission (TRC) should deal with cases of juvenile offenders, by subjecting them to a legal and judicial process while emphasizing reconciliation rather than punishment.[32]

Those in favor of prosecuting soldiers who were children at the time of their alleged crimes recognized that only a small number of persons in this category are likely to be deemed by the prosecutor of the Special Court for Sierra Leone as among those "most responsible" for serious violations. These advocates argued that the failure to determine individual legal culpability would send a message of impunity to Sierra Leone's child soldiers that would not go unnoticed in other conflict areas. They contended that, while the Convention on the Rights of the Child and other human rights and humanitarian law standards seek to protect children from exploitation and abuse, these norms were not intended to grant immunity to all persons under the age of eighteen who have committed war crimes.

The Special Court for Sierra Leone and the TRC have begun their work, and the status of children in these processes has been programmatically resolved, with consideration of contending viewpoints. The court has opted to try a small number of relatively high-profile figures from the ranks of the CDF (and the current Kabbah government), the RUF, the Armed Forces Ruling Council (AFRC), and the government of Liberia. As expected, Foday Sankoh, Sam Bockarie, and Johnny Paul Koromah (all of whom died or were killed in 2003—through uncertainty remains about Koromah's death) were indicted. In a bold and more controversial move, the court indicted and detained Chief Hinga Norman, head of the CDF and Kabbah's popular minister of interior. It has also issued a warrant for the arrest of Charles Taylor, the former rebel warlord and president of Liberia, who went into exile in Nigeria in August 2003. The work of the TRC has been less controversial, and it has provided a forum for war-affected children to tell their own stories.

Both the Special Court for Sierra Leone and the TRC are relatively new to West Africa. As their work unfolds, they raise challenging questions of ethics, politics, and law for the citizens of this subregion.[33] One such question concerns the difficulty in harmonizing indigenous norms and values with international norms and conventions. ECOWAS might soon be forced to deliberate on the implications, meaning, and value of international standards for the subregion, especially in addressing the problem of impunity. West Africa will have to deal with the application of international standards, while taking cognizance of local realities.

The situation of children affected by war remains a serious challenge for policymakers and all of West Africa's citizens. The condition of these children is a glaring sign of the deep tragedy that is unfolding in the sub-region, and a frightening indication of the degree to which human values and protective social structures have been eroded by decades of dictator-ship, corruption, and societal neglect. The condition of children in West Africa is therefore not merely a serious welfare or security issue, it is a major developmental challenge whose resolution is integral to the way that the subregion envisions its future. The urgency and commitment with which governments and older citizens in West Africa find ways of ensur-ing and nurturing stable environments for children to grow and reach their fullest potential is the ultimate test of the efficacy of the much quoted axiom "The children are the future." Given the experience of the past decade, some governments in West Africa are treating the challenge with more urgency than others. Some leaders have made progress in establishing regional structures to deal with conflicts and insecurity, and frameworks for dealing with the situation of young people are beginning to emerge in West Africa. The establishment of national commissions for children and the cre-ation of the Child Protection Unit within the ECOWAS secretariat present opportunities as well as challenges in efforts to develop a regional frame-work for the protection of children affected by armed conflicts.

Notes

1. The figure of 300,000 has been in use since 1997, but there is some debate about the accuracy of this figure, which requires further research.

2. A strong argument has been made that young people cannot be said to have voluntarily chosen to join warring factions, since the harsh sociopolitical and eco-nomic realities in war-torn countries often present them with little or no alterna-tives. See, for example, Graca Machel, "The Impact of Armed Conflict on Children: A Critical Review of Progress Made and Obstacles Encountered in Increasing Pro-tection for War-Affected Children," paper presented at a conference in Winnipeg, Canada, September 2000, p. 8.

3. The Special Representative of the UN Secretary-General on Internally Dis-placed Persons, Francis Deng, estimates that there are 40 million displaced people worldwide. It is estimated that half of these are children.

4. Thousands of French and German nationals participated in the Children's Crusade of 1212. Children have also been used in various European conflicts over the centuries. French generalissimo Napoleon Bonaparte, for example, began his military career as a boy. The United States also had a long history of using boy sol-diers between the American Revolutionary War and World War I. See, for example, Susan R. Hull, ed., *Boy Soldiers of the Confederacy* (Austin, Tex.: Eakin Press, 1998); and C. Eleanor, *Bishop, Ponies, Patriots, and Powder Monkeys: A History of America's Forces, 1776–1916* (Del Mar, Calif.: Bishop Press, 1982).

5. Graca Machel, *Impact of Armed Conflict on Children: Report of the Expert of the Secretary-General Pursuant to General Assembly Resolution 48/157* (New

York: United Nations, 1996). Before this report was published, Human Rights Watch had issued a report on the situation in Liberia titled *Easy Prey: Child Soldiers in Liberia, 1994* (New York: Human Rights Watch, 1994), and Amnesty International also wrote on the situation of children imprisoned by the military government in Sierra Leone: *Sierra Leone: Prisoners of War? Children Detained in Barracks and Prison,* Index AFR 51/06/93 (London: Amnesty International, 1993).

6. Amnesty International, *Childhood: A Casualty of Conflict,* AFR 51/69/00 (London: Amnesty International, 2000); and UNICEF, *Adult Wars, Child Soldiers: Voices of Children Involved in Armed Conflict in East Asia and the Pacific Region* (Bangkok: UNICEF East Asia and Pacific Office, 2002).

7. See Ilene Cohn and Guy S. Goodwin-Gill, *Child Soldiers: The Role of Children in Conflict* (Oxford: Clarendon Press, 1994). This source extensively discusses the reasons for children and youth joining armed forces and groups.

8. Karl Maier, "The Universal Soldier (Child Soldiers)," *Yale Review* 86 (January 1998): 70–93. The same observations are evident in the case of young people recruited by the Tamil Tigers in Sri Lanka. See, for example, Daya Somasundaram, "Child Soldiers: Understanding the Context," *British Medical Journal* 324 (25 May 2002): 1268.

9. See Krijn Peters and Paul Richards, "Why We Fight: Voices of Youth Combatants in Sierra Leone," *Africa* 68, no. 2 (1998): 185–210. For a detailed discussion of the recruitment of children and youth into armed groups across various regions, with examples from El Salvador, Ethiopia, Mozambique, Peru, Myanmar, and Sri Lanka, among others, see also Cohn and Goodwin-Gill, *Child Soldiers,* pp. 13–44.

10. Peters and Richards, "Why We Fight," p. 187.

11. Paul Richards, *Fighting for the Rainforest: War, Youth, and Resources in Sierra Leone* (Oxford: James Currey, 1996). See also Maier, "Universal Soldier."

12. See Machel, *Impact of Armed Conflict on Children;* and Somasundaram, "Child Soldiers," p. 1268.

13. Two glaring examples of this loss of state capacity in Sierra Leone are the Ministry of Social Welfare, which increasingly became irrelevant (its functions were divided and absorbed into other ministries), and the Approved School in Kingtom, an institution for rehabilitating young offenders, which fell into disuse in the 1980s.

14. People Educational Association, *Bras, Greens, and Ballheads: Interviews with Freetown "Street Boys"* (Freetown: People Educational Association, 1989). In "Universal Soldier," Karl Maier makes the point about the breakdown of traditional societies like Sande, Bundo, and Poro.

15. Richards, *Fighting for the Rainforest;* and A. B. Zack-Williams, "Child Soldiers and the Civil War in Sierra Leone," paper presented at the Development Studies Association Conference, 12–14 September 1996, University of Bath, pp. 14–16.

16. Festus Aboagye, *ECOMOG: A Sub-Regional Experience in Conflict Resolution, Management, and Peacekeeping in Liberia* (Accra: Sedco, 1999), p. 44.

17. Stephen Ellis, *The Mask of Anarchy: The Destruction of Liberia and the Religious Dimensions of an African Civil War* (London: Hurst, 1999), p. 79.

18. This was a frequently cited factor for the participation of young people on the side of the NPFL in the immediate aftermath of the invasion of Nimba county. See *Africa Report,* July–August 1990, p. 47. See also the Human Rights Watch report *Easy Prey.*

19. Ellis, *Mask of Anarchy,* p. 79. See also Bill Berkley, *The Graves Are Not Yet Full: Race, Tribe, and Power in the Heart of Africa* (New York: Basic Books, 2001), pp. 22–24.

20. Aboagye, *ECOMOG,* p. 44. See also Human Rights Watch, *Easy Prey.*

21. See, for example, 'Funmi Olonisakin, "An International War Crimes Tribunal for Africa: Problems and Prospects," *African Journal of Contemporary and International Law* 9, no. 4 (1997): 822–835.

22. The same concession was made to the RUF and the Armed Forces Ruling Council (AFRC) in the 1996 Abidjan and 1999 Lomé Accords. In neither Liberia nor Sierra Leone did a blanket amnesty guarantee peace or the compliance of rebel factions with peace accords. Sierra Leone turned out to be more fortunate than Liberia, as the machinations of Foday Sankoh, the leader of the RUF, were thwarted in May 2000. In Liberia, after a pause in fighting in 1997, war resumed barely two years later. See Adekeye Adebajo, *Building Peace in West Africa: Liberia, Sierra Leone and Guinea-Bissau* (Boulder: Lynne Rienner, 2002).

23. For details of the DDR process in Liberia during these phases, see John Mackinlay, Abiodun Alao, and 'Funmi Olonisakin, *Peacekeeping, Politicians, and Warlords: The Liberian Peace Process* (Tokyo: United Nations University Press, 2000).

24. The argument that the RUF was influenced by the pattern of war in Liberia has not gone unchallenged. For example, while a group of Sierra Leonean scholars admit that the RUF might have been influenced by the tactics of the warring factions in Liberia, some also argue that independently and unaided, the RUF and the Sierra Leone Army (SLA) could have embarked on these levels of atrocity. A stronger argument can perhaps be made that the RUF's leaders might have curtailed their actions and their treatment of children had the international community taken stronger action against those who committed grave crimes in Liberia. See Ibrahim Abdullah, "Lumpen Youth Culture and Political Violence: Sierra Leoneans Debate the RUF and the Civil War," *Africa Development* 22, nos. 3–4 (1997): 171–214 (Special Issue: "Lumpen Culture and Political Violence: The Sierra Leone Civil War").

25. Amnesty International, *Sierra Leone: Rape and Other Forms of Sexual Violence Against Women,* AFR 51/35/00 (London: Amnesty International, 29 June 2002).

26. Beverlee Bruce, "Toward Mediating the Impact of Forced Migration and Displacement Among Children Affected by Armed Conflict," *Journal of International Affairs* 55, no. 1 (Fall 2001): 35–51.

27. Amnesty International, *Childhood.*

28. It is estimated that AIDS has killed about 3.8 million children worldwide, and that 13 million children have become orphaned as a result of AIDS. In Africa, about 18.8 million people have died due to AIDS. See Machel, *The Impact of Armed Conflict on Children,* p. 14.

29. Lois Whitman and Janet Fleischman, "The Child Soldiers," *Africa Report* 39, no. 4 (July–August 1994): 65–67. For broader and more scientific studies, see Maureen A. Allwood, Debora Bell-Dolan, and Syed Arshad Husain, "Children's Trauma and Adjustment Reactions to Violent and Non-Violent War Experiences," *Journal of the American Academy of Child and Adolescent Psychiatry* 41 (April 2002): 450–458; and Salman Elbedour, Robert Ten Bensel, and David T. Bastien, "Ecological Integrated Model of Children of War: Individual and Social Psychology," *Child Abuse and Neglect* 17, no. 6 (November–December 1993): 805–1010.

30. See *Terms of Reference of the National Commission for War-Affected Children in Sierra Leone,* Office of the Special Representative of the Secretary-General for Children and Armed Conflict (OSRSG-CAAC), May 2000.

31. See the additional report of the Special Representative of the UN Secretary-General for Children and Armed Conflict to the Commission on Human Rights, submitted in accordance with General Assembly Resolution 55/79, E/CN.4/2001/76, 25 January 2001.

32. Ibid.

33. Ghana and Nigeria recently instituted Truth and Reconciliation Commissions relating to periods of military rule in both countries. Some of Nigeria's generals stonewalled and thwarted the commission at every turn, with former military rulers Generals Ibrahim Babangida (1985–1993) and Abdulsalam Abubakar (1998–1999) refusing to appear before a commission they accused of bias.

PART 3

Regional and External Actors

12

Civil Society

Yasmin Jusu-Sheriff

Notable among the many strategies and approaches being proposed and adopted in efforts to manage conflicts in West Africa are a greater recognition and use of civil society in these efforts. Kofi Annan, the UN Secretary-General, has argued that "there are few limits to what civil society can achieve."[1] Article 4 of the code of conduct of the Economic Community of West African States (ECOWAS) small arms moratorium (see Chapter 10) accords a preeminent role to civil society. With the end of the Cold War, "civil society" has been hailed by many as the new panacea for promoting democracy and preventing conflicts in Africa. Some positive developments in democratization and conflict management in West Africa over the past decade have been attributed to civil society. It is therefore understandable that ECOWAS should look to civil society to help build a Pax West Africana.

This chapter provides an analysis of the role of civil society in conflict prevention, peacemaking, and peacebuilding in West Africa. I critically examine the concept of "civil society" and assess the synergy between theoretical constructions and "actually existing [West] African civil society."[2] The chapter then analyzes four case studies of conflict management and peacebuilding efforts by civil society actors, in Liberia, Sierra Leone, Mali, and Senegal. I conclude the chapter by considering the achievements of, and constraints on, West Africa's civil society groups, as well as the opportunities for their interventions in future conflict management and democratization efforts.

Defining Civil Society

The Nature of Civil Society

Before ECOWAS's state-centric bureaucracy can escape from its familiar domain of regional economic integration and work effectively with West Africa's civil society actors on conflict management issues, it is important first to define what we mean by "civil society" and to identify the actors with which ECOWAS can collaborate to manage conflicts and promote democratic governance in West Africa. Who or what is "civil society"? Or as Crawford Young eloquently put it:

> But what precisely has ventured upon the stage? Is this truly an actor, organically constituted? Is its corporeal being only an illusion of distant perception, dissolving as one approaches? Is it merely a metaphor masquerading as a player? Is it yet another child of the anthropomorphic fertility of the social scientific imagination? Or do we spy a redemptive spirit, providentially dispatched to right a political world gone awry?[3]

Civil society is an old concept in European social and political thought to whose evolution Locke, Hegel, de Tocqueville, and Gramsci have all contributed.[4] The concept regained currency after the collapse of the communist bloc in eastern Europe in the late 1980s as new analytical and political tools were sought to explain the dynamics of new social organizations in a context in which the role and power of the state had greatly diminished.[5] "Civil society" also became an important term for understanding novel forms of social and political engagement in Africa where the postcolonial state was in retreat or on the verge of collapse after failing to deliver on the postindependence dreams of "the founding fathers" and their citizens of rapid economic transformation and material abundance.[6]

The classic conception of civil society encompasses a number of key elements. First, civil society comprises formally organized groups and associations located, according to Hegel, in the space between the state and the household.[7] Second, although these groups express and protect primary "private interests," they operate in the public sphere and usually participate in setting public rules. Third, civil society actors are autonomous of the state and, while cognizant of the legitimacy of the state, they resist its "incursions" into civic spaces.[8] Fourth, members of civil society groups are often committed to liberal democratic values and free market capitalism.[9]

While some of the elements of the classical conception of civil society may be present in the West African experience, the actual character of civil society in the subregion is far more complex and variegated.[10] Many civil society actors involving women, professionals, workers, students, religious leaders, and rural inhabitants have indisputably acted in recent times to challenge state authoritarianism, expand democratic spaces, and defend issues of public interest in many West African countries. Yet as Stephen Ndegwa points out, not all civil society groups are uniformly progressive.[11] Some are mere vehicles or stepping-stones for opposition politicians to enter into formal mainstream politics. Hence the coining of the sobriquet "next government official" to describe some representatives of nongovernmental organizations (NGOs).

Other civil society actors provide a means through which foreign countries can leverage the affairs of West African countries. Many of these groups have become sources of employment or resource appropriation in an age of job retrenchment and structural adjustment. It is therefore difficult to offer a clear and simple definition of a phenomenon that encompasses actors and organizations of all hues and origins, differentiated along ideological, class, gender, religious, and geographical lines, and performing a host of public, private, and generalized, as well as specialized, functions. Thus, according to Robert Fatton, civil society in Africa "is neither homogenous, nor wholly emancipatory; in fact it is contradictory, exhibiting both democratic and despotic tendencies. Moreover, it is conflict-ridden and prone to the devastating violence of multiple forms of particularisms. Civil society should therefore be analyzed in the plural, rather than as a uniform unitary political space."[12] Fatton's summation captures well the complexity of these issues and provides a framework, albeit an imprecise one, to situate some of the differences and "peculiarities" of West African civil society.

Reconceptualizing Civil Society in West Africa

There are many groups within African civil societies that have deep indigenous and historical roots. In precolonial Africa, there were initiation, hunter, religious, cooperative, and other associational groups that were not necessarily wedded into the local artifice of power, and that persisted throughout the colonial and postcolonial periods. These groups constituted alternative poles of power and some carved out their own autonomous "civic" space to promote or defend their specific interests. These so-called traditional groups and institutions may be marginal, but they are not disarticulated from the postcolonial African state and society, and are very much affected by the vicissitudes of state politics and policies.[13] More urbane observers in West Africa's cities regard some of the strategies and actions of these groups as "unorthodox" and even "unacceptable." But many of the contributions of civil society to public interest issues have been positive and transformative. Recent developments in Sierra Leone, Liberia, and Mali, and to a lesser extent Senegal, underscore this point.[14]

A complex interpretative framework also helps us to understand why some civil society actors in West Africa have conceived of their role as dialogical with, and complementary of, the state, rather than confrontational or oppositional to it.[15] Participants in the first Organization of African Unity (OAU)–Civil Society Conference, held in Addis Ababa in June 2001, "firmly expressed their recognition that their role in society must be one of complementing the efforts of African governments."[16] This statement runs contrary to the classical and theoretical conception of civil society.[17] Yet it comes out of the realities and political experiences of Africa: confrontation and conflict have proved to be the bane of the continent. Many civil society groups and governments have realized that managing conflicts and promoting development and democracy require the collective creative energies of the entire citizenry. As was demonstrated in the case of Mali, the country's Tuareg conflict in the 1990s posed a fundamental threat to the welfare of society, the stability of the government, and the effectiveness of civil society. This conflict transcended the differences that existed between the government and civil society, and eventually forced them to work together for the collective good. This example, however, should not obscure the reality that, just as in the classical Western framework, West Africa's civil society groups and governments are often at odds over a multiplicity of issues and approaches to tackling national and local problems.

It is almost impossible to understand the nature of civil society in West Africa without taking into consideration the extent to which civil society is a gendered space. Women became much more of a social burden in the 1980s and 1990s amid West Africa's depressing socioeconomic conditions and the eruption of violent conflicts. These conditions have pushed women into the public domain in a bid to end armed conflicts, contribute to development, and promote democracy. In Liberia, Mali, and Sierra Leone, women were at the forefront of democratization campaigns and efforts to end civil wars. Under the public spotlight, women have proved that they can be innovative, courageous, committed, hardworking, and flexible. They have combined modern and traditional strategies to build powerful coalitions across class, ethnic, and geographical lines.[18] In the process, West African women have created greater space for civil society. Men have sometimes ceded leadership roles to women based on the recognition that female activists have created new forms of commitment, credibility, and impartiality that the male-dominated political elite had previously failed to demonstrate. Women have also challenged and transcended the classical separation between the public and the private space—by voicing and politicizing issues of vital importance to them (abuse, rape, circumcision, etc.). Thus, civil society has provided, and continues to provide, an entry point for women into the largely masculine and patriarchal public domain. This has sometimes come with a high price tag, since it has often typecast activist women, exposed them to public (especially male) hostility and vilification, and limited their desire to pursue independent political careers in their own right.

Defining "civil society" in West Africa involves taking into account the hegemonic relationship between local and external actors. West African civil society groups operate neither in an international vacuum nor outside the context of global differentials in power and resources, including the historical legacy of colonial rule by European powers. Many African civil society groups are fostered by, linked to, and sometimes dependent on powerful and wealthy external countries and organizations. These external donors usually have their own agendas, which are often tailored to meet the needs and interests of their domestic sponsors and audiences rather than those of Africans. This clearly undermines the issue of autonomy in the classical conception of "civil society." By the 1980s, many western European and North American governments increasingly viewed the African state as corrupt, morally bankrupt, and of dubious legitimacy. According to Victor Azarya, "strengthening civil society has now become a deliberately designed and targeted activity of international donor organizations [and countries]."[19] Through institutions like the World Bank and the International Monetary Fund (IMF), Western donors have made the promotion of nonstate actors, particularly nongovernmental agencies and civil society groups, major pillars in their promotion of neoliberal democratization and free market economics in Africa.[20] Financial support and aid have been routed through international humanitarian and development NGOs that usually work with or through "local partners."[21] Many African civil society groups depend on external support for their survival and for pushing forward their agendas. Some scholars and many African leaders even cynically view the whole civil society phenomenon in Africa as an extension of a Western neocolonial project on the continent. In this perspective, civil society groups serve as naive "fifth columnists" for maintaining hegemonic relations with Africa.

West Africa's nongovernmental sector has revealed not only its complexities, contradictions, and limitations, but also its fluidity and dynamism over the past two decades. Many civil society groups who have either disengaged from the state or regard the public domain as outside their purview have been forced by developments over the past two decades to intervene on issues of collective national interest or significance. Thus, in nearly all West African countries, religious groups, women's groups, professional associations, and trade unions have been forced by events beyond their control to transcend their traditional confines and parochial interests to engage the state and wider society more actively.[22] Many of these actors could eventually return to their primary preoccupations once the central issues that forced them to center stage have been resolved. But can such groups still be categorized as belonging to civil society? In seeking to answer this question, we will next examine some of the concrete ways in which civil society groups have engaged the state and society in four of West Africa's conflict zones: Liberia, Sierra Leone, Mali, and Senegal.

Civil Society Interventions: Four Case Studies

Challenging Warlordism in Liberia

Liberian civil society has its roots in the struggle against presidential and True Whig Party (TWP) autocracy under the presidencies of William Tubman and William Tolbert between 1944 and 1980. For decades, the struggle to counter government authoritarianism and corruption was embodied by Albert Porte, a social commentator, teacher, and pamphleteer. His crusade against state excesses inspired and raised the political consciousness of his fellow Liberians. In the 1970s, the Movement for Justice in Africa (MOJA) and the Progressive Alliance of Liberia (PAL) joined the struggle to mobilize Liberia's civil society and to open up political space. Their activities precipitated the demise of the TWP's Americo-Liberian oligarchy and the seizure of power by Master-Sergeant Samuel Doe in April 1980 as the first indigenous leader in the country's 133-year history. Though initially positioned as voluntary associations and pressure groups, MOJA and PAL would eventually be drawn into the maelstrom of Liberian politics as political parties during the flawed democratic transition of 1985.[23] The Doe dictatorship severely restricted space for the development of civil society. Ironically, it was the outbreak of civil war in December 1989 that created new opportunities for the reemergence of civil society in Liberia.

The civil war and the collapse of the Liberian state forced several groups, particularly religious bodies, to redefine their roles and participate more actively in the civic and political spheres. The principal religious associations in Liberia—the Liberian Council of Churches (LCC) and the National Muslim Council of Liberia (NMCL)—redefined their role to include the welfare and security of Liberians within their religious and spiritual realm. The LCC and NMCL united under the umbrella of the Inter-Faith Mediation Committee (IFMC) to provide an effective voice in efforts to mediate an end to the civil war. As the violence escalated in Liberia in 1990, the IFMC undertook shuttle diplomacy between the warring factions. The immediate focus of Liberia's priests and imams was the termination of the war and the protection of the rights of citizens against the excesses of the warring factions.[24]

In June 1990 the IFMC brought together the two main Liberia factions, Doe's Armed Forces of Liberia (AFL) and Charles Taylor's National Patriotic Front of Liberia (NPFL), in Freetown in an effort to mediate an end to the war.[25] The IFMC proposals arising from this mediation effort became the basis of the plan adopted by ECOWAS leaders in Banjul in August 1990 for resolving the Liberian crisis. Throughout the seven-year conflict (1989–1996), the IFMC maintained an active, critical, but impartial voice that defended and promoted the interests and welfare of Liberia's citizens. The group met frequently with representatives of the warring parties, and organized and participated in several local and international peace conferences. The IFMC also strongly criticized the Abuja Agreement of 1995 for rewarding Liberia's warlords with government positions. After the temporary end of Liberia's civil war in 1997, the IFMC played an active role in disarmament and electoral efforts.

New civic groups emerged in Liberia in response to the war. The Catholic Justice and Peace Commission (JPC) and the Center for Law and Human Rights Education (CLHRE) were created to highlight and protest human rights violations. Both organizations documented human rights abuses and atrocities committed by the different factions. They later extended their activities to human rights education and the provision of legal services to victims of abuses. The Liberia Women Initiative (LWI) primarily devoted its attention to investigating crimes and atrocities committed against women. It drew international attention to these issues and was instrumental in putting them on the peace agenda.[26] Africa's first female head of state, Ruth Perry, who chaired Liberia's interim government between August 1996 and July 1997, had been an active member of the LWI.

Liberia's indefatigable women forced their way into the Accra Clarification Conference in 1994, from which they had initially been excluded on the grounds that they were not direct parties to the conflict. They were eventually granted official observer status and their high-profile advocacy at the peace conference served as a powerful reminder to negotiators of important interests other than those of the warlords that needed to be taken into account in any final settlement.[27] In the same year, Liberian women demonstrated in Monrovia against proposals by former U.S. president Jimmy Carter and the Special Representative of the UN Secretary-General Trevor Gordon-Somers to meet with faction leaders separately from civil society representatives on the grounds that such a meeting would lend unwarranted legitimacy to the warlords.[28]

The work of Liberia's religious and civic organizations was complemented by the emergence of a robust but fractious media in Monrovia. Newspapers like *Plain Talk, Liberia Age, The Inquirer,* and *Foto Vision* courageously strove to keep the public informed and voiced contentious opinions under the difficult conditions of civil strife.

Despite their many political differences, Liberia's civil society actors played an important role in efforts to end the country's civil war, reduce atrocities and abuses, disarm the armed factions, and organize elections.[29]

They consistently insisted on disarmament before elections and made clear that power should be obtained through the ballot box and not through bullets. After the war temporarily ended in 1997, civil society actors in Liberia's rural communities undertook cleansing ceremonies of former fighters to facilitate their reintegration into local communities.

Searching for Sustainable Peace in Sierra Leone

As in Liberia, the space for civic action against authoritarian rule in Sierra Leone contracted greatly under the one-party rule of Siaka Stevens's All People's Congress (APC) between 1968 and 1985. The APC alternatively repressed and co-opted labor, women, and other civic groups that it saw as oppositional. The opposition of Sierra Leone's civil society to autocratic rule was led during this period by university students and a few independent newspapers like the *Tablet* and *For Di People*. In 1985 the government dealt a major blow to the student movement when some of its leaders at Fourah Bay College were rusticated (see Chapter 8).

Even as the country began to return to a multiparty political system in 1990, the outbreak of a decade-long civil war in March 1991 and the search for peace that followed helped to rekindle a broader and more vibrant civil society movement in Sierra Leone. As in Liberia, the intensification of war in the mid-1990s led to closer collaboration between women's groups, religious organizations, traditional rulers, students, trade unions, the press, and other civic groups. These organizations represented a broad-based citizens' movement against the civil war and military dictatorship, and in favor of multiparty democracy and a just peace settlement in Sierra Leone.

Sierra Leone's Muslim and Christian leaders constituted themselves into the Multi-Religious Council (MRC) to advocate for peace. The National Union of Sierra Leone Students (NUSS) and the Sierra Leone Association of Journalists (SLAJ) also joined the campaign for peace. But by far the most effective civic group to emerge in the mid-1990s was the Women's Movement of Sierra Leone, led by Fatmata Boie, Yasmin Jusu-Sheriff, and Isha Dyfan. The movement, drawing its leading members mainly from the medical, legal, and educational professions as well as female church groups, became the country's most prominent antiwar group. It eventually incorporated market women and became less elitist. Sierra Leone's women enjoyed strong support from Western embassies in Freetown, particularly those of the United States and the United Kingdom. The embassies provided financial support, space for meetings, and on occasion, technical support for the group.

Traditional rulers, namely paramount chiefs, also became increasingly active in the campaign to end the civil war in Sierra Leone, through both peaceful and military means. The war ravaged many chiefdoms in the countryside, displaced people, and led to the assassination of many chiefs by Revolutionary United Front (RUF) rebels. By 1994, surviving chiefs, many of them displaced, formed a lobby group that was represented in several civil society meetings by the regent chief of Telu Bongor Chiefdom, Hinga Norman, who became deputy defense minister under the elected government of Ahmed Tejan Kabbah in 1996. The chiefs participated in different peace initiatives, but became increasingly frustrated by the lack of progress in ending the war and the escalating atrocities by rebels against their constituents and fellow chiefs. Some of the chiefs joined the effort to mobilize their constituents, especially by using local hunters and young men to form or join village- and chiefdom-level defense militias. Known in the south and east as Kamajors, and in the north as Donsos, these civil defense forces fought alongside the loyal remnants of Sierra Leone Army (SLA) and ECOWAS Cease-Fire Monitoring Group (ECOMOG) troops defending the Kabbah government from 1997 to 1999.[30] Hinga Norman played an instrumental role in galvanizing and organizing the civil defense forces, and many Sierra Leoneans were surprised by his indictment for war crimes by a special court in March 2003.

A short-lived attempt was made to incorporate all of the different civil society groups into a national peace movement in 1995 under the leadership of the country's trade unions. Over sixty religious, educational, youth, and student groups signed on to the effort, but the women's movement stayed out of this alliance. The coalition, which became known as the National Coordinating Committee for Peace (NCCP), was launched amid much fanfare. Although the NCCP was short-lived, it helped to pressure the military government in Freetown to negotiate an end to the war, organize a national conference, and return the country to civilian rule by February 1996.

The National Provisional Ruling Council (NPRC) government of Captain Valentine Strasser, which took power after a coup d'etat in April 1992, was initially hostile to the peace efforts of Sierra Leone's women's movement, and to other civil society groups. The military junta prevented the women's movement from talking to the RUF by radio in 1994. Although the NPRC subsequently permitted the Mano River Bridge peace overture by local community leaders in the subregion to proceed in 1995, the military government undermined its chances of success by launching military strikes against the rebels while the talks were being conducted.[31] The NPRC also refused to heed the NCCP's call for a national conference, though it eventually allowed a forum of civic groups to convene at Freetown's Bintumani hotel in 1995. During this period, the Bintumani conference became the dominant forum for civil society groups as well as political parties to discuss issues of national importance. Three conferences were held between 1995 and 2000. The resolutions and recommendations of these conferences were nonbinding on different governments in Freetown, but they did become an important part of the civic process of mobilizing and articulating public opinion and allowing the government to feel the pulse of the country. These efforts by Sierra Leone's resurgent civil society groups helped to push the military government to organize multiparty elections in January 1996.

The restoration of multiparty politics, however, proved to be short-lived. The democratically elected government of Ahmed Tejan Kabbah was overthrown by Major Johnny Paul Koromah in a coup d'etat in May 1997. Koromah invited the RUF to the capital, Freetown, to join his Armed Forces Ruling Council (AFRC). A Nigerian-led ECOMOG force ousted the AFRC/RUF alliance from Freetown in February 1998, but the rebels attacked the capital again with devastating vengeance in January 1999, resulting in over 3,000 civilian deaths (see Chapters 13 and 14).

This renewed violence reignited the energies of various civil society groups in their resistance to the AFRC/RUF coup. Civil society activists sought the restoration of democracy, assisted the repatriation of refugees, and supported the government-in-exile of Tejan Kabbah, who was based in Conakry, Guinea. Sierra Leone's irrepressible media made a decisive contribution during the campaign to restore the democratically elected government to power. A clandestine radio station, FM98 Radio Democracy, became a critical link between the exiled government and people in Freetown and its environs. Print journalists and news vendors, some of whom were killed during the AFRC/RUF interregnum, devised ingenious ways of opposing the junta and ensuring that their newspapers were published.[32]

Sierra Leone's students also made noteworthy contributions to restoring democratic rule,[33] and like their Liberian counterparts, these students played a leading role in the search for peace. In August 1997, Sierra Leonean students organized demonstrations in support of the Kabbah government. The military junta fired on and killed some of the demonstrators.[34] While residing in Guinea as refugees, Sierra Leonean students also volunteered to take up arms in support of the democratically elected government.

In 1997, Sierra Leonean women refugees in Guinea reconstituted the Sierra Leone Women's Forum, a network of women's groups and organizations. The forum's two main objectives were to provide support to Sierra Leonean women refugees in Guinea, and to mobilize these women for collective action to expedite a peaceful end to their exile. The group visited and helped to improve the lot of Sierra Leonean refugees in camps by advocating for better conditions for them and working with their host communities, particularly Guinean women. Guinea's minister for the promotion of women met regularly with the Sierra Leone Women's Forum in Conakry. The forum also enlisted the help of a pan-African women's NGO, Femmes-Africa-Solidarité (FAS), in building closer ties between Sierra Leonean women and their sisters in neighboring countries, particularly the Mano river neighbors of Guinea and Liberia.

If the resistance to the AFRC junta rule brought the Kabbah government and civil society groups closer together in 1997 and 1998, the search for a more durable peace settlement in Lomé in 1999 resulted in a far more complicated relationship between the government and civil society. Kabbah, and to a certain extent the United Nations Observer Mission in Sierra Leone (UNOMSIL), led by Francis Okello, relied heavily on the Inter-Religious Council of Sierra Leone (IRCSL)—a successor group of the Multi-Religious Council—to help initiate contacts, build confidence, and begin preliminary discussions between the RUF and the government.[35] The IRCSL met with, exchanged ideas with, and drew inspiration from its religious counterparts in Liberia. The role of civil society groups was deemed to be so crucial that the IRCSL and Sierra Leone's Labour Congress were granted observer status at the peace talks in Lomé.[36] Yet during the negotiations, the Kabbah government faced considerable pressure to seal a deal from the international community, especially from Jesse Jackson, the U.S. Special Envoy for the Promotion of Democracy in Africa. This led to Kabbah making substantial concessions to the RUF and the AFRC, including the granting of a general amnesty and the awarding to the rebels of several ministerial and governmental positions. These concessions exceeded the recommendations made by different civil society groups and national political parties that had met at the third Bintumani conference in June 1999. Key members of Kabbah's cabinet also opposed the peace accord. Despite vocal press opposition and street demonstrations by civic groups, Kabbah signed the Lomé Agreement in July 1999.

In spite of what they regarded as the unpalatable nature of the Lomé Agreement, Sierra Leone's civil society groups made genuine attempts at promoting peace and reconciliation between the armed factions and the civilian population. Isaac Lappia has highlighted the efforts made by chiefs and people in Gorama-Mende and Nimiyamaa chiefdoms in southern Sierra Leone to implement the Lomé Agreement's provisions on disarmament within two months of its signing.[37] The chiefs led efforts at reconciliation and the reintegration of former combatants into local communities.

In postwar Sierra Leone, civil society groups and NGOs have proliferated, though their roles and achievements remain checkered. Yet there is no doubt that civil society groups were a major, if not decisive, factor in the May 2002 elections, which resulted in a landslide victory for incumbent president Ahmed Tejan Kabbah and the humiliating defeat of the RUF. Groups like the Sierra Leone Labour Congress and the Sierra Leone Association of Journalists played an active part in voter education and election monitoring. Journalists observed the counting of ballots and, with the help of satellite and cellular phones, promptly relayed the results of the elections to the country as they were being counted and verified by the National Elections Commission (NEC). In many cases, the NEC struggled to keep up with the journalists.

Popular Peacemaking Efforts in Mali

Civil society groups intervened decisively in Mali's politics to help end the twenty-three-year dictatorship of General Moussa Traoré, to democratize the state and society, and to work for the peaceful resolution of the Tuareg secessionist rebellion in the north of the country. Traoré had seized power in 1968 and "civilianized" his military junta into a one-party regime in 1978 and 1979. Popular disaffection against his regime was manifested in two principal ways: an armed revolt by the Tuareg in the north, and popular protests by civic organization and political parties.

The "Tuareg revolt," spearheaded by the Mouvement Populaire de l'Azawad (MPA), began in June 1990 with attacks on government targets in northern Mali and a prison in Niger. Traoré's brutal military occupation of the northern region, the home of mainly Tuaregs and Arabic-speaking people, was merely one of the many complex causes of the "revolt." Northern Mali, a drought-infested region, had long been marginalized and excluded from substantial government revenues by successive colonial and postcolonial governments in Bamako. Two devastating drought cycles, which peaked in 1973–1974 and 1984–1985, disrupted the social and economic fabric of Tuareg societies, while subsequent misappropriating of food aid by the government forced many Tuaregs to move to other parts of the country or across Mali's borders.[38] Some of the young male Tuaregs found themselves in Libya, where they enlisted in Colonel Muammar Qaddafi's foreign legion. As in Sierra Leone and Liberia, some of these legionnaires became the core of the initial armed revolt against the Malian state.[39]

Civil society organizations, including trade unions, women's and students' groups, human rights, legal, and other professional associations; the fledgling independent press; and newly formed opposition parties also intensified their protests against the regime and demanded an end to the Traoré dictatorship. In December 1990, two newly established political parties with considerable support from civil society groups, the Alliance pour la Démocratie en Mali (ADEMA) and the Comité National d'Initiatives Démocratiques (CNID), organized mass antigovernment demonstrations. Traoré and his military brass hats initially responded to the crisis in the north and the popular protests in the streets of Bamako with brutal reprisals and repression. Though the regime later secured an agreement with the Tuareg rebels in January 1991 to end the violence, its credibility and legitimacy had diminished considerably. Two months later, with the support of a segment of the military and civic groups, Colonel Ahmadou Toumani Touré toppled the Traoré regime in a bid to stem the political hemorrhaging of the country.

The new government, a transitional coalition of military and civilian elements, incorporated representatives from Tuareg and civil society organizations into the political system. Despite its inclusive nature, however, civil society groups continued to pressure the transitional government to convene a national conference in order to craft a new constitution for the country and to lead Mali back to elected government. The Coordination des Associations Oeuvrant pour la Paix et le Développement au Nord,[40] a pro-peace group led by Abacar Sidibe, pushed hard for the transitional government to demonstrate more commitment in resolving the conflict in the north. General Touré convened a national conference between 29 July and 12 August 1991, which paved the way for the creation of a new constitution and the holding of national elections. The Tuareg conflict was on the agenda of the national conference, and the transitional government decided to enlist the support of Algeria in the search for a durable settlement to the crisis. This strategy involved Mali's civil society groups in the meetings and discussions that led to the signing of the national pact with the Tuareg rebels in April 1992. The pact, however, failed to end the fighting until a successful disarmament process was effected in 1995 and 1996.

The negotiation of the peace accord in 1992 proceeded in tandem with Mali's democratic transition. Alpha Oumar Konaré, a renowned historian, took office in June 1992 after emerging victorious in presidential elections. The role of civil society had been crucial in creating a legitimate and democratic dispensation in Mali.[41] Yet the new, more democratic order did not result automatically in durable peace. The 1992 national pact failed to deliver long-term peace to Mali for several reasons: inadequate public understanding of the Tuareg conflict, disaffection with the peace settlement, and the new government's inability to support financially the disarmament, demobilization, and reintegration of Tuareg rebels. The conflict flared up again and threatened the fledgling democratic process.[42] Recognizing that the political establishment in Bamako had been incapable of addressing the northern crisis, Konaré turned once more to the driving force behind the country's democratic transition—civil society—to exercise leadership in the peace process.[43] According to Cheikh Omar Diarrah, in adopting this strategy the government "changed the terms of the political debate, getting away from the sterile confrontation between political parties whose members were motivated solely by personal ambition."[44]

President Konaré made a concerted effort to reach out to, and mobilize, all segments of "modern" and "traditional" civil society—religious leaders, community leaders, women's associations, and local mediators—and to encourage their different strategies of mediation and peacebuilding.[45] Like their counterparts in Liberia and Sierra Leone, Malian women's organizations such as the Coordination des Associations et Organisations Féminines (CAFO), the Coopérative Feminine (COFEM), the Mouvement National des Femmes pour la Sauvegarde de la Paix et l'Unité Nationale (MNFSPUN), and the Association des Femmes Juristes (AFJ) all actively contributed to the peace process. So did religious and traditional leaders and rural cooperatives.

With minimal financial support from the government, extensive discussions and seventeen national consultations were organized in all regions of Mali in 1994 in a bid to build a national consensus for the peace process. These discussions were usually organized by civil society groups, and were facilitated by community elders. The consultations, which lasted for three days, were chaired by government ministers. The process focused on broad popular commitment to peace, reconciliation, restoration of law and order, resuscitation of trade and commerce, and maintenance of the sovereign unity of Mali.

The popular consensus that emerged from the work of civil society groups in Mali received the steadfast support of the Konaré government. This facilitated a final peace settlement and the willingness of former rebel soldiers to disarm, demobilize, and be reintegrated into Malian society. The destruction of weapons in the "Flame of Peace" ceremony in Timbuktu in March 1996 signaled unequivocally to Malians that the war had ended. The UN supported the Malian government in its disarmament, demobilization, and reintegration efforts: 2,390 former combatants were reintegrated into Mali's armed forces, while 9,511 former combatants benefited from socioeconomic projects established to reintegrate them back into local communities. The engagement of civil society groups in Mali's conflict management process, like the efforts of their counterparts in Liberia and Sierra Leone, had achieved remarkable success in galvanizing public support for peace and mediation efforts in northern Mali. The Malian case also revealed an unprecedented partnership between government and civic organizations in finding a solution to a problem that was deemed to be of crucial national importance.

Advocating on the Periphery of Senegal's Casamance War

In Senegal, a country with a more deep-rooted civil society tradition and a historically more open political system than Mali, Sierra Leone, or Liberia, civic groups have paradoxically had less impact on facilitating the management of the country's long-running Casamance conflict. The secessionist conflict in Casamance has become one of the most protracted of West Africa's crises. Centered on the claims of the mainly minority Joola (Dioula) of their right to self-determination, the crisis has its roots in French colonial rule. As early as 1947, the Mouvement des Forces Démocratiques de Casamance (MFDC) had begun clamoring for a separate administration and self-rule in Senegal's southern enclave.[46] After independence from France in 1960, the Casamancais complained of exclusion, marginalization, and a lack of representation in the economic and political mainstream of the country, just as the Tuaregs in Mali and the Gio and Mano in Liberia had done. Senegal's first president, Léopold Sédar Senghor, managed the Casamance problem

mainly by co-opting some of its senior leadership. The province's secessionist spirit erupted again under Senghor's successor in 1980, Abdou
Diouf. The MFDC was revived under the symbolic leadership of a Catholic
priest, Abbé Augustin Diamancoune Senghor, and in 1982 a protest occurred
against the central administration in Ziguinchor. The heavy-handed repression of the protest, including the arrest of several MFDC leaders, led to
more violent protests, which in turn invited more government repression. In
May 1990 the MFDC declared that it had resorted to armed struggle to further its goal of Casamancais independence.[47] In the 1990s, despite several
cease-fires and negotiations, the conflict intensified amid deteriorating relations between Senegal and some of its neighbors, namely Mauritania, Gambia, and Guinea-Bissau.[48] The Senegalese government accused Guinea-
Bissau of providing rear bases for the MFDC as well as being a conduit for
arms—a situation exacerbated by Guinea-Bissau's descent into civil conflict in 1998 and 1999, and Senegalese military intervention, alongside
Guinea, to support the government of João Vieira (see Chapter 13).

The worsening security situation in Casamance and the Senegambian
subregion became a source of urgent concern to civil society organizations
like the Rencontre Africaine pour la Défense des Droits de l'Homme
(RADDHO) and the Conseil Régional des Femmes pour la Paix en Casamance (CRFPC). RADDHO, a Senegalese human rights NGO, was invited
in 1995 by the MFDC to engage in "quiet diplomacy" and launch a dialogue between the rebels and the government in Dakar. The organization
called for "Peace Now" and made concerted appeals to the main opposition
leader and current president, Abdoulaye Wade, to pursue a dialogue with
the MFDC. RADDHO also participated in a project with local residents that
involved rebuilding houses destroyed by the war.[49] The CRFPC organized
a series of marches in 2001 to draw attention to the desire for peace of the
people in this volatile region and to keep the issue at the top of the government's agenda. In a bid to reinforce their demands for a peaceful resolution
of the crisis, the women's organization also held talks with the political and
military wings of the MFDC in Banjul.[50] Seyneba Malle Cisse, the leader
of the CRFPC, has noted consistently that peace is unattainable without the
development of the region. Her group is seeking to build economic capacity in the region through community credit schemes. The search for peace
also drew in Senegalese church leaders, who participated in mediation and
confidence-building efforts between the Senegalese government and the
predominantly Christian Casamancais separatists.[51] At the village level, the
Association pour la Promotion Rurale de l'Arrondissement de Nyassia has
undertaken peacemaking efforts in some of the more devastated areas of
Ziguinchor.

The government of Abdoulaye Wade eventually secured a cease-fire with
the MFDC in December 2002, but Wade, unlike Malian president Alpha

Konaré, has indicated that he is not interested in civil society mediation of the conflict.[52] There are several reasons to explain Wade's attitude. Despite the country's economic woes, the war has not been a serious financial burden on Dakar, and the Senegalese army has continued to receive financial and technical support from Western countries, particularly France.[53] Like his predecessors, Wade has sought to benefit from the divisions within the secessionist movement. The Casamancais rebels have similarly revealed a lack of political will in ending the conflict. As RADDHO's Alioune Tine observed: "The State delegation prepares a course of action, then hesitates and consequently leaves itself open to manipulation. The negotiators do not always consult the appropriate sources and are often ill-informed. To add to this, the world of the MFDC is an extremely complex one. Some are involved in valuable work, others less so. If we are honest, it is political incompetence that is holding up the peace process."[54] Most crucial, perhaps, is that unlike Sierra Leone and Liberia, the conflict in Casamance did not reach, or has not yet reached, the level of a full-scale war that affects most of the country. Thus, despite the best efforts of civil society organizations like RADDHO, the CRFPC, and a few others, the Casamance crisis has been a marginal issue for most of Senegal's citizens.

However, a more profound explanation must be sought for the lack of success by civil society groups in efforts to manage this conflict. Such an explanation is particularly important since the "modern" Senegalese civil society movement has had a significant impact in democratizing the state (which abandoned the one-party system in 1978), and in addressing human rights and gender issues such as female circumcision. The key difference between Senegal and the three other West African countries surveyed in this chapter seems to be political culture. In spite of its imperfections and repressive tendencies during the Senghor and Diouf years (1960–2000), the Senegalese political system and culture did not produce the damagingly autocratic leadership that was evident in Liberia, Sierra Leone, and Mali. Dennis Galvan attributes this to a complex mixture of the liberal political heritage of four Senegalese communes (Gorée, Dakar, St. Louis, and Rufisque), and the dependence of the country's political parties on the powerful electoral support of the Muslim brotherhoods—the Mouridiyya, Tijaniyya, and Qadiriyya.[55] The combination of these two factors has produced a formalist democratic system that is urban, competitive, and liberal, but at the same time embedded in a culture in which "familialist" (kinship) idioms foster cross-ethnic and cross-cultural networks. Thus, opposition political parties and civil society groups were tolerated by governments in Dakar, though within confined and often suffocating spaces, and were allowed to participate in the political process. To their credit, these opposition parties utilized nonviolent means to pursue political power.[56] A third explanatory factor for the country's avoidance of full-scale civil conflict is that Senegal has a history of strong and independent trade unions and professional organizations stretching back to the colonial era. Thus, civic space in Senegal is relatively more open than in the other three cases. All these factors help to explain why RADDHO and the CRFPC, not necessarily the biggest players in civil society, have had such little impact on the peace process in Casamance, and why Wade may have been reluctant to concede a major role to them.

West Africa's Civil Society: Achievements and Constraints

The above analysis has demonstrated the valuable contributions that civil society actors have made and can make to individual West African countries and the subregion as a whole. Civil society groups can contribute to the repoliticization and redemocratization of societies, manage conflicts and foster peace, and promote regional security and development. These actors have considerable expertise and experience and draw on grassroots contacts, communication networks, and resources that are often unavailable to national and international actors. Civil society groups in West Africa also face considerable constraints, including an unstable security environment, government hostility, intra–civil society competition, and donor dependency. Nevertheless, there still remains considerable scope for building on the strengths and reducing the constraints of civil society through a more cooperative attitude by subregional governments toward civil society, greater cooperation and networking among civil society, greater linkages with diaspora groups, and tapping into local sources of funding to reduce the dependence of the region's NGOs on external donors and to foster local "ownership" over peacemaking and democratization initiatives.

Civil society groups in Liberia, Sierra Leone, and Mali were able to have tremendous influence in ending dictatorship, opening up democratic space, and helping to manage conflicts. In spite of their differences, civil society actors in these countries united around common agendas, namely the promotion of peace, democracy, and security. In Liberia, NGOs tirelessly worked for peace and pushed vigorously for the elections of July 1997, though the Charles Taylor regime and new rebel factions quickly undid their good work. The overthrow of Traoré in Mali in 1991 was the culmination of the collective efforts by a coalition of civil society interests and reformist military officers. Mali's civil society actors also played a vital role in the forging of peace between the government and Tuareg rebels. Women, journalists, trade unionists, professionals, and students in Sierra Leone formed the bulwark that forced the NPRC to cede power in 1996. These groups opposed Johnny Paul Koromah's AFRC junta between May

1997 and February 1998 and promoted the restoration of democratic rule to Sierra Leone in March 1998.[57] In nearly all of these cases, these experiences were mutually transformative. They changed and strengthened civil society, the state, as well as the wider society. Despite the rhetoric of cooperation and complementarity between government and civil society, in all four countries under review, civil society had to struggle to find a direct role in these conflict management efforts. In fact, as the four case studies demonstrate, if governments had encouraged early civil society interventions, many of these regional crises may not have reached such intolerable levels of violence.

In their struggle to achieve democratic change and peace, civil society organizations were able to mobilize resources that governments could not. These groups often have very effective communication networks and can transmit information and opinions from the "periphery" (local rural communities) to the center (the capital) in a way that the subregion's lumbering governments (which are more used to speaking to, than listening to, local people) cannot.[58] Where logistical difficulties led to voters having problems exercising their civic duty (as in Liberia's Lofa county in 1997) or where the single-constituency proportional representation voting system made it harder for voters to elect their parliamentarians (as in Sierra Leone in 1996), the ability of civil society organizations to understand the situation on the ground was crucial in rectifying these situations. Moreover, civil society organizations mobilized the population in northern Mali, summoning general assemblies to meet at a time when the region was considered a "no go" area.[59]

Despite their notable achievements, however, West Africa's civil society actors still face tremendous obstacles. The subregion's conflicts may have reenergized many civil society groups, but continuing instability and violence in many parts of West Africa continue to deprive these groups of the conditions needed to promote growth and maturity. In Liberia, years of work by civil society activists and ECOMOG were undone by the intractable struggle for power between the Liberians United for Reconciliation and Democracy (LURD) faction and the Taylor regime, which waged another civil war between 1999 and 2003. Even in countries like Sierra Leone and Mali, in which peace has apparently been restored after years of conflict, many difficulties remain in entrenching fledgling pluralistic political systems. Mali's elections in 2002, which saw General Amadou Touré return to power as an elected president, were poorly organized amid allegations of vote rigging, violence, and intimidation. Similar problems were evident in the run-up to the 2002 elections in Sierra Leone, though the conduct and outcome of this poll were less contested than Mali's election.

Civil society groups and actors in West Africa have sometimes been their own worst enemies due to their fractiousness, unaccountable leadership, lack of maturity, and excessive dependence on external funding.[60] These groups have often fallen prey to the institutional weaknesses, ethnic factionalism, and patronage systems that bedevil the rest of society. Some civil society activists see their agenda as "incorporationist," namely to become attached to the state in order to share in its riches.[61] In Liberia, civil society split along factional lines: the Monrovia group (largely anti-NPFL activists in the capital) and the "Greater Liberia" group (publicly supportive of the NPFL, the faction in control of this area).[62] Even after the Liberian war temporarily ended in 1997, organizations emerged, supported by the Taylor government, that described themselves as "civil society" but whose raison d'être appeared to be the prevention of united action by the country's NGO community.[63]

The paucity or absence of local sources of funding for West African NGOs has resulted in their manipulation by cynical political elites, and also in their dependence on external donors for survival. The OAU–Civil Society Conference held in Addis Ababa in June 2001 highlighted the attendant problems of donor dependency and the constraints that such dependence imposes on the independent actions of civil society actors.[64] The dependence of NGOs on external donors fosters not only what Giles Mohan has described as "a new form of imperialism and trusteeship,"[65] but can also dilute the identity, endanger the internal democracy and accountability of these organizations, and lead to damaging competition for scarce resources among local groups. Thus, West Africa's grinding poverty and lack of employment opportunities for university graduates have led to civil society providing an environment for people with questionable motives and agendas to seek greener pastures.

Given this situation, some have suggested that it may become necessary to institutionalize civil society in order for it to function effectively.[66] Some West African governments are conscious of this problem, and are trying to rectify it. The governments of Sierra Leone, Mali, and Ghana are trying to make legal distinctions between local and international NGOs and between community-based groups and local NGOs.[67] They have also been trying to draw up legal guidelines to govern the activities of these different organizations. It is doubtful, however, whether such distinctions or guidelines will make much difference on the ground, given the administrative limitations of most West African governments and their reluctance to view civil society organizations as partners in conflict management and democratization rather than as externally funded agents that threaten sitting governments.

Governments in many West African countries are hostile, suspicious, and wary of civil society. Many government officials are reluctant to accept that civil society actors can make a useful contribution in areas previously considered the sole preserve of governments, particularly security and conflict management. This attitude is evident in the almost contemptuous manner in which the Senegalese government reacted to mediation efforts in Casamance by RADDHO.[68] Even in Mali, our most successful case of government and civil society cooperation, there are many government administrators in Bamako who are unwilling to acknowledge that ordinary people can contribute to governance efforts.[69] With so many of the government's traditional functions being privatized under structural adjustment programs led by the World Bank and the IMF, the reaction of subregional governments to a further erosion of their responsibilities is perhaps not surprising. Furthermore, government officials are wary of the political intentions and agendas of civil society actors. After all, in at least three of the four case studies—Liberia, Sierra Leone, and Mali—civil society groups have demonstrated their ability to displace entrenched regimes, and some former civil society activists are today serving as prominent government officials. This trend has reinforced the paranoid belief among many West African politicians that civil society is just another tool for their political opponents to gain power. For West Africa's political elite, the academic and theoretical distinction between civil society and political society is an illusion.

Enhancing Civil Society's Role in Democracy and Peacebuilding

There are several ways in which the role of civil society in peacebuilding and conflict management can be enhanced. The first is for civil society activists to continue to push for the creation of a more open and democratic culture and the changing of the highly competitive (and sometimes violent) nature of politics in West Africa. Politics is intended to be a means of preventing and resolving differences, but political competition in many parts of West Africa has become a major cause of conflicts.[70] Politicians and their supporters must be encouraged to pursue their ambitions through peaceful means. Civil society can help set standards for politicians preparing for public service in order to help them provide competent, honest leadership; accept defeat graciously; and become a more effective opposition. Open, disciplined, and democratic civil society organizations can provide alternative models for public life. Groups within civil society must thus be careful not to allow their individual political aspirations to subvert the freedom of speech and association that have been painfully clawed back from governments in the past decade. They must not convert the hard-won civic space into just another arena for party politicking. West African governments must also provide the space and conditions for civil society to operate without harassment.[71]

The creation of open, democratic political cultures and systems cannot be confined to individual countries in West Africa in view of the regional dimension of the subregion's political, economic, and social problems. Civil society organizations must therefore increase the linkages and networks not only between the different types of civil society actors within countries, but also across West Africa. Regional networking can provide valuable opportunities for civil society groups to contribute more effectively to conflict management and democratization efforts. Successful networking enables organizations to exchange experiences and ideas, and to pool resources and share the costs of regional initiatives. Many problems in West Africa cut across the subregion's artificial national frontiers. The conflicts in the Mano river basin and in Côte d'Ivoire are clear examples of this phenomenon. So is the Tuareg problem in Mali and Niger. The meetings and exchanges between religious and women's organizations from Liberia, Sierra Leone, and Guinea at the height of the instability in the Mano river area were valuable in sharing experiences and ideas and in coordinating strategies. Such networks and organizations can greatly enhance the national, regional, and external profile, as well as the legitimacy and authority, of civil society organizations. The obstacles to effective networking, however, should not be underestimated in a subregion in which the communication and transportation infrastructure is notoriously poor.

Facilitating the work of civil society actors in West Africa requires substantial financial resources, but much of this funding still comes from outside the region with all the political strings and implications attached to this dependence. West African civil society organizations need to generate more resources within the subregion. Membership fees, voluntary contributions, and fundraising events could help pay for basic administration and organization of events. The West African business community also represents an untapped source of resources to support the work of West Africa's NGOs. Businesspeople, big and small, already commit substantial resources to supporting politicians and greasing the palms of bureaucrats to promote their business interests. Some of these resources could support civil society groups that are working to create better political and economic practices in the subregion. ECOWAS is well placed to bring the private sector into closer cooperation with civic actors engaged in conflict management and democratization activities.

The hundreds of thousands of West Africans in the diaspora could also complement and support the work of civil society groups in the subregion. The exodus of skilled people from West African countries like Sierra Leone, Liberia, Nigeria, and Ghana, due to economic hardship and political instability, means that many actual and potential civil society activists will be operating away from their home countries. Ideally, such individuals should be encouraged to return to their countries to contribute their acquired knowledge and skills to strengthen domestic civil society. However, until conditions at home improve sufficiently to attract this skilled labor back, West African governments should try to increase (as Ghana did, particularly in the 1990s) the growing remittances of these exiles and to channel these resources into worthy political and socioeconomic projects. West African diaspora communities have played an important role in organizing events, disseminating information, mobilizing public support, and trying to influence government policies toward their countries in places like the United States and Britain.

ECOWAS and Civil Society: The Way Forward

Given its bureaucratic character, state-centric focus, and financial constraints, it appears unlikely that ECOWAS can quickly develop a significant, long-term collaborative relationship with civil society groups in West Africa. However, such a collaboration with civil society is not optional for ECOWAS; it is essential. Adebayo Adedeji maintains that ECOWAS must be revitalized to achieve its economic integration and regional security objectives. The Nigerian scholar-practitioner considers civil society to be critical to the successful realization of this project (see Chapter 2). Also critical to this revitalization is the development of a West African integration culture. ECOWAS needs the assistance of civil society groups to elucidate common subregional values that will legitimize interventions under the ECOWAS security mechanism of 1999, underpin and inform decisions to intervene, and set parameters for actions taken. A security mechanism driven "from below" by civil society may not be the outcome anticipated by the signatories of the ECOWAS security protocol of 1999, but ultimately the attainment of ECOWAS's security goals under this protocol depends on the active participation of civil society actors, which have already contributed significantly to developing its early warning system for conflict prevention.

ECOWAS may find it difficult to identify long-term civil society partners for its work in the area of conflict management. The interest of many civil society organizations may wane as conflicts end and other more pressing issues emerge. Also, the resources for particular projects related to conflict management may diminish as the priorities of external donors change. In all of these cases, ECOWAS should be prepared to be innovative and to form useful partnerships with civil society actors as a less costly conflict prevention strategy. As our cases of Liberia, Sierra Leone, Mali, and Senegal have clearly demonstrated, ECOWAS can maintain its relevance to West Africa's citizens by collaborating effectively with civil society actors to manage conflicts and promote democratization in the subregion.

Notes

1. Cited in Anatole Ayissi and Robin E. Poulton, eds., *Bound to Cooperate: Conflict, Peace, and People in Sierra Leone,* UNIDIR/2000/19 (New York: United Nations Institute for Disarmament Research, 2000), p. 5.

2. Stephen Orvis, "Civil Society in Africa or African Civil Society?" in Stephen N. Ndegwa, ed., *A Decade of Democracy in Africa* (Boston: Brill, 2001), p. 17.

3. Crawford Young, "In Search of Civil Society," in John Willis Harbeson, Donald Rothchild, and Naomi Chazan, eds., *Civil Society and the State in Africa* (Boulder: Lynne Rienner, 1994), p. 33.

4. Ibid., pp. 33–36.

5. Ibid., pp. 36–37; and Victor Azarya, "Civil Society and Disengagement," in Harbeson, Rothchild, and Chazan, *Civil Society and the State in Africa,* p. 83.

6. On state collapse in Africa, see I. William Zartman, ed., *Collapsed States: The Disintegration and Restoration of Legitimate Authority* (Boulder: Lynne Rienner, 1995); and Naomi Chazan, Peter Lewis, Robert Mortimer, Donald Rothchild, and Stephen John Stedman, *Politics and Society in Contemporary Africa* (Boulder: Lynne Rienner, 1988).

7. Michael Bratton, "Beyond the State: Civil Society and Associational Life in Africa," *World Politics* 41, no. 3 (April 1989): 407–418.

8. Robert Fatton, "Africa in the Age of Democratization: The Limitations of Civil Society," *African Studies Review* 38, no. 2 (September 1995): 67–99.

9. On further definitions of civil society, see Harbeson, Rothschild, and Chazan, *Civil Society and the State in Africa;* Jean-François Bayart, "Civil Society in Africa," in Patrick Chabal, ed., *Political Domination in Africa: Reflections on the Limits of Power* (Cambridge: Cambridge University Press, 1986), p. 109; and Joel D. Barkan et al., "Hometown Voluntary Associations and the Emergence of Civil Society in Western Nigeria," *Journal of Modern African Studies* 29, no. 3 (1991): 457–480.

10. There are some scholars who question and even dismiss the concept of civil society as a useful analytical category for Africa. See, for example, Chris Allen, "Who Needs Civil Society?" *Review of African Political Economy* 24, no. 73 (September 1997): 329–333. Yet as John Makumbe points out, there are groups that continue to define and regard themselves as part of civil society. See John Makumbe, "Is There a Civil Society in Africa?" *International Affairs* 75, no. 2 (1998): 305–317.

11. Stephen Ndegwa, *The Two Faces of Civil Society: NGOs and Politics in Africa* (West Hartford, Conn.: Kumarian Press, 1996).

12. Fatton, "Africa in the Age of Democratization," p. 93.

13. In Senegal, for example, the Muslim brotherhoods have diversified their strategies. They have responded to the decline of the local groundnut economy by increasingly facilitating the economic migration of their members to countries from which remittances can be sent. These remittances are then recycled into providing welfare services at the community level.

14. On Mali, see R. Poulton and I. Youssouf, eds., *A Peace of Timbuktu: Democratic Governance, Development, and African Peacekeeping,* UNIDIR/2000/ 19 (New York: United Nations Institute for Disarmament Research), 1998.

15. In fact, there are political theorists who do not necessarily see the state and civil society as belonging to separate spheres or in opposition. See Goran Hyden,

No Shortcuts to Progress (London: Heinemann, 1993); and Patrick Chabal, *Power in Africa: An Essay on Political Interpretation* (London: Macmillan, 1992).

16. See general report of the first OAU–Civil Society Conference, June 2001, Addis Ababa, 2001, para. 146.

17. Azarya, "Civil Society and Disengagement," pp. 85–86.

18. For an account of a number of peacemaking initiatives by African women, see United Nations High Commissioner for Refugees (UNHCR) et al., "Best Practices in Peace Building and Non-Violent Conflict Resolution," 1999.

19. Azarya, "Civil Society and Disengagement," p. 84.

20. World Bank, *Working Together: The World Bank's Partnership with Civil Society* (Washington, D.C.: World Bank, 2000); and World Bank, *Consultation with Civil Society Organisations: General Guidelines for World Bank Staff* (Washington, D.C.: World Bank, 2000).

21. Gordon Crawford, "Promoting Democratic Governance in the South," *European Journal of Development Research* 12, no. 1 (2000): 25–37. See also J. Hearns, *Foreign Aid, Democratisation, and Civil Society in Africa: A Study of South Africa, Ghana, and Uganda,* Institute for Development Studies (IDS), discussion paper no. 368, IDS, University of Sussex, 1999.

22. See Samuel Kofi Woods II, "Civic Initiatives in the Peace Process," in Jeremy Armon and Andy Carl, eds., *ACCORD: The Liberian Peace Process* no. 1 (London: Conciliation Resources, 1996); and Yasmin Jusu-Sheriff, "Sierra Leonean Women and the Peace Process," in David Lord, ed., *ACCORD: Paying the Price: The Sierra Leone Peace Process* no. 9 (London: Conciliation Resources, 2000).

23. See Amos Sawyer, *The Emergence of Autocracy in Liberia: Tragedy and Challenge* (San Francisco: Institute for Contemporary Studies, 1992).

24. Augustine Toure, *The Role of Civil Society in National Reconciliation and Peacebuilding in Liberia* (New York: International Peace Academy, April 2002).

25. Woods, "Civic Initiatives in the Peace Process," p. 29.

26. Toure, *Role of Civil Society,* pp. 1–2.

27. See UNHCR et al., "Best Practices in Peace Building," pp. 11–12.

28. Association of Female Lawyers of Liberia (AFELL) et al., "Hundreds of Victims Silently Grieving," in Meredith Turshen and Clotide Twagiramanya, eds., *What Women Do in Wartime: Gender and Conflict in Africa* (London: Zed Books, 1998), pp. 133–134.

29. Max Ahmadu Sesay, "Politics and Society in Postwar Liberia," *Journal of Modern African Studies* 34, no. 3 (1996): 406.

30. The relationship between the civil defense forces (especially the Kamajors), who are mainly rural dwellers, and the urbanites in Sierra Leone was not always amicable. Even though these forces helped ECOMOG to secure rural areas and Freetown in 1998, their members were subjected to much criticism from the urban-based press and civil society activists. In December 1998 the Sierra Leonean government, in response to calls from city dwellers, withdrew civil defense force units from defensive positions around Freetown, leaving the way open for the rebels who attacked the city on 6 January 1999. For an analysis of the Kamajors, see Patrick Muana, "The Kamajoi Militia: Violence, Internal Displacement, and the Politics of Counter-Insurgency," *African Development* 22, nos. 3–4 (1997): 77–100.

31. Jusu-Sheriff, "Sierra Leonean Women and the Peace Process," p. 43.

32. Olu Gordon, "Civil Society Against the State: The Independent Press and the AFRC-RUF Junta," in Ibrahim Abdallah, ed., *Between Democracy and Terror: The Sierra Leone Civil War* (Dakar: CODESRIA, 2003), pp. 180–198.

33. Ibid.

34. Olu Awoonor-Gordon, "Civil Society and the Struggle for Democracy," *Democracy and Development* 2, no. 5 (January–March 2001): 18.

35. For example, President Kabbah agreed to IRCSL initiatives to make radio contact with the RUF and to hold meetings with RUF leader Foday Sankoh, and later with his field commanders. See Thomas Turay, "Civil Society and Peace Building," in Lord, *ACCORD*, p. 53.

36. Some religious actors in Sierra Leone tend not to view themselves as belonging to civil society. During 2000, Haja Mariatu Mahdi of the IRCSL caused consternation at a seminar organized by Christian Aid in London by forthrightly declaring that IRCSL was not part of civil society. Ironically, Haja Mariatu was part of a delegation touring Europe to publicize the success of Sierra Leonean civil society peacemaking initiatives.

37. Isaac Lappia, "Community Based Disarmament and Post Conflict Peace Building," in Ayissi and Poulton, *Bound to Cooperate*, pp. 131–135.

38. See Poulton and Youssouf, *A Peace of Timbuktu*, pp. 23–52. On the impact of the drought, see Jonathan Derrick, "The Great West African Drought, 1972–74," *African Affairs* 76, no. 305 (October 1977): 537–586.

39. Poulton and Youssouf, *A Peace of Timbuktu*, p. 55; and Kare Lode, *Civil Society Takes Responsibility: Popular Involvement in the Peace Process in Mali* (Oslo: International Peace Research Institute, 1997).

40. The Coordination was an amalgam of three northern-based civic peace groups, the Committee for Development and Peace, the Association for Implementation of Peace and Security in the Northern Regions, and the Malian Association for the Preservation of National Unity.

41. A. Ihassane, "The Experience of Northern Mali," in Adebayo Adedeji, ed., *Comprehending and Mastering African Conflicts* (London: Zed Books, 1999), pp. 207–216; and Richard Vengroff, "Governance and the Transition to Democracy: Political Parties and the Party System in Mali," *Journal of Modern African Studies* 31, no. 4 (December 1993): 541–562.

42. Kare Lode, "The Peace Process in Mali: Oiling the Works," *Security Dialogue* 28, no. 24 (December 1997): 16.

43. Poulton and Youssouf, *A Peace of Timbuktu*.

44. Cheikh Omar Diarrah, *Le défi démocratique au Mali* (Paris: L'Harmattan, 1996), p. 286.

45. O. Traore, M. D. Maiga, and M. Hayri, "Le role du capital social et de la société civile dans la résolution du conflit du Nord-Mali," *UNDP-Mali* (Bamako: UN Development Programme, 1999), p. 174.

46. Audra Dykman, *The Reintegration of the Casamance Region into Senegalese Society,* School of Advanced International Studies (SAIS) Studies on Senegal Series (Baltimore: Johns Hopkins University, Summer 2002).

47. Ibid.

48. Ron Parker, "The Senegal-Mauritania Conflict of 1989: A Fragile Equilibrium," *Journal of Modern African Studies* 29, no. 1 (1991): 155–171.

49. Interview with Alioune Tine of RADDHO, Dakar, July 2001.

50. Interview in Walfadjri, 4 September 2001, available at www.walf.sn/archive/article.cfm?article_num=3789.

51. U. Solinas, "Intervention Precedes Legitimacy," in Monique Mekenkamp, Paul van Tongeren, and Hans Vande Veen, eds., *Searching for Peace in Africa: An Overview of Conflict Prevention and Management Activities* (Utrecht: European Platform for Conflict Prevention and Transformation, 1999), p. 288.

52. Interview with Alioune Tine of RADDHO, Dakar, July 2001.

53. "Casamance: Between War and Peace," *The Courier ACP-EU* no. 196 (January–February 2003): 77–78.

54. Interview with Alioune Tine of RADDHO, Dakar, July 2001.

55. See Dennis Galvan, "Democracy Without Ethnic Conflict: Embedded Parties, Transcendent Social Capital, and Non-Violent Pluralism in Senegal and Indonesia," paper presented at the annual meeting of the American Political Science Association, San Francisco, September 2001; and Dennis Galvan, "Francophone Africa in Flux: Political Turnover and Social Change in Senegal," *Journal of Democracy* 12, no. 3 (2001): 51–62. The religious brotherhoods, though professedly nonpolitical, constituted alternative and significant sources of nonstate power and authority. Colonial as well as postcolonial Senegalese governments have contended and reached accommodation with them. See Lucy E. Creevey, "Muslim Brotherhoods and Politics in Senegal in 1985," *Journal of Modern African Studies* 23, no. 4 (December 1985): 715–721; Irving Leonard Markovitz, "Traditional Social Structure, the Islamic Brotherhoods, and Political Development in Senegal," *Journal of Modern African Studies* 8, no. 1 (April 1970): 73–96; and David Robinson, *Paths of Accommodation: Muslim Societies and French Colonial Authorities in Senegal and Mauritania, 1880–1920* (Athens: Ohio University Press, 2000).

56. Robert Fatton, *The Making of a Liberal Democracy: Senegal's Passive Revolution, 1975–1985* (Boulder: Lynne Rienner, 1987).

57. Binta Mansaray, "Women Against Weapons: A Leading Role for Women in Disarmament," in Ayissi and Poulton, *Bound to Cooperate*, pp. 154–155.

58. Jusu-Sheriff, "Sierra Leonean Women and the Peace Process," p. 43.

59. Poulton and Youssouf, *A Peace of Timbuktu*, p. 14.

60. Makumbe, "Is There a Civil Society in Africa?" pp. 314–316. See also Nelson Kasfir, "Civil Society, the State, and Democracy in Africa," in Nelson Kasfir, ed., *Civil Society and Democracy in Africa: Critical Perspectives* (London: Frank Cass, 1998), pp. 123–140.

61. Azarya, "Civil Society and Disengagement," p. 83.

62. Toure, "Role of Civil Society," p. 12.

63. Ibid.

64. General report of the first OAU–Civil Society Conference, para. 44.

65. Giles Mohan, "The Disappointments of Civil Society: The Politics of NGO Intervention in Northern Ghana," *Political Geography* 21, no. 1 (2002): 131.

66. Harbeson, Rothschild, and Chazan, *Civil Society and the State in Africa*, p. 19.

67. Mohan, "Disappointments of Civil Society," p. 145.

68. Interview with Alioune Tine, Dakar, July 2001.

69. Poulton and Youssouf, *A Peace of Timbuktu*, p. 110.

70. Mariane C. Ferme, "Staging Politisi: The Dialogics of Publicity and Secrecy in Sierra Leone," in Jean Comaroff and John Comaroff, eds., *Civil Society and the Political Imagination in Africa: Critical Perspectives* (Chicago: University of Chicago Press, 1999).

71. Azarya, "Civil Society and Disengagement," p. 97.

13

Pax West Africana?
Regional Security Mechanisms

Adekeye Adebajo

West Africa is currently among the most volatile regions in Africa. Local brushfires have raged in the past decade from Liberia to Sierra Leone to Guinea to Guinea-Bissau to Senegal in an interconnected web of instability. But West Africa has gone further than any other African subregion in efforts to establish a security mechanism to manage its own conflicts.[1] The Economic Community of West African States (ECOWAS) Cease-Fire Monitoring Group (ECOMOG) intervention in Liberia between 1990 and 1998 was the first such action by a subregional organization in Africa relying principally on its own men, money, and military matériel. It was also the first time the United Nations had sent military observers to support an already established subregional force (see Chapter 14). The ECOMOG intervention in Sierra Leone to restore the democratically elected government of Ahmed Tejan Kabbah to power in 1998 was equally unprecedented. ECOMOG undertook a brief but unsuccessful intervention into Guinea-Bissau in 1999. Building on these three experiences, as well as the ECOWAS interventions in Côte d'Ivoire and Liberia in 2003, West Africa's leaders are currently attempting to institutionalize a security mechanism to manage future subregional conflicts.

This chapter will assess the three ECOMOG military interventions in the decade of the 1990s, in Liberia, Sierra Leone, and Guinea-Bissau. After assessing the domestic, subregional, and external dimensions of West Africa's security complex through these three cases, I will briefly analyze ECOWAS's fourth military intervention, in Côte d'Ivoire, which was launched in early 2003. The Ivorian case again highlighted the interdependence of security in West Africa and the need to adopt a regional approach to managing its interconnected conflicts. The chapter then examines the establishment of the ECOWAS security mechanism in 1999, its key institutions, its functions and principal actors, the obstacles to its effective functioning, and the prospects for its successful operationalization.

Seamen from Renaissance Africa

All three ECOMOG missions launched between 1990 and 1999, in Liberia, Sierra Leone, and Guinea-Bissau, saw subregional armies sailing to Monrovia, Freetown, and Bissau on a modern *mission civilisatrice*. But ECOMOG had embarked on journeys without maps in all three cases, unclear of its mandates and uncertain about the reception it would receive from local warlords. The ECOMOG contingents were disgorged from warships and left logistically ill-equipped to improvise peacekeeping solutions. Charles Taylor welcomed the peacekeepers with a barrage of artillery fire and mortar shells; Sierra Leone's *sobels* staged a coup d'état; Guinea-Bissau's rebel general, Ansumane Mane, continued to battle his nemesis, President João Vieira, at the seaport, even as subregional peacekeepers disembarked from a French warship.

Liberia and Sierra Leone both endured a decade of civil wars that resulted in nearly 300,000 deaths and the spilling across borders of over 1 million refugees. Liberia's civil war lasted from December 1989 to the end of 1996 and was fought mainly by eight factions.[2] It took ECOMOG's peacekeepers seven years to disarm Liberia's factions and organize elections in July 1997, which the most powerful warlord, Charles Taylor, won. ECOMOG's involvement in Sierra Leone's civil war was inextricably linked to its peacekeeping efforts in neighboring Liberia's civil war. The Revolutionary United Front (RUF) had invaded Sierra Leone from Liberia in March 1991 with the assistance of Charles Taylor's National Patriotic Front of Liberia (NPFL), resulting in several hundred Nigerian, Ghanaian, and Guinean troops being deployed to assist Sierra Leone, a fellow ECOMOG member, in defending its capital, Freetown. ECOMOG's role in Sierra Leone increased tremendously after late Nigerian autocrat General Sani Abach diverted peacekeepers from the concluding Liberia mission to Sierra Leone in an attempt to crush a military coup by the Sierra Leone Army (SLA) in Freetown in May 1997. After the putsch, the military junta invited the RUF to join its administration. A Nigerian-led ECOMOG force reversed the coup in February 1998 and restored the elected president, Ahmed Tejan Kabbah, to power. However, the unsuccessful but devastating rebel invasion of Freetown in January 1999 showed that ECOMOG was unable to eliminate the rebels as a military threat. In both Liberia and Sierra Leone, logistically ill-equipped and poorly funded peacekeeping missions were unable to defeat rebels in guerrilla warfare and a military stalemate forced political accommodation and the appeasement of local warlords.[3]

Sierra Leone's civil war was fought between successive civilian and military governments in Freetown, in alliance with civil defense groups like the Kamajors. The relationship between RUF leader Foday Sankoh and Charles Taylor, whose fighters had been trained in guerrilla warfare in Libya, was cemented by the exchange of Sierra Leonean diamonds for NPFL arms. The civil war in Sierra Leone lasted from March 1991 until a cease-fire in July 1999, and the UN Mission in Sierra Leone (UNAMSIL) eventually took over ECOMOG's peacekeeping duties.[4] The RUF attacked UN peacekeepers in May 2000, killing and holding them hostage. This led to the arrest of Foday Sankoh, who had been appointed vice president in a transitional government at a peace conference in Lomé in July 1999. UNAMSIL eventually recovered its balance, disarming Sierra Leone's factions and overseeing elections in May 2002, which Kabbah won comfortably. Sankoh and Taylor were indicted for war crimes by an international Special Court for Sierra Leone in 2003, along with Johnny Paul Koromah and Hinga Norman, the head of the Kamajors. Bockarie has since been killed in Liberia under mysterious circumstances, Sankoh died in detention, and Koromah also reportedly died in 2003.

As the military and financial bulwark of ECOMOG, Nigeria provided at least 80 percent of ECOMOG's troops (12,000 out of 16,000 in Liberia, and 12,000 out of 13,000 in Sierra Leone) and 90 percent of its funding during the military interventions in both Liberia and Sierra Leone. Its treasury released billions of dollars for both ECOMOG missions, and the country suffered an estimated 1,000 fatalities. Ghana, Guinea, Sierra Leone, and Senegal also suffered dozens of fatalities. Nigeria's military leaders were keen to portray their country as the indispensable power in West Africa in pursuit of a Pax Nigeriana: a historical quest for hegemonic leadership in Africa.[5] Nigeria's military brass hats were also concerned about the impact of the civil war on the stability of the subregion and on ECOWAS, an economic integration scheme launched with strong Nigerian leadership in 1975 (see Chapter 2). Following Abacha's death in June 1998 and a transition to civilian rule, Nigeria withdrew about 8,500 of its peacekeepers from Sierra Leone. Its remaining 3,500 troops were eventually subsumed under UNAMSIL.

Both ECOMOG interventions are often erroneously portrayed as a pursuit of parochial national interests and hegemonic bullying by Nigeria.[6] Several ECOWAS states in fact had their own specific national interests in supporting ECOMOG. Gambian dissidents fought with the NPFL in Liberia, and an unsuccessful 1981 coup in Gambia was widely believed to have been sponsored by NPFL ally Libya. Guinea, Côte d'Ivoire, and Sierra Leone were flooded with about 750,000 Liberian refugees. Fighting from Liberia and Sierra Leone spilled over into Guinea, while Liberian factions made border incursions into Côte d'Ivoire. The NPFL had Sierra Leonean dissidents within its ranks, who launched a decade-long civil war from Liberia in 1991. Guinea and Sierra Leone backed the United Liberation

Movement of Liberia for Democracy (ULIMO) faction against the NPFL, while Guinean troops fought with ECOMOG in Sierra Leone mainly in areas near the common border between both countries. Five hundred thousand Sierra Leonean refugees spilled into Guinea and Liberia, and after being elected president of Liberia in July 1997, Charles Taylor continued to support the RUF against the elected government in Freetown and ECOMOG peacekeepers. After 1999, Guinea backed former ULIMO rebels calling themselves Liberians United for Reconciliation and Democracy (LURD), who launched incursions into Liberia. Taylor also supported armed dissidents in Guinea.[7] In July 2003, Guinean-backed LURD rebels and Ivorian-backed Movement for Democracy in Liberia (MODEL) rebels reached Monrovia and forced Taylor into exile in Nigeria a month later.

Having assessed the domestic and regional dynamics of the conflicts in Liberia and Sierra Leone, it is important to analyze the role of external actors in both countries. The United States, the major external Cold War ally of Liberia's autocrat, Samuel Doe, in the 1980s, abandoned him to his fate when the civil war erupted in December 1989. Washington contributed $500 million in humanitarian assistance to Liberia during the civil war, but did not support ECOMOG substantially until near the end of its mission, when it provided crucial logistical support for disarmament. This was due in part to strained bilateral relations between Washington and Abuja, but also to U.S. aversion to becoming embroiled in African conflicts following a botched mission in Somalia in October 1993. In Sierra Leone, the country's former colonial power, Britain, has been the most influential external actor in conflict management efforts, using its position as a permanent member of the UN Security Council to mobilize international support for a 20,000-strong UN peacekeeping force in Sierra Leone. Britain, like the United States, lent mostly diplomatic and humanitarian assistance to ECOMOG's peacekeeping efforts and, until a brief military intervention in 2000 that helped stabilize a collapsing UN mission, desisted from playing a direct military role in Sierra Leone. Both interventions in Liberia and Sierra Leone illustrated the growing indifference of external actors to African conflicts in the post–Cold War era, and the rising influence of regional actors like Nigeria.

Guinea-Bissau's civil war, which took place between June 1998 and May 1999, followed the deterioration in the relationship between President João Vieira and his army chief of staff, General Ansumane Mane. The disintegration of their relationship led to the division of the country's army into rival factions, one supporting Vieira and the other Mane. In January 1998, Vieira accused Mane of providing arms to Casamance secessionists of the Mouvement des Forces Démocratiques de Casamance (MFDC) in neighboring Senegal. The president then suspended his army chief from his post. Vieira's attempt to arrest Mane in June 1998 led to an attempted coup d'état by Mane. Fighting erupted between rival factions of the army in June 1998, resulting in hundreds of deaths. Most of the army deserted to Mane, whose soldiers soon controlled an estimated three-quarters of the country. Some MFDC rebel fighters in Senegal reportedly crossed the border to join Mane.[8]

In response to these developments, Senegal, with about 2,000 troops, and Guinea, with about 400, intervened militarily in Bissau in support of Vieira. Dakar and Conakry justified their intervention on the basis of bilateral defense pacts with Guinea-Bissau. Many critics within Guinea-Bissau, however, questioned the legality of these accords, arguing that their purpose was to defend against externally instigated threats rather than to maintain internal security. Like the ECOMOG interventions in Liberia and Sierra Leone, the Seneguinean intervention was undertaken without the initial blessing of the full ECOWAS Authority of Heads of State and was of questionable legality.

A peace accord, brokered in Abuja in November 1998, called for the withdrawal of Senegalese and Guinean troops from Guinea-Bissau and the simultaneous deployment of ECOMOG observers from more neutral states.[9] By February 1999, Benin, Gambia, Niger, and Togo sent 712 troops to Guinea-Bissau, resulting in Senegal and Guinea withdrawing their troops from the country. The delay in deploying the ECOMOG force to Guinea-Bissau was due to the same logistical and financial difficulties that had plagued the missions in Liberia and Sierra Leone. The ECOMOG force in Guinea-Bissau was able to be deployed only because France provided it with logistical and financial support. Despite this assistance, the force remained weak and underfunded. Taking advantage of the ill-equipped ECOMOG force, General Mane ousted Vieira on 7 May 1999, routing his depleted forces in Bissau. ECOMOG troops did not intervene in the fighting. They were instead withdrawn from Guinea-Bissau in June 1999, due to the deteriorating security situation.[10]

The role of external actors has also been important in Guinea-Bissau. Portugal, the former colonial power, was accused of backing Mane during the civil war. France, which sponsored the largely francophone ECOMOG force to Guinea-Bissau in 1999, was keen to maintain its influence in a country that had joined the Communauté Financière Africaine (CFA) franc zone in 1997, and was considered close to Vieira and accused of providing military support to him. A small UN Peacebuilding Support Office in Guinea-Bissau (UNOGBIS) was established in 1999 to contribute to the electoral process and the implementation of the Abuja Accord, as well as to coordinate donor assistance to the country.

West Africa's Tragic Triplets

In order to understand the dynamics of the conflicts in Liberia, Sierra Leone, and Guinea-Bissau, two critical questions must be posed. First, what domestic, subregional, and external factors hampered or helped peacemaking efforts in the three countries, and what factors account for the unresolved security and political processes in all three countries? Second, how successful have efforts at conflict management been in these three cases, and what factors were responsible for similar or different outcomes in these countries? Once these questions have been addressed, we can turn our attention to the lessons that can be derived from these three cases for building sustainable peace in West Africa and, more specifically, for institutionalizing ECOMOG as a permanent security mechanism in West Africa.

In the case of Liberia, three main arguments explain the protracted conflict. First, the failure to implement thirteen peace agreements for six years was due to the proliferation of armed factions and the manipulation of ethnic rivalries and plundering of resources by rival warlords (see Chapter 9). Second, amid fears of Nigeria's hegemonic ambitions by subregional states, ECOWAS members could not agree on a common approach to managing the conflict while several subregional states backed rival factions. ECOMOG also lacked the military and financial tools and the political support—subregionally and externally—to engage the warlords in a protracted guerrilla war. Third, external actors failed to significantly support subregional efforts to manage the conflict, and were wary of ECOMOG's lack of impartiality, as well as Nigeria's repressive military regimes.

Three further arguments explain the (temporary) end of Liberia's war in 1997. First, the warlords, after being handed the spoils of office during a peace conference in Abuja in August 1995, largely cooperated with ECOMOG in disarming their fighters, with the most powerful, Charles Taylor, being confident of winning power through elections, having made peace with Nigeria. Second, subregional unity was facilitated by the fact that Nigeria no longer supported anti-NPFL factions, and francophone Burkina Faso, Côte d'Ivoire, and Niger contributed troops to a more united ECOMOG force. Third, with increased cooperation from the warlords and a more diverse subregional force, the United States and members of the European Union (EU) provided crucial logistical and financial support to ECOMOG, which facilitated the disarmament of the factions and the holding of elections in 1997, with UN support.

A similar pattern emerged in the case of Sierra Leone, where three factors explain the protracted nature of the decade-long conflict. First, a combination of diamond-plundering warlords and undisciplined militias, as well as often inept politicians and soldiers in Freetown totally dependent on external military support, produced political and military deadlock. Second, a divided ECOWAS saw different members supporting either successive governments in Freetown or rebels in the countryside, while several ECOWAS states complained about Nigeria's military dominance of the ECOMOG high command as well as its unilateral military and diplomatic actions. Third, as in Liberia, the international community starved ECOMOG and Sierra Leone of the resources and attention that may have made peace-making efforts more effective. The UN was eventually forced to take over ECOMOG's peacekeeping duties by 2000 after a democratically elected civilian regime emerged in Nigeria under Olusegun Obasanjo.

As in Liberia, it took changes at these three interdependent levels to achieve an end to the conflict in Sierra Leone. At the domestic level, after Sankoh's arrest and incarceration in May 2000, a more moderate RUF leadership emerged under Issa Sesay that implemented a new peace accord that was crafted in Abuja in November 2000 by the Special Representative of the UN Secretary-General, Olu Adeniji, and ECOWAS leaders. At the sub-regional level, the diminishing of a preponderant Nigerian role and the establishment of a peacekeeping mission under UN command made it harder for the rebels to use Nigeria's dominance as an excuse not to disarm. The UN's provision of financial support made it easier for ECOMOG states like Ghana, Guinea, and Mali to maintain their troops in Sierra Leone and for Gambia to contribute troops to the mission. Externally, Britain used its permanent seat on the UN Security Council to convince other members to establish a sizable peacekeeping mission in Sierra Leone, while its brief military intervention in May 2000 helped stiffen the resolve of a collapsing UN force. Diamond and arms sanctions imposed on Charles Taylor's regime in May 2001 also contributed tremendously to halting his support for RUF rebels and to weakening his regime.

In the case of Guinea-Bissau, three factors explain the failed ECOMOG intervention and the fragility of peacebuilding efforts in the country. First, Guinea-Bissau's two main protagonists, Vieira and Mane, negotiated agreements in bad faith that they had no intention of honoring. The support provided them by various external actors allowed them to continue waging war. Second, a military intervention by Senegal and Guinea in support of Vieira, amid security concerns in Dakar of arms trafficking to secessionists in Casamance, only hardened Mane's resolve to keep fighting. The replacement of Seneguinean forces by a more neutral but ill-equipped, underfunded, and inadequately sized ECOMOG peacekeeping force meant that the peacekeepers were unable to defend the capital when the rebel force attacked the incumbent regime. This resulted in the withdrawal of the ECOMOG force from Guinea-Bissau after only four months. Finally, despite the holding of democratic elections and the establishment of a UN peacebuilding office in Guinea-Bissau in 1999, continued political instability and concerns about the financial probity of the elected government of President Kumba Yala in Bissau dissuaded wary external donors from contributing substantially to peacebuilding efforts in the country. Yala's erratic rule was ended through a military coup in September 2003. A civilian president, Henrique Pereira Rosa, was installed to hold office until the next presidential election, scheduled for 2005.[11]

The conflicts in Liberia, Sierra Leone, and Guinea-Bissau highlight the interdependence of security in West Africa and the importance of adopting a regional approach to conflict management. The UN Inter-Agency Mission to West Africa in May 2001, led by then–Assistant Secretary-General Ibrahima Fall, recommended that the UN Security Council adopt such an approach to managing the subregion's interconnected conflicts.[12] The civil war in Liberia had led to deep political splits within ECOWAS, with francophone states opposing the Nigerian-led intervention, which had also largely involved Ghana, Guinea, Sierra Leone, Senegal, Mali, and Gambia. The Liberian civil war had been triggered from Côte d'Ivoire, and the rebels received military support from Burkina Faso (and Libya). The fighting spilled about 750,000 refugees into Côte d'Ivoire, Guinea, Sierra Leone, Ghana, and Nigeria, and military incursions were launched into Côte d'Ivoire and Guinea by Liberian factions. The continuing instability on the Guinea-Liberia border and the rebel invasion of Liberia's northern Lofa county by LURD rebels in 1999 saw governments in Conakry and Monrovia supporting rival rebel movements against each other's regimes.

The interdependence of security in West Africa was further underlined when the Taylor-backed RUF triggered a decade-long civil war in Sierra Leone through an invasion from Liberian territory in March 1991. Nigeria, Ghana, Guinea, and Mali sent troops to support the regime in Freetown. Over 500,000 Sierra Leonean refugees spilled into neighboring Guinea and Liberia as a result of this civil war. An intricate network of personal relationships and shifting alliances often determined the policies of individual states toward the conflicts in Liberia and Sierra Leone. The NPFL was backed initially by Côte d'Ivoire's Félix Houphouët-Boigny, and more substantially by Burkina Faso's Blaise Compaoré and Libya's Muammar Qaddafi. In Liberia, ULIMO was backed by Sierra Leone and Guinea, while Nigeria was accused of providing military assistance to the Armed Forces of Liberia (AFL) and the Liberia Peace Council (LPC). In Sierra Leone, governments in Abuja, Accra, and Conakry supported successive beleaguered regimes in Freetown, while Liberia and Burkina Faso—and allegedly Côte d'Ivoire—backed the RUF against ECOMOG. Nigeria, particularly after increasing its presence in Sierra Leone in 1998, provided military assistance to the Kamajors. In Guinea-Bissau, Senegal and Guinea intervened militarily in a conflict that spilled refugees into Senegal, Guinea, and Gambia. Over 3,000 refugees entered Guinea-Bissau to flee fighting in Senegal's Casamance region. The conflict in Guinea-Bissau also saw alleged arms trafficking by the MFDC, a secessionist group that used bases in Guinea-Bissau to launch attacks into Senegal. Elements of the MFDC also reportedly supported Bissau Guinean general Ansumane Mane's rebellion against Vieira.

The Crisis in Côte d'Ivoire

The descent of Côte d'Ivoire—formerly an oasis of calm amid West Africa's troubled waters—into conflict took many observers by surprise. The warning signs, however, had been evident much earlier. By the 1980s, Côte d'Ivoire, the jewel in France's West African crown, was experiencing serious economic problems. The collapse of world coffee and cocoa prices had led Côte d'Ivoire to seek assistance from the International Monetary Fund (IMF) in 1980, and in 1987 its gross domestic product fell by 3.9 percent.[13] By 1989, Abidjan had accumulated a public external debt of $14.5 billion. But, though operating an autocratic political system until the early 1990s, Ivorian leader Houphouët-Boigny had managed the political system with great dexterity and adopted an enlightened policy toward the country's large immigrant population—estimated at a quarter of the population. But Houphouët's failure to channel sufficient resources to developing the north of the country almost certainly contributed to the current crisis.[14]

The Ivorian leader died in December 1993 after thirty-three years in power. Houphouët's heirs—Henri Konan Bédié, General Robert Gueï, and Laurent Gbagbo—showed less skill and foresight than *le vieux* ("the old man") in managing the political system. Houphouët's successors instituted a xenophobic policy of *Ivoirité,* which discriminated against Ivorians of mixed parentage and "foreigners," many of whom had been born in Côte d'Ivoire or had settled in the country. The exclusion of former Ivorian premier Alassane Ouattara (who apparently had one parent born outside the country) from contesting presidential elections alienated many of his northern Muslim constituents, while Gbagbo dismissed a number of northern soldiers from the army. These tensions eventually culminated in a coup attempt by largely northern officers in September 2002 and the emergence of two rebel factions: the Mouvement pour la Justice et la Paix (MJP) and the Mouvement Populaire Ivorien du Grand Ouest (MPIGO). Gbagbo accused Burkina Faso and Liberia of fomenting the rebellion, while Taylor accused Abidjan of backing Liberia's MODEL rebels. Liberian and Sierra Leonean fighters were reported to be fighting on the side of both the government and the rebels in the Ivorian conflict. The war spilled over 125,000 Ivorian refugees into Liberia, Ghana, Guinea, Mali, and Burkina Faso.

Several mediation efforts by ECOWAS in Accra and Lomé eventually led to the brokering of the Linas-Marcoussis Accord in France in January 2003. The accord established a transitional government with a neutral prime minister, Seydou Diarra, who was mandated to oversee the disarmament of the rebels and to organize elections. Under Houphouët's leadership, Côte d'Ivoire had been accused of supporting NPFL and RUF rebels in Liberia and Sierra Leone. Some observers therefore regarded the Ivorian crisis as a case of regional chickens coming home to roost. France, which has maintained a permanent military base in Côte d'Ivoire since the country's independence in 1960 as part of its neocolonial strategy in the region, deployed about 4,000 troops to monitor the cease-fire. By early 2003, 1,288 troops from Senegal, Ghana, Niger, Togo, and Benin, known as the ECOWAS Peace Force for Côte d'Ivoire (ECOFORCE), had been deployed in the country in what represented the fourth ECOWAS military mission to a West African country in thirteen years. By November 2003, ECOFORCE—renamed the Forces of ECOWAS—numbered 1,383 troops and was deployed along the cease-fire line separating the belligerents. The UN Security Council also established the UN Mission in Côte d'Ivoire (MINUCI) in May 2003, and agreed to the deployment of seventy-six military liaison officers to support the work of French and ECOWAS peacekeepers.[15]

As with the ECOMOG mission in Guinea-Bissau, the mission in Côte d'Ivoire was largely financed and equipped by France, with other logistical and financial assistance provided by Belgium, Britain, the Netherlands, and the United States. Meanwhile, France also sought, like Britain in Sierra Leone, to use its permanent seat on the UN Security Council to secure a substantial UN peacekeeping force in Côte d'Ivoire.[16] Tensions over the Anglo-American mililtary intervention in, and occupation of, Iraq beginning in March 2003, however, contributed to Washington's reluctance to sanction a strong UN force in Côte d'Ivoire, until it relented in February 2004. Even as efforts continued to resolve the Ivorian crisis, the volcanic situation in Liberia threatened to spread its deadly lava across the subregion and to overwhelm ECOWAS's fledgling security mechanism. After weeks of fighting between Charles Taylor's government and rebels, resulting in an estimated 1,000 civilian deaths in Monrovia, a Nigerian battalion of about 1,000 troops deployed in Liberia in August 2003. These were the advance units of a 3,600-strong ECOWAS Mission in Liberia (ECOMIL). Benin, Gambia, Guinea-Bissau, Ghana, Senegal, Togo, and Mali also provided troops. The United States sent a small force of 200 soldiers to provide limited logistical support for ECOMIL, while the UN took over the peacekeeping mission in October 2003.

The UN Mission in Liberia (UNMIL) was mandated to support the implementation of the cease-fire agreement and peace process, provide assistance for security sector reform, and facilitate humanitarian and human rights assistance. By December 2003, UNMIL's total strength had reached 6,038, with the largest contingents coming from Nigeria, Bangladesh, and Guinea-Bissau. The presence of the peacekeeping force managed to stem the carnage in Monrovia, but sporadic fighting continued in Nimba, Bassa, and Bong counties at the end of 2003. At the time of writing in early 2004, UNMIL was preparing to increase its troops closer to its authorized strength of 15,000, deploy to all parts of the country, and oversee a disarmament, demobilization, and reintegration program for an estimated 40,000 combatants. National elections were scheduled for 2005.[17]

Building a New Security Architecture in West Africa

The Creation of an ECOWAS Security Mechanism

I will now assess the creation of an ECOWAS security mechanism in 1999, and suggest ways of improving its effectiveness.[18] Fresh from the successful Liberian elections five months earlier, ECOWAS leaders met in Lomé on 17 December 1997 and approved a Nigerian suggestion to establish the Mechanism for Conflict Prevention, Management, Resolution, Peacekeeping, and Security. Francophone Côte d'Ivoire and Senegal, the host and head of the all-francophone Accord de Non-Aggression et d'Assistance en Matière de Défense (ANAD) respectively, were said to have only reluctantly supported the Nigerian proposal.[19] The revised ECOWAS treaty of 1993 had envisaged the creation of a security mechanism.[20] ECOWAS foreign ministers met in Abidjan in January 1998 to endorse the plan to create a security mechanism based on ECOMOG's experiences in Liberia and Sierra Leone. At this meeting, Senegal, Togo, and Burkina Faso—all francophone states—insisted on a more restricted ECOMOG force with specially trained units remaining with their national contingents, rather than joining a permanent, centralized force.[21]

ECOWAS ministers of foreign affairs, defense, internal affairs, and security met in Yamoussoukro on 11 and 12 March 1998. The meeting set out guidelines for experts from member states and the ECOWAS executive secretariat in Abuja to prepare a draft report on the proposed security mechanism. But the Yamoussoukro meeting revealed the continuing tensions within ECOWAS and continued francophone apprehensions about Nigeria's domineering diplomatic style. Yamoussoukro was marked by a clash between Nigeria's abrasive foreign minister, Tom Ikimi, and his Senegalese counterpart, Moustapha Niasse. In a barely veiled criticism of France, which a fortnight earlier had sponsored an all-francophone military training exercise in Senegal, Ikimi criticized "foreign countries working to weaken our inter-African organizations by dividing us along anglophone-francophone lines."[22] Niasse's riposte was swift and equally undiplomatic: "No one can prevent Senegal or any other state from organizing such military maneuvers as it wishes . . . nor can anyone prevent states from training their police, gendarmerie and army or freely choosing their partners."[23] Côte d'Ivoire expressed support for the Senegalese position. These exchanges suggest that the true test of the success of the ECOWAS security mechanism will not be the signing of diplomatic protocols, but rather the management and overcoming of lingering suspicions that are legacies of the subregion's colonial divisions (see Chapter 3).

In May 1998, ECOWAS military chiefs of staff contributed ideas on the establishment of a security mechanism. A meeting of experts was held in Banjul from 13 to 22 July 1998 to prepare a draft report for the consideration of ECOWAS ministers. ECOWAS ministers of defense, internal affairs, and security met again in Banjul on 23 and 24 July 1998 to review the proposed mechanism. The ministers started their meeting by acknowledging three main problems in the ECOMOG deployments to Liberia and Sierra Leone: the mode of deployment, the composition of the force, and the command and control of the operations, especially the lack of involvement of ECOWAS members and the secretariat in managing both missions.[24]

One of the main issues of discussion in Banjul was whether prior UN Security Council authorization should be required before launching future ECOMOG interventions. ECOWAS leaders determined in the end that, based on the extreme reluctance of the Security Council to sanction UN peacekeeping missions in Liberia, Sierra Leone, and Guinea-Bissau, it would be better for ECOWAS to retain autonomy over the decision to intervene and not let the Security Council prevent ECOWAS from taking urgent action to maintain subregional stability.[25] After much discussion and refinement of these ideas, ECOWAS leaders met in Lomé in December 1999 and signed the Protocol Relating to the Mechanism for Conflict Prevention, Management, Resolution, Peacekeeping, and Security.[26] It is worth assessing this important document in some detail, since it has attempted to draw lessons from ECOMOG's experiences in Liberia and Sierra Leone and, to a lesser extent, in Guinea-Bissau.

The ECOWAS Mechanism: Institutions and Actors

Five major flaws in the three ECOMOG interventions must be corrected to ensure the smooth functioning of the ECOWAS mechanism. First, ECOMOG peacekeepers were deployed to Liberia, Sierra Leone, and Guinea-Bissau before detailed logistical and financial arrangements had been made. The peacekeepers were ill equipped and ill prepared, and not all ECOWAS members were informed before full-scale deployment occurred. Second, the ECOMOG forces in Liberia and Sierra Leone were dominated by Nigeria, resulting in a lack of subregional unity and depriving the force of important legitimacy in fulfilling its tasks. Third, the ECOMOG force in Guinea-Bissau was deployed without Nigeria, denying the peacekeepers the logistical and financial muscle of the subregion's dominant force. Fourth, the ECOMOG missions in Liberia and Sierra Leone were under the operational control of ECOMOG commanders in the field, rather than the ECOWAS secretariat in Abuja. Since these commanders, with the brief exception of Ghana's General Arnold Quainoo in 1990, were all Nigerian, as was the bulk of the troops, Nigeria's military leaders were kept closely informed of military operations on the ground. This information, however, did not always filter speedily, if at all, to other ECOWAS members and the secretariat. Finally, the ECOMOG mission in Guinea-Bissau, under a Togolese commander, Colonel Gnakoundé Berema, reported directly to Togolese leader Gnassingbé Eyadéma, the ECOWAS chairman at the time. Some of these errors appear to have been repeated in Côte d'Ivoire in 2003, where the presence of a 4,000-strong French contingent has made up for some of ECOFORCE's deficiencies and helped it to avoid the debacle of the ill-equipped ECOMOG force in Guinea-Bissau.

The ECOWAS security protocol of 1999 set out to correct these flaws. The protocol called for the establishment of the following organs: a Meditation and Security Council, a Defense and Security Commission, and a Council of Elders. The ECOWAS protocol of 1999 also called for improved cooperation in early warning, conflict prevention, peacekeeping operations, and combatting cross-border crime and trafficking in small arms and narcotics.[27] Many of these suggestions were based on ECOMOG's experiences, with the concern about cross-border crimes and arms trafficking being a direct result of the deleterious effect of civil wars on neighboring states like Côte d' Ivoire, Guinea, Sierra Leone, Liberia, and Senegal.

The Mediation and Security Council aims to accelerate decisionmaking in crisis situations by making decisions on deploying military and political missions and informing the UN and the African Union (AU) of such decisions on behalf of the ECOWAS Authority of Heads of State. Clearly inspired by the ECOWAS Committee of Nine on the Liberian crisis, the body was to have nine members elected to two-year terms. ECOWAS leaders have since increased the membership of the council to ten. Ambassadors of the ten countries in Abuja meet once a month; their foreign, defense, and internal affairs ministers meet quarterly; and their heads of state are mandated to meet at least twice a year. Decisions are to be made by a two-thirds majority of six members.[28] By April 2003, the council had met ten times to discuss security issues in Liberia, Sierra Leone, Guinea-Bissau, and Côte d'Ivoire, as well as rebel attacks along the border areas of the three Mano River Union states of Liberia, Sierra Leone, and Guinea.[29] The Mediation and Security Council also sent a delegation to New York to meet with the UN Security Council before the imposition of sanctions on Liberia in May 2001 and periodically dispatched teams to Liberia to monitor compliance with the sanctions.[30]

These decisions represent a clear effort to improve on decisionmaking and build wider subregional support for ECOMOG peacekeepers following the difficult experiences of the five-member Standing Mediation Committee that sent ECOMOG into Liberia, of the Committee of Seven on Sierra Leone, and of the Committee of Nine on Guinea-Bissau. ECOWAS leaders hope that, with a more representative and diverse group of decisionmakers, such subregional divisions as occurred in Liberia and Sierra Leone, and to a lesser extent in Guinea-Bissau, can be avoided for future peacekeeping missions. But the ECOWAS mechanism does not state what would occur if the Mediation and Security Council failed to secure two-thirds support for future peacekeeping missions, a serious omission that will need to be corrected if future subregional divisions are to be avoided.

The Defense and Security Commission is to advise the Mediation and Security Council on mandates, terms of reference, and the appointment of force commanders for future military missions. The commission, made up of army chiefs of staff, police chiefs, and experts from foreign ministries, immigration, customs, narcotics, and border control, is also to advise the Mediation and Security Council on administration and logistics support for military operations.[31] But the commission could end up duplicating rather than complementing the work of domestic ministries and other ECOWAS organs. Existing subregional institutions appear better placed to perform an advisory role without having to create an additional layer of bureaucracy that could render decisionmaking unnecessarily cumbersome. The Defense and Security Commission met for the first time in July 2000, with ECOWAS members pledging troops to a permanent ECOMOG standby force (discussed below). General Cheick Diarra, ECOWAS's deputy executive secretary, has traveled around West Africa to determine potential standby forces and to gauge their level of preparedness for future deployment. Training bases for the new ECOMOG force have also been identified in Côte d'Ivoire and Ghana, while plans are proceeding for establishing a military planning cell within the ECOWAS secretariat.

The Council of Elders consists of eminent personalities from Africa and outside the continent, including women, traditional, religious, and political leaders appointed on an ad hoc basis. Seventeen of its thirty-two members met for the first time in Niamey, Niger, from 2 to 4 July 2001. At the meeting, former Nigerian head of state General Yakubu Gowon was elected as the council's chairman, with Niger's Ide Oumarou and Burkina Faso's Alimata Salambere elected as vice chairmen. In Niamey, ECOWAS's executive secretary at the time, Lansana Kouyaté, and his deputy, General Diarra, briefed the Council of Elders on their mandate and on the progress of the ECOWAS security mechanism. Council members urged the ECOWAS secretariat to expand its membership to ensure that all members of the subregional body were represented. They also appealed to members to implement the protocol related to the community levy for financing the work of the mechanism.[32] Council members have since been sent by ECOWAS to observe elections in Gambia, Sierra Leone, and Zimbabwe.

Though traditional leaders and civil society activists can and do contribute immensely to the management of conflicts at the local level (see Chapter 12), the three ECOMOG interventions of the 1990s, in Liberia, Sierra Leone, and Guinea-Bissau, offer cautionary tales as to the efficacy of such efforts on a nationwide basis during civil wars in which warlords control most of the country. Despite various efforts to involve traditional rulers and civic groups in mediation efforts in all three countries, it was clear that the key to the resolution of the war often lay with warlords and rebel groups, who were usually unwilling to lay down their arms. Thus, while the involvement of civil society actors in mediation efforts may serve a useful purpose, its efficacy as a method of resolving national conflicts should not be overestimated.

The ECOWAS security mechanism of 1999 further proposed that the powers of the organization's executive secretary, currently Mohamed Chambas, be broadened, giving him the authority to take initiatives for the prevention and management of conflicts, including fact-finding, mediation, facilitation, negotiation, and reconciliation of parties. A deputy executive secretary for political affairs, defense, and security, General Diarra, was appointed to manage field operations in support of cease-fires and/or peace agreements.[33] Diarra has been particularly active in peacemaking efforts in Côte d'Ivoire and Liberia. His role will be important in coordinating activities between the ECOWAS secretariat and field missions, and will hopefully help avoid the experiences of ECOMOG's interventions in Liberia, Sierra Leone, and Guinea-Bissau, in which military commanders often reported directly to their own leaders rather than to the ECOWAS secretariat.

A damaging error of the ECOMOG interventions that the 1999 protocol attempts to rectify is the appointment of a special representative of the executive secretary to peacekeeping missions authorized by ECOWAS. This is an effort to ensure a high-level diplomatic presence on the ground and better coordination and information-sharing between the ECOWAS secretariat and peacekeeping missions in the field. The special representative is expected to lead peacemaking efforts and coordinate the humanitarian and peacebuilding operations of ECOWAS, international organizations, and nongovernmental organizations (NGOs).[34] This idea seems particularly sensible since in Liberia, Sierra Leone, and Guinea-Bissau, delicate diplomatic tasks were often left in the hands of military commanders who were ill equipped and untrained to handle such matters. These problems also took away from the commanders' time to focus on purely military and security issues.

The ECOMOG experiences, however, suggest that in the future it might be worth considering making the deputy executive secretary a full executive secretary with his or her own separate organization, which can be physically close to, but bureaucratically separate from, ECOWAS. This would allow ECOWAS to concentrate on its raison d'être of regional integration while recognizing the crucial link between security and economic integration. Such an arrangement can be seen in Europe, with the European Union (EU) and the Western European Union (WEU) playing complementary but separate roles that allow each to concentrate on its own area of specialization. Under the ECOWAS protocol, the executive secretary could end up being overburdened with security tasks that prevent his or her total concentration on economic integration issues. The two Liberia experiences in particular, but also those in Sierra Leone, Guinea-Bissau, and Côte d'Ivoire, demonstrate how much ECOWAS's attention can be diverted from its economic goals to focus on security issues.

ECOWAS's Early Warning System

As envisaged in the ECOWAS security protocol of 1999, an observation and monitoring center is currently being established within the ECOWAS secretariat. The EU is funding this project, and the director of the center, its program manager, and the heads of ECOWAS's four zonal bureaus have now been recruited. But the EU insisted that recruitment be done according to its own bureaucratic rules, and not those of ECOWAS, revealing how donors can sometimes act in a heavy-handed manner even as they claim to support "ownership" of subregional mechanisms by local actors. ECOWAS's observation center consists of two departments, the Department of Operations, Peacekeeping, and Humanitarian Affairs (DOPHA) and the Department of Political Affairs and Security (DPAS). The first aims to formulate and implement all military, peacekeeping, and humanitarian operations, while the latter is mandated to organize, manage, and provide support for political activities related to conflict prevention as well as to formulate and implement policies on cross-border crime, the proliferation of small arms and light weapons, and the control of drug trafficking.

ECOWAS's protocol also calls for a peace and security observation mechanism as well as an early warning system, with information bureaus, collectively known as ECOWATCH, established in four reporting zones based in Banjul (to cover Cape Verde, Gambia, Guinea-Bissau, and Senegal), Cotonou (to cover Benin, Nigeria, and Togo), Monrovia (to cover Ghana, Guinea, Liberia, and Sierra Leone), and Ouagadougou (to cover Burkina Faso, Côte d'Ivoire, Mali, and Niger). From these four zonal headquarters, officials are expected to assess political (human rights, democracy), economic (food shortages), social (unemployment), security (arms flows, civil-military relations), and environmental (drought, flooding) indicators on a daily basis.[35] By April 2002, these bureaus had been established. Programmers and analysts had been recruited, equipment purchased, and the U.S. European Command in Germany was helping ECOWAS to establish an effective communications system.

One encouraging development of ECOWAS's early warning system is the involvement of civil society actors in its establishment. The African Strategic and Peace Research Group (AFSTRAG), a small Nigerian-based research and policy institute, established a project on developing ECOWAS's early warning system with a forum of twenty-six mostly West African NGOs under a West African Network for Peacebuilding (WANEP), which met in Abuja from 24 to 27 March 2001 to discuss the potential contributions of civil society groups to ECOWAS's early warning system.

While the observation system and plans surrounding it are all laudable goals, these tasks will need to be reduced and made more focused to reflect better the political realities of West Africa. Monitoring human rights, press freedom, and civil-military relations would have been politically impossible for the ECOWAS secretariat, for example, under a repressive regime like that of Nigeria's General Abacha between 1993 and 1998. In a subregion in which twelve of the sixteen leaders in 1998 initially came to power through a military coup, such political tasks seem simply beyond the authority of international civil servants working at the behest of governments. It would appear more sensible for the observation mechanisms to focus on less politically sensitive issues, like economic, social, and environmental indicators, while perhaps leaving some of the more sensitive political analysis to civil society groups.

The Institutionalization of ECOMOG

Based largely on the experiences of ECOMOG, the ECOWAS protocol of 1999 called for the establishment of a standby force of brigade size consisting of specially trained and equipped units of national armies ready to be deployed at short notice. All fifteen ECOWAS states have pledged one battalion each to the proposed force. It now remains to be seen whether this pledge can be translated into reality. The main tasks of the force will involve observation and monitoring, peacekeeping, humanitarian intervention, enforcement of sanctions and embargos, preventive deployment, peacebuilding operations, disarmament and demobilization, and policing, including antismuggling and anticriminal activities.[36] These were among the tasks that ECOMOG attempted to perform in Liberia, Sierra Leone, and Guinea-Bissau. The proposed subregional force is to embark on periodic training exercises to enhance the cohesion of its troops and compatibility of its equipment. ECOMOG's soldiers will also undertake training exchange programs in West African military training institutions, as well as external training involving the UN and the AU. Four thousand troops from Benin, Burkina Faso, Chad, Côte d'Ivoire, Niger, Togo, and Ghana have already taken part in war games in Burkina Faso and Togo in May 1998, with Nigeria involved in the military planning.[37]

Despite these encouraging developments, it is important to examine three important issues related to the new West African peacekeeping force: first, the criteria for mandating military interventions; second, the importance of distinguishing between keeping and enforcing peace; and third, the danger of the force becoming a defense pact for the protection of subregional autocrats. The proposed ECOMOG force is to be used in four cases: first, aggression or conflict within a member state; second, a conflict between two or more member states; third, internal conflicts that threaten to trigger a humanitarian disaster, pose a serious threat to subregional peace and security, result in serious and massive violation of human rights, and/or follow the overthrow or attempted overthrow of a democratically elected government; and fourth, any other situation that the Mediation and Security Council deems appropriate.[38]

While the first two scenarios for justifying military interventions were included in the ECOWAS Protocol on Mutual Assistance and Defense of 1981, the third scenario is a conscious attempt to provide legal cover for future interventions, based on ECOWAS's four military interventions. In Liberia, Guinea-Bissau, and Côte d'Ivoire, ECOWAS intervened militarily by arguing that the situation had threatened a humanitarian disaster and posed a threat to subregional peace and security. In Sierra Leone, ECOMOG had restored a democratically elected government to power after its overthrow by soldiers. The interventions in Liberia (1990) and Sierra Leone (1998) were controversial and questioned on legal grounds, even by some ECOWAS members.

It must also be recognized that decisions to intervene in the internal affairs of countries will be profoundly influenced by the concrete political interests of member states. Unlike the collective security system of the UN, whose universal membership often allows it to send peacekeepers from countries that have no direct interest in the conflicts to be settled, ECOWAS does not have this luxury. The organization will have to find a way of excluding countries whose presence is strongly opposed by the parties to the dispute. It might sometimes have to borrow troops from outside its own subregion, as it did in Liberia with the Organization of African Unity and UN peacekeepers and as it has done in Sierra Leone, where ECOMOG was subsumed under a UN peacekeeping mission while retaining a subregional core of peacekeepers. Such innovative divisions of labor will have to be devised for future interventions. Future subregional peacekeeping operations must learn from the Liberia and Sierra Leone experiences the importance of diversifying troop-contributing contingents to include both ECOWAS and non-ECOWAS members to avoid charges of Nigerian or anglophone domination.

Political discretion will also have to be exercised in decisions to intervene in conflicts even when ECOWAS's criteria for intervention have been met. It is clear that if a military regime were to take power with popular support from a democratically elected but politically discredited civilian regime, as occurred, for example, in Nigeria with General Muhammadu Buhari's coup in December 1983, an ECOMOG intervention force would be practically impossible to deploy. Likewise, if a military coup were to succeed in a francophone state with popular domestic support or tacit French and francophone support, a Nigerian-led ECOMOG intervention would be fraught with political and military risks that could lead to the force being regarded as a foreign invasion. It is significant that Nigeria, which had led ECOMOG missions in Liberia and Sierra Leone, has been noticeably absent from the French-backed ECOFORCE in Côte d'Ivoire.

Military interventions by ECOWAS will always have to be determined on a case-by-case basis. The requirement of a two-thirds majority is an important check that allows for a blocking minority. The experts meeting in Banjul in 1998 to discuss the ECOWAS mechanism did not suggest alternatives to break this possible deadlock for fear of creating negative loopholes that could be exploited by member states.[39] But this still leaves ECOWAS in a quandary: its ability to act in critical humanitarian emergencies for the benefit of the entire community can potentially be obstructed by the veto of a minority of four states on the Mediation and Security Council defending parochial and partisan interests.

The ECOMOG intervention in Liberia parallels such a scenario, with Burkina Faso and Côte d'Ivoire opposing ECOMOG due largely to their own interest in seeing an NPFL victory. Under the ECOWAS protocol of 1999, ECOMOG would probably not have found the six votes necessary to intervene in Liberia. With eight out of fifteen members in ECOWAS, the Francophonie possesses the most united, though not monolithic, political bloc in the organization. This relationship has been cemented through close cooperation in the institutions of the franc zone, often under French leadership. It does not seem difficult to imagine four francophone states saying "*non*" to a future Nigerian-led intervention that they perceive to be against their own interests.

It is also important to establish conceptual clarity in determining the mandate of the proposed subregional force. The ECOWAS security protocol of 1999 talks of peacemaking, peacekeeping, and peacebuilding, but neither explicitly defines these terms nor addresses the issue of peace enforcement, which occurred in both Liberia and Sierra Leone. This suggests a certain conceptual confusion. It seems that peace enforcement has simply been subsumed into peacekeeping without differentiating clearly traditional peacekeeping—which involves defensive, lightly armed troops monitoring an agreed peace and defending themselves only when attacked—from peace enforcement action—involving offensive, heavily armed troops imposing peace against recalcitrant parties.[40] This distinction will need to be more clearly defined for future ECOMOG missions, since such decisions will be crucial in determining the needs and mandate of forces to be dispatched into conflict zones.

Finally, the fourth criterion for intervention, which leaves the situation under which military interventions can occur to the discretion of the Mediation and Security Council, introduces the possibility, expressed particularly by many West African civil society actors,[41] of the manipulation of the ECOWAS mechanism by self-serving dictators. The fear is that autocratic subregional leaders who have lost the support of their citizens could convince their fellow leaders to sanction interventions to protect their regimes. Such an allegation was leveled against ECOMOG, and particularly Nigeria, in relation to Liberian leader Samuel Doe when its peacekeepers entered Liberia in 1990. Similar accusations were made against Senegal and Guinea for their military support of João Vieira after an attempted coup in 1998. ECOWAS could face similar charges of trying to protect Laurent Gbagbo's regime in Côte d'Ivoire.

Of Men, Money, and Military Matériel

Many of the institutions proposed by the 1999 protocol represent an important step to improving ECOWAS's ability to manage conflicts, but they will also be expensive to staff. Based on the experience of member states in failing to pay their dues to maintain existing ECOWAS institutions, there are genuine grounds for skepticism as to whether these institutions will receive consistent funding. This will require greater commitment from member states as well as more detailed financial arrangements to ensure continued funding both from within and outside the subregion.

All three ECOMOG interventions clearly exposed the logistical weaknesses of West Africa's armies. Improving the effectiveness of such forces requires the following: serviceable weapons, good communications equipment, tactical mobility and logistical support, knowledge of basic doctrine, individual skills training, and realistic exercises involving whole units. Convoy escort operations through hostile territory during military interventions are best undertaken with the support of scout and attack helicopters. West African peacekeepers do not have such assets in significant quantities. Attacks against resisting forces in urban areas are difficult without access to precise-fire weaponry such as attack helicopters, gunships, and night-vision equipment.

For operations to establish order in even relatively small countries, over 10,000 troops are likely to be needed. ECOMOG had roughly this number at the height of its peacekeeping missions in Liberia and Sierra Leone, while it had only 712 peacekeepers in Guinea-Bissau and initially sent less than 1,500 troops to Côte d'Ivoire and Liberia in 2003. In 1996, ECOMOG's military planners calculated that they would need at least

18,000 troops to fulfill their peacekeeping and disarmament tasks satisfactorily in Liberia. In the end, they had to settle for 10,500. Logistical support in the form of weaponry, transportation, and communications equipment will still need to be provided by external actors for the foreseeable future. There is also a continuing need for support in the form of trucks, transport helicopters, water purification equipment, tents, uniforms, and boots. Costs for such equipment could reach $1 billion for a total force of 30,000 to 50,000, but this could be the only way of ensuring that a military force could operate autonomously and successfully once it was deployed.[42]

Several subregional military analysts have suggested that ECOWAS establish strategic reserves of equipment that can be used for peacekeeping missions, much like the UN's central depot in Italy.[43] But this issue was discussed in Banjul in 1998 by the experts who drafted the ECOWAS security mechanism, and they decided that it would be too risky to establish military reserves that could be stolen and used if conflict broke out in the country in which such equipment had been stored.[44] General Maxwell Khobe, the late ECOMOG task force commander in Sierra Leone, offered some sensible ideas for overcoming ECOWAS's logistical deficiencies. Khobe suggested, among other things, the standardization of the equipment, arms, ammunition, training standards, and doctrine of ECOMOG's standby forces; the establishment of an ECOMOG standing command staff to harmonize military policies; and the creation of an ECOMOG support command with ships and airlift capability.[45] As noted above, the implementation of these ideas will require both financing and political will.

The issue of financing is particularly important to the building of ECOMOG's proposed force. The ECOWAS protocol of 1999 foresees troop-contributing countries bearing financial costs for the first three months of military operations, whereupon the ECOWAS secretariat takes over the costs of the mission. The initial agreement for the ECOMOG mission in Liberia was for each contingent to fund its own troops for the first month of the mission, after which time all ECOWAS members were to assume responsibility for the force. But Nigeria ended up footing about 90 percent of the costs, and francophone countries opposed to ECOMOG were unwilling to contribute to a mission they did not support. Similarly in Sierra Leone, Nigeria shouldered much of the financial burden for the mission. In Guinea-Bissau, France underwrote the financial costs of the peacekeepers, providing stipends, transportation, and some communication equipment. France, Britain, Belgium, the Netherlands, and the United States largely financed the ECOWAS force in Côte d'Ivoire. Under the ECOWAS protocol, funds for the security mechanism are to be raised from the annual budget until a community levy comes into existence. Funding is also expected to be provided by the UN, international agencies, the AU, and voluntary contributions and grants from bilateral and multilateral sources.[46]

This is an unsatisfactory system that does not correct a critical flaw in ECOMOG's peacekeeping efforts. All three ECOMOG missions clearly demonstrated the importance of securing financial support *before* embarking on a military intervention. The ECOMOG missions in Liberia and Sierra Leone cost the Nigerian treasury billions of dollars (though a large part of these funds was embezzled by corrupt generals). Such costs can prove a disincentive to future interventions in a subregion saddled with a crippling external debt. Tanzania and Uganda withdrew their contingents from the peacekeeping mission in Liberia in 1995 in large part because their financial and logistical needs were not being met. Other ECOWAS states declined to contribute troops to ECOMOG due to the costs of maintaining peacekeepers in Liberia, Sierra Leone, Guinea-Bissau, and Côte d'Ivoire.

The Nigerian-led OAU intervention in Chad was forced to withdraw from the country in 1982 largely because of the deteriorating security situation in Ndjamena and the force's lack of sufficient funding and logistical support.[47] In 1997, only Nigeria, Benin, and Côte d'Ivoire had paid their ECOWAS dues in full, and since 1975 only these three countries and Togo have contributed regularly to the ECOWAS budget. By July 1992 the arrears to the ECOWAS budget were equivalent to three years of its operating budget,[48] while unpaid arrears stood at $38.1 million in December 1999. The ECOWAS secretariat's move from Lagos to Abuja in 1998 was delayed by seven years due to lack of funds, and its staff are irregularly paid. The Nigerian government had to loan ECOWAS money to pay its personnel in September 1998.[49] This hardly appears to be a promising basis for securing financial support for a future ECOMOG force. A sounder financial base must be built through the acceleration of the community levy in order for ECOWAS's security mechanism to be successful. The fact that only three out of ECOWAS's fifteen states had ratified its security protocol by August 2002 also suggests a continuing lack of political will in implementing subregional initiatives.

In concluding this section, I will briefly assess efforts by three external actors—France, Britain, and the United States—to contribute to building ECOWAS's security capacity. France has invited nonfrancophone states to participate in its Renforcement des Capacités Africaines de Maintien de la Paix (RECAMP) military program and has established a peacekeeping training center in Côte d'Ivoire. The evolving French role in Africa, involving a less unilateral use of force than witnessed in the last four decades, coincides with an increasing but limited U.S. and British security role in Africa (see Chapter 15).[50] Britain deployed a small military contingent in Sierra Leone in 2000, which trained a new national army, and supported a poorly equipped UN force. London has also established an African peacekeeping training support program involving officer training projects in

Ghana, South Africa, and Zimbabwe. The United States has provided military assistance to Benin, Ghana, Mali, and Senegal, as part of its 1996 African Crisis Response Initiative (ACRI)—now renamed the African Contingency Operations Training Assistance (ACOTA)—to strengthen the military capabilities of African states for regional peacekeeping. But with a total annual contribution of only about $20 million to selected African states, ACRI did not contribute significantly to ECOWAS's logistical deficiencies. Washington also trained five battalions, three Nigerian, one Ghanaian, and one Senegalese, for participation in the UN mission in Sierra Leone in 2000.

Critical voices in Africa have argued that external security initiatives have not been coordinated, that Africans have not been adequately consulted on these initiatives, and that emphasis on training is misguided, since logistical and financial support is more essential for African peacekeepers. At a meeting organized by ECOWAS and the New York–based International Peace Academy (IPA) in Dakar in August 2002, experts, including five former ECOMOG commanders, stressed the need for ECOWAS to prioritize security sector reform as a conflict prevention strategy. The failure to do so in Liberia was seen as the major reason for the reeruption of the civil conflict in 1999. The Dakar meeting also stressed the importance of sharing posts within the ECOMOG high command so as to avoid the Nigerian dominance of senior military positions, as occurred in Liberia and Sierra Leone.[51] ECOWAS must avoid becoming overdependent on external funding for its operations, since this could compromise its independence of action and lead to funding shortfalls due to changing donor priorities. The ECOWAS security mechanism has received funding from the AU and several donor governments. The OAU gave ECOWAS $300,000 for its deployments in Sierra Leone and Liberia. The EU, the U.S. Agency for International Development (USAID), and the governments of Britain, Canada, Japan, and Germany have also made contributions in support of the ECOWAS mechanism.

Armed Humanitarianism

The ECOWAS security mechanism foresees humanitarian and logistical support being provided by the subregional body.[52] Based on the ECOMOG experiences, however, it is obvious that such resources are in short supply within West Africa. ECOMOG did play a role in revitalizing ports, electricity stations, and communication facilities in Liberia and Sierra Leone, while its engineers rebuilt some roads and bridges.[53] This experience could provide a foundation for future missions. But in the humanitarian field, ECOWAS simply lacks the resources and experience provided by UN agencies and the NGO community, while in the area of logistics, such basic equipment as radios, tents, medical equipment, boots and uniforms, as well as trucks and helicopters, had to be provided by the United States, France, and the EU.

It would seem sensible for future ECOMOG missions to emulate the division of labor established in Liberia, where ECOMOG concentrated on disarmament and providing security for humanitarian convoys, while leaving the bulk of humanitarian tasks in the hands of UN agencies and NGOs. Although the ECOWAS protocol of 1999 foresees a peacebuilding role for ECOMOG, a division of labor between ECOWAS and international actors would appear to be more realistic at this stage. ECOWAS could take the lead in elections, supported by the UN and other groups, while ECOMOG, or preferably the better-resourced UN, provides security after completing disarmament. But the reintegration of fighters and food-for-work projects are better left to the UN, the World Bank, and the EU, which have both the experience and the resources, though sometimes not the political will, to undertake these tasks.

Toward a Pax West Africana

West Africa remains today among the world's poorest and most conflict-prone subregions. Four ECOWAS states—Guinea, Guinea-Bissau, Liberia, and Sierra Leone—all of them significantly involved in recent conflicts, are among the ten poorest countries in the world. Despite these difficulties, there are some rays of hope in West Africa's apparently bleak security prospects. ECOWAS has survived for nearly three decades despite its members' political and cultural divisions and economic disparities. Following four unprecedented military interventions (and a fifth intervention in Liberia in 2003, a mission now under UN control), the organization has managed to overcome many obstacles to establish one of the world's first subregional security mechanisms. Mali and Niger have imaginatively used civil society groups and government mediation to manage their long-running Tuareg problems. ECOWAS's citizens travel visa-free and work throughout its fifteen countries. Highways have been built linking Lagos to Nouakchott and Dakar to Ndjaména. A West African gas pipeline is under construction. A semblance of democratic rule appears to be emerging in Benin, Cape Verde, Ghana, Nigeria, Senegal, and Sierra Leone. There are plans afoot to create a common currency and an ECOWAS court of justice, while a subregional parliament has been established in Abuja and now meets regularly.

There is a glimmer of hope in the birth of a new security mechanism in West Africa. ECOWAS has finally started to fulfill the ambition of establishing a Pax Africana in its subregion by creating an indigenous system for managing its own conflicts.[54] Usually, theory and conceptualization precede practice in the establishment of security structures. In ECOWAS's case, however, the practice of five subregional interventions has preceded theory. This gives ECOWAS a golden opportunity to draw from its experiences in Liberia, Sierra Leone, Guinea-Bissau, and Côte d'Ivoire to build an effective security mechanism. The lessons of these cases must be properly learned if a Pax West Africana is to be achieved in this troubled subregion.

Notes

1. See ECOWAS, *Protocol Relating to the Mechanism for Conflict Prevention, Management, Resolution, Peacekeeping, and Security,* Lomé, 10 December 1999.

2. For accounts of the Liberian civil war, see Colonel Festus Aboagye, *ECOMOG: A Subregional Experience in Conflict Resolution, Management, and Peacekeeping in Liberia* (Accra: Sedco, 1999); Adekeye Adebajo, *Liberia's Civil War: Nigeria, ECOMOG, and Regional Security in West Africa* (Boulder: Lynne Rienner, 2002); Abiodun Alao, John Mackinlay, and 'Funmi Olonisakin, *Peacekeepers, Politicians, and Warlords: The Liberian Peace Process* (Tokyo: United Nations University Press, 1999); Stephen Ellis, *The Mask of Anarchy: The Destruction of Liberia and the Religious Dimensions of an African Civil War* (London: Hurst, 1999); Karl Magyar and Earl Conteh-Morgan, eds., *Peacekeeping in Africa: ECOMOG in Liberia* (London: Macmillan, 1998); Klaas Van Walraven, *The Pretence of Peace-Keeping: ECOMOG, West Africa, and Liberia, 1990–1998* (The Hague: Netherlands Institute of International Relations, 1999); and Margaret Vogt, ed., *The Liberian Crisis and ECOMOG: A Bold Attempt at Regional Peacekeeping* (Lagos: Gabumo Press, 1992).

3. For further details on ECOMOG's military shortcomings, see Herbert Howe, "Lessons of Liberia: ECOMOG and Regional Peacekeeping," *International Security* 21, no. 3 (Winter 1996–1997); Cyril Iweze, "Nigeria in Liberia: The Military Operations of ECOMOG," in M. A. Vogt and A. E. Ekoko, eds., *Nigeria in International Peacekeeping, 1960–1992* (Lagos: Malthouse Press, 1993); and Robert Mortimer, "From ECOMOG to ECOMOG II: Intervention in Sierra Leone," in John W. Harbeson and Donald Rothchild, eds., *Africa in World Politics: The African State System in Flux,* 3rd ed. (Boulder: Westview Press, 2000).

4. For accounts of the Sierra Leone conflict, see Ibrahim Abdullah and Patrick Muana, "The Revolutionary United Front of Sierra Leone: A Revolt of the Lumpen-proletariat," in Christopher Clapham, ed., *African Guerrillas* (Oxford: James Currey, 1998); Adekeye Adebajo, *Building Peace in West Africa: Liberia, Sierra Leone, and Guinea-Bissau* (Boulder: Lynne Rienner, 2002); *African Development* 22, nos. 2–3 (1997) (Special Issue: "Youth Culture and Political Violence: The Sierra Leone Civil War"); John Hirsch, *Sierra Leone: Diamonds and the Struggle for Democracy* (Boulder: Lynne Rienner, 2001); Mark Malan, Phenyo Rakate, and Angela McIntyre, *Peacekeeping in Sierra Leone: UNAMSIL Hits the Home Straight* (Pretoria: Institute for Security Studies, 2002); William Reno, *Warlord Politics and African States* (Boulder: Lynne Rienner, 1998); and Paul Richards, *Fighting for the Rainforest: War, Youth, and Resources in Sierra Leone* (Oxford: James Currey, 1996).

5. For a fuller explanation of Pax Nigeriana, see Adebajo, *Liberia's Civil War,* pp. 43–48.

6. See, for example, Neil Macfarlane and Thomas Weiss, "Regional Organizations and Regional Security," *Security Studies* 2, no. 1 (Autumn 1992); and Robert Mortimer, "ECOMOG, Liberia, and Regional Security in West Africa," in Edmond Keller and Donald Rothchild, eds., *Africa in the New International Order: Rethinking State Sovereignty* (Boulder: Lynne Rienner, 1996).

7. See International Crisis Group (ICG), *Tackling Liberia: The Eye of the Storm,* Africa Report no. 62 (Freetown: ICG, 30 April 2003).

8. Economist Intelligence Unit, Country Report, "Guinea-Bissau," 1st Quarter 2000, p. 30.

9. See United Nations, *Report of the Secretary-General Pursuant to Security Council Resolution 1216 (1998) Relative to the Situation in Guinea-Bissau,* UN Doc. S/1999/294, 17 March 1999, pp. 1–2.

10. See Adebajo, *Building Peace in West Africa,* pp. 111–136; Eric G. Berman and Katie E. Sams, *Peacekeeping in Africa: Capabilities and Culpabilities* (Geneva: UN Institute for Disarmament Research, 2000), pp. 128–138; and Comfort Ero, "The Future of ECOMOG in West Africa," in Jakkie Cilliers and Greg Mills, eds., *From Peacekeeping to Complex Emergencies: Peace Support Missions in Africa* (Johannesburg: South African Institute of International Affairs, 1999), pp. 67–69.

11. See *Report of the Secretary-General on Developments in Guinea-Bissau and on the Activities of the UN Peacebuilding Support Office,* UN Doc. S/2003/1157, 5 December 2003.

12. See the United Nations, *Report of the Inter-Agency Mission to West Africa: Towards a Comprehensive Approach to Durable and Sustainable Solutions to Priority Needs and Challenges in West Africa,* UN Doc. S/2001/434, 2 May 2001.

13. See Femi Aribisala, "The Political Economy of Structural Adjustment in Côte d'Ivoire," in Adebayo Olukoshi, Omotayo Olaniyan, and Femi Aribisala, eds., *Structural Adjustment in West Africa* (Lagos: Nigerian Institute of International Affairs, 1994); and Yves A. Fauré, "Côte d'Ivoire: Analysing the Crisis," in Donal B. Cruise O'Brien et al., eds., *Contemporary West African States* (Cambridge: Cambridge University Press, 1991).

14. For a background to the current crisis, see Abdoulaye Bathily, "La crise ivoirienne: Elements pour situer ses origines et ses dimensions sous-régionales," *Democracy and Development* 3, no. 2 (2003): 93–99; and Jeanne Maddox Toungara, "Prospects for Peace in Ivory Coast," statement to the U.S. House of Representatives Committee on International Relations Subcommittee on Africa, 12 February 2003.

15. See *Second Report of the Secretary-General on the UN Mission in Côte d'Ivoire,* UN Doc. S/2003/1069, 4 November 2003.

16. See United Nations, *Report of the United Nations Secretary-General on Côte d'Ivoire,* UN Doc. S/2003/374, 26 March 2003.

17. See *First Progress Report of the Secretary-General on the UN Mission in Liberia,* UN Doc. S/2003/1175, 15 December 2003.

18. This section on building a new security architecture has been adapted from Adebajo, *Building Peace in West Africa,* pp. 145–163.

19. Personal interview with General Ishola Williams, Lagos, 6 August 1999.

20. See Article 58 of the *Revised ECOWAS Treaty,* 1993.

21. Desmond Davies, "Peacekeeping African Style," *West Africa* no. 4190 (4–17 May 1998): 413.

22. Cited in Mortimer, "From ECOMOG to ECOMOG II," p. 200.

23. Ibid., p. 200.

24. *ECOWAS Draft Mechanism for Conflict Prevention, Management, Resolution, Peacekeeping, and Security,* Meeting of the Ministers of Defense, Internal Affairs, and Security, Banjul, 23–24 July 1998, pp. 2–3.

25. Personal discussions with Margaret Vogt, director of the International Peace Academy's Africa Program at the time, who headed the team of experts in Banjul.

26. See ECOWAS, *Protocol Relating to the Mechanism for Conflict Prevention, Management, Resolution, Peacekeeping, and Security.*

27. Ibid., p. 7.

28. Ibid., p. 10.

29. Mohamed Chambas, "The Security Council and ECOWAS: Facing the Challenges of Peace and Security in West Africa," address to the UN Security Council, New York, 11 April 2003.

30. Mohamed Chambas, "Operationalizing the ECOWAS Mechanism for Conflict Prevention, Management, Resolution, Peacekeeping, and Security," address at a policy forum organized by the International Peace Academy in New York, 29 April 2002.

31. ECOWAS, *Protocol Relating to the Mechanism for Conflict Prevention, Management, Resolution, Peacekeeping, and Security,* pp. 14–15.

32. Inaugural Meeting of the ECOWAS Council of Elders, *Final Communiqué,* Niamey, 2–4 July 2001, pp. 2–4.

33. ECOWAS, *Protocol Relating to the Mechanism for Conflict Prevention, Management, Resolution, Peacekeeping, and Security,* p. 13.

34. Ibid., p. 23.

35. Ibid., pp. 17–19.

36. ECOWAS, *Protocol Relating to the Mechanism for Conflict Prevention, Management, Resolution, Peacekeeping, and Security,* pp. 16–17.

37. See Ebow Godwin, "'Cohesion Kompienga 98,'" *West Africa* no. 4191 (18–31 May 1998): 474–475.

38. ECOWAS, *Protocol Relating to the Mechanism for Conflict Prevention, Management, Resolution, Peacekeeping, and Security,* pp. 19–20.

39. I thank Lateef Aminu, one of the experts in Banjul, for this point, which I learned during an interview in Lagos on 6 August 1999.

40. See Boutros Boutros-Ghali, *An Agenda for Peace* (New York: United Nations, 1992); and Alan James, *Peacekeeping in International Politics* (London: Chatto and Windus, 1990).

41. This point was made particularly forcefully at an International Peace Academy (IPA)/Council for the Development of Social Science Research in Africa (CODESRIA) seminar of African civil society actors in Senegal. See IPA/CODESRIA, *War, Peace, and Reconciliation in Africa,* November–December 1999, available at www.ipacademy.org.

42. I thank my coauthor, Michael O'Hanlon, for the observations in this and the previous paragraph, in Adekeye Adebajo and Michael O'Hanlon, "Africa: Toward a Rapid-Reaction Force," *SAIS Review* 17, no. 2 (Summer–Fall 1997): 153–164.

43. Aboagye, *ECOMOG,* p. 300; and personal interview with General Emmanuel Erskine, New York, 21 June 1999.

44. I thank Lateef Aminu for this point.

45. Maxwell Khobe, "The Evolution and Conduct of ECOMOG Operations in West Africa," in Mark Malan, ed., *Boundaries of Peace Support Operations: The African Dimension,* Institute for Security Studies (ISS) Monograph no. 44 (Pretoria: ISS, February 2000), pp. 118–119.

46. ECOWAS, *Protocol Relating to the Mechanism for Conflict Prevention, Management, Resolution, Peacekeeping, and Security,* p. 25.

47. See, for example, Margaret Vogt and Lateef Aminu, eds., *Peacekeeping as a Security Strategy in Africa: Chad and Liberia as Case Studies,* 2 vols. (Enugu: Fourth Dimension, 1996).

48. Daniel Bach, "Institutional Crisis and the Search for New Models," in Réal Lavergne, ed., *Regional Integration and Cooperation in West Africa: A Multi-dimensional Perspective* (Ottawa: International Development Research Council, 1997), p. 85.

49. Berman and Sams, *Peacekeeping in Africa,* p. 146.

50. See Jendayi Frazer, "The African Crisis Response Initiative: Self-Interested Humanitarianism," *Brown Journal of World Affairs* 4, no. 2 (Summer–Fall 1997): 103–118; Eboe Hutchful, "Peacekeeping Under Conditions of Resource Stringency," in Cilliers and Mills, *From Peacekeeping to Complex Emergencies,* pp. 113–117; Paul Omach, "The African Crisis Response Initiative: Domestic Politics and Convergence of National Interests," *African Affairs* 99, no. 394 (January 2000): 73–95; and Rocklyn Williams, "Beyond Old Borders: Challenges to Franco–South African Security Relations in the New Millennium," *African Security Review* 8, no. 4 (1999): 3–19.

51. IPA/ECOWAS, "Operationalizing the ECOWAS Mechanism for Conflict Prevention, Management, Resolution, Peacekeeping, and Security," Dakar, August 2002, available at www.ipacademy.org.

52. ECOWAS, *Protocol Relating to the Mechanism for Conflict Prevention, Management, Resolution, Peacekeeping, and Security,* pp. 25–27.

53. I thank General Ishola Williams, one of the experts in Banjul in 1998, for this insight.

54. Ali Mazrui, *Towards a Pax Africana* (Chicago: University of Chicago Press, 1967).

14

The United Nations

James O. C. Jonah

There is currently widespread appreciation of the need for effective cooperation between the United Nations and regional organizations in the security field. This is a welcome change of attitude and focus when one considers the dominant debate in the early years of the UN's creation in 1945 over the wisdom of employing regional arrangements—rather than the UN—to manage regional disputes.

While the UN Charter makes adequate provisions, in Chapter VIII, for collaboration between the UN and regional organizations, there were strong disagreements in the post-1945 years about whether the UN Security Council or regional organizations should have primacy over resolving regional disputes. This debate had its roots in the planning for a new global organization to replace the discredited League of Nations while World War II still raged. Two schools of thought dominated this debate: on the one hand, the British prime minister, Winston Churchill, expressed a clear preference for regional security arrangements to be the centerpiece of the postwar global security order; on the other hand, Cordell Hull, the U.S. secretary of state, worked strenuously for a global security arrangement within the context of the new United Nations.[1]

Washington's view prevailed over London's as evidenced by the U.S.-inspired Dumbarton Oaks proposals, which became the basic document at the San Francisco Conference in 1945, where the Latin American states successfully argued for a more explicit recognition of regional security arrangements as a condition for accepting the UN Charter. The provisions contained in Chapter VIII are due mainly to the efforts of these states.[2] Unfortunately, it was also in Latin America, particularly at the time of the Guatemalan crisis of 1954, that controversy raged about the differing or complementary roles of the UN and the Organization of American States (OAS) in the resolution of regional disputes. While the UN Security Council conceded that the OAS should have the primary role in managing regional conflicts, it nevertheless accepted that individual members of the OAS should not be denied their sovereign right to resort to the Council if they so desired.

Amid the euphoria of African independence in the early 1960s, African states initially, perhaps somewhat naively, placed great hopes in the UN as the global security organ that would deal with all the security problems on the continent. However, owing to their bitter experiences during the Congo crisis (1960–1964), when the superpowers sought to manipulate the United Nations Organization Mission in the Congo (MONUC) to their own advantage,[3] many African governments became more pragmatic and less naive about the UN's role in managing regional conflicts, particularly after the establishment of the Organization of African Unity (OAU)—now the African Union (AU)—in 1963.[4] The new African approach to managing conflicts was forcefully elaborated during the debate in the UN Security Council on the Stanleyville incident of 1964 in the Congo.[5] Many African states argued that whenever there was a dispute involving members of the OAU, the pan-continental organization would use its best efforts to resolve the crisis. They argued further that disputes between OAU members and non-OAU members should be referred directly to the UN Security Council or the General Assembly.

A major snag in this position was the reluctance of the OAU to intervene in civil conflicts in Africa, even when they resulted in enormous loss of lives and destruction of property. The OAU Charter, like the UN Charter, did not allow interference in the internal affairs of member states. But many Western countries expressed dissatisfaction that the OAU refrained from tackling cases like the protracted civil war in Sudan that has raged since the 1950s, the Nigerian civil war of 1967 to 1970, and the massive human rights abuses in Uganda under the autocratic leadership of the self-styled "field marshall" Idi Amin in the 1970s. Since the OAU refused to deal with these internal disputes, the UN was also reluctant to take up these issues. As earlier noted, the difficult experiences of the Congo crisis of the 1960s, when the UN became embroiled in Cold War rivalries, were an important deterrent to UN intervention in Africa. This history largely explains why the UN took so long to intervene in the Somalia dispute in the early 1990s.

With the passage of time and the end of the Cold War, the OAU relaxed its position and showed greater willingness to deal with internal disputes in Africa.[6] While this shift was occurring at the OAU, the UN Security Council developed a greater reluctance to intervene in African disputes. Although this trend began at the end of the 1980s, it became more pronounced after the UN's debacle in Somalia in 1993.[7]

It is important to note a significant practice that has gradually developed over the years in the relationship between the UN and regional organizations, especially the OAU. It is now commonplace for the UN Secretary-General to address annual summit meetings of the OAU. In addition, there are now regular meetings at the organizational and technical levels between the UN secretariat and those of regional organizations. There are increasingly frequent exchanges of information and ideas between the UN and regional organizations. The UN has also collaborated with the OAU in peacekeeping missions in Rwanda in 1993 and Ethiopia/Eritrea in 2000.

Having briefly provided a context for understanding the relationship between the UN and regional organizations, this chapter will now focus attention on the relationship between the UN and the Economic Community of West African States (ECOWAS) in conflict management in Liberia and Sierra Leone, and to a lesser degree in Guinea-Bissau. I will assess the UN's contributions to peacemaking in Liberia and Sierra Leone and, very briefly, its peacebuilding efforts in Guinea-Bissau. A major goal of the chapter will be to examine the difficulties in the cooperation between ECOWAS and the UN in these three cases in the political, military, and humanitarian spheres. I conclude the chapter by offering some policy lessons for improving cooperation between ECOWAS and the UN for future missions in West Africa.

ECOWAS and the UN in Liberia

ECOWAS's Early Challenges

It is only by examining current events through the context just provided that one can fully appreciate the steps taken by subregional organizations in Africa to find solutions to their own problems. The start of the Liberian civil war in December 1989 coincided with the end of the Cold War. As this brutal war continued, neither the UN nor the wider international community made any effort to bring succor to the suffering people of Liberia. In a real sense, the world was standing idly by while the Liberian civil war produced unprecedented butchery in the subregion and resulted in the destabilization of neighboring states as a result of the spillover of about 750,000 refugees across Liberia's borders.[8]

ECOWAS, although primarily an economic organization (see Chapters 2, 3, and 4), searched for ways and means to find a solution to the crisis in Liberia. Under the leadership of Nigeria, a 1981 security protocol on mutual assistance in defense matters that had laid dormant for a decade was controversially dusted off in a bid to transform ECOWAS into a security instrument. The entry of ECOWAS into the security arena was not widely appreciated at first. In fact, there was widespread criticism when ECOWAS, through its cease-fire monitoring group, ECOMOG, intervened in Liberia in August 1990 (see Chapter 13). The response of ECOMOG leaders was simple: the situation in Liberia presented a grave threat to the stability of West Africa, and member states could not tolerate the kidnapping and killing of foreign nationals. Furthermore, the civil war was causing a massive outflow of refugees into neighboring countries, which in turn presented an overwhelming burden on these states and threatened their own security. An additional consideration, which was not voiced at the time but was discussed in closed diplomatic circles, was the apparent discovery of a plan by Libyan-trained rebel groups—the National Patriotic Front of Liberia (NPFL) and the Revolutionary United Front (RUF)—to take over the subregion by toppling sitting regimes through armed rebellions. Among Charles Taylor's NPFL fighters were citizens of Sierra Leone, Burkina Faso, and Gambia, and some of these rebels planned to invade neighboring countries from Liberia, as the RUF successfully did in March 1991. ECOMOG's leaders were equally determined to prevent their regimes from becoming subregional dominoes at the mercy of multinational rebels.

Prior to the establishment of ECOMOG, the first request for technical assistance to establish a peacekeeping force in Liberia was made to the UN by the ECOWAS secretariat in Lagos. Although the informal request was made to me as the UN Undersecretary-General for Special Political Questions, Javier Perez de Cuellar, the UN Secretary-General at the time, was kept fully informed. In a sense, the planning for the establishment of ECOMOG was done with the full knowledge and collaboration of senior officials of the UN secretariat in New York. The UN Security Council itself had its first informal consultations on Liberia on 3 August 1990. No specific action was taken at the time.

A major initiative was undertaken by Sir Dawda Jawara, then chairman of ECOWAS and Gambia's president, when Perez de Cuellar received Omar Sey, Gambia's foreign minister, in New York on 10 August 1990. Sey had brought de Cuellar a message from Jawara to which was attached the final communiqué of the ECOWAS Standing Mediation Committee summit meeting in Banjul from 6 to 7 August 1990, which had taken the decision to dispatch ECOMOG to Liberia.

In a letter dated 13 August 1990, the UN Secretary-General informed the Security Council that Sey had told him that ECOMOG would function in full accordance with the UN Charter. The Gambian foreign minister argued that ECOMOG's sole objective would be to stop the senseless slaughter taking place in Liberia, to establish a durable cease-fire, and to save lives. The decision by the ECOWAS summit in Banjul to establish an Interim Government of National Unity (IGNU), Sey continued, was mainly to ensure the holding of "free and fair" elections. Gambia's foreign minister requested the support of members of the UN Security Council for ECOMOG's peace-keeping mission in Liberia. He indicated that ECOWAS would welcome any financial and material support from the international community.

De Cuellar, in an August 1990 letter responding to Sey's letter, expressed his personal views to the UN Security Council: he supported the decision taken by ECOWAS, hoped that ECOMOG would not only stabilize the situation but also save lives, and argued that the establishment of the peacekeeping force was vital to the UN's humanitarian relief efforts in Liberia. The Secretary-General also put on record the informal cooperation between the UN secretariat and the ECOWAS secretariat when he stated that "the [UN] Secretariat would do [its] utmost to provide advice and technical assistance to ECOWAS on the modalities for the establishment and the functioning of its peacekeeping force."[9]

The UN Security Council discussed the Secretary-General's letter in informal sessions, but regrettably took no action on Liberia. Under the prevailing practice of the Council, members would usually be guided by the views of its African members on conflicts affecting the continent before contemplating any action. At the time that the Liberia issue was before the Council, its three African members—Côte d'Ivoire, Ethiopia, and Zaire (now the Democratic Republic of Congo)—at first did not favor UN involvement in the crisis. Côte d'Ivoire was supporting the NPFL, and along with Ethiopia and Zaire, reflexively opposed external interference in the internal affairs of an African state, in line with the OAU's historical non-interventionist principles. However, on 15 January 1991 the Ivorian mission in New York wrote to the president of the Security Council, Zaire's Bagbeni Adeito Nzengeya, drawing attention to the final communiqué of the first extraordinary session of ECOWAS heads of state and government, which had met in Bamako, Mali, from 27 to 28 November 1990. At the Bamako meeting, a peace agreement had been signed to establish a ceasefire, disarm fighters, and create a broad-based interim government. Shortly after Bamako, the Ivorian permanent mission requested a meeting of the UN Security Council to endorse the establishment of ECOMOG as a legitimate subregional peacekeeping force and to obtain international support for its efforts in Liberia.

The Bamako Peace Meeting

The Bamako meeting of November 1990 was an important step in laying a solid foundation for cooperation between the UN and ECOWAS over the Liberia issue. Prior to this meeting, the establishment of ECOMOG had been highly controversial within ECOWAS. Out of the initial troop-contributing members of ECOMOG, only Guinea was a francophone state; the four others—Ghana, Nigeria, Sierra Leone, and Gambia—were anglophone.

It is a sad fact of African diplomacy that historical colonial influences have often divided African states along linguistic lines—as was the case initially with ECOMOG. A linguistic divide was clearly evident: almost all of ECOWAS's francophone states—nine out of sixteen member states—expressed unhappiness about the establishment of ECOMOG without their explicit consent. In fact, some of these states asserted that ECOWAS had no mandate to establish the force. Nigeria was accused of pursuing hegemonic ambitions to dominate West Africa. Charles Taylor's NPFL took full advantage of these divisions and continually raised doubts about the legality of the ECOMOG force.

The well-attended Bamako meeting, however, contributed greatly to creating a consensus among ECOWAS members on Liberia. As chairman of ECOWAS, President Jawara gave a detailed report at the meeting of the steps taken by ECOWAS's Standing Mediation Committee (Gambia, Ghana, Mali, Nigeria, and Togo), and explained the reasons behind the establishment of ECOMOG. Following discussions on his report, the extraordinary ECOWAS summit decided to endorse the decision to establish ECOMOG. Once this decision was taken, Charles Taylor had no choice but to accept ECOMOG formally, although he continued to criticize the preponderance of Nigerian influence within the peacekeeping force. Bamako created a clear basis for the UN Security Council to recognize ECOMOG as a legitimate force acceptable to all ECOWAS states. This may explain why Côte d'Ivoire, which had been lukewarm toward ECOMOG before the Bamako meeting, was prepared to engage the UN Security Council on Liberia after all of ECOWAS's members had endorsed the establishment of the peacekeeping force in Bamako.

On 22 January 1991, the UN Security Council met to consider Abidjan's request. At the conclusion of the Council's deliberations on Liberia, the president of the Security Council, Ambassador Nzengeya, stated: "The members of the Security Council commended the efforts made by the ECOWAS Heads of State and Government to promote peace and normalcy in Liberia. The members of the Security Council call upon the parties to the conflict in Liberia to continue to respect the ceasefire agreement which they have signed and to cooperate fully with ECOWAS to restore peace and normalcy in Liberia."[10] Even though the Council did not go further than the president's statement, these developments nevertheless created the necessary political space for the UN Secretary-General to cooperate with ECOWAS and ECOMOG.

At this initial stage, cooperation took the form of Perez de Cuellar responding positively to ECOWAS's request to dispatch a diplomatic envoy to participate in all ECOWAS summits and ministerial meetings, alongside senior officials from the OAU secretariat in Addis Ababa. In my capacity as the UN Undersecretary-General for Political Affairs dealing with African problems, I attended all of ECOWAS's meetings on Liberia held in various West African capitals. I was always widely consulted by ECOWAS leaders on how best to proceed in implementing the peace plan for Liberia, and on how ECOWAS could most effectively cooperate with the UN Security Council. Through my attendance at these meetings, the UN Security Council and Secretary-General were kept fully informed about all the essential details of ECOMOG's involvement in Liberia. At a later stage, the UN Secretary-General adopted the practice of dispatching special envoys, not only to ECOWAS summits and ministerial meetings, but also to individual West African heads of state to discuss how the UN could best assist the implementation of the ECOWAS peace plan for Liberia. A similar arrangement of employing a UN special envoy was repeated during ECOWAS's involvement in Sierra Leone after 1997.

The Cotonou and Akosombo Accords

There were occasions in Liberia when the political relationship between the UN and ECOWAS experienced severe strain. The signing of the Akosombo Agreement on 12 September 1994, as a supplement to the 1993 Cotonou Accord, came as a surprise to senior officials at the UN secretariat in New York. Although the Special Representative of the UN Secretary-General, Trevor Gordon-Somers, participated in the Akosombo meeting, the UN secretariat was puzzled by the signing of an agreement that was seen as unbalanced in favor of Liberia's warlords. Gordon-Somers also failed to explain why the accord had been signed. The Cotonou Agreement of 25 July 1993, in contrast, had been a significant achievement. It was signed by all three Liberian factions—the IGNU, the NPFL, and the United Liberation Movement of Liberia for Democracy (ULIMO). While reaffirming the call for a cease-fire, Cotonou called for the establishment of a single Liberian National Transitional Government (LNTG), which would have three branches—legislative, executive, and judicial. The accord further called for the expansion of ECOMOG through the inclusion of additional contingents from within and outside West Africa. It was the Cotonou Agreement that called for an important monitoring role for the UN through the deployment of 368 military observers who, together with ECOMOG, would oversee implementation of the accord.

The Politics of ECOWAS-UN Cooperation in Liberia

The acceptance of ECOMOG by all members of ECOWAS did not end the bickering over the actions and performance of the peacekeeping force. In this context, it is important to note that an attempt was made in the early stages of the ECOMOG presence in Liberia to replace ECOMOG with a

UN force. It would appear that when Côte d'Ivoire approached the UN
Security Council in January 1991, it had hoped for just such an outcome. In
its absence, the government in Abidjan began to explore other options.
Amara Essy, the Ivorian foreign minister and the former long-serving permanent representative of his country in New York, who had intimate
knowledge of the internal workings of the labyrinthine UN bureaucracy,
met with Marrack Goulding, UN Undersecretary-General for Special Political Affairs, on 14 August 1991 in New York to explore the details of a possible UN intervention in Liberia. Essy acknowledged that, while he was
aware that the problem in Liberia was principally an internal civil war, he
was frustrated that the UN was marginalizing Africa as evidenced by the
lack of any concrete action by the world body in Liberia. The Ivorian foreign minister noted that, in contrast, the UN had taken concrete actions in
Nicaragua, Haiti, and El Salvador, thereby giving some international legitimacy to these problems. Essy informed Goulding that he had discussed
the same matters and expressed similar views to Lawrence Eagleburger, the
deputy U.S. secretary of state, in Washington. The Ivorian diplomat concluded his discussions with Goulding by informing him that his president,
Félix Houphouët-Boigny, wanted the UN to take over ECOMOG's peacekeeping responsibilities.

Due to my intimate knowledge of ECOWAS's internal discussions
through attending closed-door meetings on Liberia, I knew that it would be
difficult to replace ECOMOG with a UN peacekeeping force. In fact, many
attempts to bring in the UN to assist ECOMOG's peacekeeping efforts during previous meetings had failed. There was a prevailing view among many
of its member states that ECOWAS must be careful not to jeopardize any
success in Liberia by bringing in the UN. The same view was expressed by
ECOWAS member states when plans were being made to deploy a UN
force in Sierra Leone in 1999.

Nevertheless, ECOWAS members sought the political support of the
Security Council. On 19 November 1992 a delegation of nine ECOWAS
foreign ministers participated in the Council's debate on Liberia.[11] At the
conclusion of the deliberation, the Security Council adopted Resolution 788
(1992), which, inter alia, called for the imposition of a mandatory arms
embargo against Liberia and the appointment of a Special Representative of
the Secretary-General. In pursuance of this resolution, Trevor Gordon-
Somers, a Jamaican economist, was named Special Representative of the
Secretary-General for Liberia.

Only very reluctantly did ECOWAS members accept the dispatch of UN
observers to Liberia in September 1993. Nicéphore Soglo, the president of
Benin and ECOWAS chairman at the time, had to be convinced that the presence of UN observers could help meet the concerns of Charles Taylor's NPFL,
which was refusing to disarm to ECOMOG, particularly the Nigerians. Taylor

had proposed disarming to ECOMOG's Ghanaian contingent. This arrangement was unacceptable to the ECOMOG high command. It was at this stage that, in my capacity as UN Special Envoy of the Secretary-General, I suggested that UN observers might oversee the process of disarmament and ensure the impartiality of ECOMOG. The NPFL delegation accepted this arrangement, and Soglo, at a closed meeting of the ECOWAS summit in Cotonou on 25 July 1993, called on me to make the case to the other ECOWAS leaders. Following an exchange of views on the matter, the summit agreed to request the UN to provide 250 to 300 military observers who, together with ECOMOG, would monitor and supervise the military aspects of the Cotonou Agreement. There was, however, consensus within ECOWAS that the UN should not replace ECOMOG as the principal peacekeeping force in Liberia.

When I reported back to UN headquarters on the request for UN observers, I encountered stiff opposition. An informal exchange of views with key members of the Security Council and formal discussions in the secretariat revealed serious reservations about allowing a UN operation to coexist alongside a regional force. This had never happened in the history of UN peacekeeping. During his meeting with Amara Essy in August 1991, Marrack Goulding had made clear to the Ivorian foreign minister that the UN tries to avoid undertaking peacekeeping operations with regional groups. Similar problems arose when the UN agreed to assume ECOMOG's peacekeeping responsibilities in Sierra Leone in 1999.

Despite the strong reservations of the new UN Secretary-General, Boutros Boutros-Ghali, and some of his senior officials, in the end the Egyptian scholar-diplomat, in a bid to enhance the UN's cooperation with ECOWAS, did recommend to the Security Council the acceptance of ECOWAS's request for UN observers. The Council responded by adopting Resolution 813 (1993), which enabled the Secretary-General to dispatch a technical mission to Liberia in August 1993 to determine the needs of a possible deployment of UN observers to Liberia. When the technical mission made its recommendations on the establishment of the United Nations Observer Mission to Liberia (UNOMIL), it was with the clear understanding that the unarmed military observers would be protected by ECOMOG in the exercise of their duties and functions. UNOMIL was established in accordance with UN Security Council Resolution 866 of 22 September 1993 with the following fivefold mandate: investigating cease-fire violations; monitoring compliance with a UN-imposed arms embargo, disarmament, and demobilization; observing and verifying elections; coordinating humanitarian assistance; and reporting on major violations of international law.[12] With this understanding, the Security Council approved the dispatch of UNOMIL to Liberia. This was the first time that the UN had ever deployed military personnel to work alongside an already established regional force in the field.

At the time that UNOMIL was established, the original concept of operation required 368 UN military observers to deploy around Liberia at border crossings, entry points, and sea and air ports, and to monitor and supervise ECOMOG peacekeepers in the implementation of their disarmament tasks. The assumption was that ECOMOG would be similarly deployed and colocated with, and provide security for, UNOMIL. In the event, owing to logistical and financial constraints on ECOMOG, it deployed to only about 15 percent of Liberian territory and was unable to guarantee the security of UNOMIL's peacekeepers.

The expectation that ECOMOG would protect UNOMIL was dashed during the bloody fighting in Monrovia in April and May 1996. In light of the total breakdown of law and order in Liberia's capital, the UN drastically reduced its presence and kept only about 100 military observers in Liberia until the end of its mission in 1997. As a result of the events of 1996, Boutros-Ghali appointed me as his Special Envoy to review the situation in Liberia, especially the cooperation between ECOMOG and UNOMIL on the ground. The findings and lessons learned during this mission may have influenced UN arrangements for the protection of its military observers in Sierra Leone.[13] Despite the chaos in Liberia in 1996, UNOMIL was functioning fairly well and cooperating with ECOMOG. The arrangement between ECOMOG and UNOMIL was viewed by both the UN and ECOWAS to be a viable model for similar missions in future. The UN presence in Liberia provided the opportunity for the world body to assist ECOWAS in Liberia's electoral process.

Even though UNOMIL staff were generally satisfied with the cooperation between ECOMOG and the UN in Liberia, there were areas of difficulties that are important to highlight. In Liberia, and later in Sierra Leone, ECOMOG officials viewed with envy, and sometimes anger, the disparity in logistics and equipment (vehicles, functioning radios, and other communications equipment) as well as financing of UN observers, who, unlike the ill-equipped ECOMOG forces, were not involved in fighting Liberia's factions and were exposed to much less danger in the field. UNOMIL officers, usually of the rank of captains, majors, or sometimes colonels, were usually paid their salaries by their respective governments. In addition, they received per diem allowances from the UN in excess of $100, compared to the $5 daily stipend of ECOMOG peacekeepers, which often arrived late. These factors tended to breed discontent between both sides. ECOMOG officers did not understand why the UN could not meet at least some of their basic costs and share some of their equipment with the subregional peacekeeping force.[14]

Perhaps the greatest threat to cordial relations between ECOWAS and the UN was the question of financial support. ECOWAS leaders have never understood the unwillingness of the UN Security Council to fund the

ECOMOG peacekeeping operations in Liberia and Sierra Leone. In particular, they have argued, correctly in my view, that the Security Council should have been more supportive of ECOMOG in recognition of the valuable role that its peacekeepers played in saving lives and property in both Liberia and Sierra Leone. ECOWAS leaders often noted that, in the absence of ECOMOG at crucial stages, both countries would have been plunged into greater chaos. They recall with pride that, without ECOMOG's efforts and sacrifices, involving over 1,000 fatalities in Liberia and Sierra Leone and billions of dollars, the entire West African subregion would have gone up in flames. Why then, they ask, is the UN Security Council unwilling to play its part in providing the necessary funding to ECOMOG? ECOWAS leaders tend to dismiss as mere excuses all explanations that the UN maintains a rigid stance against funding any operation that is not under its direct command and control.

The implications of this divergence of views between the UN and ECOWAS over funding of peacekeeping missions was played out in Sierra Leone in May 2000 with near-fatal consequences. The Nigerian government bore about 90 percent of the costs of the ECOMOG missions in Liberia and Sierra Leone. The government of Ghana also made major financial sacrifices. Former Ghanaian president Jerry Rawlings once complained to me that some of his senior military officers were upset that Rawlings was allocating Ghana's limited military resources to the upkeep of its ECOMOG contingent in Liberia instead of channeling the resources to the much more urgent needs of the Ghanaian army at home. It was this continuing financial burden that led ECOWAS troop-contributing countries constantly to threaten the withdrawal of their troops from the ECOMOG missions in Liberia and Sierra Leone. The UN Security Council rebuffed Boutros-Ghali's proposal in February 1995 to establish a large UN peacekeeping force in Liberia under which ECOMOG would have been subsumed.[15]

ECOWAS and the UN in Sierra Leone

From ECOMOG to UNAMSIL

A Nigerian-led ECOMOG force had reversed a military coup in May 1997 in Sierra Leone and restored to power the elected government of Ahmed Tejan Kabbah in March 1998. A rebel invasion of Freetown in January 1999 highlighted the frustrations and deficiencies of ECOMOG's ill-equipped peacekeepers, who suffered hundreds of casualties. The newly elected Nigerian government of Olusegun Obasanjo in 1999 argued that a civilian government in Abuja would be unable to sustain the level of financial support for ECOMOG in Sierra Leone, which it estimated at $1 million a day.

Nigeria and its ECOWAS allies from Ghana, Guinea, and Mali once more explored the possibility of the UN making substantial financial contributions to ensure the continuation of ECOMOG's peacekeeping role in Sierra Leone. When these efforts were rebuffed, Nigeria announced that it would withdraw its troops from Sierra Leone. It was clear that the premature withdrawal of ECOMOG, particularly the Nigerian contingent, would spell grave danger for Sierra Leone. Evidence has since surfaced that RUF leader Foday Sankoh premised his calculations for a military takeover of the country on the withdrawal of ECOMOG. Undoubtedly, it was the start of the withdrawal of the Nigerian contingent that triggered the May 2000 events in Freetown, when the RUF, in spite of its pledge to uphold the Lomé Agreement of July 1999, almost took over the country from the elected government of Ahmed Tejan Kabbah, in which I served as finance minister.[16]

It is true that individual members of the UN Security Council, particularly Britain and the United States, and some members of the European Union (EU), made some efforts to provide some funding—especially logistical support or training to ECOMOG contingents. But these meager efforts could not compensate for the glaring difference between ECOMOG's poorly equipped and maintained troops and the fully equipped and maintained troops of the United Nations Observer Mission in Sierra Leone (UNOMSIL), which had been working alongside ECOMOG since August 1998. When UN Assistant Secretary-General Hedi Annabi briefed the Security Council in informal consultations on 29 December 1999, he observed that Nigeria had indicated its intention to withdraw from ECOMOG because it was unwilling to stay in Sierra Leone in circumstances where there would be two different forces, mandates, commands, and conditions of service. Under the Lomé Agreement, the cooperation between ECOMOG and the proposed United Nations Mission in Sierra Leone (UNAMSIL) had been envisaged as follows: ECOMOG would protect Freetown and its environs and undertake any military enforcement actions, while the UN would take care of the rest of the country.

The failure to provide a financial solution to ECOMOG's problems provoked anger within the force. ECOMOG officers realized that, under these circumstances, the peacekeeping mission would be forced to withdraw from Sierra Leone. They wanted to stay, but could not find a basis for doing so. ECOMOG leaders suggested a plan under which the entire ECOMOG force would be taken over by the UN. They were politely told by the UN secretariat that this was not an option. Furthermore, there was resistance within the UN secretariat and Security Council to the idea that the new UN peacekeeping force be headed by a senior Nigerian military officer. The subsequent compromise offered by UN Secretary-General Kofi Annan was the post of Special Representative of the UN Secretary-General to a Nigerian diplomat, Oluyemi Adeniji. Anyone who followed the debate about the division of labor between ECOWAS and the UN in Sierra Leone closely would not have been surprised that the Indian UN force commander, General Vijay Jetley, had a difficult time in Sierra Leone. The bitterness felt by ECOMOG officers toward UNAMSIL was real, and no matter who the UN commander had been, he would have faced difficulties with ECOMOG's senior officers. ECOMOG and some other ECOWAS members felt strongly that the UN was attempting to steal the glory from the subregional peacekeepers after they had borne the brunt of the dangers of protecting Sierra Leone from rampaging rebels for three years.

The problems in the relationship between the UN and ECOMOG in Sierra Leone were not made easier by the ambivalent attitude of Sierra Leoneans toward ECOMOG. The Kabbah government strongly supported the idea of keeping ECOMOG in Sierra Leone, although it realized that such an arrangement would mean a lack of funding from the UN. Many Sierra Leoneans initially erroneously believed that the UN would dispatch a robust peacekeeping force to their country with a mandate to repel the rebels from their strongholds in the eastern diamond areas and the north. They had developed this unrealistic expectation when the case was made by senior UN officials to replace ECOMOG with a UN force. Even though the majority of Sierra Leoneans appreciated and supported ECOMOG, there was a clear preference, particularly in the local press, for the creation of a UN force. Sierra Leoneans, like Somalis and Rwandans, later turned against the UN when it refused to fight on the grounds that it had no mandate to do so. Only the small British contingent of about 800 troops that was sent to Freetown in May 2000 and helped to stabilize UNAMSIL enjoyed universal public support. Many Sierra Leoneans appreciated the decisive manner with which the British forces routed the notorious "West Side Boys" after their comrades had been taken hostage by the militia in September 2000.

The Politics of the ECOMOG Intervention in Sierra Leone

There was one occasion when the visit of an ECOWAS ministerial committee to New York caused bitter acrimony between the subregional body and the UN. The ECOWAS Ministerial Committee of Five (Côte d'Ivoire, Ghana, Guinea, Liberia, and Nigeria) was visiting New York and consulting with UN Security Council members and the Secretary-General at the same time that ECOMOG's largely Nigerian peacekeepers intervened to remove the military junta from Freetown in February 1998. There were accusations by Security Council members that the ministers had deceived the UN by failing to inform its members of ECOMOG's imminent entry into Freetown. As Sierra Leone's permanent representative to the UN at the time, I maintained, throughout the period of the coup, very close contact with the ECOMOG team at Lungi airport and was fully informed of the circumstances of this intervention. I was monitoring developments hourly with the ECOMOG command at Lungi and can confirm that the ECOWAS foreign ministers were unaware of the developing military situation in Freetown. The Nigerian ECOMOG force commander, General Timothy Shelpidi, had earlier given a free hand to the local commander at Lungi—Colonel Maxwell Khobe (also a Nigerian)—to intervene militarily at any time of his choosing under the strategy of defense-offense. There was no deception of the UN by ECOWAS ministers. In fact, the majority of the ECOWAS ministers in New York were publicly opposed to a military intervention in Sierra Leone. The intervention was carried out almost single-handedly by the Nigerian contingent, ably assisted by loyal Sierra Leonean army troops and civil defense forces.

It is important to counter another basic criticism of ECOMOG's intervention in Freetown in 1998. It has often been argued that ECOMOG had no direct authorization from the UN Security Council to use force in Sierra Leone. In order to address this issue accurately, one must necessarily revisit the way in which the UN Charter provisions were crafted at Dumbarton Oaks and approved at San Francisco in 1945. The overarching principle of the UN Charter is collective security.[17] Accordingly, member states must expect support from the UN Security Council if they are under armed attack, and the Council is obligated to come to their assistance. In return, and due to the expectation of the principle of "collective security" being upheld to protect their sovereignty from armed attack, member states renounced the threat or use of force in settling disputes. Nevertheless, it was recognized that there might be occasions when a state may be under imminent armed attack and the Security Council may not have the means immediately to provide collective security. In such cases, member states are allowed to use the provisions of Article 51 of the UN Charter and act in self-defense. This act, however, was conditional on immediately reporting the situation to the Security Council in the expectation that the Council would take action. These are the problems underlying the use of force under the UN Charter, and they are applicable to regional arrangements.

The key question that the Sierra Leone case raises, however, is this: If, contrary to the UN Charter, Council members fail to provide collective security to an endangered member state, can one blame a state that decides to use force in its own defense? This is the dangerous implication of the tendency of some Security Council members' constant assertion that the Council cannot act in all situations in which peace and security are threatened. Incidentally, the failure of the Council to act to rescue small and weak states is making more credible, in some quarters, the arguments by private security firms or "mercenaries," such as Executive Outcomes, that they can provide security to vulnerable states more effectively than the UN and regional organizations.[18] The Sierra Leone case was worthy of Security Council intervention because the May 1997 coup and the RUF itself were externally supported, and the OAU had called for ECOWAS to remove the junta from power at its June 1997 summit.

The Abidjan Accord

In Sierra Leone, an uneasy relationship developed between ECOWAS—under the leadership of Côte d'Ivoire—and the Special Representative of the UN Secretary-General in Sierra Leone, Berhanu Dinka, over tactics and procedures in implementing the Abidjan peace accord of November 1996 between the Kabbah government and the RUF. Dinka, appointed in February 1995, enjoyed the full confidence of the Kabbah government. He was regarded as a model international civil servant who intimately understood the nature of the problem in Sierra Leone. Dinka was keenly aware, however, that the Kabbah government had no confidence in Akyaaba Addai-Sebo, the representative of the London-based nongovernmental organization (NGO) International Alert. Based on Sierra Leonean government intelligence sources, Addai-Sebo was regarded as a close ally of the RUF and was therefore seen as incapable of acting as an impartial negotiator. The Kabbah government, however, made it clear that it had no objection to Addai-Sebo acting as an adviser to the RUF in peace negotiations.

The tension between Dinka and Abidjan was due, in the view of the Kabbah government and the UN, to the very close relationship between Addai-Sebo and Amara Essy, the foreign minister of Côte d'Ivoire. Owing to mutual suspicions, both the Ivorian government and the UN, as well as the RUF, perhaps inadvertently, undermined each other, which in turn adversely affected their mediation efforts in Abidjan. Even after the May 1997 coup, Addai-Sebo did everything to advance the cause of the RUF and to sabotage all of Dinka's peacemaking efforts.

Lomé: No Justice, No Peace?

In contrast to the divisions surrounding the Abidjan Agreement of November 1996, the ECOWAS-UN negotiating team in Lomé in May 1999 worked well together. However, some elements of the Sierra Leonean government, as well as the UN secretariat, felt that the government negotiation team showed inordinate interest in the signing of a peace agreement without taking proper cognizance of the nature of the dispute or the record of the RUF in reneging on earlier accords. It was only after the conclusion of the negotiations and the preparation of the peace documents that it became public knowledge that the UN secretariat was dissatisfied with the Lomé Accord, particularly the provisions on amnesty for war crimes committed by RUF rebels. At the signing ceremony, Francis Okelo, the Special Representative of the UN Secretary-General to Sierra Leone, was authorized by Kofi Annan to enter a reservation with regard to Lomé's amnesty clauses. It has subsequently been revealed that the officials dealing with Sierra Leone in the UN secretariat were not privy to the details of the negotiations in Lomé. Many humanitarian NGOs severely criticized the Lomé Accord's amnesty provisions.

The Politics of Sanctions: Liberia and Sierra Leone

The UN and ECOWAS disagreed about the imposition of sanctions against Liberia as well as the UN's refusal to buy arms from warring factions in furtherance of the disarmament and demobilization processes in Liberia and Sierra Leone. On the issue of sanctions, ECOWAS leaders and officials argued that the imposition of sanctions or conducting of trials under an international tribunal would deter rebels from making peace and handing over their weapons. In particular, they believed that Liberian president Charles Taylor, who played an important role in pressing the RUF to sign the Lomé Accord, should be seen as a useful partner for peace in Sierra Leone and should therefore not be the object of any UN sanctions. Several members of the UN Security Council, led by Britain and the United States, disagreed with this position. There was a strong belief among key members of the UN Security Council and secretariat that Charles Taylor had been masquerading as an impartial mediator, while continuing to fuel the war in Sierra Leone. They therefore argued for diamond, arms, and travel sanctions against Liberia, which were imposed in May 2001. Taylor was later indicted for war crimes by the Special Court for Sierra Leone and departed for exile in Nigeria in August 2003.

The Politics of Elections: Liberia and Sierra Leone

Another area of cooperation between ECOWAS and the UN was the organization and supervision of elections in Liberia and Sierra Leone. This complex process has three components—military, political, and humanitarian. On the political side, this relationship has already been assessed. However, there remains another area in which the UN and ECOWAS did not cooperate fully. In Liberia, although a crucial ECOWAS summit in Abuja in September 1996 drew extensively from my experience as head of the electoral commission in Sierra Leone in the conduct of elections under difficult circumstances, it was unclear what role ECOWAS wanted the UN to play in the Liberian elections. This became clearer only after Boutros-Ghali received Nigeria's foreign minister, Tom Ikimi, in New York in September 1996. At this meeting, Ikimi delivered a message from the ECOWAS chairman,

General Sani Abacha, on the recently concluded ECOWAS summit in Abuja. This message clearly stated that the ECOWAS Committee of Nine (Benin, Burkina Faso, Côte d'Ivoire, Gambia, Ghana, Guinea, Nigeria, Senegal, and Togo) would have the sole responsibility for finding peace in Liberia. While welcoming the UN's assistance in the peace process, Abacha's message on the conduct of elections in Liberia was this: "Though elections have been held in some other countries of the world under crisis situations, their circumstances are quite different from the situation in Liberia. The United Nations would be requested to work with ECOWAS to provide necessary assistance and support in the process leading to the conduct of free and fair elections in Liberia."[19]

The essence of this message was that the elections in Liberia would be conducted by ECOWAS itself with the assistance of the UN. The view at the ECOWAS summit, however, as reflected in the statements of the majority of subregional leaders, was for the UN to conduct the elections, in close collaboration with ECOWAS. This was also the strong expectation of Liberia's active civil society groups, who were lobbying on the fringes of the summit hall in Abuja. Many of Liberia's political parties expressed disappointment with this outcome, but the UN could do nothing about it. The UN accepted Abacha's decision and tried to see how best it could be of assistance to ECOWAS.[20] This decision was largely based on Abacha's determination not to have the UN steal the glory from success in Liberia from subregional peacekeepers who had sacrificed enormously in seven years of lonely peacekeeping.

Regrettably, the joint coordination mechanism envisioned in Boutros-Ghali's 19 March 1992 report to the UN Security Council involving the UN, ECOWAS, and Liberian parties was never created. The mechanism was expected to have been the basis on which the UN and ECOWAS would, in full partnership, monitor the progress of the electoral process, identify gaps in this process, coordinate observer teams, and jointly certify whether the elections were "free and fair." At UNOMIL's initiative, a less formal mechanism known as the "Standing Committee" was established in May 1997, bringing together the Liberian Election Commission, the UN, ECOWAS, and international donors.

The UN did not expect a flawless election in Liberia under the prevailing circumstances. However, it should be noted that the electoral calendar adopted by ECOWAS had ten days fewer than Kofi Annan had advised as the minimum period necessary to enable the holding of credible elections in Liberia. ECOWAS's calendar was also at least nineteen days short of the Liberia Election Commission's original assessment of the time that would be required to organize and conduct credible elections. To help ease the problems created by the compressed calendar, ECOWAS provided substantial technical and logistical assistance to the Liberian Election Commission.[21]

An area of fruitful cooperation in preparation for the elections in Liberia was the disarmament process, which was critical to the conduct of the elections. Pakistan's Major-General Sikandar Shami, UNOMIL's chief military observer at the time, noted that once donors had helped ECOMOG to increase its strength with the addition of three military battalions, thus raising its overall strength to almost 11,000 troops, UNOMIL and ECOMOG jointly redeployed their forces in a manner that not only overcame existing shortcomings but also enhanced a feeling of security among Liberians. The appointment of the dynamic Nigerian general Victor Malu as ECOMOG force commander in August 1996 also increased international confidence in the subregional force. UNOMIL bolstered ECOMOG's deployment in Lofa county, which had comprised only a single 100-man company at Voinjama. Other such redeployments saw ECOMOG establish a presence in virtually every county in Liberia. Similarly, with the arrival of additional resources, UNOMIL was able to increase its own bases in Liberia from ten to sixteen.

In furtherance of cooperation and coordination, ECOMOG and UNOMIL decided to continue with the disarmament of Liberia's factions along two simultaneous tracks. While ECOMOG mounted a series of raids to recover weapons forcibly, UNOMIL kept open its disarmament sites for combatants who chose to surrender their weapons voluntarily. As a result, while UNOMIL collected an additional 458 weapons and 27,000 pieces of ammunition, ECOMOG seized approximately 6,000 weapons and 150,000 rounds of ammunition.

The unexpected lack of total cooperation between the UN and ECOWAS in the conduct of Liberia's elections revealed to senior UN officials an aspect of a problem that had caused great irritation within ECOMOG and by extension within ECOWAS. Whether in the ECOWAS Committee of Nine on Liberia (or the Ministerial Committee of Five on Sierra Leone), UN representatives were constantly bombarded with complaints of Nigeria's "heavy-handedness" in the peace process and in ECOMOG's military operations. In fact, in my capacity as Special Envoy of the UN Secretary-General, I was dispatched to Liberia in 1996 to examine these concerns and report back to the UN Secretary-General, who in turn reported to the Security Council.

With respect to the 1996 elections in Sierra Leone, ECOWAS was not involved. The UN made significant contributions to Sierra Leone's Interim Electoral Commission (INEC), which I headed. UN support greatly enhanced INEC's capacity. In the actual conduct of the elections, the responsibility for conducting the poll remained with INEC, but the UN provided the umbrella for an international observer team, which included the Commonwealth and the OAU. Despite sporadic violence in parts of the country, this election was undoubtedly the most democratic in the history of

Sierra Leone up to that point, and marked the transition from military to civilian rule.[22]

In contrast to the 1996 elections in Liberia, both ECOMOG and UNAMSIL were very much involved in the conduct of the elections in Sierra Leone in May 2002. The UN made substantive financial contributions to the electoral commission in Sierra Leone and provided crucial logistical support for the balloting. By the time of this election, there was no ECOMOG force in Sierra Leone, since the key contingents, such as the Nigerians, had been absorbed into UNAMSIL. The security provided by UNAMSIL's 20,000 peacekeepers throughout the country made it possible for many more Sierra Leoneans to cast their ballots in peace and tranquillity. This was in sharp contrast to the violence that had adversely affected the 1996 elections. ECOWAS sent a delegation from its Council of Elders to observe the elections, which were judged to have been free and fair.

The Politics of Humanitarianism: Liberia and Sierra Leone

On the humanitarian side, there were some difficulties in the relationship between the UN and ECOMOG. The UN had envisaged ECOMOG's role to be to facilitate the delivery of humanitarian assistance to vulnerable populations in Liberia. When ECOMOG, through its intelligence operations, discovered in 1993 that some international NGOs were helping to transport arms and supplies to the NPFL, it set out to interdict such supplies and conducted bombing raids on supply lines and bases. As a result, several NGOs approached the UN's Department of Humanitarian Affairs to urge a halt to the bombings by ECOMOG on the ground that civilian targets were being hit. The humanitarian arm of the UN therefore became a critic of ECOMOG in Liberia, as it would later become in Sierra Leone.

ECOMOG's force commander in 1992 and 1993, General Adetunji Olurin, visited the UN secretariat in 1993 to explain ECOMOG's actions.[23] The political side of the UN secretariat showed greater understanding of ECOMOG's position than the UN's humanitarian department, which was very vocal in its criticism of the West African peacekeepers. Some argued that ECOMOG's decision to suspend cross-border humanitarian assistance from Côte d'Ivoire to NPFL-held areas was a direct result of the UN's increased political profile and involvement in regional politics. Many humanitarian workers, within and outside the UN, had believed that, with the appointment of Trevor Gordon-Somers as the UN Special Representative to Liberia in November 1992, all humanitarian operations would be subsumed under a political initiative mounted in partnership with ECOWAS. After the UN established a political presence in Liberia, international agencies, however, experienced considerable interference and encountered difficulties in fulfilling their tasks.

The propensity for conflict between international humanitarian organizations and peacekeeping forces in all parts of the world complicated the relationship between the UN's humanitarian staff and ECOMOG. It was perhaps inevitable that, given their separate mandates and sometimes conflicting agendas—ECOMOG's obsession with security, the humanitarian groups' obsession with free movement and access to populations—both actors would become embroiled in disputes. More often than not, these differences of view can be found within the UN and its agencies in the field. The observation that some of the UN's political and military personnel did not share the criticism of ECOMOG by the UN's humanitarian staff also held true in the case of Sierra Leone.

In Liberia, these disputes led to the removal of the head of the United Nations Special Coordinating Office for Liberia (UNSCOL), Ross Mountain. UNSCOL had been created in July 1990 to facilitate and coordinate the UN's relief operations involving the World Food Program (WFP), the United Nations Children's Fund (UNICEF), the World Health Organization (WHO), and the office of the United Nations High Commissioner for Refugees (UNHCR). Ross Mountain was severely criticized by Amos Sawyer's interim government and ECOMOG for what they perceived to be his close relationship with the NPFL.

In Sierra Leone, the humanitarian community was unhappy with the imposition of economic and military sanctions on the country by both the UN Security Council and ECOWAS. They therefore launched a campaign to secure some exemptions from the sanctions for essential supplies. Throughout the conflict in Sierra Leone, the humanitarian organizations were misunderstood and often bitterly criticized by the government and people alike. The major bone of contention was related to the fact that the humanitarian NGOs were in constant touch, as they should have been, with the population under RUF control. Accordingly, many Sierra Leoneans considered these NGOs to be sympathetic to the rebels.

With the invasion of Freetown by rebel forces in January 1999, the relationship between ECOMOG and the government of Sierra Leone on the one hand, and the humanitarian NGO community on the other, worsened. The UNHCR strongly objected to actions taken by the government in Freetown and ECOMOG against the International Committee of the Red Cross (ICRC), particularly when their communication equipment was confiscated by the government, with the assistance of ECOMOG. Donor governments strongly supported the humanitarian NGOs and called on the government of Sierra Leone to change its policy and allow the NGOs to continue with their humanitarian activities without obstruction.

It took an extended period of negotiations before a modus operandi was achieved and NGOs resumed their humanitarian activities. In order to explain the role of humanitarian NGOs in Sierra Leone to the general public, the government in Freetown, assisted by ECOWAS representatives, carried out an information campaign that clarified that the delivery of humanitarian assistance to rebel-held areas by these organizations was to support vulnerable populations and was not in any way a sign of support for the rebels.

The Diplomacy of ECOWAS-UN Relations: Liberia and Sierra Leone

The political relationship between ECOWAS and the UN was less contentious than in the humanitarian field. As earlier noted, the UN Secretary-General used several methods to foster cooperation between the two organizations. As Undersecretary-General for Political Affairs and the UN's Special Envoy, I was involved with ECOWAS leaders in promoting the peace process in Liberia. The UN Special Representatives in Liberia and Sierra Leone also played indispensable roles in moving the peace process forward in both countries. There was a clear convergence of views between senior officials of ECOWAS and the UN Special Envoy on how to proceed with the peace process in both countries. One reason for this close and fruitful cooperation was the mutual respect and confidence displayed by both sides. For example, in the case of Liberia, as UN Special Envoy I was allowed to attend all the closed-door meetings of ECOWAS leaders. They often treated me as someone they could trust and confide in. They were always confident that I would convey their views and interests fully and correctly to the UN Secretary-General and to the Security Council. In addition, they relied on me at these meetings to explain the complexities of the UN system and the type of support that ECOWAS could expect to obtain from the UN.

Similarly, the UN Special Representatives in Liberia and Sierra Leone were drawn into discussions with key local and subregional actors on implementing various peace agreements. Their views were canvassed, and together with ECOWAS's political representatives on the ground, they planned strategies together. To take one example, Trevor Gordon-Somers visited Liberia and neighboring states in March 1993 and had extensive consultations with all of Liberia's factions. These contacts led to negotiations that were sponsored by the UN, the OAU, and ECOWAS in Liberia in March 1993 and culminated in the most comprehensive peace agreement of the Liberian war, signed by Liberia's parties in Cotonou on 25 July 1993.

Cooperation between the UN and ECOWAS in the political and security fields also took another form. ECOWAS leaders sought to enhance this cooperation by periodically dispatching groups of ECOWAS foreign ministers to New York to consult directly with members of the Security Council and the UN Secretary-General. To address the conflicts in Liberia and Sierra Leone, ECOWAS leaders created two ministerial committees: the ECOWAS Committee of Nine for Liberia and the ECOWAS Committee of

Five for Sierra Leone. These two ministerial committees made a number of visits to New York for often useful consultations. They briefed the Security Council under the "Arrias formula"—for example in November 1997 on Sierra Leone—and once or twice made formal statements to open sessions of the Security Council. On the basis of these contacts, the Security Council gained better appreciation of the ebb and flow of developments in both Liberia and Sierra Leone and was able to make decisions based on perspectives garnered from diplomats working on the ground.

Pax Nigeriana in Liberia and Sierra Leone

Despite the accolades showered on ECOMOG by some analysts for its successes in Liberia and Sierra Leone, it should be admitted that it was principally a Nigerian achievement. Nigeria has a comprehensive and achievable policy objective in Africa and was prepared, particularly under the military regimes of Generals Ibrahim Babangida and Sani Abacha (1985–1998), to make whatever sacrifices were necessary to attain its leadership goals in Liberia and Sierra Leone. No one should take lightly the principles of Nigerian foreign policy to protect the interests of Africans on the continent (see Chapter 13). Perhaps there is a need to recognize Nigeria as a "benign hegemon" on the continent.

However, if Nigeria is to achieve its leadership ambitions, it will be necessary in the future for its leaders to take into account the contributions of other African states. This was not always the case in Liberia and Sierra Leone. Nigeria's domineering leadership sometimes irritated other countries, particularly its dominance of the ECOMOG high command as well as the alleged lack of consultation with senior military officers of other troop-contributing countries. One unfortunate mistake at the start of the ECOMOG operation in Liberia in 1990 was the way in which the first ECOMOG force commander—Ghana's General Arnold Quainoo—was replaced by a Nigerian commander—General Joshua Dogonyaro. Even though this change turned out to be effective, it should have been carried out with more tact and consultation.

A more serious and persistent complaint was the brusque manner in which Tom Ikimi, Nigeria's foreign minister from 1995 to 1998, was said to have executed his task as chairman of both the Committee of Nine on Liberia and the Committee of Five on Sierra Leone. It was widely felt that Ikimi had a personal desire to downplay the UN's role in the electoral process in Liberia. During negotiations at ECOWAS ministerial meetings over Sierra Leone, Ikimi often sought to downplay the role of the Sierra Leonean representative, Foreign Minister Shirley Gbujama, in the discussions on how to remove the military junta that had seized power in Freetown in May 1997. Ikimi's actions were not well received by the Sierra Leonean delegation.

Nigeria's foreign minister also took a curious position at the OAU summit in Harare, Zimbabwe, in June 1997. As the representative of Sierra Leone, I had urged the summit to denounce the military coup of May 1997 and called for the forcible removal of the unconstitutional regime. In response, Ikimi made a statement that could have been interpreted as a justification for the coup. He asserted that elections should not have been held in Sierra Leone in February 1996, arguing that these elections caused the problems that resulted in the May 1997 coup. This view directly contradicted the position of the UN, which had coordinated support for the holding of the elections in February 1996.

ECOWAS and the UN in Guinea-Bissau

Having focused largely on the two cases of Liberia and Sierra Leone, it is important to note briefly the cooperation between ECOWAS and the UN in Guinea-Bissau. Developments in Guinea-Bissau present a different case when compared to Liberia and Sierra Leone. Following the pattern in Liberia and Sierra Leone, ECOWAS took the initiative in tackling the deteriorating security situation in Guinea-Bissau.[24] The conflicting parties were brought to Abuja, Nigeria, where on 1 November 1998 the government of João Bernardo Vieira and the military junta of General Ansumane Mane signed the Abuja Agreement (S/1998/1028, annex) that provided for, inter alia, a government of national unity, the deployment of an ECOWAS Military Observer Group interposition force (ECOMOG), and the withdrawal of foreign troops (Senegal and Guinea had sent troops to support Vieira in 1998).

The UN assistant secretary-general for Political Affairs at the time, Ibrahima Fall, participated in the Abuja meeting, and on the basis of the UN Secretary-General's report, the Security Council, by its Resolution 1216 (1998), endorsed the Abuja Accord on 21 December 1998. Perhaps in light of its experience in Liberia and Sierra Leone, the Council requested that ECOMOG should provide it with reports on Guinea-Bissau at least once a month. The Council also called on the UN Secretary-General, Kofi Annan, to cooperate with ECOWAS in its peacekeeping tasks and to report back to it on progress in Guinea-Bissau. But while the Council demanded that ECOMOG submit periodic reports to it, the UN was reluctant to provide the necessary financial assistance for ECOMOG to fulfill its tasks in Guinea-Bissau.

An ECOWAS ministerial delegation visited UN headquarters and met with the Secretary-General in December 1998 to appeal for financial and technical assistance to enable ECOMOG to accomplish its tasks in Guinea-Bissau. Unfortunately, despite the convening in Geneva in May 1999 of a donor's meeting, the pledged financial assistance did not arrive due to continuing political instability in Guinea-Bissau. The Security Council's calls for funds to be provided to a trust fund also failed to yield substantial support.

After a military coup by General Mane removed Vieira from power on 7 May 1999 in violation of the Abuja Agreement, ECOMOG troops were withdrawn from Guinea-Bissau. Interestingly, the UN did not move quickly to deploy a peacekeeping force in Guinea-Bissau as it later did in Sierra Leone in 1999 after the departure of the bulk of ECOMOG peacekeepers. Annan, on at least two separate occasions, informed the Security Council that the government of Guinea-Bissau had requested the deployment of UN military observers.

After elections in 1999, the UN assisted the government of Guinea-Bissau through its Peacebuilding Support Office (UNOGBIS), which was established in April 1999 under the leadership of Samuel Nana-Sinkam. UNOGBIS has played a useful role in Guinea-Bissau. For example, it helped to stabilize the situation at the time of the failed coup in November 2000, during which General Mane was killed. The office also contributed, along with the United Nations Development Programme (UNDP), to the conduct of a "free and fair" election in Guinea-Bissau in November 1999, as well as to the presidential runoff in January 2000, which Kumba Yala won, before being toppled by a military coup in September 2003.

Learning Lessons

This chapter has highlighted some of the lessons learned in the cooperation between ECOWAS and the UN, and offered suggestions about how to tackle these problems. In concluding the chapter, I highlight two important issues—defining the proper division of labor between ECOWAS and the UN, and financing future regional peacekeeping operations—that, if not urgently addressed, will continue adversely to affect the security cooperation between ECOWAS and the UN.

From Burden Shedding to Burden Sharing

All evidence from Liberia and Sierra Leone would suggest that it is possible to have a UN peacekeeping force in coexistence with a regional force if proper arrangements have been made regarding the division of labor between both organizations. The frequent assertion that hybrid forces do not work in the field of peacekeeping may be too hasty a judgment to make. Many of these comments were made following ECOMOG's withdrawal from Sierra Leone by 2000, but as this chapter has made clear, such comments did not take sufficient account of the circumstances surrounding ECOMOG's withdrawal. After all, UNOMIL, despite its shortcomings, did work fairly well with ECOMOG in Liberia.

It is of vital importance that the UN work closely with regional forces at the operational level. Such cooperation provides credibility and can inspire confidence in local populations that the international community cares about peace in their country. The presence of a UN force alongside a regional force can also help foster pressure for accountability from regional peacekeepers. In the case of Liberia, the deployment of UNOMIL helped to resolve a sticking point in the negotiations regarding the disarmament and demobilization of the armed factions in 1993. Furthermore, the UN was able to act as an "honest broker" in assisting ECOWAS and Liberia's parties to break a major political stalemate by establishing an international panel of inquiry that investigated the massacre of about 600 people near Harbel in June 1993. The initial assessment by ECOWAS and IGNU was that the NPFL had committed the massacre. The international panel of inquiry, however, fingered elements of the Armed Forces of Liberia (AFL). As a result, the UN gained credibility as an impartial actor in the eyes of the NPFL.

We have also seen from the cases of Liberia and Sierra Leone that the UN and ECOWAS can cooperate effectively in promoting negotiations among the parties to a dispute. The necessary requirements, however, are that both groups must select their representatives with great care. These negotiators must be well tested and experienced. The UN, in particular, should return to the long-established tradition of appointing Special Representatives who are experienced negotiators. The world body must use high-quality leaders with sound management skills and a high degree of competence and integrity. Such individuals must believe in the concept of the international civil service and not just be highly connected individuals in search of a well-paid job. In this connection, it may be advisable to include in the team of negotiators an AU representative, as was the case in Liberia when the late Reverend Canaan Banana served as the OAU's Eminent Person between 1993 and 1997.

The UN's Inter-Agency Task Force on West Africa recommended the establishment of a UN Office for West Africa in May 2001. This office has now been established in Dakar, Senegal, and Mauritanian diplomat Ahmedou Ould-Abdallah was appointed as the Special Representative of the UN Secretary-General in 2002 to head it. The establishment of this office could prove advantageous for cooperation between the UN and ECOWAS. The UN office has been mandated to assist the strengthening of ECOWAS's peacekeeping and electoral capacities and to collaborate with civil society actors in West Africa in their governance and democratization efforts. The office is also mandated to assist the UN and its subregional offices in coordinating strategies in West Africa; monitor and report on political, humanitarian, and human rights developments; harmonize the UN's activities with those of ECOWAS; monitor ECOWAS's decisions and activities; and support national and subregional peacebuilding efforts.[25] The establishment of this office is a recognition of the need to adopt a regional approach to conflict management in West Africa; if used effectively, this office could provide a potentially invaluable tool for managing ECOWAS-UN relations and coordinating the UN's activities in West Africa.

Financing Future Peacekeeping Operations

Finally, one cannot overemphasize the crucial importance of finding a durable solution to the financing of regional forces, whether or not they are deployed alongside a UN force. I have argued in this chapter that ECOMOG was a decisive force in the maintenance of relative stability in West Africa. As such, ECOMOG has played a vital role for the UN Security Council as well as the organization as a whole. There is therefore an essential obligation on the international community to ensure that regional forces like ECOMOG are provided with the logistical and financial wherewithal to accomplish their peacekeeping tasks. There is nothing in the UN Charter that prohibits the financing of regional peacekeeping forces by the United Nations. A proper reading of Chapters VII and VIII, along with creative diplomacy, can provide suitable formulae through which the UN Security Council can begin to make arrangements for financing regional peacekeeping forces.

It is true that Security Council members, in their individual capacities, have assisted ECOMOG in the areas of operational effectiveness, training, logistics, and in rare cases, equipping national contingents and paying stipends to troops (France, for example, equipped and provided stipends for the ECOMOG force in Guinea-Bissau). I am here proposing that the Security Council undertake serious discussions with regional organizations like ECOWAS with a view to providing long-term and practical financing of regional peacekeeping operations on the ground. In Sierra Leone, the problems of UNAMSIL could have been considerably eased if the terms of the Lomé Accord of July 1999 had been maintained with respect to ECOMOG's peacekeeping role. In both Liberia and Sierra Leone, ECOMOG gave ample evidence of its readiness to fight if provoked by the rebels. Even though, at times, ECOMOG sustained heavy casualties, there were no loud calls by its troop-contributing countries to withdraw their forces. This posture contrasts sharply with that of the UN. The constant reluctance of UN peacekeepers to engage with rebels after suffering casualties, as evidenced by events in Somalia in 1993 and Rwanda in 1994, is not only a result of problems relating to specific Security Council mandates authorizing peacekeeping missions, but also clearly reflects the reluctance of troop-contributing countries to put their soldiers in harm's way and have them return home in body bags. In this regard, the Brahimi Report of 21 August 2000 notes: "There are many tasks which United Nations peacekeeping forces should not be asked to undertake and many places they should not go. But when the United Nations does send its forces to uphold the peace, they must be prepared to confront the lingering forces of war and violence, with the ability and determination to defeat them."[26] The report goes on:

> Impartiality for United Nations operations therefore means adhering to the principles of the Charter: where one party to a peace agreement clearly and incontrovertibly is violating its terms, continued equal treatment of all parties by the United Nations can in the best case result in ineffectiveness and in the worst may amount to complicity with evil. No failure did more to damage the standing and credibility of United Nations peace keeping in the 1990s than its reluctance to distinguish victim from aggressor.[27]

If UN peacekeepers cannot and will not fight, then the UN has an obligation to finance a regional force that will do so. Rebel forces respect only a peacekeeping or peace enforcement force that will fight. Experience has demonstrated that the only reliable deterrent to a determined rebel force is a well-armed force that will not hesitate to fight if provoked. In the context of the UN peacekeeping force in the Middle East in 1974, former UN Secretary-General Kurt Waldheim once addressed UN troops in Cairo by reminding them that peacekeeping is not a picnic.

Notes

1. The U.S. undersecretary of state, Sumner Welles, sympathized with Winston Churchill's plan to establish regional organizations. On 22 May 1943, Churchill proposed that postwar collective security could be best maintained by three regional councils and a supreme world council. In line with this framework, Welles fleshed out in greater detail a regional plan for collective security. However, U.S. Secretary of State Cordell Hull opposed the regional concept put forward by Churchill and Welles and proposed instead a universal organization in which all "peace-loving" states, regardless of size or strength, would be represented on an equitable basis. Hull's concept of a universal approach gained wider support when he replaced Welles as chairman of the Advisory Committee on Problems of Foreign Relations in January 1943.

2. Ruth B. Russell and J. Nuther, *A History of the United Nations Charter* (Washington, D.C.: Brookings Institution, 1958).

3. See Georges Abi-Saab, *The United Nations Operation in the Congo, 1960–1964* (Oxford: Oxford University Press, 1978); Catherine Hoskyns, *The Congo Since Independence, January 1960–December 1961* (London: Oxford University Press, 1965); Conor Cruise O'Brien, *To Katanga and Back: A UN Case History* (London: Hutchinson, 1962); Indar Jit Rikhye, *Military Adviser to the Secretary-General: UN Peacekeeping and the Congo Crisis* (London: Hurst, 1993); and Brian Urquhart, *A Life in Peace and War* (New York: W. W. Norton, 1987).

4. See Yassin El-Ayouty and I. William Zartman, eds., *The OAU After Twenty Years* (New York: Praeger, 1984); Yassin El-Ayouty, ed., *The Organization of African Unity After Thirty Years* (London: Praeger, 1994); Z. Cervenka, *The Organization of*

African Unity (London: Julien Friedman Press, 1977); Kwame Nkrumah, *Africa Must Unite* (London: Heinemann, 1963); Amadou Sesay, ed., *The OAU After Twenty-five Years* (Cambridge: St. Martin's, 1990); and Immanuel Wallerstein, *The Politics of Unity* (New York: Vintage Books, 1967).

5. UN Doc. S/PV 1176, 15 December 1964, p. 2.

6. See Adekeye Adebajo and Chris Landsberg, "The Heirs of Nkrumah: Africa's New Interventionists," *Pugwash Occasional Paper* 2, no. 1 (January 2001); Chris Bakwesegha, "Conflict Resolution in Africa: A New Role for the Organization of African Unity?" in Gunnar Sorbo and Peter Vale, eds., *Out of Conflict: From War to Peace in Africa* (Uppsala: Nordiska Afrikainstitutet, 1997), pp. 79–96; Solomon Gomes, "The OAU, State Sovereignty, and Regional Security," in Edmond Keller and Donald Rothchild, eds., *Africa in the New International Order: Rethinking State Sovereignty and Regional Security* (Boulder: Lynne Rienner, 1996); International Peace Academy, *Report of the Joint OAU/IPA Task Force on Peacemaking and Peacekeeping in Africa* (New York: International Peace Academy, March 1998); *OAU-IPA Seminar on Peacemaking and Peacekeeping*, Addis Ababa (New York: International Peace Academy, November–December 1998); and Monde Muyangwa and Margaret Vogt, *An Assessment of the OAU Mechanism for Conflict Prevention, Management, and Resolution, 1993–2000* (New York: International Peace Academy, November 2000).

7. See Hussein Adam, "Somalia: A Terrible Beauty Being Born?" in I. William Zartman, ed., *Collapsed States: The Disintegration and Restoration of Legitimate Authority* (Boulder: Lynne Rienner, 1995), pp. 69–78; Walter Clarke and Jeffrey Herbst, eds., *Learning from Somalia: The Lessons of Armed Humanitarian Intervention* (Boulder: Westview Press, 1997); John L. Hirsch and Robert B. Oakley, *Somalia and Operation Restore Hope: Reflections on Peacemaking and Peacekeeping* (Washington, D.C.: U.S. Institute of Peace Press, 1995); and Mohamed Sahnoun, *Somalia: The Missed Opportunities* (Washington, D.C.: U.S. Institute of Peace Press, 1994).

8. See Colonel Festus Aboagye, *ECOMOG: A Subregional Experience in Conflict Resolution, Management, and Peacekeeping in Liberia* (Accra: Sedco, 1999); Adekeye Adebajo, *Liberia's Civil War: Nigeria, ECOMOG, and Regional Security in West Africa* (Boulder: Lynne Rienner, 2002); Abiodun Alao, John Mackinlay, and 'Funmi Olonisakin, *Peacekeepers, Politicians, and Warlords: The Liberian Peace Process* (Tokyo: United Nations University Press, 1999); Stephen Ellis, *The Mask of Anarchy: The Destruction of Liberia and the Religious Dimensions of an African Civil War* (London: Hurst, 1999); Karl Magyar and Earl Conteh-Morgan, eds., *Peacekeeping in Africa: ECOMOG in Liberia* (London: Macmillan, 1998); Klaas Van Walraven, *The Pretence of Peace-Keeping: ECOMOG, West Africa, and Liberia (1990–1998)* (The Hague: Netherlands Institute of International Relations, 1999); and Margaret Vogt, ed., *The Liberian Crisis and ECOMOG: A Bold Attempt at Regional Peacekeeping* (Lagos: Gabumo Press, 1992).

9. Letter of the Secretary-General dated 13 August 1990 and addressed to the president of the Security Council. This letter was circulated to Council members but was not published as a UN document.

10. UN Doc. S/PV.2974, 22 January 1991, p. 9.

11. UN Doc. S/PV.3138, 19 November 1992.

12. UN Doc. S/PV.3281, 22 September 1993. See also UN Doc. S/26422 and Add. 1, 9 September 1993.

13. *Case Study 1: Cooperation Between the United Nations and the Economic Community of West African States (ECOWAS): UNOMIL/ECOMOG* (New York: UN Lessons Learned Unit, Department of Peacekeeping Operations, February 1998).

14. See Clement Adibe, "The Liberian Conflict and the ECOWAS-UN Partnership," *Third World Quarterly* 18, no. 3 (1997); Binaifir Nowrojee, "Joining Forces: UN and Regional Peacekeeping—Lessons from Liberia," *Harvard Human Rights Journal* 18 (Spring 1995); and 'Funmi Olonisakin, "UN Co-operation with Regional Organizations in Peacekeeping: The Experience of ECOMOG and UNOMIL in Liberia," *International Peacekeeping* 3, no. 3 (Autumn 1996).

15. See United Nations, *Ninth Progress Report of the Secretary-General on the United Nations Observer Mission in Liberia,* UN Doc. S/1995/158, 24 February 1995, p. 12.

16. For accounts of the Sierra Leone conflict, see Ibrahim Abdullah and Patrick Muana, "The Revolutionary United Front of Sierra Leone: A Revolt of the Lumpenproletariat," in Christopher Clapham, ed., *African Guerrillas* (Oxford: James Currey, 1998); Adekeye Adebajo, *Building Peace in West Africa: Liberia, Sierra Leone, and Guinea-Bissau* (Boulder: Lynne Rienner, 2002); *African Development* 22, nos. 2–3 (1997) (Special Issue: "Youth, Culture, and Political Violence: The Sierra Leone Civil War"); John Hirsch, *Sierra Leone: Diamonds and the Struggle for Democracy* (Boulder: Lynne Rienner, 2001); Mark Malan, Phenyo Rakate, and Angela McIntyre, *Peacekeeping in Sierra Leone: UNAMSIL Hits the Home Straight* (Pretoria: Institute for Security Studies, 2002); William Reno, *Warlord Politics and African States* (Boulder: Lynne Rienner, 1998); and Paul Richards, *Fighting for the Rainforest: War, Youth, and Resources in Sierra Leone* (Oxford: James Currey, 1996).

17. Inis Claude Jr., *Power and International Relations* (New York: Random House, 1962).

18. See, for example, Jakkie Cilliers and Peggy Mason, eds., *Peace, Profit, or Plunder? The Privatisation of Security in War-Torn African Societies* (Pretoria: Institute for Security Studies, 1999); Greg Mills and John Stremlau, eds., *The Privatisation of Security in Africa* (Johannesburg: South African Institute of International Affairs, 1999); and Abdel-Fatau Musah and J. Kayode Fayemi, eds., *Mercenaries: An African Security Dilemma* (London: Pluto Press, 2000).

19. General Abacha's message was hand-delivered and was not published as a UN document.

20. *UNOMIL's Electoral Observation: Final Report* (Monrovia: UN Electoral Division, September 1997).

21. See, for example, Terrence Lyons, *Voting for Peace: Post Conflict Elections in Liberia* (Washington, D.C.: Brookings Institution, 1998).

22. Howard W. French, "West African Surprise: Suddenly, Peace Takes Root in Sierra Leone," *New York Times,* 5 May 1996, p. 1.

23. Lindsay Barrett, "The Relief Game," *West Africa,* 17–23 May 1993, pp. 816–818.

24. See Adebajo, *Building Peace in West Africa;* Eric G. Berman and Katie E. Sams, *Peacekeeping in Africa: Capabilities and Culpabilities* (Geneva: UN Institute for Disarmament Research, 2000); and Comfort Ero, "The Future of ECOMOG in West Africa," in Jakkie Cilliers and Greg Mills, eds., *From Peacekeeping to Complex Emergencies: Peace Support Missions in Africa* (Johannesburg: South African Institute of International Affairs, 1999).

25. United Nations, *Report of the Inter-Agency Mission to West Africa: Towards a Comprehensive Approach to Durable and Sustainable Solutions to Priority Needs and Challenges in West Africa,* UN Doc. S/2001/434, 2 May 2001, p. 15.

26. UN Doc. A/55/305-S/2000/809, 21 August 2000, p. 8.

27. Ibid., p. 9.

15

France, Britain, and the United States

Kaye Whiteman and Douglas Yates

The interplay of French, British, and U.S. security roles in West Africa has related very much to two major phenomena in the second half of the twentieth century: decolonization and the Cold War. Both sprang from global power shifts that followed World War II, a cataclysm that left the two major colonial powers in Africa—Britain and France—economically debilitated and in no position to maintain their global empires.[1] The U.S. superpower, now equipped with a nuclear arsenal, was nevertheless locked in an ideological and strategic confrontation with its global rival, the Soviet Union, that prevented it from developing a coherent African strategy.[2] The respective policies of the three major Western powers in Africa must be considered in light of these larger developments in the structure of the international system.

It is instructive to compare and contrast the comportment of these three powers over the course of the last six decades. The United States, having no colonies in the region, and only a whisper of a legacy in Liberia, left Africa to North Atlantic Treaty Organization (NATO) allies, pushing, but not too hard, for them to decolonize. In their larger strategy of "containment," policymakers in Washington left responsibility for the African "southern flank" (a low priority in strategic planning) to their counterparts in London and Paris. The U.S. provided military support to its NATO ally Portugal, which helped it to maintain its colonies in Angola, Guinea-Bissau, and Mozambique. But a contrast between the French and British approaches, amounting to an almost Manichean dichotomy, revealed important "psychonationalist" differences in the postwar period.

Strategic Legacies of Decolonization, 1945–1960

Divergent Postwar Models

The United States had led the Allied victory in World War II and was thereafter in a position of uncontested global economic and military power within the Western alliance. But the United States was not sufficiently fluent in African politics (the State Department did not even have a "Bureau of African Affairs" until decolonization necessitated its creation in 1958). A more narrowly defined U.S. Africa policy, especially as far as West Africa was concerned, remained essentially one of working through the colonial powers in the capital cities of Europe.[3] But the British, having played an important part in the victory over Nazi Germany, were mainly experiencing honorable fatigue, and were ready, imperceptibly, to foreclose on the whole British empire.

The mood induced by World War II led to a reaffirmation of self-determination through the creation of the United Nations in 1945 and brought a Labour government to power in London that was ready to tackle Indian independence. British prime minister Winston Churchill, victorious in the war, would have found it hard to contemplate the loss of India, the "jewel in the crown" of the British empire, had he retained office. The Labour Party, under Clement Attlee, had no such problem. Still, after Indian independence in 1947, the rest of the decolonization process was inevitable.

The French, for their part, had not had a good war. General Charles de Gaulle and the "Free France" movement he led had at least saved their honor, but after the war a succession of governments and the French army, backed for a long time by a wide segment of public opinion, fought grimly and vainly to hold on to the mainstays of the French empire, first in Indochina, then in Algeria. The French had lost almost all of Indochina during the war to Ho Chi Minh and his charismatic revolutionary movement, and they tried desperately and unsuccessfully to regain control after 1945. The British had mounted a somewhat similar reassertion of their position in the Malaya peninsula, but this had not been such a hopeless situation, and they were apparently more successful than their French counterparts in building up a local elite.

The single most important difference that marks postwar decolonization is that the British ultimately yielded when they found they had to, but the French fought two long, destructive, and futile wars in Indochina and North Africa. British strategists were cushioned by the pretenses and hypocrisies of the new Commonwealth, but were clever enough to foresee its future as a developmental organization. The French were not able to enjoy such illusions. Their savage eight-year war against Algerian independence (1954–1962) proved to be more disastrous than its Vietnamese counterpart had been for the French military, worse even than the 1954 humiliation at Dien Bien Phu. This was because Algeria was closer to home. It was a French *département,* not a colony. Algeria was defined as a southern extension of France—a deadly combination of what Ulster and Rhodesia represented for the British.

Absence/Presence of Defense Accords

Nothing illustrates the differing positions of the two European colonial powers better than their contrasting attitudes to the Suez crisis of 1956, when a tripartite invasion of Gamal Abdel Nasser's Egypt by Britain, France, and Israel was forced into a humiliating retreat by U.S. president Dwight Eisenhower. Even now, the British see this as their major end-of-empire climacteric, when real loss of power was brought home conclusively. But the French had only regarded Suez as a failed maneuver, and could never really understand why the British were engaged in such moral agonizing. What the Suez crisis marked definitively for both countries was the reality of the hegemony of the United States, which had pulled the rug out from under its British allies by exposing their economic weakness. The great powers of the Old World were forced to cede preeminence to the superpower of the New World. By coincidence, the Suez crisis was almost immediately followed by Ghanaian independence in 1957. This was a symbol that the British approach in Africa was paying off. It also helped the French to see that in giving way in Africa, they could save their position. Africa's central importance to postwar France was aptly summed up by former French president François Mitterrand, who said in 1957: "Without Africa, France will no longer have a history in the twenty-first century."[4]

British gradualism contrasted with the twists and turns of French policy, where independence had at first been ruled out, and even autonomy, when it finally came, progressively balkanized the two major colonial federations—Afrique Occidentale Française (AOF) and Afrique Equatoriale Française (AEF). In 1958, de Gaulle returned to the Elysée palace, and in the heat of the Algerian war he still vainly hoped that half-measures like the Communauté Française would keep a form of control over France's African colonies. But Algeria threatened the very existence of the French state. Once de Gaulle took the momentous and statesmanlike decision in 1960 to abandon the French settlers, the *pieds noirs,* he made every effort to guard what he could of France's sphere of influence in sub-Saharan Africa. There was, for example, no question of fighting to hold on to French-run Cameroon, where a communist-inspired rebellion had broken out in 1955. This was in any case not a French colony, but a UN trust territory, which made its own independence inevitable, and independence, allied to French military response, undercut the rebels' position. Moreover, the independence of Kwame Nkrumah's Ghana had a profound effect on the region. In particular it bolstered *enfant terrible* Sékou Touré's famous 1958 "*non*" in French Guinea to what de Gaulle had called "a certain kind" of independence in his community proposal.

Despite aspects of Nkrumah that France profoundly distrusted, at least the successful independence of Ghana in 1957 did encourage the French to have a little more confidence in the possibility, if not the viability, of independence. The pace certainly quickened thereafter. Nigeria's effortless slide to independence in 1960 occurred as the French were going through the process in their remaining African territories. But there was from this time a fundamental difference in the French and British attitudes toward security in Africa. Having been fully responsible for security in all of its territories until 1960, France had been able, and indeed had even said that it felt obliged, to establish instant African national armies, even though there had been very little preparation for the full independence that came almost unexpectedly in 1960. Paris also immediately constructed a remarkable neocolonial network of defense agreements with the vast majority of its former sub-Saharan African territories. Though Britain had enjoyed a similar responsibility for security in Ghana, Nigeria, Sierra Leone, and Gambia before the disbanding of the "Royal West African Frontier Force" in 1959, the only attempt that it made at a French-style "defense cooperation" was with Nigeria, an agreement that was abrogated soon after independence in 1961 following student demonstrations against the pact and growing political hostility.

African Security Policy During the Cold War, 1960–1989

French Neocolonialism

Throughout the Cold War, France consistently sought a much higher security profile in Africa than either Britain or the United States. The French took advantage of the balkanization of their federations and the establishment of a congeries of fragile ministates, all in urgent need of protection from possibly hostile neighbors (not to mention domestic popular revolt). For thirty-five years, French security policy proved to be a unique phenomenon in Africa that permitted active intervention and excited the admiration of some strategists as a valid postcolonial model, though in reality it resembled classic neocolonialism. Even today, there is a French military presence that casts a strategic net over the continent. But its scope has been much reduced in recent years, and the will to use military force in the way it was wielded in the past has waned almost to the point of impotence.

Of course, security was but one of the three essential material props of the French sphere of influence in Africa. These were, first, the monetary zone of the Communauté Financière Africaine (CFA); second, the "cooper-ation accords" for development, education, and culture; and third, "defense accords." These props were tied integrally into the overall structure known generically as *la coopération* (a term in the international development lex-icon popularized by the French), devised by the Gaullists in 1960 and 1961. While de Gaulle established a ministry of cooperation to handle the devel-opmental side of this Africa-centered foreign policy, the system also gave the ministry of defense a defined but constrained role in conducting secu-rity operations and providing tactical support, when needed, in the former African colonial federations. The central policy actor, however, was the Elysée, since Africa fell into de Gaulle's famous constitutional *domaine réservée*. The key architect of de Gaulle's Africa policy was the new "sec-retary-general for African and Malagasy affairs," Jacques Foccart, whose famous network outside the official security organizations—*le réseau Foc-cart*—provided essential support for running francophone Africa as a chain of enclaves of enduring French influence.[5]

With these instruments, France was able to maintain, alone among the major foreign powers, a remarkable string of military bases, with airports and naval installations from Djibouti in the east to Dakar in the west, and from Libreville in the south to Fort Lamy (later Ndjaména) in the north. At their zenith, these bases housed more than 12,000 troops. These military forces were parlayed by the French into justifying their role as a middle-ranking major world power with a seat on the UN Security Council. France took great comfort from knowing that it could, if it wished, contribute to operations with its allies. This tended to figure into NATO's strategic think-ing whenever planners in Brussels or Washington factored Africa into their Cold War calculations. Between 1960 and 1995, however, what should be described as the neocolonial interventions of France had little to do with protecting Africa from the foreign menace of the Soviet Union. Almost all of these interventions related to internal affairs of the states in question. If one were to count all the minor unpublicized engagements of French troops in Africa, especially in the 1960s, it would run into dozens, if not more than a hundred. Some were simply backups for fledgling armies. Others were part of ongoing efforts to crush domestic rebellions.

The French intervention in Gabon in 1964 was the first major indica-tion that France was willing to invoke its defense accords and use serious force to make or unmake African governments. There were many others, some of them lower profile, on a continuous basis, as in Mauritania and Cameroon in the 1960s, and some of them of a higher profile, like Sene-gal. French troops were known to have propped up President Léopold Senghor's regime there on at least three occasions between 1960 and 1968.[6]

Again, precisely because the French were so prone to intervene mili-tarily in Africa, it was conspicuous when they failed to do so. This was most blatant when the French did nothing to prevent the assassination of

Sylvanus Olympio in Togo in 1963 despite reportedly having some prior intelligence. Also, de Gaulle conspicuously ignored the appeals of Abbé Fulbert Youlou for French military support during the Trois Glorieuses (Three Glorious Days) in Congo-Brazzaville in 1963—the intervention in Gabon six months later was perhaps an effort by France to prove to its other allies that the defense agreements still had muscle. There were other occasions where the French allowed certain puppets to fall from power because they were no longer worth saving: a classic example was Maurice Yameogo in Upper Volta (now Burkina Faso) in 1966.

Then there were countries like the coup-prone Dahomey (now Benin), where even the French recognized the futility of military intervention. Likewise, in the Central African Republic (CAR), the French did not even try to prevent the 1966 coup by Colonel Jean-Bédel Bokassa. They later lived to regret this decision, and flew David Dacko in the back of one of their military aircrafts when they overthrew the self-declared Emperor Bokassa I from his throne in 1979. This latter event proved to be France's most conspicuous neocolonial unmaking of a government in the whole postindependence era. Although most observers approved of Bokassa's removal, "Operation Barracuda" was still a major public exposure of the bankruptcy of French security policy in Africa, and the whole experience helped to sow the seeds of a change in French policy.[7] There were other cases where the French, through their own inaction, may have discreetly encouraged the military to take power. This may have happened in Niger when they allowed the army to oust Hamani Diori after he crossed French uranium interests in 1974.[8] It was almost certainly the case with the coup in 1975 against François Tombalbaye in Chad.

The Chad Case

Chad was in fact the most dramatic case history of France's security role in Africa, experiencing more interventions in the postcolonial period than any other African country. France's military relations with Chad go back to the battle of Kousseri in 1900, in which the local religious leader, Rabeh, was defeated and the last vast area of the southern Sahara opened up to French military conquest. When the French resistance army mounted its reconquest of the country from the African southern flank in 1943, France's military presence in Chad became even more entrenched. The northern préfectures of Borkou, Ennedi, and Tibesti, constituting one-third of the territory of Chad, were under military administration for the whole colonial period up to 1960. But after the war, Chad remained (along with the CAR) the poorest and most neglected of France's African territories.[9] Faced with an antitax revolt in central Chad in 1965 and a serious uprising of the Toubou in the Tibesti plateau in 1968, Jacques Foccart convinced de Gaulle to order a massive military intervention in Chad only a month before he resigned from the presidency in 1969. Because of the close interconnected nature of France's former West African colonies, and the wave of military coups just preceding this decision, "it was a major test of France's guarantee to African states close to her."[10]

After the arrival of Georges Pompidou in the Elysée palace in 1969, military intervention in Chad was briefly palliated by an ambitious administrative reform program in 1972. Pompidou took a very different view of France's role than his predecessor. Unlike de Gaulle, he was a civilian, less grand and more pragmatic in nature. Pompidou was particularly disturbed by the idea that any French lives should be lost in this desolate former African colony. "*Mort pour le Tchad*" became an ironic expression during the Pompidou years.[11] As time went on, however, the reform program was abandoned. Wherever the French military remained, it was claimed they were not there to protect the military regime, but only to guarantee the "security" of the country.

When Valéry Giscard d'Estaing was elected president in 1974, there were some grounds for believing that a change of policy would ensue. Giscard, a former finance inspector who had neither sprung from the Gaullist circles nor displayed much interest in African affairs until then, was aware of all the criticisms being made of Jacques Foccart's clandestine network in Africa. He smartly removed Foccart from the African *cellule* in the Elysée, but replaced him with another discreet security operative, René Journiac, who happened to have served as Foccart's deputy. Soon, Giscard found that the clothing of Gaullist Africa policy was rather comfortable. Chad was one of his first testing grounds. The coup against François Tombalbaye in 1975 was one byproduct, followed erratically by the request to withdraw French troops. Military "cooperation" assistance remained. The popular impact of the kidnapping of French archaeologist Françoise Claustre[12] heightened awareness of Chad's problems, and Giscard ordered air strikes against the Tibesti rebels in 1977 in a bid to prevent the collapse of the new military government under Félix Malloum.

By 1978, Giscard's France was being called the "*gendarme d'Afrique*" because of Chad and other interventions, notably in Shaba (in the former Zaire). But Giscard could not prevent the descent of Chad into a state of civil conflict. The supreme irony of his presidency was that despite all his posturing, Giscard was unable to do anything about Libyan moves into Chad in 1980 as part of a spurious union with Goukouni Weddeye and the transitional government. In the wake of the disastrous flirtation with his hunting companion, Jean-Bédel Bokassa of the Central African Republic, Giscard became disillusioned with Africa in his last eighteen months in office. He thus left François Mitterrand to pick up the policy pieces after the socialists came to power in 1981.

The next phase of the protracted war in Chad saw Hissen Habré installed to power in 1982, with U.S. backing, in a bid to thwart Libyan influence in the country. Three Nigerian-led peacekeeping missions failed to stem the conflict between 1979 and 1982, and the peacekeepers were forced to withdraw without achieving their goals.[13] Mitterrand was initially a bit squeamish about Habré, who had a reputation for ruthlessness. When it seemed, however, that the Libyan-backed forces might take over the capital city of Ndjaména, U.S. president Ronald Reagan sent his emissary, General Vernon Walters, to see Mitterrand to persuade him to send French troops to the country. Reagan's advisers believed that French troops would be better suited than U.S. soldiers for fighting in Chad. This was an ironic illustration of the United States forcing the French to live up to what they had always declared to be their special responsibilities in Africa.

The subsequent dispatch of 3,000 French troops to Chad under the code name of "Operation Manta" in 1983 was, at the time, France's biggest postcolonial intervention in Africa. The operation was partly motivated by France's fears of losing its sphere of influence in Chad (as much to the United States as to Libya) and partly out of Mitterrand's desire to demonstrate his ability to take decisive action on African issues in the manner of his predecessors. After saving Habré's regime, Mitterrand tried to disengage from Chad, but was unable to do so after legislative elections brought Jacques Chirac to power as prime minister during the first *cohabitation* government from 1986 to 1988. Chirac implemented "Operation Sparrowhawk" (Epervier), which remains in place today. In 1990, Habré was overthrown by a former army chief, Idriss Déby, with close links to the French military, as well as to the Sudanese and the Libyans. Ironically, when French soldiers in Abéché conspicuously failed to block the path of invading troops from Sudan in the east, Habré's fate was sealed. The Cold War was over, and Habré was the first victim of the new "wind of change" blowing through Africa.

Gallic Hyperactivity, British Passivity

By the beginning of the 1960s, there was a fundamental difference between British and French policies in Africa. While the French were doing their best to remain in a disguised neocolonial state, the British only very reluctantly recognized that they had to respond to the appeals coming from the governments of the newly independent states in East Africa (Tanzania, Uganda, and Kenya) and were faced with mutinies in the wake of the Zanzibar revolution of 1964. Ironically, de Gaulle used the preemptive moves by the British as a precedent for the much larger and more controversial intervention in resource-rich Gabon in 1964. A successful military coup had overthrown Leon M'Ba, a puppet of French timber interests and member of the "*réseau Foccart*," and replaced him with opposition leader Jean-Hilaire Aubame, suspected of having pro-U.S. sympathies.[14]

Gabon marked the first important postindependence manifestation of the "other Cold War" in Africa: the Franco-American rivalry. Largely subterranean, this competition occasionally surfaced without warning to complicate the otherwise complicit Africa policy of the two Western powers. In the case of Gabon, the struggle was over major oil reserves that the French had discovered in the late 1950s and to which U.S. oil companies were denied access.[15] The tiny equatorial enclave of Gabon witnessed a blast of paranoid fury against *les Anglo-Saxons* trying to take over French interests, an example of what Roland Marchal has dubbed "the Fashoda syndrome."[16] What was unusual about this paranoia was the way in which French strategists confused and conflated not only the Americans and the British, but worse, the anglophone Africans—often included in sweeping statements about Anglo-Saxons. These reactions were emotionally rooted in France's wartime experience, especially in the bitterness of Gaullist humiliations at the hands of the British and the Americans. The United States had on several occasions, to the great irritation of the French, provided food aid to the left-leaning regime of Guinea's Sékou Touré, whom the French had done their best to destabilize, notably in supporting the failed Portuguese-inspired mercenary landings in Conakry in 1970.[17]

These feelings came up again during the Nigerian civil war of 1967–1970 when the French supported Biafra, although not to the point of recognition, while the two most influential French client states, Côte d'Ivoire and Gabon, did go as far as to recognize the secessionist republic and provide French arms to the Biafran regime.[18] Despite the wrapping of its motives in humanitarian terms, the French position was also an effort to undermine a country that represented a rival pole of attraction in its West African sphere of influence (see Chapter 13). Nigeria was for the Gaullists a privileged domain of their British rivals. But for Ivorian leader Félix Houphouët-Boigny, the idea of a federation represented a route that he had rejected when he participated in the balkanization of the two French colonial federations in West and Equatorial Africa. All these perceptions seriously misunderstood Nigeria's priorities, especially as articulated during its civil war.

The British reaction to the international context of the Nigerian civil war was in fact in keeping with their general inclination to maintain a low profile, even when forced to center stage. For if the Lyndon Johnson and Richard Nixon administrations in Washington were content to leave the British to take the lead, the government of Harold Wilson in London was still hesitant in the role. The British limited their support to arms, and grudgingly supplied even that. Wilson was beset with Rhodesia's Unilateral Declaration of Independence in 1965, where military intervention had been conspicuously ruled out. As the Nigerian civil war ground on, Downing

Street (the prime minister's residence) became increasingly vulnerable to pressures from the media and public opinion that was stirred up in support of the Biafran cause. This meant that British support for Nigeria was kept to the minimum necessary in order not to destroy a postwar relationship with Lagos. Nixon was subjected to the same pressures during the 1968 U.S. election campaign, but maintained a low-key neutral line once in office. This also meant in the end that many Nigerian federalists felt, perhaps unjustly, that Britain had been no ally at all. British passivity during this crisis was in fact a reflection of the indifference that successive British governments felt toward any overseas commitment of armed forces in postcolonial Africa.[19]

The 1960s were the years of Britain's great disengagement "east of Suez" that pervaded all aspects of foreign policy. African soldiers continued to train at Sandhurst military academy, and there was always going to be a lucrative trade in arms and equipment, but the notion of "intervention"—especially in West Africa—was far from anyone's mind. This rule of thumb was maintained for several decades. There may well be some evidence that implicates the U.S. Central Intelligence Agency (CIA), as well as the British and French secret services, in at least encouraging the overthrow of Kwame Nkrumah in Ghana in 1966, but such evidence has remained vague and inferred rather than provable.[20] If the French, rather than the British, had been the former colonial rulers of Nigeria, how much more significant would their role have been in West Africa?

The succession of coups and attempted coups in anglophone Nigeria, Ghana (subsequent to 1966), Sierra Leone (1967), and Gambia (1981) were mostly homegrown affairs. The nearest that Britain ever came to real "intervention" in its former West African colonies was the use of the Special Air Services to rescue Lady Chilel Jawara from the Libyan-backed rebels of Kukoi Samba Sanyang in Gambia in 1981. But it was Senegalese troops—supported logistically by the French—who effectively restored Sir Dawda Jawara as president. Such an exercise would have been outside the scope of British policy at the time. It was only during the Falklands war with Argentina in 1982 that the value of the deep-water ports of Banjul and Freetown, and indeed, of Dakar airport, was brought home to London. British defense strategists started to look more closely at West Africa, and glanced enviously at the French, who seemed able, at that time, to organize military strategy so much better. Dakar has also recently been an essential staging post for British troops after the May 2000 intervention in Sierra Leone (discussed below).

U.S. Proxy Wars

U.S. policy in Africa during the Cold War was largely centered on central and southern Africa, though Washington also had a special historical relationship with Liberia. The Congo crisis of 1960–1965 was the defining event of U.S. military policy toward Africa during this period. By the summer of 1960, the Eisenhower administration had concluded that Congolese premier Patrice Lumumba was an "African Castro," a Soviet client, and thus an enemy of the most dangerous type. The recruitment of Joseph Mobutu by the CIA followed by Lumumba's assassination in 1961 led to increased U.S. support for the UN peacekeeping force in the Congo, which eventually crushed the Katanga rebellion in 1963.[21]

U.S. support for Congolese unity eased to some extent the African hostility to U.S. policy that had been generated by Lumumba's murder. With the defeat of Lumumba's followers and the reintegration of secessionist Katanga, the Congo settled into corrupt, oppressive, pro-U.S. quasi-stability that rested on two pillars: first, UN troops, numbering about 20,000 (withdrawn in 1964); and second, the Congolese army under Colonel Mobutu. To suppress a subsequent rebellion, however, the United States backed a third element: mercenaries, mainly from South Africa and Rhodesia, using the precedent of French and Belgian mercenaries, who had been the main prop of Moise Tshombe's secession effort in Katanga. U.S. officials justified the use of mercenaries by arguing that the rebels were receiving "outside" military assistance. But the rebels obtained only small amounts of military aid from African countries, the Soviet Union, and China. Only Cuba sent troops— under the legendary Che Guevara, who arrived in 1965 and left after only seven months.

After the Congo crisis, the main drift of U.S. policy in Africa (especially as the war in Vietnam took its toll) was that Africa was an area better left to its former European colonial powers. At any rate, Africa was a realm of pure realpolitik, not a traditional Cold War theater. In the early 1970s, when U.S. secretary of state Henry Kissinger shaped a global foreign policy, new fears about Soviet expansionism developed in southern Africa. The policy was based on the dubious premise that South Africa and Portugal were the most effective bastions against communist expansion in Africa. It compounded a basic error of U.S. policy in Africa—supporting Pretoria's ingenuous and misleading claim that African nationalism could be equated with communism—with a myopic support of Portuguese colonialism.

After the collapse of Portuguese fascism in 1974 resulted in the coming to power the following year of the Movimento Popular de Libertação de Angola (MPLA), a Marxist movement, Washington supported rebel forces of the União Nacional para a Independência Total de Angola (UNITA) under Jonas Savimbi and even mercenary forces of the Frente Nacional de Libertação de Angola (FNLA) under Holden Roberto. This was done through supply lines in Zaire (now the Democratic Republic of Congo), and through South African troops. The French and Belgians, with U.S. logistical support, stepped in to assist Mobutu during the two Shaba crises in

1977 and 1978 when the Front National de la Libération du Congo (FNLC) crossed the border from Angola.[22]

For a brief but frenetic ten days in May 1978, all kinds of outlandish thoughts were discussed at a NATO meeting about "recolonizing" Africa. Cold War paranoia was reinforced by purported threats to strategic raw materials. These fears eventually gave way to common sense, and French and Belgian troops in Shaba were soon replaced by African troops from Morocco and Senegal. After these episodes, U.S. military interventions in Africa lacked a central base of action. The United States continued to intervene militarily through proxy wars against Soviet rivals in Angola and Mozambique, as well as Ethiopia and Somalia. Washington tended to play a tactical support role for interventions by France and South Africa throughout the remainder of the Cold War period. Still, U.S. provision of arms and other support to Savimbi during Ronald Reagan's presidency, from 1980 to 1988, was arguably the most significant element in keeping Angola's civil war going, in spite of the direct commitment of South African troops at certain periods.

In West Africa, policy toward Liberia had always been something of an anomaly, given the longevity of U.S. interests in the country. "Liberia is the only country in Africa," wrote Gus Liebenow, "which has enjoyed a sustained relationship with the United States over a period of more than 160 years."[23] Founded by freed black American slaves in 1847, Liberia remained under the yoke of a corrupt, nepotistic Americo-Liberian oligarchy through most of the twentieth century. The country's constitution, currency, and flag were modeled on those of the United States. Monrovia, the capital, took its name from James Monroe. The United States was Liberia's main trading partner. Black American officers headed the Liberian Frontier Force. U.S. industrial giant Firestone established the world's largest rubber plantation in the country. During the Cold War, Liberian presidents William Tubman and William Tolbert remained staunch U.S. allies. Liberia hosted 3,000 American expatriates. Firestone, Goodrich, Uniroyal, Bethlehem Steel, Chase Manhattan, and Citibank all had a presence in Liberia. U.S. private investments in the country were worth around $350 million. By 1980, when Master-Sergeant Samuel Doe staged his successful coup, over 52 percent of government revenue in Liberia came from just two U.S. firms.

At first, the United States cut aid and direct foreign investment in response to Doe's assassination of members of the ancien régime. But when the Soviet Union, Cuba, and Libya warmly greeted the new regime, strategic calculations led Washington to send its assistant secretary of state for African affairs, Richard Moose, to Monrovia for high-level talks with Doe. After this visit, Moose recommended increased economic and military aid. Eliminating radical elements in his cabinet, Doe shut down the Libyan embassy in 1981. He established relations with Israel, and became a strident defender of U.S. policies at the UN. Ronald Reagan invited Doe for an official state visit to Washington in 1982 (referring to him as "Chairman Moe"). One year later, Reagan described him (more accurately) as "a dependable ally—a friend in need."[24] In 1985, Doe closed down the Soviet embassy in Monrovia. He authorized the United States to use Liberia as a staging ground for its rapid deployment force, and a transit point for arms to UNITA rebels in Angola. Doe became a key ally in U.S. efforts to thwart Libya's regional ambitions. In return the CIA granted Doe special security protection, and the Reagan administration stepped up aid to Liberia, finally totaling over $500 million in the 1980s, including an annual $14 million in military assistance. While the United States had no colonies in Africa, Liberia was a special case in the region, and Doe was arguably "Uncle Sam's Frankenstein."[25]

Current Military Strategies, 1990–2003

"Françafrique"

The major shift in France's Africa policy in recent times has been the de-emphasis of military influence to the advantage of economic neocolonialism, all under the guise of an official policy of "democratization."[26] It is generally accepted that the rhetorical emphasis on "democratization" started at the Francophone African summit in La Baule in 1990, when, before an assembly of loyal African "dinosaurs" like Omar Bongo of Gabon and Félix Houphouët-Boigny of Côte d'Ivoire, François Mitterrand, aware of the way the democratic wind was blowing, announced that his country's generous *coopération* assistance would mainly be given to those who, like former autocrat Matthieu Kérékou—after the national conference in Benin in 1989—were engaging in political reforms, notably in the direction of democracy.

Mitterrand's speech must be interpreted in the light of the fall of the Berlin Wall in 1989 and the end of the Cold War. Propping up tyrants and dictators had certainly become more controversial since La Baule. But security crises in the Gulf of Guinea have equally made it increasingly difficult to protect French nationals working in its oil and mineral enclaves. While preserving the loyal autocrat Omar Bongo in power against serious democratic opposition, the French military intervention in Gabon in 1991 also illustrated the problem of implementing the idealist rhetoric of La Baule.[27] For, behind the invoking of the defense cooperation accords, and thus the old political relationship between France and francophone Africa, this intervention was at heart a cynical economic move to evacuate Elf-Gabon personnel and to protect French oil investments at Port Gentil. As

Omar Bongo put it a few years later, "Africa without France is like a car without a driver. France without Africa is like a car without fuel."[28]

In the post–Cold War era, economic imperialism replaced military imperialism and proxy wars. France was willing to spill French blood in the protection of tangible national interests. Resources could be used to justify intervention in Françafrique. But the real challenge to the spirit of La Baule presented itself not in resource-rich Gabon, but in dirt-poor Togo in 1991. French policymakers had to decide whether to use troops to protect a nascent francophone African democracy movement in Lomé against the old autocratic dinosaur, Gnassingbé Eyadéma. Would France invoke its defense treaties to oust one of the very men who had provided so much "stability"? In too many interventions, the French had supported men who had either acquired power through the *réseau Foccart* or who had come to power through a military coup and were out of touch with the new democratic era. Eyadéma, assassin of Olympio and a dyed-in-the-wool dictator, was humiliated by the national conference in 1991, and appeared to be on his way out like Hissen Habré in Chad and Moussa Traoré in Mali. As Eyadéma prepared to use force to recover his personal rule in Togo, the French actually sent troops to neighboring Benin in a vain attempt to warn him off. But faced with real threats from Eyadéma as to what might happen if any French troops landed in Lomé, the French blinked first. The Lomé office of prodemocracy prime minister Joseph Kokou Koffigoh was blasted by rockets, and the Togolese democracy movement went into a retreat from which it has yet to recover.[29] What had happened to the spirit of La Baule?

The era of French prime minister Edouard Balladur, from 1993 to 1995, proved to be a defining moment in Franco-African relations. Balladur, a dry financial technocrat with absolutely no African connections (unusual among the French political class), pushed through two key reforms in his period in power. Although these reforms had been resisted by the "cooperation lobby," Mitterrand, sick with prostate cancer and already entangled in the debacle of Rwanda in 1994, proved unable to block them. The first major concession in September 1993 was that the oversight of the economies of France's former colonies in Africa, which had always been done in Paris, was to be passed to the Washington institutions—the International Monetary Fund (IMF) and the World Bank. This was a bow to the power of superior resources, but was still a great psychological blow to France's "special relationship" with Africa. The main immediate reform resulting from this power shift was the 50 percent devaluation of the CFA franc in January 1994. This had long been urged on both France and the franc-zone members by the two Bretton Woods institutions, but had been resisted as a cutting of the umbilical cord linking Paris with its former colonies. Symbolically, this devaluation occurred a month after the death of Houphouët-Boigny, the main minder of the Françafrique "special relationship." It took a full-fledged liquidity crisis in the franc zone to precipitate it, and was followed by huge transfers from the IMF to the zone to ensure the success of the operation. But Françafrique would never be the same again.

Though outside our principal West African area of focus, the real contradiction in the old way of doing things was seen, above all, in the disastrous personal policy of the Mitterrands' father-and-son presidential team toward the unfolding genocide in Rwanda in 1994. This event would have far-reaching consequences for France's overall Africa policy. Jean-Christophe ("*Papamadit*")[30] Mitterrand had been named by his father to run the African cell in the Elysée, where, despite the very real differences between the socialists and the Gaullists on domestic issues such as nationalization and privatization, Jean-Christophe learned, like his predecessor Journiac, that the Gaullist clothes in Africa were made to be worn.[31] The Elysée actively supported the Hutu regime of Juvénal Habyarimana, which was pro-French and actively opposed to the "anglophone" Tutsi rebels in neighboring Uganda. The Rwandan genocide was partly the result of U.S. and British passivity and French neocolonialism.[32] "Opération Turquoise" in 1994 was France's desperate effort to reclaim some lost honor from this sordid episode. Ostensibly humanitarian, this military operation is widely perceived, even in France, as having provided cover for the flight of Hutu *génocidaires*. France's support of the Hutu regime was the last throw of the policy of supporting friends no matter what, and was bitterly resented as the loss of a chunk of the French sphere of influence to English-speaking Tutsis. "Anglophobia is very much a part of French political culture," Roland Marchal has explained: "It developed among the left-wing parties as a reaction to American hegemony and among the conservative parties because the conservatives gave vital support to the Gaullist case and to national values."[33]

But the reality on the ground was that France had only about 6,500 troops spread at bases throughout the African continent at the century's close, and was becoming increasingly unwilling to use them. The speed with which, when compelled to intervene to protect the spuriously democratic regime in the Central African Republic in 1995 and 1996, the French replaced their presence with a largely West African peacekeeping mission from Burkina Faso, Chad, Gabon, Mali, Senegal, and Togo indicated the frame of mind in Paris, reinforced by the deaths of French soldiers and the burning of the French cultural center in Bangui. This was one intervention too many. Similarly in lusophone Guinea-Bissau, a member of the CFA franc zone since 1997, the French cultural center was destroyed by an angry crowd in May 1999 after the unpopular president, João Vieira, sought shelter there.

Major military reforms were initiated by President Jacques Chirac in 1996 that involved serious economies and foreshadowed more cutbacks in Africa. French troops were reduced from around 8,000 to 6,500, and the military bases in the CAR were closed. More important, there seemed to be no stomach for direct intervention anymore, the real test case being the refusal to intervene to support President Henri Konan Bédié in Côte d'Ivoire in December 1999. Again, this was a country in which France had always said it was ready to intervene, and there was serious pressure from Chirac's advisers to do something, if only to save the credibility of Franco-African defense accords. The reality of the situation, however, was that intervention would have been disastrous, and events overtook the hapless Bédié.[34] They also overtook the credibility of France's security net in Africa.

When the socialists returned to the Matignon (the prime minister's residence) in 1997, reluctance became the hallmark of France's Africa policy. Prime Minister Lionel Jospin was a very different type of socialist than his predecessor, Mitterrand, whose token progressive stance in 1981 and 1982 had regressed into a kind of "neo-Gaullism." With so many bonds having been broken, and with so many guardians of the special relationship (Houphouët-Boigny, Mobutu, Mitterrand, Foccart) having passed on, there was clearly an opening for a policy change. In one of the most far-reaching policy statements on its post–Cold War Africa policy, Hubert Védrine, France's former foreign minister, explained:

> The policy that I am following with [Cooperation Minister] Charles Josselin consists of adapting to the evolving realities and mentalities while maintaining a strong engagement—in contrast to most other western countries. For most western countries, it is not even considered worthwhile to have an Africa policy, except for a humanitarian one. But we just do not think that it is enough to give a little aid and make ritual condemnations of democratic setbacks, and for the rest, tell the Africans to "work it out yourselves!" This kind of distanced posture is not ours. France—Europe—ought to have an Africa policy. In the past, our policy was often formulated in the spirit of rivalry with other western countries present in Africa, notably Britain. Today we are doing everything in our power to overcome such sterile competition, and to take a more concerted approach. Our engagement with the African continent cannot be done alone. With whom can we cooperate? With the Americans for peacekeeping, and in Europe, with the British, the Belgians, and the Portuguese.[35]

"The other major change," continued Védrine, "is that we do not involve ourselves any more in internal crises. Since the arrival of Lionel Jospin at Matignon, we have consistently resisted pressures to intervene."

This does not mean, however, that the new French policy in Africa will automatically lead to a withdrawal of French troops from the region. When asked if France would close down its military bases in Africa, Védrine replied:

You must see our presence there in an evolutionary perspective. I don't know when it will end. The five French bases remain an element of stability. They have been used in the past for old-style interventions. Today, all that is finished. Our bases now serve only as training centers for the armed forces of the host countries or regional peacekeeping forces, and in the event they are needed, for the evacuation of expatriate communities. Leaving will not stabilize the situation! If the Africans have a different point of view, then we'll talk about it. But we should not be obsessed with liquidation.[36]

Perhaps the best example of the new use of French military bases in Africa as training centers is the Renforcement des Capacités Africaines de Maintien de la Paix (RECAMP) concept. Similar to the U.S. African Crisis Response Initiative (ACRI), the RECAMP concept sets out to enable African countries, under the aegis of the UN and the African Union (AU), to participate in peacekeeping operations on the African continent. RECAMP emphasizes preparation of African battalions for peacekeeping operations as part of a regional brigade-level military component. Acting under a joint UN-AU mandate, this brigade is designed to stabilize crises by preventive deployment, and to respond to open crises through the restoration of peace. It is also designed to protect threatened populations and to contribute to humanitarian relief efforts. The military component of RECAMP is supposed to have only a temporary status, in line with the UN "standby forces" concept.[37]

In a remarkable parallel to U.S. missions with ACRI (discussed below), France has used RECAMP to participate in the financing and training of around 1,500 African military officers. Paris also created a peacekeeping training center in Côte d'Ivoire in 1997 and provided equipment for a Senegalese peacekeeping battalion that deployed in Guinea-Bissau in 1998. The first test of the RECAMP concept was the multinational "Exercise Guidimakha" of 1998, involving some 3,500 military personnel from France, Senegal, Mali, Mauritania, Cape Verde, Gambia, Ghana, and Guinea-Bissau, with one infantry platoon and one aircraft each contributed by the United States and Britain, and one aircraft provided by Belgium. France also provided logistical support to largely francophone peacekeepers to deploy in the Central African Republic in 1997 (eventually under the UN) and largely francophone peacekeepers (from Benin, Niger, Togo, and Gambia) to deploy in Guinea-Bissau in 1999 (under the Economic Community of West African States [ECOWAS]).

If one accepts Védrine's evolutionary perspective, then French military bases in Africa will eventually become tactical support and training centers for African armies in the twenty-first century. It remains to be seen, however, how this will work in practice should a real crisis occur. In 2002,

RECAMP participated in military training with the Southern African Development Community (SADC) in Tanzania, proving that military maneuvers are possible across the anglophone/francophone divide. The United States had already seen the strategic advantage of the French military base in Djibouti during the 1991 Gulf War, and today has established a large presence there in its hunt for fleeing Al-Qaida terrorists.

The most recent French intervention in Côte d'Ivoire, in 2002, suggests that good old-fashioned military intervention may never go out of fashion. In January 2003, France, with 2,500 troops (later increased to 4,000) monitoring a tenuous cease-fire in Côte d'Ivoire, convened a meeting of all Ivorian parties in Paris in a bid to find a negotiated settlement to a growing civil war that has seen three rebel groups occupying the northern and western parts of the country. The United States and Britain both lent significant support to French military and diplomatic efforts in Côte d'Ivoire. The declared primary motive of these efforts was to protect French citizens, but the French military presence has once again indirectly helped prop up the fragile central government of the divisive Laurent Gbagbo. There were suggestions of replacing the French buffer force with one from ECOWAS, and Senegal, Ghana, Niger, Togo, and Benin deployed 1,288 troops in early 2003 to support French military efforts in Côte d'Ivoire.

But it remains unclear whether ECOWAS can overcome its logistical and financial problems (see Chapter 13), and whether France is truly prepared to disengage from the jewel in its West African crown. Following the Paris peace accord of January 2003, which called for a transitional government with representation by rebel groups and early elections in Côte d'Ivoire, angry Ivorian demonstrators attacked the French embassy and French-owned businesses in Abidjan, and many French citizens were evacuated. The demonstrators carried anti-French and pro-American placards and called for U.S. intervention in the crisis. While such an intervention is practically impossible, these actions could yet reignite paranoid concerns about Washington within policymaking circles in Paris. They have also required an explicit pronouncement by the new Gaullist government of its vision of French foreign policy in its traditional sphere of influence.

In an open speech that he delivered in June 2003 at the Institut des Hautes Études de Défense Nationale (IHEDN) in Paris, then–French foreign minister Dominique de Villepin invoked what he called the "three clear principles" that guide France's Africa policy. The first is to support "legitimate" powers. Villepin made it clear that, for him, *la légitimité* is more than being elected. "Legitimacy is also measured by the conditions of the exercise of power." The voting urns, he made precise, "confer a mandate, not immunity." The second principle is "the respect for national sovereignty and territorial integrity." In Villepin's eyes, the sanctity of existing borders remains "an absolute imperative." Finally, the third principle that

Villepin privileged is "systematic support for African peace talks" *(média-tions)*. He emphasized that if France is to intervene militarily, it is not "to impose an external solution," but "to support efforts" being made in a parallel fashion on the African continent. Legitimacy, territorial integrity, and military intervention: *Plus ça change, plus c'est la même chose?* ("The more things change, the more they stay the same?")

The British Intervention in Sierra Leone

The protection of democratically elected governments is still very much a security issue in the post–Cold War era. The British and French converged on the issue of democratization (along with the European Union [EU] and the World Bank). A month after Mitterrand's famous democracy speech in La Baule, British foreign secretary Douglas Hurd made the same point in a speech to the House of Commons on 9 June 1990, about democracy being a prerequisite of development. Britain also took the issue to the Commonwealth, where the Harare declaration at the Commonwealth Heads of Government meeting in the Zimbabwean capital in 1991 specifically made democracy and human rights Commonwealth principles. The Millbrook Declaration at the 1995 Commonwealth Heads of Government meeting in New Zealand reinforced the principles, and tied them to action following Nigeria's suspension from the organization in the wake of the execution of Ken Saro-Wiwa and eight of his fellow Ogoni activists by the military government of General Sani Abacha.

There were no security implications as such, but it was evidence of the raising of Britain's profile in Africa at this time. The practicing of democratic values was something African countries themselves were increasingly concerned with, and was arguably one of the main influences behind the British intervention in Sierra Leone in 2000. What has been insufficiently remarked upon has been the unusual, indeed unexpected, way in which, as the French were disengaging, the British were beginning to raise their profile in Africa after decades of disinterested passivity. It began to look as if both countries were trading places—that the British were becoming more interventionist as the French were becoming finally less so. It was the more unusual, although not so surprising, that it should have been a Labour government doing it, and that London was to find high-minded policy reasons for the intervention.[38]

There are many curious aspects to the British intervention in Sierra Leone. Critics dismissed Tony Blair's "ethical foreign policy" and put the motivation down to "diamond politics," but for Blair and his former foreign secretary Robin Cook in the Foreign and Commonwealth Office, the intervention had an ethical component (much as some imperial interventions benefited from the moral fervor of both antislavery and antiheathenism).

There is a touch of Victorian muscular Christianity about Blair. His only personal connection with Sierra Leone was through his father, who worked there for a time, but a strong personal connection it was, on his own admission. In acknowledgment of their moral left-wing constituency, Labour governments in Britain have always been prone to increase development aid, although this has traditionally been well behind the French figure in terms of percentage of gross national product, and has also always been lower in percentage terms in Africa. But Labour governments had never before been involved in military interventions in Africa.

The presence of Clare Short, identified closely with left-wing "Old Labour" principles, as head of a separate ministry—the Department for International Development—with a seat in the cabinet, was seen as an indication of the way in which Britain's Africa policy might be shaped. Before her controversial resignation in 2003 over Iraq policy, Short was one of the champions of the Sierra Leone intervention; indeed she was probably the most influential voice in the British cabinet in taking the decision to go in. Short shared the desire of her prime minister—who has made it a theme of his second term in office, having declared Africa a "scar on the world's conscience"—to prioritize assistance to the continent. This was most clearly evidenced by Blair's historic visit to Nigeria, Ghana, Sierra Leone, and Senegal in February 2002 and his energetic support for the New Partnership for Africa's Development (NEPAD), a development plan championed most vociferously by the leaders of South Africa, Nigeria, Senegal, and Algeria (see Chapter 6). The transition to democracy in South Africa in 1994 also meant that, for the first time in five decades, morality coincided with Britain's powerful financial and investment interests there. The importance of the antiapartheid struggle in Labour Party mythology went pleasantly hand in hand with the business realpolitik of "New Labour." The return of Nigeria to the democratic fold in 1999, ending the pariah status of the General Sani Abacha years (1993–1998), also reinforced the moving of Africa up the scale of British priorities, although it probably remains true that South Africa under President Thabo Mbeki remains Blair's most-favored African partner.

Sierra Leone, however, has been the real catalyst of the change in British policy toward Africa. It was a terrible coincidence that Major Johnny Paul Koromah's coup in May 1997 occurred in the same month that Tony Blair came to power in Britain. The appallingly violent nature of the Revolutionary United Front/Armed Forces Ruling Council (RUF/AFRC) regime, with its thuggery, looting, and on the part of the RUF, its record of maiming and mutilation, made decisionmaking easier in some respects. For this was one of the few examples of a regime being so disgusting that no member of the international community wanted to recognize it, and the British led the way in isolating it in international fora. Blair indeed made a point of inviting Sierra Leone's deposed president, Ahmed Tejan Kabbah, to the Commonwealth Heads of Government meeting in Edinburgh in 1997 to head the delegation from Sierra Leone, even though Kabbah was only the "president of Lungi airport." Nevertheless, it was still ultimately the politics of gesture, and something practical had to be done on the ground to back up British words.

There is some temptation to surmise that the strongest reason for the British making Sierra Leone such a high national priority was that it became an issue in domestic politics at Westminster after the "Sandline affair" in 1998. The whole experience of the involvement of the private security firm Sandline (which in the old days would have been simply called a group of "mercenaries") blew up as one of those Westminster issues with which both the media and the opposition, and even government backbenchers, run. When the full details of the covert presence of Sandline in Sierra Leone emerged, it appeared that attempts had been made to cover up the incidental role it had played in the Nigerian-led countercoup that restored Kabbah to power in March 1998.[39]

There was considerable political fallout, and Sandline became known as one of the major missteps of Robin Cook's four years as British foreign secretary.[40] The affair became even more embarrassing when it was revealed that the British high commissioner in Freetown, Peter Penfold, by taking his role too seriously, may have become proactively involved with Sandline. But in what Tony Blair dismissed as the "hoo-ha," there were glimpses of the prime minister's personal interests. And there seems little doubt that the attention Sierra Leone received, the most coverage the normally ignored country has received in its forty years of existence, at Westminster and in what is still misleadingly called "Fleet Street," created the political crucible that helped forge subsequent British policy. The British intervention in Sierra Leone in May 2000, when about 800 troops flew in and secured the airport and then much of western Freetown, was dramatic in its completeness. This was dictated by the official need to rescue British nationals as well as the tottering United Nations Mission in Sierra Leone (UNAMSIL) (see Chapter 14). And there was an unofficial need to save the Kabbah government from falling once more at the hands of the RUF. Although this intervention was greeted at the time with considerable publicity, and not a little skeptical criticism (especially from those who detected "mission creep"), the fact that British troops were present in West Africa for over two years elicited barely a whisper from either the mass media or the politicians back in London. Even the announcement in August 2000 of their partial withdrawal aroused little interest.

Sierra Leone became a curiously forgotten affair, yet it has probably been the most significant British intervention in Africa in recent years, and certainly of its kind. London's relations with the reenergized UN mission (which the British intervention force had refused to be part of, although cooperating closely with it) remained deliberately ambiguous, springing from an aversion to divided command. There were nonetheless many serious challenges, especially arising from the training of a new army, in a situation in which British and other trainers were forced to use many of the unreliable soldiers from the old army, as well as other forces and militias. The slow recovery of territorial control was not an easy exercise, and it was not surprising that elections had to be delayed until May 2002. These difficulties were partly compensated for by the smooth conduct of the presidential and legislative elections in which Tejan Kabbah was returned to a second term in a landslide victory.

Even at the beginning of the British intervention in 2000, there were powerful justifications, notably preventing the RUF from seizing power, and the shoring up of a collapsing UN operation, but four years later, there is much more to be said. At the time of writing, the "stability graft" seems to have worked miraculously. British troops have been substantially withdrawn after the successful completion of elections in May 2002, leaving only a group of advisers. The British seem, so far, to have clocked up a remarkable success in Sierra Leone, which may well serve as a benchmark for new-style interventions in Africa. There is no doubt that the French have taken due note of the British precedence, as evidenced by their confident action after the September 2002 outbreak of rebellion in Côte d'Ivoire. French decisiveness, however, may simply reflect the new assertiveness that followed Chirac's victory in both presidential and parliamentary elections in 2002.

One key statement of this period was the observation in 2000 of former French foreign minister Hubert Védrine that "it is paradoxical to see that while we are working to disengage our Africa policy from what was contestable about it in the past, the British have allowed themselves to run an operation in Sierra Leone comparable to what France used to do from De Gaulle to Mitterrand. And everybody is applauding them for it! But the British know that they will not be able to resolve the problems of Sierra Leone and its neighbors through a military operation of this kind."[41] Events in both Sierra Leone and Côte d'Ivoire may already have overtaken this comment. Notwithstanding such a warning by the Quai d'Orsay (the French foreign ministry), the cooperative reaction of the Elysée to the deployment of British troops in West Africa has been interesting, leading one to wonder if there is not a measure of welcome for the newfound British security interest in the region. Some skeptics, however, have not seen the role of the European powers in such a positive light, noting that Sierra Leone was a traditional British sphere of influence, just as Côte d'Ivoire remains one for the French. For them, these interventions represent a new form of neocolonialism.

Even before the British intervention in Sierra Leone, there was a clear desire progressively to increase coordination of the Africa policies of Britain and France. The first joint statement on Africa was made by British premier John Major and French president Jacques Chirac in 1995. But the two most important recent statements on Africa policy have been St.-Malo in 1998 and its follow-up at Cahors in 2001. St.-Malo was the critical one, as it came in the context of real efforts by London and Paris to coordinate defense policy within the context of the EU, followed by the famous Cook-Védrine visit to Accra and Abidjan in 1999: more *entente cordiale* than Fashoda. This was followed by a (Jack) Straw-Védrine visit in 2002 to the Great Lakes, an area where there was much greater Franco-British sensitivity. The culmination of all this cooperation is, of course, the joint EU intervention force in Bunia, eastern DRC, where French paratroopers landed on 10 June 2003, to be joined by British peacekeeping forces in what is heralded as Europe's first excursion of this kind outside the framework of NATO.

Anyone curious at the reasons for such newfound Anglo-Gallic amity needs to remember that the British and the French have been cooperating in the context of Brussels (site of the EU secretariat) for the past thirty years. In the early years of the Lomé Convention of 1975, this bilateral relationship was not without serious friction, but over the years, the tensions have become overlaid with the practicalities of forging a development policy among fifteen member states (it will become even harder after ten central European members join the EU in 2004). The European Union's increased political cooperation and foreign policy coordination after the treaties of Maastricht in 1992 and Amsterdam in 1997 have provided a permanent forum for contact and negotiation, and have provided any number of international alibis when bilateral relations have become difficult. These will continue on a more political plane with the implementation of the Cotonou Accord—the successor to the Lomé Convention—in 2000, with their reinforced democracy and human rights clauses.

This change has been notably evident in the proactive EU reaction to the crisis in Zimbabwe in 2001 and 2002, where the British have found a much more strident response to abuses of democracy and human rights than the Commonwealth, in spite of the principled utterances of the Harare Declaration of 1991 and the Commonwealth's Ministerial Action Group. This is likely to be the model for political interventionism in the future.

America's Post-Somalia "Exit Strategy"

"Regionalization" of African peacekeeping is an important cornerstone of current U.S. security strategy on the continent. In the beginning of the

1990s, after the success of the United Nations Technical Assistance Group (UNTAG) peacekeeping force in Namibia in 1989 and 1990, the unchallenged military might of the United States seemed to justify a new pattern of involvement in peacekeeping operations. But U.S. president George Bush Sr.'s decision to launch "Operation Restore Hope" in Somalia in December 1992 only proved Washington's inexperience in direct African military interventions. The second United Nations Operation in Somalia (UNOSOM II) failed when U.S. forces were drawn into clan warfare with a Somali warlord, Mohammed Farah Aideed, for which they were ill prepared, and which reached its climax when eighteen U.S. soldiers were killed and eighty-four were wounded in October 1993.[42] Although an estimated 1,000 Somalis, including women and children, died during the October incident in Mogadishu, Hollywood chose only to mythologize the American deaths in the heavily ideological film *Blackhawk Down*.[43]

The principal U.S. intervention in Africa since the end of the Cold War, "Operation Restore Hope," was a disaster. Under domestic pressure and congressional criticism, President Bill Clinton withdrew U.S. troops and stringently restricted the use of U.S. troops in future UN operations. Even after the peaceful transition to democracy in South Africa in 1994 appeared to justify increased U.S. investments in Africa, the Clinton administration stood back and watched the Rwandan genocide occur in tandem with Nelson Mandela's election in April 1994, while declaring that it was not prepared to spill American blood in Rwanda.

Following the debacle in Somalia, Clinton ordered the far-reaching presidential review of peacekeeping policy PDD-25, which outlined three main principles: first, the objectives of an operation must be clearly defined in the national interest of the United States and ensured continuing public and congressional support; second, the commitment of U.S. troops cannot be "open-ended" and consequently an "exit strategy" must be in place before troops are deployed; and third, operations involving U.S. forces must have "acceptable" command and control arrangements.[44] PDD-25 effectively ended any hopes of future major U.S. peacekeeping missions in Africa. After Somalia, Washington called for "African solutions to African problems," meaning that the United States would spend some of the money for African soldiers to shed all of the blood in African wars. Eboe Hutchful has demonstrated that the division of labor between U.S. support and African soldiers has resulted in a "growing tendency to backyard peacekeeping" that raises a new set of issues and questions, different from those that have traditionally driven peacekeeping research. Is such "lean peacekeeping" sustainable?[45]

In 1996, U.S. secretary of state Warren Christopher proposed the creation of the African Crisis Response Initiative, under which the United States would work with Western allies and African nations to enhance

African peacekeeping and humanitarian relief capacity.[46] Through the ACRI program, Washington has offered training and equipment to African countries that are ostensibly committed to democratization and civilian rule. The United States conducted initial training with battalions from Senegal, Uganda, Malawi (1997), Mali, Ghana (1998), and Benin (1999). So far, ACRI has helped train around 8,000 African troops in peacekeeping activities that include convoy escorts, logistics, negotiation techniques, command and control, and protection of refugees. After the election of George W. Bush in 2000, ACRI was under review. A Democratic initiative had to face the test of an alteration of power. According to then–deputy assistant secretary of state for African affairs, William Bellamy, the Bush administration "remains committed to continuing the kind of political-military engagement with African militaries that ACRI has established," but "ACRI's future is under review."[47] But at an annual cost of $20 million, ACRI is not much of a commitment. Neither ACRI—now renamed the African Contingency Operations Training Assistance—nor RECAMP has been tested in a major crisis. Moreover, these types of training programs that seek to "regionalize" African crises are also a way of *not* seriously committing U.S. troops.

On 27 May 2001, while flying on a plane to Budapest after his first trip to Africa as secretary of state, Colin Powell was asked by a reporter how the United States would respond to another Rwanda-style genocide in Africa. Powell replied:

> I think it is still the best policy for us to provide assistance to nations that are willing to put forward forces from the region. I don't think the United States will be able to be the court of first resort whenever there's a crisis like this . . . send in the American Army . . . to put down the conflict . . . because we're the biggest and we have the most capability. . . . [W]e have found that our forces are quite extended and we have to have a clear understanding of the missions we are going into.[48]

Only belatedly near the end of Liberia's seven-year civil war in 1996 did the United States contribute substantial logistical and financial support to the Nigerian-led ECOWAS Cease-Fire Monitoring Group (ECOMOG) mission in Liberia, a country with which the United States had special historical ties and a state that was a staunch ally of the United States during the Cold War. The deterioration of bilateral relations between Washington and Abuja under the military regime of General Sani Abacha also contributed to the refusal of the United States to provide substantial support to ECOMOG's efforts in Liberia. Following Nigeria's democratic transition in 1999, a $20 million bilateral military training agreement called "Operation Focus Relief" was signed in July 2000 after a visit to Nigeria by then–defense secretary William Cohen, shortly before President Clinton's visit to

Abuja in September 2000. The program trained Nigerian peacekeepers for participation in the UN mission in Sierra Leone. Ghanaian and Senegalese contingents were also trained for UNAMSIL under this program.

"Operation Focus Relief" was a step in advance of ACRI/ACOTA and is still a subject of some controversy in Nigeria, especially as there are suspicions that the full terms of the accord may not have been revealed. It is felt, in some quarters in Nigeria, that any such activities should be subsumed under the mechanisms of the African Union and ECOWAS and not run parallel to them. Nigeria's civilian government under Olusegun Obasanjo, however, has said that it would welcome "any direct assistance from the US in the form of finance, equipment and training that can enhance Nigeria's role in regional peacekeeping."[49] Public criticisms of aspects of "Operation Focus Relief" that were felt to have compromised Nigeria's national security reportedly contributed to the removal from office of Nigeria's chief of army staff, General Victor Malu, in May 2001.

President George W. Bush faced tremendous pressure, during a visit to Africa in July 2003, to launch an intervention to douse the flames of civil war that were threatening to engulf Liberia. In August 2003 the United States sent a warship to Liberia to provide logistical support to a Nigerian-led peacekeeping force. Though few U.S. soldiers were involved in peacekeeping on the ground, Africa had once more found a way of forcing the United States back onto its former Cold War stomping ground in what many agreed would be an exceptional case rather than a renewed trend of U.S. interventionism on the continent.

Conclusion: Africa After 11 September 2001

In the wake of the attacks on the World Trade Center and Pentagon in September 2001, the problems of security in West Africa have been demoted from regional issues requiring "small-scale contingencies of limited duration" to marginal concerns of a nation at war. The United States is concerned with its own security first, and its global "war on terrorism" has been imposing its own exigencies. Countries seeking to ingratiate themselves with Washington have enthusiastically embraced the terms of reference of this "war," while denying that they have any mercenary motive in mind. Some leaders, such as Charles Taylor, declared their own "wars on terrorism" against domestic opponents. Senegal's Abdoulaye Wade hosted an "antiterrorism" summit of African leaders in Dakar in October 2001. The Chequers summit a month earlier, involving Tony Blair and six African leaders, also produced an antiterrorism declaration, which rather eclipsed the British premier's desire to use the meeting as a platform to express his support for the Millennium African Plan, eventually unveiled in October

2001 as the New Partnership for Africa's Development.[50] Support for NEPAD may well be an acid test of how far the post–11 September international environment can be manipulated to the advantage of the African continent.

East Africa, particularly in view of the suspicions that have surrounded Somalia and Sudan, as well as U.S. embassy bombings in Nairobi and Dar es Salaam in 1998 and the terrorist attack on a hotel in Mombasa in November 2002, is much nearer any possible theater of the new U.S. "war" than West Africa. For better or for worse, West Africa appears to be more on the margins of the "war on terrorism," although there are concerns in many Western capitals about the prevalence of Islam in the subregion. President George W. Bush's proposed trip to Africa (Nigeria, Kenya, South Africa, and Mauritius) in January 2003 was postponed amid a growing U.S. troop deployment in the Gulf to launch a "preemptive" war against Iraq. This was another clear sign of the low priority that Africa has been traditionally accorded in Washington. As Peter Schraeder noted: "The net result of White House and congressional neglect of Africa . . . is that the Bush administration's foreign policy towards Africa . . . essentially will be delegated to the high-level bureaucrats and political appointees within the executive branch."[51] In the U.S. "war on terrorism," certain West African states may not have the means to impose the kind of security controls that Washington desires. In West Africa, Nigeria, Senegal, and Côte d'Ivoire are the most important countries that may be at the front lines of such a "war," but smaller countries like Mali, Niger, and Burkina Faso may be equally vulnerable.

The world has seen, in the invasions of Afghanistan in 2002 and then Iraq in 2003, the beast of U.S. unilateralism rear its ugly head. True, it was only a single administration, and it may not be representative of anything more than George W. Bush and his hawkish advisers. But perhaps Africans should be wary that their collective security may be sacrificed on the altar of "Yankee" realpolitik. When African states refused to vote for Bush's war in Iraq in the UN Security Council in 2003, Washington simply ignored them. The great imponderable of the future is whether an occult and ill-defined "war on terrorism" will create new priorities that could bring unlikely actors into the arena and produce strange realignments. Its strategic need for friends and its fear of enemies may reduce the future Africa policies of the United States to a parody of the old "our-son-of-a-bitch" mentality of the Cold War era, and this approach may even bring the European allies of the United States tumbling back into African security situations. The British and the French may find it even harder to pursue their own divergent policies now that the bipolar system has become unipolar, and the great division of the international system appears, from some perspectives, to have reclassified all states into those who are *for,* and those who are *against,* the "hyperpower."

Notes

1. Ali A. Mazrui, ed., *Africa Since 1935,* General History of Africa, vol. 8 (Berkeley: University of California Press, 1993), pp. 705–723; and Prosser Gifford and W. M. Roger Louis, *The Transfer of Power in Africa: Decolonization, 1940–1960* (New Haven, Conn.: Yale University Press, 1982).

2. For histories of early U.S. policy toward Africa, see Waldemar Nielson, *The Great Powers and Africa* (New York: Praeger, 1969); Vernon McKay, *Africa in World Politics* (New York: Harper & Row, 1963); Richard D. Mahoney, *JFK: Ordeal in Africa* (Oxford University Press, 1983); and Henry F. Jackson, *From the Congo to Soweto: U.S. Foreign Policy Toward Africa Since 1960* (New York: Morrow, 1982). For more recent historical reviews, see Zaki Laïdi, *The Super Powers and Africa: The Constraints of a Rivalry, 1960–1990* (Chicago: University of Chicago Press, 1990); and Michael Clough, *Free at Last? U.S. Policy Toward Africa and the End of the Cold War* (New York: Council on Foreign Relations Press, 1992).

3. For example, U.S. Central Intelligence Agency (CIA) station chief Larry Devlin recruited Mobutu in Brussels, not Léopoldville. See John Stockwell, *In Search of Enemies: A CIA Story* (New York: W. W. Norton, 1978).

4. Quoted in Christopher M. Andrew, "France: Adjustment to Change," in Hedley Bull, ed., *The Expansion of International Society* (Oxford: Clarendon Press, 1984), p. 337.

5. Foccart's legend was examined by French investigative journalist Pierre Péan, whose book *L'homme de l'ombre: Jacques Foccart* (Paris: Fayard, 1990) is a classic. Two volumes of the memoirs of Jacques Foccart, as told to Philippe Gaillard, have been published under the title *Foccart parle* (Paris: Fayart/Jeune Afrique, 1993, 1995). Four out of five volumes of Foccart's diaries have also been published by Fayart/Jeune Afrique. These books have done much to cultivate the legend and are a very important, if partisan, source.

6. In 1960 on the occasion of the breakup of the Mali Federation, in 1962 at the time of the "coup" of Mamadou Dia, and in May 1968 during the student-worker demonstrations.

7. The unusual relationship between Bokassa and Giscard remains one of the most bizarre episodes in Franco-African relations. Giscard's lack of judgment in choosing such a grotesque figure as a key friend and ally was astonishing. The "diamonds affair" was probably one of the principal reasons why Giscard lost the 1981 election, and it is even said that when Bokassa, in June 1979, struck René Journiac with his silver-topped cane, that it was this, rather than the earlier massacre of schoolchildren, that finally persuaded Giscard to overthrow the self-declared emperor.

8. The coup happened shortly after Pompidou died, when there was a power vacuum in Paris, and Foccart was not sure of his own position. It had always been said, however, that Diori was one of the leaders that the French would try to save, and the assassination of Diori's wife during the coup must have added to the loss of credibility.

9. Chad's sentimental position in Gaullist mythology came from the fact that its Guyanese governor, Felix Eboué, had been the first to declare for the Free French in 1940 and, along with Cameroon, was the main base from which General Leclerc's division staged the reconquest of France from the "southern flank" and ended in Berchesgarten 1945.

10. John Chipman, *French Power in Africa* (Oxford: Basil Blackwell, 1989), p. 126.

11. The expression *"Mort pour la France"* appears on countless public monuments in memorial of those who died in the two world wars.

12. Mme Claustre was kidnapped by Hissen Habré, then one of the leaders of the Front Nationale pour la Libération du Tchad (Frolinat), and was held hostage for two years. Her husband, Pierre Claustre, who tried to secure her release but ended up also being held hostage, has written an account of the two-year drama, *L'affaire Claustre: Autopsie d'une prise d'otages* (Paris: Karthala, 1990).

13. See Michael P. Kelly, *A State in Disarray: Conditions of Chad's Survival* (Boulder: Westview Press, 1986); René Lemarchand, *The Green and the Black: Qadhafi's Policies in Africa* (Bloomington: Indiana University Press, 1988); and Margaret Vogt and Lateef Aminu, eds., *Peacekeeping as a Security Strategy in Africa: Chad and Liberia as Case Studies* (Enugu, Nigeria: Fourth Dimension, 1996).

14. See Charles Darlington and Alice Darlington, *African Betrayal* (New York: David Mackay, 1968).

15. See Douglas Yates, *The Rentier State in Africa: Oil-Rent Dependency and Neo-Colonialism in the Republic of Gabon* (Trenton, N.J.: Africa World Press, 1996).

16. Roland Marchal, "France and Africa: The Emergence of Essential Reforms?" *International Affairs* 74, no. 2 (1998).

17. Sékou Touré, usually considered an ally of Moscow, had notably gratified the United States by refusing flyover rights to the Soviet Union during the 1962 Cuban missile crisis. This had been due, it was said, to his good personal rapport with John F. Kennedy. See notably John H. Morrow, *First American Ambassador to Guinea* (New Brunswick, N.J.: Rutgers University Press, 1968).

18. Olusegun Obasanjo, *My Command* (London: Heinemann, 1980); John Stremlau, *The International Politics of the Nigerian Civil War, 1967–1970* (Princeton: Princeton University Press, 1977); R. Faligot and P. Krop, *La piscine* (Paris: Seuil, 1985); and Pierre Péan and Jean-Pierre Séréni, *Les émirs de la République* (Paris: Stock, 1983).

19. Suzanne Cronje, *The World and Nigeria* (London: Sidgwick and Jackson, 1972).

20. An article by Paul Lee in *West Africa,* 19–25 November 2001, pp. 11–15, marshals, without much academic rigor, some of the circumstantial evidence available, including from U.S. official records.

21. CIA station chief in Léopoldville, Lawrence Devlin, who recruited Mobutu, has testified on more than one occasion to this fact (those interested should see the 1999 documentary *Mobutu: Roi du Zaïre* by Thierry Michel). The best account of U.S. Congo policy at this time can be found in Stephen R. Weissman, *American Foreign Policy in the Congo, 1960–1964* (Ithaca: Cornell University Press, 1974).

22. There was an outbreak of macho reporting of the Kolwezi affair in Europe. See, for example, Pierre Sergent, *La légion saute sur Kolwezi* (Paris: Presses de la Cité, 1978).

23. Gus Liebenow, *The Evolution of Privilege* (Ithaca: Cornell University Press, 1969), p. 3.

24. Paul Gifford, *Christianity and Politics in Doe's Liberia* (Cambridge: Cambridge University Press, 1993), p. 234.

25. Adekeye Adebajo, *Liberia's Civil War: Nigeria, ECOMOG, and Regional Security in West Africa* (Boulder: Lynne Rienner, 2002), pp. 33–36.

26. On Françafrique, see François-Xavier Verschave, *La Françafrique: Le plus long scandale de la République* (Paris: Stock, 1998).

27. On the French military intervention in Gabon in 1991, see David Gardinier, "Gabon: Limited Reform and Regime Survivial," in John F. Clark and David E. Gardinier, eds., *Political Reform in Francophone Africa* (Boulder: Westview Press, 1997), pp. 145–161.

28. *Jeune Afrique*, 25–31 January 1996, p. 11.

29. See John R. Heilbrum, "Togo: The National Conference and Stalled Reform," in Clark and Gardinier, *Political Reform in Francophone Africa*, pp. 225–245.

30. "Father told me."

31. See Jean-François Bayart, *La politique africaine de François Mitterrand* (Paris: Karthala, 1983).

32. Howard Adelman and Astri Suhrke, eds., *The Path of a Genocide: The Rwanda Crisis from Uganda to Zaire* (New Brunswick, N.J.: Transaction, 1999); Henry Kwami Anyidoho, *Guns over Kigali* (Accra: Woeli, 1999); Gerard Prunier, *The Rwandan Crisis: History of a Genocide* (New York: Columbia University Press, 1995); Organization of African Unity, *The International Panel of Eminent Persons to Investigate the 1994 Genocide in Rwanda and the Surrounding Events,* July 2000; and United Nations, *Report of the Independent Inquiry into the Actions of the United Nations During the 1994 Genocide in Rwanda,* UN Doc. S/1999/1257, 16 December 1999.

33. Marchal, "France and Africa," p. 365.

34. During the rule of President Houphouët-Boigny (1960–1993), it had always been supposed that the French would intervene militarily to save him should he ever run into trouble. The evidence that emerged in December 1999 of the existence of a tunnel linking the presidency in Cocody to the French embassy next door, through which Bédié, his family, and close colleagues escaped, bears this out. Bédié was not, however, Houphouët-Boigny; nor did he have the prescience of his predecessor, who, it was said, would never have allowed such a situation to develop in the military.

35. Author's translation, cited in Stephen Smith and Jean-Pierre Tuquoi, "Nous ne nous ingérons plus dans les crises internes," *Le Monde,* 10 June 2001, p. 2.

36. Ibid.

37. Eric G. Berman and Katie E. Sams, *Peacekeeping in Africa: Capabilities and Culpabilities* (Geneva: UN Institute for Disarmament Research, 2000); Eboe Hutchful, "Peacekeeping Under Conditions of Resource Stringency," in Jakkie Cilliers and Greg Mills, eds., *From Peacekeeping to Complex Emergencies: Peace Support Missions in Africa* (Johannesburg: South African Institute of International Affairs, 1999), pp. 113–117; and Rocklyn Williams, "Beyond Old Borders: Challenges to Franco–South African Security Relations in the New Millennium," *African Security Review* 8, no. 4 (1999): 3–19.

38. Adekeye Adebajo, *Building Peace in West Africa: Liberia, Sierra Leone, and Guinea-Bissau,* International Peace Academy Occasional Paper Series (Boulder: Lynne Rienner, 2002); Comfort Ero, *Sierra Leone's Security Complex,* Conflict, Security, and Development Group Working Paper no. 3 (London: Centre for Defence Studies, King's College, June 2000); and John Hirsch, "War in Sierra Leone," *Survival* 43, no. 3 (Autumn 2001): 145–162.

39. Did the British show some ambivalence about the fact that it was General Abacha who had had the nerve to sustain the ECOMOG troops through to victory in Freetown? Tony Lloyd, Foreign and Commonwealth Office minister at the time, when asked what he thought of the Nigerian operation, said curtly, "Two cheers" (conversation with Kaye Whiteman, February 1998).

40. Foreign Affairs Select Committee, 1998–1999, vols. 1–2, House of Commons, London, 1999.

41. Cited in ibid.

42. Hussein Adam, "Somalia: A Terrible Beauty Being Born?" in I. William Zartman, ed., *Collapsed States: The Disintegration and Restoration of Legitimate Authority* (Boulder: Lynne Rienner, 1995) pp. 69–78; Walter Clarke, "Failed Visions and Uncertain Mandates in Somalia," in Walter Clarke and Jeffrey Herbst, eds., *Learning from Somalia: The Lessons of Armed Humanitarian Intervention* (Boulder: Westview Press, 1997); Alex de Waal, *Famine Crimes: Politics and the Disaster Relief Industry in Africa* (Oxford: James Currey, 1997); John L. Hirsch and Robert B. Oakley, *Somalia and Operation Restore Hope: Reflections on Peacemaking and Peacekeeping* (Washington, D.C.: U.S. Institute of Peace Press, 1995); and Mohamed Sahnoun, *Somalia: The Missed Opportunities* (Washington, D.C.: U.S. Institute of Peace Press, 1994).

43. See the CNN documentary *Blackhawk Down* (title taken from the movie), in which one of the Delta Force troops explains, "It kind of sucked for the women, but I have no regrets" (17 February 2002).

44. See Mats Berdal, "Peacekeeping in Africa," in Oliver Furley and Roy May, eds., *Peacekeeping in Africa* (Aldershot, England: Ashgate), pp. 55–56.

45. Hutchful, "Peacekeeping Under Conditions of Resource Stringency," pp. 97–98.

46. See Adekeye Adebajo and Michael O'Hanlon, "Africa: Toward a Rapid-Reaction Force," *SAIS Review* 17, no. 2 (Summer–Fall 1997): 153–164; Jendayi Frazer, "The Africa Crisis Response Initiative: Self-Interested Humanitarianism," *Brown Journal of World Affairs* 4, no. 2 (Summer–Fall 1997): 103–118; and Paul Omach, "The African Crisis Response Initiative: Domestic Politics and Convergence of National Interests," *African Affairs* 99, no. 394 (January 2000): 73–95.

47. USIS, *Africa News Report,* 16 July 2001.

48. USIS, *Africa News Report,* 11 June 2001, p. 7.

49. Cited in Bassey E. Ate, "Redesigning Foreign Policy for National Transformation: The Nigerian American Bilateral Partnership," paper presented at the conference "Nigeria and the World After Forty Years," organized at the Nigerian Institute of International Affairs, Lagos, 5–6 December 2001.

50. See, for example, International Peace Academy, *NEPAD: African Initiative, New Partnership?* (New York: International Peace Academy, September 2002).

51. Peter Schraeder, "'Forget the Rhetoric and Boost the Geo-Politics': Emerging Trends in the Bush Administration's Foreign Policy Towards Africa, 2001," *African Affairs* 100, no. 400 (July 2001): 394.

PART 4

Conclusion

16

West Africa's Post–Cold War Security Challenges

Ismail Rashid

At the end of the twentieth century, the peoples of West Africa found them-selves at the depths of despondency, with their dreams of a bright post-colonial future morphing into tragic nightmares. They now live in one of the poorest, most volatile, and most conflict-ridden regions in the world. The greatest challenge for the inhabitants and governments of West Africa is how to contain and resolve the ongoing violent conflicts, forestall the outbreak of new ones, and develop security frameworks that can guarantee durable peace. This volume has contributed to tackling this central chal-lenge by critically analyzing the origins and dynamics of different conflicts in West Africa. It has examined the role of national, regional, and external actors in engendering these conflicts and in building peace. The different contributions in the book have focused more specifically on issues such as regional integration, regional peacekeeping efforts, politics and governance, civil/military relations, rebel movements, the political economy of conflict, the proliferation of small arms and light weapons, the impact of war on youth and children, the role of civil society in conflict management, and the impact of the UN and other external actors such as France, Britain, and the United States on the region's security.

In investigating and analyzing these issues, the contributors to this vol-ume have attempted to provide a much more textured historical and analyt-ical view of the origins and the dynamics of the varied conflicts in West Africa than can usually be found in the literature. They have generally sought to counter the unfair and sometimes jaundiced perspectives of these conflicts as being either "primordial" and barbaric or driven primarily by the logic of greed and plundering. The authors in this volume have sought to demonstrate that the origins of West Africa's wars, though complex and multifarious, are rooted primarily in the political exclusion, economic impoverishment, and social alienation of the vast majority of the region's citizens by autocratic regimes. The ensuing violent conflicts from these failures of governance and erosion of state capacity should be seen partly as complex responses to these problems, and partly as counterhegemonic challenges to despotic regimes. Many of the contributors to this volume maintain that West African conflicts are not simple or static, but are shaped by the specific historical experiences, social contexts, as well as different agendas of the contending forces within countries in conflict. As they evolve, the character of the conflicts, the motivations of the contending factions, and their strategies continuously change. The struggle for resources, rather than being solely an end in itself as some scholars have contended, should be situated within these changing political, socioeconomic, and cultural dynamics.

This volume has also underscored the devastating toll of conflicts on the lives of West Africa's inhabitants, on the functioning of vital state institutions, and on the stability of societies within affected and neighboring countries. The contributors have sought to demonstrate how, in some conflict-ridden countries like Liberia and Sierra Leone, vital security institutions like the army, under the stress of autocracy and war, became predatory armed factions, just like the rebel insurgents that they were employed to fight. The degradation of security structures not only accelerated the disintegration of the state, but also led to the proliferation of arms and the fostering of a "culture of violence." Whether drawn in as victims or agents, this violence has taken a terrible toll on the lives, welfare, and development of young people.

Even as many contributors to this volume have emphasized the need for a more nuanced analysis of the internal logic of West Africa's conflicts, they have also argued that the region's tragedies did not emanate solely from internal developments. They point out that external actors also played a crucial role in nurturing the context for conflicts, as well as in unleashing the "dogs of war" on West Africa. The book illustrates the extent to which former colonial rulers as well as Cold warriors manipulated regional politics and organizations for their own parochial interests by establishing military bases, propping up autocratic regimes, and initiating policies that were inimical to the political and economic development of West Africa. These manipulative acts tended to circumscribe the possibility of nonviolent popular challenges to autocratic regimes. Once conflicts erupted, foreign arms merchants and mercenaries were quick to establish international bazaars to hawk their arms and fighting skills to contending factions, as well as benefit from looted natural resources. Several of the contributors to this book have shown that certain African countries have been equally complicit in fanning the flames of conflicts by providing military training, arms, and bases for insurgent factions, and by repeatedly thwarting peace processes.

Many of the contributors have also pointed out that, despite the undeniable value of external intervention in managing some conflicts, the primary impetus for peace must come from within the region. The role of the Economic Community of West African States (ECOWAS) in creating a regional peacekeeping and enforcement mechanism, the ECOWAS Cease-Fire Monitoring Group (ECOMOG)—an attempt at achieving a Pax West Africana—stands out in this regard. The establishment of ECOMOG, regardless of the parochial interests and dissensions that were vested in it, reflected unprecedented courage, initiative, and independence from the region's traditionally jaded leadership. Supported mainly by Nigerian men, money, and matériel, ECOMOG made genuine, though checkered efforts to arrest the spiraling violence in Liberia, Sierra Leone, Guinea-Bissau, and more recently Côte d'Ivoire. Learning from the limitations and failures of the different ECOMOG missions, and recognizing the need for clear principles, policies, and guidelines, West African leaders subsequently adopted the ECOWAS Protocol Relating to the Mechanism for Conflict Prevention, Management, Resolution, Peacekeeping, and Security in Lomé in December 1999.

If ECOMOG exemplified a conflict resolution initiative "from above," this volume has underlined that civil society represented peacebuilding efforts "from below." Despite their own internal contradictions and meager resources, civil society groups, especially those spearheaded by women and religious and traditional leaders, demonstrated their tremendous value in reenergizing the populace, opening up democratic spaces, empowering women, and contributing to the management of conflicts in different countries across the region. In Mali, where the government of Alpha Konaré acknowledged their value, civil society groups played a significant role in managing the Tuareg insurrection. In Sierra Leone and Liberia, where civil society received ambiguous recognition from governments and armed factions, civic leaders helped to build peace constituencies among the masses to bring the contending factions to the negotiating table, as well as to support disarmament, reintegration, and reconciliation efforts. The two-decade Casamance conflict, in which the Senegalese government has refused to countenance the role and value of civil society organizations and actors, has proved to be one of the more intractable conflicts in West Africa.

Long-Term Security Challenges

Ensuring long-term regional security and stability is not simply about ending violent conflicts, reining in armed military factions, and ensuring stable political regimes. Durable peace also entails creating secure environments for individual citizens and groups to live peaceful, fulfilling, and rewarding lives. Within this environment, the ability of individuals and groups to satisfy their basic needs, develop their potential, and realize their aspirations without suppressing those of others must be ensured by national governments. To achieve these objectives, the contributors to this volume have identified six broad areas in which some concrete steps have been taken, but in which lessons still need to be learned and more decisive action taken by subregional governments and citizens. These areas include, first, conflict prevention and resolution and peacebuilding; second, promoting democracy and good governance; third, mainstreaming and integrating youth and children into stable societies; fourth, establishing stable civil-military relations and stemming the flow of illicit arms within West Africa; fifth, fostering regional cooperation and integration; and sixth, developing meaningful relationships between ECOWAS and civil society groups as well as the UN and other external actors.

Conflict Prevention, Resolution, and Peacebuilding

It is obvious that the most urgent security challenge in West Africa is to silence the guns, stop the killings, and end the violence. Without peace and stability, meaningful development and integration are impossible. As noted above, significant achievements have been recorded by ECOWAS in the area of conflict management. As regional leaders continue to tackle the thorny problems of Liberia and Côte d'Ivoire, they must bear in mind seven important considerations. First, each conflict has its own specific sets of triggers, actors, and dynamics, and the resolution of conflicts therefore requires nuanced approaches and a profound understanding of the idiosyncrasies of each case. Even with the lessons learned from previous cases, there is no panacea for managing regional conflicts. The specific set of factors or strategies that made conflict resolution and peacebuilding possible in Mali and Sierra Leone might be absent, or have little effect, in Liberia and Côte d'Ivoire. Second, the overall strategy must be national, regional, and external in conception and implementation, and therefore pull together the diverse experiences and resources of a variety of multinational and national institutions. Third, regional peacekeeping mechanisms such as ECOMOG in Liberia, Sierra Leone, and Guinea-Bissau; the ECOWAS Peace Force for Côte d'Ivoire (ECOFORCE); and the ECOWAS Mission in Liberia (ECOMIL) must be provided with sufficient training, resources, and logistical support to be able to contribute effectively to conflict management and the establishment of stability in West Africa. ECOWAS must move quickly to operationalize fully all aspects of its security mechanism of 1999, including the Council of Elders, the Defense and Security

Commission, the Mediation and Security Council, and its early warning system. Fourth, the crafting and implementation of peace agreements must involve all contending factions and neighboring states, as well as all external actors with a stake in the outcome of the conflict. Yet, as has been repeatedly demonstrated, effective means must still be found to ensure that these parties implement peace accords that they have signed. "Spoilers" must be made to realize that they will face regional and externally imposed sanctions if they do not fulfill their pledges. Fifth, and perhaps most important, peace processes and agreements must have some kind of mass support within local communities in order for them to be effectively implemented. The role of civil society organizations, which can draw on a wide range of popular experiences, energies, and networks, is crucial to these efforts. Women must be a critical part of these processes, and their involvement should not be limited just to raising popular concerns; they must also be integrated into long-term peacebuilding strategies. Sixth, the international donor community must recognize that conflict resolution and peacebuilding can never be done cheaply, quickly, and haphazardly. As clearly demonstrated by the cases of Liberia, Sierra Leone, Guinea-Bissau, Mali, and in stark contrast, the Balkans, sufficient resources must be provided in a timely manner at crucial points in the peace process. Finally, the price that peacemakers have been prepared to pay to buy peace by appeasing powerful warlords in places like Liberia and Sierra Leone has often been too high and sometimes even counterproductive. Blanket amnesties, which have often fostered a culture of impunity, must not be extended to faction leaders and fighters who have committed egregious human rights violations and crimes against humanity. In the same vein, ECOWAS's leaders need to sanction and shame those countries and regional leaders who fuel conflicts and play the role of "spoilers."

Democratic Regimes and Good Governance

Since the roots of West Africa's current crisis lie in a four-decade history of autocratic governance, political exclusion, and unrepresentative institutions, these are precisely the areas in which the task of constructing a secure and stable foundation for the subregion's long-term security architecture must begin. West African elites, both civilian and military, must learn valuable lessons from the fact that continued repression—especially in a situation in which states are weak and socioeconomic conditions are deteriorating—tends to be counterproductive. Former military leaders like Nigeria's Olusegun Obasanjo, Benin's Matthieu Kérékou, and Mali's Amadou Touré have learned that ballots rather than bullets are more legitimate and democratic routes to power. The democratic process in West Africa is still fragile, and more energy needs to be expended before it can become entrenched.

To achieve this, five steps must be taken at the national, subregional, and continental levels. First, it is imperative that the current processes of democratization in parts of West Africa (involving regular elections, political plurality, popular participation, and the expansion of freedom of expression and association) be nurtured, consolidated, and deepened. Deepening democratic processes necessitates going beyond periodic elections to ensuring the promotion of fundamental human rights and the rule of law, the decentralization and devolution of power, the empowerment of women, the creation of credible and independent judiciaries, the reform of inefficient bureaucracies, the development of independent legislative bodies, and the fostering of knowledgeable, effective, and independent mass media. Second, countries such as Guinea and Togo that are lagging behind in the process of democratic reform should be encouraged as well as pressured to keep pace with changes in other parts of West Africa. Third, national governments and ECOWAS must create the enabling environment for civil society to grow. Civil society groups should be able to mobilize resources independently and collaborate with governments, ECOWAS, and international organizations and actors on projects of national and regional importance. Fourth, ECOWAS and the African Union (AU) should continue to promote a regional and continental commitment to democracy and the preservation of human rights, to reject illegal seizures of power, and to strengthen the capacity of West African citizens to resist repressive regimes. To this end, several institutions emanating from recent continental and regional protocols, such as the ECOWAS Council of Elders and the AU's continental parliament and court, should be made functional and relevant to the lives of ordinary citizens. ECOWAS and the AU must develop norms and values of governance that regional leaders abide by and through which their citizens can hold them accountable. Fifth, the ultimate objective of these different democratic political processes, policies, and institutions should be the transformation of a national, regional, and continental "political culture" from one in which citizens are alienated from the state to one in which they genuinely govern themselves and are arbiters of their own future. Thus the emphasis should be not on good governance, but on *democratic* governance through which citizens can freely debate, negotiate, and design the nature of their society and their common future.[1]

The Challenge of Youth

Central to ensuring the stability of democratic regimes and promoting good governance practices in West Africa is the challenge represented by the subregion's youth. As highlighted in several chapters in this volume, youth (whether under the direction of others or of their own volition) have demonstrated tremendous capacity for conceiving and participating in counterhegemonic projects against entrenched and autocratic regimes. The challenge of youth in West Africa transcends their involvement in violence. It also includes their use as sex objects, forced laborers, couriers and consumers of illegal drugs, and victims of infectious diseases such as HIV/ AIDS. With the adoption of the ECOWAS security mechanism in 1999 and the Accra Declaration and Plan of Action in 2000, ECOWAS has taken the initial steps to meet this challenge. The subregional body has followed up these pronouncements with the establishment of a Child Protection Unit in its secretariat to provide a regional institutional framework for the protection of children affected by armed conflict. Ghana during the era of Jerry Rawlings (1981–2000), and Burkina Faso under Thomas Sankara's rule (1983–1987), offered creative ways in which young people can be drawn into mainstream politics. The recent Ghanaian establishment of a National Commission for Children and Sierra Leone's creation of a National Commission for War-Affected Children further indicate that some countries have begun trying to translate some of these agreements into reality. Clearly, more needs to be done to deal fully with the impact of conflict on children and to integrate West Africa's youth into mainstream society and politics. Meeting these challenges must begin with the conception of young people not only as victims, but also as conscious agents and full citizens. Their vital role in ensuring the generational transmission and transformation of national cultures and politics, and the sustainability of regional economic and social development, must be acknowledged. West African governments must also strengthen their commitment to international and regional resolutions, conventions, and agreements on the rights and status of children, especially those impacted by conflict. Thus the specific interests and needs of youth and children must be reflected in the political agenda, economic development, and resource allocation in national and regional budgets.

Civil-Military Relations and the Security Sector

The degeneration of security agencies and the concomitant proliferation of illicit small arms and light weapons are a crucial part of the toxic mélange of West Africa's violent conflicts. The choices made by security agencies in this subregion have been crucial in determining the extent to which states have descended into chaos. In Ghana, Mali, and Nigeria, there have been instances where the military chose either to thwart fissiparous developments or withdraw from politics to save the state from collapse. Since these security forces, especially the military and police, have been involved in fueling instability, mainly through their involvement in politics, there needs to be an urgent depoliticization of the military. West African armies must not be able to make claims to political power and, like other national institutions, must be subordinated to broad democratic processes and elective institutions. Politics in this subregion must also be demilitarized so that armies do not become partisan and repressive instruments of autocratic regimes. This will mean, at both the national and the regional levels, serious security sector reform and more stringent control of arms flows. The main security agencies—namely the military, paramilitary, and police forces—in some cases need to be reorganized, retrained, equipped, and properly remunerated to carry out their essential tasks of protecting civilians and maintaining public law and order. The failure to ensure that security forces were properly reconstituted, trained, and organized after Charles Taylor's electoral victory in 1997 paved the way for Liberia's regression to war in two short years. The current military and police retraining and reorganization experiment in Sierra Leone, underwritten largely by the British and the UN, will hopefully be more effective in promoting stable civil-military relations.

However, West Africa's security sector challenges also need to be conceptualized more broadly. This debate needs to move beyond the narrow confines of the military and police to include government-supported militias such as the civil defense forces in Sierra Leone, and irregular community defense forces like the Bakassi Boys and the Oodua People's Congress in Nigeria. These groups participate in activities that directly or indirectly impinge on law and order and public safety. Finally, security sector reform must involve coordinated national, regional, and external strategies that improve the consolidation and implementation of international agreements like the three-year ECOWAS Moratorium on the Importation, Exportation, and Manufacture of Light Weapons of 1998 (renewed in 2001), designed to track arms production, export, and usage in West Africa.

Regional Integration and Cooperation

As demonstrated by historical and contemporary experiences in Europe, as well as global developments with the increasing creation of trade blocs in North America and Asia, regional cooperation and integration offer a viable means for meeting West Africa's security challenges. Regional cooperation and integration are not an option, but a necessity. Over nearly three decades of trying to build ECOWAS into a dynamic regional organization and to establish a common market within West Africa, four key lessons have become apparent. First, West African governments need to transcend the traditional "anglophone" and "francophone" division that emerged during colonialism and calcified during the postindependence era. This historical division has resulted in the creation of competing and overlapping regional organizations, all ostensibly geared toward achieving the same purpose of uniting the countries of West Africa.

Second, smaller countries must confront the apprehension that Nigeria, West Africa's largest and most powerful state, will impose a suffocating hegemony and domination on the region. Nigeria itself must establish domestic stability and learn to treat its neighbors with respect if its leadership ambitions are to be taken seriously by others. Nigeria's leaders will need to assure other regional states that the country's aspirations, role, and actions as a regional hegemon will be beneficial and not detrimental to them. The tremendous sacrifice that Nigeria has made in lives and resources to bring peace, stability, and democracy to Sierra Leone and Liberia, and its willingness to contribute heavily to regional security, can be underlined as part of this assurance.

Third, the policies, institutions, and activities of ECOWAS and the African Union must be harmonized. Continental initiatives like the Conference on Security, Stability, Development, and Cooperation in Africa (CSSDCA) and the New Partnership for Africa's Development (NEPAD) can only be effectively implemented at the regional level if they are effectively coordinated with subregional organizations like ECOWAS. Fourth, the process of regional cooperation and integration in West Africa must be prioritized by governments and made relevant to peoples across the subregion. Regional integration must produce tangible results for the masses of ordinary people on the ground. Learning from the experiences and lessons of the past three decades, West African governments must accept one single organization, ECOWAS (which encompasses the greatest number of countries and peoples and transcends all of the historical and cultural divisions in the subregion), as the sole motor of integration in West Africa. ECOWAS should create a common currency and absorb the largely francophone Union Economique et Monétaire Ouest Africaine (UEMOA) and other smaller regional groupings under a common umbrella. ECOWAS must also learn from the experiences of UEMOA, which has been able to create a more dynamic common currency zone, common fiscal and customs policies, and common institutions. ECOWAS should work more effectively with regional civil society networks on governance and security issues, especially in the area of providing early warning assistance in developing popular responses to conflict management. Through civil society actors, ECOWAS can connect with the masses as well as help deepen current processes of democratization in West Africa.

Ultimately, the success of regional integration will depend largely on the unwavering commitment and support of citizens and member states for the ECOWAS project. Success hinges on the acceptance and the embedding in the consciousness of the region's 230 million people that an integrated regional community is an attractive, desirable, and beneficial aspiration. West African citizens have to understand that ECOWAS can produce a common regional citizenship, underwritten not only by a single currency and shared sets of fiscal and economic institutions, but also by common humanitarian values and a common political culture. If ECOWAS is to be the main vehicle for achieving these objectives, its members must make the necessary financial contributions to maintain its fiscal viability, support the effective functioning of its secretariat and institutions, and implement its agreements and policies in a timely fashion. Furthermore, it is imperative that governments and citizens regard West Africa as their own sphere of influence, and not as an appendage or object of others, particularly former colonizers and global powers.

International Relations

West Africans cannot attain viable and meaningful integration without engaging the challenge of the emerging global order and the impact of international multinational organizations such as the United Nations, the International Monetary Fund, the World Bank, the Commonwealth, the Francophonie, and powerful external actors such as the United States, France, and Britain. Many of the conflicts examined in this volume erupted within the cusp of the breakdown of the old Cold War era and the post–11 September 2001 U.S.-driven antiterrorism global order. Even within this transitional and newly emerging global framework, international institutions and actors remain an integral part of the unfolding dynamics and the management of conflicts as well as the building of long-term security in West Africa.

With very few exceptions, the policies of the international financial institutions have tended to exacerbate rather than ameliorate the economic and social crisis facing Africa since the "lost decade" of the 1980s. In insisting on restructuring, privatization, and pruning of social services in the midst of a severe socioeconomic crisis, the Bretton Woods institutions inadvertently pushed certain countries in the region toward violent conflicts or exacerbated current wars. Also, in defending particular interests, Western powers, particularly France and the United States, supported several autocratic governments and helped stifle the possibility of nonviolent democratic transitions. Once West Africa's conflicts erupted in the 1990s, the absence of the old Cold War proxy support helped shaped the nature of the conflicts and the strategies of the different factions, who found new ways of mobilizing resources by plundering accessible and valuable natural resources.

External actors, however, supported and sustained these conflicts in complex ways. By associating with or covertly supporting certain armed factions, external business interests not only financially benefited from West Africa's conflicts, but also ensured the inflow of the resources necessary to sustain such wars. More positively, the United States provided crucial financial and logistical support for regional conflict resolution and peacekeeping efforts in Liberia in 1996. Britain, France, and Portugal have also played important roles in advocating and ensuring international intervention in Sierra Leone, Côte d'Ivoire, and Guinea-Bissau. The British military intervention in Sierra Leone in 2000 was crucial in stabilizing a dangerous situation and strengthening a crumbling UN peacekeeping mission. The United Nations Mission in Sierra Leone (UNAMSIL) has so far proved to be a crucial instrument for disarmament and demobilization, underwriting peace and ensuring stability in Sierra Leone. It remains unclear whether Britain's presence in Sierra Leone will be a short-term reflexive reaction or part of a more coherent long-term engagement, as has been the case with France over the past four decades. The limited U.S. intervention in Liberia in August 2003 may also prove to be a temporary flash in the pan.

Given the paradoxical roles of external actors and the need for stable long-term security arrangements in West Africa, subregional governments and external actors need radically to redefine their roles and relationships with each other. External actors and institutions must realize that meaningful dialogue and partnerships and the creation of a secure regional environment cannot be built on former imperial legacies and renewed forms of asymmetrical power relationships. France, the most active external actor in the region, has to accept that it can indeed have a "future history"—François Mitterrand's words—with Africa, but not one that continues to be based on perpetual domination and overbearing hegemony. The same can be said about Britain, Portugal, and the world's new "hyperpower," the United States. U.S. policymakers must realize that the global status that the country aspires to comes with serious international responsibilities and obligations. They must be aware that security and prosperity for U.S. citizens also imply and entail security and prosperity for peoples in other parts of the world. Supporting economic development and integration in, and increased and fairer trade with, regions like Africa is surely a cheaper and more effective conflict prevention strategy for external actors like the United States than constantly waging far-flung wars.

In the crucial areas of peacekeeping and peacebuilding, a clear and equitable relationship and division of labor need to be worked out between regional and external actors. In Sierra Leone, the UN mission replaced ECOMOG, which for three years (1997–2000) had borne the brunt of peacekeeping and peace enforcement. A significant reason for the reversal of much of ECOMOG's sacrifices in Liberia and Sierra Leone was the failure of the international community to provide resources for peacebuilding. This remains a major problem in reconstruction efforts in West Africa. Significantly, with the backing of the United States, Britain, and other Security Council members, the UN provided Sierra Leone with the necessary resources to end a decade-long civil war by 2002, though many peacebuilding challenges still remain. UNAMSIL absorbed a significant number of former ECOMOG troops, but the subsequent tussle for command and leadership of the mission highlights the need to work out more clearly the relationship, division of labor, and modus operandi between regional and external forces. UNAMSIL's eventual success in ending Sierra Leone's war contains potentially valuable lessons for Liberia, Guinea-Bissau, and Côte d'Ivoire.

The establishment of a UN regional office in Dakar in 2002 is a positive step toward ensuring the establishment of the nexus between governance and security and bringing the world body closer to the citizens and governments of West Africa. ECOWAS should devise a strategic framework indicating areas of priority and the necessary steps to build effective cooperation between itself and the UN in the field of conflict management. Furthermore, both organizations should pay closer attention to festering low-level communal and regional conflicts in Casamance and the Niger Delta.

* * *

This volume, written largely by African scholars and practitioners, has made four major contributions to understanding and managing West Africa's post–Cold War security challenges. First, it has provided retrospective and critical insights into regional efforts at integration and cooperation by examining the evolution of rival subregional organizations, focusing particularly on ECOWAS, which has primary responsibility for promoting regional integration and security in West Africa. Second, the book has provided a comprehensive diagnosis and analysis of the origins, character, dynamics, and political economy of West Africa's most violent conflicts, particularly the cases of Liberia and Sierra Leone. The volume has also dealt with the conflicts in Guinea-Bissau, Mali, Côte d'Ivoire, Senegal's Casamance, and Nigeria's Niger Delta. Third, the study has provided diverse perspectives on the international dimensions of conflicts, highlighting both the negative and the constructive impact of external actors on West Africa's security complex. Finally, the volume has provided concrete policy challenges that must be confronted in order to ensure long-term regional security and stability in West Africa. We hope that this book will complement the tremendous courage, resilience, and initiatives that have been shown by West Africa's masses as they try to make sense of the recent decade of troubles and strive to build a peaceful and prosperous subregion for future generations.

Note

1. Thandika Mkandawire, *Our Continent, Our Future* (Dakar: CODESRIA, 1999), p. 133.

Acronyms

AAF-SAP	African Alternative Framework to Structural Adjustment Program for Socio-Economic Recovery and Transformation
ACOTA	African Contingency Operations Training Assistance
ACRI	African Crisis Response Initiative (now ACOTA)
ADB	African Development Bank
ADEMA	Alliance pour la Démocratie en Mali
AEC	African Economic Community
AEF	Afrique Equatoriale Française
AFJ	Association des Femmes Juristes (Mali)
AFL	Armed Forces of Liberia
AFRC	Armed Forces Ruling Council (Sierra Leone)
AFSTRAG	African Strategic and Peace Research Group
AIDS	acquired immunodeficiency syndrome
ALF	African Leadership Forum
ANAD	Accord de Non-Aggression et d'Assistance en Matière de Défense
AOF	Afrique Occidentale Française
APC	All People's Congress (Sierra Leone)
APRM	African Peer Review Mechanism
AU	African Union
BBC	British Broadcasting Corporation
BCEAO	Banque Centrale des Etats de l'Afrique de l'Ouest
BEAC	Banque des Etats d'Afrique Centrale (now CEMAC)
CAFO	Coordination des Associations et Organisations Féminines (Mali)

CAR	Central African Republic
CCR	Centre for Conflict Resolution
CDF	Civil Defense Force (Sierra Leone)
CEAO	Communauté Economique de l'Afrique de l'Ouest
CEDAW	Convention to Eliminate All Forms of Discrimination Against Women
CEMAC	Communauté Economique et Monétaire d'Afrique Centrale
CFA	Communauté Financière Africaine
CIA	Central Intelligence Agency (United States)
CLHRE	Center for Law and Human Rights Education (Liberia)
CNID	Comité National d'Initiatives Démocratiques (Mali)
CNN	Cable News Network
COCOM	Coordinating Committee on Multilateral Export Controls
CODESRIA	Council for the Development of Social Science Research in Africa
COFEM	Coopérative Feminine (Mali)
COMESA	Common Market for Eastern and Southern Africa
CPU	Child Protection Unit (ECOWAS)
CRC	Central Revolutionary Council (NPFL faction)
CRFPC	Conseil Régional des Femmes pour la Paix en Casamance (Senegal)
CSGSP	Convergence, Stability, Growth, and Solidarity Pact
CSSDCA	Conference on Security, Stability, Development, and Cooperation in Africa
DDR	disarmament, demobilization, and reintegration
DFID	Department for International Development (UK)
DOPHA	Department of Operations, Peacekeeping, and Humanitarian Affairs (ECOWAS)
DPAS	Department of Political Affairs and Security (ECOWAS)
DRC	Democratic Republic of Congo
EAC	East African Community
ECA	Economic Commission for Africa (UN)
ECB	European Central Bank
ECCAS	Economic Community of Central African States
ECOFORCE	Economic Community of West African States Peace Force for Côte d'Ivoire
ECOMIL	Economic Community of West African States Mission in Liberia
ECOMOG	Economic Community of West African States Cease-Fire Monitoring Group
ECOWAS	Economic Community of West African States

EEC	European Economic Community
EMS	European Monetary System
EMU	European Monetary Union
ERP	economic recovery plan
EU	European Union
FAL	Final Act of Lagos
FAS	Femmes-Africa-Solidarité
FNLA	Frente Nacional de Libertação de Angola
FNLC	Front National de la Libération du Congo
Frolinat	Front Nationale pour la Liberation du Tchad
G8	Group of Eight
GDP	gross domestic product
HIV	human immunodeficiency virus
HSGIC	Heads of State and Government Implementation Committee (NEPAD)
ICRC	International Committee of the Red Cross
IFMC	Inter-Faith Mediation Committee (Liberia)
IGAD	Intergovernmental Authority on Development
IGNU	Interim Government of National Unity (Liberia)
IHEDN	Institut des Hautes Études de Défense Nationale
IMF	International Monetary Fund
INEC	Interim Electoral Commission (Sierra Leone)
INPFL	Independent National Patriotic Front of Liberia
IPA	International Peace Academy
IRCSL	Inter-Religious Council of Sierra Leone
JPC	Justice and Peace Commission (Liberia)
LCC	Liberian Council of Churches
LDF	Lofa Defense Force (Liberia)
LNTG	Liberian National Transitional Government
LPA	Lagos Plan of Action
LPC	Liberia Peace Council
LURD	Liberians United for Reconciliation and Democracy
LWI	Liberia Women Initiative
MAP	Mass Awareness and Participation (Sierra Leone)
MAP	Millennium Africa Recovery Program
Mercosur	Southern Cone Common Market
MFDC	Mouvement des Forces Démocratiques de Casamance (Senegal)
MINUCI	United Nations Mission in Côte d'Ivoire
MJP	Mouvement pour la Justice et la Paix (Côte d'Ivoire)
MNFSPUN	Mouvement National des Femmes pour la Sauvegarde de la Paix et l'Unité Nationale (Mali)
MODEL	Movement for Democracy in Liberia

MOJA	Movement for Justice in Africa (Liberia)
MONUC	United Nations Organization Mission in the Congo
MOSOP	Movement for the Survival of the Ogoni People
MPA	Mouvement Populaire de l'Azawad (Mali)
MPIGO	Mouvement Populaire Ivorien du Grand Ouest (Côte d'Ivoire)
MPLA	Movimento Popular de Libertação de Angola
MRC	Multi-Religious Council (Sierra Leone)
NACCIMA	Nigerian Association of Chambers of Commerce, Industry, Mines, and Agriculture
NAFTA	North American Free Trade Agreement
NATO	North Atlantic Treaty Organization
NCCP	National Coordinating Committee for Peace (Sierra Leone)
NEC	National Elections Commission (Sierra Leone)
NEPAD	New Partnership for Africa's Development
NGO	nongovernmental organization
NIEO	New International Economic Order
NMCL	National Muslim Council of Liberia
NPFL	National Patriotic Front of Liberia
NPRAG	National Patriotic Reconstruction Assembly Government (Liberia)
NPRC	National Provisional Ruling Council (Sierra Leone)
NUSS	National Union of Sierra Leone Students
OAS	Organization of American States
OAU	Organization of African Unity
OECD	Organization for Economic Cooperation and Development
OMVS	Organisation pour la Mise en Valuer du Fleuve Senégal
OPEC	Organization of Petroleum-Exporting Countries
PAL	Progressive Alliance of Liberia
PANAFU	Pan-African Union
PCASED	Programme for the Coordination and Assistance for Security and Development (UNDP)
PDCI	Parti Démocratique de Côte d'Ivoire
PPP	Progressive People's Party (Liberia)
PRC	People's Redemption Council (Liberia)
PTA	Preferential Trade Area for Eastern and Southern African States
PTSD	posttraumatic stress disorder
RADDHO	Rencontre Africaine pour la Défense des Droits de l'Homme (Senegal)
RDA	Rassemblement Démocratique Africain

RECAMP	Renforcement des Capacités Africaines de Maintien de la Paix
RUF	Revolutionary United Front (Sierra Leone)
SACU/CMA	Southern African Customs Union/Common Monetary Area
SADC	Southern African Development Community
SADCC	Southern African Development Coordination Conference (now SADC)
SALWs	small arms and light weapons
SAP	structural adjustment program
SLA	Sierra Leone Army
SLAJ	Sierra Leone Association of Journalists
SLPP	Sierra Leone People's Party
SSD	State Security Defense (Sierra Leone)
STD	sexually transmitted disease
TCR	Taxe de Coopération Régionale
TEU	Treaty on European Union
TRC	Truth and Reconciliation Commission (Sierra Leone)
TWP	True Whig Party (Liberia)
UDAO	Union Douanière de l'Afrique de l'Ouest
UDEAC	Union Douanière et Economique de l'Afrique Centrale
UDEAO	Union Douanière et Economique de l'Afrique de l'Ouest
UEMOA	Union Economique et Monétaire Ouest Africaine
ULAA	Union of Liberian Associations in the Americas
ULIMO	United Liberation Movement of Liberia for Democracy
ULIMO-J	ULIMO under Roosevelt Johnson
ULIMO-K	ULIMO under Alhaji Koromah
UMOA	Union Monétaire Ouest Africaine (now UEMOA)
UN	United Nations
UNAIDS	United Nations Joint Program on HIV/AIDS
UNAMSIL	United Nations Mission in Sierra Leone
UNDP	United Nations Development Programme
UNHCR	United Nations High Commissioner for Refugees
UNICEF	United Nations Children's Fund
UNITA	União Nacional para a Independência Total de Angola
UNMIL	United Nations Mission in Liberia
UNOGBIS	United Nations Peacebuilding Support Office in Guinea-Bissau
UNOMIL	United Nations Observer Mission to Liberia
UNOMSIL	United Nations Observer Mission in Sierra Leone
UNOSOM	United Nations Operation in Somalia
UNSCOL	United Nations Special Coordinating Office for Liberia
UNTAG	United Nations Technical Assistance Group

USAID	U.S. Agency for International Development
VOA	Voice of America
WAMI	West African Monetary Institute
WAMZ	West African Monetary Zone
WANEP	West African Network for Peacebuilding
WEU	Western European Union
WFP	World Food Program
WHO	World Health Organization

Bibliography

Abdullah, Ibrahim. "Bush Path to Destruction: The Origin and Character of the Revolutionary United Front/Sierra Leone." *Journal of Modern African Studies* 36, no. 2 (1998).

Abdullah, Ibrahim, and Patrick Mauna. "The Revolutionary United Front: A Revolt of the Lumpenproletariat." In Christopher Clapham, ed., *African Guerrillas.* London: James Currey, 1998.

Abdullah, Ibrahim, et al. "Lumpen Youth Culture and Political Violence: Sierra Leoneans Debate the RUF and the Civil War." *Africa Development* 22, nos. 3–4 (1997). Special Issue: "Lumpen Culture and Political Violence: The Sierra Leone Civil War."

Abi-Saab, Georges. *The United Nations Operation in the Congo, 1960–1964.* Oxford: Oxford University Press, 1978.

Aboagye, Festus. *ECOMOG: A Subregional Experience in Conflict Resolution, Management and Peacekeeping in Liberia.* Accra: Sedco Enterprise, 1999.

Adamolekun, Ladipo. *Sékou Touré's Guinea: An Experiment in Nation Building.* London: Methuen, 1976.

Ade-Ajayi, J. F. "Africa's Development Crisis in Its Historical Perspective." In Bade Onimode and Richard Synge, eds., *Issues in African Development: Essays in Honour of Adebayo Adedeji at Sixty-Five.* Ibadan, Nigeria: Heinemann, 1995.

Adebajo, Adekeye. *Building Peace in West Africa: Liberia, Sierra Leone, and Guinea-Bissau.* Boulder: Lynne Rienner, 2002.

———. *Liberia's Civil War: Nigeria, ECOMOG, and Regional Security in West Africa.* Boulder: Lynne Rienner, 2002.

Adebajo, Adekeye, and Chris Landsberg. "The Heirs of Nkrumah: Africa's New Interventionists." *Pugwash Occasional Paper* 2, no. 1 (January 2001).

———. "South Africa and Nigeria as Regional Hegemons." In Mwesiga Baregu and Christopher Landsberg, eds., *From Cape to Congo: Southern Africa's Evolving Security Challenges.* Boulder: Lynne Rienner, 2002.

Adebajo, Adekeye, and Michael O'Hanlon. "Africa: Toward a Rapid-Reaction Force." *SAIS Review* 17, no. 2 (Summer–Fall 1997).

Adedeji, Adebayo. "Africa and the Single European Act 1992." Paper submitted to the seminar "Europe 1992," organized by the Union Bank of Nigeria Plc, 12 June 1990.

――――. "Africa, the Third World, and the Search for a New Economic Order." Turkeyen Third World Lectures, Georgetown, Guyana, November 1976.

――――. "Comparative Strategies of Economic Decolonisation in Africa." In Ali Mazrui and C. Wondji, eds., *Africa Since 1935: UNESCO General History of Africa,* vol. 8. Oxford: Heinemann, 1993.

――――, ed. *Comprehending and Mastering African Conflicts: The Search for Sustainable Peace and Good Governance.* London: Zed Books, 1999.

――――. "Prospects for Regional Economic Cooperation in West Africa." *Journal of Modern African Studies* 8 (July 1970).

Adedeji, Adebayo, and Bamidele Ayo, eds. *People-Centred Democracy in Nigeria? The Search for Alternative Systems of Governance at the Grassroots.* Ibadan, Nigeria: Heinemann Educational Books and African Centre for Development and Strategic Studies, 2000.

Adekanye, J. 'Bayo. *The Retired Military as an Emergent Power Factor in Nigeria.* Ibadan, Nigeria: Heinemann Educational Books, 1999.

Adeleke, Ademola. "The Politics and Diplomacy of Peacekeeping in West Africa: The ECOWAS Operation in Liberia." *Journal of Modern African Studies* 33, no. 4 (1995).

Adelman, Howard, and Astri Suhrke, eds. *The Path of a Genocide: The Rwanda Crisis from Uganda to Zaire.* New Brunswick, N.J.: Transaction, 1999.

Adibe, Clement. "The Liberian Conflict and the ECOWAS-UN Partnership." *Third World Quarterly* 18, no. 3 (1997).

Adonai, J. L., and Kokou Fagla. "Une frontière débordée par la vie." *L'Autre Afrique* 2 (August 2001).

Afolayan, A. A. "Immigration and Expulsion of ECOWAS Aliens in Nigeria." *International Migration Review* 22, no. 1 (1988).

African Development. Vol. 22, nos. 2–3 (1997). Special Issue: "Youth, Culture, and Political Violence: The Sierra Leone Civil War."

Agbese, Pita. "Options for Democratic Control of the Military." Paper presented at the workshop "The Military Question in West Africa," Hill Station Hotel, Jos, Nigeria, 15 July 2000.

Ajala, Adekunle. "Background to the Establishment, Nature, and Structure of the Organisation of African Unity." *Nigerian Journal of International Affairs* 14, no. 1 (1988).

Ake, Claude. *Democracy and Development in Africa.* Washington, D.C.: Brookings Institution, 1996.

Akindele, R. A. "The Organisation of African Unity, 1963–1988: An Introductory Overview." *Nigerian Journal of International Affairs* 14, no. 1 (1988).

Alao, Abiodun. *Security Reform in Democratic Nigeria.* Conflict, Security, and Development Group Working Paper no. 2. London: Centre for Defence Studies, King's College, February 2000.

Alao, Abiodun, John Mackinlay, and 'Funmi Olonisakin. *Peacekeepers, Politicians, and Warlords: The Liberian Peace Process.* Tokyo: United Nations University Press, 1999.

Allen, Chris. "Understanding African Politics." *Review of African Political Economy* 22, no. 65 (September 1995).

Andrew, Christopher M. "France: Adjustment to Change." In Hedley Bull, ed., *The Expansion of International Society.* Oxford: Clarendon Press, 1984.

Anyang' Nyong'o, Peter, ed. *Popular Struggles for Democracy in Africa*. London: Zed Books, 1987.

Asante, S. K. B. *African Development: Adebayo Adedeji's Alternative Strategies*. Ibadan, Nigeria: Spectrum, 1991.

———. "ECOWAS/CEAO: Conflict and Cooperation in West Africa." In R. I. Onwuka and A. Sesay, eds., *The Future of Regionalism in Africa*. London: Macmillan, 1985.

———. "Ghana-Nigeria Fast-Track for the West African Integration Process: Problems and Prospects." Paper presented at the workshop "West African Integration: The Way Forward," organized by the Legon Centre for International Affairs and Friedrich Ebert Stiftung, Ho, Ghana, November 2000.

———. *The Political Economy of Regionalism in Africa: A Decade of the Economic Community of West African States (ECOWAS)*. New York: Praeger, 1986.

———. *Regionalism and Africa's Development: Expectations, Reality, and Challenge*. London: Macmillan, 1997.

———. *The Strategy of Regional Integration in Africa*. Accra: Gold-Type, 1996.

Asante, S. K. B., and Alex Abankwa. *A Study of the Impact of the West African Economic and Monetary Union (UEMOA) on Ghana*. Consultancy report, Accra, October 1999.

Ate, Bassey E. "Redesigning Foreign Policy for National Transformation: The Nigerian American Bilateral Partnership." Paper presented at the conference "Nigeria and the World After Forty Years," organized at the Nigerian Institute of International Affairs, Lagos, 5–6 December 2001.

Austin, Kathi. "Illicit Arms Brokers: Abiding and Abetting Atrocities." *Brown Journal of World Affairs* 9, no. 1 (Spring 2002).

Ayoob, Mohammed. *The Third World Security Predicament: State Making, Regional Conflict, and the International System*. Boulder: Lynne Rienner, 1995.

Azar, E. E. "Protracted International Conflicts: Ten Propositions." In E. E. Azar and J. Burton, eds., *International Conflict Resolution: Theory and Practice*. Boulder: Lynne Rienner, 1986.

Bach, Daniel. "Francophone Regionalism or Franco-African Regionalism?" In Daniel C. Bach and Anthony M. Kirk-Greene, eds., *States and Society in Francophone Africa*. London: Macmillan, 1995.

———. "Institutional Crisis and the Search for New Models." In Réal Lavergne, ed., *Regional Integration and Cooperation in West Africa: A Multidimensional Perspective*. Ottawa: International Development Research Council, 1997.

———. "The Politics of West African Economic Co-operation: CEAO and ECOWAS." *Journal of Modern African Studies* 21, no. 4 (1983).

———. "Regional Domination and Power Conversion in Africa: Soft and Hard Hegemony." Paper presented at the annual meeting of the African Studies Association, Nashville, 2000.

———. "Regionalization in a Comparative Perspective: Soft Structural Hegemony, Transstate Regionalization, and Deterritorialization in Africa." Paper presented at the forty-third annual convention of the International Studies Association, New Orleans, La., 2002.

———. "Revisiting a Paradigm." In Daniel C. Bach, ed., *Regionalization in Africa: Integration and Disintegration*. Oxford: James Currey, 1999.

Bangura, Yusuf. "Strategic Policy Failure and Governance in Sierra Leone." *Journal of Modern African Studies* 38, no. 4 (2000).

———. "Understanding the Political and Cultural Dynamics of the Sierra Leone War: A Critique of Paul Richards's *Fighting for the Rainforest*." In Ibrahim

Abdullah and Yusuf Bangura, eds., *African Development* 22, nos. 2–3 (1997). Special Issue: "Youth Culture and Political Violence: The Sierra Leone Civil War."

Bayart, Jean-François. *"Bis repetita:* La politique africaine de François Mitterrand de 1989 à 1995." Paper presented at the colloquium "La politique extérieure de François Mitterrand à l'épreuve de l'après-guerre froide," Centre d'Études et de Recherches Internationales, Paris, 13–15 May 1997.

———. *La politique africaine de François Mitterrand.* Paris: Karthala, 1983.

———. *The State in Africa: The Politics of the Belly.* London: Longman, 1993.

Bayart, Jean-François, Stephen Ellis, and Beatrice Hibou. *The Criminalization of the State in Africa.* Oxford: James Currey, 1998.

Baynham, Simon. "The Subordination of African Armies to Civilian Control: Theory and Praxis." *Africa Insight* 22, no. 4 (1992).

Berdal, Mats, and David M. Malone, eds. *Greed and Grievance: Economic Agendas in Civil Wars.* Boulder: Lynne Rienner, 2000.

Berkeley, Bill. *The Graves Are Not Yet Full: Race, Tribe, and Power in the Heart of Africa.* New York: Basic Books, 2001.

Berman, B., and John Lonsdale. *Unhappy Valley: Conflict in Kenya and Africa.* London: James Currey, 1992.

Berman, Eric G., and Katie E. Sams. *Peacekeeping in Africa: Capabilities and Culpabilities.* Geneva: UN Institute for Disarmament Research, 2000.

Berman, Harold. *Law and Revolution: The Formation of the Western Legal Tradition.* Cambridge: Harvard University Press, 1983.

Brown, M. Leann. "Nigeria and the ECOWAS Protocol on Free Movement and Residence." *Journal of Modern African Studies* 27, no. 2 (1989).

Cain, Kenneth L. "The Rape of Dinah: Human Rights, Civil War in Liberia, and Evil Triumphant." *Human Rights Quarterly* 21 (May 1999).

Cartwright, John. *Politics in Sierra Leone.* Toronto: University of Toronto Press, 1971.

Cervenka, Z. *The Organisation of African Unity.* London: Julien Friedman Press, 1997.

Chabal, Patrick, and Jean-Pascal Daloz. *Africa Works: Disorder as Political Instrument.* London: James Currey, 1999.

Charlton, Roger, and Roy May. "Warlords and Militarism in China." *Review of African Political Economy* 16, nos. 45–46 (Summer 1989).

Cheema, Shabbir G., and Dennis A. Rondinelli. "Decentralization and Development: Conclusions and Directions." In Shabbir G. Cheema and Dennis A. Rondinelli, eds., *Decentralization and Development: Policy Implication in Developing Countries.* Beverly Hills, Calif.: Sage, 1983.

Chipman, John. *French Power in Africa.* Oxford: Basil Blackwell, 1989.

———. "Managing the Politics of Parochialism." In M. Brown, ed., *Ethnic Conflict and International Security.* Princeton: Princeton University Press, 1993.

Cilliers, Jakkie, and Peggy Mason, eds. *Peace, Profit, or Plunder? The Privatisation of Security in War-Torn African Societies.* Pretoria: Institute for Security Studies, 1999.

Claeys, Anne-Sophie, and Alice Sindzingre. "The Impact of the Monetary Union on Developing Countries: The Case of the Franc Zone." In Franck Amalric and Marikki Stocchetti, eds., *The European Union Facing Global Responsibility: Past Records, Future Challenges.* Rome: Society for International Development, 2001.

Claustre, Pierre. *L'affaire Claustre: Autopsie d'une prise d'otages.* Paris: Karthala, 1990.

Clough, Michael. *Free at Last? U.S. Policy Toward Africa and the End of the Cold War*. New York: Council on Foreign Relations Press, 1992.

Cohen, Herman. *Intervening in Africa: Superpower Peacemaking in a Troubled Continent*. New York: St. Martin's, 2000.

Cohn, Ilene, and Guy S. Goodwin-Gill. *Child Soldiers: The Role of Children in Conflict*. Oxford: Clarendon Press, 1994.

Coleman, James, and Belmont Brice. "The Military in Sub-Saharan Africa." In John Johnson, ed., *The Role of the Military in Underdeveloped Countries*. Princeton: Princeton University Press, 1962.

Collier, Paul. "Africa's External Economic Relations, 1960–1990." *African Affairs* 13, no. 3 (July 1991).

———. "Doing Well out of War: An Economic Perspective." In Mats Berdal and David M. Malone, eds., *Greed and Grievance: Economic Agendas in Civil Wars*. Boulder: Lynne Rienner, 2000.

———, ed. *Regional Integration and Trade Liberalization in Sub-Saharan Africa*. Vol. 1, *Framework, Issues, and Methodological Perspectives*. New York: St. Martin's, 1997.

Collier, Paul, and Anke Hoeffler. "Justice-Seeking and Loot-Seeking in Civil War." Washington, D.C.: Development Economics Research Group, World Bank, February 1999. Mimeo.

Cousens, Elizabeth M., and Chetan Kumar. *Peacebuilding as Politics: Cultivating Peace in Fragile Societies*. Boulder: Lynne Rienner, 2001.

Cox, Robert W. *Production, Power, and World Order: Social Forces in the Making of History*. New York: Columbia University Press, 1987.

Cronje, Suzanne. *The World and Nigeria*. London: Sidgwick and Jackson, 1972.

Darlington, Charles, and Alice Darlington. *African Betrayal*. New York: David Mackay, 1968.

Davenport, Michael. *Identification Study for Reinforcing the Capacity of the ECOWAS Secretariat*. London: March 2000. Mimeo.

Decalo, Samuel. *Coups and Army Rule in Africa*. 2nd ed. New Haven, Conn.: Yale University Press, 1990.

———. "Not by Democracy Alone." *Journal of African Policy Studies* 1, no. 3 (1995).

Deng, Mading Francis. "State Collapse: The Humanitarian Challenge to the United Nations." In I. William Zartman, ed., *Collapsed States: The Disintegration and Restoration of Legitimate Authority*. Boulder: Lynne Rienner, 1995.

de Waal, Alex. *Famine Crimes: Politics and the Disaster Relief Industry in Africa*. Oxford: James Currey, 1997.

———, ed. *Who Fights Also Cares? War and Humanitarian Action in Africa*. Asmara: Africa World Press, 2000.

Diamond, Larry, Juan Linz, and Seymour Martin Lipset. *Democracy in Developing Countries*. Vol. 2, *Africa*. Boulder: Lynne Rienner, 1988.

———. "What Makes for Democracy." In Larry Diamond et al., eds., *Politics in Developing Nations: Comparing Experiences with Democracy*. Boulder: Lynne Rienner, 1995.

Durch, William. *Constructing Regional Security: The Role of Arms Transfers, Arms Control, and Reassurance*. New York: Palgrave, 2000.

ECOWAS (Economic Community of West African States). *Economic Community of West African States: 2000*. Interim report by the executive secretary, ECW/CM XLVVI/2, Abuja, 2000.

———. *Evaluation of Implementation of the Moratorium During the First Three Years (3) (1998–2001)*. Meeting of Ministers of Foreign Affairs, Dakar, 17 December 2001.

————. *Executive Secretary's Reports: Twenty-fifth Anniversary Report*. Abuja: ECOWAS, 2000. Available at www.ecowas.int/sitecedeao/english/regional.htm.

————. *Le progrès continu dépend d'un effort soutenu: Rapport intérimaire du Secrétaire Exécutif M. A. Bundu*. Lagos: Executive Secretariat, November 1992.

————. *Treaty of ECOWAS*. Abuja: ECOWAS Secretariat, 1993. Available at www.ecowas.int/sitecedeao/english/stat-1.htm.

Elaigwu. J. I., and Ali Mazrui. "Nation-Building and Changing Political Structures." In Ali Mazrui and C. Wondji, eds., *Africa Since 1935*. Berkeley: University of California Press, 1993.

El-Ayouty, Yassin, ed. *The Organization of African Unity After Thirty Years*. London: Praeger, 1994.

El-Ayouty, Yassin, and I. William Zartman, eds. *The OAU After Twenty Years*. New York: Praeger, 1984.

Ellis, Stephen. "Liberia 1989–1994: A Study of Ethnic and Spiritual Violence." *African Affairs* 94, no. 375 (April 1995).

————. *The Mask of Anarchy: The Destruction of Liberia and the Religious Dimensions of an African Civil War*. London: Hurst, 1999.

Ero, Comfort. "The Future of ECOMOG in West Africa." In Jakkie Cilliers and Greg Mills, eds., *From Peacekeeping to Complex Emergencies: Peace Support Missions in Africa*. Johannesburg: South African Institute of International Affairs, 1999.

————. *Sierra Leone's Security Complex*. Conflict, Security, and Development Group Working Paper no. 3. London: Centre for Defence Studies, King's College, June 2000.

Esedebe, P. Olisanwuche. *Pan-Africanism. The Idea and Movement, 1776–1963*. Washington, D.C.: Howard University Press, 1982.

European Commission. *The European Union, the Countries of West Africa, and WAEMU*. Brussels: European Commission, 1997.

Evans, Peter, Dietrich Rueschemeyer, and Theda Skocpol, eds. *Bringing the State Back In*. Cambridge: Cambridge University Press, 1985.

Fahnbulleh, H. Boima. *Disarmament and the International Community in the Resolution of the Liberian Civil War*. Monrovia: Yandia Press, 1994.

Faligot, R., and P. Krop. *La piscine*. Paris: Seuil, 1985.

Featherstone, Kevin. "The Political Dynamics of Economic and Monetary Union." In Laura Cram, Desmond Dinan, and Neill Nugent, eds., *Developments in the European Union*. New York: St. Martin's, 2000.

Fine, Jeffrey, and Stephen Yeo. "Regional Integration in Sub-Saharan Africa: Dead End or Fresh Start?" In Ademola Oyejide, Ibrahim Elbadawi, and Paul Collier, eds., *Regional Integration and Trade Liberalization in Sub-Saharan Africa*. Vol. 1, *Framework, Issues, and Methodological Perspectives*. New York: St. Martin's, 1997.

Foccart, Jacques. *Tous les soirs avec de Gaulle*, vol. 1. Paris: Fayard, 1997.

Frazer, Jendayi. "The Africa Crisis Response Initiative: Self-Interested Humanitarianism." *Brown Journal of World Affairs* 4, no. 2 (Summer–Fall 1997).

Furley, Oliver. "Introduction: Africa—The Habit of Conflict." In Oliver Furley, ed., *Conflict in Africa*. London: I. B. Tauris, 1995.

Gaillard, Philippe. "A feu la coopération." *Jeune Afrique,* 10–16 February 1998.

————. *Foccart parle*. 2 vols. Paris: Fayard/Jeune Afrique, 1995, 1997.

Gardinier, David. "Gabon: Limited Reform and Regime Survivial." In John F. Clark and David E. Gardinier, eds., *Political Reform in Francophone Africa*. Boulder: Westview Press, 1997.

Gershoni, Yerkutiel. "From ECOWAS to ECOMOG: The Liberian Crisis and the Struggle for Political Hegemony in West Africa." *Liberian Studies Journal* 18, no. 1 (1993).

———. "Military and Diplomatic Strategies in the Liberian War." *Liberian Studies Journal* 22, no. 2 (1997).

Gifford, Paul. *Christianity and Politics in Doe's Liberia.* Cambridge: Cambridge University Press, 1993.

Gifford, Prosser, and W. M. Roger Louis. *The Transfer of Power in Africa: Decolonization, 1940–1960.* New Haven, Conn.: Yale University Press, 1982.

Glaser, Antoine, and Stephen Smith. *Ces messieurs Afrique.* Vol. 1, *Le Paris: Village du continent noir.* Paris: Calmann-Lévy, 1992.

———. *Ces messieurs Afrique.* Vol. 2, *Des réseaux aux lobbies.* Paris: Calmann-Lévy, 1997.

Goldsworthy, David. "Civilian Control of the Military in Black Africa." *African Affairs* 80, no. 318 (1981).

Gomes, Solomon. "The OAU, State Sovereignty, and Regional Security." In Edmond Keller and Donald Rothchild, eds., *Africa in the New International Order: Rethinking State Sovereignty and Regional Security.* Boulder: Lynne Rienner, 1996.

Gowon, Yakubu. "The Economic Community of West African States: A Study of Political and Economic Integration." Ph.D. thesis, Warwick University, February 1984.

Grindle, Merilee S. *Challenging the State: Crisis and Innovation in Latin America and Africa.* Cambridge: Cambridge University Press, 1996.

Gusfield, Joseph. "Tradition and Modernity: Misplaced Polarities in the Study of Social Change." *American Journal of Sociology* 72 (January 1967).

Haas, Ernst B. *The Uniting of Europe.* Stanford: Stanford University Press, 1968.

Hardin, Russell. *One for All: The Logic of Group Conflict.* Princeton: Princeton University Press, 1995.

Harris, David. "From 'Warlord' to 'Democratic' President: How Charles Taylor Won the 1997 Liberian Elections." *Journal of Modern African Studies* 37, no. 3 (1999).

Harris, Katherine. *African and American Values: Liberia and West Africa.* Lanham, Md.: University Press of America, 1985.

Hartung, William D., and Bridget Moix. *Deadly Legacy: U.S. Arms to Africa and the Congo War.* New York: World Policy Institute, January 2000.

Hayward, Fred. "Sierra Leone: State Consolidation, Fragmentation, and Decay." In Donal B. Cruise O'Brien et al., eds., *Contemporary West African States.* Cambridge: Cambridge University Press, 1991.

Heilbrum, John R. "Togo: The National Conference and Stalled Reform." In John Clark and David Gardinier, eds., *Political Reform in Francophone Africa.* Boulder: Lynne Rienner, 1997.

Hettne, Björn. "The New Regionalism: A Prologue." In Björn Hettne, Andrés Inotai, and Osvaldo Sunkel, eds., *The New Regionalism and the Frontiers of Security and Development,* vol. 4. London: Macmillan, 2000.

Heyer, Judith, Pepe Roberts, and Gavin Williams, eds. *Rural Development in Tropical Africa.* New York: St. Martin's, 1980.

Hirsch, John. *Sierra Leone: Diamonds and the Struggle for Democracy.* Boulder: Lynne Rienner, 2001.

———. "War in Sierra Leone." *Survival* 43, no. 3 (Autumn 2001).

Hlope, Stephen S. *Class, Ethnicity, and Politics in Liberia: A Class Analysis of Power Struggles in the Tolbert and Tubman Administrations from 1944–1975.* Washington, D.C.: University Press of America, 1979.

Hoeffler, Anke. "Economic Determinants of Conflict." *Bulletin of the Conflict, Security, and Development Group* (Centre for Defence Studies, King's College) no. 16 (2002).

Hogg, Ian V., and John S. Weeks. *Military Small Arms of the Twentieth Century.* 4th ed. Northfield, Ill.: DBI, 1981.

Holsti, Kalevi. "Political Causes of Humanitarian Emergencies." In E. Wayne Nafziger, Frances Stewart, and Raimo Väyrynen, eds., *The Origins of Humanitarian Emergencies: War and Displacement in Developing Countries.* 2 vols. Oxford: Oxford University Press, 2000.

Hoskyns, Catherine. *The Congo Since Independence, January 1960–December 1961.* London: Oxford University Press, 1965.

Huband, Mark. *The Liberian Civil War.* London: Frank Cass, 1998.

Hugon, Philippe. *La zone franc à l'heure de l'euro.* Paris: Karthala, 1999.

Human Rights Watch. *The New Racism: The Political Manipulation of Ethnicity in Côte d'Ivoire.* New York: Human Rights Watch, August 2001.

Huntington, Samuel. *The Soldier and the State: The Theory and Practice of Civil-Military Relations.* Cambridge: Harvard University Press, 1957.

Hutchful, Eboe. *Ghana's Adjustment Experience: The Paradox of Reform.* Oxford: James Currey, 2002.

———. "Military Issues in the Transition to Democracy." In Eboe Hutchful and Abdoulaye Bathily, eds., *The Military and Militarism in Africa.* Dakar: CODESRIA, 1998.

———. "Oil Companies and Environmental Pollution in Nigeria." In Claude Ake, ed., *The Political Economy of Nigeria.* Ibadan, Nigeria: Longman, 1985.

———. "Peacekeeping Under Conditions of Resource Stringency." In Jakkie Cilliers and Greg Mills, eds., *From Peacekeeping to Complex Emergencies: Peace Support Missions in Africa.* Johannesburg: South African Institute of International Affairs, 1999.

———. "Pulling Back from the Brink: Ghana's Experiences." In Gavin Cawthra and Robin Luckham, eds., *Security Structures and Democratic Governance in Conflict-Torn Societies.* London: Zed Books, 2003.

———. "Understanding the African Security Crisis." In Abdel-Fatau Musah and J. Kayode Fayemi, eds., *Mercenaries: An African Security Dilemma.* London: Pluto Press, 2000.

Hutchful, Eboe, and Abdoulaye Bathily, eds. *The Military and Militarism in Africa.* Dakar: CODESRIA, 1998.

Hveem, Helge. "Political Regionalism: Master or Servant of Economic Internationalization?" In Björn Hettne, Andrés Inotai, and Osvaldo Sunkel, eds., *Globalism and the New Regionalism,* vol. 1. London: Macmillan, 2000.

Igué, John O., and Bio Soulé. *L'état-entrepôt au Bénin: Commerce informel ou solution à la crise?* Paris: Karthala, 1992.

Ihonvbere, Julius. "Are Things Falling Apart? The Military and the Crisis of Democratization in Nigeria." *Journal of Modern African Studies* 34, no. 2 (1996).

Ihonvbere, Julius, and Terisa Turner. "Africa in the Post Communist Era: Constraints, Pressures, and Prospects for the Twenty-First Century." *Round Table* no. 328 (October 1993).

Ilchman, Warren, and Ravindra C. Bhargava. "Balanced Thought and Economic Growth." In Fred W. Riggs, ed., *Frontiers of Development Administration.* Durham, N.C.: Duke University Press, 1971.

IPA (International Peace Academy). *The Infrastructure of Peace in Africa: Assessing the Peacebuilding Capacity of African Institutions.* New York: IPA, September 2002.

———. *NEPAD: African Initiative, New Partnership?* New York: IPA, September 2002.

———. *Report of the Joint OAU/IPA Task Force on Peacemaking and Peacekeeping in Africa.* New York: IPA, November–December 1998.

IPA and ECOWAS. *Toward a Pax West Africana: Building Peace in a Troubled Sub-Region.* New York: IPA, September 2001.

Jackson, Henry E. *From the Congo to Soweto: U.S. Foreign Policy Toward Africa Since 1960.* New York: Morrow, 1982.

Jebuni, Charles D., Olawale Ogunkola, and Charles C. Soludo. "A Case-Study of the Economic Community of West African States." In Ademola Oyejide, Ibrahim Elbadawi, and Stephen Yeo, eds., *Regional Integration and Trade Liberalization in Sub-Saharan Africa.* Vol. 3, *Regional Case Studies.* London: Macmillan, 1999.

Johnson-Thomas, Brian. "Anatomy of a Shady Deal." In Lora Lumpe, ed., *Running Guns: The Global Black Market in Small Arms.* Norwegian Initiative on Small Arms Transfers and the International Peace Research Institute. London: Zed Books, 2000.

Kahler, Miles. *Decolonization in Britain and France: The Domestic Consequences of International Relations.* Princeton: Princeton University Press, 1984.

Kandeh, Jimmy D. "Politicization of Ethnic Identities in Sierra Leone." *African Studies Review* 35, no. 1 (April 1992).

Kaplan, Robert. "The Coming Anarchy." *Atlantic Monthly* 271, no. 2 (February 1994).

———. *Ends of the Earth: A Journey at the End of the Twenty-First Century.* New York: Random House, 1996.

Keen, David. "Crime and Access to Resources." In E. Wayne Nafziger, Frances Stewart, and Raimo Väyrynen, eds., *War, Hunger, and Displacement: The Origins of Humanitarian Emergencies.* Oxford: Oxford University Press, 2000.

———. *The Economic Functions of Violence in Civil Wars.* Adelphi Paper no. 320. Oxford: Oxford University Press, 1998.

———. "Incentives and Disincentives for Violence." In Mats Berdal and David M. Malone, eds., *Greed and Grievance: Economic Agendas in Civil Wars.* Boulder: Lynne Rienner, 2000.

———. "The Political Economy of War." In E. Wayne Nafziger, Frances Stewart, and Raimo Väyrynen, eds., *War, Hunger, and Displacement: The Origins of Humanitarian Emergencies.* Oxford: Oxford University Press, 2000.

———. "A Rational Kind of Madness." *Oxford Development Studies* 25, no. 1 (1997).

Kelly, Michael P. *A State in Disarray: Conditions of Chad's Survival.* Boulder: Westview Press, 1986.

Kennes, Walter. *Competing in the Big League: Small Developing Countries and Global Markets.* London: Macmillan, 2000.

Kilson, Martin. *Political Change in a West African State.* Cambridge: Harvard University Press, 1966.

Koroma, Abdul Karim. *Sierra Leone: The Agony of a Nation.* Freetown: Andromeda, 1996.

Kramer, Reed. "Liberia: A Casualty of the Cold War's End?" *CSIS Africa Notes* no. 174 (July 1995).

Laïdi, Zaki. *The Super Powers and Africa: The Constraints of a Rivalry, 1960–1990.* Chicago: University of Chicago Press, 1990.

Lambert, Michael C. "Violence and the War of Words: Ethnicity vs. Nationalism in the Casamance (Senegal)." *Africa* 68 (Fall 1998).

Landsberg, Chris. "From African Renaissance to NEPAD . . . and back to the Renaissance." *Journal of African Elections* 1, no. 2 (September 2002).

Leaning, Jennifer, and Sam Arie. *Human Security: A Framework for Assessment in Conflict and Transition*. Washington, D.C.: U.S. Agency for International Development/Complex Emergency Response and Transition Initiative, December 2000.

Le Billon, Philippe. "The Political Economy of Resource Wars." In Jackie Cilliers and Christian Dietrich, eds., *Angola's War Economy: The Role of Oil and Diamonds*. Pretoria: Institute for Security Studies, 2000.

Lelart, Michel. "The Franc Zone and European Monetary Integration." In Daniel Bach, ed., *Regionalization in Africa: Integration and Disintegration*. Oxford: James Currey, 1999.

Lemarchand, René. *The Green and the Black: Qadhafi's Policies in Africa*. Bloomington: Indiana University Press, 1988.

Lewis, Peter. "From Prebendalism to Predation: The Political Economy of Decline in Nigeria." *Journal of Modern African Studies* 34, no. 1 (1996).

Liberty, C. E. Zamba. "Butuo: A Lilliputian Testament to a Struggle." *Liberian Studies Journal* 23, no. 1 (1998).

Liebenow, Gus. *The Evolution of Privilege*. Ithaca: Cornell University Press, 1969.
———. *Liberia, the Quest for Democracy*. Bloomington: Indiana University Press, 1987.

Lock, Peter. "Africa, Military Downsizing, and the Growth of the Security Industry." In Jakkie Cilliers and Peggy Mason, eds., *Peace, Profit, or Plunder: The Privatization of Security in War-Torn African Countries*. Halfway House, South Africa: Institute for Security Studies, 1999.

Lodgaard, Sverre, and Carsten F. Rønnfeldt, eds. *A Moratorium on Light Weapons in West Africa*. Oslo: Norwegian Initiative on Small Arms Transfers, May 1998. Available at www.nisat.org/publications.

Loescher, Gil, and Laila Monhan, eds. *Refugees and International Relations*. Oxford: Oxford University Press, 1989.

Lowenkopf, M. *Politics in Liberia: The Conservative Road to Development*. Stanford: Stanford University Press, 1976.

Lucas, Emma T. "Sexual Abuses as Wartime Crimes Against Women and Children: The Case of Liberia." *Liberian Studies Journal* 22, no. 2 (1997).

Luckham, Robin. *The Nigerian Military: A Sociological Analysis of Authority and Revolt, 1960–1967*. Cambridge: Cambridge University Press, 1971.

Lumpe, Lora. *Civil Society Support for the Program for Coordination and Assistance on Security and Development*. Norwegian Initiative on Small Arms Transfers, Bamako, Mali, March 1999. Available at www.nisat.org/west%20africa/civil_society_support_for_the.htm.

Lumumba-Kasongo, Tukumbi. "Social Movements and the Quest for Democracy in Liberia: MOJA and Its Transition into a Political Party." In M. Mamdani and Ernest Wamba-dia-Wamba, eds., *African Studies in Social Movements and Democracy*. Dakar: CODESRIA, 1995.

Lyons, Terrence. *Voting for Peace: Post Conflict Elections in Liberia*. Washington, D.C.: Brookings Institution, 1998.

Machel, Graca. "The Impact of Armed Conflict on Children: A Critical Review of Progress Made and Obstacles Encountered in Increasing Protection for War-Affected Children." Paper presented at a conference in Winnipeg, Canada, September 2000.

Mackinlay, John. "War Lords." *RUSI Journal* 143, no. 2 (April 1998).

Madsen, Wayne. *Genocide and Covert Operations in Africa, 1993–1999.* Lewiston: Edwin Mellen Press, 1999.

Magyar, Karl, and Earl Conteh-Morgan, eds. *Peacekeeping in Africa: ECOMOG in Liberia.* London: Macmillan, 1998.

Mahoney, Richard D. *JFK: Ordeal in Africa.* Oxford: Oxford University Press, 1983.

Makgoba, Malegapuru William, ed. *African Renaissance.* Cape Town: Tafelberg, 1999.

Malan, Mark, Phenyo Rakate, and Angela McIntyre. *Peacekeeping in Sierra Leone: UNAMSIL Hits the Home Straight.* Pretoria: Institute for Security Studies, 2002.

Mamdani, Mahmood. *Citizen and Subject: Contemporary Africa and the Legacy of Late Colonialism.* Princeton: Princeton University Press, 1996.

Mamdani, Mahmood, and Ernest Wamba-dia-Wamba, eds. *African Studies in Social Movements and Democracy.* Dakar: CODESRIA, 1995.

Manning, Patrick. *Francophone Sub-Saharan Africa.* 2nd ed. New York: Cambridge University Press, 1998.

Marchal, Roland. "France and Africa: The Emergence of Essential Reforms?" *International Affairs* 74, no. 2 (1998).

Marchesin, Philippe. "La politique africaine de la France en transition." *Politique Africaine* 71 (October 1998).

———. *L'aide publique au développement en 1997.* Observatoire permanent de la coopération française. Paris: Karthala, 1997.

Martin, Guy. "France's African Policy in Transition: Disengagement and Redeployment." In Luis Ondo Ayang et al., eds., *Mélanges euro-africains en hommage au Professeur Max Liniger-Goumaz,* vol. 1. Madrid: Editorial Claves para el Futuro, 2001.

———. "Francophone Africa in the Context of Franco-American Relations." In John W. Harbeson and Donald Rothchild, eds., *Africa in World Politics: Post–Cold War Challenges,* 2nd ed. Boulder: Westview Press, 1995.

Masson, Paul, and Catherine Pattillo. *Monetary Union in West Africa (ECOWAS): Is It Desirable and How Could It Be Achieved?* International Monetary Fund (IMF) Occasional Paper no. 204. Washington, D.C.: IMF, 2000.

Mazrui, Ali A., ed. *Africa Since 1935.* General History of Africa, vol. 8. Berkeley: University of California Press, 1993.

———. *The African Condition.* New York: Cambridge University Press, 1980.

———. *Soldiers and Kinsmen in Uganda: The Making of a Military Ethnocracy.* London: Sage, 1975.

McCarthy, Colin. "SACU and the Rand Zone." In Daniel Bach, ed., *Regionalization in Africa: Integration and Disintegration.* Oxford: James Currey, 1999.

McGowan, Pat, and Thomas Johnson. "Sixty Coups in Thirty Years: Further Evidence Regarding African Military Coups d'Etat." *Journal of Modern African Studies* 24, no. 3 (1986).

McIntrye, Angela, Kwesi Aning, and Prosper Addo. "Politics, War, and Youth Culture in Sierra Leone: An Alternative Interpretation." *African Security Review* 11, no. 3 (2002).

McRae, Rob, ed. *Human Security and the New Diplomacy: Protecting People, Promoting Peace.* Montreal: McGill-Queen's University Press, 2001.

Meagher, Kate. "Informal Integration or Economic Subvention: The Development and Organization of Parallel Trade in Sub-Saharan Africa." In Réal Lavergne, ed., *Regional Integration and Cooperation in West Africa: A Multidimensional Perspective.* Ottawa: International Development Research Council, 1997.

Melvern, Linda. *A People Betrayed: The Role of the West in Rwanda's Genocide.* New York: Zed Books, 2000.

Milenky, Edward S. "Developmental Nationalism in Practice: The Problems and Progress of the Andean Group." *Inter-American Economic Affairs* 25, no. 3 (1971).

Mills, Greg, and John Stremlau, eds. *The Privatisation of Security in Africa.* Johannesburg: South African Institute of International Affairs, 1999.

Mittelman, James H., and Richard Falk. "Global Hegemony and Regionalism." In James H. Mittelman, ed., *The Globalization Syndrome: Transformation and Resistance.* Princeton: Princeton University Press, 2000.

Mkandawire, Thandika. "Crisis Management and the Making of Choiceless Democracies." In Richard Joseph, ed., *State, Conflict, and Democracy in Africa.* Boulder: Lynne Rienner, 1999.

———. "Shifting Commitments and National Cohesion in African Countries." In Lennart Wohlegemuth et al., eds., *Common Security and Civil Society in Africa.* Stockholm: Afrikainstitutet, 1999.

———. "The Terrible Toll of Post-Colonial 'Rebel Movements' in Africa: Towards an Explanation of the Violence Against the Peasantry." *Journal of Modern African Studies* 40, no. 2 (June 2002).

Momoh, Abubakar. "Popular Struggles in Nigeria." *African Journal of Political Science* 1, no. 2 (1996).

Mondjanagni, A. C., ed. *People's Participation in Development in Black Africa.* Douala, Cameroon: Pan-African Institute for Development, 1984.

Montague, Dena. "The Business of War and the Prospects for Peace in Sierra Leone." *Brown Journal of World Affairs* 9, no. 1 (Spring 2002).

Morrow, John H. *First American Ambassador to Guinea.* New Brunswick, N.J.: Rutgers University Press, 1968.

Mortimer, Robert. "From ECOMOG to ECOMOG II: Intervention in Sierra Leone." In John W. Harbeson and Donald Rothchild, eds., *Africa in World Politics: The African State System in Flux,* 3rd ed. Boulder: Westview Press, 2000.

Mukonoweshuro, Eliphas. *Colonialism, Class Formation, and Underdevelopment in Sierra Leone.* Lanham, Md.: University Press of America, 1993.

Musah, Abdel-Fatau. "Small Arms: A Time Bomb Under West Africa's Democratization Process." *Brown Journal of World Affairs* 9 (Spring 2002).

Musah, Abdel-Fatau, and J. Kayode Fayemi, eds. *Mercenaries: An African Security Dilemma.* London: Pluto Press, 2000.

Muyangwa, Monde, and Margaret Vogt. *An Assessment of the OAU Mechanism for Conflict Prevention, Management, and Resolution, 1993–2000.* New York: International Peace Academy, November 2000.

Nafziger, E. Wayne, and Juha Auvinen. "The Economic Causes of Humanitarian Emergencies." In E. Wayne Nafziger, Frances Stewart, and Raimo Väyrynen, eds., *The Origins of Humanitarian Emergencies: War and Displacement in Developing Countries.* 2 vols. Oxford: Oxford University Press, 2000.

Naldi, Gino J. *The Organization of African Unity: An Analysis of Its Role.* 2nd ed. London: Mansell, 1999.

Nkrumah, Kwame. *Africa Must Unite.* London: Heinemann, 1963.

Nowrojee, Binaifir. "Joining Forces: UN and Regional Peacekeeping—Lessons from Liberia." *Harvard Human Rights Journal* 18 (Spring 1995).

Nugent, Paul, and Anthony I. Asiwaju. "Introduction: The Paradox of African Boundaries." In Paul Nugent and Anthony I. Asiwaju, eds., *African Boundaries.* London: Pinter, 1996.

OAU (Organization of African Unity). *The International Panel of Eminent Persons to Investigate the 1994 Genocide in Rwanda and the Surrounding Events*. July 2000.
———. *Treaty Establishing the African Economic Community*. Abuja, 3 June 1991.
Obasanjo, Olusegun. *My Command*. London: Heinemann, 1980.
Obasanjo, Olusegun, and Felix Mosha, eds. *Africa: Rise to Challenge*. New York: African Leadership Forum, 1993.
Obi, Cyril. *Structural Adjustment, Oil, and Popular Struggles: The Deepening Crisis of State Legitimacy in Nigeria*. CODESRIA Monograph Series no. 1. Dakar: CODESRIA, 1997.
Olojede, Iyabo, Banji Fajonyomi, Ighodalo Akhape, and Suraju Mudashiru. *Nigeria: Oil Pollution, Community Dissatisfaction, and Threat to National Peace and Security*. Occasional Paper Series vol. 4, no. 3. Harare: African Association of Political Science, 2000.
Olonisakin, 'Funmi. "An International War Crimes Tribunal for Africa: Problems and Prospects." *African Journal of Contemporary and International Law* 9, no. 4 (1997).
———. "UN Co-operation with Regional Organizations in Peacekeeping: The Experience of ECOMOG and UNOMIL in Liberia." *International Peacekeeping* 3, no. 3 (Autumn 1996).
Omach, Paul. "The African Crisis Response Initiative: Domestic Politics and Convergence of National Interests." *African Affairs* 99, no. 394 (January 2000).
Oman, Charles. *Globalisation and Regionalization: The Challenge for Developing Countries*. Paris: Organization for Economic Cooperation and Development, 1994.
Onwuka, Ralph. "The Role of ECOWAS in Ensuring a Working Peace System." In A. A. Owusekun, ed., *Towards an African Economic Community: Lessons and Experiences from ECOWAS*. Ibadan: Nigerian Institute of Social and Economic Research, 1986.
Onwuka, R. I., and A. Sesay, eds. *The Future of Regionalism in Africa*. London: Macmillan, 1985.
Péan, Pierre. *L'homme de l'ombre: Jacques Foccart*. Paris: Fayard, 1990.
Péan, Pierre, and Jean-Pierre Séréni. *Les émirs de la République*. Paris: Stock, 1983.
Plessz, Nicholas. *Problems and Prospects of Regional Integration in West Africa*. Montreal: McGill University Press, 1968.
Pollis, Adamantia, and Peter Schwab, eds. *Human Rights: New Perspectives, New Realities*. Boulder: Lynne Rienner, 2000.
Poulton, R., and I. Youssouf, eds. *A Peace of Timbuktu: Democratic Governance, Development, and African Peacekeeping*, UNIDIR/2000/19. New York: United Nations Institute for Disarmament Research, 1998.
Prah, Kwesi, ed. *African Languages for the Mass Education of Africans*. Cape Town: Centre for Advanced Studies of African Society, 1995.
———. *Between Distinction and Extinction: The Harmonisation and Standardisation of African Languages*. Cape Town: Centre for Advanced Studies of African Society, 1998.
———. *Mother Tongue for Scientific and Technological Development in Africa*. Cape Town: Centre for Advanced Studies of African Society, 1993.
Puetz Detlev, and Joachim von Braun. "Parallel Markets and the Rural Poor in a West African Setting." In Michael Roemer and Christine Jones, eds., *Markets in Developing Countries: Parallel, Fragmented, and Black*. San Francisco: Institute for Contemporary Studies Press, 1991.
Rashid, Ismail. "Subaltern Reactions: Lumpens, Students, and the Left." *African Development* 22, nos. 2–3 (1997).

Regan, Patrick. *Internal Wars and Foreign Powers: Outside Intervention in Inter-state Conflicts*. Ann Arbor: University of Michigan Press, 2000.

Reno, William. *Corruption and State Politics in Sierra Leone*. Cambridge: Cambridge University Press, 1995.

———. "Reinvention of an African Patrimonial State: Charles Taylor's Liberia." *Third World Quarterly* 16, no. 11 (1995).

———. *Warlord Politics and African States*. Boulder: Lynne Rienner, 1998.

Rice, Edward E. *Wars of the Third Kind: Conflict in Underdeveloped Countries*. Berkeley: University of California Press, 1988.

Rich, Paul B. "Warlords, State Fragmentation, and the Dilemma of Humanitarian Intervention." *Small Wars and Insurgencies* 10, no. 1 (Spring 1999).

Richards, Paul. *Fighting for the Rainforest: War, Youth, and Resources in Sierra Leone*. Oxford: James Currey, 1996.

———. "Rebellion in Liberia and Sierra Leone: A Crisis of Youth?" In Oliver Furley, ed., *Conflict in Africa*. London: I. B. Tauris, 1996.

Rimmer, Douglas. "Le Nigeria ne sera pas, dans l'Afrique de demain, une puissance économique et politique significative." *Marchés Tropicaux et Méditerranéens* no. 3000 (9 May 2003).

Rivière, Claude. *Guinea: The Mobilization of a People*. Ithaca: Cornell University Press, 1978.

Rondinelli, Dennis A., John R. Nellis, and G. Shabbir Cheema. *Decentralization in Developing Countries: A Review of Recent Experience*. World Bank Staff Working Paper no. 581. Washington, D.C.: World Bank, 1983.

Russell, Ruth B., and J. Nuther. *A History of the United Nations Charter*. Washington, D.C.: Brookings Institution, 1958.

Sawyer, Amos. "Children, Governance, and Development: Toward a Framework for Protecting the Rights of West Africa's Children." Paper presented at the conference "War-Affected Children in West Africa," sponsored by UNICEF and the governments of Ghana and Canada, Accra, 27–28 April 2000.

———. *The Dynamics of Conflict Management in Liberia*. Occasional Paper no. 12. Accra: Institute of Economic Affairs, 1997.

———. *Effective Immediately: Dictatorship in Liberia, 1980–1986: A Personal Perspective*. Bremen, Germany: Liberian Working Group, 1987.

———. *The Emergence of Autocracy in Liberia: Tragedy and Challenge*. San Francisco: Institute for Contemporary Studies Press, 1992.

Schiff, Rebecca. "Civil-Military Relations Reconsidered: A Theory of Concordance." *Armed Forces and Society* 22, no. 1 (1995).

Schraeder, Peter. "'Forget the Rhetoric and Boost the Geo-Politics': Emerging Trends in the Bush Administration's Foreign Policy Towards Africa, 2001." *African Affairs* 100, no. 400 (July 2001).

———. "France and the Great Game in Africa." *Current History,* May 1997.

———. "The U.S. and France in Africa: Competition or Collaboration?" Paper presented at the forty-second annual meeting of the African Studies Association, Philadelphia, 11–14 November 1999.

Sesay, Amadu. "The Mano River Union: Politics of Survival or Dependence?" In R. I. Onwuka and A. Sesay, eds., *The Future of Regionalism in Africa*. London: Macmillan, 1985.

———, ed. *The OAU After Twenty-five Years*. Cambridge: St. Martin's, 1990.

Sesay, Amadu, Olusola Ojo, and Orobola Fasehun. *The OAU After Twenty Years*. Boulder: Westview Press, 1984.

Shaw, Timothy, and Clement Adibe. "Africa and Global Developments in the Twenty-First Century." *International Journal* 51 (Winter 1995–1996).

Short, Clare. Keynote address at the symposium "Security Sector Reform and Military Expenditure," London, 17 February 2000. Available at www.dfid.gov.uk.

Smaldone, Joseph P. "Mali and West African Small Arms Moratorium." In Jeffrey Boutwell and Micheal T. Klare, eds., *Light Weapons and Civil Conflict: Controlling the Tools of Violence.* Carnegie Commission on Preventing Deadly Conflict. Lanham, Md.: Rowman and Littlefield, 1999.

Smith, Tony, ed. *The End of European Empire: Decolonization After the Second World War.* Lexington, Mass.: D. C. Heath, 1975.

Snow, Donald M. *Uncivil Wars: International Security and the New Internal Conflicts.* Boulder: Lynne Rienner, 1996.

Sohlmans, Staffan. "The Wassenaar Arrangement and the Moratorium for West Africa." Henri Dunant Centre, 5 May 1999. Available at www.nisat.org/west%20africa/wassenaar_arrangements_and_the_mo.htm.

Stockwell, John. *In Search of Enemies: A CIA Story.* New York: W. W. Norton, 1978.

Stremlau, John. *The International Politics of the Nigerian Civil War, 1967–1970.* Princeton: Princeton University Press, 1977.

UN (United Nations). *Case Study 1: Cooperation Between the United Nations and the Economic Community of West African States (ECOWAS): UNOMIL/ECOMOG.* New York: UN Lessons Learned Unit, Department of Peacekeeping Operations, February 1998.

———. *Ninth Progress Report of the Secretary-General on the United Nations Observer Mission in Liberia.* UN Doc. S/1995/158, 24 February 1995.

———. *Report of the Economic and Social Council for 2000.* UN Doc. A/55/305-S/2000/809, 21 August 2000.

———. *Report of the Independent Inquiry into the Actions of the United Nations During the 1994 Genocide in Rwanda.* UN Doc. S/1999/1257, 16 December 1999.

———. *Report of the Inter-Agency Mission to West Africa: Towards a Comprehensive Approach to Durable and Sustainable Solutions to Priority Needs and Challenges in West Africa.* UN Doc. S/2001/434, 2 May 2001.

———. *Report of the Panel of Experts Appointed Pursuant to Security Council Resolution 1408, Paragraph 16, Concerning Liberia.* UN Doc. S/2002/470, 19 April 2002.

———. *Report of the Panel of Experts Appointed Pursuant to UN Security Council Resolution 1306 (2000), Paragraph 19, in Relation to Sierra Leone.* UN Doc. S/2000/1195, 20 December 2000.

———. *Report of the Special Representative of the Secretary-General for Children and Armed Conflict: Mr. Olara A. Otunnu, to the Commission on Human Rights, Submitted in Accordance with General Assembly Resolution 55/79.* E/CN.4/2001/76, 25 January 2001.

———. *UNOMIL's Electoral Observation: Final Report.* Monrovia: UN Electoral Division, September 1997.

UNDP (United Nations Development Programme). *Human Development Report 2001.* New York: Oxford University Press, 2001.

———. *UNDP and Governance: Experiences and Lessons Learned.* New York: UNDP Management Development and Governance Division, 1998.

———. Emergency Response Division. Small arms brochure section on Mali's "'Security First' Approach to Conflict Resolution and Development." Available at www.undp.org/erd/archives/brochures/small_arms/sa3.htm.

UNDPKO (United Nations Department of Peacekeeping Operations). *Case Study 1: Cooperation Between the United Nations and the Economic Community of*

West African States (ECOWAS): UNOMIL/ECOMOG. New York: UN Lessons Learned Unit, February 1998.

UNECA (United Nations Economic Commission for Africa). *African Alternative Framework for Structural Adjustment Programs for Socio-Economic Recovery and Transformation.* Addis Ababa: UNECA, 1989.

UNICEF (United Nations Children's Fund). *The State of the World's Children, 1990–1999.* New York: UNICEF, 1999.

Urquhart, Brian. *A Life in Peace and War.* New York: W. W. Norton, 1987.

Uvin, Peter. *Aiding Violence: The Development Enterprise in Rwanda.* West Hartford, Conn.: Kumarian Press, 1998.

Van Creveld, Martin. *The Transformation of War.* New York: Free Press, 1991.

Van de Goor, Luc, Kumar Rupesinghe, and Paul Sciarone, eds. *Between Development and Destruction: An Enquiry into the Causes of Conflict in Post-Colonial States.* London: Macmillan, 1996.

Van Walraven, Klaas. *The Pretence of Peace-Keeping: ECOMOG, West Africa, and Liberia (1990–1998).* The Hague: Netherlands Institute of International Relations, 1999.

Verschave, François-Xavier. *Complicité de génocide? La politique de la France au Rwanda.* Paris: La Découverte, 1994.

———. *La Françafrique: Le plus long scandale de la République.* Paris: Stock, 1998.

———. *Noir silence: Qui arrêtera la Françafrique?* Paris: Editions des Arènes, 2000.

Vogt, Margaret, ed. *The Liberian Crisis and ECOMOG: A Bold Attempt at Regional Peacekeeping.* Lagos: Gabumo Press, 1992.

Vogt, Margaret, and Lateef Aminu, eds. *Peacekeeping as a Security Strategy in Africa: Chad and Liberia as Case Studies.* Enugu, Nigeria: Fourth Dimension, 1996.

Wallerstein, Immanuel. *The Politics of Unity.* New York: Vintage Books, 1967.

Wampah, H. A. K. "Future Plans for the ECOWAS Monetary Zone." Paper presented at the seminar "European Monetary Union and the Euro: A Learning Experience for ECOWAS," Accra, April 2002.

Wauthier, Claude. *Quatre présidents et l'Afrique: De Gaulle, Pompidou, Giscard d'Estaing, Mitterand.* Paris: Editions du Seuil, 1995.

Welch, Claude. "Civil-Military Agonies in Nigeria: Pains of an Unaccomplished Transition." *Armed Forces and Society* 21, no. 4 (1995).

Wesley, M. *Casualties of the New World Order: The Causes and Failure of UN Missions to Civil Wars.* London: Macmillan, 1997.

Whiteman, Kaye. "The Man Who Ran Françafrique." *National Interest* 49 (Fall 1997).

Williams, Rocklyn. "Beyond Old Borders: Challenges to Franco–South African Security Relations in the New Millennium." *African Security Review* 8, no. 4 (1999).

Wood, Brian, and Johan Peleman. "Making the Deal and Moving the Goods: The Role of Brokers and Shippers." In Lora Lumpe, ed., *Running Guns: The Global Black Market in Small Arms.* Norwegian Initiative on Small Arms Transfers and the International Peace Research Institute. London: Zed Books, 2000.

World Bank. *Governance: The World Bank's Experience.* Washington, D.C.: World Bank, 1994.

Yates, Douglas. *The Rentier State in Africa: Oil-Rent Dependency and Neo-Colonialism in the Republic of Gabon.* Trenton, N.J.: Africa World Press, 1996.

Zack-Williams, A. B. *Tributors, Supporters, and Merchant Capital: Mining and Underdevelopment in Sierra Leone.* Aldershot, England: Avebury, 1995.

Zartman, I. William. "African Regional Security and Changing Patterns of Relations." In Edmond J. Keller and Donald Rothchild, eds., *Africa in the New International Order.* Boulder: Lynne Rienner, 1996.

The Contributors

Ibrahim Abdullah is a historian who specializes in colonial and post-colonial history. He has published in the area of African social/labor history and has taught in universities in the United States, Canada, Nigeria, South Africa, and Sierra Leone. He has edited an anthology on the decade-long conflict in Sierra Leone, titled *Between Democracy and Terror: The Sierra Leone Civil War* (2003). He is currently working on a book-length project titled *Youth, Culture, and Counter-Hegemony in Sierra Leone.*

Adekeye Adebajo is executive director of the Centre for Conflict Resolution in Cape Town, South Africa. From 2001 to 2003, he was director of the Africa Program at the International Peace Academy (IPA) in New York and adjunct professor at Columbia University's School of International and Public Affairs (SIPA). He served on United Nations missions in South Africa, Western Sahara, and Iraq. He is the author of *Building Peace in West Africa: Liberia, Sierra Leone, and Guinea-Bissau; Liberia's Civil War: Nigeria, ECOMOG, and Regional Security in West Africa;* and coeditor (with Chandra Sriram) of *Managing Armed Conflicts in the Twenty-First Century.*

Adebayo Adedeji has been a proponent and architect of regional integration in Africa since the early 1970s, beginning with the establishment of the Economic Community of West African States (ECOWAS). Between 1971 and 1975, he was Minister of Economic Reconstruction and Development in Nigeria. During his tenure as Executive Secretary of the UN Economic Commission for Africa from 1975 to 1993, Adedeji led the development of the Preferential Trade Agreement (PTA), which later became the Common

Market for Eastern and Southern Africa (COMESA). Presently, Professor Adedeji is the director of the African Centre for Development and Strategic Studies, a think-tank based in Ijebu Ode, Nigeria.

Kwesi Aning received a Ph.D. from the University of Copenhagen, Denmark. During this period, he was a guest scholar at the Centre for Peace Research and Conflict Resolution in Denmark, and the National War College in Nigeria. Since 1998, Kwesi Aning has taught at several universities worldwide, including the European Peace University, Austria, and Fourah Bay College, Sierra Leone. He is currently a senior researcher at an Accra-based think-tank, African Security Dialogue and Research, and teaches a graduate course at the Legon Centre for International Affairs. He has published extensively in scholarly journals and contributed book chapters.

S. K. B. Asante, formerly a principal regional adviser to governments on regional economic cooperation and integration at the Cabinet Office of the United Nations Economic Commission for Africa, received his Ph.D. from the London School of Economics and Political Science, University of London. He is currently an international consultant. A specialist in regionalism and African development strategies, Asante has authored five books on African development, regionalism, and pan-Africanism, and over 100 book chapters, monographs, and articles in scholarly journals. He is a fellow of the Ghana Academy of Art and Sciences.

Daniel C. Bach is a director of research at the French National Centre for Scientific Research. He is attached to the Centre d'Etude d'Afrique Noire and teaches at the University of Bordeaux. He holds a D.Phil from Oxford University, and has taught in Nigeria, Canada, the United States, and Japan. He has written extensively on Nigerian federalism, regionalization processes in Africa, and the interactions between Africa's regionalization and the globalization of the world economy. His current research focuses on Africa and international relations theory.

Comfort Ero is Policy and Planning Officer with the United Nations Mission in Liberia (UNMIL), following a stint as project director, West Africa Office, International Crisis Group. Prior to that she was research fellow with the Conflict, Security and Development Group at the Centre for Defence Studies, King's College, London. From 1998 to 1999 she was research associate at the International Institute for Strategic Studies in London. She has written extensively on African regional security issues.

Eboe Hutchful, a Ghanaian political scientist, is professor of African Studies at Wayne State University in Detroit, Michigan, and a director of

African Security Dialogue and Research (ASDR), an NGO based in Accra, Ghana. He is currently involved in research and advocacy in the area of civil-military relations and security sector governance and reform. He is the author and coeditor of several books and a large number of journal articles, including *The Military and Militarism in Africa* (1998), with Abdoulaye Bathily, and *Ghana's Adjustment Experience: The Paradox of Reform* (2002). He is also member and chair of the African Leadership Forum's Experts Group on Security, Demilitarization, and Development in Africa.

James O. C. Jonah is currently a senior fellow at the Ralph Bunche Institute for International Studies at the City Univeristy of New York Graduate Center where he is completing his memoirs. These cover thirty years of experience in the United Nations Secretariat where he rose to the rank of Under Secretary-General for Political Affairs. Prior to this, Jonah served his country, Sierra Leone, as minister of finance, development, and economic planning and as Permanent Representative of Sierra Leone to the United Nations.

Yasmin Jusu-Sheriff is a barrister with a law degree from Oxford University. A noted campaigner for women's rights, she is credited with establishing the first all-female law firm in Sierra Leone. She is a member of several local and international women's organizations, including the Sierra Leone Women's Forum (SLWF), Femmes Africa Solidarité (FAS), and the Mano River Women's Peace Network (MARWOPNET). Jusu-Sheriff served as the first Executive Secretary of the Truth and Reconciliation Commission.

Jimmy D. Kandeh is associate professor of political science at the University of Richmond. He has published several articles on Sierra Leone, Liberia, and The Gambia, and he is the author of the forthcoming book entitled *Coups from Below: Armed Subalterns and State Power in West Africa.*

Christopher Landsberg is the director of the Centre for Policy Studies (CPS) in Johannesburg and the cofounder of the Centre for Africa's International Relations at the University of the Witwatersrand, Johannesburg. During 2000–2001 he was deputy chair of the board of directors of CPS. He coedited, with Mwesiga Baregu, *From Cape to Congo: Southern Africa's Evolving Security Challenges* (Lynne Rienner, 2003). He has published widely on Africa's international relations, particularly in the areas of governance, democracy promotion, development, and peace and security.

Angela Ndinga-Muvumba is a senior program officer with the International Peace Academy's (IPA) Africa Program. Prior to joining IPA, she worked with the Association François-Xavier Bagnoud, the UN Development Programme, and the UN Development Fund for Women. She has taught courses in U.S. foreign policy and political geography at Farleigh Dickinson University and published articles in *The World Today, West Africa,* and on *Africana.com.* Her current research focuses on the HIV/AIDS pandemic's impact on African development and democratization processes.

'Funmi Olonisakin is a visiting senior fellow at the African Security Unit, International Policy Institute, King's College, London. Prior to this, she worked in the Office of the United Nations Special Representative of the Secretary-General for Children and Armed Conflict. She has been a MacArthur Foundation post-doctoral fellow at the Department of War Studies, King's College, London, and a research associate at the Institute for Strategic Studies, University of Pretoria. She has conducted extensive research on regional security issues in Africa. She is the author of *Reinventing Peacekeeping in Africa* (2000) and coauthor of *Peacekeepers, Politicians, and Warlords* (1999), among other publications.

Ismail Rashid teaches in the history department and Africana Studies program at Vassar College. His primary teaching and research interests are popular anticolonial resistance and contemporary conflicts in West Africa. His recent publications include articles in *Africa Development; Slavery and Abolition;* and the *Canadian Journal of African Studies* and "Millenarianism and Mahdism: Idara and Bubuya Revolt Revisited," in Toyin Falola (ed.), *Ghana in Africa and the World* (2002).

Amos Sawyer is associate director and research scholar at the Workshop in Political Theory and Policy Analysis, a policy research center, at Indiana University. He holds a Ph.D. in political science from Northwestern University and has served in several teaching and research capacities, including dean of the College of Social Sciences at the University of Liberia. He has written extensively on conflict resolution and governance challenges in Africa. He served as chairman of Liberia's constitution-drafting commission in the early 1980s and led the first interim government of Liberia during the outbreak of violent conflict between 1990 and 1994. He also chairs the board of directors of the Center for Democratic Empowerment, which he founded in 1994.

Kaye Whiteman was managing editor at the weekly *West Africa* until 1999. Whiteman has been in journalism and communications for over forty years. Early in his career he was deputy editor of *West Africa* and then spent almost ten years as an information officer in the Commission of the European Community in Brussels, before returning to *West Africa*. He is now a full-time freelance writer on African affairs. In Nigeria he worked with Business Media, which merged with the daily financial newspaper *Business Day* (Nigeria), for whom he still writes.

Douglas Yates teaches political science and law at the American University of Paris, the American Graduate School of International Relations and Diplomacy, and the Université de Cergy-Pontoise. Since the publication of *The Rentier State in Africa: Oil-Rent Dependency and Neocolonialism in the Republic of Gabon* (1996), Yates has published extensively on France's Africa policy, with a particular emphasis on the oil business in the Gulf of Guinea. A frequent contributor to *West Africa* magazine, Yates has also researched and spoken extensively around the subcontinent.

Index

About the Book

Among the world's most unstable regions, West Africa in the last decade has experienced a web of conflicts with profound and wide-ranging effects. *West Africa's Security Challenges* is the first comprehensive assessment of the resulting mix of setbacks and progress.

The authors provide a context for understanding the region's security dilemmas, highlighting the link between failures of economic development, governance, and democratization on the one hand, and military insecurity and violent conflicts on the other. The role of key regional and external actors in foiling—and sometimes fueling—conflicts is also examined. The result is an analysis that is not only academically rigorous, but also relevant to current policy debates.

Adekeye Adebajo is executive director of the Centre for Conflict Resolution at the University of Cape Town, South Africa. Previously director of the Africa Program at the International Peace Academy and adjunct professor at Columbia University's School of International and Public Affairs (SIPA), he is author of *Building Peace in West Africa* and *Liberia's Civil War* and coeditor of *Managing Armed Conflicts in the Twenty-First Century*. **Ismail Rashid** is assistant professor of history and Africana studies at Vassar College in the United States. His research focus includes pan-Africanism and social conflicts in contemporary Africa.